The Cambridge Encyclopedia of
Russia and the Soviet Union

Consultant Editors

John Bowlt
Associate Professor, Slavic Department
University of Texas at Austin;
Director (and Head, Visual Arts Section)
Institute of Modern Russian Culture
Blue Lagoon, Texas

H. B. F. Dixon
Lecturer in Biochemistry
University of Cambridge
Fellow of King's College, Cambridge

The Cambridge Encyclopedia of
RUSSIA AND THE SOVIET UNION

General Editors

Archie Brown
Lecturer in Soviet Institutions
University of Oxford,
Fellow of St Antony's College, Oxford

John Fennell
Professor of Russian
University of Oxford,
Fellow of New College, Oxford

Michael Kaser
Reader in Economics
University of Oxford,
Professorial Fellow of St Antony's College, Oxford

H. T. Willetts
Lecturer in Russian History
University of Oxford,
Fellow of St Antony's College, Oxford

CAMBRIDGE UNIVERSITY PRESS
Cambridge London New York New Rochelle
Melbourne Sydney

Editorial Director: James R. Clark
Managing Editor: Barbara Horn
Executive Editor: Elizabeth Kaser
Designer: Terry Smith
Maps: Swanston and Associates
Diagrams: Martin Causer
Index: Douglas Matthews

Published by the Press Syndicate of the University of Cambridge,
The Pitt Building, Trumpington Street, Cambridge, CB2 1RP
32 East 57th Street, New York, NY 10022, USA,
296 Beaconsfield Parade, Middle Park,
Melbourne 3206, Australia

Created, designed and produced by
Trewin Copplestone Books Limited, London

© Trewin Copplestone Books Limited, 1982

First published by Cambridge University Press 1982

Library of Congress catalogue card number: 81–9965

British Library Cataloguing in Publication Data
The Cambridge encyclopedia of Russia and the Soviet Union
    1. Russia–Dictionaries and encyclopedias
    I. Brown, Archie
    947'.003   DS705

ISBN 0 521 23169 8

Set in Linotron Plantin and Univers by Tradespools Ltd, Frome
Separation by Scanplus Ltd, London
Made and printed in Italy by New Interlitho S.P.A., Milan

Contributors

A. B. P.   **Dr A. Polonsky**
Reader in International History, London School of Economics and Political Science

A. E. R. F.   **Professor Ann Farkas**
Brooklyn College, City University of New York

A. F.   **The late Alan Ferguson**
Lecturer in the History of the South Slavs, School of Slavonic and East European Studies, University of London

A. G. S.   **Dr A. G. Sherratt, FSA**
Assistant Keeper, Ashmolean Museum of Art and Archaeology, Oxford

A. H.   **Dr Ann Helgeson**
Senior Research Fellow, Department of Economics, University of Essex

A. H. B.   **Archie Brown**
Lecturer in Soviet Institutions, University of Oxford; Fellow of St Antony's College, Oxford

A. K.-W.   **Dr A. Kemp-Welch**
Lecturer in Politics, University of Nottingham

A. M.   **Alastair McAuley**
Senior Lecturer in Economics, University of Essex

A. McD.   **Dr Adrian McDonald**
Lecturer, School of Geography, University of Leeds

A. M. C.   **Aldyth M. Cadoux**

A. N.   **Professor Alec Nove, FBA**
Department of International Economic Studies, University of Glasgow

A. P.   **Dr Alex Pravda**
Lecturer in Politics, University of Reading

B. H.   **Dr Basil Haigh, FIL**
Formerly Physician to HM Embassy, Moscow

B. R.   **Professor Bernard Rudden**
Professor of Comparative Law, University of Oxford; Fellow of Brasenose College, Oxford

C. A. J.   **C. A. Johnson**
Senior Lecturer in Russian, University of Leeds

C. C.   **Dr Catherine Cooke**
Lecturer in Design, The Open University

C. D   **Dr Charlotte Douglas**
Department of History of Art, Ohio State University

C. H.   **Dr Caroline Humphrey**
Lecturer in Social Anthropology, University of Cambridge; Fellow of King's College, Cambridge

C. N. D.   **Christopher Donnelly**
Senior Lecturer, Soviet Studies Research Centre, Royal Military Academy, Sandhurst

D. B.   **Dr Derek Bailey, FCMA**
Lecturer in Accounting, University of Birmingham

D. H.   **Professor David Hooson**
Department of Geography, University of California, Berkeley

D. J.   **Professor David Joravsky**
History Department, Northwestern University

D. J. B. S.   **Dr D. J. B. Shaw**
Lecturer in Geography, University of Birmingham

D. L.   **Professor David Lane**
Department of Sociology, University of Birmingham

D. R.   **D. J. Richards**
Head of Department of Russian, University of Exeter

D. S. M. W.   **Dr D. S. M. Williams**
Lecturer in the History of Asiatic Russia, School of Slavonic and East European Studies, University of London

E. G.   **Dr Elizabeth Garnsey**
Research Associate, Department of Applied Economics, University of Cambridge

E. L.   **Evan Luard**
Supernumerary Fellow of St Antony's College, Oxford; formerly Joint Parliamentary Under-Secretary, Foreign and Commonwealth Office and UK Delegate to the United Nations General Assembly

E. V. **Dr Elizabeth Valkenier**
Senior Fellow, Russian Institute, Columbia University

F. C. M. K. **Dr Faith C. M. Kitch**
Lecturer in Russian Language and Literature, School of Slavonic and East European Studies, University of London

F. O'D. **Dr Felicity O'Dell**
Formerly Research Fellow, Social and Political Sciences Committee, University of Cambridge

G. A. **Dr Gregory Andrusz**
Senior Lecturer, Department of Sociology, Middlesex Polytechnic, Enfield

G. E. S. **Dr G. E. Smith**
Lecturer in Geography, University of Cambridge

G. M. H. **Professor G. Melvyn Howe**
Department of Geography, University of Strathclyde

G. R. S. **Dr Gerald R. Seaman**
Associate Professor in Musicology, University of Auckland

G. T. **Dr Gregory F. Treverton**
Assistant Director, International Institute for Strategic Studies, London

G. W. **Dr Gregory Walker, ALA**
Head of Slavonic Section, Bodleian Library, Oxford

G. Wh. **Colonel Geoffrey Wheeler, CIE, CBE**
Formerly Director, Central Asian Research Centre, London

H. B. F. D. **Dr H. B. F. Dixon**
Lecturer in Biochemistry, University of Cambridge; Fellow of King's College, Cambridge

H. H. **Dr H. Hanak**
Reader in International Relations, School of Slavonic and East European Studies, University of London

H. L. **Dr H. Leeming**
Reader in Comparative Slavonic Philology, School of Slavonic and East European Studies, University of London

H. M. P. **Professor H. M. Powell, FRS**
Professor Emeritus of Chemical Crystallography, University of Oxford

H. S. **Dr H. Shukman**
Lecturer in Modern Russian History, University of Oxford; Fellow (and Director, Russian and East European Centre), St Antony's College, Oxford

H. T. W. **H. T. Willetts**
Lecturer in Russian History, University of Oxford; Fellow (formerly Director, Russian and East European Centre), St Antony's College, Oxford

I. G. **Dr Igor Golomstock**
Art historian; formerly Lector in Russian, University of Oxford

I. P. F. **I. Paul Foote**
Lecturer in Russian, University of Oxford; Fellow of Queen's College, Oxford

J. A. **Colonel Jonathan Alford**
Deputy Director, International Institute for Strategic Studies, London

J. B. **Dr Jennifer Baines**
Formerly Research Fellow, Somerville College, Oxford

J. C. **Dr Julian Cooper**
Research Fellow, Centre for Russian and East European Studies, University of Birmingham

J. D. **Dr J. C. Dewdney, FRSGS**
Reader in Geography, University of Durham

J. E. B. **Professor John Bowlt**
Slavic Department, University of Texas at Austin; Director, Institute of Modern Russian Culture, Blue Lagoon, Texas

J. H. **Dr Jana Howlett**
Lecturer in Russian, University of Cambridge

J. M. B. **Dr J. M. Boyd**
Director, Nature Conservancy Council, Edinburgh

J. M. K. **Dr Michael Kitch**
Formerly Lecturer in Romanian History, School of Slavonic and East European Studies, University of London

J. N. **Professor J. Nutting, FIM**
Head of Department of Metallurgy, University of Leeds

J. P. **Dr Judith Pallot**
Lecturer in the Geography of the USSR, University of Oxford; Student of Christ Church, Oxford

J. R. **Dr James Riordan**
Senior Lecturer in Russian Studies, University of Bradford

K. D. **Dr Karen Dawisha**
Lecturer in Politics, University of Southampton

K.-E. W. **Professor K.-E. Wädekin**
Professor of East European and International Agrarian Policy, Justus-Liebig University, Giessen

K. G. **Kenneth W. Gatland, FRAS**
Editor, *Spaceflight*

L. H. **Dr L. Hirszowicz**
Senior Research Officer, Institute of Jewish Affairs, London

L. J. S. **Professor Leslie Symons**
Department of Geography, University College of Swansea

L. L. **Professor Lionel W. Longdon**
Department of Mathematics and Ballistics, Royal Military College of Science, Shrivenham

L. S. **Professor Leonard Schapiro, CBE, FBA**
Emeritus Professor of Political Science with Special Reference to Russian Studies, London School of Economics and Political Science

M. A. N. **Dr M. A. Nicholson**
Lecturer in Russian and Soviet Studies, University of Lancaster

M. B. **Professor Milka Bliznakov**
Professor of Architecture and Urban Design, Virginia Polytechnic Institute and State University

M. C. **Mary Chamot**
Formerly Assistant Keeper, Tate Gallery, London

M. D. **Martin Dewhirst**
Lecturer in Russian Language and Literature, University of Glasgow

M. F. **The Reverend Michael Fortounatto**
Precentor and Choir Master, Cathedral of the Assumption and All Saints, London

M. G. P. **Dr Michael Priestley**
Lecturer, H. H. Wills Physics Laboratories, University of Bristol

M. H. **Dr Muriel Heppell**
Senior Lecturer in the Medieval History of Orthodox Eastern Europe, School of Slavonic and East European Studies, University of London

M. H. L. **Professor M. H. Lader, FRCPsych**
Professor of Clinical Psychopharmacology, University of London

M. H. S. **M. H. Shotton**
Lecturer in Russian, University of Oxford; Fellow of St Catherine's College, Oxford

M. K. **Michael Kaser**
Reader in Economics, University of Oxford; Professorial Fellow of St Antony's College, Oxford

M. M. **Dr Mary McAuley**
Senior Lecturer, Department of Government, University of Essex

M. M. F. **Mariamna Fortounatto**

M. R. B. **Michael Binyon**
Moscow correspondent, *The Times*, London

M. T. **Dr M. Teich**
Fellow of Robinson College, Cambridge

M. V. G. **Michael Glenny**
Formerly Lecturer in Russian Language and Literature, University of Birmingham; translator

N. D. C. G. **Professor Nigel Grant**
Department of Education, University of Glasgow

N. G. **Noël Goodwin**
Associate Editor, *Dance and Dancers*

N. J. R. W. **N. J. R. Wright, FGS**
Formerly Cambridge Arctic Shelf Programme, Department of Geology, University of Cambridge

N. S. **Dr Norman Stone**
Lecturer in History, University of Cambridge; Fellow of Trinity College, Cambridge

O. C. **Professor Olga Crisp**
School of Slavonic and East European Studies, University of London

P. D. R. **Dr P. D. Rayfield**
Senior Lecturer and Head of Department of Russian, Queen Mary College, University of London

P. G. **Professor P. Gray, FRS, FRIC**
Head of Department of Physical Chemistry, University of Leeds

P. H. **Dr Philip Hanson**
Reader in Economics, Centre for Russian and East European Studies, University of Birmingham

P. M. **Patrick Moore, OBE, FRAS**
Formerly Vice-President, British Astronomical Association; Honorary Member, Astronomic-Geodetic Society of the USSR

P. R. **Peter Reddaway**
Senior Lecturer in Political Science, London School of Economics and Political Science

R. A. **Dr Ronald Amann**
Senior Lecturer in Soviet Politics and Science Policy, Centre for Russian and East European Studies, University of Birmingham

R. A. F. **Dr R. A. French, FRGS**
Senior Lecturer, Department of Geography, University College, London

R. D. P. **Professor Richard Portes**
Head of Department of Economics, Birkbeck College, University of London

R. H. **Dr Raymond Hutchings, FRGS**
Formerly Visiting Professor of Economics, University of Texas at Austin

R. I. K. **Dr Ronald I. Kowalski**
Lecturer in Russian/Soviet History, Worcester College of Higher Education, Worcester

R. J. H. **Dr Ronald Hill**
Associate Professor of Political Science and Fellow, Trinity College, Dublin

R. P. **Dr Roger Parsons, FRS, FRIC**
Director, Laboratoire d'Electrochimie Interfaciale, (CNRS), Meudon, Hauts-de-Seine

R. P. B. **Dr Roger Bartlett**
Senior Lecturer, Department of Russian Studies, University of Keele

R. T. **Dr Richard Taylor, FRHistS**
Lecturer in Politics and Russian Studies, University College of Swansea

R. W. D. **Professor R. W. Davies**
Centre for Russian and East European Studies (formerly Director), University of Birmingham

S. F. **Dr Simon Franklin**
Research Fellow, Clare College, Cambridge

S. H. **The Reverend Dr Sergei Hackel**
Reader in Russian Studies, University of Sussex

S. M. **Dr Simon Mitton, FRAS**
Formerly Secretary of the Cambridge Institute of Astronomy; Fellow of St Edmund's House, Cambridge

S. M. W. **Dr S. M. Walters**
Director, Cambridge University Botanic Garden; Fellow of King's College, Cambridge

S. W. **Dr Stephen White**
Lecturer, Department of Politics, University of Glasgow

T. B. **Dr Terence Boddington**
Department of Physical Chemistry, University of Leeds

T. E. A. **Dr Terence Armstrong**
Reader in Arctic Studies; Deputy Director, Scott Polar Research Institute, University of Cambridge; Fellow of Clare Hall, Cambridge

T. M. R. **Dr T. M. Ryan**
Lecturer in Social Policy, University College of Swansea

T. T. R. **Tamara Talbot Rice**
Specialist in Byzantine and Islamic art and architecture

V. G. T. **Professor V. G. Treml**
Department of Economics, Duke University, Durham, N.C.

W. M. M. **Dr Mervyn Matthews**
Reader in Soviet Studies, University of Surrey

W. H. Z. **Dr W. H. Zawadzki**
Formerly Research Fellow, Wolfson College, Oxford

W. N. **Dr Walter Newey**
Lecturer, Department of Geography, University of Edinburgh

TRANSLITERATION

Cyrillic alphabet		Latin alphabet
А	а	a
Б	б	b
В	в	v
Г	г	g
Д	д	d
Е	е	e
Ё	ё	e
Ж	ж	zh
З	з	z
И	и	i
Й	й	y
К	к	k
Л	л	l
М	м	m
Н	н	n
О	о	o
П	п	p
Р	р	r
С	с	s
Т	т	t
У	у	u
Ф	ф	f
Х	х	kh
Ц	ц	ts
Ч	ч	ch
Ш	ш	sh
Щ	щ	shch
	ъ	
	ы	y
	ь	'
Э	э	e
Ю	ю	yu
Я	я	ya

In proper names initial E- (with occasional exceptions for familiar names) is rendered Ye-terminal -ый and -ий are simplified to -y (Dostoevsky) and -ия to -ia (Sofia); well-known Russian names are given in the form in which they have become familiar to English-speaking readers (Nicholas II, Peter the Great, Alexander Solzhenitsyn)

Contents

List of maps

Select glossary

AA	Autonomous area (okrug); the lowest nationality-based administrative division; part of a kray or oblast
apparat	The administrative personnel of the Party or the state
ASSR	Autonomous Soviet Socialist Republic; a nationality-based division of a Union Republic; administratively comparable to an oblast
AR	Autonomous region (oblast); a nationality-based administrative division; part of a kray or Union Republic
BAM	Baykal-Amur Railway
CCP	Chinese Communist Party
CEC	Central Executive Committee of the Congress of Soviets
Cheka (Vecheka)	All-Russian Extraordinary Commission (of the Council of People's Commissars) for combating Counter-Revolution, Sabotage and Speculation; the state security and intelligence organ, 1917–22
Comecon (CMEA)	Council for Mutual Economic Assistance; the economic grouping of the USSR, six East European states, Cuba, Mongolia and Vietnam
Cominform	Communist Information Bureau, 1947–56
Comintern	The Third (Communist) International, 1919–43. Its headquarters was in Moscow
CPSU	Communist Party of the Soviet Union
DOSAAF	Voluntary Society for Aid to the Army, Air Force and Navy
FRG	Federal Republic of Germany
GDR	German Democratic Republic
glavk	Chief administration within a ministry or under the Council of Ministers
Glavlit	Directorate for Literary and Publishing Affairs; the official censorship organ
GlavPUR	Political Directorate of the Armed Forces
GOELRO	State Commission for the Electrification of Russia
Gosbank	State Bank
Gosplan	State Planning Committee (Commission)
Gossnab	State Committee on Material-Technical Supply
GPU	State Political Administration; the state security and intelligence organ, 1922–3 (*see* OGPU)
guberniya	A pre-revolutionary administrative division of the Russian Empire (translatable as 'province')
GUGB	Main Administration for State Security, 1934
GULag	Main Administration for Camps; under the MVD (and since 1958 redesignated GUITU) it administers the penal detention system
KGB	Committee for State Security, established in that form 1954
kray	Territory; a division of a Union Republic and administratively comparable to an oblast; generally containing one or more nationality-based territorial divisions
LSR	Left Socialist Revolutionaries
MGB	Ministry for State Security, 1946–53
mir	Village commune
MKhAT	Moscow Arts Theatre
MVD	Ministry of Internal Affairs; state security and intelligence organ, 1953–4
NEP	New Economic Policy, 1921–8; initiated by Lenin
NKGB	People's Commissariat for State Security, 1943–6
NKVD	People's Commissariat for Internal Affairs; state security and intelligence organ, 1934–43
nomenklatura	List of responsible posts and of suitable holders of them; refers especially to appointments requiring approval of Party organs
NS	New Style or Gregorian calendar. Imperial Russia continued to use the Julian (Old Style) calendar which had been superseded in all other European states in the 17th or 18th centuries. In the 20th century both the Julian and Gregorian style were frequently used jointly in newspapers and elsewhere (written, for example, as 9/22 March). A Soviet decree (26 January 1918) fixed 1 February 1918 (OS) as 14 February 1918, and thus the New Style came into force
oblast	Region; an administrative division of a Union Republic; it may contain an autonomous area (AA)
OGPU	Unified State Political Administration; the state security and intelligence organ, 1923–34
okrug	An autonomous area (AA)
OS	Old Style or Julian calendar; *see* NS
Politburo	Political Bureau of the Central Committee of the CPSU
rayon	An administrative district within a republic, kray, oblast, okrug or city (and, in a general sense, any zone)
RSFSR	The Russian Soviet Federative Socialist Republic
SALT	Strategic Arms Limitation treaty and talks (between the USSR and the USA)
samizdat	'Self-publishing'–the clandestine circulation of writings
Sovnarkom	Council of People's Commissars (CPC)
SR	Socialist Revolutionary Party
SSR	Soviet Socialist Republic, one of the fifteen comprising the Soviet Union
uezd	A pre-revolutionary administrative division of a province (*guberniya*) (and translatable as 'county')
verst	1.07 km, 0.55 miles
Vesenkha	Supreme Economic Council
VUZ	A higher education institution
zemsvto	Pre-revolutionary elected organ of local government
— and ..	In tables, respectively, nil or negligible; not available

Index

An asterisk against a word in the text indicates that there is an entry on this subject, or substantial further reference to it, which can be found elsewhere in the book by consulting the index

TERRITORY AND PEOPLES

Mountains, an Armenian landscape by Martiros Sar'yan, 1923

(1)

(2)

(3)

(4)

(5)

(6)

The evolution and structure of the landscape

Tectonic structure

The varied landforms within the territorial vastness of the Soviet Union assume the shape of a colossal amphitheatre. The towering Caucasus, Pamir, Tyan-Shan, Altay, Sayan and Far East mountain ranges along the southern and eastern borders slope down to the vast East European (Russian) Plain, the West Siberian Plain and the Turan-Caspian Lowland. However, such a simple pattern of peripheral mountains and plains belies a complex geological structure and evolutionary history.

The land area at present occupied by the USSR comprises two large, very ancient and deep-seated stable blocks or continental platforms: the east European (Russian) platform in the west and the Siberian platform in the east. Both are composed of extremely tough igneous and metamorphic rocks of Pre-Cambrian (Archaean) age lying at varying depths below geologically more recent strata. These basal

(1) On the tundra-taiga borderline in north Siberia (Pre-Cambrian zone). (2) The mountains surrounding Lake Baykal (Caledonian zone. (3) Landscape of eroded mountains–the Urals (Hercynian zone). (4)The Lena in its flat lower reaches, Yakutia (Mesozoic zone). (5) The mountains of the Caucasus from the Georgian Military Highway (Alpine zone). (6) The Karakum desert near Chardzou, Turkmenia

Pre-Cambrian zone

EAST EUROPEAN PLATFORM
1 Baltic shield
2 Belorussian rise
3 Ukrainian shield
4 Voronezh block
5 Black Sea Basin
6 North Ukrainian Basin
7 East Russian Basin
8 Moscow Basin
9 Caspian Basin

SIBERIAN PLATFORM
10 Anabar shield
11 Aldan shield
12 Tungus Basin

Caledonian zone

EASTERN SECTION
13 Baykal region
14 Western Trans-Baykal region

WESTERN SECTION
15 Yenisey range
16 Sayan Mountains
17 Minusinsk Basin
18 Kuznetsk Basin

Hercynian zone

UPLANDS
19 Novaya Zemlya
20 Ural Mountains
21 Central Kazakhstan
22 Altay
23 Tyan-Shan
24 Taymyr Peninsula
25 Severnaya Zemlya

Hercynian zone (continued)
LOWLANDS
26 Ural-Siberian depression
27 Irtysh Basin
28 Turgay depression
29 Amu-Darya Basin
30 Syr-Darya Basin
31 Fergana Basin
32 Chu Basin
33 Balkhash Basin
34 Khatanga depression

Mesozoic zone

SIBERIA AND MARITIME COUNTRY
35 Verkhoyansk range
36 Chersky range
37 Anadyr range
38 Kolyma range
39 Dzhugdzhur range
40 Sikhote-Alin'
41 Eastern Trans-Baykal region

CENTRAL ASIA
42 Mangyshlak Mountains
43 Bol'shoy Balkhan range

Alpine zone

MOUNTAIN BORDER
44 Carpathians
45 Crimea
46 Caucasus
47 Kopet-Dag
48 Pamirs
49 Sakhalin
50 Kamchatka
51 Koryak range

Source: adapted from *Bol'shoy sovetsky atlas*, vol. I, Moscow, 1937

KEY

Tectonic zones classified by past periods of mountain building

 Alpine zone   Mesozoic zone

ROCKS OF THIS PERIOD DEEPLY BURIED BY LATER DEPOSITS

Hercynian zone

Caledonian zone

Pre-Cambrian zone

ROCKS OF THIS OR EARLIER PERIODS AT OR NEAR SURFACE

Hercynian zone

Caledonian zone

Pre-Cambrian zone

TECTONIC ZONES

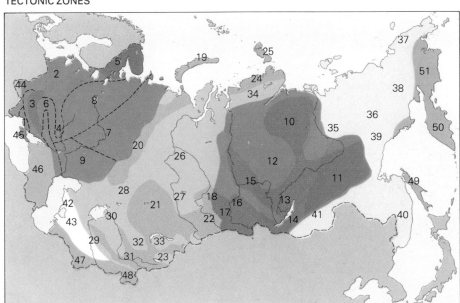

complexes have proved, in general, to have been resistant to later fold or mountain-building movements and overlying deposits are almost horizontal and only slightly disturbed. Occasionally the ancient foundations outcrop at the surface as 'shield' areas. In European Russia they are exposed in Karelia and Azov-Podolia; in Siberia, in the Aldan and Anabar shields.

The broad belt of Palaeozoic (Primary) strata between the two great platforms was folded in Hercynian times. These structures are exposed at the surface in the low ranges of the Ural Mountains and in the Kazakh Uplands (which also contain some Caledonian elements) but are buried beneath younger sediments in the West Siberian Lowland. Structural elements of Mesozoic (Secondary) age occur in eastern Siberia and the Soviet Far East. They include the great geosyncline or depression (marking an ancient fold in the strata) through which the Lena River flows.

Along the southern and eastern margins of the Pre-Cambrian, Palaeozoic (Caledonian and Hercynian) and Mesozoic structural zones lies part of the great belt of Cainozoic (Tertiary, Alpine) folding – originally the northern border of the great Tethys geosyncline. Within the USSR it includes a small section of the eastern Carpathians, the Crimean Mountains, Caucasus, Kopet-Dag and Pamirs. Volcanic activity here belongs to the recent geological past and earth movements and extinct volcanoes (such as Mt Elbrus) are common. A second belt of more recent Cainozoic formations borders the earlier tectonic zones along the Pacific seaboard. Within Soviet territory the belt includes the Koryak ranges, Kamchatka, Sakhalin, the Kuril Islands and the coastal ranges of Sikhote-Alin'; it is composed of fold mountains with which are associated much seismic and volcanic activity.

The Pre-Cambrian platforms lie deep below the lowlands of the European part of the USSR and beneath low but well-dissected plateau blocks in Siberia. Where exposed at the surface these and other areas of ancient folding (such as the Ural Mountains) represent but vestigial remains of former greatness. They are usually low in altitude with exposed roots and inverted relief. In contrast, in areas of Cainozoic folding, denudation has had only a relatively short time in which to work, tectonic structures are conformable and landscapes youthful in character. Slopes are steep and mountain peaks high and jagged; upfolds continue to form the mountain summits, and downfolds the intervening valleys.

Past periods of mountain-building are of undoubted importance in the evolution of the landscapes, but possibly of greater significance were the frequent alternating advances and withdrawals of the sea, which occurred particularly west of the Urals. During these movements sedimentary strata were alternately laid down, largely giving rise to the variety in age and character of the surface deposits over much of the country.

Glaciation

The ice ages of Pleistocene (Quaternary) times were the last major event in the evolution of the landscape. The four major advances and retreats of the ice-sheet from centres in Scandinavia, northern Karelia, Novaya Zemlya, the northern Urals and the Altay, Sayan, Pamir and Caucasus mountains, have left an indelible mark. The

LIMITS OF GLACIATIONS AND PERMAFROST

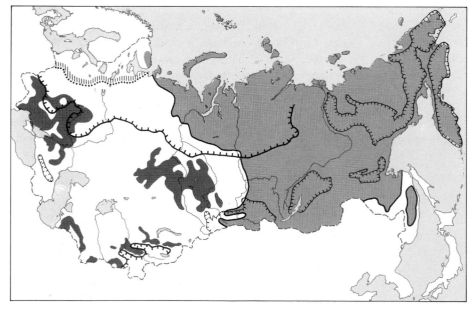

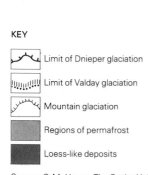

KEY

⌢⌢⌢ Limit of Dnieper glaciation

|ıllıllıl| Limit of Valday glaciation

⌢⌢⌢ Mountain glaciation

▨ Regions of permafrost

■ Loess-like deposits

Source: G. M. Howe, *The Soviet Union*, 2nd edn, London 1979

second (Oka) glaciation was the most extensive: it penetrated southwards to the edge of the Central Russian Upland with a great lobe down the basin of the Don River and thence along the foot of the Volga Upland to the middle Ural Mountains. There was a contemporary (Dem'yanka) glaciation in western Siberia but this did not extend so far south as over the plains to the west. A lobe of ice associated with a third glaciation (Dnieper), from a mainly Scandinavian source, penetrated well south along the Dnieper Lowland. The fourth glaciation (Valday) did not extend as far south as the Dnieper-Don stage, neither did it affect Siberia, but because it was the last it has left most evident traces and accounts for many features of the landscape. Near the ice centres, particularly in more northerly latitudes, the effects of the ice were mainly erosive: as it crept over the land surface soils were removed and hollows gouged out of the bedrock which are now occupied by myriads of lakes, as in Karelia. Beyond, in northern European USSR and southwards to the limit of the ice-sheets, is a region of glacial deposition with extensive dumps and spreads of morainic deposits such as boulder clay, glacial sands and gravels and terminal moraines. These deposits have impeded drainage and left behind a diffuse drainage* pattern, innumerable ponds and lakes and extensive swamps and marshes. Beyond the southernmost limit of the ice front is a broad region of water-eroded relief and finely graded and sorted deposits laid down by melt-water streams and wind action; these now form spreads of deep, fertile loess.

Permafrost

Many landforms and processes owe their origin to permafrost or perennially frozen ground, which underlies about 47 per cent (9 million sq km) of the territory of the USSR in a relatively narrow coastal strip north of the Arctic Circle in European Russia, a broader zone in western Siberia and almost the whole of the country east of the Yenisey River, to the Pacific. The upper, so-called 'active layer' thaws in summer and is up to 2m thick; the perennially frozen layer beneath may be more than 1000m thick. Patterned ground, pingos or frost boils and thermokarst topography marked by sinks and other irregularities are examples of the surface effects of permafrost. The impervious perennially frozen layer retains moisture near the surface and encourages solifluction – mudflows and landslides on slopes.

Relief

The surprising variety of landforms and scenery is the result of a long and complex geological history, of unremitting surface erosion and of deposition and erosion by sea, river and ice. Even so, such is the territorial immensity of the country that the relief units which comprise it appear vast, monotonous and unchanging and extend for thousands of kilometres. The over-all pattern is one of extensive lowlands and tablelands girdled by great ranges of mountains.

The East European (Russian) Lowland extends from the western frontiers of the country to the Urals and from the Arctic Ocean to the Black Sea and the Caspian Sea, covering almost the whole of European Russia. Its average elevation is 100–200m above sea-level, although there are parts where altitudes of 300–400m are attained. Hilly terrain such as the Valday Hills, Central Russian Uplands and Volga Upland alternates with practically flat lowlands such as the Dnieper, Oka-Don and Black Sea lowlands.

The Valday Hills, north-west of Moscow, are a jumbled mass of hills where a dissected carboniferous limestone escarpment is crossed by a terminal moraine and other glacial debris. The highest summits are more than 300m and form the drainage divide between the headwaters of the four main river systems of the area – Volga, Dnieper, Western Dvina (Daugava) and Msta, which are connected at their sources in a vast bog. The Central Russian Upland is a heavily dissected loess-covered plateau with many recent and developing ravines. Its average height is 230–250m and the highest points in the Tula district reach 290m. The Volga Heights, which reach 350m and stretch almost meridionally along the west bank of the Volga from Gorky to Volgograd, like the Central Russian Upland, form an asymmetrical plateau which descends comparatively steeply in the east to the valley of the Volga.

The broad depression of the Dnieper Lowland (50–150m), principally occupying the plain on the left bank of the Dnieper, separates the Volyno Podol'sk shield from the Central Russian Upland. During the Dnieper glaciation the lowlands were occupied by a lobe of the ice-sheet which left them extensively covered with sands and clays, with swamps and a poorly developed drainage system. These conditions prevail in the Pripyat Marshes of the Polesye Lowland, but on the lower Dnieper the lowland, which extends east of the Dnieper for more than 150km, has long dried out. The alluvial Oka-Don Lowland (160–180m) fills the broad depression between the eastern slopes of the Central Russian Upland in the west and the Volga Heights in the east. Broad river terraces covered with loess-like sandy soils are the principal landscape form. The Black Sea Lowland is a relatively thin belt (100–200km) stretching along the northern shores of the Black Sea and the Sea of Azov, and including the Crimean Plain. The surface, which only occasionally exceeds 100m, is flat and loess-covered, and in places reaches the coast in cliffs up to 30m high.

The Kola-Karelian region in the extreme north-west of European Russia lies wholly within the shield area of Pre-Cambrian crystalline rocks. It is an area of ice-scoured plateaux, mostly below 300m, although the massif of the Khibiny Mountains in the Kola Peninsula reaches more than 900m at one point. The numerous lakes are a legacy of the Quaternary glaciations.

The Ural Mountains, which separate the European and Asian parts of the USSR, comprise a composite and much denuded north-south mountain system, broken by transverse valleys. These mountains, generally 300–800m high (highest peak Mt Narodnaya, 1894m), appear as no more than a gentle swelling within the vast Russian-West Siberian Plain. The West Siberian Plain extends from the Arctic Ocean to the steppes of Kazakhstan and eastwards 200km to the Yenisey. It is only insignificantly above sea-level, its highest points are mostly below 200m and in parts even below 100m. This, the largest area of level land on the earth, is drained by the mighty rivers Ob', Irtysh and Yenisey which cause extensive flooding in the spring.

Soviet Central Asia is almost essentially the Turan-Caspian Lowland which lies to the south of the West Siberian Plain and beyond the low Turgay Plateau. It is an area of inland drainage extending from the shores of the Caspian Sea to the mountains of Central Asia, which tower to heights of 5000–7000m. The region consists of flat plains around the northern shores of the Caspian Sea and clayey and dune-covered deserts – the Karakum and Kyzylkum – separated by the Ust-Urt Plateau. An abrupt change in the landscape takes place east of the Yenisey River. Here the greater part of the countryside is taken up by the heavily dissected and thickly forested Central Siberian Plateau, 400–1000m, bordered to the south by the mountains of southern Siberia and to the east by the trough-like valleys of the Lena and Vilyuy. In north-eastern Siberia the character of the landscape changes yet again. This extensive and imperfectly explored territory, bounded to the east by the mountains of the Pacific margins, is mainly highland country, including high ranges (1800-3000m) around the Verkhoyansk and Kolyma tablelands.

The Soviet Far East is a comparatively narrow strip of land extending from north-east to south-west for practically 4500km. In the north the rugged Dzhugdzhur Range along the Sea of Okhotsk separates the region from Siberia proper; in the south the low (600–1000m) ranges of the Sikhote-Alin' system face the Sea of Japan. Structurally associated with the outer ranges of the Sikhote-Alin' and separated by the Gulf of Tartary is Sakhalin, a mountainous island formed of two parallel chains with a central depression. The Koryak Range, Kamchatka (with 30 active volcanoes) and the Kuril Islands are part of the arc-shaped system which runs the length of the east coast of Asia to form a section of the 'fiery girdle of the Pacific'.

Not only eastern Siberia and the Soviet Far East are characterized by mountains; a highland belt of Alpine-type fold mountains and associated plateaux also encircles the Russian Lowland, Soviet Central Asia and the West Siberian Plain in the south and east. In the south-west are the Ukrainian Carpathians, 1000–1800m high; the relatively low Crimean Range (reaching 1500m) on the southern margins of the peninsula is a further link in the southern mountain belt. The Caucasus, extending between the Black and Caspian seas, is a system of ranges of which the highest is Mt Elbrus (5642m). East of the Caspian Sea the Kopet-Dag attains 800m in Soviet territory but

lies mainly in Iran, where the greatest elevations are reached. The cloud-shrouded and permanently snow-covered Pamir-Alay and the Tyan-Shan Mountains with summits rising to over 6000m (Mt Communism, 7495m) are some of the highest in the USSR. These ranges are interspersed with deep valleys and rounded highlands. Between the Tyan-Shan and the Altay mountains lies the relatively low Dzhungarian Gate, the historic gateway from China across Mongolia to the Kazakh steppes and thence to the Volga. The Altay Mountains in southern Siberia are followed eastwards by the high ranges, tablelands and depressions of the Western and Eastern Sayan Highlands in the west and the Yablonovy and Stanovoy ranges in the east, the whole area forming a complex of rounded ranges and basins.

G.M.H.

Rivers and drainage

Several of the world's greatest rivers are within the USSR. The Ob'-Irtysh river system and the Yenisey, at 5410km and 5540km respectively, are the longest in Eurasia, while the Volga (3960km) is the longest and one of the most intensively-used rivers in Europe. Although most of the country drains into six river systems, it has over 100 000 rivers exceeding 10km. Some 200 000 lakes account for over 20 per cent of the world's freshwater lake storage. Most of these are in the north-western USSR, in the Kola-Karelia region, but the bulk of the freshwater storage (23 000cu km or 80 per cent) is in Lake Baykal in the south of eastern Siberia and famed for its great depth (at 1620m it is the deepest continental water body) and for the diversity and biological uniqueness of its wild life.

Annual precipitation on to the USSR totals some 8500cu km of

The river Ob' near Tomsk, Siberia

which some 4700cu km becomes surface run-off, most of which drains into the Arctic Ocean. Significant amounts drain internally to the Caspian and Aral seas, or into the largely enclosed Black Sea, and only a little reaches the Baltic Sea and the Pacific Ocean. To the west of the Urals the Volga, rising in the Valday Hills north-west of Moscow, drains a catchment of some 1 360 000sq km into the Caspian (the largest inland sea in the world: area 371 000sq km, maximum depth 1025m). To the east of the Caspian and almost directly south of the Urals, the Aral Sea, the fourth largest inland sea, receives the flow of the Amu-Darya and Syr-Darya. These rivers rise in the mountains of the Pamir, Hindu Kush and Alay but only half of their catchment represents stream-flow source areas; the remainder, such as the Karakum, represents areas where evaporative losses exceed stream-flow additions. The natural flow of both rivers varies considerably – for example, the wet year 1969 provided double the flow of 1968. The increased withdrawal of water (mainly for irrigation) is reflected in the reduction of the inflow to the Aral Sea to below 70 per cent of the 1926–50 average.

Immediately east of the Urals, the West Siberian Plain is drained by the Ob'-Irtysh river system, which, with a drainage area of 3 479 000sq km, is the largest in the USSR and sixth in the world. The extreme eastern edge of the Siberian Plain is drained by the Yenisey, which flows some 5540km when measured along the Selenga-Baykal-Angara tributaries. It draws the bulk of its stream-flow from the Mid-Siberian Plateau, an elevated area on average 600m high, most of the remainder of which is drained by the Lena. Although it is significantly shorter than the Yenisey, the Lena's drainage area is

almost as large – 2 425 000sq km as compared with 2 580 000sq km – and it also rises close to Lake Baykal and flows to the Arctic Ocean at the Laptev Sea. The East Siberian upland is drained in part by the Lena but because of its complex topography (a north-facing horseshoe of mountains with a lake-studded, low-lying, ill-drained centre through which the Kolyma flows) and because it has sea outlets to the north, east and south – the East Siberian Sea, the Bering Sea and the Sea of Okhotsk – the drainage is complex and relatively small-scale. The drainage in the Soviet Far East is via the river Amur. Atypically in the USSR, it drains an eastern run-off slope and for much of its 2800km length it forms the boundary with China. Like both the Yenisey and the Lena, the Shilka, one of the Amur's major tributaries, rises in the Baykal region.

The distribution of these water volumes is uneven both temporally and spatially. Almost all the rivers have a considerable snow-melt component which results in the bulk of their flow being released in late spring and early summer floods. Even the Amur, which has summer/autumn monsoon rainfall floods, also has a spring snow-melt flow. Over 80 per cent of the annual run-off of the USSR occurs in areas where less than 20 per cent of the population resides. Past increases in the demand for water (a tripling during 1960–80) have been satisfied by controlling the flow of the Volga and the minor rivers west of the Urals, which has promoted transport use of these rivers and generated hydroelectric power. Increased evaporation in storage and the losses in irrigation and other uses have, however, markedly reduced the inflow totals to the Caspian Sea, so affecting its hydrologic, chemical and biological status that it may follow the

MAIN DRAINAGE FEATURES

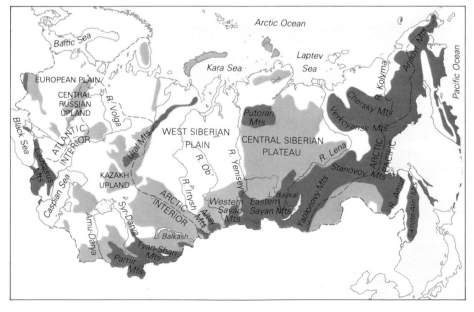

KEY

▨ Uplands

▨ Mountains

----- Divides: Atlantic; Arctic; Interior; Pacific

Source: after P.E. Lydolph, *Geography of the USSR* (New York, London, 1970)

A new irrigation canal in Turkmenia

Climate

The extent of latitude provides a range of temperature from the frigid Arctic north to the warm subtropical south, while the vast west-east dimension, situated mainly within middle latitudes, results in the predominance of extreme features of climatic continentality, marked by great contrasts between mean winter and summer temperatures, and brief transitional spring and autumn seasons, together with generally moderate or low mean levels of precipitation. The heat received from direct solar radiation increases from north to south in accordance with the increase in the noon elevation of the sun, but this is modified by the greater cloudiness of the European region resulting from the effect of the greater frequency of depressions in that area as compared with Siberia, an area remote from the Atlantic Ocean, which is the chief source of moisture. Temperatures thus range from less than 10°C in the extreme north in July to over 25°C in the extreme south of the country.

Winter is the dominant season; the climate becomes influenced by the development of a continental air mass which forms an anticyclonic ridge of high pressure over the 50th parallel, spreading out in all directions to give very low temperatures to almost all the country and generate cold, dry winds. The Siberian region, far from the moderating effects of mild westerly Atlantic air-streams, becomes colder and colder eastwards; thus Oymyakon, at latitude 63° north in eastern Siberia, has the lowest absolute temperature anywhere in the northern hemisphere: −67.7°C. The northerly latitude of part of the USSR contributes to the severity of winter: much of the land is sub-Arctic, lying north of the 60th parallel. In addition, the great mountain barrier in the south excludes warm tropical air, but there is no such relief barrier in the north so that cold polar air has almost complete access to the great lowland areas of the country. Only in the far south, as for instance on the Black Sea coast of the Crimea and in the Transcaucasian area, are winter temperatures above freezing. Winter snowfall is deep, particularly in the west, produced by the occasional passage of depressions – which also bring brief thaws. But the duration of the snow cover is still long, varying from about 160 days at Leningrad to 80 days at Kiev. In the very high

Black Sea in developing anaerobic putrid lower layers. Future domestic and industrial demand for water is expected to grow, particularly given the tentative plans to expand the irrigated area from 17 million ha in 1976 to 40 million ha in 2000. Annual freshwater consumption in the long term could reach 800cu km, or 2.3 times that of 1979.

The demand for water induces two forms of water shortage: in Central Asia and southern Kazakhstan there is a direct deficit of water; while in the rivers and seas of the southern run-off slopes of the European USSR, although run-off exceeds long-term water use, the diminishing flows of water to inland water bodies necessitate flow augmentation if unacceptable environmental* effects of diminishing levels are to be halted. The Soviet response to problems of water resources* has been storage to reduce temporal variations in flow, and inter-basin transfer to aid deficient regions. By the end of the century artificial reservoirs are expected to yield 800cu km of usable storage (a 50 per cent increase on that currently available) and to permit control of one-fifth of total annual run-off.

North-south transfer within the European USSR has mainly used the Volga and Kama rivers as conduits to take waters from the north-flowing Sukhona, Onega, Pechora and Vychegda rivers. The complete implementation could yield some 60cu km annually which, although insufficient to reverse the environmental degradation of the Caspian Sea, would go a long way towards arresting this. There are proposed east-west transfers mainly from the Ob'-Irtysh system to the Kama in the north and to the north Aral Basin in the south; the Ob'-Irtysh Canal at Pavlodar already allows the irrigation of four million ha. A larger scheme to reverse the flow of the Tobol' by draining the Ob'-Irtysh at Tobol'sk is unlikely to be implemented as it would flood much of the oil and gas zones of Siberia.   *A.McD.*

KEY

Winter temperatures	Summer temperatures	Precipitation
∿ January isotherms	⎯ July isotherms	⎯ Mean annual precipitation (cm)
▨ Over 0°C	■ Over 32°C	▨ Over 80 cm
▨ Under −40°C	▨ Mountain areas	▨ 40–80 cm

Source: J.P. Cole and F.C. German, *A Geography of the USSR*, London, 1970

WINTER TEMPERATURES

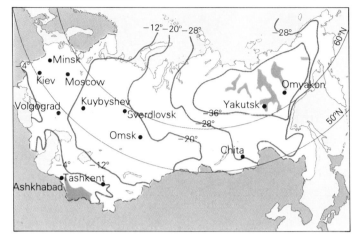

SUMMER TEMPERATURES

PRECIPITATION

Top: early winter in Kirov, in the central European RSFSR. Above: summer in the taiga south of Irkutsk

mountains of the south, the snow and ice last all the year, and in the Moscow region the Moskva and Oka rivers freeze before December and remain frozen until mid-April.

In spring the anticyclone weakens as the great land mass warms rapidly; the snow melts, the rivers thaw and by midsummer a broad belt of warmth with temperatures between 20°C and 16°C extends across the country from the west to mid-Siberia. The highest summer temperatures in the whole country occur in subtropical areas such as Georgia and in the hot dry areas of Central Asia where, for example, Tashkent records a July mean of over 25°C.

Summer is the season of highest precipitation, except in the Black Sea region where moist air from the Mediterranean produces mainly autumn and winter rains. The Atlantic is the principal source of precipitation, producing a central belt of moderate amount (400–600mm) from which there is a decrease eastwards, southwards and northwards. Summer rainfall in eastern Siberia is low and irregular but the driest region is the desert zone east of the Caspian Sea where less than 100mm are recorded. Summer monsoon rains occur in the Far East from the Pacific source region, but the mountainous relief of that area restricts the heaviest falls to maritime areas, minimizing their effect in eastern Siberia.   *W.N.*

Vegetation and soil

The vegetation and soil constitute two of the principal renewable natural resources★ of the USSR, as they form the basis of its agriculture★ and of the supply of many types of organic raw materials. The natural selection exerted by the environment since the end of the Pleistocene glaciations has resulted in a vegetation cover characterized by certain major plant types: soil and flora correspond to a north-south gradation in temperature, rainfall and other

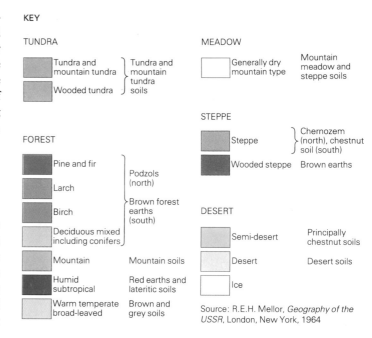

KEY

TUNDRA

Tundra and mountain tundra ⎫
Wooded tundra ⎬ Tundra and mountain tundra soils

FOREST

Pine and fir
Larch } Podzols (north)
Birch
Deciduous mixed including conifers } Brown forest earths (south)
Mountain — Mountain soils
Humid subtropical — Red earths and lateritic soils
Warm temperate broad-leaved — Brown and grey soils

MEADOW

Generally dry mountain type — Mountain meadow and steppe soils

STEPPE

Steppe } Chernozem (north), chestnut soil (south)
Wooded steppe — Brown earths

DESERT

Semi-desert — Principally chestnut soils
Desert — Desert soils
Ice

Source: R.E.H. Mellor, *Geography of the USSR*, London, New York, 1964

VEGETATION AND SOIL

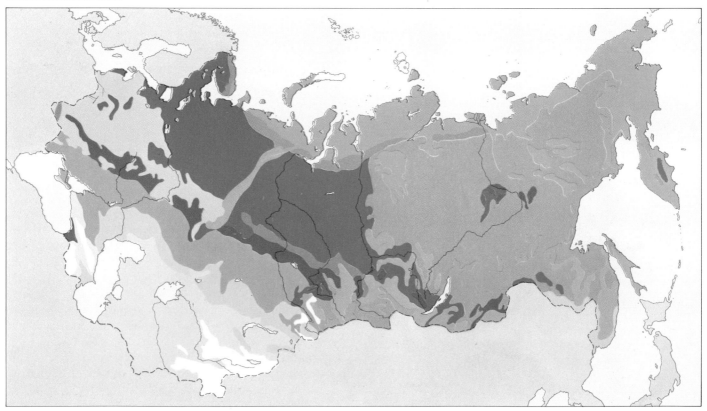

elements. In the Far North are the treeless cold deserts or tundras. Farther south, higher temperatures and a longer growing season have allowed the formation of great forested zones. South again, the forests are succeeded by steppes or temperate grasslands more suited to sub-humid conditions. The steppe grasslands in turn gradually yield to semi-desert and to desert. This succession is of course modified in mountainous areas.

Each of these vegetation belts is closely related to a particular type of soil, the formation of which depends upon five factors – the parent rock material, the climate,* the living organisms (vegetation and fauna*), the structure* of the land and the time involved in soil development. The interaction of these factors gives rise to distinctive soil layers, commonly considered as the surface soil, the subsoil and the substratum of rock material. Much of the Soviet Union is lowland, substantially uniform topographically and geologically. The influence of climate and vegetation upon soil formation is thus exceptionally clear, as the other physical factors of geology and relief which would have modified the climatic influence are generally constant. The soil types correspond closely to the zones of vegetation established by interacting climatic elements and form broad belts

generally parallel with each other except in mountain areas, where the more rapid variations in physical factors (climate and relief) produce a vertical zonation of soil and vegetation.

The tundra

Climate: Arctic; soil type: gleysols

The tundra or cold desert covers almost all the extreme north of the European and Siberian USSR but also extends southwards into mountainous areas such as the Far East. Winters are very long and cold, with short days so that the subsoil remains permanently frozen. The vegetation is confined to a shallow upper soil layer, the 'active layer', which thaws only during the brief two-month summer; usually it is waterlogged, as moisture cannot drain through the solidly frozen permafrost* beneath. The soil thus lacks air and hence bacteria and other agents of decomposition. An acid, peaty layer tends to form on the surface above a lower horizon of blue clay (termed the gleyed layer), but the layers are usually disturbed by frost action, which may also thrust stones upwards to the surface where they form circular or polygonal groups. The low fertility, scanty precipitation and brief growing season exclude all plants but mosses,

SCHEMATIC CLIMATE CHANGES AND VEGETATION AND SOIL PROFILES OF THE EUROPEAN USSR

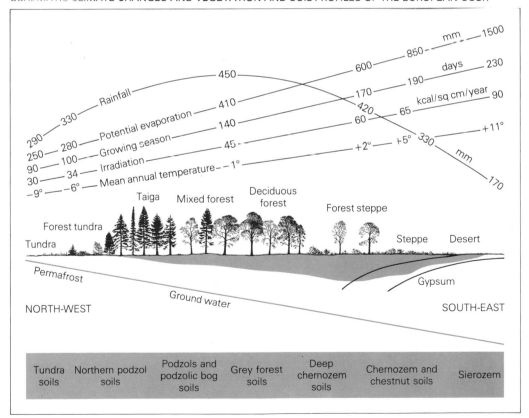

Source: after H. Walter, *Vegetation of the Earth in Relation to Climate and the Eco-physiological Conditions*, New York, 1973

lichens, perennial shrubs, grasses, sedges and other flowering herbs. Almost all plants are dwarfed, no taller than a few cm, commonly with a prostrate growth-habit, so that there is some protection from wind-chill or desiccation. Many herbs bear bright flowers in summer when growth of vegetation is rapid during the constant daylight, allowing the accumulation of food reserve for the renewal of growth in the following spring. This plant life supports an important and abundant animal population of which some are endangered by human pressures; some species are resident, others migrate into the tundra in spring. Cultivation is minimal but there are extensive natural pastures for reindeer-herding, an important meat-producing indus-try in the Soviet Far North.

The boreal forest or taiga

Climate: sub-Arctic; soil type: podzols

The tundra passes gradually southwards into a zone of transition: the wooded tundra or forest tundra, where groups of tree species alternate with areas of tundra. This margin between the forest proper and the tundra coincides approximately with the July isotherm of 10°C and extends southwards as the climate becomes more severe in the central Siberian region.

The boreal forest covers almost all the sub-Arctic northern part of the USSR and is the largest coniferous forest in the world, containing almost half the total world reserves of exploited softwood timber within a vast area extending from the international boundary in Europe to the shores of the Pacific Ocean in the east. Among the needle-leaf coniferous species, pine and spruce are the most valuable for industrial purposes and cover large areas of the west, in the European region, but larch dominates the forests of eastern Siberia and the Soviet Far East. However, the taiga area has also considerable stands of deciduous trees such as birch and aspen which commonly replace the conifers after forest fires or severe logging operations; it also has a rich fauna.

Although limited areas of the taiga have been cleared for pasture or crop production, neither its climate nor its soil favour agriculture. The soils are characteristic of coniferous vegetation and climatic conditions of low temperature and high humidity. Surface organic matter, composed of plant litter, forms a layer of raw, acid humus; the constant downward seepage of moisture causes a process of leaching (eluviation) whereby mineral nutrients from the surface layers are washed downwards, producing a sterile layer just under the surface; lower, an iron-pan often impedes drainage and restricts growth of plant roots.

Forest is often absent in areas of very poor drainage – depressions or flat plains near rivers where the excess moisture prevents tree growth but favours the formation of deep, acid peat from the remains of bog moss vegetation. Such bogs and marshes abound in the western part of the taiga, exemplified by the vast Vasyugan'e swamp

area of western Siberia. Some peat deposits are utilized for thermal electricity generation, and the drained areas are used for agriculture.

The mixed forest

Climate: cool temperate continental; soil type: cambisols

South and west of the taiga the central region of the European low-land consists of mixed forests comprising a mosaic of stands of coniferous trees, such as pine, and broad-leaf deciduous species (lime, oak, elm and maple), but as the latter species occupied the more fertile soils they have largely been cleared for agriculture. This region has a longer growing-season than that of the taiga, with a warm summer (Moscow's July mean is 19°C), but winters are long and snowfall is heavy.

The soils associated with the deciduous woodlands are leached but the podzolization is less pronounced than that of the taiga soils, and although acid they have a richer organic upper layer and are moderately fertile. The brown podzolic soils in the north of the region grade, southwards of Moscow and Gorky, into the grey forest clays and loams (orthic luvisols) of the broad-leaf forest and wooded steppe.

The steppes and wooded steppe

Climate: cool temperate continental; soil type: orthic luvisols

Southwards of a line running approximately from Kiev, Kursk, Tula to Ulyanovsk, as the climate becomes warmer and drier the vegetation changes to a transitional belt of forest-steppe and then to steppe or prairie grassland, today widely replaced by crops. These two zones constitute much of the country's most fertile farmland; they appear also east of the Urals, in Siberia, where they are narrower. The forest-steppe consists of predominantly oak woodland among areas of grassland, both much modified by agriculture. The oaks are the remaining fragments of the central European deciduous forest which has developed a fertile soil, the grey forest soil; originally formed beneath grassland, these soils are weakly leached in the upper layer but have a deep, nutrient-rich clayey lower layer.

With decreasing precipitation and increasing summer heat to the south-east, the forest-steppe is replaced by fertile steppe or prairie grassland. The natural vegetation of the steppe was a rich cover of grasses, sedges, legumes and other flowering herbs, densest in the moister north and known as the meadow steppe, more open in the drier south where the grasses form tussocks and there are fewer herb species. The soils are the famous chernozems (Russian 'black earths') named after the black or dark-grey organic matter of their upper layer, which was formed by the decay of the dense network of grass roots, together with the activity of the abundant soil fauna. Intense activity of bacteria in spring releases nitrogen, calcium and other plant nutrients, which remain close to the surface as leaching is counteracted by evaporation and transpiration. In the north, however, where precipitation is higher, some leaching does occur, producing a soil known as leached chernozem. The parent material is usually loess, a wind-blown deposit rich in lime. The natural fertility of these soils may be reduced by the frequency of droughts; they are also affected by wind or water erosion unless adequate plant cover is maintained – hence the policy of planting trees to serve as windbreaks or 'shelter-belts'.

Desert and semi-desert

Climate: arid continental; soil type: xerosols and yermosols

A further increase in aridity southwards is accompanied by less abundant vegetation and consequently a shallower humus layer in the soil. These features characterize the southern chernozems, which however, grade to the south into the chestnut soils (kastanozems), occurring in the extreme south of the Ukraine and extending eastwards north of the Caspian Sea into Siberia. Chestnut soils have an upper layer of dark-brown organic matter, formed by a plant cover of grasses, short herbs and small shrubs, the latter often salt-tolerant and drought-resistant.

The extreme south, occupied by the Central Asian republics, is an intensely dry region, very hot in summer and cold in winter with a low and irregular rainfall. The plant cover is scanty and there is much bare sand and rock. Many plants are either ephemerals, lying dormant until an occasional shower moistens the soil, or drought-resistant shrubs and grasses. The grey desert soils (xerosols), have a thin humus content, a layer of lime or gypsum close to the surface and may be fertile if irrigated. But large areas east of the Caspian Sea have only a loose cover of rock fragments, coarse sand or clay; these are raw mineral soils (yermosols) and often contain accumulations of salt, drawn up to the surface by evaporation of saline ground-water.

The subtropics

Climate: humid subtropical; soils: red podzolic (acrisols)

South of the main ranges of the Caucasus, largely in the Georgian SSR, the natural vegetation was broad-leaved warm-temperate forests, very rich in species and luxuriant in character, most of which was sustained by acrisols – acid, leached, well-drained soils reddish in colour due to the abundance of iron-oxides. These areas, when cleared of forest, yield crops of tea and citrus fruits. Eastwards in Azerbaijan, where the climate is drier and often colder in winter, in the lower Kura valley there is a natural steppe region with steppe or desert soils requiring irrigation for crop production.

The Caucasus

In the mountains there is a succession of vegetation and soils from the lower to the higher slopes, related to changes in temperature, precipitation and gradient; but these differ according to aspect, for the northern slopes are influenced by arid conditions and the

southern slopes by humid subtropical conditions. The warm-temperate forests on the Georgian side give place upwards to mountain coniferous forests on podzols, and above these are alpine meadows, rocky tundras which extend to the high snowfields, and glaciers. The much drier north slopes bear steppe vegetation and soils but with increasing precipitation there are mountain forests, and above them the alpine meadows and tundras extending upwards to the snow line – lower on this slope with its colder winter when snow lies longer.   *W.N.*

Fauna

Owing to the variety of environmental conditions encountered within the USSR and its great latitudinal extent, the fauna is extremely varied. In the high Arctic are the polar bear (*Thalarctos maritimus*), Arctic fox (*Alopex lagopus*), musk-ox (*Ovibos moschatus*), lemming (*Lemmus* and *Dicrostonyx* sp.), snowy owl (*Nyctea scandiaca*), raven (*Corvus corax*) and ptarmigan (*Lagopus lagopus*). The wild reindeer (*Rangifer tarandus*) of much of the tundra* has been crowded out from its grazing grounds by the domesticated reindeer and its numbers are decreasing. Elk (*Alces alces*), bear (*Ursus* sp.) and many small fur-bearing animals such as the sable (*Martes zibellina*), squirrel

The brown bear (*Ursus arctos*)

Manchurian tigers

(*Sciurus vulgaris* and *S. fuscombens*), fox (*Vulpes* sp.), marten (*Martes martes*) and ermine (*Mustela erminea*) frequent the taiga* in European Russia, Siberia and the Far East. The musk-rat, introduced from Canada in 1930, has adapted well to the swampy environment. The mixed forest zone of the European USSR has been much depleted of wild life by man. The roebuck (*Capreolus capreolus pygargus*), wolf, fox and squirrel are still common, but the brown bear and badger (*Meles meles*) less so. The beaver (*Castor fiber*) is found in the marshes of the west. Wild life in the extensively cultivated steppe-lands has been sadly depleted and many species such as wild horses, cattle and the marmot have been exterminated while others, such as the saiga antelope (*Saiga tatarica*), have migrated into the semi-desert regions. The dormouse, hamster, mole-rat, ground-squirrel remain, however, as do several species of birds including the great bustard or strepet (*Otis tarda*). The ground-squirrel (*Citellus fulvus, C. pigmaeus*), jumping mice and other rodents together with the gazelle (*Gazella subgutturosa*) frequent the semi-deserts and deserts. The Volga delta is no longer rich in wild-fowl but cormorants (*Phalacrocorax carbo*), geese and egrets are numerous. Mountain fauna is made up of a great variety of species. In the Causasus, for example, the wild life includes mountain goats (*Capra aegagrus, C. ibex caucasica, C. ibex severtzovi*), the chamois, red deer and roe-deer and mountain sheep. Northern taiga and southern species are found in the Far East of the country. These include the Manchurian and Caspian tigers (*Panthera tigris altaica* and *P. tigris virgata*), leopard (*Panthera pardus orientalis*), raccoon dog (*Nyctereutes procyonoides ussuriensis*), an endemic Manchurian hare (*Lepus mandschuricus*), elk, musk-deer, sable and brown bear. Environmental protection* legislation to cover the conservation of a wide range of species, including insects and soil fauna, was passed in 1981.   *G.M.H.*

Natural resources

With approximately 22.4 million sq km of territory, or about 16 per cent of the world's total land area, the USSR is richly endowed with natural resources. Not all, however, are well located with respect to the distribution of population and economic activity, nor have they always been utilized in the wisest possible manner. Only about 10.7 per cent of the territory, for example, can be used for arable farming, though the natural hayland (2.6 per cent), pasture (14.2 per cent) and the reindeer pastures of the north (14.8 per cent) are also of agricultural significance. Expansion of the arable areas at the expense of swamp and marsh (8.5 per cent of the territory) and of forest and scrubland (37.2 per cent) has had some limited success. The remaining 12.0 per cent of the territory is classified as unsuitable or unoccupied land. Despite the size of the country, the authorities became very concerned during the 1970s at the amount of agricultural land being taken for construction purposes; in the late 1960s, for example, over 100000ha of arable land per year were being lost to non-agricultural uses. More stringent legislation, however, has reduced this annual loss to about half that figure.

Forest reserves

The extensive forests constitute over one third of the world's total forest area accessible for exploitation. The actual forested area is some 747 million ha, representing 79000 million cu m of timber; of

this 84 per cent is coniferous, and about 80 per cent of the annual cut comes from the boreal forest zone of the north. By far the greater part (515 million ha) lies in the remoter Asiatic part of the country, although here the harsher climate* produces a thinner stand and a much slower annual growth rate. The timber industry is oriented towards the more accessible forests, and 70 per cent of all timber is classified as mature or over-age.

Rich resources of fauna* exist: of the 125–130 thousand known species found, special importance attaches to commercial land game, over 40 species of which live mainly in the forest zone (marten, sable, squirrel, lynx, wolverine, ermine, beaver and others). The tundra* (polar fox and northern reindeer) and taiga* together provide about 80 per cent of all the furs and 90 per cent of the forest game.

Water resources

One of the most important of the USSR's resource problems is that of water. Although receiving about 10 per cent of the world's precipitation, and possessing about one-eighth of the world's surface run-off, the USSR's water resources are extremely unevenly distributed. Considerable areas suffer from an over-abundance of water, especially in the forest zone. Peat bog, however, makes a small but important contribution to the energy* supply – the USSR estimates claim 60 per cent of the world's peat resources. A much greater problem for the authorities is aridity: 30 per cent of the territory, especially in Central Asia and the southern European area, has only 2 per cent of the total surface water resources. Of the annual surface run-off, 62 per cent is lost to the Arctic Ocean and 20 per cent to the Pacific, leaving only 18 per cent, corresponding with the internal and Atlantic drainage* basins, available for 80 per cent of the population. Water shortages are common not only in the southern regions, but also in many industrialized and urbanized areas further north. Though it is estimated that only some 20 per cent of the reliable annual surface run-off is currently utilized, inter-basin transfers are becoming increasingly necessary if water shortages are to be avoided.

Minerals

The Soviet Union provides for most of its own needs in minerals claiming, for example, to possess half of the world's reserves of iron ore. Much of its metallic deposits are in convenient locations: three-quarters of its iron is in the European area, including the Urals, and the same is true of manganese (of which the USSR has the world's greatest reserves), chromite, tungsten, titanium and molybdenum, although other ferro-alloys, especially nickel and cobalt, are in remote areas of the north. Information on non-ferrous minerals is scarce, but the USSR appears to be well endowed in copper, lead, zinc, gold,* silver, diamonds, asbestos, mercury and antimony; supplies of bauxite and tin appear to be less abundant.

Energy resources

Most of the country's energy* resources are found in the eastern part but 75 per cent of the population and 80 per cent of industry (both in fixed assets and value of output) are located in the west. The east,

Left: log-rafting on Lake Onega, Karelia. Right: open-cast iron ore extraction at Kounrad, Kazakhstan

for example, has 90 per cent of Soviet coal reserves; estimates suggest that the country possesses one-third of the world's proven and almost two-thirds of potential reserves, of which 66 per cent is hard coal. The USSR also boasts 11.4 per cent of the world's hydroelectric power potential with 54 per cent in Siberia, 20 per cent in Central Asia and Kazakhstan and 18 per cent in the European area. Much of this potential, especially that in the east, is unrealizable at present. Reserves of hydrocarbons are also believed to be very extensive, although once again distribution is very much oriented towards the east. If the resources of East Siberia and the Far East are excluded, as being relatively much less explored and far less exploited than the deposits elsewhere in the country, 58 per cent of hydrocarbon resources are located in West Siberia (oil and gas), 22 per cent in Central Asia (gas), 10 per cent in the Volga-Urals zone (oil), 6 per cent in the southern Caspian area (oil) and 4 per cent in the south of the European part of the country (gas).   *D.J.B.S.*

KEY

	Asbestos		Antimony
Ab	Asbestos	Sb	Antimony
Au	Gold	Sn	Tin
Cu	Copper	U	Uranium
D	Diamonds	Zn	Zinc
F	Fluorspar		
Hg	Mercury		
M	Mica		
Pb	Lead		

Source: after P. E. Lydolph, *Geography of the USSR*, Elkhart Lake, 1979

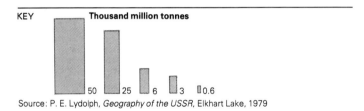

KEY   **Thousand million tonnes**

50   25   6   3   0.6

Source: P. E. Lydolph, *Geography of the USSR*, Elkhart Lake, 1979

KEY

■ Hard coal deposit and mining centre   ▢ Brown coal deposit and mining centre

Numbers next to coal-fields represent estimated production costs in roubles per standard tonne (7 million kcal)
Source: P. E. Lydolph, *Geography of the USSR*, Elkhart Lake, 1979

IRON ORE RESERVES

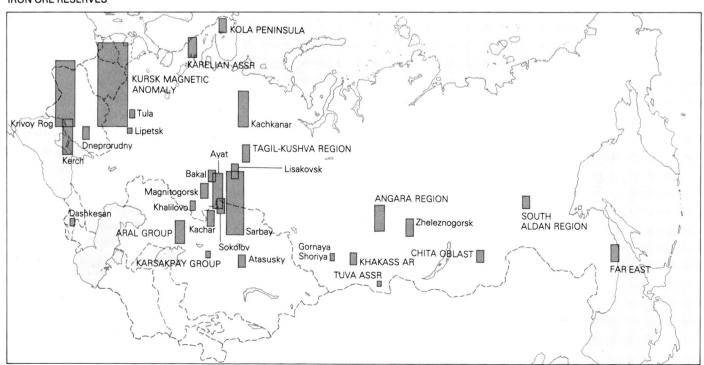

LOCATION OF MINERALS

COAL AND LIGNITE BASINS AND MINING LOCATIONS

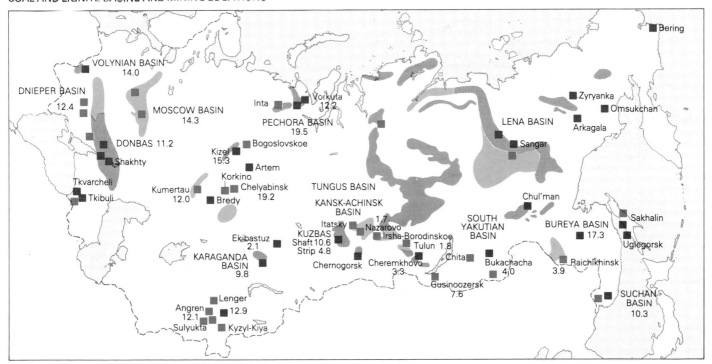

KNOWN OIL- AND GAS-BEARING SEDIMENTARY AREAS, OIL- AND GAS-FIELDS AND MAIN PIPELINES

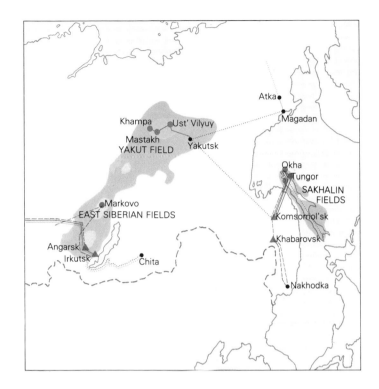

KEY

International boundary	Oil trunk pipelines under construction
Known sedimentary areas	Oil trunk pipelines planned
Main oil areas	Oil products pipelines
Main gas areas	Oil products pipelines under construction
Oil-fields	Oil products pipelines planned
Gas-fields	Natural-gas trunk pipelines
Oil refineries	Natural-gas trunk pipelines under construction
Oil trunk pipelines	Natural-gas trunk pipelines planned

KEY   **Kilometres of gullies per square kilometre**

0–0.2 km	0.5–1.0 km
0.2–0.5 km	Mountainous areas

Source: P. R. Pryde, *Conservation in the Soviet Union*, Cambridge, 1972

Environmental protection

Despite central planning★ and ownership of the major means of production, the Soviet Union has not avoided environmental disruption, probably because of a commitment to rapid economic growth, a failure to put a price on such resources as water and land, and lack of coordination and foresight. Also important has been a belief, especially under Stalin,★ in the inexhaustible nature of many natural resources★ and in man's ability to modify nature to suit his own purposes. Environmental disruption in the USSR takes many forms, among them pollution, waste and errors of planning.

Pollution is a serious problem in many industrialized areas though the USSR has so far escaped the worst aspects of air pollution associated with the use of the automobile; 450 cities have air-pollution monitoring, and legislation for cleaner air took effect in 1981. Rivers★ and inland water bodies, on the other hand, are frequently badly polluted in industrial regions. In 1980 the All-Union Research Institute for Water Conservation completed a study of 15 seas and lakes and 26 large rivers, and put forward proposals for pollution control.

The waste of natural resources greatly concerns the authorities, especially since remoter and more expensive resources are now having to be developed as the more accessible are exhausted; cam-

EXTENT OF GULLY EROSION IN THE WESTERN USSR

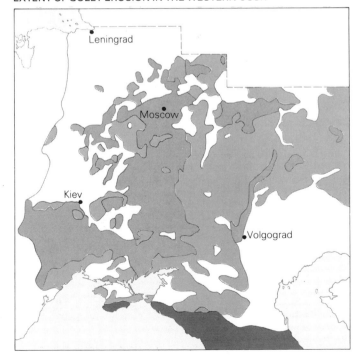

paigns have particularly been directed at the saving of energy* and water. While consumer waste is as yet less rampant than in Western economies, it causes some concern.

The planned modification of the environment frequently has negative as well as positive consequences – for example, the loss of agricultural land to hydroelectric power schemes. More worrying are those manifold negative consequences which seemingly result from a lack of foresight by planners and engineers: reductions in the water table and forest fires caused by drainage schemes; secondary salinization of the soil produced by unwise irrigation techniques; dust storms and declining water run-off resulting from the cultivation of some semi-arid areas. Even more serious are wind and gully erosion in the 'black earth' regions produced by careless methods of cultivation (5–20 per cent of the soils of these areas have been seriously affected). The gradual contraction of the Caspian and Aral seas in consequence of the damming of their river supplies and the withdrawal of water for irrigation, domestic and industrial uses has attracted worldwide attention.

Although decrees on the conservation of the environment date back to the earliest years of Soviet power, it was not until the late 1950s and early 1960s that concern at the environmental consequences of industrialization became widespread. Between 1957 and 1964 all 15 Union Republics adopted comprehensive laws on the management and conservation of natural resources. Various sections of republican criminal codes have also been adapted to provide penalties for infringements of conservation laws; Communist Party* pronouncements and numerous government decrees have publicized certain aspects. Of special significance have been the legislative bases adopted for the management of land (1968), water (1970), minerals (1975) and forest (1977) which have provided the framework for further legislation. Natural landscapes are increasingly protected in the growing number of nature preserves and reserves,* and since the 1970s in the national parks; in 1974 endangered species of plants and animals were listed in the 'Red Book' – *Krasnaya kniga* – and international collaboration in ecological research* has increased.

Control over conservation exists at many levels. An All-Union State Committee for Hydrometeorology and Environmental Control was established in 1978 and the USSR Ministry of Agriculture has long had a Chief Administration for the Conservation of Nature, the Hunting Economy and Nature Reserves. Permanent commissions on conservation exist in both chambers of the Supreme Soviet, and the Union Republics have state committees on conservation, although their detailed roles appear to vary. Scientific and advisory work is undertaken by the USSR Academy of Sciences* and its various agencies; the Society for the Conservation of Nature, founded in 1924, has an important advisory role. The State Committee for Science and Technology (established 1965) of the USSR Council of Ministers has a subsidiary council for complex problems of the

natural environment and rational use of natural resources.

The planning of natural resource use is within the competence of the State Planning Committee (Gosplan), which has a section dealing with environmental protection. In the early 1970s, ministries and organizations began to include conservation measures in their annual plans, subject to Gosplan's approval, and Latvia drew up the first complex plan for use and conservation of natural resources in 1975. The eleventh Five-year Plan (to 1985) proposes to treble capital investment in environmental protection. Conservation is the responsibility of the agency concerned with each branch – at the federal level such as the State Committee on Forestry, the Ministry of Reclamation and Water Resources, the Ministry of Fisheries, and the Ministry of Agriculture, and at the republican level the Ministry of River Navigation. Local soviets* also have a limited conservation mandate within their administrative districts. In conservation, as elsewhere, the detailed competence of the various authorities is not always clear; legislation and reform in the 1970s have been devoted with notable success to a clarification of roles, a tightening of control, and an improvement in agencies of inspection. *D.J.B.S.*

The settlement of northern Eurasia

The settlement of northern Eurasia began with the 'Neolithic revolution', which introduced agriculture and the necessity of permanent residence. About the start of the 5th millennium BC the first agriculture appeared on present-day Soviet territory, in the extreme south of Turkmenistan. From here agriculture, based on irrigation and settled societies with early urban forms, spread to the river valleys of Central Asia. A second penetration of Neolithic agriculture and a settled way of life came into European Russia from the Danubian lands, the Tripol'e culture of the 3rd millennium BC. Thereafter a succession of agricultural societies, living in permanent villages, occupied the forest-steppe* zone and gradually penetrated northwards into the zone of mixed forest.* Last in this succession were the East Slav* tribes, who had spread through the mixed forest of European Russia by the 6th century AD. The open steppes north of the Black Sea remained the home of successive nomadic* peoples, although some, notably the Khazars,* farmed and founded towns.

The Slavs steadily colonized the forests; slash-and-burn cultivation supported small village kinship communities, linked into tribal groupings. Near the southern forest margin, the frontier with the

KEY

⊡— Present-day USSR boundaries   ⊞ Defensive lines (with date)

Design by R. A. French

DEFENSIVE LINES ON RUSSIA'S EXPANDING FRONTIERS OF SETTLEMENT, 1550–1800

steppe peoples, the villages were characteristically fortified with ditches and earthen banks, topped by wooden palisades. Some of these fortified places, the seats of chieftains, grew into towns as tribute from the adjacent regions provided surpluses for craft manufacture and trade. The formation of the Kievan★ state in the 9th century stimulated the processes of forest clearance for agriculture, the establishment of new villages and urban foundation. By 1238 there were nearly 300 Russian towns, each focused around a fortified kremlin or citadel; Russian village settlement extended north to the Gulf of Finland and east to the middle Volga.

The Tatar★ invasion long retarded Russian settlement, but as Tatar power declined colonization was resumed. At first movement was northwards into the largely unpopulated basins of the White and Kara seas, away from the Tatar threat. Monasteries,★ such as that at Archangel, often formed the nuclei of new towns, but severities of climate★ and soil★ conditions greatly limited rural settlement. In the mid-16th century Ivan the Terrible's★ defeat of the Tatars of Kazan' and Astrakhan' opened the way southwards and eastwards to Russian expansion.★ The southern frontier of Russian colonization into the steppe was protected by successive, lengthy defensive lines from Tatar raids; many towns began existence as fortresses guarding Muscovy's★ southern flank. The rich 'black earth' soil encouraged intensive agricultural settlement in villages strung out along the steppe rivers; much larger than the hamlets of the forests to the north, these villages spawned daughter villages in side valleys, as settlement intensified after the Russians reached the Black Sea coast in the 18th century. Often Germans★ and other foreigners were settled by the government in large 'plantation' villages of regular layout, while private landowners transferred serfs to their new, extensive steppe estates.

Eastwards, Yermak's Cossacks in the later 16th century had opened the way to colonize Siberia. In explorations★ motivated initially by the wealth of furs, Russian settlers had reached the Pacific by the mid-17th century. Wooden forts guarding the long river routes eastward rapidly acquired town status as centres of the fur trade, but it was only in the 18th and even more 19th centuries that there was large-scale agricultural settlement of more favourable areas in southern Siberia by official colonists, runaway serfs and persecuted religious★ groups.

The 19th century saw the tardy start to industrialization★ in Russia and, with it, numerous urban foundations based on manufacturing. In the central region earlier serf workshop centres became textile towns; on the Donbas coal-field a group of mining and metallurgical towns emerged. The ancient Baltic ports, important since Hanseatic times, were now rivalled by new Black Sea ports. Serf emancipation★ was decreed in 1861 but it was only with the 1906 Stolypin★ agrarian reforms that rural settlement began to undergo a major change. Peasants could opt out of common-field cultivation, enclose their

own holdings and build their house on the enclosure. The traditional, tightly nucleated Russian village began to be replaced in some areas (notably in the Baltic lands★) by widely dispersed individual farmsteads. However, before this process had much effect, the 1917 Revolution★ and the collectivization★ of agriculture after 1928 halted and even reversed it. The Soviet government (in its General Scheme of Settlement★) has actively pursued a policy of consolidating small, rural settlements into larger places, provided with all modern services, where the Marxist★ aim of abolishing differences between urban and rural living standards might be achieved. Ultimately it is hoped to reduce the 469 253 rural settlements of 1970 to only 175 000. Meanwhile the rapid pace of Soviet industrialization has in 60 years created more new towns than the whole pre-revolutionary period and has developed new industrial areas, especially in Asiatic parts of the country.   *R.A.F.*

Mortality and fertility

In the absence of really large-scale immigration or emigration,★ population growth since the 1917 Revolution★ has been almost entirely a product of natural increase – the balance between births and deaths. Over the past 63 years, the total population has increased by nearly two-thirds, rising from 163 million in 1917 to 265 million in 1980, a magnitude exceeded only by that of China (900 million) and of India (600 million) and some 40 million greater than that of the USA (220 million). In both relative and absolute terms, growth has been appreciably more rapid than in the rest of Europe over the same period, suggesting the persistence of a certain demographic vitality among the Soviet population. Yet, although growth over-all has been rapid by European standards, it has been subject to pronounced fluctuations and has been sometimes checked by disasters, in particular the civil war,★ collectivization★ in the early 1930s and, above all, the Second World War,★ to which at least 20 million additional deaths may be attributed. Without these events, the Soviet population would by 1980 have been well over 300 million. Superimposed on these fluctuations in growth rates has been a long-term trend towards slower population growth, particularly marked since about 1960 when the gap between the USSR and other European

KEY

Urban

Rural

Years for which no data have been published

Source: *Narodnoe khozyaystvo SSSR*, various years

NUMBER OF BIRTHS AND DEATHS PER ANNUM

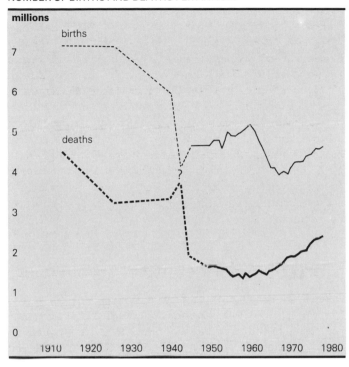

ANNUAL EXCESS OF BIRTHS OVER DEATHS

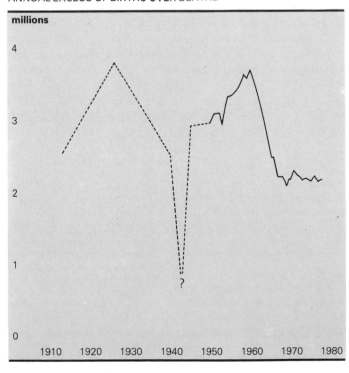

BIRTH AND DEATH RATES

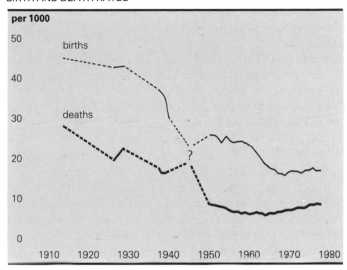

NATURAL INCREASE RATE

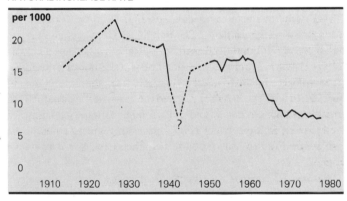

URBAN, RURAL AND TOTAL POPULATION

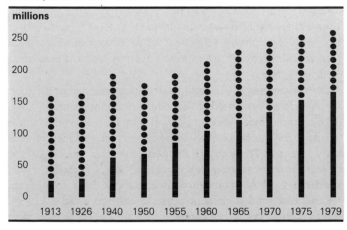

states in this respect has become much narrower. Finally, throughout the whole period since 1917 there have been marked regional variations in population growth-rates – partly the result of migration★ movements but also of regional differences in the rate of natural increase, which became increasingly pronounced in the 1960s and 1970s. While information on fertility and mortality for much of the Soviet period is fragmentary (birth-rate and death-rate figures have been regularly published only since 1950) general trends may be distinguished.

Before the First World War both birth- and death-rates were well above the European average. With mortality declining more rapidly than fertility, the natural-increase rate accelerated, reaching 1.6 per cent in 1913. After the upheavals of 1914–21, when mortality was exceptionally high and fertility much reduced, pre-war trends were re-established and natural increase rose to a peak of just over 2 per cent in 1926. Thereafter, fertility and mortality continued their slow decline, but the rate of natural increase remained above 1.5 per cent per year throughout the inter-war years; during 1917–40, the population increased by nearly 20 per cent, from 163 to 194 million.

The Second World War produced a massive rise in mortality accompanied by a reduced birth-rate. The population declined by about 8 per cent during the 1940s, and the pre-war level was not achieved until 1955. The early post-war years saw a return to relatively high fertility – the birth-rate remained above 25 per 1000 throughout the 1950s – and exceptionally low mortality due partly to the population's youthful age structure and partly to improvements in standards of medical care,★ although infant mortality remains high and has been rising in the 1970s. In 1950, 80.7 of children below the age of one year died for every 1000 born alive; at its lowest in 1971 the rate had fallen to 22.9. Although official data were not published after 1974, when the rate had reached 27.9, some age-specific death rates were published until 1976, for which year a rate of 31.1 could be calculated (more than double the 14 of the UK and the 15 of the USA). The rise in infant deaths may well be influenced by the high rate of abortion.

The 1960s saw a dramatic decline in the birth rate from 24.9 per 1000 in 1960 to 17.0 per 1000 in 1969, due largely to a shortage of women of child-bearing age as the small birth cohorts of the war years entered the reproductive age-groups, but at the same time an increasing proportion of Soviet married couples were adopting the Western 'small family habit'; both abortion (particularly) and contraception★ contributed to this reduction in family size.★ In the 1920s and early 1930s, abortion was freely available to Soviet women and was the most widely used method of birth control. In 1936, however, legal abortion became much more difficult to obtain and increasing numbers resorted to illegal operations until 1955 when the law was relaxed and the number of legal abortions increased enormously – probably exceeding the number of live births since

1960; it is not uncommon for a woman to have had four or five abortions. In the 1970s the supply and quality of contraceptives has been improved in an attempt to reduce the number of abortions, while family allowances★ and other services for mothers and children have been increased to encourage population growth.

During the 1970s the birth-rate has slightly increased (18.3 per 1000 in 1979) due entirely to the larger supply of young parents from the large birth cohorts of the late 1940s and early 1950s, but the death-rate simultaneously edged slowly upwards owing to the greater proportion of elderly people (10.1 per 1000 in 1979); the natural-increase rate has thus remained stable at 8–9 per 1000 – well above the growth-rates of Western Europe, where in several countries population growth came to a halt in the early 1970s.

These recent changes in fertility and mortality rates have caused a marked decline in the growth of the population – the annual excess of births over deaths reached a peak of 3.7 million in 1960 but by 1969 it had fallen to 2.1 million, and was the same in 1979 – but have not affected all sections of the population to the same degree; pronounced regional contrasts in the rate of natural increase are associated primarily with the ethnic factor. Fertility decline, while affecting all ethnic groups to some extent, has been much greater among the Russians and other European groups than among many minorities – the Muslim★ groups of Central Asia still have very high birth-rates. Birth- and death-rate data are published on a regional and not an ethnic basis, but the influence of the ethnic factor is clear. In the RSFSR in 1978, the birth-rate was only 18.2 and the death-rate 9.7 per 1000 and thus the rate of natural increase was only 8.5 per 1000. At the other extreme, the Tadzhik SSR rates were 37.5, 8.3 and 29.2 per 1000. The effect of this differential fertility will be to raise the share of Union Republics with Muslim traditions to one-quarter of the Soviet

A Turkmen 'Heroine Mother' with her husband and 16 children

POPULATION OF THE USSR AT CENSUS DATES

Union Republics and their constituent territorial administrative divisions[1]	15 January 1970	17 January 1979	1970–1979
	thousand	thousand	percentage increase
Russian Soviet Federative			
Socialist Republic (RSFSR):	130 090	137 552	6
Kaliningrad	732	806	10
North-west:	12 160	13 275	9
Leningrad oblast	1 436	1 519	6
Leningrad city	3 950	4 588	16
Archangel:	1 402	1 467	5
Nenets AA	39	47	21
Vologda	1 296	1 310	1
Murmansk	799	965	21
Novgorod	722	722	0
Pskov	876	850	−3
Karelian ASSR	714	736	3
Komi ASSR	965	1 118	16
Central:	27 663	28 947	5
Bryansk	1 582	1 507	−5
Vladimir	1 512	1 581	5
Ivanovo	1 338	1 321	−1
Kalinin	1 718	1 649	−4
Kaluga	995	1 007	1
Kostroma	871	804	−8
Moscow oblast	5 774	6 360	10
Moscow city	7 071	8 011	13
Orel	931	892	−4
Ryazan'	1 412	1 362	−4
Smolensk	1 106	1 121	1
Tula	1 953	1 907	−2
Yaroslavl'	1 400	1 425	2
Volga-Vyatka:	8 348	8 343	0
Gorky	3 683	3 695	0
Kirov	1 726	1 662	−4
Mari ASSR	685	703	3
Mordvin ASSR	1 030	990	−4
Chuvash ASSR	1 224	1 293	6
Central Black Earth region:	7 997	7 797	−3
Belgorod	1 261	1 305	4
Voronezh	2 527	2 478	−2
Kursk	1 474	1 399	−5
Lipetsk	1 224	1 225	0
Tambov	1 511	1 390	−8
Volga:	18 377	19 393	6
Astrakhan'	868	915	5
Volgograd	2 324	2 475	7

POPULATION OF THE USSR AT CENSUS DATES (*continued*)

Union Republics and their constituent territorial administrative divisions[1]	15 January 1970	17 January 1979	1970–1979
	thousand	thousand	percentage increase
RSFSR, Volga (*continued*)			
Kuybyshev	2 752	3 093	12
Penza	1 536	1 504	−2
Saratov	2 454	2 560	4
Ul'yanovsk	1 225	1 269	4
Bashkir ASSR	3 819	3 848	1
Kalmyk ASSR	268	293	9
Tatar ASSR	3 131	3 426	10
North Caucasus:	14 285	15 487	8
Krasnodar kray:	4 511	4 814	7
Adyge AR	386	404	5
Stavropol' kray:	2 306	2 539	10
Karachay-Cherkess AR	345	369	7
Rostov	3 832	4 081	7
Dagestan ASSR	1 429	1 627	14
Kabardino-Balkar ASSR	589	675	15
North Osetin ASSR	553	597	8
Chechen-Ingush ASSR	1 065	1 154	8
Urals:	15 184	15 568	3
Kurgan	1 085	1 080	−1
Orenburg	2 050	2 089	2
Perm':	3 024	3 011	0
Komi-Permyak AA	212	173	−18
Sverdlovsk	4 319	4 454	3
Chelyabinsk	3 289	3 440	5
Udmurt ASSR	1 417	1 494	5
West Siberia:	12 110	12 959	7
Altay kray:	2 670	2 675	0
Gorno-Altay AR	168	172	2
Kemerovo	2 918	2 958	1
Novosibirsk	2 505	2 618	5
Omsk	1 824	1 955	7
Tomsk	786	866	10
Tyumen':	1 407	1 887	34
Khanty-Mansi AA	272	569	109
Yamalo-Nenets AA	80	158	98
East Siberia:	7 464	8 158	9
Krasnoyarsk kray:	2 962	3 198	8
Taymyr AA	38	44	16
Khakass AR	446	500	12
Evenki AA	13	16	23
Irkutsk:	2 314	2 560	11
Ust'ordinsky Buryat AA	146	133	−9

Population

POPULATION OF THE USSR AT CENSUS DATES (*continued*)

Union Republics and their constituent territorial administrative divisions[1]	15 January 1970	17 January 1979	1970–1979
	thousand		*percentage increase*
RSFSR, East Siberia (*continued*)			
Chita	1 145	1 233	8
Aginsky Buryat AA	66	69	5
Buryat ASSR	812	901	11
Tuva ASSR	231	266	15
Far East:	5 780	6 819	18
Primorsky kray	1 722	1 978	15
Khabarovsk kray:	1 346	1 565	16
Jewish AR	173	190	10
Amur	793	938	18
Kamchatka:	287	378	32
Koryak AA	31	34	10
Magadan:	352	466	32
Chukot AA	101	133	32
Sakhalin	616	655	6
Yakut ASSR	664	839	26
Ukrainian SSR	47 136	49 757	6
Donets-Dnieper:	20 059	21 045	5
Dnepropetrovsk	3 344	3 640	9
Donetsk	4 894	5 160	5
Zaporozhe	1 775	1 946	10
Kirovograd	1 260	1 251	−1
Voroshilovgrad	2 749	2 788	1
Poltava	1 706	1 741	2
Sumy	1 505	1 463	−3
Kharkov	2 826	3 056	8
South-west:	20 694	21 578	4
Vinnitsa	2 132	2 046	−4
Volynia	975	1 016	4
Zhitomir	1 626	1 597	−2
Transcarpathia	1 057	1 154	9
Ivano-Frankovsk	1 250	1 333	7
Kiev city	1 632	2 144	31
Kiev oblast	1 836	1 924	5

[1]Oblast except where otherwise stated

POPULATION OF THE USSR AT CENSUS DATES (*continued*)

Union Republics and their constituent territorial administrative divisions[1]	15 January 1970	17 January 1979	1970–1979
	thousand		*percentage increase*
Ukrainian SSR, South-west (*continued*)			
L'vov	2 428	2 583	6
Rovno	1 048	1 121	7
Ternopol'	1 153	1 163	1
Khmel'nitsky	1 616	1 558	−4
Cherkass	1 536	1 547	1
Chernigov	1 560	1 502	−4
Chernovtsy	845	890	5
South:	6 383	7 134	12
Crimea	1 814	2 184	20
Nikolaev	1 148	1 242	8
Odessa	2 390	2 544	6
Kherson	1 031	1 164	11
Uzbek SSR:	11 963	15 391	29
Karakalpak ASSR	702	904	29
Kazakh SSR	12 850	14 685	14
Belorussian SSR	9 003	9 559	6
Azerbaijan SSR:	5 111	6 028	18
Nakhichevan ASSR	202	239	18
Nagorno-Karabakh AR	149	161	8
Georgian SSR:	4 688	5 016	7
Abkhaz ASSR	487	506	4
Adzhar ASSR	310	355	15
South Osetin AR	100	98	−2
Moldavian SSR	3 572	3 948	11
Tadzhik SSR:	2 900	3 801	31
Gorno-Badakhshan AR	98	127	30
Kirgiz SSR	2 933	3 529	20
Lithuanian SSR	3 129	3 399	9
Armenian SSR	2 493	3 031	22
Turkmen SSR	2 158	2 759	28
Latvian SSR	2 365	2 521	7
Estonian SSR	1 357	1 466	8
Total USSR	241 748	262 442	9

Source: *Narodnoe khozyaystvo SSSR v 1970 godu*, Moscow, 1971; *Narodnoe khozyaystvo SSR v 1978 godu*, Moscow, 1979

population by the end of the century. Demographic projections prepared by the Foreign Demographic Analysis Division of the US Bureau of the Census in 1977 forecast a rise in the population of Central Asia, Kazakhstan and Azerbaijan from 38.35 million on 1 July 1970 to 73.63 million in the year 2000 – an increment of 92 per cent. Since the 1970 total includes all residents of the Union Republics, a more accurate comparison may be with the 35.08 million recorded at the 1970 census as having the mother-tongue of an ethnic group with a Muslim tradition. The US projection of the total Soviet population showed an increase from 242.76 million to 308.89 million, or only 27 per cent. As a consequence, those living in Union Republics which have a Muslim tradition would constitute 24 per cent of the total, against 16 per cent in 1970 and 18 per cent at the 1979 census.   *J.D.*

Migration and emigration

'Russia's history is the history of a country colonizing itself', wrote the historian V. O. Klyuchevsky (1841–1911). In the 18th and 19th centuries Russian eastward expansion* paralleled the American westward thrust. As Napoleon was entering Moscow the Russian Empire was actually establishing a small settlement in northern California. The colonies on the west coast of North America were abandoned by the mid-19th century, but Russian and Soviet expansion continued into the present century. By about 1960 the boundary between the settled core and the sparsely populated periphery of the USSR was stabilizing but the Soviet population is more mobile than ever. Over 12 million people (about 5 per cent of the population) change their place of residence every year, effecting a gradual redistribution within the settled zone.

Inter-regional redistribution

Migration statistics are collected in towns by the internal passport* departments of the militia* (where migrants are required to register), but are published only for the 19 large economic regions of the USSR and much regional detail is consequently lost or obscured. Without access to the original data we have to resort to an elaborate indirect method in which population change between census dates (1959 and 1970 in this case) is assumed to be the net result of migration after the effects of mortality are allowed for. This procedure shows that inter-oblast migration over the period 1959–70 resulted in the net relocation of about 8 million persons (excluding children born during the period). If movements offset by others in the opposite direction were to be counted – that is, the gross movement – probably some 40 million were affected. The geography of the migration shows the southward drift of the population, the enormous and isolated growth

of Moscow oblast and those containing the cities of Leningrad, Kiev and Minsk, and the relative unimportance of Siberia in the over-all population redistribution. None of these three observations can be said to conform with the official view of how the Soviet population distribution should be changing: the southward movements have tended to exacerbate the problem of surplus labour in regions such as the North Caucasus and Central Asia; the growth of the three largest cities has been expressly deplored and fought; and the massive move to the east envisioned by Khrushchev* has simply not materialized.

The era of step-by-step migration from village to small town to large town within a relatively small area is ending and inter-urban movement is now responsible for most changes in regional distribution. Migrants are no longer village youths for whom even the most meagre urban amenities represent luxury – they are urbanites from birth and their movement is often motivated by a search for a more sophisticated life.

In contrast to the thousands of commodities in the Soviet economy which are centrally allocated, labour is not. Since migration is largely not subject to direction by the authorities except as regards industrial location and expansion (and therefore new jobs), it is impossible to say that the geographical distribution of labour* is planned. During the years of rapid industrialization* before the Second World War there were generally effective controls to individual movement (through the internal passport system, for example), but most have been abolished or weakened and the Soviet citizen is largely free to move at will. Between the censuses of 1959 and 1970 more than three million moved from north to south, but only a few between east and west. Central Asia and Kazakhstan have gained rather more net migrants than were lost from Siberia and the Far East. This southward movement was not centrally planned and may be considered irrational as regards distribution of economic activity, but it reflects the individual residence preferences of the migrant population in the atmosphere of thaw after Stalin.* The RSFSR, where roughly two-thirds of Soviet industrial fixed capital is located, lost over two million migrants to other republics, the capitals of which attracted large numbers.

The five large zones of net loss during 1959–70 are contiguous and form a broad belt in the middle and northern latitudes of the USSR. The negative pole in the Soviet migration field is in the Urals and Upper Volga zone. Losses from the Urals and Siberia reflect the weak development of residential and social amenities; many settlements resemble 'company towns' where housing, shopping and cultural facilities depend on the largesse of the controlling industrial ministry.* The losses in European Russia were largely absorbed by Moscow and Leningrad oblasts (one in seven net migrants in 1959–70 went to Moscow oblast), but there was still a net outflow of some 800 000 to more southerly regions. As in the 19th century, emigration continues from the Western Ukraine and Belorussia.

A quayside group of Russian migrants at the Pacific port of Nakhodka

The positive pole of migration attraction is possibly in the North Caucasus, which might be compared to California in migrant-drawing power and in climatic and social attractiveness; by Russian standards, it has a pleasant, warm climate* and its impressive scenery attracts many Soviet tourists. The southern fringe of the European USSR gained nearly 1.3 million migrants. The Southern Ukraine attracted migrants both to its developed industrial base in the Don Basin and the Dnieper Bend and to the climatic and physical amenity of the Crimea. The migration of nearly 900 000 into Kazakhstan was a source of some satisfaction to economic planners: new mineral and fuel resources* are being exploited and cities have sprung up in the wilderness. The Volga zone, the centre of an oil-boom in the 1950s, has since sustained its growth because of its central location and environmental attraction, but prospects for the new oil zones of the 1970s in West Siberia are not as promising.

The net migration shown (in thousands of persons) took place from one region to another between the censuses of 1959 and 1970 of the population (urban and rural) aged 10–79 years in 1970. Thus, for example, balancing inward against outward migration, 286 000 moved into the Baltic region between 1959 and 1970, and 182 000 left Belorussia. These regions do not in all cases conform to the Soviet official regional divisions.   Design by Ann Helgeson

INTER-REGIONAL MIGRATION, 1959–70

BELORUSSIA −182

BALTIC +286

SOUTH UKRAINE +1274

WEST UKRAINE −526

EUROPEAN RUSSIA −802

NORTH CAUCASUS +834

VOLGA +525

URALS and UPPER VOLGA −1708

SIBERIA −1064

FAR EAST +113

TRANS CAUCASUS +84

KAZAKHSTAN +878

CENTRAL ASIA +375

Rural-urban movement

The movement from village to town reached massive proportions in the post-war period and only in the late 1970s showed signs of slowing down with the diminishing rural population. During 1959–70 there was a net rural-to-urban redistribution of some 20 million for whom housing and services had to be provided by already hard-pressed urban administrations. The rates at which this is occurring are above average in the north–especially the RSFSR and more recently Belorussia–and below average in the south. The Soviet rural population is split roughly equally between north and south but over two-thirds of rural out-migration in the 1960s was from villages in the north.

The relative immobility of the Muslim* Central Asian rural population is a problem for Soviet planners. The extremely high rates of fertility* in Central Asia and low rates among the Slavic* population are generating regional labour surpluses and deficits. Only if Central Asians see some advantage in migration to Siberia or European Russia could this maldistribution be redressed, yet the rural population seems even reluctant to move to Central Asian cities. Moreover, the Slavs are themselves migrating out of labour-deficit

regions such as Siberia and the Urals into Central Asia: in 1970 only one-third of wage-earners in Kazakhstan, Kirgizia, Tadzhikistan, Turkmenia and Uzbekistan were members of the nationality after which their republic is named.

Migration of young people

The young are always and everywhere the most mobile, but in the USSR the proportion of migrants aged under 30 is particularly large. In the 1960s over half of the population redistribution that came about

KEY

Rural gain

More than 30 per cent loss

20–30 per cent loss

10–20 per cent loss (national mean 19 per cent)

Less than 10 per cent loss

The migration shown took place between 1959 and 1970 of the rural population aged 10–79 years in 1970 (expressed as a percentage of the rural population of that age-group in 1965)

Design by Ann Helgeson

MIGRATION FROM THE COUNTRYSIDE SINCE 1959

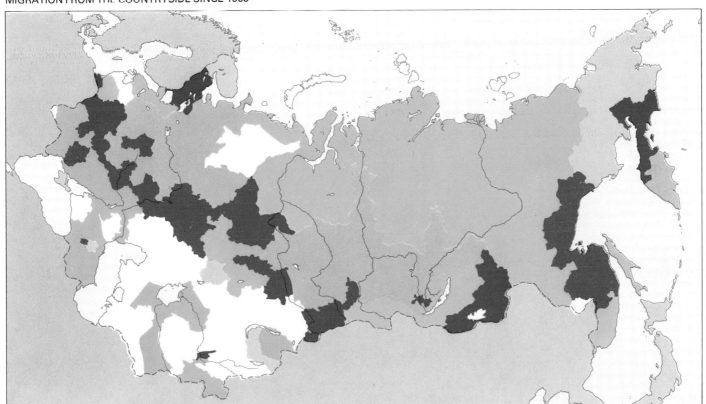

through migration, and two-thirds of the rural-urban movement, fell within this age-group. Young people in their twenties did not take part in the southward population movement as did older migrants; unlike the older groups they caused growth rather than decline in the eastern regions. The inclinations of this group fit in well with the interests of economic development in the east. It has become something of a tradition – for whatever reasons – for young persons before settling down to spend some time in the Far North or east working on prestigious and highly remunerative construction projects, sometimes under harsh living conditions: this has assisted Siberian development. The official channels of migration – the Organized Recruitment of Workers (Orgnabor) – and the compulsory placement of university and technical school graduates largely concentrate their attention on youth. In recent years the Komsomol* has directed young brigades to work on construction projects in the eastern regions. From the 1980s, however, this age-group will decline rather dramatically in numbers among the Slavic population and the rapidly growing metropolitan centres of the western part of the country hold out competing attractions.

KEY

SLAV

| 1 Russian | 3 Belorussian |
| 2 Ukrainian | |

TURKIC

4 Uzbek	10 Bashkir
5 Kazakh	11 Khakass
6 Azeri	12 Chuvash
7 Turkmen	13 Yakut
8 Kirgiz	14 Karakalpak
9 Tatar	

LATVIAN, LITHUANIAN

| 15 Latvian | 16 Lithuanian |

FINNO-UGRIC

| 17 Estonian | 19 Komi |
| 18 Karelian | 20 Mari |

CAUCASIAN

| 21 Georgian | 23 Chechen |
| 22 Armenian | |

MONGOL

| 24 Kalmyk | 25 Buryat |

IRANIAN

| 26 Tadzhik | 27 Osetin |

MOLDAVIAN

PEOPLES OF THE NORTH

28 Nentsy	31 Chukchi
29 Khanty-Mansi	32 Other national
30 Evenki	minorities of the
	north

SPARSELY INHABITED TERRITORIES

Source: P. E. Lydolph, *Geography of the USSR*, Elkhart Lake, 1979

ETHNIC GROUPS IN THE USSR

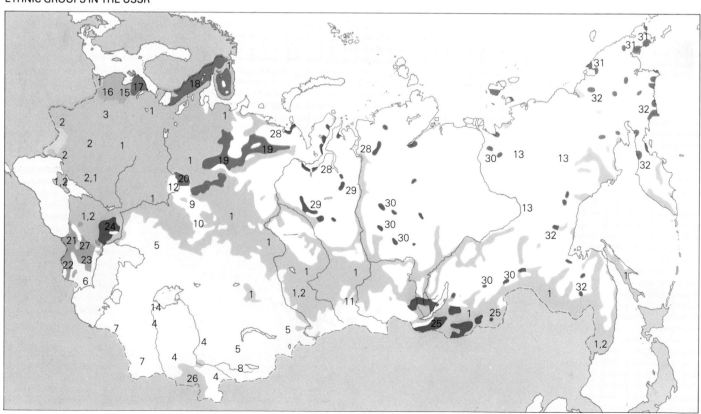

NATIONALITY COMPOSITION OF THE USSR (1979 CENSUS)

Ethnic groups	Population million
Russians	137.4
Ukrainians	42.3
Uzbeks	12.5
Belorussians	9.5
Kazakhs	6.6
Tatars	6.3
Azeris	5.5
Armenians	4.2
Georgians	3.6
Moldavians	3.0
Lithuanians	2.9
Tadzhiks	2.9
Turkmen	2.0
Germans	1.9
Kirgiz	1.9
Jews	1.8
Chuvash	1.8
Latvians	1.4
Bashkirs	1.4
Mordvinians	1.2
Poles	1.2
Estonians	1.0
Others	9.8
Total population	262·1

Emigration from the USSR

Émigré* numbers compared to the volume of internal migration are still negligible – since 1960 about 150 000, of whom the majority are Jewish,* have emigrated. During 1968–80 some 250 000 Jews left the USSR, the majority going to Israel. In the same period over 60 000 Soviet Germans emigrated to either West or East Germany and thousands of dissidents left voluntarily or involuntarily. *A.H.*

The Slav peoples: Russians, Ukrainians, Belorussians

The Slavonic peoples of Eastern Europe and Asia, all of which are Indo-European, can be divided into three branches: the Western Slavs (Czechs, Slovaks, Poles), the South Slavs* or Yugoslavs (Serbs, Croats, Slovenes, Macedonians and Bulgarians) and the Eastern Slavs (Russians, Ukrainians, Belorussians). The 189.2 million Eastern Slavs are by far the most numerous branch – Russians 137.4 million, Ukrainians 42.3 million and Belorussians 9.5 million according to the census of 1979. The Russians and Ukrainians are the largest and second largest nationalities in the USSR, but the Belorussians ceded third place to the Uzbeks (12.5 million) in the 1960s.

Until modern times the term 'Russian' (*Russhy, Ruskaya*) was often indiscriminately applied to all Eastern Slavs. Between the 10th and 12th centuries the political, economic and cultural centre of Rus'* was Kiev* and its inhabitants were known as Rusichi. As political conditions came to emphasize their linguistic and cultural divergence, distinctions were made by the Slavs between Little Russians (Ukrainians), Great Russians (Russians) and White Russians (Belorussians).

The Eastern Slavs had settled by the 9th century in the approximate areas they inhabit in modern Europe, and their distribution – with the Ukrainians and Belorussians on the verges of Central Europe and Poland and the Russians to their east – determined their eventual cultural and linguistic differentiation. They absorbed Norsemen (Varangians), Tatars,* Mongols* and Finns, which left linguistic traces but did not alter their Slav identity fundamentally. Political divisions for much of the period before the 19th century stimulated the formation and development of three distinct Eastern Slav languages,* which have, however, remained mutually intelligible. Geopolitical factors determined which of the three peoples

Source: after T. Rakowska-Harmstone, 'The dialectics of nationalism in the USSR', *Problems of Communism*, xxiii, no. 3; data from *Naselenie SSSR*, Moscow, 1980. (The total of 262.1 million falls short of the total population enumerated at the census — 262.4 million. It is thought that the difference represents citizens of foreign states resident in the USSR) remained territorially static. While the Russians were able to expand eastwards with few constraints other than technology and climate,* the Ukrainians and the Belorussians have continued to comprise compact ethnic units. The present borders of the Ukrainian and Belorussian republics approximate to the national boundaries of the two peoples but neither is nationally homogeneous. Ethnic Ukrainians represented 74.9 per cent of the population of their republic in 1970 and 73.6 per cent in 1979, while Belorussians constituted 81.0 per cent of theirs in 1970 and 79.4 per cent in 1979. There are Belorussian communities in Latvia, Lithuania and the Byałystok district of Poland, while the Ukrainian SSR contains as many as 80 national minorities, including Russians (21 per cent), Belorussians (0.8 per cent) and Moldavians (0.6 per cent). In the inter-war period parts of Belorussia and of the Ukraine were under Polish rule while other areas inhabited by Ukrainians belonged to Czechoslovakia and Romania. These areas passed to the USSR as a result of the Second World War. Six million Ukrainians in Poland, one million in Romania in Northern Bukovina and Bessarabia* and 500 000 Ukrainians of Czechoslovakia were thus added to the Ukrainian Soviet Socialist Republic (SSR).

The population density of the vast Russian Soviet Federative Socialist Republic (RSFSR) is much lower than that of the other republics, but 8 of the USSR's 18 cities of more than one million inhabitants (1979 census) are in the RSFSR: Chelyabinsk 1.03, Gorky 1.34, Kuybyshev 1.22, Leningrad 4.59, Moscow 8.01, Novosibirsk 1.31, Omsk 1.01 and Sverdlovsk 1.21. The others are situated in the Ukraine (Dnepropetrovsk 1.07, Donetsk 1.02, Kiev 2.14, Kharkov 1.44 and Odessa 1.05) and Belorussia (Minsk 1.28), while four are located in non-Slav republics (Baku 1.55, Tashkent 1.78, Tbilisi 1.07 and Yerevan 1.02).

Ethnic Russians comprise 82.6 per cent of the population of the RSFSR. A majority still inhabit European Russia, although the colonial expansion* into Siberia, Central Asia, the Far East and Far North has accelerated their over-all numerical increase. In this century the industrialization* of the 1930s and the shift of industries eastwards during the Second World War generated the formation of new population centres. A sizeable majority of Siberia's population inhabit the thin arable belt across central and southern Siberia. Russian migration* to Siberia between 1870 and 1914 almost tripled the population of the area; since then, the development of cities such as Omsk, Krasnoyarsk and Irkutsk has accounted for an even greater increase, and a high proportion of the 800 new cities and towns of the USSR are Russian-populated and situated in central and southern Siberia. Caucasia and Central Asia have witnessed an equally dramatic influx of Russians. Since the establishment of the USSR the Slav peoples have increased numerically by over 53 per cent, but it is they who have suffered most fatalities in time of war.   *A.F.*

The Baltic peoples: Lithuanians, Latvians, Estonians, Karelians

The Lithuanian, Latvian, Estonian and Karelian peoples are located on the eastern shores of the Baltic Sea. All four ethno-linguistic groups have been granted official nationality status by Moscow. Over 90 per cent of the 2.8 million Lithuanians, 1.4 million Latvians and 1.0 million Estonians resided within the boundaries of their respective republics at the 1979 census while the remainder are to be found mainly in the towns of the RSFSR, Belorussia and the Ukraine. In contrast, the Karelians, whose national territory was down-graded from a Soviet Socialist Republic (SSR) to an Autonomous Soviet Socialist Republic (ASSR) in 1956, have only half their 138 000 total within the Karelian ASSR. Sizeable Karelian communities are also located in Kalinin and Murmansk oblasts, the Leningrad area and in neighbouring Finland.

The national languages* of the Latvians and Lithuanians belong to the Baltic group, an Indo-European sub-group. Although Latvians and Lithuanians are unintelligible to each other, both languages are characterized by a similar lexical development and structure. The more northerly located Estonians and Karelians belong to the Finno-Ugric language group, a branch of the Uralic language family.

In terms of cultural development, the Estonians have more in common with their southern neighbours than with the Karelians. The character of the Estonian, Latvian and Lithuanian languages and cultures owes much to the rise of nationalist* movements in the last quarter of the 19th century and to their parallel literary revivals, continuing through the period of statehood as Baltic republics* (1918–40). The Lutheran* religion in 19th-century Estonia and

Estonians in a cafe in Tallinn

Latvia also influenced the high level of literacy found among the indigenous peasantry. Lutheranism in Estonia and Latvia, and Catholicism* in Lithuania set these peoples apart from their eastern Slav neighbours. The only exception to this synonymity between ethnicity, language and religion was a large Catholic community in Eastern Latvia (Latgalia), an area occupied by Poland in the 16th century. Cut off from coastal Latvia, Latgalia developed a regionalism manifest in dialect, religion and rural institutions – the latter characterized by the *mir* (village community) whereas the individual farmstead was usual in the rest of Latvia, in Estonia and in Lithuania. Within the Estonian ethno-linguistic community there is also another small ethnographic group, the Setu, who inhabit south-east Estonia and areas adjacent to Pskov oblast and who are Orthodox Christians,* not Lutheran.

Left: a Lithuanian girl in national dress. Below: Latgalian women, Latvia

The Karelians, with close linguistic and cultural ties to neighbouring Finland, have a less distinctive social and cultural identity than the other three Baltic peoples. This is partly explained by the drift of Karelians to other regions of the USSR, and the predominance of Russians who outnumber the eponymous nationality by six to one in the ASSR itself. Outnumbered as they are, most Karelians are necessarily bilingual.

The Lithuanians, Latvians and Estonians have also seen their predominance within their respective republics challenged. Since the final incorporation of the three republics into the Soviet Union in 1944, the immigration of Russians and to a lesser extent Ukrainians and Belorussians has continued steadily. As in Karelia, one of the main reasons behind such an influx was industrialization. In contrast to the Karelian ASSR, however, the Lithuanians, Latvians and Estonians are still the predominant nationality groups within their republics and do not possess such a high percentage of their nationality group speaking Russian as their mother tongue. However, bilingualism is increasingly becoming the norm among these peoples. With one of the lowest rates of natural population increase in the USSR, the highly urbanized Latvians and Estonians have declined in numerical importance within their own republics. By 1979 Latvians constituted 53.7 per cent of their republic's population while Estonians registered 64.7 per cent. With a lower level of economic development and slightly differing demographic structure, Lithuania has not to the same extent witnessed these population changes although trends in immigration* and the direction of the Lithuanian economy would tend to imply that the Lithuanians as a proportion of the total in their republic – 80 per cent – may well begin to decline. In all three republics the urban areas particularly show a higher level of bilingualism, which reflects the migrants' preference for the Baltic cities and the pressure on the indigenous population to communicate in a more widely understood language.

G.E.S.

The Caucasian peoples

Turkic* and Iranian* peoples apart, the Caucasus presents a living museum of languages and peoples who have lived there since pre-history. They consist of the Armenians, whose language is Indo-European and whose republic lies on the Turkish border, the north-west Caucasians, the Abkhaz and Adyge of the high Caucasus on the Black Sea littoral; the Nakh peoples (primarily the Chechen and Ingush) of the northern slopes of the central Caucasus; the Kartvelians, principally the Georgians, south of the west and central Caucasian range; and the 30 or so Dagestani peoples of the eastern Caucasus and Caspian littoral. The ethnic and linguistic affinities of the Caucasians are still uncertain. Their languages have in common a phenomenally rich consonantal system, noted for the 'imploded' consonants and the great grammatical complexity in verbs and nouns and in syntax. But they differ from each other as sharply as they do from Indo-European or Turkic. The 'Japhetic' theory that presupposes a common origin is still widely accepted, but unproven; attempts to link them to Basque, Etruscan or lost ancient Anatolian languages are still speculative.

The Armenians once had a kingdom that stretched from the Mediterranean to the Caucasus. A millennium of disasters has reduced them to a Soviet republic where about 1.5 million speak Armenian. They have been Gregorian Christians (of the Armenian Church★) with their own alphabet and literature since the 4th century AD. Another 1.5 million Armenians are widely scattered through the USSR. Soviet Armenians enjoy prosperity and some unofficial freedoms in economic and religious fields and in contacts with émigré★ communities. They speak the eastern dialects of Armenian, different enough from the western Armenian spoken by emigrés to make comprehension uncertain. Armenian is intermediate between Iranian and Slavonic in the Indo-European family; its basic features owe much to Caucasian and Anatolian influences.

The north-west Caucasians consist of the Abkhaz (and related Abazin) in the Abkhaz Autonomous Soviet Socialist Republic (ASSR) (part of the Georgian Soviet Socialist Republic (SSR)) and of the Circassians, who are now classified as the Adyge (sharing an autonomous republic with the Turkic Karachay) and the Kabarda (sharing an autonomous republic with the Turkic Balkar). The 91 000 Abkhaz in the USSR are outnumbered in their own republic, a cause of some ethnic friction. Their language is probably the 'fastest' phonically in the world, complete information, such as word root and tense, often being conveyed by a single consonant. Abkhaz is a recent literary language. The Circassian languages differ considerably from Abkhaz: 80 000 speak Adyge and 235 000 Kabarda, which is thus the fifth most populous group of the Caucasus.

The Nakh peoples are concentrated in the Chechen-Ingush ASSR of the Russian republic (RSFSR). The Chechens number 746 000 and the

PEOPLES OF THE CAUCASUS

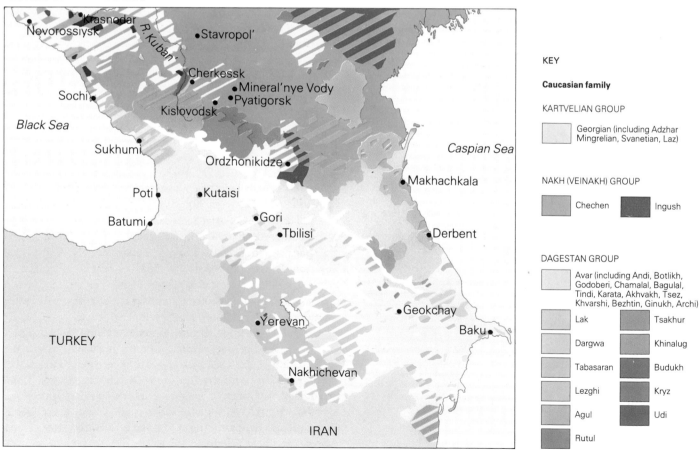

KEY

Caucasian family

KARTVELIAN GROUP

Georgian (including Adzhar Mingrelian, Svanetian, Laz)

NAKH (VEINAKH) GROUP

Chechen   Ingush

DAGESTAN GROUP

Avar (including Andi, Botlikh, Godoberi, Chamalal, Bagulal, Tindi, Karata, Akhvakh, Tsez, Khvarshi, Bezhtin, Ginukh, Archi)

Lak   Tsakhur

Dargwa   Khinalug

Tabasaran   Budukh

Lezghi   Kryz

Agul   Udi

Rutul

Ingush, badly depleted by deportation in 1944, 186000. The two languages, closely related, are thriving new literary languages with local newspapers and radio.

The Kartvelian peoples (from *k'artveli*, the Georgians' self-appellation) consist of 3.6 million Georgians of whom 3.4 million are in their own republic, perhaps 200000 Mingrelians or Zan (known as Laz in neighbouring parts of Turkey) and 34000 Svans in the high Caucasus north of Kutaisi. Mingrelian is no longer a literary language; Svan, noted for its archaic structure and folk lore, has never attained literary status. The Georgians have had an independent kingdom or kingdoms since the days of Herodotus. Despite domination by Mongols, Persians and Turks, they evolved a powerful Christian* culture from the 4th century AD. Not until 1801 did they become a protectorate, and then a province, of the Russian Empire. In 1917 they achieved an independent republic, recognized by the League of Nations shortly before the Red Army* incorporated it into the USSR in February 1921. Their language has had its own alphabet since at least 450 AD and soon gave rise to a literary medium whose

richness is out of all proportion to the number of speakers. Their culture and ethos have been forged out of disparate elements: the sophisticated polyphonic music of the western plains; the heroic folk lore of the mountain tribes; Oriental and, via Russia, European influences.

The one-million strong Dagestani peoples are linked by their history of ferocious resistance to Russian encroachment and their Muslim* (often Shi'a) piety. Most live in the Dagestan ASSR of the RSFSR. Each valley of the north-east Caucasus has its own language, often restricted to a few hundred families. Nevertheless, five peoples are extensive enough to have evolved recent literary languages. (There exist traces of Caucasian Albanian, or Udi, from the 7th century AD.) The 483000 Avars* had an inter-tribal dialect, Bolmat'-s, which facilitated the rise of a vigorous literary language for most Dagestanis. The Dargwa (287000), the Lezghi (383000), infamous as slave- and cattle-raiders on Georgia's north-east borders, as well as the 100000 Lakk and 75000 Tabasaran, all have literary languages.

The largely fictitious autonomy of the Caucasian peoples has, however, real benefits in keeping minority languages alive as media for everyday communication, education,* radio* and television.* Bi- and tri-lingualism has always been normal in the Caucasus; now the *lingua franca* tends to be Russian instead of Turkish. Russia's dominance is, albeit slowly, eroding even such old-established languages as Georgian, but the process—like that of Russian colonization—is negligible here in comparison with its effects in Siberia or in the European republics.   *P.D.R.*

The Turkic peoples

Over 90 per cent of the Turkic* peoples of the USSR are historically of the Muslim faith, and over 90 per cent of these inhabit Soviet Central Asia and the Kazakh Soviet Socialist Republic (SSR). The remainder of the Turkic Muslims* live in the Caucasus and the Volga region. The Gagauz and Chuvash living in Europe and the Yakuts and Tuvinians living in East Asia have never been affected by Islam.* Physical features common to all the Turkic peoples are hard to discern, and the only common cultural feature is language. With the exception of those spoken by such non-Muslim peoples as the Gagauz and Yakuts, the Turkic languages strongly resemble one another, most of them being to some extent mutually intelligible. Under the Soviet regime all the Turkic languages have been greatly developed and provided with literary forms, which now use varieties of the Cyrillic alphabet. Smaller groups of Turkic peoples are: the Muslim Kumyks, Karachays, Balkars and Nogays living in the North Caucasus, and the partly pagan and partly Christian Khakass and Altays of southern Siberia.

Caucasian family (*continued*)

ADYGE-ABKHAZ GROUP

Adyge — Abkhaz
Kabarda — Abazin
Circassian

Indo-European family

SLAVONIC GROUP

Russian — Ukrainian

IRANIAN GROUP

Ossete — Tat (including Mountain Jews)
Kurd — Talysh

OTHER INDO-EUROPEAN GROUPS

Armenian — Greek

Altay family

TURKIC GROUP

Azeri — Karachay
Kumyk — Balkar
Nogay — Turkmen

MONGOLIAN GROUP

Kalmyk

Semitic-Hamitic family

SEMITIC GROUP

Assyrian

Source: *Narody Kavkaza*, Moscow, 1960, Vol. 1

An Uzbek riding his donkey in Bukhara

Uzbeks

The Uzbeks are the largest Turkic people in the USSR and the largest in the world after the Turks of Turkey. They are the third most numerous nationality in the USSR. Of the total of 12.5 million, 85 per cent live in the Uzbek SSR (formed in 1924) in which they constitute 69 per cent of the population. The remainder are more or less equally divided between the adjoining SSRs. Their name was probably derived from Uzbek, one of the khans of the Golden Horde. In the 15th century the Uzbeks occupied the country between the lower Volga and the Aral Sea. Moving south early in the 16th century, they conquered the settled regions of Bukhara and Samarkand and, later, Urgench and Tashkent, and eventually became mixed with the earlier settlers in these regions, including the ancient Iranian population of Khorezm and Soghdia. They constituted more than half of the former khanate of Khiva, and a third of that of Bukhara. Originally nomads,* the Uzbeks have been sedentary for the last three centuries. Outside the USSR there are also over one million Uzbeks in Afghanistan and about 8000 in the Sinkiang-Uygur Autonomous Region of China.

Tatars

Of the total of 6.3 million about 1.5 million Tatars live in the Tatar Autonomous Soviet Socialist Republic (ASSR) and about one million in the Bashkir ASSR; 649 000 live in the Uzbek SSR, 313 000 in the Kazahk SSR and smaller numbers in the Kirgiz, Tadzhik and Turkmen SSRs and in the Mordva, Udmurt, Chuvash and Yakut ASSRs. Other Tatar elements are widely scattered throughout the RSFSR. A distinct Tatar community numbering about 250 000 and known as the Krym (Crimean) Tatars inhabited the former Crimean Tatar ASSR (now part of the Ukrainian SSR) until they were expelled in 1945 for alleged collaboration with the German invaders. Only a few Krym Tatar families have been allowed to return to their homeland; the remainder are believed to be living in the Uzbek SSR in whose Tatar population they are probably included.

Kazakhs

Of the 6.6 million Kazakhs, 81 per cent inhabit the Kazakh SSR of which they comprise only 36 per cent of the population. The Kazakhs were originally constituted an ASSR in 1920, which was raised to the status of SSR in 1936. Under the tsarist administration the Kazakhs were known as Kirgiz, the real Kirgiz being called Kara Kirgiz. The origin of the Kazakhs is obscure, their name not appearing in Turkic language records until the 11th century. The historian V. V. Bartol'd describes them as 'Uzbeks who in the 15th century detached themselves from the bulk of their nation and consequently had not taken part in the conquest of the Timurid kingdom'. The three 'hordes' into which the Kazakhs formed themselves after the break-up of the Golden Horde in the 15th century were distributed over a vast steppe area including Lake Balkhash, the north and central part of what is now the Kazakh SSR, and in the western part of the latter near the Caspian Sea and the Ural River. Although now largely stabilized, the Kazakhs were originally nomadic and since the coming of the Russians there have been large migrations* of them between Russian and Chinese territory. In addition, about 500 000 live in the Sinkiang-Uygur Autonomous Region of China.

A Kazakh girl from
Alma-Ata

Azeris

Of the 5.5 million in the USSR, 86 per cent live in the Azerbaijan SSR, of which they constitute 78 per cent of the population, and the remainder in the Georgian and Armenian SSRs and the Dagestan ASSR. During the tsarist regime the Azeris were known as Tatars, with whom they have no ethnic connection. Originally of Caucasian stock, they came under Muslim influence in the 7th century and were conquered by the Seljuks in the 11th century. They were incorporated in the Safavid Iranian empire in the 16th century and their territory began to attract the attention of Russia in the 18th century, being finally annexed at the beginning of the 19th century. After the Revolution* the Azeris achieved a brief independence in 1918, but were overrun by the Red Army* in 1920 and formed into the Azerbaijan Soviet Republic. This was at first included in the Transcaucasian Federal Republic but in 1936 was constituted an SSR. During the Iranian occupation the Azeris adopted the Shi'a rite to which they still adhere. The republic adjoins the Iranian province of Azerbaijan in which live about another four million Azeris.

Turkmens

Of the total of 2.0 million Turkmens 93 per cent live in the Turkmen SSR, of which they constitute 65 per cent of the population. The remainder live in the Uzbek SSR. The Turkmens are the most distinctive Turkic people in the USSR. Their origin is obscure but their long-shaped heads suggest intermingling with some ancient non-Turkic stock. Tradition connects them with the Oguz tribes, to which the Seljuk and Osmanli Turks also belonged. Until the 1880s the Turkmens were under varying degrees of domination by the khanates of Khiva and Bukhara, and by Iran where some 250 000 of them still live. After the final Russian conquest in the 1880s, a large

Elders of a collective farm in Kalinsk rayon, Turkmenia

Kirgiz labourers employed in railway construction, c. 1908

part of their territory was constituted the oblast of Transcaspia. Originally semi-nomadic, the Turkmens are now mainly stabilized. Several thousands inhabit northern Afghanistan.

Kirgiz

Of the total of 1.9 million Kirgiz in the USSR, 89 per cent live in the Kirgiz SSR of which they constitute 48 per cent of the population. The origin of the present-day Kirgiz is obscure but they are probably of mixed descent from the Kirgiz who inhabited the upper reaches of the Yenisey River between the 6th and 9th centuries, and various invading Mongol and Turkic tribes. The Kirgiz came finally under Russian domination in 1876. Under the Soviet regime they were first constituted an autonomous oblast in 1924, an ASSR in 1926 and an SSR in 1936. There are also some 70 000 Kirgiz in the Sinkiang-Uygur Autonomous Region of China.

Karakalpaks

The vast majority of the 303 000 Karakalpaks living in the USSR are concentrated in the Karakalpak ASSR (part of the Uzbek SSR since 1936), originally formed in 1925 as an autonomous oblast within the Russian republic (RSFSR). They are closely allied to the Kazakhs both ethnically and linguistically. Their main occupation is agriculture and fishing.

Uygurs

A national minority numbering 211 000, the Uygurs live mainly in the Alma-Ata oblast of the Kazakh SSR and in the Fergana valley. They originate from what is now the Sinkiang-Uygur Autonomous Region of China.

Bashkirs

Numbering in all about one and a half million, the Bashkirs live mainly in the Bashkir ASSR, where they constitute about one-quarter of the population. Muslims since the 14th century, they came under Russian domination in the 16th century. In 1917 a Bashkir nationalist government was formed but in 1919 it joined the Bolsheviks* and was constituted an ASSR.

Gagauz

The majority of the total of 173 000 Gagauz live in the Moldavian SSR. There are also small groups living in the Zaporozhe oblast of the Ukraine, in the North Caucasus and in the Kazakh SSR. Their origin is not clear. Those now living in the USSR are Orthodox Christians* who migrated from Turkish territory during the 18th and 19th centuries. Their language is Turkic, but they have no other affinities with the Turkic peoples.

Chuvash

The majority of the 1.7 million Chuvash live in the Chuvash ASSR and constitute about three-quarters of its population. They are thought to be descended from the medieval Volga Bulgarians. Their territory was annexed to Russia with the conquest of Kazan' in 1552. They became Orthodox Christians and all traces of Islamic civilization have disappeared. Although their language is Turkic it is strongly aberrant. Since 1940 it has been written in a modified Cyrillic script.

Yakuts

The largest people of the Altaic family, the 328 000 Yakuts* live in the Yakut ASSR (founded in 1922) and the remainder in neighbouring areas of east Siberia. They have been subject to Russia since the 17th century. Their language is Turkic but strongly aberrant: it is now written in a modified form of the Cyrillic character.

Yakuts at Tomtor in the Soviet North

A Tuvinian family

Tuvinians

The majority of the 166 000 Tuvinians live in what was the independent People's Republic of Tannu Tuva between 1921 and 1944; incorporated in the USSR in October 1944, it was designated the Tuvinian autonomous region (AR) until 1961, when it became an ASSR. Their Turkic language has been written in the Cyrillic character since 1940. They are Lamaist Buddhists.*   *G.Wh.*

The Iranian peoples

Small Iranian communities are Kurds (116 000), Tats (22 000) and Talysh living in Transcaucasia, and Baluchis in the Tadzhik SSR.

Tadzhiks

Of the total of 2.9 million, some 77 per cent live in the Tadzhik Soviet Socialist Republic (SSR), of which they constitute 59 per cent of the population. Of the remainder 595 000 live in the Uzbek SSR and 23 000 in the Kirgiz SSR. The Tadzhiks are without doubt the oldest ethnic element in Central Asia, being the descendants of the ancient Soghdian and Bactrian population. But traces of ancient Iranian civilization are no more marked in them than in the Uzbeks, except among the so-called mountain Tadzhiks of the Gorno-Badakhshan autonomous region (AR). Before 1921 the Tadzhiks were mainly concentrated in the khanate of Bukhara, but they also made up a large part of the so-called Sarts (a term no longer in use) living in the Fergana, Zeravshan and Gissar valleys. Their language closely resembles the Dari spoken in Afghanistan. Many Tadzhiks are bilingual in Tadzhik and Uzbek. The Tadzhiks mainly follow the

Tadzhiks at an open-air teahouse—the *topchan* dais is characteristic of every Central Asian village

Sunni (Muslim★) rite but some of the mountain elements follow the Ismaili Shi'a rite. There are over two million Tadzhiks in northern Afghanistan and a few thousand also in the Sinkiang-Uygur Autonomous Region of China.

Ossetes

An Iranian people numbering about 500 000, the Ossetes mostly live either in the North Osetin ASSR or in the South Osetin AR. They are descended from the medieval Alans. In the 18th century they came under strong Russian influence and were annexed to Russia early in the 19th century. They are mostly Orthodox Christians★ but there is a small Sunni Muslim element.   *G. Wh.*

The Mongol peoples

The Mongol peoples of the USSR fall into two large groups: the Buryats and the Kalmyks. Although other Asian peoples such as the Tuvinians,★ Altays and some of the Evenki have been strongly influenced by Mongol culture, their languages are not from the Mongol group and hence they must be considered separately. Only a very small percentage of the Mongol peoples count Russian as their native language; although there has been a strong Russian influence in dress, living habits, the striving for education and the abandoning by young people of religion, both Buryats and Kalmyks retain a certain national culture.

Buryats

The Buryats numbered 353 000 in 1979, most living in the Buryat Autonomous Soviet Socialist Republic (ASSR), to the south and east of Lake Baykal. Other groups live to the west of the lake in the Ust'-Ordynsk autonomous area (AA), and in the east, in the Aginsk Buryat AA. Some tens of thousands of Buryats also live in Mongolia and in the north-west of China.

In the 17th century, the Buryats were a series of loosely-connected nomadic★ pastoralist tribes. Many of them had been subject to the Mongol khans,★ but after a border was established between Mongolia and Russia the majority decided to stay on the Russian side. They were under the indirect rule of the tsarist government, and kept many of their own traditions. Their early religion, shamanism, was superseded by lamaism during the 19th century in the eastern parts of Buryatia—despite the border, the Mongolian influence was still strong.

The basis of the Buryat economy was livestock herding, and the eastern Buryats continued to be nomadic until after the Revolution.★ The western Buryats were strongly influenced by Russian culture, developed an agricultural tradition and a more settled life, and even were converted in a rather superficial way to Orthodox Christianity.★ Ousted by Russian peasant settlers from their lands west of Lake Baykal, they began to migrate to the other side, and the eastern Buryats in their turn moved even further, towards Mongolia and Manchuria. A fairly large migration★ of this kind took place after the civil war★ in the 1920s. Today, both western and eastern Buryats have a diversified economy and are settled in villages and towns. They conduct mixed farming in the rural areas, and some are employed in engineering and other industries in the towns along the Trans-Siberian Railway.

A Buryat family

Kalmyks

The Kalmyks, like the Buryats, speak a dialect of Mongolian. They numbered 147 000 in 1979. Most of them now live in the Kalmyk ASSR, near the mouth of the Volga where it enters the Caspian Sea, in an area of grassland steppe suitable for the nomadic pastoralism which used to form the basis of their economy.

The Kalmyks previously lived in Western Mongolia (Dzhungaria) and fled from there to the Volga region in the early 17th century under pressure from feudal wars. By the 18th century they had been converted from shamanism to lamaism, their cultural links still being primarily with Mongolia. Later, under pressure from the tsarist government, some fled back over the steppes as far as China, an immense trek in which many lost their lives. The remaining 13 000 Kalmyks were registered in the Astrakhan' province of the Russian Empire. Like the Buryats, the Kalmyks were ruled indirectly and had their own tribal princes. After the Revolution nomadism gradually became less important as agriculture was taken up, and after collectivization★ in the 1930s it ceased altogether. As with the Buryats, lamaism was essentially destroyed during this period, leaving only a few token monasteries.

During the Second World War★ part of Kalmykia was occupied by the Germans, and as a punishment for alleged disloyalty on the part of the Kalmyks, Stalin's★ government abolished the Kalmyk ASSR in 1943 and expelled its population to various parts of Siberia. The republic was re-established in 1957, and most of them were allowed to return to it. The Kalmyks now have a diversified economy: mixed farming, with some industry around the capital town of Elista. *C.H.*

The peoples of the north

The indigenous peoples of the Soviet north are both more diverse and more numerous than those of Arctic and sub-Arctic America. Soviet ethnographers use the phrase 'the small peoples of the north', which connotes 26 peoples but excludes the two largest northern groups, the Komi and Yakuts.★ These are listed here with three others (Mordva, Udmurt, Mari) who, although not normally considered northern, round out the Finno-Ugrian peoples. The Estonians and Karelians are also Finno-Ugrians, but are grouped under Baltic peoples.★

At the beginning of the Soviet period the larger among these peoples were the dominant groups in their homelands, but since a massive immigration★ of Russian settlers, all except the Komi-Permyaki are minority groups in their local administrative areas, even those areas which bear their name. The occupation of these peoples is briefly characterized, but this is only a general indication; an increasing number of Soviet citizens in all national groups move into industrial and professional jobs having no special relationship to their national background.

It may be wondered what chances of survival the smaller peoples will have. The Soviet contention that many were dying out under tsarism may be justified in some cases, but reversal of that trend is not spectacular, for the increase in numbers between 1926 and 1970 was under 10 per cent. It is likely that there has been much assimilation into Russian or other immigrant groups. However, about a third of the peoples numbering under 30 000 have received written languages

Left: a Kalmyk Buddhist monk before the Revolution. Right: a Komi girl of Ozel village, Komi ASSR

THE PEOPLES OF THE SOVIET NORTH

Peoples[1]	1970 census	1979 census
URALIAN FAMILY		
Finno-Ugrian peoples		
1 Mordva (Mordvinians)	1 262 670	1 192 000
2 Udmurty (Votyaks)	704 328	714 000
3 Mariytsy (Mari, Cheremis)	598 628	622 000
4 Komi-Zyryane (Zyrians)	321 894	327 000
5 Komi-Permyaki (Permians)	153 451	151 000
6 Khanty (Ostyaks) ⎱ (Ob' Ugrians)	21 138	20 900
7 Mansi (Voguls) ⎰	7 710	7 600
8 Saami (Lapps, Sami)	1 884	1 900
Samoyedic peoples		
9 Nentsy (Samoyeds)	28 705	29 900
10 Sel'kupy (Ostyak Samoyeds)	4 282	3 600
11 Nganasany (Tavgi Samoyeds)	953	900
12 Entsy (Yenisey Samoyeds)	300	..
ALTAIC FAMILY		
Turkic peoples		
13 Yakuty (Yakuts)	296 244	328 000
14 Dolgany (Tya-kikhi)	4 877	5 100
15 Tofa (Tofalary, Karagas)	620	800

Peoples[1]	1970 census	1979 census
ALTAIC FAMILY (continued)		
Tungus-Manchurian peoples		
16 Evenki (Tungus)	25 149	27 500
17 Eveny (Lamuts)	12 029	12 300
18 Nanaytsy (Nanay, Golds)	10 005	10 500
19 Ul'chi (Nani)	2 448	2 600
20 Udegeytsy (Udekhe)	1 469	1 500
21 Orochi (Nani)	1 089	1 200
22 Negidal'tsy (El'kan Beyenin)	537	500
23 Oroki (Ul'ta)	under 500	—
PALAEOASIATIC PEOPLES		
24 Chukchi (Luoravetlan)	13 597	14 000
25 Koryaki	7 847	7 900
26 Nivkhi (Gilyaks)	4 420	4 400
27 Itel'meny (Kamchadals)	1 301	1 400
28 Eskimosy (Eskimoes)	1 308	1 500
29 Kety (Yenisey Ostyaks, Yeniseians)	1 182	1 100
30 Yukagiry (Odul, Detkil')	615	800
31 Aleuty (Aleuts)	441	500

[1]The numbers refer to those on the map; the names of peoples are those currently used in the USSR, with alternatives in parenthesis

Source: *Naselenie SSSR po dannym vsesoyuznoy perepisi naseleniya 1979 goda*, Moscow, 1980

DISTRIBUTION OF NORTHERN PEOPLES IN THE USSR

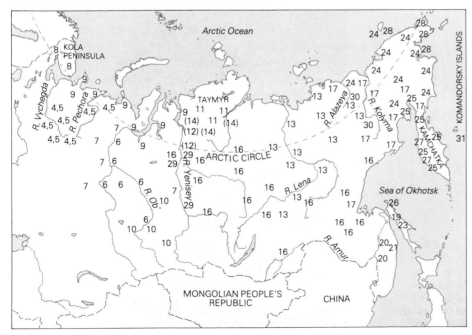

The numbers refer to the table 'Peoples of the Soviet north'; the numbers in brackets signify the last known location of peoples no longer listed in the census returns
Source: after R. St J. Macdonald, ed., *The Arctic Frontier*, Toronto, 1966

in Soviet times, and the outlook for their cultural survival must be rated brighter.

The Uralian family live in northern Russia, in Europe or in north-west Siberia. The Finno-Ugrian peoples are predominantly pastoralists. The most southerly members – Mordva, Udmurt, and Mari – are the most numerous, and their importance was recognized by the establishment in each case of an Autonomous Soviet Socialist Republic (ASSR) on the group's homeland (the Volga and Kama basin). They have played a role in the history of the Russian plain since earliest historical times, making contact with Russian principalities and city states. Further north, in the boreal forest,* live the Komi (also as an ASSR) and their less numerous cousins, the Komi-Permyaki. All are quite sophisticated peoples, a significant proportion of their members having higher education.* The remaining members of the Finno-Ugric group are the Khanty and Mansi, collectively known as Ob' Ugrians, two related peoples who were until recently mainly hunters and fishers, with some interest in reindeer-herding. Finally, the Saami tend reindeer in the vicinity of Murmansk; they are related ethnically and linguistically to the Lapps (Sami) of Scandinavia.

The remaining group in the Uralian family are the Samoyedic peoples. The name Samoyed was dropped for the peoples (it implies 'cannibal' in Russian), but is retained for the group. They live on or near the coast on the Barents and Kara seas, and are still primarily hunters, fishers, and reindeer herders.

In the Altaic family, the most important are the Yakuts,* who are pastoralists living in the middle Lena basin. They have had close contact with the Russians for three centuries and are well educated; many have entered the professions. Yakut language and culture appear to thrive. The language is Turkic,* the Yakuts being the most north-easterly of the Turkic-speaking peoples. Others in the north are the Dolgany, reindeer-herders of Taymyr who speak Yakut but are of mainly Tungus origin, and a very small group, the Tofa, who are now mostly fur-farmers and live near Irkutsk.

The other Altaic group are the Tungus-Manchurians, reindeer-herders, hunters and fishers of the Far East forests. The largest are the Evenki (formerly called Tungus, the name now used for the group), who range across a huge belt of territory from the Yenisey to the Pacific and into Manchuria. Their cousins, the Eveny, live to the north-east, on the shores of the Sea of Okhotsk and the Arctic Ocean, while the remaining members inhabit the lower Amur valley and (the Oroki) the island of Sakhalin.

The Palaeoasiatic peoples live chiefly in the far north-east and also are hunters, fishers and reindeer-herders. The term was coined to embrace peoples whose languages belonged to none of the major groups. In fact the Chukchi, Koryak, and Itel'men languages are related, thus giving some unity to the peoples of the Chukotka and Kamchatka peninsulas. The Eskimoes and Aleuts are the Asiatic

Top: Khanty children in winter dress, Tege, Tyumen' region. Left: Saami schoolchildren at a German lesson in Lovozero village, Murmansk region. Below: Evenki reindeer herdsmen in Verkhoyansk rayon, the 'pole of cold' of the northern hemisphere

representatives of those two related peoples whose main populations are in North America although they are believed to have originated in Asia. The Yukagiry, on the Kolyma River, have largely been assimilated into neighbouring groups. The Nivkhi are separated physically as well as linguistically and live on Sakhalin. The Kety, living on the Yenisey, are even more widely separated and their provenance (or language affiliation) has always been something of a mystery.
T.E.A.

The Jews

The Jews are a recognized Soviet nationality. According to the 1970 census they numbered 2.15 million, but only 1.81 million at that of 1979. There were 5 million Jews in Russia in 1897, 2.7 million within the reduced boundaries of the USSR in 1926 and 3 million in 1939; about 4.8 million within the enlarged USSR in 1941 (of whom about 2.5 million perished in the Second World War); and 2.3 million in 1959. They are dispersed throughout the country; the majority inhabit the Russian republic (RSFSR) (701 000), the Ukraine (634 000), Belorussia (135 000), Uzbekistan (100 000) and Moldavia (80 000). Some 90 per cent of Soviet Jewry are Ashkenazi whose ancestral language is Yiddish; the Oriental Jews inhabit Dagestan and the Caucasian and Central Asian republics. There were in 1979 10 166 Jews (5.4 per cent of the local population) in the Jewish autonomous region (AR) Birobidzhan, which is part of the Khabarovsk territory (kray) in the RSFSR.

The Jews are an overwhelmingly urban population: about 98 per cent inhabit urban areas; about a quarter inhabit the three largest cities (Moscow, Leningrad, Kiev). They are a highly educated population: in 1970 239 per 1000 of all Jews, and about one-third of the Jews employed in the national economy, had a higher education. Though only 0.8 per cent of the population, Jews constituted in 1975 4.1 per cent of all employees with higher education and 1.4 per cent of employees with specialist secondary education. They are strongly represented among scientific workers, lawyers, doctors, cultural and artistic workers, writers and journalists. But they are few in the Party and state apparatus,* the military, the security forces and the diplomatic service – a reversal of the situation in the first decades of the Soviet regime. The rapid decline of the number of Jewish students and postgraduates since 1970 indicates that their role in the economy and scholarly life is bound to be reduced likewise.

Soviet Jewry is a declining population, because of small family-size and loss through mixed marriages and assimilation. In 1968–80 about 250 000 Jews emigrated,* the majority to Israel. In 1979 83.3 per cent declared Russian as their mother tongue, while only 14.2 per cent so declared their national language and a further 5.4 per cent

declared the national language as their second tongue; 70.4 per cent gave Yiddish as their mother tongue in 1926. According to Soviet estimates, there were approximately 60 000 observing Jews in 1979, although the number of people feeling a certain affinity with Jewish religion and custom is much greater; 69 synagogues were known to exist in 1977 (according to Soviet figures, 92), compared with 451 in 1959 and 1103 (in a smaller territory) in 1926.

The Jews became part of the Russian Empire after the Polish partitions under Catherine I.* It was in the former Polish territory that the important movements of Hassidism, Zionism and Jewish socialism emerged. Under the tsars they were subject to many disabilities, and they suffered great losses in the Russian civil war.* The Soviet regime offered them equality and rapid upward mobility, as well as a regimented secular national culture. Simultaneously, it eliminated their predominant bourgeois and petty bourgeois occupations, suppressed the Jewish political parties and the Hebrew language, and severely restricted their religious* life. But these basically non-discriminatory, though repressive, policies began to change in the third decade of Soviet rule, in the sense that, successively, Jewish schools and the teaching of the Yiddish language were eliminated, the Jews were increasingly excluded from politically sensitive occupations, discrimination was introduced in many other fields, and Jewish institutions and culture were suppressed. This policy reached a climax in Stalin's* last years (1948–53), when political campaigns against Jewish nationalism and 'cosmopolitanism' were followed by the closing-down of all Jewish institutions and publications, the arrest of many individuals and the execution on 12 August 1952 of 24 prominent Jewish leaders and writers. The notorious 'doctors' plot' was fabricated in Stalin's final months and this was accompanied by the expulsion of thousands

Jews gathered in front of the Moscow synagogue on a Sabbath afternoon

from their jobs and increasing anti-Jewish tension in the country.

Some improvements occurred under Stalin's successors, but the discriminatory policy was not fundamentally reversed. A Yiddish literary journal was launched in 1961 (7000 copies in 1978); a limited amount of Jewish theatrical activities, some of them professional, has been permitted; in 1970–9 an average of six Yiddish books have been published yearly, in translation into Russian or other Soviet languages, and about 130 such books appeared during that decade. In the later 1960s and the 1970s, under the impact of the 1967 Six-Day War in the Middle East and the emergence of Soviet dissent,* a Jewish movement of emigration to Israel developed and an unofficial Jewish culture appeared in the form of *samizdat** Jewish publications in Russian, the teaching of Hebrew and the holding of seminars. At the same time, the official propaganda against Israel and Zionism was intensified and in many cases acquired anti-semitic features.   *L.H.*

The Moldavians

Among the nationalities of the USSR, the Moldavians are the most artificial. Ethnically, linguistically and culturally Moldavians are indistinguishable from Romanians. Romanian inhabitants of the USSR were designated a separate and distinct nationality–Moldavians–as a ploy in the longstanding dispute between Russia and Romania over the disposition of Bessarabia.* In 1924, six years after Romania incorporated Bessarabia, the Moldavian Autonomous Soviet Socialist Republic (ASSR) was formed as part of the Ukrainian Soviet Socialist Republic (SSR). Within its frontiers were most, but not all, of the Romanians living east of the Dniester, who made up some 30 per cent of its population. From the outset, the republic was intended to formalize Soviet opposition to Romania's annexation of Bessarabia and to pose as the nucleus of a 'reunited' Moldavia. Acting on the secret protocols of the German-Soviet Pact of August 1939, the USSR annexed Bessarabia, together with northern Bukovina and, on 2 August 1940, established the Moldavian SSR. The new republic consisted of most of Bessarabia and the western portions of the original republic. Overrun and occupied by Romanian forces in June 1941, the Moldavian SSR was returned to the USSR by the Soviet-Romanian Armistice Convention of 1944, which was subsequently confirmed by the Romanian peace treaty of 1947. The post-war settlement has provided a *de jure*, though not a *de facto*, solution to the Bessarabian and Moldavian issues.

In 1979 the Moldavian SSR had a population of 3.95 million of whom 2.5 million (64 per cent) were Moldavians. The Moldavian inhabitants of the republic represent 85 per cent of all Moldavians in the USSR. The Moldavian SSR records the highest birth-rate (20.1 per 1000 in 1978), but at 9.8 per 1000 it no longer exhibits the lowest death-rate of the European republics. Its population density is the highest in the USSR, although its degree of urbanization is the lowest among Union Republics.

Available evidence about educational achievement, occupational patterns and political participation suggests that the Moldavians are an underprivileged majority in their republic. Despite the growth of educational facilities, in 1971 the Moldavian SSR had the next to lowest proportion (among all republics) of inhabitants attending or completing secondary or higher education–only 39.7 per cent. Moldavians held relatively few places in higher educational institutions; limited access to education was reflected in employment. Less than a third of the republic's 'white collar' employees in 1959 were Moldavians; comparable data for 1970 are not available, but in 1971 they accounted for only 0.26 per cent of 'scientific workers' in the entire USSR although they made up 1.1 per cent of the population. Data on Party membership by nationality is meagre, but again it indicates that Moldavians are among the more under-represented of republic nationalities. Estimates of Communist Party membership for 1963 set the Moldavian proportion at 34 per cent and the Russian at 36 per cent; in 1972 Moldavians comprised only 0.4 per cent of the total membership of the CPSU.* Official explanations of the under-representation of Moldavians in the republic's élite groups stress the shortcomings of the schools in rural areas, particularly in Russian language instruction. But this overlooks the effects of an educational and cultural policy designed to sever links between Moldavian and Romanian culture and to ensure the dominance of Russian cultural forms.

There is no Moldavian language distinct from Romanian, and the Cyrillic script in which Romanian is printed in the USSR is a clumsy obfuscation. The authorities have steadily replaced 'Moldavian' with Russian as the language of instruction in the republic, especially in institutions of higher education. Although the Moldavian SSR has a full complement of theatres, orchestras, libraries, museums and an Academy of Sciences, its cultural activities, apart from folk music* and dance,* are managed by non-Moldavians. Denied links with Romania to which they had always been peripheral, in favour of Russification, the Moldavians live in a cultural limbo.

Official statements reflect some anxiety at the resilience of traditional Romanian attitudes, in which anti-Russian and anti-semitic sentiments prevail. Concern seems to have grown since the mid-1960s when Romania challenged the supranational pretensions of the USSR and officially revived traditional nationalist ideology and aspirations. At moments of severe strain in its relationship with the USSR, the Romanian government has hinted obliquely that the Bessarabian* question might be reopened. Alone of the Union Republics, the Moldavian SSR thus has a counterpart in the Soviet sphere in Eastern Europe whose relationship with the USSR seems to determine the course of Moldavian affairs.   *J.M.K.*

The Germans

The oldest settled German communities within the Russian Empire* were the Baltic Germans, descendants of the medieval Teutonic knights and their followers. The Baltic provinces passed to Russia in the 18th century; the privileged position of the German noble and urban classes, derived from Polish and Swedish charters, was eroded in the 19th, and finally lost after the 1917 Revolution,* when the Baltic peoples* formed independent republics. In 1940–1, pursuant to the German-Soviet pact of August 1939, the Baltic Germans were all transferred to Germany when the USSR took control of the Baltic states.* A second, small, group of Russian Germans included descendants of those who entered Russia at different times as military, technical or cultural specialists, or for entrepreneurial or commercial purposes. Most present-day Soviet Germans, however, are descended from immigrant peasant farmers, who settled principally on the lower Volga, near Saratov, and around the Black Sea. The immigration policy initiated in 1762 by Catherine II,* involving a variety of nationalities, continued during the early 19th century. In the 1870s land shortage and the cancellation of special privileges started a process of partial re-emigration,* chiefly to the Americas, which has continued intermittently ever since. After 1917 the Volga Germans were the first Soviet ethnic minority to be organized as a separate entity, in the Workers' Commune of the Volga Germans (1918), transformed in 1924 into the Autonomous Soviet Socialist Republic (ASSR) of the Volga Germans. Many Soviet German communities suffered severely in the civil war,* and in the great southern famine of 1921–2. Thereafter until 1941 they shared the common life and experiences of the USSR. With the outbreak of war with Germany, however, Germans were deported eastwards: the total number of such German deportees is estimated at between 650 and 700 thousand. The Volga German ASSR was abolished. Deportation of the Ukrainian German population was cut short by the advance of the German armies, who then removed remaining Soviet Germans westwards, into Poland and Germany. After 1944–5 many were returned to the USSR and sent to join their fellows in the north or in Central Asia. Rehabilitation of the Soviet Germans came in decrees of 1955 and 1964; but permission to return to areas of former settlement has never officially been granted. In their present principal areas of settlement – the Komi ASSR and Urals region in the north, the Central Asian republics and south-western Siberia – Soviet Germans live largely scattered among other nationalities. Since 1955 German-language schools have been established in areas with significant German population, and some very limited religious facilities have been allowed. An all-Union German-language newspaper, *Neues Leben*, founded in 1956, has been followed by some local German-language newspapers and by radio broadcasts. In the Komi ASSR Germans are involved in the timber industry, elsewhere primarily in agriculture. A technical and intellectual stratum has also emerged, and a significant minority has become assimilated to the dominant culture. The 1979 census showed 1.9 million German citizens of the USSR, of whom 57 per cent (67 per cent in 1970) gave German as their first language.　　　*R.P.B.*

1979 CENSUS DATA ON MINORITIES OF FOREIGN ORIGIN

	thousand
Germans	1936
Poles	1151
Koreans	389
Bulgarians	361
Greeks	344
Hungarians	171
Romanians	129
Turks	93
Finns	78
Persians	31
Citizens of foreign states	351

Source: *Naselenie SSSR po dannym vsesoyuznoy perepisi naseleniya 1979 goda*, Moscow, 1980

A collective farm board in a Korean settlement, Uzbekistan: Koreans are the third largest minority of foreign origin

The Gipsies

According to the 1979 census there were 209 000 Gipsies living in the Soviet Union but the real figure may be closer to 500 000. The discrepancy arises partly because the nomadic life of many Gipsies makes it difficult to record their numbers accurately, and partly because parents sometimes register their children not as Gipsies but as members of the eponymous nationality.* According to censuses, their population has trebled over 50 years, despite the killing of many thousands in the German-occupied areas during the Second World War* (the nomadic Gipsies were classified with Jews*). Most Soviet Gipsies live in European Russia, Belorussia, the Ukraine and the Baltic republics.* They arrived in two waves: the first from the south, via the Balkans in the 15th and 16th centuries and the second via Germany and Poland in the 16th and 17th centuries; by the early 18th century a small number had established themselves in Siberia. Soviet Gipsies speak Romani, which derives from the Indo-Aryan branch of the Indo-European family of languages* and is common to all Gipsies (who call themselves 'Rom'), but each group has been influenced by the language of the surrounding people. Because the majority passed through the Byzantine Empire in the Middle Ages, their language has a strong Balkan influence. Despite living in widely scattered communities, the Gipsies seem to have resisted linguistic assimilation.

Before the Revolution,* the Gipsies lived mainly by horse-trading (men) and fortune-telling (women), but also undertook blacksmithing, woodwork and basket-making. Most were wandering people, but they regularly visited peasant markets and festivals, and some settled in St Petersburg* and Moscow, where they gained a living as singers, fiddlers and dancers.

A separate group of about 8000 Gipsies lives in Central Asia; they call themselves 'Mugat', but are known as 'Lyuly' by the Uzbeks* and 'Dzhugy' by the Tadzhiks.* Most of them speak two languages: either Uzbek or Tadzhik, and their own argot, which is a mixture of Tadzhik and the secret language of the wandering people of Central Asia, a language which goes back to the Middle Ages. These Gipsies have no legends about their origin, which scholars suppose to have been Indian, but their dark physical features and the custom of tattooing the forehead suggest a southern origin. They formerly lived in patrilineal groups descended from a common ancestor, in winter gathering in particular neighbourhoods at the edges of towns, and in summer moving off through the countryside. In addition to the usual Gipsy occupations, they specialize in folk medicine.

Because of the Gipsies' lack of a regular work tradition, it has been difficult for the Soviet authorities to include them in the socialist economy.* An all-Gipsy collective farm called 'Kommunism' soon disintegrated, and even in farms where Gipsies were mixed with other people the Gipsy section often gave up and moved away. However, there are now several collective farms with Gipsy brigades whose members have settled houses, send their children to school and make use of Soviet institutions such as medical help and bank loans.

Many have, nevertheless, resisted attempts to settle them in permanent jobs. In 1956 a decree of the Supreme Soviet* made it an offence punishable by 'corrective labour' for a Gipsy to live a nomadic life. Such measures have had little effect, and they are not rigorously enforced; only partial success has been achieved in persuading Gipsies to educate their children. Large numbers still maintain their wandering traditions and live in tents.

The Gipsies' most noted influence on Soviet culture is perhaps in music.* The vogue for Gipsy revelry began in the late 18th century when Count G. A. Orlov brought a Gipsy choir from Moldavia to perform for Catherine II,* and throughout the 19th century Gipsy singers, dancers and musicians were among the most popular entertainers, whether in noble houses (many of whose owners maintained their own Gipsy troupes) or in the taverns and restaurants of Moscow and St Petersburg. Yet the 'Gipsy romance' – the most widely known and performed genre of 'Gipsy' song from the mid-19th century to the present – is in fact a Russian invention, with no roots in native Gipsy tradition. After the Revolution Gipsy troupes were at first criticized as artificial creations of the old aristocratic culture, but from the late 1920s they were encouraged to develop their own culture. Two Romani journals were established (*Rómany Zórya* in 1927, and the monthly *Nevo Drom* in 1929), and Romani school textbooks appeared. Publishing in Romani lapsed after the Second World War until the early 1970s. In 1931 the 'Romen' Gipsy theatre* was founded, and after a shaky start–the initial problem was to find Gipsies with the education and experience to run it–it has become one of the most popular theatres in Moscow. *S.F.&C.H.*

The Mikhay Gipsy family conformed to the 1956 decree prohibiting nomadism

HISTORY

Peter I, founder of the Russian Empire:
Falconet's statue (1782) erected in St
Petersburg by Catherine the Great

The earliest peoples

Nomadism

Although in its earlier prehistory Russia was a frontier region, remote from the main centres of economic and cultural development in the Old World, it came to play a crucial role in history as the birthplace of a new way of life which profoundly affected surrounding areas: steppe nomadism.

It was in the early fourth millennium BC that the tribes living in the lower reaches of the rivers flowing through the Ukrainian steppes–Dnieper, Dniester and Don–began to use the herds of wild horses which roamed the dry areas in between as more than a source of meat. Finds from the site of Dereivka, near Kiev, include fragments of horse-bits, indicating that these animals were used for the first time for riding. This innovation produced major changes in this area. People spread on to the steppe areas, using their new mobility to keep herds of sheep and using solid-wheeled wooden carts (drawn by oxen) which were first constructed by groups living on the fringes of Near Eastern civilization in the Caucasus. The dead were buried in round mounds which can still be seen in enormous numbers on the steppes.

In some of these, models or actual remains of carts have been found, as in the famous find in the Tri Brata tumulus on the Kalmyk Steppe. Metal objects in these graves show connections with the flourishing metal-working area of the Caucasus. Settlements of this period, such as Usatovo and Mikhaylovka near Odessa, show that wealthy communities lived in defended settlements.

The way of life which crystallized in the Ukraine was the key to the occupation of the dry zone which stretched eastwards across to the Altay. Movements of population, probably speaking Indo-European* languages, carried communities of millet-farmers and sheep herders who used the horse and the Bactrian camel for transport in a wave of eastward expansion. Archaeologically these are represented by the Andronovo and Karasuk cultures, which are known as far east as the Minusinsk depression (along the upper Yenisey river) in the early second millennium BC. It was the southern wing of this movement, around the eastern side of the Caspian, which brought Indo-European languages into Iran and ultimately as far south as India. The combination of horses and wheeled vehicles led to the first construction of the light chariot by the people of the steppes, whose military advantage allowed them to penetrate deeply into the older urban civilizations to the south. By the middle of the second

THE ORIGINS OF NOMADISM

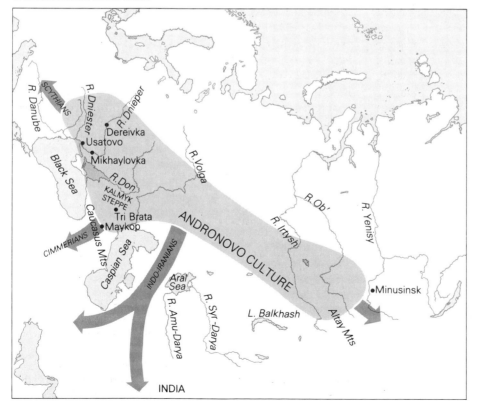

KEY

Area of origin of pastoral nomadism

Later migrations of pastoral nomads

Design by A. G. Sherratt

millennium BC wheeled vehicles of steppe origin were in use in China by the founders of the first Chinese state, the Shang dynasty.

This Indo-European domination of the steppes (whose later representatives were the historically-recorded Scythians,* Sarmatians* and Sakas) came to an end only in the first millennium AD when groups of oriental origin reversed the eastward flow of population to appear in history as invading Huns,* Avars,* and Khazars.*   *A.S.*

Scythians and Sarmatians

Russian history proper can be said to begin along the northern shore of the Black Sea and in the steppe beyond. Here it was that the peoples of southern Russia came into contact with the Ancient World of Greece and Rome through the Greek colonies which began to appear along the Black Sea coast from about the 7th century BC. The Greek historian Herodotus, who lived in the 5th century BC, spent some time in the Greek colony of Olbia at the mouth of the river Bug and left a valuable description of the surrounding region and its population. The knowledge provided by this account and by other fragmentary writings of the same period has been verified and greatly augmented by archaeological evidence from excavations carried out both in imperial* Russia and, on a larger scale, in the Soviet Union. The excavation of burial-mounds in southern Russia has proved a rich source of information. Material from the so-called 'frozen tombs' of Pazyryk in Siberia has proved even more valuable. Although outside the Scythian area of influence, much of this material bears a striking similarity to finds in southern Russia, and provides evidence in support of references in Herodotus. The earliest in the succession of peoples who appeared in southern Russia from about the year 1000 BC in the course of waves of invasion from Asia are thought to have been the Cimmerians; it appears that they spoke an Indo-European language and ruled southern Russia from about 1000 BC to 700 BC. The Scythians, a new wave of invaders, defeated them and destroyed their state. The new rulers, who spoke an Iranian* language, held sway in southern Russia from the 7th to the end of the 3rd century BC; according to Herodotus, their dominions extended from the Danube to the Don and from the shore of the Black Sea a 20-day journey northwards. At its greatest extent the Scythian state probably stretched south of the Danube and across the Caucasus into Asia Minor.

The Scythians lived the life typical of nomads. They were effective in warfare and established a strong military state, so strong that not even the Persians could defeat them in their own territory. Herodotus describes their state as a tribal confederation ruled by the 'royal Scythians', who always provided the monarch and 'counted all other Scythians their slaves'. He also distinguishes the 'Scythian-farmers' and the 'Scythian-pastoralists', although it seems unlikely that the whole population of the region was Scythian. Some historians think that the successive waves of invaders formed only the ruling group in

southern Russia while the bulk of the population was indigenous and continued a steady development of culture.

Some time in the 3rd century BC the Scythians were displaced by the Sarmatians, another wave of Iranian-speaking nomads from Central Asia, who ruled until the beginning of the 3rd century AD. Sarmatian social organization and culture was similar in many ways to the Scythian, and they seem to have fitted easily into the culture and economy of the region.

It was during the Scythian–Sarmatian period that the interaction between Greek civilization and the nomadic way of life led to the appearance in the steppe and on the shores of the Black Sea of a highly-developed culture known as the Graeco-Iranian. The nomads brought a distinctive art and craftsmanship, especially in metal-work, and an original style in decorative art* known as the Scythian animal style. They made no sustained effort to destroy the Greek colonies of southern Russia, but traded with them and developed other close contacts, thus making a distinctive contribution to classical civilization, and leaving their imprint on the land that was to become known as Russia.

Goths

Sarmatian rule in the steppe region north of the Black Sea was brought to an end in about AD 200 by the Goths, Germanic invaders from the north-east, probably from the region of the Baltic. They were divided into several tribes, of which the most important were known as the Ostrogoths and the Visigoths. The Ostrogothic empire in southern Russia reached its zenith under Hermanric (who reigned from about AD 350 to 370) when it stretched from the Black Sea to the Baltic. Little is known of their system of administration, and their cultural level was probably considerably lower than that of southern Russia, to which they had little to contribute. About AD 362 the Goths penetrated the Crimea where they established town-like settlements and buried their princes and other notables in graves which often closely resemble earlier Scythian burial-mounds.

Huns

The empire of Hermanric was shattered by the Huns, who descended upon the Goths about AD 370. The Huns, who came in a mass migration from Central Asia, are thought to have been originally a Turkish-speaking people with the addition of large groups of Mongols,* but by the time they reached central Europe they were a much more mixed group containing large Iranian and Germanic elements they had conquered and absorbed in the course of their irresistible surge along the great steppe road from Asia into Europe. Although one of the most primitive peoples to break into southern Russia, the Huns had sufficient energy and military ability not only to conquer the region, but to go on to play a vital part in the period of the 'Great Migrations' in Europe. They penetrated deep into France and, although defeated at the battle of Châlons in 451, invaded Italy. But with the sudden death of their leader, Attila, in 453, the primitive and poorly-organized Hunnic empire quickly disintegrated.

Avars
The Avars were another Turkic/Mongol group from Asia, whose invasion of southern Russia in 558, like that of the Huns, changed the whole political system of east-central Europe. It caused a new wave of migrations of Germanic and Iranian tribes, although on a more limited scale than the general displacement caused by the Huns. The centre of the Avar empire lay in the basin of the middle Danube, and at the height of their power their sway extended to eastern Russia. Control of Russia was lost after about a hundred years, but the Avar state lasted about two and a half centuries, in the course of which it threatened Byzantium and waged wars in the west against the empire of Charlemagne. In the end the Avar state quickly fell to pieces and disappeared virtually without trace, the common fate of politically and culturally weak nomad empires.

Khazars
The next organized power to emerge in Russia dates from the 7th century. This was the state of the Khazars, which covered the region of the lower Volga and the south-eastern Russian steppe. They were yet another Turkish-speaking people from Asia, whose arrival split up a powerful tribal confederation known as Great Bulgaria, which had occupied the region of the lower Volga and north Caucasus since the collapse of the Hunnic empire; one group settled in the Balkans, to be absorbed by the Slavs and give its name to present-day Bulgaria, while another went north-east and eventually established a prosperous trading state on the middle Volga. The Khazar state lay in an even more favourable position across important trade routes, and the Khazars, although originally a nomadic people, built towns, developed commerce and played an important role in the international politics of the period. They fought stubbornly against the Arabs and succeeded in blocking the spread of Islam★ into Europe. In the 8th and 9th centuries the ruler and the upper class embraced Judaism★–another curious development in an unusual history. The Khazar state survived until about the year 1000, although it never really recovered from the shattering series of blows dealt it by the Kievan prince Svyatoslav★ in 965.

Slavs
The history of the peoples and cultures of southern Russia before the 9th century AD forms an essential background to Kievan★ Russia, but the inhabitants of the Kievan state who became known as Russians were not Scythians, Huns or Khazars–they were Slavs.★ The first written references to the Slavs occur in early classical writers such as Pliny the Elder, and it is now assumed by many historians that Slavs

composed a significant part of the population of southern and central Russia from the time of the Scythians. Surviving the successive invasions and migrations, they make their appearance in the Russian Primary Chronicle,★ where at the dawn of Kievan history a number of East Slavonic tribes are shown paying tribute to the Khazars.

D.S.M.W.

The land of Rus′

The Russian Primary Chronicle
The Russian Primary Chronicle (edited in the early 12th century) opens with the intention to reveal 'the origins of the land of Rus′ . . . the source from which the land of Rus′ had its beginning'. However, faced with a distant and undocumented past, the chronicler had to content himself with a stylized introduction to Russian history, much of which resembles myth or saga. He was not to know that he would thereby kindle a controversy which has yet to run its course.

According to the chronicle, three Scandinavian (Varangian) brothers, Ryurik, Sineus and Truvor, came with their followers to the land of Rus′ (*c*.860–2) in answer to an invitation from the local east Slav tribes: 'Our whole land is great and rich, but there is no order in it. Come to rule and reign over us.' Whether the brothers came from Denmark or Sweden remains unclear. Even less clear is the meaning of the term Rus′, which is applied to them, as well as to their host land. But perhaps the most crucial question which remains unanswered concerns the extent of their influence and that of their successors on the Slavs who allegedly invited them to come.

The chronicle suggests that the land was 'great and rich'. Yet another long-standing controversy relates to the source of this apparent wealth. Were the peoples of Rus′ principally engaged in agriculture or in trade? Archaeology tends to provide support for the former; the literary sources give preference to the latter. In either case, the new Varangian overlords undoubtedly imposed order by taxation. They also sought to increase prosperity by extending and safeguarding trade routes. Chief among these (and perhaps the lure which brought them to Rus′) was the Dnieper-Black Sea route 'from the Varangians to the Greeks' which linked Scandinavia with the fabled wealth of Constantinople.

The lure of Constantinople
Thus Ryurik's associates Askol′d and Dir seized the township of Kiev (860) and used it as their base for an ambitious attack on Constantinople itself. The assault was not brought to a successful conclusion, but the Byzantines were never to forget it. It forced them to take cognizance of their bellicose northern neighbours and to plan for their containment.

It is not clear whether Askol'd and Dir became Christians before their death at the hands of Ryurik's councillor Oleg (882). But the eventual baptism of the Kievan rulers Ol'ga and Vladimir was undoubtedly consonant with Byzantium's desire to reduce the risk of any further such incursions.

Meanwhile, however, Oleg (882–912) followed Askol'd and Dir to Mikligard (as the Norsemen named the Byzantine capital). His expedition of 907 (if the evidence of the Russian chronicle is to be accepted) was successful enough to result in a favourable Russo-Byzantine treaty (911). Under Ryurik's son Igor' (913–95) two more expeditions were launched against Constantinople (941 and 944), which resulted in a second treaty. Though somewhat less advantageous to the Russians than the first, it still provides evidence of the extent to which the two parties valued each other's trade and collaboration.

The baptism of Igor''s widow Ol'ga (regent 945–64) under the sponsorship of the Byzantine emperor himself indicated the way towards even closer collaboration. In connection with this event she was received by him in Constantinople (957). But her example was followed by few, and certainly not by the Kievan state as a whole.

Ol'ga was widowed as the result of local Slav (Drevlian) resentment at her husband's main alternative source of income, tribute. The Drevlians had been required to pay an exceptionally heavy tribute after an earlier uprising against Igor'. In 945 they rose once more, captured Igor' and executed him. In the chronicle Ol'ga is remembered almost as much for the terrible revenge which she took on the Drevlians – she killed their envoys, burned their town and put 5000 of its inhabitants to death – as for her subsequent conversion to the religion of mercy and peace.

Svyatoslav (962–72)

Askol'd and Dir had captured Kiev from the Khazars,* whose empire lay to the south-east, centred on the Volga basin. Ol'ga's son Svyatoslav was to go further and to undermine the empire itself. He was a brilliant tactician – in the years 963–6 and again 968–9 he moved tirelessly from one victory to another – but he was deficient in strategy: he failed to exploit his dismemberment of Khazaria and moreover failed to compensate for it. In the process a buffer state vanished and Rus' was subjected to endless inroads from nomads who replaced the Khazars – at first the Pechenegs, subsequently the Polovtsy (Cumans). The Pechenegs demonstrated their new strength by killing Svyatoslav himself (971) as he returned from an abortive attempt to extend his power to the Balkans. Earlier, he had intended to make Pereyaslavets on the Danube his capital (967), unabashed by the resulting confrontation with the combined forces of Bulgaria and Byzantium.

Svyatoslav's three sons were left to resolve their differences as to who should rule in Kiev. For Kiev, rather than Novgorod (where Ryurik settled), had by now acquired a pre-eminence which it was to retain, if only in theory, for many years to come. According to the Russian Primary Chronicle, it had been designated 'the mother of Russian cities' by Oleg as long ago as 882; the same chronicle contained a legend to the effect that its future site had once been blessed by no less a visitor than the apostle Andrew.

Vladimir I (980–1015)

The would-be successors' struggle for power (unlike many that were to follow) was comparatively brief. Prince Vladimir emerged the sole survivor. In an attempt to unite the Rus' lands he fostered the creation of a pagan pantheon at Kiev. He furthered their stabilization by regulating the collection of tribute from the various provincial capitals, in each of which he placed one of his twelve sons to rule. He also sought to counteract the work of Svyatoslav by building a line of forts to the east as a protection against the Pechenegs. Instead of over-extending his frontiers to the west, he attempted to stabilize them by conquest of the 'Cherven' cities' from Poland (981).

All this provides evidence of an astute mind, though it hardly prepares for that demonstration of statesmanship which was to ensure his lasting fame and bring Rus' firmly within the bounds of the Byzantine 'commonwealth'.

The conversion of Rus'

The creation of an indigenous pantheon could bring few benefits in the field of foreign relations. The Khazars had been converts to Judaism;* the eastern Bulgars were Muslim;* the homeland of the Varangians had recently turned to western Christianity, as had the Poles and Hungarians; to the south and south-west lay the Orthodox* world, in the midst of which Svyatoslav had hoped to settle. The acceptance of any one of the great monotheistic religions would facilitate new alliances and further trade. Vladimir seems to have pondered the options for some time. Ultimately, he chose to follow his grandmother's example in his acceptance of Orthodox Christianity. This choice was diplomatically the more attractive since support for the Byzantine emperor (Basil II) brought him the coveted reward of the emperor's sister in marriage. Vladimir's baptism (about 987–9) was the necessary prelude to such a match.

In the event, the emperor was reluctant to proceed with his part of the bargain: Vladimir needed to capture the Crimean city of Kherson from the Byzantines (989) to prompt the despatch of his bride. He returned to Kiev later that year with the necessary zeal and support to initiate the accelerated (and often forcible) conversion of his subjects. It was a turning-point in Russian history.

The Russian Primary Chronicle paints an excessively laudatory portrait of the Christian Vladimir. But there is no reason to doubt the sincerity with which he accepted the new faith, nor the efficiency with which he established and disseminated it. Kiev was soon graced with a stone cathedral (990–6), church statutes were elaborated (996/1007–11) and bishoprics were established. However, the new faith was not enough to ensure amity among Vladimir's offspring. His death (1015) immediately provoked or exacerbated the kind of internecine strife which became a depressingly familiar feature of early Russian political life.

Yaroslav the Wise (1036–54)

The Kievan throne was seized by Svyatopolk (1015–19). According to the subsequently elaborated narratives, it was he who immediately ordered the assassination of his rivals Boris, Gleb and Svyatoslav. If only on this account, Yaroslav of Novgorod disputed Svyatopolk's succession. The ensuing war (with Yaroslav supported by Varangians, Svyatopolk by Poles and Pechenegs) ended in victory for Yaroslav (1019).

But Yaroslav did not thereby become sole ruler of the Russian territories. Most important among his remaining rivals was Mstislav of Tmutarakan', whose successful struggle with Yaroslav (1024–6) ended in an agreement to divide the country, using the Dnieper as frontier. Yaroslav retained Novgorod, Kiev and the right (west) bank: Mstislav's territory extended from the left bank to include Chernigov and Pereyaslavl', as well as Tmutarakan'. Only Mstislav's death without issue (1036) reunited these equally significant areas.

Yaroslav's unchallenged reign proved to be an exceptional one. Though remarkable as much for consolidation as for innovation, it was to earn him the sobriquet *mudryy*, 'the wise'. Kiev gained notably in grandeur and prestige. Adam of Bremen (d. 1074) went so far as to call it 'the rival of Constantinople's realm, the brightest ornament of the Greek [Orthodox] world'. Under Yaroslav began the construction of its great St Sophia cathedral (1037–46). This was to be the seat of Kiev's metropolitan (the head of the Church), normally the legate of Constantinople. However, at one stage Yaroslav sponsored the election of a native Russian (Ilarion) to this exalted post (1051–2), as if to demonstrate his independence of the Byzantine world. Possibly by way of redress, he arranged the marriage of his son to a Byzantine princess (1052). It was one of many such marriages by which Yaroslav sought to establish or cement good relations with the outside world. His immediate family was linked to the royal families of Sweden, Norway, Poland, Hungary, France and Germany.

Yaroslav's work in the legal sphere was to prove more lasting than his diplomacy. Early in his career (about 1016) he had seen to the codification of Russian law (*Pravda russkaya*); this was revised and amplified two decades later. Although it began life as a local Novgorodian codex, it was to serve Russian law-makers as a source and model for centuries to come.

The troubled succession

Regrettably, Yaroslav probably elaborated no legislation or guidelines concerning the complex succession to his throne. Though some kind of rota system may have been followed by his immediate successors, this would seem to have been the result of their pragmatic decisions rather than of any preconceived plan. Thus the death of Yaroslav presented a challenge to centralized government in the Kievan realm, a challenge which it was ill-prepared to withstand. Only by the mutual agreement of Yaroslav's three most powerful successors – Izyaslav, Svyatoslav and Vsevolod – was fragmentation of the realm delayed. All three ruled successively in Kiev: Izyaslav, the eldest, with two significant interruptions, both caused by the popular discontent which he had provoked (1054–68, 1069–73 and 1077–8). Like Svyatopolk before him, Izyaslav regained his throne with Polish help in 1069. But neither Poles nor Germans were anxious to offer him support in his second exile, from which he returned briefly only on his supplanter's death.

That only one of Yaroslav's sons (Vsevolod) remained to rule in the years 1078–93 by no means ensured stability. Troubles were compounded by the appearance of a new enemy in the steppe. The defeat of the Pechenegs in Yaroslav's time had simply made way for the Polovtsy who from 1061 were to harass the Russian principalities. Worse, they were later to be employed by one principality against another.

The reign of Svyatopolk II (1093–1113) produced no resolution of Russia's political problems, despite the unprecedented attempt to bring them to a conference table (Lyubech, 1097). At first a reconciliation of the various princes and power groups seemed indeed to have been achieved; but the very participants of the conference soon suspected one another of conspiracy, and the treacherous arrest and blinding of Yaroslav's grandson Vasil'ko (1097) revealed the fragility of that same year's agreements.

Vladimir Monomakh (1113–25)

Ironically, it was one of the staunchest defenders of the Lyubech accord who was to deviate from it and thus offer Kievan Rus' the security and stability which had evaded it for so long.

Vladimir Monomakh's reign in Kiev began democratically with an invitation from the Kievan *veche* (city assembly). The riots which preceded and provoked the invitation (as well as those which followed Monomakh's initial refusal to serve) were ended by his promptly effected social and fiscal reforms. His military prowess had already been displayed in his successful campaigns against the Polovtsy – notably in 1111. Such campaigns were to be continued by his son Yaropolk (1116 and 1126). But the authority of Vladimir rested on more than the ability to wage war or conduct diplomacy. It is clear that his personal integrity was a cohesive force of paramount importance. Some indication of its character is provided by the magnificent *Testimony* (*Pouchenie*), incorporated into the Russian Primary Chronicle, which was edited and revised in his reign.

The decline of Kiev

However, the days of Kiev's primacy were numbered. Monomakh's sons Mstislav (1125–32) and Yaropolk (1132–9) were able to follow successfully in their father's footsteps, but the succeeding years saw endless disputes and power struggles involving a prize of ever-decreasing value. Chernigov had long been an alternative centre of power. In the western regions, Galicia and Volynia (to be united in 1199) tended ever more to go their own way. In the north-west, Novgorod had always retained a certain independence; it had its own trade connections via the Baltic with the west, and its mercantile concerns, as well as its distinctive form of government, were to further its separate development. Nowhere was the *veche* and its council to gain such status, nowhere was the prince to become so much its servant.

The city of Vladimir

Kiev could no longer hope to influence (let alone control) Novgorod after 1136, and a hitherto comparatively obscure principality of the north-east began to manifest its pretensions in this respect by the mid-12th century. With the accession of the most forceful of Monomakh's grandsons, Andrey, to the throne of Rostov and Suzdal' (1157–74), the centre of gravity was to move to his newly established capital Vladimir on the Klyaz'ma. The succeeding half-century saw Vladimir's embellishment as rival and supplanter of Kiev. Its impressive Cathedral of the Assumption (*Uspenskiy sobor*)★ (1158–60/1185–9) still stands as a memorial to Andrey's ambitions, which were fully shared by his successor, Vsevolod III (1176–1212). The decline of Kiev was calculatedly emphasized by Andrey, who captured and sacked the old capital in 1169 but spurned it as his seat.

The end of Kievan Rus'

In due course Vladimir itself suffered depredations and decline. Six years before the death of Vsevolod III, a 'supreme emperor' had been proclaimed in the Far East: in Mongolian his title read 'Chingis [or Genghis] Khan'. By 1223 his advance battalions entered Polovtsian territory from the south on a victorious reconnaissance for the main

THE FRAGMENTATION OF KIEVAN RUSSIA, 1054–1238

KEY

The twelve principalities of Russia in 1100

Source: M. Gilbert, *Russian History Atlas*, London, 1972

Mongol* army. A combined force of Russians and Polovtsy was defeated by them on the Kalka river (1223). The Mongols' subsequent withdrawal should have engendered no complacency for they were to return in full force (1237). Ultimately only a few western cities were to escape the broadcast destruction which established Mongol suzerainty and ushered in a new age. *S.H.*

The Mongol conquest

In the autumn of 1237 a Mongol army led by Batu, grandson of Genghis Khan, swooped down upon the Russian city of Ryazan'. This was the beginning of the Mongol invasion of the 'western lands', the final stage in a programme of conquest planned by an assembly of Mongol chieftains in 1206. Batu's army then proceeded methodically through north-eastern Russia, capturing and sacking many cities, including Vladimir on the Klyaz'ma, which fell in February 1238. By the time the Mongols (or Tatars* as they are more commonly known in the Russian sources) arrived there Prince Yury Vsevolodovich, grand prince of Vladimir, had left the town (trusting that its strong walls would protect it) and retreated northwards with his army. He hoped that a long march of pursuit would weaken the invaders; but he underestimated the toughness and endurance of the Mongol horsemen, who could spend long hours in the saddle with little need for food or rest. When Batu's army caught up with Yury on the banks of the river Sit' the Russians were defeated and Yury himself was killed. Batu then turned west, towards the wealthy commercial city of Novgorod. However Novgorod was saved by a change in the weather: in 1238 the spring thaw came unusually early, making the ground too swampy for Batu's mounted troops to advance.

Mounted Mongol archers crossing a frozen river (from a Persian illuminated manuscript, *c.* 1300)

During the year 1239 Batu undertook no major campaigns; then in the summer of 1240 he struck again, this time in a south-westerly direction. The cities of Chernigov and Pereyaslavl' were captured and sacked, and finally Kiev itself, in December 1240. This completed the conquest of Russia and inaugurated the period of Mongol overlordship described in Russian chronicles as the 'Tatar yoke', which was to last for nearly two and a half centuries. At the same time as the Russians faced the Mongol onslaught they were also threatened from the west, by the armies of Sweden and the Teutonic Knights, who attacked Novgorod in 1240 and Pskov in 1242. Both attacks were repulsed by the prince of Novgorod, Alexander Nevsky (so called for his victory over the Swedes on the Neva River, 1240) his second victory being the famous Battle of the Ice on Lake Peipus. The scale of this engagement has probably been exaggerated, but this has not lessened Alexander Nevsky's importance as a warrior hero and cult figure.

The Tatar yoke

After 1240 the whole of what was formerly Kievan Russia became part of the vast Mongol empire, of which it formed the western section. Batu, now its khan, or ruler, established his capital at Saray near the mouth of the Volga. At first this was a large camp, since the Mongols continued to follow their nomadic life-style, but in time it became more like a conventional town, with settled inhabitants. The khan and his entourage at Saray were known collectively as the Golden Horde (from the word *orda*, meaning camp). The Golden Horde did not administer the conquered territory as a single unit, a fact which was to influence the future course of Russian history. The middle Dnieper area was ruled directly from Saray by Mongol officials, while the rest of Russia remained under the control of its princes, as vassals of the Golden Horde. This meant that each prince had to go to Saray, make a formal act of obeisance to the khan and then receive a *yarlyk* or patent authorizing him to rule his principality, though under the watchful eye of a resident Mongol overseer called a *baskak*. The *yarlyk* had to be renewed every time there was a new prince or khan, so that visits to Saray became part of the normal pattern of life for the Russian princes. Sometimes they would spend many months there, competing for the khan's favour by means of bribes and flattery, since this was the surest way to political success in their quarrels with each other. Only two princes, Daniil of Galicia and Alexander Nevsky's brother Andrey, attempted serious military resistance; but both were forced into submission by Mongol counter-attacks.

To the ordinary people Mongol rule meant two things: financial tribute and compulsory military service. The Mongols, who used the decimal system, at first demanded a tenth of everything. Later the tribute was commuted to money payments, assessed separately for towns and rural areas. The tribute was first collected by tax-farmers, then subsequently, after the reign of Khan Mengu-Temir (1266–79), by specially appointed tax-gatherers. Finally under Khan Uzbeg (1313–41) the duty of collecting taxes became the prerogative of the leading Russian princes. For military service the Mongols conscripted ten per cent of the male population; they also forced many skilled craftsmen to work for them. In order to make accurate assessments for the purpose of taxation and conscription the Russian population was 'counted', in four successive stages, during the second half of the 13th century.

The heavy burden of taxation and conscription, following after the devastation caused by the invasions, had a depressing effect on the economy of the Russian lands. Outside the city of Novgorod, which reached the height of its prosperity during the 14th and 15th centuries, commerce declined and the Russian economy became more agrarian in character. As a result landowners became the most important social and economic group in the community; this has led Soviet historians to describe this period of Russian history as 'feudal'. (It must be noted, however, that this term does not mean the same as it does when applied to western Europe in earlier centuries.)

The Church under Mongol rule

The period of Mongol rule proved important in the development of the Orthodox Church* in Russia. Khan Mengu-Temir issued a *yarlyk* exempting all church lands from taxation, and all people working on them from military service. The Church thus became a specially privileged institution. The reason for this was that it was part of Mongol tradition, preserved in a document known as the Great Yasa, 'to respect the learned and wise men of all peoples', and the monks and priests of the Orthodox Church were so regarded in the lands subject to the Golden Horde. In time these privileges proved to be double-edged: they strengthened the Russian Church as an institution, and thus helped it to keep alive such cultural activities as chronicle-writing and icon-painting;* but increasing wealth also led to worldliness and corruption among some of the monks and clergy. Moreover in time princes began to covet church lands, which caused tension between secular rulers and church authorities.

Although the Russian Church continued to be a single unit of ecclesiastical administration controlled by a metropolitan appointed and consecrated by the patriarch of Constantinople, from the beginning of the 14th century onwards it became more national in character: a number of Russian metropolitans were appointed, and Russian princes made determined efforts to secure the election of favoured candidates. At times this caused tension with the patriarchs of Constantinople, but the formal tie of dependence continued until 1448, when a synod of Russian bishops elected one of their own number as metropolitan because of their opposition to the act of union with the Western Church signed at the Council of Florence in 1439. From then on the Russian Church had its own head. There were also attempts to establish a separate area of jurisdiction with its own metropolitan in the west Russian lands which had been wrested from the Mongols and conquered by the Lithuanians during the 14th century. But these attempts did not prove to be permanent.

Monastic* life flourished during the period of Mongol rule: at least 180 monasteries are known to have been founded, including the famous Trinity Monastery of St Sergy, founded by St Sergy of Radonezh, and the Solovetsky Monastery founded in 1429 on an island in the White Sea. Both these houses, and many others, owed their foundation to a revival of the ascetic ideals and practices of early Christian monasticism, of which St Sergy was a notable exponent. As many monasteries were founded in hitherto uninhabited areas, they performed an important economic role by attracting settlers and opening up new lands to agriculture.   *M.H.*

Alexander Nevsky, *c.* 1220–63 (from a 17th-century mural in the Archangel Cathedral, the Kremlin, Moscow)

The rise of Moscow

In the years after the Mongol* conquest the process of political fragmentation and resultant inter-princely strife continued, a fact which helped the Golden Horde to maintain its supremacy. However, in the course of the 14th century, one principality achieved a position of political predominance: this was Moscow.

At the time of the Mongol invasions Moscow was a relatively minor city of the grand principality of Vladimir, which did not acquire the status of a separate principality with its own prince until 1301, when it was assigned to Daniil, a younger son of Alexander Nevsky. It was then a modest 500 square miles (about 1300 sq km) in extent, which his descendants were to increase thirtyfold. However, territorial expansion was not the only factor in Moscow's rise to power. While it was quite small in area one of its early rulers, Ivan I (1325–40), usually known as *Kalita* or 'Moneybag', acquired the coveted *yarlyk* for the

office of grand prince of Vladimir, though he had to share it with Prince Alexander Vasil'evich of Suzdal' until the latter's death in 1331. This title conferred special prestige on its holder since he was considered the most senior of all the Russian princes. For some years this *yarlyk* had been ferociously contested between the princes of Moscow and those of Tver', who belonged to a more senior branch of the prolific Ryurikovichi (the descendants of Ryurik); and it was only after Ivan I had helped the Golden Horde to suppress a popular revolt in Tver' in 1327 that he was finally granted the *yarlyk* as a reward. From then on it was held almost exclusively by the princes of Moscow, though not always without a struggle. The Moscow princes also benefited from their position as the chief financial agents of the Golden Horde, and from the transference of the seat of the metropolitan of the Russian Church to Moscow after 1328.

During the middle decades of the 14th century the Golden Horde itself became prey to internal dissensions, a fact which proved advantageous to the Russian principalities, especially Moscow.

THE RISE OF MOSCOW, 1261–1533

Ivan I

KEY

▨	Principality of Moscow by 1462
▨	Further expansion of Moscow by 1533

Source: M. Gilbert, *Russian History Atlas*, London, 1972

Palace (or tent) revolutions were frequent, and between 1360 and 1380 there were 25 khans, some of whom reigned only a few weeks. In such circumstances the Golden Horde was in no position to enforce the payment of tribute, much of which went into the coffers of the prince of Moscow. However, later in the century a vigorous grand vizier named Mamay assumed effective power at Saray and demanded the payment of arrears, organizing a punitive expedition to enforce his request. The prince of Moscow at this time was Dmitry Ivanovich, a grandson of Ivan I. Although he was somewhat reluctant to risk a military confrontation with the Mongols, when he heard that their army was advancing towards Moscow he decided to resist it, with help from some other Russian princes. The armies met at Kulikovo Field near the river Don on 8 September 1380, and after a hard-fought battle the Russians emerged victorious; in honour of this victory Prince Dmitry came to be known as Dmitry Donskoy ('Victor of the Don'). The battle of Kulikovo certainly did not mean the end of the 'Tatar yoke'; indeed two years later a Mongol army raided and burnt Moscow and re-enforced the payment of tribute for some years. But the victory of Kulikovo is rightly considered an important landmark in Russian history because it shattered the legend of the military invincibility of the Mongols.

During the rest of the reign of Dmitry Donskoy and those of his successors Vasily I (1389–1425) and Vasily II (1425–62) Moscow further increased its territory and maintained its political predominance, in spite of a prolonged internal dynastic conflict during the reign of Vasily II. It was his son Ivan III and his grandson Vasily III who were destined to bring all the east Russian lands under their rule, and lay the foundations of a united Russian state   *M.H.*

Ivan III (1462–1505)

Ivan III, sometimes known as Ivan the Great, became grand prince of Moscow and Vladimir in 1462. Although he inherited a territory many times larger than that of his ancestor Prince Daniil Alexandrovich, there were even larger areas of the future Russian state which lay outside his control. It was to be his major achievement to bring these under his rule. They comprised two different types of territory: appanages within Muscovy granted to his four younger brothers, and independent principalities ruled by their own princes, descended, like Ivan III himself, from different branches of the Ryurikovich dynasty. The most important of these principalities were Yaroslavl', Rostov, Ryazan' and Tver', Moscow's ancient rival.

Territorial unification
In the task of territorial unification Ivan III displayed both political acumen and diplomatic skill, but he was also helped by good luck.

Ivan III

For example two of his brothers, Yury and Andrey the Younger, died without heirs and their appanages reverted to Ivan. Uglich, the appanage of Andrey the Elder, was confiscated because he refused to participate in a campaign against the Kazan' Tatars.* The regions outside Muscovy were likewise acquired by varied means: the princes of Yaroslavl' and Rostov renounced their sovereign rights in return for financial compensation (in 1463 and 1474 respectively); Tver' was annexed in 1485 when its prince tried to make an alliance with Casimir IV of Poland (thus breaking the terms of a previous treaty with Moscow); Ryazan' came under Ivan's control (though not formally annexed) as the result of a dynastic marriage, arranged between its heir, Prince Vasily Ivanovich and Ivan III's sister in 1464.

Perhaps Ivan III's most difficult task was the subjugation of the city-republic of Novgorod, which controlled a vast colonial territory. Although nominally part of the grand principality of Vladimir, Novgorod had long been autonomous, governed by officials appointed by its own *veche*.* Relations with the suzerain princes of Moscow had often been tense, but it was Ivan III who finally abolished the political privileges of Novgorod. The circumstances of the final confrontation in 1477 were complicated, and Ivan III was able to take advantage of social and political dissensions within the city which provided him with an opportunity for intervention.

The acquisition of so much new territory raised problems of administration. Ivan III tried to centralize this as much as possible, by appointing provincial governors responsible to himself, known as *namestniki*. In some cases, however, their powers were modified by local charters making specific administrative and judicial arrangements for those areas. A few of these have survived, for example the Beloozero Charter of 1488, which provides for some participation by elected local inhabitants. In 1497 he issued a *Sudebnik* or law-code to establish uniform legal norms throughout his dominions.

An artist's reconstruction of a street in 14th-century Novgorod

Border consolidation

Ivan III pursued a vigorous foreign policy in relation to his immediate neighbours, the Tatar khanates and the grand principality of Lithuania, itself dynastically linked to the kingdom of Poland. In the middle of the 15th century the once-powerful Golden Horde split up into three separate units: the Crimean Tatars (under the suzerainty of the Ottoman Empire after 1475), the Kazan' khanate and the so-called Great Horde, or remnants of the Golden Horde. Although the overlordship of the Golden Horde had become merely nominal even before Ivan III's accession, and was formally renounced in 1480, the Tatars remained dangerous neighbours because of their frequent and destructive raids into Russian territory. Ivan III attempted to neutralize this danger in two ways: he cultivated friendly relations with the Crimean Tatars and made a treaty of alliance with their khan Mengli-Girey in 1480; in the case of Kazan' he intervened in its internal political power struggles with a view to securing subservient and pro-Russian khans. Several military expeditions against Kazan' were organized for this purpose during Ivan III's reign. His policy towards Lithuania was more aggressive, since he regarded the Dnieper area which the Lithuanians had conquered from the

Mongols as part of his territorial patrimony. At first activities against Lithuania were limited to border skirmishes, the so-called 'small war' of 1487–94, in which Ivan III was not even officially involved; but from 1500 to 1503 there was a period of open warfare in which Russian troops had considerable success, though they failed to take the important city of Smolensk. The war was concluded by a six-year truce, leaving Russia in possession of all the territory it had occupied.

Ivan III's last years were darkened by quarrels within his family as to who should succeed him, the main protagonists being Elena, the wife of his deceased eldest son Ivan, and his masterful second wife Sofia Paleologue (niece of the last Byzantine emperor), each of whom desired the succession of her own son. Ivan finally decided in favour of his eldest son by Sofia, who succeeded him as Vasily III in 1505. *M.H.*

Vasily III (1505–33)

Under Vasily III the administration of the Russian state was consolidated and its territory further extended, notably by the annexation of Ryazan' and Pskov (formerly a subsidiary town of Novgorod), and the capture of Smolensk. The circumstances following the annexation of Pskov gave rise to the dictum describing Moscow as the Third Rome,★ and thus by implication the heir of the Byzantine Empire recently conquered by the Ottoman Turks. The famous words occur in a letter written by the monk Filofey, member of a monastery near Pskov, urging Vasily III to be less harsh in his treatment of the citizens of that town. *M.H.*

Left: Vasily III. Right: Ivan IV. Far right: boyars at the court of Emperor Maximilian II

Ivan IV – the Terrible (1533–84)

When Vasily III died in 1533 he was succeeded by his eldest son, Ivan, then only three years old; hence a regency was necessary. In 1547 Ivan IV announced that he was of age to govern, and his first official act was to have himself crowned tsar in a ceremony closely modelled on that used for the coronation of the Byzantine emperors, his crown being the legendary Cap of Monomakh, said to have been presented to Ivan's ancestor Vladimir Monomakh by his own imperial grandfather, Constantine IX. Ivan IV, generally known as Ivan the Terrible (though this word does not accurately render the Russian word *Groznyy* by which he was known and some historians term him 'The Dread') possessed qualities which promised well for his task as ruler of Russia, including physical energy, a keen intelligence and an awareness of the needs of his large but backward realm. Unfortunately these were counterbalanced by an over-exalted sense of the importance of his office, suspicion of others amounting to paranoia, and violent and uncontrolled aggressiveness.

His reign began with a series of useful administrative, legal and military reforms, including the promulgation of a revised *Sudebnik* in 1550. In this task the tsar was assisted by a group of able advisers known as the Chosen Council. But this 'good phase' did not last: in 1565 Ivan IV's morbid suspicion of all those around him, especially the boyars (representatives of the titled and non-titled senior nobility and aristocracy), caused him to divide his country into two parts, one of which was placed under his complete personal dictatorship. This was known as the *oprichnina*, 'special court territory' or 'realm apart'. Within this area the tsar's will was enforced by the *oprichniki* or members of the 'special court'. Before long their activities spread beyond the boundaries of the *oprichnina* and subjected the entire Russian land to a reign of terror, culminating in a large-scale massacre of the citizens of Novgorod in 1569 (on the pretext of treasonable plotting with the king of Poland), and a similar pogrom in Moscow in 1572. The activities of the *oprichniki* then gradually diminished, but not before they had inflicted immense physical and psychological damage on the country.

Ivan IV's reign opened well in the sphere of foreign policy. His grandfather's attempts to curtail the aggressive activities of the Tatar khanates by means of alliances and pro-Russian puppet rulers had broken down, and it was clear that bolder measures were necessary. Ivan IV therefore undertook three campaigns against the Kazan' khanate with a view to annexing its territory; the third of these, in 1552, was successful. Some of his advisers thought that he should then have turned against the Crimean Tatars; but he preferred to pursue a policy of westward expansion* at the expense of Lithuania and the Livonian Order who controlled the Baltic coast. This involved him in a complex series of military operations known as the Livonian War (1558–83). In spite of some setbacks, a considerable amount of territory was occupied by the Russian armies; but all this was lost when the recently elected Polish king Stephen Bathory organized a series of determined counter-offensives, 1578–81.

Ivan IV's strong desire for more contact with the West, in which he anticipated Peter the Great,* also caused him to welcome Richard Chancellor and the English sailors who made their way overland from the mouth of the Northern Dvina River to Moscow in 1553. This resulted in the establishment of regular trade with England conducted by the Muscovy Company, founded in 1555.   *M.H.*

Fedor I (1584–98)

Ivan IV* was succeeded by his eldest surviving son Fedor. He was intensely interested in religious observances and had little taste or aptitude for the task of government. These were consequently left to his advisers, especially his brother-in-law, the boyar Boris Godunov.* Under his direction Russia gradually recovered from the stresses of the years preceding Fedor's accession, and further progress was made in the economic development and colonization of Siberia, which had begun under Ivan IV. Fedor's reign also saw the gradual erosion of the freedom of movement of the peasantry, which had been guaranteed, though on a restricted basis, by the *Sudebniki* of 1497 and 1550. This process was closely linked with the increase in the number of *pomest'e* estates (land granted in return for military service) for which it was essential to secure an adequate labour force. *M.H.*

Fedor I

Boris Godunov (1598–1605)

Fedor I's* death in 1598 marked the end of the Ryurikovich dynasty. The succession problem was solved by the election of Boris Godunov as tsar, by an assembly known as the *Zemsky sobor* (Assembly of the Land);* although this consisted mainly of boyars, ecclesiastical dignitaries and service gentry, it also included some representative elements. Boris Godunov proved an intelligent and efficient ruler, but nevertheless he was not popular; the older nobility resented his authority, and he was suspected of having contrived the murder of Ivan IV's* youngest son Dmitry, who had died in mysterious circumstances in 1591. Boris hoped that his son might succeed him; but in fact his sudden death in 1605 was followed by a prolonged succession crisis, only finally resolved by the election of Mikhail Romanov* as tsar in 1613. *M.H.*

Boris Godunov

The Time of Troubles

The years between the death of Boris Godunov* and the accession of Mikhail Romanov* is usually known as the *Smutnoe vremya* (Time of Troubles).* This was a period of civil war in which the issues were very confused, since the search for a ruler was complicated by smouldering social discontent, political tensions and the dynastic ambitions of the king of Poland. The prominent part played by successive pretenders claiming to be the tsarevich Dmitry was symptomatic of the deep-seated malaise in Russia at that time. *M.H.*

The early Romanovs

During the period 1613–82 Russia was ruled by three tsars: Mikhail Romanov (1613–45), his son Aleksey (1645–76) and his grandson Fedor III (1676–82). Seen in retrospect, this time appears relatively calm and uneventful compared with the tumultuous and dynamic periods which preceded and followed. However, it was by no means a time of stagnation; old problems continued to exercise the minds of rulers and their advisers, and important new developments in home and foreign policy were initiated.

The first task of Mikhail Romanov after his election was the restoration of internal order; this included the expulsion of the Poles and Swedes who had occupied Moscow and other places during the Time of Troubles.* It was also necessary to regulate the government's relations with the Cossacks, who had played an active part in the recent unrest, and to restore the country's shattered economy. This involved increasing the financial burdens of the already oppressed peasantry; there was also further economic development in Siberia, which in 1637 acquired its own *prikaz* or government office. During the earlier part of his reign Mikhail Romanov was much influenced by his masterful father, Patriarch Filaret, who had been forced to retire to monastic life by Boris Godunov.*

In foreign policy the most important development during this period was the continuation of Russia's westward territorial expansion* into the middle and lower Dnieper area now generally known as the Ukraine. This was closely linked with the government's relations with the Dnieper and Zaporozhian Cossacks who inhabited the region. Nominally subjects of the king of Poland, the Cossacks were Orthodox* in religion and disinclined to submit to any kind of rigid governmental control. In 1653 Bogdan Khmel'nitsky, the elected *hetman* or leader of the Zaporozhian Cossacks offered to place his followers, who then included the Dnieper Cossacks, under the suzerainty of Tsar Aleksey instead of that of the king of Poland. After some hesitation this offer was accepted. Not surprisingly it led to war between Russia and Poland, the progress of which was complicated by the intervention of Poland's inveterate enemy Sweden, and dissensions amounting to civil war among the Cossacks themselves. This war was concluded by the Treaty of Andrusovo in 1667, which left Russia in control of the left bank of the Dnieper, including Kiev.

The *Zemsky sobor* (Assembly of the Land)

An interesting aspect of this period of Russian history was the participation of the *Zemsky sobor*. It met ten times in Mikhail's reign and several times during that of Aleksey, who consulted it in 1653 on the issue of accepting suzerainty over the Zaporozhian and Dnieper Cossacks. Though not empowered to initiate legislation, it could present petitions, and much of the content of the enlarged law-code of 1649 known as the *Sobornoe ulozhenie* was based on such petitions.

The Old Believers Schism

The reign of Aleksey saw the first and only major conflict between the secular and ecclesiastical power in Russia, which culminated, in 1668, in the formal deposition of Patriarch Nikon.* He had tried to introduce changes in ritual designed to bring the Russian Church into conformity with other Orthodox communions, particularly the Greek. Though seemingly trivial on the surface, Nikon's reforms and his manner of introducing them symbolized deeper changes in the Russian Church and roused strong opposition among the more conservative elements. Some of these eventually broke away and formed a schismatic group known as the Old Believers.*

Top right: Aleksey Mikhaylovich. Right: Patriarch Nikon

Enserfment

All these developments contain some element or promise of progress in the Russian state; but the position of the peasants remained economically and culturally backward, while their legal status further deteriorated as a result of the removal of any time limit for reclaiming runaway peasants, which was included in the *Sobornoe ulozhenie* of 1649. This completed the process of the enserfment* of the Russian peasantry, which lasted until 1861. The discontent of the peasants with their hard conditions led to frequent desperate attempts to seek escape by flight, and occasionally to uprisings. One of these, under the leadership of the Cossack Sten'ka Razin in 1670–71, reached the dimensions of a major rebellion, which was brutally suppressed. Thus Russia at the threshold of its modern age carried a heavy burden which must inevitably hinder progress.   *M.H.*

Right: Peter the Great's half-sister Sofia. Below: Peter the Great as a ship's carpenter

Peter the Great (1682–1725)

The death of Fedor III* in 1682 left no clear heir to the throne, and brought to a head conflict between the factions at court. The election as tsar of 10-year-old Peter, son of Aleksey Romanov's* second wife, was overturned in a bloody *coup d'état*. Peter's half-sister Sofia seized power as regent, creating her sickly brother Ivan co-tsar with Peter.

In the following years Peter was kept away from court and left largely to his own devices. This unorthodox education freed him from the constraints of Muscovite tradition, and gave scope both to his great energy and to the passion for things military which were to become hallmarks of his reign. Discovery of an old boat led to a fascination with ships and the sea, and ultimately to the creation of a powerful navy.* The 'toy regiments' recruited for his amusement from among noble companions and serving-boys helped him to overthrow Sofia in 1689, and later became the Guards regiments which formed the élite of his modernized army. Only after his mother's death in 1694 did Peter personally take up the reins of government, and it was characteristic that his first major undertaking was military: an attack upon the Turkish fortress of Azov in 1695.

The technical problems which he encountered before he was able to reduce Azov in 1696, as well as a desire to revitalize the international alliance of the 1680s against the Turks, took Peter on a 'Grand Embassy' to Western Europe in 1697–8. The journey proved seminal. It showed Peter that the anti-Turkish alliance was dead, and turned his eyes northwards to the Swedish territories on the Baltic: with Augustus of Poland he planned an attack on Sweden which opened the Great Northern War (1700–21). It showed him, too, the wealth and the power of the world beyond Muscovy's* borders.

Reforms

The tasks of fighting Sweden, and of modernizing his country along advanced, Western, lines, became Peter's two major preoccupations of the next 25 years. Each fed upon the other. 'War was the mother of the Petrine reforms' in so far as it compelled Peter to change the country's governmental and economic structure, in order to withstand the power of Charles XII of Sweden and to underpin the huge land and sea forces which Muscovy built up. The decisive battle of the war was Peter's crushing victory over Charles at Poltava (1709); although in 1711 he suffered near-disaster on the river Pruth at the hands of the Turks, with whom Charles had taken refuge. The end came in 1721, with the Treaty of Nystad, which showed the balance of power decisively in Muscovy's favour. To mark the peace, Peter assumed the title of emperor: Muscovite Russia became the Russian Empire.

But if military imperatives hastened the transformation of Muscovy, Peter's wars were themselves only means to a greater end which that transformation also served, the establishment of Russia as a great power in the European mould of the times. His broader aspirations are represented by the elegant Western architecture of his new port and capital, St Petersburg,* founded in 1703 on territory captured from Sweden, and by the Academy of Sciences,* set up in 1725 after previous consultation with G. W. Leibnitz.

Renewal and expansion of the armed forces were followed by reforms in almost every sphere. The central government administration was reorganized into a system of boards or Colleges; coordination of administration and policy was vested in a new Senate. The Russian Orthodox Church* was subordinated to the state: a Holy Synod* under a lay Procurator replaced the patriarchate (established in 1589). Attempts to reorganize provincial and municipal government remained unsuccessful. More effective were Peter's efforts to mobilize the financial and human resources of the nation. The capitation or 'soul' tax, levied on every male subject, nobles and clergy excepted, finally solved the government's constant need for greater tax revenue. The upper classes were also pressed into more effective service. The Inheritance Law of 1714 and the Table of Ranks (1724) provided a closely coordinated service structure for the nobility. Under Peter their position as land- and serf-owners was consolidated, but so were their obligations to the state.

Peter's reforms were conducted at first on an *ad hoc* basis, under the pressures of the time; after Poltava he had the leisure, and the experience, to be more systematic. His measures were informed by a rationalistic, pragmatic spirit which reflected the political wisdom of contemporary Europe; they reached down to the minutiae of popular daily life; and they contributed to a strengthening of state power at home which was as great as the influence on the international scene achieved through the defeat of Sweden. However, the range and the speed of change were bound to provoke opposition, even though little

that Peter did was totally without precedent. His ruthless subjection of all classes to the vastly expanded demands of the state, his subjugation of the Church, his insistence on Western forms and skills, all produced discontent and resistance. The most important of several popular opposition movements was Bulavin's Cossack revolt of 1707–8. Among the upper classes conservative dissent was kept in check by brutal police methods, but crystallized around the feckless heir apparent, the Tsarevich Aleksey. Confrontation between father and son led finally to the death of Aleksey under interrogation and torture in 1718, and Peter changed the law of succession to safeguard his work. The new law of 1722, repealed only at the end of the century (1797), provided for the monarch to choose his own heir. But Peter's death in 1725 was too sudden to allow him to make the choice. *R.P.B.*

Catherine I (1725–7)

The grandees around the throne at once sought to fill the vacuum left by the absence of an official successor. The crown now passed to Peter's widow, his second wife Catherine (Martha Skavronska, Catherine I), an illiterate peasant woman from Livonia. Captured in Peter's early Baltic campaigns, she was the mistress of Field-Marshal Sheremet'ev, then of Peter's close assistant Prince Aleksandr Menshikov, before moving to Peter's own bed and subsequently becoming his wife and empress. Now she owed her elevation essentially to Menshikov and to the Guards regiments which he brought to the palace to acclaim her. Menshikov was also of common birth; and during Catherine's reign he was all-powerful. The social origin of the new rulers symbolized once again the way in which Peter had upset the outward forms and traditions of Muscovy, while the intervention of the Guards in the succession set a fashion for the rest of the century. *R.P.B.*

Catherine I

Peter II (1727–30), Anna (1730–40)

Under Catherine, who took no interest in matters of state, power had been exercised by a Supreme Privy Council in which Menshikov★ played an important role. The Council retained power under her successor Peter II (1727–30), the young son of the ill-fated Tsarevich Aleksey, although Menshikov lost his position. On Peter II's sudden death from smallpox in 1730, the Privy Councillors decided to offer the throne to Peter I's★ niece Anna, Dowager Duchess of Courland, who lived in her Baltic duchy in poverty-stricken obscurity; they took the opportunity to impose upon Anna conditions which would ensure her dependence upon them. Initially Anna accepted the Council's 'Points' or proposals; but finding that they lacked the support of the majority of the nobility, who feared oligarchy more than a single absolute ruler, she tore up the 'Points' in a melodramatic confrontation with the Councillors, and assumed full autocratic powers. In return for their support, the nobility gained improvements in the conditions of their service to the state. Anna's reign (1730–40) has generally been seen as a dark period in imperial Russia's history, marked by the corrupt and oppressive rule of her German favourite Biron (Bühren) and his associates, and by heavy financial burdens on the population. Life at Court was characterized by the ruler's shallow and perverted tastes, shown in her liking for dwarfs and monsters (a penchant shared with her uncle Peter I). There were, however, lighter and more positive sides: this was also a time of cultural development, with the introduction of opera★ into Russia, from Italy, under court patronage. Russia made its weight felt in Europe in the crisis over the Polish succession (1733–5); a successful war with Turkey (1735–9) regained Azov, lost by Peter in 1711.

Anna died childless in 1740, leaving the crown to her infant great-nephew Ivan Antonovich (Ivan VI), under the regency of his mother Anna Leopol'dovna and her husband the Duke of Brunswick. Biron's initial domination of the new regent was broken within months by a coup, which did not, however, end the prominence of Germans at the head of the government. But in November 1741 a further coup, backed by the Guards and financed with French money, brought Peter I's daughter Elizabeth★ to the throne. *R.P.B.*

Elizabeth (1741–61)

Like her immediate predecessors, Elizabeth took little interest in political affairs. Her particular contribution was to encourage the Western luxury and expensive tastes which had already begun to show themselves under Anna,★ and which accorded well with

Empress Elizabeth

Elizabeth's extravagant pleasure-seeking and love of social life. In the absence of firm guidance from the sovereign, influence was still exercised by favourites and men of confidence. Until his fall in 1758 A. Bestuzhev dominated foreign affairs, while the Shuvalov family– Aleksandr, Petr, Ivan–became prominent in internal government. Petr Shuvalov interested himself in social and economic matters, to the country's and his own personal advantage. Ivan was a noted patron of the arts and sciences. Together with Russia's 'universal genius' M.V. Lomonosov,★ he was instrumental in the founding of Moscow University in 1755. Lomonosov, son of a White Sea fisherman, made a name in many fields, as poet, historian, scientist, ending his days in 1765 as a prominent cultural administrator and an Academician.★ The new university was followed by the establishment of the first Russian theatre★ (1756) and of an Academy of Fine Arts★ (1757). These and other developments heralded the cultural efflorescence of the last decades of the century. In international affairs Russia's position continued to grow stronger. The Swedish declaration of war in 1741 rapidly proved futile. Russia's part in the international complications of the Austrian succession was a relatively minor one, but in the Seven Years War (1756–63) Elizabeth's determined hostility to Frederick of Prussia and the campaigns against him of the Russian armies were instrumental in bringing Prussia to its knees. Final victory, however, eluded Elizabeth. To Frederick's great relief she died late in 1761. *R.P.B.*

Peter III (1761–2)

Peter III, born in Holstein and brought to Russia as grand prince and heir apparent, was Elizabeth's* nephew and successor. Maladjusted and boorish, Peter had an unconcealed scorn for things Russian, and was a fervent admirer of Prussia. He not only withdrew Russian forces from the anti-Prussian coalition, but at once gave up all Russia's conquests and pledged his support for Frederick. Such blatant disregard for Russia's interests, as well as Peter's attitude to the established government and the national church, provoked intense resentment. Some measures of Peter's government were notably liberal, and of considerable importance: a Manifesto freeing the nobility from compulsory service; decrees on trade; concessions to the Old Believers.* But these did not save him. In June 1762, his wife Catherine, whose own position was jeopardized by Peter's infatuation with a mistress whom he threatened to marry, mounted a coup with the help of her lover and his brothers, popular Guards officers. Peter abdicated, and was murdered soon after.   *R.P.B.*

Catherine the Great (1762–96)

Catherine II was a German princess, married at the age of 15 to the grand prince Peter III,* and consequently had no title at all to the Russian throne. In the event she became one of 18th-century Russia's most successful rulers, and her long reign covered an important period in Russian history. Her strong personality and vivid private life have attracted many biographers. Traditionally she has been included among the so-called Enlightened Despots, absolute monarchs who in the age of the Enlightenment tried to apply the ideas of the time to the task of government. However, the ideas most influential in the absolute governments of 18th-century Europe, as recent scholarship has shown, were not those of the French Enlightenment, but of the early German Enlightenment and the German political economists of the time (the 'cameralist' school), whose concerns were essentially with the wealth and strength of the state.

Social and political reform

Catherine has frequently been damned for her social policies, and for the hypocritical way in which she allegedly masked oppressive measures with fine gestures and resounding phrases. Her critics call 18th-century Russia a 'gentry monarchy', and point to Catherine's reign as the Golden Age of the Russian nobility and the apogee of serfdom. The usurper on the throne, they argue, safeguarded her position by giving the nobles new privileges and *carte blanche* in their

relations with the peasantry. This view of Catherine has more recently been challenged by scholars who see the empress as an effective monarch responding to the problems of ruling a vast and underdeveloped country. The rise of the nobility and their liberation from the severe constraints imposed on them by Peter I* was a long process, to which the concessions of Anna,* Elizabeth* and especially Peter III, with his Manifesto of 1762, had all contributed. It reflected not only the power of the nobility over the throne, but also the growing strength and capacity of the bureaucratic administrative system and the professional army.

Despite the rapid growth of the bureaucracy, however, the nobility as a class was still essential to the government of the empire. The great peasant revolt led by Ye.I. Pugachev (1726–75) in 1773–5 showed the necessity of involving the noble landowners in the maintenance of

Catherine the Great

law and order in the countryside. Catherine's provincial reform of 1775, which gave a significant role to the gentry, sought to provide a solution to long-standing problems of provincial government; but its rapid introduction was a response to the Pugachev revolt. The 1785 Charter to the Nobility finally completed the establishment of the nobility as a separate estate within Russian society, with extensive and exclusive privileges. In the same period, however, Catherine issued a similar Charter to the Towns of the Empire, and worked on the draft of another for the state peasantry: in short, she was moving towards the organization of Russian society along the lines of west European estates. The social group ignored here were the serfs,★ the landowners' peasants, who had suffered a steady decline in their rights and status parallel to the rise of the gentry. That process, too, was largely complete before 1762; and if Catherine did little to meet

Ye. I. Pugachev incarcerated in a cage

the immediate grievances of the peasants, and even increased them, it was she personally who initiated the discussion of their situation within society which began seriously in the 1760s: the first comprehensive attack on serfdom, published in 1763, was authorized by the empress herself.

The difficulties of reform were fully demonstrated by the clashes of interest in the famous Legislative Commission of 1767; Pugachev showed the possible consequences of any loss of control. In her political theory Catherine was eclectic; but her policies aimed basically to maximize all the resources of the country, and so its wealth and power. To this end she actively encouraged trade and industry; agriculture was much discussed, but little improved. An important object of state policy, equally pursued by other European governments, was the expansion of the population. Her concern with the peasant question should be seen from this point of view, just as interests of state dictated reliance on the nobility as an instrument still necessary to the greater strength and security of the country.

In many respects, Catherine's reign was a turning-point; existing trends were brought to completion and foundations laid for the 19th century. The position of the major social classes was fixed until the peasant emancipation★ of 1861. Economic developments were the fruit of Peter I's beginnings, while the foundation of Odessa (1794) on the Black Sea laid the basis for Russia's great 19th-century southern trade. In cultural affairs, the latter decades of the century saw a great flowering: the cultural and educational demands made on the nobility by the new Petrine service structure and Russia's openness to the West now produced an élite interested in literary pursuits. The development of a modern literature★ accompanied an increasing interest in European intellectual currents and the application to Russia of the new ideas: Russia too was involved in the Enlightenment. And from it sprang radical political criticism of the Russian system. A. N. Radishchev (1749–1802), in his *Journey from St Petersburg to Moscow* (1790), combined the form of Laurence Sterne's *Sentimental Journey* with a fierce attack on the institutions of serfdom and autocracy. Following the outbreak of the French Revolution, however, Catherine was no longer open to such ideas: Radishchev, 'the father of Russian radicalism', was condemned to death, a sentence commuted to exile in Siberia.

Territorial safeguards

In foreign affairs, Catherine II's reign likewise marks a turning-point. On her accession in 1762 she withdrew Russian support from Frederick II, but did not renew hostilities against him. Common Russian and Prussian interest in Poland led eventually to the three partitions (with Austria) of 1772, 1793 and 1795 and established a long tradition of Russian–Prussian cooperation; the extinction of Poland as a nation state in 1795 ended a centuries-old conflict on Russia's western borders. Catherine's two Turkish wars of 1768–74 and 1787–91, together with the annexation of the Crimea in 1783, finally removed the Tatar threat to Russian security, and irreversibly established Russian control over the northern coast of the Black Sea. A last effort by Sweden in 1787–8 to reassert its power in the Baltic, taking advantage of Russia's involvement with Turkey, failed completely. *R.P.B.*

Paul (1796–1801)

Catherine II* was succeeded by her son Paul. Resentful at long years in the shadow of his mother and her favourites, and unbalanced like his (putative) father, Peter III, Paul exercised a capricious tyranny over court and country. His treatment of the nobility and some measures with respect to the lower classes have sometimes gained him undeserved credit as a friend of the common people. However, both the vagaries of his foreign policy, in Russia's dealings with France, and his unpredictable and humiliating treatment of government and military at home made his rule intolerable, even to his son and heir the grand prince, Alexander. With Alexander's consent, a coup deposed Paul on 1 March 1801; during a scuffle with the conspirators he was strangled. *R.P.B.*

Emperor Paul

Alexander I (1801–25)

Alexander I (1777–1825) came to the throne as a result of the murder of his father, Paul,* in 1801. He was obliged to begin his reign with undertakings to restore for the nobles their status under Catherine the Great.* But his own inclinations were romantic, and he tended towards the ideals of the European Enlightenment. In 1802 and 1803 he established a 'Secret Committee' in which four close friends, including the Polish Prince Adam Czartoryski, discussed methods of bringing enlightenment to Russia. But social reform, especially in the question of serfdom,* was beyond even the tsar's powers; and the reforms were mainly concerned with matters of government, in which the efficiency of the Senate in its executive and legislative functions was improved and a beginning was made towards harmonious ministerial government.

Alexander I

Alexander's reign was dominated by foreign affairs. Russia had vacillated between French and English connections under Tsar Paul,* but Alexander opted for an English and Austrian alliance in January 1805, largely because he feared Napoleon's ambitions in Germany and the eastern Mediterranean. This policy failed, in a series of Allied defeats which ended with the battle of Friedland in summer 1807. Alexander then opted for alliance with Napoleon, which was promoted after a meeting on the river Niemen at Tilsit. Relations between France and Russia worsened over Polish and economic matters, and Napoleon invaded Russia in June 1812. His army, 600 000 strong, was over twice as large as the Russian armies, but it was badly supplied and was prone to disease. It gradually pushed back the Russian forces (which, contrary to legend, did not deliberately retreat), but losses were such that Napoleon had to fight a major battle outside Moscow, Borodino, with only 100 000 men. He entered Moscow, which–in circumstances that have never been clarified–burnt down. He stayed on, hoping that the tsar would come to terms. But Alexander, buoyed up by a great wave of patriotic emotion, would not do so. Napoleon retreated, in ever-worsening circumstances, and re-crossed the Niemen with only 30 000 men. In the next three years, Russian forces dominated Europe and took a prominent part in the fall of the Napoleonic Empire.

M. M. Speransky

A. A. Arakcheev

Alexander wavered between extremely religious conservatism and the Enlightenment of his youth. But the Russian situation was such that serious reform made little headway. Alexander's main reforming statesman, M. M. Speransky (1772–1839), was dismissed in 1812 because he offended powerful conservative, aristocratic interests (he had written: 'There are no truly free persons in Russia except beggars and philosophers'); the dominant voice in the latter part of Alexander's reign was that of the militarist A. A. Arakcheev (1769–1834). Alexander's liberalism was confined to the conquered lands of Finland (taken from Sweden in 1808) and Congress Poland, to which he gave a constitution. He died in 1825, though thought by some merely to have hidden away from the burdens of rule.   *N.S.*

Nicholas I (1825–55)

Alexander I's* successor, his brother Nicholas, was of much harsher character. He was a lover of Prussia, and wished to keep a large police establishment. He was known as 'the gendarme of Europe' and Russia's role throughout his reign (and especially in 1848) was highly conservative. Russian armies crushed revolt in Poland in 1830–1 and in Hungary in 1848. They did intervene in the Balkans against Turkey and in favour of small Balkan peoples of Orthodox* faith, but the intervention was limited. Nicholas was mainly concerned to keep the peace in Europe, a freedom that enabled him to expand Russia's frontiers in the southern Caucasus* at Persian expense, and to a lesser extent in Central Asia.*

The 'Decembrists'

At home Nicholas imposed a rigid, bureaucratic rule. He was challenged at the outset of his reign by a conspiracy of army officers, known as the 'Decembrists' from the date of their uprising, 14 December 1825, who had picked up doctrines of European liberalism and were full of ideas for a free, constitutional, federative Russia. But these officers were not efficient, nor did they have any serious support. Their uprising, centred on Senate Square outside the Winter Palace, soon fizzled out, and the leaders were either hanged or exiled for lengthy terms in Siberia. Thereafter, Nicholas imposed strict censorship,* to which many literary figures, including Pushkin,* fell victim.

Serfdom and emancipation

Nicholas maintained serfdom,* which embraced almost four-fifths of the population, whether as serfs of the nobles or of the state. He, and many other Russians, appreciated that serfdom was corrupting both the serfs and their owners by preventing the establishment of a free class of prosperous farmers, and driving much of the peasant population towards shiftlessness and alcohol.* But if he abolished serfdom, the nobles would no longer maintain administration, discipline and taxation; would not the country then fly apart? His assistant P. D. Kiselev (1788–1872) ameliorated conditions for the state serfs, but the effect was limited. Nicholas continued to rule through the police, reorganized (under A. K. Benckendorff (1783–1844)) as Third Section of the Tsar's Chancery, and the army.* Little was done for education; his aim was a static society: 'glitter at the top, rot at the bottom' was one comment on it.

Emancipation proclaimed to serfs on the Prozorov estate, Moscow province, 1861

But change came just the same. The economy was gradually shifting, with the towns expanding (in 1864 there were three times as many towns with a population of 50 000 as in 1830) and the population doubling between 1800 and 1860 (when it reached 60 million). Many nobles were unable to keep pace, and three-quarters of their serfs were mortgaged to the state by 1855. Moreover, Europe no longer tolerated the Russian claim to dominate the Near East. In 1854 Great Britain and France came to the support of Turkey, and landed troops in the Crimea.* Sebastopol, a Russian naval base in the Black Sea, was captured. Nicholas I, dismayed that his Austrian ally had abandoned him, died, and his son Alexander II* made peace in 1856.   *N.S.*

Alexander II (1855–81)

Russia had reached a considerable crisis. Its foreign policies were a failure, and the 'Black Sea Clauses' of the peace treaty prevented it from moving warships into or out of the Black Sea. The peasantry were becoming restive, and agrarian protests against serfdom* grew in scale. Finance was in disarray, for the state could not sustain for ever the burden of supporting a noble class whose mortgages accounted, in 1859, for 450 million roubles of the 750 million in circulation. In the circumstances, Alexander II, though himself a man of conservative inclinations, saw no alternative but radical reform.

In 1861 emancipation of the serfs was proclaimed. No longer would the peasants formally belong to a nobleman. But personal freedom was only a start, for there remained many complicated questions. Now that the nobles no longer directly administered serfs, who would do this job? How much land should the former serfs be given? Should the nobles have compensation? These questions were not satisfactorily solved, though a better effort was made than some idealists imagined. The peasants acquired (with very great regional variations) roughly two-thirds of the land they had previously worked, and they undertook to pay 'redemption dues' of annual cash payments to the state, which advanced compensatory lump sums to the nobles. Not surprisingly, the peasants protested, and efforts to recover redemption payments were not successful. Even 40 years later (when they were written off) the payments were in arrears. The state also limited peasants' freedom: they were included in village communes which owned the land and assigned parts of it to individual peasants, generally according to their families' size. This was administratively convenient, and suited the peasants' own ways in much of the country, but it acted as a block on rural economic progress, for a man could not count on having the same land for even half of his working life. Russian agriculture,* though capable of producing great quantities of grain for export, was never as efficient as Western agriculture, and there were some devastating famines.

Alexander II had to create a new bureaucracy, for which he also created schools and colleges; the State Bank came into existence in 1859; elected county councils (*zemstva*) were set up in 1864 to deal with local administration, and the system of taxation was overhauled. Many Russians hoped that Alexander would go further, and grant a constitution, but in the tsar's view Russia was simply too large and too varied to allow any other system of rule but autocracy – certainly not rule by a small noble class. He grew irritable when constitutional changes were suggested by *zemstvo* leaders, two of whom he exiled. His reforms therefore stopped short, and this encouraged radical opposition to tsarism.

There was no coherent popular protest for most of the 19th century, and the opposition movements of intellectuals and some of the nobility were necessarily confined in scope. Opposition was also divided in aim. German liberalism and Hegelianism acted as a spur for the 'Westerners', at their head Petr Chaadaev (1793–1856), in the 1840s; the Decembrists had anticipated this inspiration from the West. In the 1850s and 1860s the opposition was particularly shaped by Alexander Herzen, whose journal-in-exile, *The Bell*, was even read by the tsar, and who aimed at a synthesis of Russian tradition with Western ways which, in pure form, he despised. Counter to these traditions ran the ideas of the 'Slavophils' (especially A. S. Khomyakov, 1804–60) who despised legal forms and advocated Slav institutions: a free Russia based on the village commune and the old Russian form of parliament. Such opposition necessarily remained academic, and literary: the exiles, with their confused finances, opinions and (still more) private lives, were typical of it.

In the 1860s there arose a more popular opposition, based on the 'intelligentsia' – a phrase that now began to be used to describe educated, rebellious young people usually of lower middle-class extraction. Expansion of the educational system, though not generous (and considerably less than in other European countries), had been forced on the tsarist state by the needs of modernity. It created a number of aspiring and educated young people who did not have secure employment, and who lived from hand-to-mouth. They had no stake in existing society, and yet had lost their roots. The result was a plethora of dissident doctrines. With N. G. Chernyshevsky (1828–89) there arrived an opposition movement, populism, that had lost touch even with the Herzen-inspired opposition movements of the earlier period. Chernyshevsky and his like rejected religion, order, the family. They were, in Turgenev's* word, 'nihilists'.

The limitation of Alexander II's reforms was such that more and more of these young people were driven into a radical opposition. In the 1870s they attempted to carry their doctrines 'to the people', and they went out to the villages in an effort to convince the peasantry. They failed. The peasants were suspicious of all townsmen, and did not take kindly to the women students. The populists succeeded in arousing the peasantry only when they happened on traditional grievances, expressed in traditional ways (a pretender-tsar, for instance). Elsewhere the peasantry handed them over to the police. In despair, a section of the populists established a terrorist organization, 'Land and Liberty', which plotted assassinations. The most successful of these was the shooting by Vera Zasulich, of General Trepov, police chief of St Petersburg, in 1878. She was pronounced not guilty by a sympathetic jury, which caused the tsar to whittle down the entire jury system. Efforts were made against the tsar himself, culminating in his assassination in March 1881.   *N.S.*

The assassination of Alexander II

Alexander III (1881–94)

Alexander III absorbed the lesson of his father's murder, and resolved that there should be no further liberalizing measures. Thereafter, a vicious circle developed: the government became harsher and regarded liberal reforms as merely an incitement to greater opposition; while the opposition was pushed further and further towards extremism. The constitutional experiment with which Alexander II* had been toying on the eve of his death was shelved. Alexander listened to his adviser K. P. Pobedonostsev (1827–1907), an uncompromising highly religious reactionary, whose beliefs were of a type unfamiliar in Europe since the mid-17th century. Efforts were made to resuscitate the declining nobility by, for example, the provision of mortgages through a Land Bank (1883), and to provide greater police-coverage in the towns and the countryside. The activities of the *zemstva* (county councils) were cut back. In the short run, this policy succeeded, and active opposition inside the country collapsed.

The 1880s brought considerable economic change. As Russia developed railways, it was able to export grain and to stimulate metallurgical extraction and working. The state lacked capital, but by the 1890s it was able to acquire considerable capital from abroad, especially France, and its resources began to be seriously exploited – with some 260 foreign companies well to the fore. Native Russian capitalists did exist, notably in the Moscow area, where the textile industry became quite advanced, but on the whole they were clumsy and parasitical. This again developed into a vicious circle. The government retained a somewhat cumbersome measure of state control, mainly because it did not trust the capitalists on their own; and the capitalists responded by developing a bureaucratic, rather than an entrepreneurial, mentality. Where they were menaced (as in the depression of 1900–3) they responded, not by technological inventiveness, but by cartellization and price-fixing, often at the expense of employment and wages. Russian industry* and banking therefore became highly monopolistic, and corruption seems to have played a considerable part. Foreign skills and capital were therefore important to the progress that Russian industry unquestionably made in the 1890s. In 1897 Russia conformed to world practice and adopted the gold* standard, under the finance minister S. Yu. Witte.* This procured foreign investment, but did so, it has been suggested, at the expense of native credit-institutions. The Russian worker was badly-paid, was forbidden to form unions,* and then had to pay high prices for the goods he needed. Any threat from workers could easily be checked by an influx of fresh labour from the countryside, where agriculture* underwent a similarly patchy development.

The peasant commune (*mir*) was far from being an ideal base for agrarian capitalism, and yet it continued to flourish in the latter part of the century. To some extent, government policy was responsible: the government needed the administrative services of the village elders, and therefore left them in charge of the community. But it was mainly the interests of the bulk of the peasantry that kept communes together in most of European Russia. The commune gave a man land when he had mouths to feed from it, and, by the same token, hands to work it. At a time when population* was rising fast (from 60 million in 1860 it rose to 130 million in 1905) and land was under pressure, the commune carried out an obvious service in the short run. The difficulty was of course that no peasant without hereditary tenure had much interest in developing his land, and agriculture remained very backward. A few noble estates did well, and in some areas where communal tenure was weak there were adequately efficient independent farmers. Grain made up two-fifths of Russia's exports in the late 19th century, but the agricultural problem was quite as serious for the tsars as it was for their successors.

Alexander III responded with timid efforts to promote peasant property (a Peasants' Land Bank being established in 1885) but he tended to head off peasant discontent in the direction of the Jews* or the non-Russian peoples;* an aggressive, Panslav foreign policy was another part of the system. The tsars had tried to confine Jews to the Pale of Settlement in eastern Poland and White Russia, but the Jewish and non-Jewish populations did clash, and from 1881 onwards there was a series of pogroms against the Jews. Jewish emigration, fostered by railways, went ahead, but even as late as 1891 measures of almost 18th-century style were being used against Jews (for instance, their expulsion from Moscow and Kiev). The Jewish population responded by producing its own nationalism and social-democratic opposition (the *Bund*). Similarly Russian agents acted against the lesser peoples of the empire–Poles, Ukrainians,* even Baltic Germans* whose university at Dorpat near Riga was Russified. This reaction stimulated native nationalist movements. It should be said, however, that in most cases these nationalistic movements were not separatist. A sense of religious* community set limits to the animosity between Russians and Ukrainians, in particular.   *N.S.*

Nicholas II (1894–1917)

Alexander III* died in 1894, but his son and successor, Nicholas II, was far from perceiving a need for political liberalization. He was himself of a narrow, authoritarian disposition, and in this he had the support of his German-born wife, Alexandra. Latterly, he took advice of similar type from the 'mad monk', Rasputin, who claimed almost miraculous healing powers which he used on the haemophilic tsarevich. In his early years Nicholas followed Pobedonostsev's

The imperial family at Tsarskoe Selo, January 1916

advice, and later he lent a willing ear to old-fashioned reactionaries. In the early years of his reign there was some justification for this. After all, the empire had remained at peace, its economy had been growing satisfactorily, and its frontiers had been prodigiously expanded,* in Central Asia, the south and now at the expense of China. More, it had been able to pose as champion of Panslavism and Orthodoxy,* having defeated the Turks in war in 1878, and having promoted the independence of small Slavonic states in the Balkans. Nicholas could see no reason for change, and he dismissed a *zemstvo* petition to this effect as 'senseless dreaming'. His 23-year reign was to end in the cataclysm of war and revolution in 1917; he himself was shot with his family at Yekaterinburg in July 1918. His association with autocratic reaction, though not perhaps as consistent as some have contended, has reflected unfavourably upon him to this day.

Socialism and Marxism

Opposition necessarily became all the more extreme, and this time it had a real base among the people. Industrial development created a proletariat in the cities which lived in conditions of squalor. In St Petersburg, rents were higher than anywhere else in Europe, and in spring many of the underground dwellings were flooded. Until 1900, the death-rate* remained higher there than the birth-rate,* which did not prevent a constant influx of rural labour seeking any work at all. Socialist doctrines began to spread among the working class despite considerable police harassment. At the same time, a substantial part of the dissident intelligentsia moved towards Marxism.* The chief Russian Marxist, G. V. Plekhanov (1857–1918), propagated the doctrine particularly among exiles, but inside Russia many middle-class youths were attracted.

Among them was Vladimir Il'ich Ul'yanov, subsequently known under his pseudonym, Lenin;* he was son of an inspector of schools, and his brother was executed in 1887 for attempting to assassinate the tsar. Lenin adopted a rigid Marxism, was exiled to Siberia for some years, and in 1900 emigrated to Austria and Switzerland. He was responsible for pushing Russian social democracy into extremism.

The Social Democratic Labour Party had been formally founded in 1898, but most of the founders were then arrested, and it was not until 1903 that a real foundation was possible, in conferences held at Brussels and London. Many of the founders wanted to collaborate with middle-class liberalism. Lenin opposed this; he preferred alliance with the peasantry, however primitive, and his methods involved creation of a highly centralized band of political fanatics who would somehow anticipate the will of the workers before it even consciously existed. Underhand political skills gave him a majority of votes on a decisive issue, and his followers (Bolsheviks,* from the Russian for 'majority' that might also stand as a code for 'extremists') were distinguished from the 'minority' (Mensheviks), less adamant on isolation. Non-Marxist dissidents founded the Socialist Revolutionary Party in 1902, a section of which turned to terrorist acts, assassinating some leading officials.

Defeat by Japan

Depression affected Russian industry and agriculture in the first years of the 20th century, and Witte was dismissed from his post as finance minister as working-class agitation and, still more, agrarian unrest began in 1903. The tsar's reaction was, as before, to head off discontent. He had a ready-made cause in the Far East.* Russian expansion in Korea and Manchuria had proceeded as the Chinese empire disintegrated and foreign powers became involved. The Japanese regarded their interests in Korea as paramount, and many of them wished for some control of northern China, particularly Manchuria, as well. Russian interests were involved in a northern and southern Manchurian railway, to link up Russian Asia with the new port of Vladivostok. Several highly-placed Russians also had ambitions in Korea, and hoped to control the ice-free port of Port Arthur. Russian and Japanese interests clashed, and tsarist diplomacy was both too incompetent and too ambitious to compromise. Accordingly, the Japanese concluded alliance with Great Britain in 1902 and launched a surprise attack on the Russian positions in Port Arthur in February 1904.

The Russo-Japanese war* was a considerable humiliation for the tsar. His armies were badly supplied along the then defective Trans-Siberian Railway, and they were also badly led. One general, A.N. Kuropatkin, failed to appreciate that, in the days of quick-firing gunnery, cavalry charges would be a disaster; and no one understood trench warfare. The Manchurian armies were defeated, and Port Arthur itself surrendered. In May 1905 the Baltic Fleet,* which had sailed round the world, was defeated by the Japanese at the Straits of Tsushima, and in August 1905 peace was concluded, on terms disadvantageous to Russia, in the USA.   *N.S.*

The pseudo-parliamentary period: 1905–14

By 1904, when war with Japan broke out, Russia was in ferment. The professional classes, identified with the *zemstvo* movement, were demanding representative government, and organizing themselves to become the Constitutional Democratic Party (Kadet). The land hunger and poverty of the peasants was exploding in violence and arson. The students, influenced by all shades of revolutionary thought–Marxist,★ populist, anarchist–were demonstrating against the government's educational policies, and its refusal to grant autonomy to the universities. Among the working class, economic and political demands, formulated since the 1880s under Marxist guidance, had created a strike movement which by 1904 achieved mass proportions.

'Bloody Sunday'

In August 1904 the Minister of the Interior was assassinated. With the army in the Far East,★ the government seemed weak and the police disoriented. The turbulence increased. On Sunday 9 January 1905 (OS), a huge procession of workers with their families, led by the priest/police-agent Fr Gapon (1870–1906), marched to the Winter Palace in St Petersburg to present a pious petition to an absent tsar. After giving warnings to disperse, the troops fired into the crowds, killing at least 200. Throughout Russia and in the West, 'Bloody Sunday' provoked outrage.

Appeasement and repression

Nicholas II★ offered consultative representation, provoking further demands by this show of weakness, worsened by disasters in Manchuria and the total loss in May of the Russian Fleet at Tsushima.

In August peace was concluded at Portsmouth, USA, and the government offered the opposition movement a legislative assembly–the Duma. It was to be elected on a restricted suffrage and satisfied nobody. The unrest continued, culminating in a general strike which paralysed the empire from 7 to 17 October (OS). The police were unable to cope, and the strikers escalated their demands: constituent assembly, civil rights, the 8-hour day; then, as professional revolutionaries came to the fore, democratic republic, amnesty, arming of the workers.

The movement in St Petersburg was led by a soviet,★ or council, which began as a central coordinating strike committee and developed into the spokesman for the entire revolutionary labour movement. Nevertheless, when the government arrested all 562 deputies in December, the workers did not react.

In Moscow, meanwhile, the local Bolsheviks★ had been campaigning ardently for armed uprising, and when by December sufficient arms had been collected, an insurrection was staged, only to be crushed by government troops after a week's bloody fighting.

The revolution had reached its zenith with the general strike in October and thereafter the government was regaining lost ground. Having granted civil liberties and promised a democratically elected assembly, Nicholas II brought his army back from the war and set about 'pacifying' the country.

Left: Father Gapon.
Right: strikers at Yartsevo (Smolensk region), 1905

The October Manifesto had split the opposition movement. Moderates advocated the peaceful reconstruction of the country on the basis of the Manifesto and formed themselves into the Octobrist Party. Liberals were now prepared to cut their ties with the revolutionaries and adopt parliamentary methods, but were not satisfied with the scope of the concessions and formed themselves into the Kadet Party, with the aim of working legally towards full constitutional government. The Prime Minister, S. Yu. Witte (1849–1915), was unable to attract liberals or moderates into his cabinet, because they could not countenance the traditional tsarist methods being employed to crush the revolution. Under Witte's successor, P. A. Stolypin (1862–1911), the gallows, nicknamed 'Stolypin's necktie', were in constant use, and field courts martial were the normal means used by him for the summary trial and execution of thousands of insurrectionaries in 1906–7.

The repressions were accompanied by a powerful upsurge of Russian chauvinism and violent anti-semitism. Aided, even prompted by the police, pogromists wreaked vengeance on the Jews for the humiliations recently heaped upon the tsar and the Russian people, in war and revolution. The post-1905 period saw the greatest waves of Jewish emigration.*

The Duma

The Duma was to be elected by all classes, though the franchise was indirect. Laws would be passed only with Duma approval, though legislation also required the approval of the State Council and the tsar.

The first two Dumas (1906 and 1907) were unworkable. The first reflected the temper of recent events and was hence powerfully liberal, with a token number of the extreme left, since the Socialist Revolutionaries, and the Bolsheviks and Mensheviks* had at first boycotted the elections, thus losing much support to the Kadets. Stolypin knew cooperation from such an assembly was impossible and dissolved it after two months. The second Duma came with stronger left-wing and conservative elements, a token extreme right and a weakened Kadet centre. Again, the government was unable to find support in the assembly and it was dissolved after three months.

Stolypin's reforms

Stolypin had a vast programme of legislation, including land reform, freedom of religion,* inviolability of the person, civic equality, workers' national insurance, income-tax reform, *zemstvo* reform, introduction of *zemstva* into the western provinces, compulsory primary education,* secondary- and high-school reform, and police reform, none of which he felt able to risk in the Duma. By the simple act of temporarily suspending the Duma and invoking Article 87 of the Fundamental Laws, which permitted the government to legislate when the Duma was not in session, Stolypin was able to pass most of his legislation, though he would have preferred to grace it with the air of constitutionality the Duma could have provided.

To this end, in June 1907 he altered the electoral law and achieved a third Duma that provided him with support from the Octobrists and the Right, greatly reduced the Kadets and all but eliminated the socialists and national groups. The third Duma ratified Stolypin's

The meeting of the first Duma, 1906

P.A. Stolypin

War and revolution

The patriotic upsurge accompanying Russia's entry into the First World War★ gave way to anxiety when it was seen that the country was poorly prepared and no match for Germany. The absolutist psychology of the tsar, barely touched by the pseudo-parliamentary★ experience, dictated that war was the business of government. Only after persistent efforts on the part of liberal politicians and industrialists, and after serious military defeats, did Nicholas II agree to allow some degree of public organization of the war effort.

Relations between the tsar, who from mid-1915 was supreme military commander, and his critics sharpened as defeat followed defeat, and the country's economic position grew worse, with galloping inflation, transport chaos and food shortage.

With the tsar at GHQ, the empress's mismanagement of the ministers, and her close relationship (for her son's sake) with the notorious Rasputin, made the imperial family a clear target for the opposition, who by the end of 1916 were openly proclaiming that Russia's misfortunes were the result of either treason or stupidity in high places. Duma spokesmen were saying the tsar must go. Even bureaucrats and military leaders saw this as the only way to save the war effort and the monarchy.

Revolution

On 23 February 1917 (OS) bread riots occurred in Petrograd (St Petersburg until 1914), spreading quickly to working-class quarters where the violence increased. Two days later some regiments of the vast garrison, consisting of peasant raw recruits and convalescent troops from the front, joined the rioters. The next day the Duma★ elected a Provisional Committee of moderate, liberal and radical leaders. Later that day, strikers and revolutionaries formed the Petrograd Soviet of Workers' Deputies in the Tauride Palace, where the new Provisional Committee also sat. One of its deputy chairmen was A. F. Kerensky (1881–1971), also a member of the Provisional Committee.

The government lost its head. The ministers were arrested, and the tsar, totally isolated from his supporters, did not oppose the revolutionary government, and on 2 March (OS) abdicated. His brother and heir, Michael, refused the crown unless it were given to him by a democratically elected constituent assembly and thus the Romanov★ dynasty was at an end. The Provisional Government, which now emerged, immediately enacted liberal laws, abolishing the police and replacing them by a people's militia.★

Also on 2 March, the Soviet issued its Order no. 1, calling for the establishment of soviets★ (revolutionary councils) in army units to monitor officers. This, combined with the shock of the tsar's abdication and (despite war conditions) the total freedom of speech,

land reform, which permitted peasants to leave the commune freely, and which encouraged those willing to try independent farming, so furthering his aim of building Russia's rural stability on a class of free, prosperous farmers.

Before 1914 Russian nationalism grew rabid, reaching a climax in the Beilis Affair (1913), when the accusation of ritual murder against a Jew aroused widespread indignation at home and abroad. The Right saw Russia's traditional institutions declining, and in Stolypin's increasing power a threat to the tsar's personal standing. In 1911 Stolypin was assassinated, probably by a police agent.

Elections in the following year produced a fourth Duma much like the third. Though the government had majority support, the opposition parties maintained continual criticism of state policy, and even of court life—criticism that established the strained relations that would deteriorate to the point of collapse between the government and its critics during the First World War.★   *H.S.*

generated an atmosphere of political anarchy so rampant that Lenin★ could call the Russia of 1917 the freest country in the world.

Lenin had spent the war in Swiss exile, returning to Russia only in April, with the aid of the German government. Lenin's wartime propaganda was for persuading the belligerent armies to turn the imperialist war into civil war, and this policy, in the context of 1917, meant attacking the new regime in Russia for its determination to prosecute the war to a successful conclusion.

Having displaced the old regime through its incompetence in war, the Provisional Government was committed to improving Russia's fortunes, despite the reluctance of the soviets, swollen by deserters and troops unwilling to go to the front. At first, the Petrograd Soviet, and the local Bolshevik leaders, took the line that they would support the new government 'in so far as its actions were not counter-revolutionary'. In spirit, the Soviet and the crowds which thronged it were for immediate peace.

Lenin was to exploit this gap, which divided the interests of the two organs of power that coexisted since March, by advocating defeatism in the rear and fraternization at the front. He brought the Petrograd Bolsheviks into line, and with large funds channelled to him by the Germans via his agents in Scandinavia he mounted a virulent campaign against the government, against the war, and in favour of the transfer of all power to the soviets. Although the Bolsheviks were a minority in the soviets, Lenin's purpose was to use this potential weapon to knock the government off balance.

Erosion of the Provisional Government

In May a new coalition came into being, when the foreign and war ministers, P. N. Milyukov (1859–1943) and A. I. Guchkov (1862–1936), the most committed to war, resigned. The government now promised to make peace without annexations or indemnities–the Soviet's socialist formula–but was still compelled by patriotic inertia to defend the country and the Revolution, a policy which appeared, especially to the troops, as contradictory. Also in May, a new wave of returning professional revolutionary internationalists, Bolshevik and Menshevik, flooded the Petrograd Soviet, stiffening its militancy.

In July the liberals resigned from the government, the Galician offensive collapsed, with the troops deserting wholesale, and thousands of armed soldiers, sailors and workers poured on to the streets of the capital shouting 'all power to the soviets'. The Soviet declined to seize power and, unsure of the government's military support, Lenin, too, hesitated to lead the armed mobs.

To press the government's fragile political advantage at this moment, Kerensky, now Prime Minister as well as war and navy minister, caused documents to be published, albeit prematurely, alleging that Lenin's party had been receiving money from the Germans to conduct defeatist and fraternization agitation. Tipped off

Banner with republican slogans displayed by a Russian regiment at the front, 1917

in advance, Lenin had gone into hiding in Finland, but the revolutionary masses, who now saw in the July demonstrations a German-backed manipulation of their revolution, turned against the Bolsheviks, and the Bolshevik Red Guards were disarmed.

Kerensky and the army commander L. G. Kornilov (1870–1918) agreed now to demonstrate the government's strength and resolve by a show of force against the mobs in the capital, aimed at restoring discipline in the army and submission in the Soviet. But while Kornilov's troops were moving towards Petrograd, Kerensky, fearing that he might be overthrown by Kornilov, reversed his orders. The troops and Kornilov were confused and demoralized, but not before the Soviet, panicked by Kerensky, had rearmed the Bolshevik Red Guards. From this moment the Provisional Government had no credible forces at its disposal.

Trotsky's coup

By September the Bolsheviks had majorities in the Petrograd and Moscow Soviets, and Lenin was frantically urging them to seize power, but it was Trotsky (Lev Davidovich Bronstein, 1879–1940), President of the Petrograd Soviet, who planned and executed the coup. On 24 October (os) the garrison troops acknowledged the Soviet as sole power, and next day the Peter and Paul Fortress with its arsenal went over to the Soviet. The seizure of the Winter Palace took place that night. The Provisional Government, intimidated by a blank shot from the cruiser *Aurora*, refused to use force in its own defence. Five soldiers, one sailor, and no defenders were killed, and the October Revolution was an accomplished fact.   *H.S.*

Lenin in power

Bolsheviks and socialists

When the II All-Russian Congress of Soviets opened at 11 p.m. on 25 October 1917 (OS) the total strength of the Bolsheviks and their supporters was 370 or 380 out of 650, but their position was much fortified when the socialist delegates walked out in protest against the Bolshevik coup. The Congress voted at 5.30 a.m. the following morning to vest power in an all-Bolshevik Council of People's Commissars, headed by Lenin.* The Bolsheviks had already by 10 October won majorities in the Petrograd and Moscow soviets* and in other urban centres, and for some time earlier Lenin, from his Finnish hiding-place, had been bombarding his colleagues with calls to seize power. In the end the uprising was fixed to coincide with the Congress meeting, largely owing to the insistence of Trotsky* that the coup must be clothed with the legitimacy of a transfer of power to the soviets—as against Lenin's view that power should be seized as soon as possible. The evidence suggests that the decision to launch the operation was taken only at the last minute.

Although Lenin always had in mind a seizure of power by his party, Trotsky's plan to make it appear as a soviet take-over was fully justified, since both the workers in the capital and Bolshevik delegates to the Congress itself supported a coalition of socialists and Bolsheviks as represented in the Congress of Soviets. Under threat of a strike from the Union of Railway Workers the Bolsheviks agreed to a coalition with the breakaway Left Socialist Revolutionaries (LSR), which proved to be short-lived. The 'neutrality' of the Petrograd garrison ensured that there was virtually no resistance in the capital; in Moscow the conflict lasted a little longer.

Bolshevik propaganda had fully supported the convening of a Constituent Assembly to decide the future of Russia, and had blamed the Provisional Government* for delaying the elections. These were duly held on the days it had appointed, 12 and 13 November, and all the evidence suggests that the vast majority of the electorate voted freely. The Bolsheviks secured about one-quarter of the total votes cast; half the country voted for socialism and against bolshevism. When the Constituent Assembly opened on 5 January 1918, it rejected by 237 votes to 136 a Bolshevik declaration endorsing the first decrees adopted by the All-Bolshevik Council of People's Commissars. The Bolsheviks and their LSR allies then walked out, and on the following day the Red Guards refused to admit the remaining delegates to the adjourned meeting of the Assembly. About a week later the III All-Russian Congress of Soviets, the elections to which had been carefully rigged, approved by an

Top: *Izvestia*, 27 October 1917, announces the decree on peace.
Right: voting in elections for the Constituent Assembly, 1917

overwhelming majority the forcible dispersal of the last freely elected representative body in Soviet history to date.

Civil war and the Red Terror

One of the first acts of the II Congress of Soviets was to adopt a decree on peace, which the Central Powers at first ignored. But on 2 December 1917 an armistice was signed, and after protracted negotiations in which the Powers increased the severity of their terms, violent dissensions appeared among the Bolshevik leaders, many of whom demanded a 'revolutionary war'. Peace was eventually signed on crippling economic terms at Brest-Litovsk on 3 March 1918 (NS). One result of the peace was the end of the coalition with the LSR who were incensed both by the capitulation to Germany and by Bolshevik policy towards the peasants. On 6 July the German ambassador was assassinated by a member of the LSR, and small-scale revolts by that party took place in Moscow and Petrograd. Thereafter it was forced out of existence, though many of its adherents joined the Bolsheviks (Communist Party★ as they became after March 1918).

The second result was civil war. During July there were several anti-communist insurrections, and anti-communist forces began their advance into the heart of Russia. On 30 August an attempt was made on Lenin's life, and the Bolsheviks inaugurated the mass arrests and executions, accompanied by the suppression of virtually all surviving non-Bolshevik newspapers, known as the Red Terror.

The civil war lasted in effect from the summer of 1918 until November 1920, when the last of the anti-Bolshevik (or White) forces under General P. N. Wrangel (1878–1928) were evacuated from the south of Russia. Apart from the attack in the south, where General A. I. Denikin (1872–1947) had preceded Wrangel as commander, Admiral A. V. Kolchak (1870–1920) allied with the Czech Legion attacked from Siberia, while in the north-west General Yudenich's thrust got very near to Petrograd by October 1919. The approach of the White forces to Yekaterinburg (now Sverdlovsk) where the former emperor Nicholas II★ and his family were held in captivity, motivated the communists' decision to kill the emperor, his wife and children, his doctor and three servants on 16 July 1918. Communist

The Revolution triumphs over a panic-stricken crowd of capitalists, officers and clergy (a poster of 1917)

Lenin and Ya.M. Sverdlov (1885–1919) at the unveiling of a monument to Marx and Engels in Moscow, 1918

fortunes varied in the course of the war, but the ultimate victory meant a great lift to their self-confidence. Victory was mainly due to three factors. The first was the energy and organizing ability of Trotsky as People's Commissar for War, who rebuilt the demoralized Imperial Army* into the Red Army,* making use in the process of tens of thousands of former officers. The second was the fact that the peasant population, though it did not support the communists, disliked them less than the White forces, whose policy was to restore the land acquired by peasants under the Bolsheviks to its former landlords. The third factor was the presence of enthusiastic communists at key points to maintain drastic discipline and morale. The much-publicized Allied intervention was originally motivated by the desire to restore the eastern front which had collapsed owing to Bolshevik policy, thus enabling the Germans to move troops to the west. Although ill-planned, ill-supported and militarily of virtually no importance, this intervention played a big part in communist propaganda as a rallying call against a hostile capitalist West.

War Communism*

The period of extreme communization which lasted from mid-1918 until spring 1921 was called 'War Communism'. It is uncertain whether this was a deliberate ideological plan or a series of improvisations in response to events. The Bolsheviks had inherited enough chaos from the Provisional Government: their own measures considerably added to it. In October nationalization of land, with the right of cultivation assured to the peasants, unleashed anarchy in the villages; in the following month industry was disorganized by a decree on workers' control. Before long stringent economic centralization was introduced, and workers' control was abandoned in favour of disciplinary management. The problem of food shortage was the most acute: compulsory requisitioning of food from the peasants was soon decreed, and class war broke out in the villages on the setting up of 'committees of the poor'. The immediate response of the peasants was to reduce production, and to try to unload their products on the extensive black market. But in time their resistance took on military form and by the end of 1920 a virtual guerrilla war was in operation in parts of the country. About half the work-force left the towns for the villages. An attempt to nationalize almost the entire industry of the country did not prevent economic collapse: by 1921 gross output had fallen to less than a third on the average, and foreign trade had disappeared – in part owing to the Allies' blockade. The sufferings of the population through death, famine, disease, civil war and communist terror were enormous.

Internal dissension

It is not surprising that with this background the new regime should have been faced with serious opposition. The forces opposed to the Revolution mostly rallied to the various White armies. The liberal parties were quite early on destroyed by murder, arrest and exile. The two main socialist parties, the Mensheviks and the Socialist Revolutionaries (SR), were never (except for a few months) outlawed, and indeed throughout the civil war continued to return fair-sized contingents in elections to the soviets. But, as their criticism of the communists became more vocal, they were increasingly harassed and impeded in their political aims by arbitrary violence and deprived of their press. The accusation of counter-revolutionary violence levelled against them was untrue. The SR did for some months attempt to collaborate with one of the governments set up by the White forces, but soon abandoned both that attempt and general political activity. The Mensheviks relied expressly on strictly constitutional means, and expelled individuals who took part in violence. The conclusive proof that the socialist parties were not counter-revolutionary (though certainly anti-communist) is provided by the fact that many thousands of their adherents were left at their official posts throughout the civil war and only afterwards removed from public service. The reasons for their destruction by arrest, exile, and – in the case of the SR – by a show trial in 1922, were their increasingly effective and popular criticism of Communist Party policy, and arbitrary violence.

Within the Party also critical factions developed in 1920 – such as the Democratic Centralists* who demanded more autonomy for the communists in the soviets, and the Workers' Opposition who claimed more independence for trade union* communists. In March 1921 the crews and garrison at the naval base of Kronstadt revolted, demanding an end to communist monopoly of power and more freedom for workers and peasants. Faced with crisis, Lenin presented the X Congress of the Communist Party with a series of measures which reflected the Party's panic in face of the threat to its sway. At the same time the Kronstadt rebels were mown down with heavy casualties, with the full support of the Congress including the members of the opposition factions. Lenin's measures, apart from the New Economic Policy (NEP),* included the prohibition of factions on pain of expulsion, severe limitations on freedom of discussion within the Party, and a call for the suppression of the socialist parties (the Mensheviks had, indeed, for some time been advocating a policy very similar to NEP).

Reorganization of the state

After the Bolshevik seizure of power, legislative authority was technically vested in a Central Executive Committee, in session between the intermittent All-Russian Congresses of Soviets. In practice, legislative power was exercised more often by the Council of People's Commissars, and by the Council of Workers' and Peasants' Defence, of which Lenin was also the Chairman; its main tasks were the supply of the Red Army and the militarization* of the population and industry for civil war needs. As for the legal system,* the entire body of law left intact by the Provisional Government, as well as the bar and the judiciary, were abolished by decree, and on 24 November 1917 Revolutionary Tribunals were set up. These were directed to decide cases by their 'revolutionary conscience' but even after 1922, when codes of civil and criminal laws were promulgated, a great deal of discretion was left in the hands of the courts and of the, often, lay judges who presided over them. Also, on 6 December 1918 the All-Russian Extraordinary Commission of the Council of People's Commissars for Combating Counter-Revolution, Sabotage and Speculation, known as Vecheka, was set up. Although its authority was, by the decree, limited to investigation and confiscation of property and ration cards, the Vecheka soon assumed the powers of imprisonment and execution without trial. Administrative arrests were followed by deportation and consignment to prison camps* for forced labour, where conditions were appalling.

The first Constitution* of the RSFSR was adopted on 10 July 1918. Its characteristic features were: indirect elections to the soviets, inequality of franchise, disfranchisement of certain classes and omission of any reference to the real force in government – the Communist Party. It included clauses guaranteeing civil rights, but provided no method for their enforcement. A new but similar Constitution was adopted on 6 July 1923, embodying the 'voluntary' union of the Ukrainian, Belorussian and Transcaucasian SSRs into the Union of Soviet Socialist Republics (USSR). Since the will that decided for union was that of the local Communist Parties only, its voluntary nature is open to doubt. The mortally ill Lenin warned his party in 1922 against excessive Great Russian chauvinism in the treatment of national minorities. Yet in 1921 Lenin had apparently authorized the invasion by the Red Army of Menshevik-controlled Georgia in support of a rebellion staged by local communists – in flagrant breach of the treaty of 7 May 1920 between Georgia and the RSFSR.

Lenin suffered his first stroke in May 1922, and thereafter could work only intermittently until March 1923. In April 1922 Stalin,* with Lenin's full approval, had become General Secretary of the Central Committee of the CPSU.* By the end of 1922 Lenin had expressed doubts about Stalin's fitness for the post (in a letter to the forthcoming Party Congress, which Stalin succeeded in suppressing) but when he died on 21 January 1924 Lenin had not suggested his own successor. *L.S.*

Stalin gains ascendancy

At Lenin's* death, the immediate succession fell to G. Y. Zinoviev (real name Radomysl'sky, 1883–1936), L. B. Kamenev (real name Rozenfel'd, 1883–1936) and I. V. Stalin (real name Dzhugashvili, 1879–1953). The son of a Georgian shoemaker, Stalin was expelled in

1899 from the Tiflis Orthodox seminary as a Marxist agitator and became a full-time professional revolutionary in 1901. He first attracted Lenin's attention in 1905, became a member of the Bolshevik Central Committee in 1912, and was from then on one of the most prominent Bolshevik leaders inside Russia.

Trotsky,* with whom Stalin clashed during the civil war,* had made many enemies in the Party, and had already been defeated in debate in the Party organs which Stalin largely controlled. Stalin also enjoyed the full support of the right wing of the Party, headed by N. I. Bukharin (1888–1938), since until 1928 he fully supported NEP* of which Bukharin was then the main advocate. The opposition of Zinoviev and Kamenev was easily routed by the XIV Congress of the CPSU* at the end of 1925, the composition of which was manipulated by Stalin as General Secretary. Trotsky was already defeated and discredited on theoretical issues such as 'Socialism in One Country' versus 'World Revolution'. Early in 1926 he joined with Zinoviev and

Below: leading communists, including Trotsky, on the temporary Lenin mausoleum, November 1924. Bottom: N. I. Bukharin with Mariya Ulanova, Lenin's sister, in the offices of *Pravda*, May 1924

Kamenev in a United Opposition against Stalin's growing dictatorship. Events soon showed that the struggle was hopeless, owing to Stalin's control over the organs of the Party through his Secretariat.* In such conditions, the Left Opposition to NEP, which probably commanded much support in the Party, was irrelevant. On 14 November 1927 Trotsky and his supporters were expelled from the Party and exiled, and the following year Trotsky was ejected from the USSR.

Trotsky's dictatorial practices, together with the fact that he was a Jew, made it unlikely that he could ever rally wider support in the Party – quite apart from the obstacle of Stalin's control of the apparatus.* Bukharin, described by Lenin as 'the favourite of the Party', was in quite a different position. The policy which he advocated, and which Stalin for a time seemed to support, was squarely based on Lenin's thoughts, as expressed in his last writings. NEP, according to Lenin, was in no sense a temporary device in order to secure a breathing-space: it was part of a plan designed to last 'not centuries, but generations'. The Bolsheviks* had in 1917 been 'forced' to take power in circumstances in which the population was not ripe for socialism.* The period of reconciliation between town and country which NEP offered would provide an opportunity for the peasants to acquire political maturity, and to learn by experience the virtues of cooperation: in no circumstances, according to Lenin, should this be forced. NEP was popular with many sections of the population: it repaired the ravages of the civil war* – the level of previous production in agriculture was reached by 1925, while the real wages of workers in terms of purchasing power rose to 108.4 per cent of the 1913 level in 1926/7. Intellectual life enjoyed a freedom that it has never known since. There was therefore every incentive for a man as jealous of political rivals as Stalin to eliminate Bukharin and his supporters when once their alliance against the Left Opposition was no longer necessary to him.

Stalin's primary motive in ending NEP may have been not so much the desire to remove Bukharin as economic and political considerations. The economic argument was the alarming drop in grain supplies to the towns. The peasants were eating better and were, as usual, reluctant to sell grain unless compelled while industry was providing few products for them in exchange; attempts at the beginning of 1928 to stimulate deliveries were unsuccessful. Again, all were agreed that both collectivization* of agriculture and industrialization* of the country were desirable: the debatable question was one of pace. Bukharin, who accepted Lenin's time-scale of 'generations', believed that capital should be extracted from the peasants by first developing light industries which would produce the kind of goods that the peasants would buy in exchange for their produce. Supporters of the Left Opposition believed in some kind of compulsion against the peasants, although no one advocated the all-out war against 100 million people that Stalin unleashed, at the cost of millions of their lives and of long-term damage to agriculture. Apologists for Stalin have sometimes justified his policy on the grounds that it was necessary in order to ensure rapid industrialization in face of the rising menace of attack by Germany – but this looks like being wise after the event.

It is not known exactly when Stalin decided on the 'Third Revolution' – enforced collectivization of agriculture and industrialization at breakneck speed. Clear signs of the impending change appeared by the spring of 1928. But rumours of the ending of NEP were indignantly denied, and Stalin proceeded with great caution in the face of known opposition inside the Party. He also showed great skill in outmanoeuvring Bukharin and the right wing of the Party leadership. This operation occupied the whole of 1928. By the XVI Party Conference in April 1929 Bukharin and his supporters had been condemned: they were later expelled from the Politburo. At this Conference the ambitious First Five-year Plan and a policy of rapid collectivization of agriculture were adopted unanimously. For nearly five years thereafter the Party was to be engaged in open war against a terrorized, hostile and desperate people. By 10 March 1930 over half of all farms had been collectivized in a campaign which had lasted only five months, and engaged at the outset 25 000 Party workers. On 2 March 1930 Stalin, in a *Pravda* article which referred to 'dizziness from success', attempted to divert odium from his policy on to the subordinates who carried out his orders. But the respite which followed was only temporary, and the XVI Party Congress, in June and July 1930, urged a further determined struggle. To make it more effective for the control of industry, this Congress also reorganized the apparatus of the Communist Party, which by then numbered over one million, having quadrupled since October 1917.   *L.S.*

Stalin's autocracy

Immediately after Stalin* gained political ascendancy, he set about the social and economic transformation of the country. A hectic process of state-building took place, in which much that is now familiar in the Soviet scene was born. Large-scale ministries and collective farms were formed, vast construction sites started to cover the countryside with towns and industry, and the repressive organs extended outwards, including their major manifestation: the growing GULag* empire of concentration camps, forced labour camps and transit prisons. All levels of society changed places: peasants became workers, millions of whom migrated* annually to the towns (until stopped by the restoration of the internal passport*), workers poured into offices and the swelling ranks of lower administration, and the top echelons coalesced into an amorphous and privileged élite, misleadingly entitled the 'Soviet intelligentsia'.

But this was not the work of Stalin alone. His 'great break' of 1929 quite consciously harnessed the energies of younger Party cadres, of Komsomols* and even schoolchildren, in a gigantic effort to reshape the culture and economy of the countryside. They formed 'raiding parties' of 'light cavalry' which transformed every area of social life, from grain requisitioning to philosophy, into the struggle with 'alien tendencies' and 'class enemies' on each particular 'front'. However carefully they were oriented by the Party leadership, such forces had an identity of their own, and formed part of the social basis for Stalinism. In addressing them, Stalin and other oligarchs were appealing to a quite authentic, if often suppressed, stream of the original bolshevism.*

Since 1921 the whole pattern of policy had been retreat: a mixed economy, peasant agriculture, compromise with 'bourgeois special-ists' and a prospect of socialism that would take (in Lenin's* words) 'years and years'. Stalin's policies promised advance at last, enacted with much of the rhetoric and militancy of the civil war period, but literally too: for younger cadres this was their own civil war, the one against the peasantry.

Stalin and the Party

Stalin's leadership transformed the CPSU* into a mass organization, whose size had swelled from 1.3 million (1928) to 3.5 million (when recruitment was halted) in January 1933. Of these, the first intake was primarily of workers. Over a million production and transport workers were admitted in 1930–1, with mass applications often received from workshops and even factories in the first stage of the Five-year Plan. By April 1930, 48.6 per cent of Party members were manual workers. But the target of one worker for every two communists was not achieved; thereafter 'proletarian' enrolment fell away, simultaneously with the reduced status of the 'working class' in the official definitions of society. Peasant intake also rose in the early months to reach a high point of one new recruit in five during 1930. Most came from the newly-constituted collective farms whose Party cells and 'political departments' formed the new focus of Party influence in the countryside. All was not well in these first stages; Stalin's *Pravda* article 'Dizzy with success' (March 1930) being an attempt to blame 'excesses' of collectivization* on the fervour of local Party workers. Further indication of resistance may be seen in the fact that some 40 000 individual peasants (uncollectivized) still held Party membership in January 1931. This was not the last of the political difficulties with the countryside.

But out of the recruitment policies which Stalin pursued there soon emerged a third and most decisive element. As the dust settled, it became clear that the beneficiaries of the incipient Stalin order were neither the working class nor least of all the peasantry. At the heart of this new policy, which found expression in Party membership quite early on, was the appeal to a new stabilizing factor:

a new 'middle' in Soviet society,* and one through which it could properly be said that the country was being ruled. This third estate, which lumped together such disparate strata as the local adminis-trators, factory managers, technical intelligentsia and 'specialists', both old and new, rose steadily as a proportion of Party membership through the 1930s. Among industrial managers, Party members increased from 15 per cent (1930) to 70 per cent (1933), and among top officials in agriculture, the jump was from 15 per cent (1930) to 83 per cent (1933). In the central apparatus of state, the Party soon came to achieve predominance – even saturation – while at some crucial levels of local government, such as the rayon (district), it reached an average of 97 per cent. Thus Party members of this rank became a vital link between the political leadership and the society they were administering.

Stalin and society

At the first stage of Stalin's ascendancy, in which 'proletarian' forces were unleashed originally against the Party's right and thereafter upon the whole society, positive discrimination was exercised in their favour. Access to higher education* was thought vital to a working class which would treble in size (from 6 to 20 million) during the 1930s. The special faculties which prepared workers for universities were vastly expanded from an annual intake of 160 000 to some 511 000 students by 1933. A new technical intelligentsia was similarly recruited after 1928 according to a stringent *numerus clausus* on class lines, and a series of show trials of 'wreckers' between 1928 and 1931 served as a reminder that 'bourgeois' technical specialists were capable of sabotage and every ingenious trick to destroy the country's industrial effort.

In July 1931, Stalin suddenly reversed this line, and denounced the 'specialist-baiting' and anti-intellectual discrimination which he had earlier fostered. In parallel pronouncements he laid down theoretical bases for inegalitarianism: the 'new stage' he had inaugurated needed specialist skills, and was willing, he clearly hinted, to pay for them. Quality of work, not social origin, would be the new basis of reward and discrimination. A similar line was followed, in April 1932, towards the cultural intelligentsia, when militant and proletarian associations in literature* and the arts* were suddenly disbanded, and replaced (on orders of the Central Committee)* by more broadly-based bodies: the cultural unions.

Such a shift in policy was well-grounded in economic necessity, and reflected the determination to produce greater balance, proportion, internal consistency and realism in the targets for the Second Five-year Plan (1933–37). It also reveals the relationship between Stalinism and society. Whereas, at the previous stage, Stalin had sought to mobilize the pre-existing elements who most opposed – and now destroyed – the remnants of the NEP* society, at the second stage (from 1931-2 on) he showed himself a conscious social manipulator, breaking with his previous supporters, and looking ahead towards the stabilizing policies which would enable him to rule a now-transformed country with some greater degree of assurance and regularity. This shift in attitude, however, may also have been determined by a change in Stalin's personal political position.

Opposition to Stalin

While no outright opposition to Stalin emerged before the XVII Party Congress, there had previously been significant rumblings of discontent behind the scenes. During 1929 all leaders were 'Stalinist' in that they upheld basic tenets: collective farming imposed at whatever cost (at least 6 million peasant deaths during the resulting famines); industrial development by force where necessary; and forced labour by the growing camp and prison populations. Yet despite these original assumptions, opposition started to appear. Already during 1930, serious divisions on policy could be discerned within the Stalinist leadership. Two top officials of the Party and governmental apparatus, S. I. Syrtsov (1893–1937) and V. V. Lominadze (1897–1935), appear to have drawn up a secret manifesto, which condemned the violent repression of the peasantry, the megalomania of such large industrial projects as the Stalingrad tractor factory, and Stalin's autocratic conduct. Little had come of this before they were expelled from the Party as a 'left-right bloc' in December 1930.

In the summer of 1932 a new opposition document appeared, the Ryutin manifesto, some 200 pages of analysis which was disseminated quite widely in upper Party circles. It argued that N. I. Bukharin's (1888-1938) warnings against adventurist economic policies had been vindicated, proposed an economic retreat, including scaled-down investments and dismantling of the collective farm system, a general amnesty, and reinstatement of expelled Party members. Much of the text was devoted to criticism of Stalin, whose personal vindictiveness and power-seeking were held to be the ruin of the Revolution. Stalin responded with extreme vehemence and is said to have demanded the death penalty for the ringleaders, a request refused by the Politburo,* among whom the Leningrad Party secretary, S. M. Kirov (1886–1934), is reported to have been particularly firm. No doubt other leaders were united in the expectation that, if the request had been granted, they would be potential victims, and Stalin himself seemed to imply this in the famous telegram of September 1936, which told the security organs* that they were 'four years behind' in the work of exposing enemies within the Party.

The XVII Party Congress (the 'Congress of Victors') assembled in January 1934 ostensibly to celebrate the defeat of 'enemies of socialism' in the Soviet Union. Collective agriculture had been established, industrial production put on a firm footing and above all, as Stalin's speech insisted, the hopes expressed abroad that the 'Soviet experiment' would founder had themselves been confounded. But there were other murmurings behind the scenes, of which the most important concerned Stalin's personal position.

During 1933 a new set of tendencies had emerged within Soviet society, that may be summarized as the call for order. Much earlier than anyone could have anticipated, the new social structure – with its growing hierarchies and inequalities – had begun to settle down, exerting pressures, even perhaps demands of its own. In the cultural sphere, as championed by Gor'ky,* these took the form of a campaign for 'quality' and a rejection of the shoddy literary standards of the First Five-year Plan. In education, this involved an end to the *numerus clausus*, renewal of academic standards and a largely conservative school reform. From the Soviet establishment, with its swelling organs of administration, came the call for routine, predictability, the laying-down of directives and even of legal regulations. Of the latter, Kirov seems to have been champion. He warned that the agricultural administration was ineffective, calling for the abolition of its much-hated political departments (a measure enacted later in 1934). Further, he condemned 'extremism' in dealing with the countryside, particularly the punitive expulsion from collective farms, which amounted often to sentence to death by starvation. Kirov probably intended to restrict the sweeping powers of the secret police in their usurped judicial role (widened in a circular of July 1929) to the functions simply of arrest and preliminary investigation. Finally, though not publicly expressed at the Congress, came criticism of Stalin's leadership, implying that any restoration of legality would have to begin at the top. Voting figures are not known, but Stalin was demoted from the post of General Secretary, while Kirov was promoted and was to move from

Stalin and his team, 1934; S. M. Kirov on extreme right

Leningrad to a position alongside him in the Moscow Secretariat*
– a transfer prevented by Kirov's assassination in December 1934.

The Great Terror

The Kirov murder was the signal for a new stage in Soviet history, one
of mass repression which began in earnest in 1936, and did not
subside until 1939. Paradoxically, the descent into lawlessness was
accompanied by public gestures of legality. Promulgation of the
Stalin Constitution* ('the most democratic in the world') took place
simultaneously with the great purges and trials of 1936. Bukharin, its
main author, appears genuinely to have believed that legal limits
could be put on Stalin's power; he contemplated a project (articulated
on a foreign journey of 1936) of setting up a 'second party' of loyal
socialist intellectuals who would criticize the status quo from an
independent viewpoint. Stalin had other ideas. Rather than sanction
a second party he resolved to rule without one.

Until the end of 1934 Soviet policies came, nominally at least, from
the Party and were confirmed by periodic meetings of its oligarchs
and upper echelons. These upper ranks were a prime target of
subsequent repression – 70 per cent of the Central Committee elected
at the XVII Congress was executed during the following five years. Of
ordinary delegates, some 1108 were arrested or executed in the same
period, and only 59 of the original 1966 reappeared as delegates to the
next Congress in 1939. Analysis of those purged within the Party
shows that terror moved steadily closer to the centres of power. This
was signalled by the first 'show trial' of top leaders (G. Ye. Zinoviev
(1883–1936), L. B. Kamenev (1883–1936) and 14 others) in the
summer of 1936. Those of other leaders (G. L. Pyatakov (1890–
1937), K. Radek (1885–1939) and 'accomplices') followed in
January 1937, while Bukharin and others (including A. I. Rykov
(1881–1938), Kh. G. Rakovsky (1873–1938) and G. G. Yagoda
(1891–1938)) were retained for the grand finale in 1938. Terror
against the Party was renewed at the Party Plenum of February 1937,
where Stalin and supporters forced through – against various
doubters – a resolution which demanded further 'intensification of
struggle' against 'enemies of the people'. That opened the door to
mass arrests in all sections of society, though particular attention was
certainly given to leading groups: top administrators, managers, the
intelligentsia, military officers and so on.

Of total arrests, above 8 million (about 5 per cent of the population)
is a likely figure. Of those arrested, some 800 000 (one in ten) were
probably executed, while the remainder faced incarceration or
transportation to the camp system. As to the death-rate in camps, a
figure of 10 per cent in 1933, rising to 20 per cent in 1938, is probably
conservative, but even so would mean a death rate annually of well
over one million persons for the purge years. Given that 10 years was a
standard sentence, it can easily be seen that only a small fraction of
those convicted can have survived.

Stalin's use of power

Four instruments were essential to Stalin's rule. First was his mastery
of the Party through its apparatus* – a tendency which worried
Lenin, who had promoted him – and his consequent ability to select
delegates to the Party Congresses which would choose him. As the
Party institutions atrophied during the later 1930s, he relied ever
more closely on his private secretariat. Second, was a compliant
Procuracy* – a quite familiar feature of old Russia – and the willingness of jurists to subordinate themselves to his orders. Of these, the
most infamous was A. Ya. Vyshinsky (1883–1955), Chief Prosecutor
in the 'show trials'. Stalin's third instrument was the secret police,
who came to constitute a state within the state, omnipresent, and
significantly entrusted (after the suicide of Stalin's second wife,
Nadezhda Alliluyeva, in November 1932) with the management of
his households. Last, at the apex of the terror system, was the GULag:
which quite quickly grew to be a basic element of his rule and, not surprisingly, the word with which Stalinism has become synonymous.

Nevertheless, terrifying and destructive though it was, this period
still produced achievements. The 1930s saw the USSR industrialize,
largely through its own resources, and such show pieces as the
Moscow Metro railway system, the gigantic power-stations in the
Urals and the machine-building combines were concrete evidence of
what could be done. Other of the 'prestige projects' – such as the
White Sea/Baltic Canal – were economically worthless, and
amounted to pyramids in honour of Stalin, after whom the largest
were named. Throughout the decade, therefore, waste was accompanied by construction. Only after truths about the labour camps
became widely known – ignored at the time but finally accepted in the
Khrushchevian 'thaw'* – could attention turn to the balance-sheet of
Stalin's achievement: despite the madness of his methods, the main
elements of a modern state were formed.   *A.K.-W.*

The Moscow Metro system: a monument to the Stalinist era

The USSR at war

The state of the nation on the eve of war

On the eve of war the ordinary Soviet citizen could, it seemed, look forward to a period of relative stability. Real wages* were still lower than in 1926 and would remain so until 1952. Many items of food were in short supply: the massacre of livestock during collectivization* had left the country with fewer cattle than in 1913. The prison camps* of Central Asia, Siberia and the Far North were choked with slave labourers. But the population at large, especially the office-holders and the educated, had been, as a Soviet writer would later put it, 'frightened once and for all' by the Great Terror,* and were reliably subservient. Police activity had therefore been reduced. Stalin* himself said that there would in future be no need for mass purges. (He should have added that the population would none the less be systematically culled both to refresh their memories of 1936–8 and to provide cheap labour for industries and areas which held little attraction for free workers.) Collectivization and the Five-year Plans,* for all the waste and confusion of the early 1930s, had laid the foundations of a modern economy. Stalin had silenced those of independent standing who might challenge his authority; exile did not save his sternest critic, Trotsky,* who was murdered on Stalin's orders in Mexico in June 1940. The central organs of government were staffed with his creatures, the middle levels of authority in all sectors with people who had made themselves accomplices in the bloodletting and who joined loudly in the rites of the Stalin cult. Science,* culture and education* were by now as tightly controlled, and as rigidly subordinated to central planning,* as were industry and agriculture.* It might appear that the country could concentrate on the two huge tasks which Stalin had set it – overtaking the leading capitalist countries in economic performance and producing by education and indoctrination 'Soviet man',* a new type of human being fit to live in the communist society of the future. Many in the USSR were ready to believe that the 'Stalin Constitution',* though scarcely relevant to the present, was a genuine blueprint for a happier future. Many were prepared to overlook, as temporary tactical necessities, glaringly unsocialist or inhumane features of the system: the draconian labour legislation, the fees charged in the higher classes of schools, the special shops selling to the privileged goods inaccessible to other citizens, and even the corrective labour camps, the full horror of which seems to have been concealed with remarkable success from the population at large.

In June 1941 the 'sudden and perfidious' attack by his recent partner ruined Stalin's hopes of a period of intensive economic development and social engineering.

The course of the war

In the early stages of the war the Soviet regime was preserved by the mistakes of the enemy and by luck rather than by its own efforts. Though it is scarcely credible that Hitler* took the ever-suspicious Stalin by surprise, he certainly found him ill-prepared. The Great Purge had weakened the Soviet armed forces. The first Soviet commanders in the three main sectors were incompetent old civil war* hacks. In the western regions – and particularly in the Ukraine and Belorussia – the inhabitants at first often welcomed the German

THE SOVIET UNION'S WESTERN BORDERS, 1939–45

KEY

——— 1939	– – – 1941	═══ 1945

Source: A. E. Adams, I. M. Matley and W. O. McCagg, *An Atlas of Russian and East European History*, London, 1967

invaders as liberators. By November 1941, one of the three main invading armies was outside Leningrad (which the Germans never succeeded in taking, although millions died in the beleaguered city), the second was 20 miles from Moscow, and the third deep in the Ukraine. Moscow, however, was saved by Hitler's own miscalculation in diverting armour from the central sector to the other two, and by the early onset of a very severe winter. The Soviet regime retained its main centre of command and communications, and succeeded in evacuating to the rear some 1500 industrial enterprises, the output from which, together with the material aid supplied by the Allies, ensured that in the last two years of the war the Soviet forces were better armed and equipped than the enemy. In 1942 the German drive towards Baku, intended to cut off Soviet oil supplies, was checked, and Hitler made his second great mistake in concentrating too much of his strength on Stalingrad–an objective of more symbolic than strategic importance. The defeat of Field-Marshal von Paulus at Stalingrad (January 1943), and the capture of his huge army, was the turning-point in the war. In the next 18 months the Soviet armies recovered all the territory taken by the Germans, and thereafter swept westward and southward into Romania, Bulgaria, the Baltic states, Poland, Hungary, Austria and Czechoslovakia. On 22 April 1945 Soviet forces surrounded Berlin, and linked up with American troops on the Elbe. The unconditional surrender of Germany to the Allies followed on 7 May. On 8 August (two days after the USA had dropped an atomic bomb on Hiroshima) the USSR joined in the last phase of the war against Japan and rapidly captured the Japanese forces in Manchuria, to justify the territorial gains promised at the Yalta Conference.

The war had inflicted enormous losses, human and material, on the USSR: 20 million killed (half of them civilians or prisoners), 1710 urban centres destroyed, 25 million people left homeless, thousands of enterprises and thousands of kilometres of railway put out of action.

The territories under German occupation
Still grosser than Hitler's military blunders were the political errors committed by the German authorities in the occupied territories. Those Ukrainians, Belorussians and–a smaller proportion of their national group–Russians who met the invader with the symbolic 'bread and salt' hoped in vain for deliverance from the most objectionable features of the Soviet system. Though the German commanders often recommended more tactful and realistic treatment of the local population, the SS (the Nazi Party troops) and the political authorities on the whole favoured ruthless exploitation and the ultimate extermination of Slavic 'submen'. The Law for Restoration of Private Land (February 1942) did not in fact result in the general dismantling of collective farms. The Orthodox Church*– regarded as a potential focus for nationalist feeling and, like all forms of Christianity, ideologically as detestable to Nazis as to communists–was not allowed to resume its old place in the life of the people. The execution of civilian hostages, the massive levies for forced

Kerch, 1941: 8000 civilians were shot in this field by Germans withdrawing under Russian counter-attack

labour in Germany and elsewhere, and the ruthless ill-treatment of prisoners of war held in the occupied areas helped to convince the local population that they had exchanged a bad master for a worse. The powerful Ukrainian nationalist* movement from mid-1943 onwards considered itself at war with both Nazis and communists. By the autumn of 1943, 10 per cent of German fighting troops in the USSR were engaged against partisan units – many of which were also viewed with suspicion and anxiety from Moscow. Though the Germans had in their hands a sufficient number of Soviet volunteers to launch an anti-communist crusade in the USSR itself, and a general of proven talent willing to command it (General A. A. Vlasov (1900–46), captured outside Leningrad in July 1942), they decided that the enterprise might rebound upon them.

The patriotic revival

Stalin, for his part, showed great psychological acumen in his handling of the Soviet population. Although the regime since its inception had propagated 'militant atheism' and at times actively persecuted believers, he recognized the importance of the Orthodox Church as a focus of patriotic feeling by receiving Metropolitan Sergius in September 1943, and permitting the re-establishment of the Holy Synod.* Writers and artists* were allowed a measure of creative freedom unknown since the late 1920s. Foreign cultural imports – particularly films* – were accepted for their entertainment value, with little regard to ideological content. Propaganda for the home front centred around 'patriotic' rather than narrowly communist themes: more was heard of old Russia's military heroes – Alexander Nevsky,* A. V. Suvorov (1729-1800), M. I. Kutuzov (1745–1813) – than of Marx and Engels. Guards regiments and divisions were set up again, specifically military decorations (the Orders of Suvorov and Kutuzov) introduced, epaulettes and saluting (both previously regarded as symbols of the old caste system) were brought back. Stalin promoted his most successful commanders marshals, and himself took this title, as well as the unique style of 'Generalissimus'. The abolition (in March 1943) of the Comintern* convinced many at home and abroad that Russian nationalism had finally triumphed over communist internationalism. *H.T.W.*

The reversion to Stalinist normality

The great victories of 1943–5 might seem to have demonstrated conclusively the loyalty of the bulk of the Soviet population and of the army in particular, and to have shown that the regime was firmly and efficiently in control of the country and its resources. It had certainly raised Soviet power and Stalin's* personal authority (indeed, his personal popularity) to an unprecedented level. But if the Soviet peoples expected that after the war the leadership would reward their tremendous efforts by relaxing its heavy political and economic pressures upon them, they were to be disappointed.

After the Second World War Stalin was, if anything, still more morbidly obsessed with problems of security, internal and external, than he had been before. Those sections of the population which had passed out of Soviet control during the war – and this included prisoners of war and those deported to forced labour in the Third Reich, as well as civilians who had lived under German occupation – were automatically suspect, as were the inhabitants of newly annexed regions. Tribunals with powers of summary punishment followed in the wake of the liberating Soviet armies, condemning to execution or imprisonment not only actual traitors but others who had done no more than continue to teach Soviet schoolchildren, or live in their own homes with German soldiers billeted upon them. Perhaps the most tragic of Stalin's victims were the displaced persons forcibly repatriated to the USSR by its Western allies.

Population transfers for reasons of security modified the ethnic map of the USSR. In 1941, in the path of the German advance, the Volga Germans* had been moved from what had been their home for nearly two centuries. After the German retreat, the Soviet authorities uprooted whole peoples – the Crimean Tatars,* the Caucasian* Chechen Ingush and the Kalmyks* – alleged to have collaborated with the occupier. Mass deportations from the Baltic republics* helped to clear the way for Russian immigration.* The persecution of 'homeless cosmopolitan' writers and critics, during the campaign to restore ideological discipline in the arts, opened up a new era of official anti-semitism.

Post-war reconstruction* of the country's battered and distorted economy was in itself a task which might have taken a decade. Stalin, however, proclaimed a much more ambitious and exacting programme: a series of Five-year Plans* to treble pre-war industrial output and 'guarantee our motherland against all eventualities'. Relations between the USSR and its wartime allies had deteriorated quickly as communist regimes were installed by force or fraud in Eastern and Central Europe. Soviet propagandists proclaimed once again the division of the world into two camps, and the alleged threat of an 'imperialist' onslaught on the USSR was used to justify the narrow concentration of Soviet economic resources on heavy industry and military production.* Progress in these sectors was impressive. By 1948 the country had basically reconstructed its war-damaged industries, and expansion thereafter was rapid. By 1949 the USSR had acquired a nuclear* weapon. Light industry, and more particularly agriculture,* were starved of capital to make all this possible. Meat, fats, sugar, flour, clothing and footwear were always in short supply. The war-devastated cities of the Ukraine, the mid-Volga region and South Russia were rebuilt with remarkable speed, but in the congested older cities the housing* shortage grew increasingly acute.

THE SOVIET UNION IN EASTERN EUROPE, 1945–8

Source: M. Gilbert, *Russian History Atlas*, London, 1972

KEY

Territory annexed by the USSR, 1939–40 and re-incorporated in 1945

Former German and Czechoslovak territory annexed by the USSR in 1945

States liberated by the Soviet army, and/or in which communist regimes came to power between 1945 and 1948

Soviet occupation zones in Austria (evacuated 1954) and Germany

British, French and United States occupation zones

The iron curtain in 1948

Eastern and southern frontiers of 'Western Territories' incorporated into Poland in 1945

Nowhere were increased investment and generous incentives more necessary than in agriculture, and nowhere were they so heartlessly denied. The means by which Stalin hoped to increase agricultural output – higher norms for compulsory deliveries, tighter labour discipline, administrative reorganization, grandiose schemes to 'transform nature' by for instance raising great shelter belts in the path of the drying east winds, and generalizing 'ley rotation' farming – were utterly ineffectual, and the country was in sight of a grave crisis of supply on the eve of his death.

In the ageing dictator's last years the stultifying effect of what his successors would call 'the cult of the personality' became more and more obvious in all sectors of public life. To judge from its coverage in the Soviet press, by far the most important event in the immediate post-war period was the 70th birthday of J. V. Stalin in 1949. His prejudices and whims governed the activities not only of administrators but of scholars, writers, artists and scientists: incalculable damage to Soviet agriculture, as well as to science, was caused by his unqualified support of the pseudo-genetics* of Lysenko, and the development of automation* in the USSR was impeded by his conviction that 'cybernetics is a bourgeois delirium'. In 1949 *Pravda* for several days devoted its centre pages to polemical articles on linguistic science, in preparation for a pronouncement of stunning banality on this subject by J. V. Stalin. His only significant contribution to the proceedings of the XIX Congress of the CPSU* in 1952 (the first since 1939) was a comically crude pamphlet on 'The Economic Problems of Socialism'.

Stalin's jealous and vainglorious insistence on his own intellectual and political supremacy had more sinister results than these. In 1949 he authorized the execution of N. A. Voznesensky (1903–50), a member of the Politburo* and chairman of the State Planning Commission, and a number of other senior officials. The 'Leningrad Affair' (as it is called, since several of those concerned had connections with Leningrad and with Zhdanov,* who had been in charge of the city during the war) was a warning that even the highest office-holders could be summarily destroyed if they aroused Stalin's suspicions. In 1952 it appeared that others might shortly follow Voznesensky into oblivion. At the XIX Party Congress in October the Politburo was enlarged and renamed 'Presidium'. According to Khrushchev,* in his 'secret speech' of 1956, this was in preparation for the elimination of older leaders in favour of 'less experienced' persons. It became obvious that Stalin was contemplating bloodshed when in January 1953 *Pravda* reported that nine doctors had confessed to the murder of Zhdanov and to plotting against other prominent persons on the orders of the US intelligence services. When Stalin died two months later, these charges were dropped and the police officials and false witnesses responsible for them were punished.   *H.T.W.*

The Khrushchev years

Collective leadership

After the death of Stalin* no single individual attained the dictatorial power which he had wielded during the last 20 years or more of his life. The collective leadership which was established in the first two years following Stalin's death on 5 March 1953 was a product not so much of agreement among his heirs as of disagreement on policy issues and of personal rivalry among the leaders. The struggle for power which took place behind the cloak of collective leadership was, moreover, one between powerful bureaucratic machines as well as between leaders. Those who immediately emerged as potential supreme leaders were G. M. Malenkov (b.1902) who, as Chairman of the Council of Ministers, headed the government; L. P. Beria (1899–1953), Minister of Internal Affairs and head of the security police (later the KGB*); and N. S. Khrushchev (1894–1971), a Party secretary who quickly became *de facto* head of the Party organization and who in September 1953 was officially accorded the title of First Secretary of the Central Committee of the Communist Party (CPSU).* It was not difficult for a majority of central Party leaders and government ministers to agree on the need to keep the security police in a much more subordinate role than it had played under Stalin. Beria's ambitions threatened this policy and though the secret-police chief tried to add political support to the coercive force he could

The pall-bearers at Stalin's funeral (including N. A. Bulganin, V. M. Molotov, G. M. Malenkov, L. P. Beria)

command by attempting to appeal to the non-Russian nationalities, both Malenkov and Khrushchev had much stronger followings at the centre (where power in the Soviet Union was – and still is – concentrated). In July 1953 it was announced that Beria had been arrested and in December it was officially confirmed that he had been executed.

Malenkov initially had the upper hand over Khrushchev and until mid-1954, when alphabetical order was adopted, the former's name headed the list of members of the Central Committee's Presidium (Politburo* until 1952, and again since 1966). But already before the end of 1953 Khrushchev had apparently taken over from Malenkov primary responsibility for agricultural policy and he championed the claims of heavy industry as against Malenkov's attempt to place a new emphasis on the consumer goods sector. By so doing, Khrushchev no doubt won additional support from the powerful bureaucratic agencies whose interests he thus served. In February 1955 Malenkov was forced to resign his chairmanship of the Council of Ministers and engage in self-criticism, whereby he took the blame for the failures of past agricultural policy and accepted that the foundation of the economy* on heavy industry was correct.

N. A. Bulganin (1895–1975) took Malenkov's place as Chairman

G. M. Malenkov, former Soviet Prime Minister, in London, 1956

of the Council of Ministers and he, in turn, was replaced as Minister of Defence by the war hero, Marshal G. K. Zhukov (1896–1974). Khrushchev's standing within the leadership was becoming greater, but was by no means unchallengeable. Partly no doubt to strengthen his own position in relation to such senior rivals as Malenkov and V. M. Molotov (b.1890) and partly because of his genuine revulsion against Stalin's style and methods of rule, Khrushchev took the initiative – and the risk – of denouncing the man to whom, in his years as supreme leader of the country, god-like qualities had been attributed. Malenkov and Molotov (as well as Khrushchev's mentor, L. M. Kaganovich, b.1893) were more intimately involved in some of Stalin's worst excesses than Khrushchev had been and so stood to lose more from an exposure of Stalin's misdeeds. Khrushchev was far from having been without sin in Stalin's time, but with characteristic boldness he was prepared to cast the first stone.

The XX Party Congress and de-Stalinization

The scene of Khrushchev's attack on Stalin was the XX Congress of the CPSU held in February 1956. In a four-hour speech in closed session at the end of the Congress (which was issued in only a limited Soviet edition for Party workers, but which none the less soon became widely known throughout the USSR and Eastern Europe and was shortly published in full in the West) Khrushchev attacked the cult of Stalin's personality and drew attention to many of the injustices and crimes he had perpetrated. In his discussion of the Terror,* Khrushchev limited himself to deploring the execution and imprisonment on trumped-up charges of Party members and did not concern himself with the fate of non-members of the CPSU. Nevertheless, this breakthrough into relative frankness had momentous consequences. It contributed to a freer intellectual atmosphere within the Soviet Union itself, though it came as a great shock to many communists and helped to stimulate unrest in Eastern Europe (especially in Hungary and Poland) and dissension within the international communist movement.

Though these consequences of the XX Congress undoubtedly caused great concern within the Party leadership, they did not deter Khrushchev from returning to the de-Stalinization theme at the XXII Party Congress in 1961. There in open session he made points which he had included only in his 'secret speech' of 1956, and other speakers provided further details of Stalin's crimes. Symbolically, Stalin's body was removed from the mausoleum in Red Square where it had lain, since his death in 1953, alongside Lenin's. Places which had been named after Stalin ceased to bear the name of the discredited leader; even the famous Stalingrad became Volgograd. These changes had been preceded in the mid-1950s by the much more important release and rehabilitation of hundreds of thousands of political prisoners and the posthumous rehabilitation of others, though the process was far from complete.

The anti-Party group crisis

The struggle for power between Khrushchev and his rivals came to a head in June 1957 when his leading opponents combined to outvote him in the Presidium (Politburo) and made a determined attempt to remove him. The seven-to-four majority against Khrushchev included such important leaders as Malenkov, Molotov, Kaganovich and Bulganin. Malenkov and Molotov had taken somewhat different policy lines in the recent past and the coalition was united in little but their desire to be rid of Khrushchev. His opponents were, however, labelled 'the anti-Party group' by Khrushchev and it is true that Khrushchev's support lay, above all, in the Party apparatus,★ since a majority of the secretaries at the Central Committee of the CPSU, Union Republican and regional levels had been appointed during his incumbency as First Secretary of the Central Committee and looked to him as their patron. Khrushchev, backed by A. I. Mikoyan (1896–1978) among the most senior of Politburo members and by Marshal Zhukov, insisted on taking the dispute to a plenary session of the Central Committee which supported him against the majority of the Presidium. This victory enabled Khrushchev to strengthen his position by ousting from the Party leadership (in 1957–8) Malenkov, Molotov, Kaganovich and Bulganin, among others, and when Bulganin was relieved also of his chairmanship of the Council of Ministers in 1958, Khrushchev himself took over the post and headed both Party and government from then until his removal from the political scene in October 1964.

Khrushchev's record

Though Khrushchev will probably be remembered above all for his contribution to the cause of de-Stalinization, he was not averse to imposing his own views on his colleagues and his policies were marked by inconsistency and over-optimism. The inconsistency was especially notable in cultural policy and was symbolized by his refusal, on the one hand, to allow publication of Boris Pasternak's★ novel, *Doctor Zhivago* (and his forbidding Pasternak to accept the Nobel Prize for Literature in 1958) and, on the other, by Khrushchev's personal approval for publication of Alexander Solzhenitsyn's★ *One Day in the Life of Ivan Denisovich* in 1962.

In foreign policy Khrushchev took the important step of recognizing that war between states with 'different social systems' was not inevitable; he was very conscious of the destructive power of nuclear weapons. At the same time his heavy emphasis on nuclear★ rather than conventional forces helped to lose him the support of the Soviet military. Similarly, his tolerance of attacks on Stalin and the Stalin period alarmed the KGB and conservative Party officials and helped to undermine his support in those quarters.

In other areas Khrushchev combined reformist initiatives with a tendency to push particular policies too far. He upgraded the status of agriculture★ within the Soviet economy, but his division in 1962 of regional Party organs into industrial and agricultural sections – partly to promote 'campaigning' in agriculture – alienated many in the Party apparatus. Nevertheless, the living standards of the mass of the people received far more attention under Khrushchev than they had under Stalin. Having earlier supported the claims of heavy industry in the course of his struggle against Malenkov, Khrushchev, in the years of his ascendancy, put his own weight behind the effort to make life easier for the Soviet citizen. One reflection of this was the massive house-building★ programme, notwithstanding the fact that the quality of the hastily-built apartment blocks left much to be desired.

A new Party Programme adopted in 1961 set over-ambitious targets to be met by 1980; the Programme is still in force within the CPSU, but its over-optimistic elements are quietly ignored. In addition to approving the Programme, the XXII Congress of the CPSU in 1961 approved new Party Rules. These are also, in the main, still in force, but one disturbing innovation was rescinded at the first post-Khrushchev Party Congress (the XXIII in 1966). This was Article 35 which stated that at each regular election not less than a quarter of the membership of the Central Committee and its Presidium, not less than one-third of the Union Republican Central Committees and of the regional Party committees, and not less than one half of the membership of town and district Party committees and of primary Party organization★ committees or bureaux must be renewed. It was widely held that Khrushchev had introduced the compulsory percentage turnover in order to be able to move people from Party office at will, while maintaining himself and his supporters in positions of authority by invoking the escape clause which safeguarded the position of those of especially great prestige and ability. (A much less specific sentence on systematic renewal was added to Article 24 when the Rules were revised at the XXIII Congress, a change which strengthened the security of tenure of Party office-holders.)

The fall of Khrushchev

Khrushchev's style of rule helped to lose him the support he had earlier built up. It is evident from his own memoirs as well as from the writings of his Soviet critics that he took many important decisions alone and that latterly he frequently put more reliance upon his personal advisers than upon officials within the appropriate Party and government agencies. Some of his personal initiatives – notably the decision to put missiles★ in Cuba★ in 1962 – were also fraught with danger and when they turned out to be less than wholly successful, it was clear where responsibility lay.

A coalition of Khrushchev's disgruntled Party colleagues, with the evident support of other élite groups such as the military and the KGB, finally brought his remarkable political career to an end. There was no repetition of the 1957 events when Khrushchev attended the Central Committee session on 14 October 1964. This time the top

N. S. Khrushchev, June 1966

leadership (Politburo and Secretariat★) were united against him and the Central Committee had no longer any collective desire to come to his support. Ostensibly, Khrushchev 'retired' on grounds of old age – he was 70 – and failing health, but the subsequent almost complete exclusion of his name from the Soviet press, as well as attacks in which he was clearly the unnamed target, made plain to Soviet citizens that he had been toppled against his will.

Khrushchev's career and personality were not lacking in contradictions. He was a hard and ruthless politician who yet possessed a warm humanity; a Stalinist from his youth who did more than anyone to shake the foundations of Stalinism; a poorly educated worker of peasant origin who had a sharp intelligence and a remarkable capacity for learning (not least from his trips to the West); and a true believer in the goal of a humane world communism who did not hesitate to send tanks into Budapest to crush with armed force the Hungarian uprising★ of 1956.   *A.H.B.*

The Brezhnev era

The re-establishment of collective leadership
Of the two highest political positions in the country held by Khrushchev,★ the more powerful post – First Secretary (in 1966 renamed General Secretary,★ a return to the nomenclature of Stalin's★ time) of the Central Committee of the CPSU★ – went to L. I. Brezhnev (b.1906) and the chairmanship of the Council of Ministers★ to A. N. Kosygin (1904–80). It is one measure of the re-establishment of collective leadership that until 1980 both men, by this time in their mid-70s, held the same posts, and that there were

two other survivors of Khrushchev's Presidium★ still holding Politburo★ membership (as well as secretaryships of the Central Committee): M. A. Suslov (b.1902) and A. P. Kirilenko (b.1906). Under this leadership the division of labour among the various Party and governmental bodies became more clear-cut, and though Party controls, in a broad sense, remained as strong as ever, there was less arbitrary interference by the leadership in the work of specialist institutions. Brezhnev, unlike Khrushchev, accepted that he could not take personal decisions in every policy area from foreign policy to family law and from agriculture to literary culture.

Brezhnev's enhanced status
While Brezhnev did not come to wield the individual power of a Khrushchev, still less that of a Stalin, he gradually strengthened his position in relation to his colleagues and acquired a greater prominence in the 1970s than he had had in the 1960s, becoming the leading Soviet spokesman on foreign affairs and overshadowing Kosygin who had earlier often engaged in 'summit talks' on behalf of the Soviet Union. Brezhnev was also able to strengthen his position within the Politburo by securing the promotion to full membership of such protégés and supporters as F. D. Kulakov (1918–78), D. A. Kunaev (b.1911) and V. V. Shcherbitsky (b.1918) in 1971, and K. U. Chernenko (b.1911) in 1978, and by removing from the leadership such potential opponents as P. Ye. Shelest (b.1908) in 1973, A. N. Shelepin (b.1918) in 1975 and N. V. Podgorny (b.1903) in 1977.

The removal of Podgorny facilitated a further enhancement of Brezhnev's position – the chairmanship of the Presidium of the Supreme Soviet (a post which Podgorny had held since 1965 when he succeeded Mikoyan). This was the first time in Soviet history that a Party General Secretary had combined that post with the formal headship of state and though it was a less powerful combination of offices than Khrushchev's combining the Party leadership with the chairmanship of the Council of Ministers, in terms of status it increased the distance between Brezhnev and his colleagues. Brezhnev, indeed, became the recipient of a whole series of official honours★ – for example, the Lenin Peace Prize, 1973; Marshal of the Soviet Union, 1976; the Order of Victory (the highest military honour), 1978; and the Lenin Prize for Literature (for his memoirs), 1979. While the leadership changes of the 1970s were to Brezhnev's advantage, and his public honours surpassed those accorded to Khrushchev, it is noteworthy that since 1964 turnover in the Politburo, Secretariat★ and Central Committee (and among Party officials generally) has been much slower than under either of Brezhnev's predecessors. This no doubt reflects both his more cautious, consensus-seeking style and the desire of his colleagues to maintain some counterweights to him within the leadership.

L. I. Brezhnev at the XXV CPSU Congress, 1976

Reversal of Khrushchev's policies

Under Brezhnev's leadership, many of Khrushchev's policies were modified or even reversed. A number of his administrative reforms were speedily annulled. Military expenditure* was increased. Attacks upon Stalin and the Stalin period became virtually forbidden, though the great purges were not so much exonerated as ignored. In these respects, the attitudes of Brezhnev and his colleagues have been more conservative than that of their ebullient predecessor. In foreign affairs, a policy of extending Soviet influence without taking undue risks (with the possible exception of the military intervention in Afghanistan* in 1979) has been pursued. Determination to uphold the status quo in Eastern Europe was exemplified by the armed intervention of August 1968 in Czechoslovakia* which put a stop to the reformist course on which the leadership of the Czechoslovak Communist Party had embarked.

The early 1970s saw a substantial improvement in Soviet relations with the USA and with Western European countries (notably, the FRG). The signing of the Helsinki Agreement (the Final Act of the Conference on Security and Cooperation in Europe on 1 August 1975) marked the achievement of an important Soviet goal – the official acceptance by Western powers of the division of Europe and of the borders which had existed *de facto* since the end of the Second World War. Other provisions of the Agreement – on human rights, cultural cooperation and dissemination of information – caused the USSR some embarrassment, especially in the light of the election of Carter as President of the United States in 1976 and the stress which he laid on the human rights issue. In 1980 Soviet-American relations reached their lowest ebb of the Brezhnev years with the USA cutting grain shipments to the Soviet Union and boycotting the Olympic Games* in response to the Soviet action in Afghanistan.

Party membership trends

The CPSU has grown rapidly in the post-Stalin years, both in absolute numbers and as a proportion of the population. In the Brezhnev – as distinct from Khrushchev – period, however, an apparently successful effort has been made to slow down the rate of membership* increase. The leaders of the CPSU had criticized the Communist Party of Czechoslovakia in 1968 for, among other things, letting the Party become too large (almost 12 per cent of the total population) and it was clearly felt in Moscow that Party discipline and controls could be endangered by excessive growth.

THE GROWTH OF THE CPSU UNDER KHRUSHCHEV AND BREZHNEV

	Population of the USSR *millions*	Party membership	Party membership as a percentage of population
1952	184.8	6 707 539	3.62
1957	201.4	7 494 573	3.72
1964	226.7	11 022 369	4.86
1973	248.6	14 330 525	5.76
1981	266.6	17 480 000	6.56

So far as the social composition* of the CPSU is concerned, the post-Stalin years have seen an increased proportion of workers entering the Party and a falling percentage of peasants and 'white-collar' workers (even though the prospect of a well-educated specialist becoming a Party member remains vastly greater than the chance of the average worker following suit). The emphasis of the Party leadership on the desirability of recruiting a higher proportion of workers is reflected in the statistics on membership trends.

THE CHANGING SOCIAL COMPOSITION OF THE CPSU (PERCENTAGES)

	1956	1961	1964	1967	1971	1976	1979	1981
Workers	32.0	34.5	37.3	38.1	40.1	41.6	42.7	43.4
Peasants	17.1	17.5	16.5	16.0	15.1	13.9	13.2	12.8
'White-collar' employees and others	50.9	48.0	46.2	45.9	44.8	44.5	44.1	43.8

The Soviet Union in the 1970s

The Soviet economy grew more slowly in the 1970s than in the 1960s, but there were, none the less, significant improvements in production* and productivity in both industry and agriculture,* and a measure of levelling-up of incomes was achieved. The progress in agriculture of the post-Khrushchev years was from a very low starting-point and so by the end of the 1970s many provincial towns still suffered from severe shortages of meat and of dairy products. Indeed, there were signs that not only money wages* but

Above: Soviet leaders at May Day celebrations 1979– L. I. Brezhnev and A. N. Kosygin flanked by D. F. Ustinov and M. A. Suslov.
Right: Leningrad metal workers examine the draft of the new Constitution in 1977

expectations had increased faster than the supply of products, and the consequences of inflationary pressure were to be seen in a number of official price* rises (including the doubling of taxi fares and of the cost of restaurant meals) and, still more, by the rise in peasant market and black market prices. Basic foodstuffs on sale in Soviet shops were still, however, heavily subsidized by the state, so that, for example, meat (where available) and bread cost no more in 1980 than they had in 1953.

Such political changes as were introduced during the decade were of a gradual and piecemeal nature. One which was much heralded by the Soviet mass media was the promulgation in 1977 of a new Soviet Constitution* to replace the Stalin Constitution* of 1936. A more informative document than its predecessor, it also provided a more accurate reflection of Soviet political reality (most notably with its emphasis on the CPSU as 'the leading and guiding force of Soviet society'), but on a number of contentious issues it opted for compromise, in keeping with the predominant tendency of that decade in Soviet domestic politics. The ageing leadership eschewed both a return to Stalinism and any real attempt at radical reform. By 1980 the average age of the Politburo was over 70, and the average age of the top leadership within that body, over 75. The very fact that a number of prominent politicians were able to grow old together and stay in office reflected the tranquillity and relative stability of the Brezhnev years, in comparison with domestic politics in any previous period of Soviet history. At the same time, it would appear that the septuagenarian leaders were leaving many difficult choices to their successors. *A.H.B.*

RELIGION

A centre of Russian Orthodoxy: the Cathedral of the Assumption at the Monastery of the Trinity and St Sergius, Zagorsk

The Russian Orthodox Church

The beginnings of Russian Christianity may be traced back to the 9th century, but the evidence is fragmentary. A 'Russian' diocese seems to have been established by the Byzantines in 867, though its location is not certain. In 944 there were Russian Christians among the signatories of a Byzantine-Russian treaty; by the middle of the 10th century (c.955) the regent of Kiev,★ Princess Ol'ga (c.890–969) was herself baptized. However, her own baptism was not the prelude to an immediate conversion of her people. On the contrary, the Kievan realm was to experience something of a pagan revival under her son Svyatoslav★ (942–72) and, even more markedly, under the young Vladimir★ (d.1015), her grandson. Under Vladimir, indeed, there was an attempt to create a new Nordic pantheon, with Perun (the god of thunder) at its head. It was the same Vladimir who was to demolish its monuments and desecrate its shrines in the last decade of the century. For the new pantheon proved to be an anachronism.

Conversion

The principality of Kiev was surrounded by powerful neighbours, each of whom had accepted one of the great monotheistic religions in the course of the preceding century. Vladimir must have perceived that his country's political and economic–not to mention spiritual–welfare depended on conversion to one or another of these faiths, whether Judaism,★ Islam★ or Christianity. His investigations persuaded him that Byzantine Christianity had most to offer.

Negotiations with Constantinople led to Vladimir's marriage to the emperor's sister (989) and to its necessary precondition, his baptism

The baptism of the Russians, from *The Chronicle of Constantine Manasses*

(988). It was a baptism which was to determine the religion of the Russian people for centuries to come.

At the outset 'conversion' was the policy of an élite, which showed no hesitation in promoting it by force. Although the new religion spread with remarkable speed and Rus'★ was soon able to display all the marks of a flourishing Christian civilization, paganism was to linger for many a century, however covertly, especially in the rural areas.

Rus' inherited a fully-developed Christian tradition from the Byzantine world. The converts were not expected to engage in any major theological controversies (the age of the great Ecumenical Councils had come to an end with the Council of 787). Nor were they required to devise new liturgical forms. For their worship and instruction the Byzantines provided them even with a corpus of Slavonic translations. The new faith was communicated in a language which was accessible to the local population, an important factor in its diffusion and acceptance.

Organization

It remains unclear which diocese of the new Church had precedence until 1037. The matter is complicated by the existence of several

Eleventh-century mosaic of Aaron, St Sophia Cathedral, Kiev

missionary centres prior to the conversion of the Kievan realm. But although there were briefly to be metropolitans in Chernigov and Pereyaslavl' even in the second half of the 11th century, the appointment of a metropolitan of Kiev (Feopempt) in 1037 determined the location of the primatial see throughout the pre-Mongol period and its designation for some time after. Under Kiev at least seven other dioceses were soon established; their number was to rise to 15 by the time of the Mongol conquest.* The first metropolitan was a Greek, as were most of his successors for some time to come. An exception, such as the Russian Metropolitan Ilarion, was not likely to gain the approval of Constantinople. Ilarion remained in office for barely a year (1051–2). Not until the 15th century did the Russian Church begin to take decisions in such matters entirely for itself: formally, it remained a province of the patriarchate of Constantinople until at least 1448.

As members of that patriarchate the Russians were party to Constantinople's ever-increasing estrangement from Rome, of which the Schism of 1054 was but one expression. The 'missionary' inroads of the Swedes (1240) and the Baltic Teutonic Knights (1242), successfully resisted by Alexander Nevsky* (c.1220–63), were to confirm their worst suspicions of the heretical West.

Early monasteries and first saints

The Kievan Monastery of the Caves (1051) grew up around two saintly figures, Antony (d.1072/3) and Feodosy (d.1074). If not the first, it was certainly the most important of the early monastic foundations. These were to number 68 by the time of the Mongol invasion. Almost all had an urban location and a commitment to their secular environment. They were valued for their educational, artistic and philanthropic work, as well as for their spiritual life.

The growing maturity of the Church was demonstrated by the canonization of several saints. First among these were the princes Boris and Gleb (d.1015); their feast was celebrated three times a year. Feodosy, who attended the translation of their relics in 1072, was soon to follow them into the ranks of saints (1108). Vladimir himself was not to be canonized until 1240, the very year in which his old capital was sacked by the Mongols. Thus began a new and sombre period.

Mongol toleration

The devastation which accompanied the Mongol invasion affected the Church no less than any other institution. But the toleration of the Mongol rulers for all religions (which was to outlive their subsequent conversion to Islam) led them to safeguard, even to enhance the position of the Church. Its beliefs and practices were to be respected; moreover it was to be exempt from all taxation. The tolerance of one khan even led to the establishment of a new see at the Mongol capital of Saray (1261).

Kiev-Vladimir-Moscow

The sack and consequent decline of Kiev persuaded Metropolitan Maksim (d.1305) to transfer his residence to the city of Vladimir. For less obvious reasons, his successor Petr (d.1326) moved to the as yet unimportant township of Moscow (1325). In due course the alienation of Kiev (it fell under Polish-Lithuanian dominion) provided yet one more reason for the metropolitan to change his title to that of 'Moscow and all Rus'' (1458). A separate metropolitanate of Kiev was established, first under Roman auspices (1458), then under Constantinople (1470).

Monastic revival

The most significant church figure of the 14th century was not a metropolitan but a humble monk, Sergy of Radonezh (1314–92). Around his hermitage in the wilds 70 km north-east of Moscow (at the place subsequently named after him Sergiev Posad, now Zagorsk) was to develop one of the greatest of Russian monasteries, dedicated to the Holy Trinity (and eventually also to its saintly founder). Sergy's work provided the stimulus for a revival of monastic life. New foundations proliferated, by contrast with the pre-Mongol period, in areas which were hardly populated, even unexplored. In Sergy's lifetime there were perhaps 50 new monastic houses; the number was to be trebled within a century of his demise.

The monastic colonizers often acted as missionaries. None made such an impact as the great missionary of the Zyrian (Komi*) people, Stefan of Perm' (1340–96), who translated the Scriptures and the liturgy into the local language and created a Zyrian alphabet for the purpose. He followed in the footsteps of SS Cyril and Methodius (the 9th-century apostles of the Slavs,* creators of a Slavonic alphabet) and paved the way for the missionary translators of later centuries, particularly the 19th. Unlike many a later Russian missionary, however, St Stefan resolutely refused to have his work exploited in the interests of the Russian state.

Rome-Constantinople-Moscow

The independence of the Muscovite Church was hastened, though it was not determined by the formal (and short-lived) reunion of Rome and Constantinople—the Catholic and Orthodox Churches—brought about at the Council of Ferrara-Florence (1438–9). Metropolitan Isidor of Moscow had been a member of the Council and party to its decisions. But Moscow would have none of them. On his return to Moscow Isidor was at first imprisoned by the grand prince (1441), then allowed to flee the country. Isidor, while residing as cardinal in Rome, remained nominally metropolitan of Moscow until his death (1463). But his replacement had been chosen long before, and by the Russian Church alone—without even a token preliminary reference to Constantinople. Metropolitan Iona (d.1461), the new metropolitan in Moscow, became head of an effectively independent (autocephalous) Orthodox Church in 1448.

Constantinople was soon to fall to the Turks (1453). In Muscovy it was bruited about that this was a punishment for acceptance of the Union with Rome. The termination of Byzantium's political independence, together with the growth of Muscovy's power and self-esteem, encouraged the Russians to seek unequivocal validation of their Church's independence. The century which began with the monk Filofey's attempt to popularize the concept of Moscow the Third Rome (as successor to the Second Rome, Constantinople) ended with the Second Rome's acceptance of Moscow's patriarchal status (1589). The first patriarch of Moscow and all Rus' (1589–1605) was to be Metropolitan Iov of Moscow, formerly archbishop of Rostov. His patriarchate was allotted fifth place in order of precedence by the ancient Eastern patriarchates in 1593; it retains this position to the present day.

Imperial throne, Cathedral of the Assumption, Kremlin, Moscow

Church and State: the 16th century

The negotiations which led to the patriarchate's establishment had been conducted by the tsar. In the course of the 16th century the Church had become ever more closely identified with the State, despite the proclamation by the Moscow *Stoglav* ('hundred chapters') Council of 1551 to the effect that the Byzantine principle of 'symphony' between Church and State was to be followed. An attempt to secularize monastic landholdings in the early years of the century had come to nothing—though there had been some support for such a policy from among 'Non-possessor' monks, such as Nil Sorsky (1433–1508), as well as from the would-be beneficiaries of the secular world. However, the victor in the dispute between 'Possessors' and 'Non-possessors', Abbot Iosif of Volokolamsk (1439–1515), nevertheless sought to further the ever-increasing authority of the State. Ivan IV was to demonstrate its power most brazenly: at one stage he not only dismissed the metropolitan of Moscow Filipp (1568), but had him strangled. Moves to canonize Metropolitan Filipp began within 21 years of his death. His name was soon to be added to the calendar of Russian saints which had been so greatly augmented under the auspices of his persecutor-to-be and at the initiative of the enterprising Metropolitan Makary (1481–1563). At the Councils of 1547 and 1549 the Church had approved the canonization of no less than 39 new Russian saints.

The Time of Troubles

The Time of Troubles★ (*Smuta*) at the beginning of the 17th century involved the heroic 16-month long defence of St Sergy's Trinity monastery against a besieging army of 30 000 Polish invaders (1608–9) and, at a different level, the repulse by the Russian Church of Catholic overtures and machinations. The aged Patriarch Germogen (1606–12) died witnessing to the integrity of Orthodoxy. His successor Patriarch Filaret (*c*.1554–1634) was to pursue a markedly anti-Catholic policy. The West-Russian Orthodox hierarchs under Polish rule had earlier accepted Union with Rome at yet another Council (Brest, 1596) at which the Uniat Church was created. Filaret, a prisoner of the Poles for the eight years preceding his enthronement (1619), had no intention of tolerating such arrangements. Filaret occupied a curiously privileged place in the state since he was also father (and mentor) of the new tsar, Mikhail Romanov.★ He therefore took the title of Great Lord (*Velikiy gosudar'*).

Nikon's reforms

In the mid-century a later patriarch, Nikon (1605–81), was also to insist on this title in an attempt to assert not only the equality, but the supremacy of the Church in Church-State relations. His policies, and in particular his autocratic manner of pursuing them, led to disarray in Church and State alike. Indeed, their mutual relations were to be affected for centuries to come. Nikon's reign may be seen as a watershed in the history of the Russian Church. His failure to establish (he would have argued, re-establish) the primacy of the Church cleared the way for the ecclesiastical reforms of Peter the Great.★

The Ecclesiastical Regulation

At the death of Patriarch Adrian (1690–1700), Peter let the patriarchate lapse. He gave his support successively to two clerics of a Protestant orientation, Metropolitan Stefan Yavorsky (1658–1722) and Archbishop Feofan Prokopovich (1681–1736). The latter was to prove all-important as the effective author of Peter's *Ecclesiastical Regulation* (1720). It was a document drawn up in camera by the emperor's nominee. Although it was subsequently signed by the Russian bishops and other senior clergy, these were no longer free agents (as the document itself made plain). Their successors remained subordinate and largely subservient until the end of the empire.

The Holy Synod

The *Regulation* established an Ecclesiastical College (*Kollegium*) which was almost immediately renamed Holy Synod; neither adjective could disguise the fact that this was essentially a government department. Charged with its oversight was a secular administrator, the Chief Procurator or *Ober-Prokuror*. Significantly, this was a German title, with no roots in Orthodox history. For Peter's entire programme for the subjugation and administration of the Church was unashamedly borrowed from the West. In particular, he turned for guidance to the Lutheran G. W. Leibnitz (1646–1716).

Education

Paradoxically, while the administration took on a Protestant appearance, the Church initially provided its future leaders with an education which was based principally on Catholic models. Throughout the 17th century the Ukraine (strongly influenced by the Catholic West) had provided Muscovy with teachers and scholars, many of them trained under Uniat auspices. The integration of much of the Ukraine and Muscovy (1654) and the transfer of the Kievan metropolitanate from Constantinople to Moscow (1685–7) served to confirm this tendency.

The syllabus of the Helleno-Greek Academy of Moscow (1685) followed a scholastic pattern. Its first masters were the Greek brothers Ioaniky and Sofrony Likhud, who had gained their doctorates in Padua. Perhaps appropriately, the Academy eventually took the name Slavo-Latin (1700–75) before becoming Slavo-Greco-Latin (1775–1814). This was to make way for the Moscow Ecclesiastical Academy at Sergiev Posad (1814). Three other institutions had also gained the title of Academy by this time: Kiev (1701), St Petersburg and Kazan' (1797). All four were to survive until the Revolution of 1917; two of them (at Leningrad and Zagorsk)

were to be re-established after the Second World War.

Secularization of monasteries

The secularization of monastic properties which had been successfully resisted by Abbot Iosif of Volokolamsk was undertaken by Catherine II★ soon after her accession to the throne (1762–4). The Church was deprived of extensive landholdings and of almost two million serfs, and thus became the more dependent on the state. The unfortunate metropolitan of Rostov, Arseny Matseevich (1696–1772) was one of the few to protest against the actions of the government. He was demoted and imprisoned.

Elders

Yet an inner revival of monastic life was on the horizon. Poverty was exactly what Bishop Tikhon of Zadonsk (1724–83) sought and propagated; his humble way of life was to be remembered with more affection than Metropolitan Arseny's naive triumphalism. But none was to gain more renown than the meek recluse Serafim of Sarov (1759–1833). His radiant ministry served as a reminder that the Church was left inwardly unscathed by the administrative and fiscal reforms which had come its way.

The influence of the Moldavian Elder Paisy Velichkovsky (1722–94) was to transform the life of a number of monasteries in the course of the 19th century. He translated the recently compiled *Philokalia* ('Love of Beauty') into Slavonic (1793), propagated the use of the Jesus Prayer and ensured that the institution of spiritual elders (*startsy*) gain widespread approval. The great monastery at Kozel'sk, Optina Pustyn', was to become a renowned centre for *startsy* until its closure in the 1920s. Among its most revered elders were the *startsy* Leonid (1768–1841), Makary (1788–1860), Amvrosy (1812–91) and Nektary (1856–1928).

19th-century missions

Although it used the designation *Russian* Orthodox, the Church had come to minister to a considerable variety of ethnic groups both within the borders of the empire and beyond its confines. Not only Zyrians but Tatars,★ Chuvash,★ Cheremis, and Votyaks were among the tribes or nationalities which provided converts in their tens of thousands. The missionary enterprise had its disreputable aspect as an arm of Russian imperialism. But there were saintly figures among missionaries and converts alike. Russian missions abroad left their mark in Alaska (from 1794) and Japan (from 1861). Among the great missionaries of the 19th century mention should be made of Archimandrite Makary Glukharev (1792–1847) of the Altay mission; Metropolitan Innokenty Veniaminov (1797–1879), who worked in Kamchatka, Alaska and the Aleutian Isles; and Archbishop Nikolay Kasatkin (1836–1912), the first saint of the now autonomous Orthodox Church of Japan.

The Established Church to 1917

Few voices were raised in protest against the restrictions under which the Church had to operate in the 19th century, and even these were muted by censorship.* Among those who accepted the status quo the most noteworthy were the statesmanlike metropolitan of Moscow, Filaret Drozdov (1782–1868) and the devout but ultra-conservative Chief Procurator K. P. Pobedonostsev (1827–1907). But the revolutionary events of 1905 gave impetus to reformers; there was new hope for a restoration of the Church's independence from the state. Removal of numerous restrictions from the hitherto under-privileged (and not infrequently persecuted) non-Orthodox religious bodies of the empire (1905) encouraged the Orthodox to work towards a Council of the Russian Orthodox Church. It seemed lamentable that a body of such age, dignity and size should not be permitted to regulate its own affairs. By 1914 it possessed 73 dioceses, 54 174 churches (not to mention a comparable number of chapels) and 1025 monastic foundations. With its 291 hospitals and its 35 528 parish schools it had a social as well as a liturgical role to perform, though it favoured the latter. But the tsar remained obdurate and convened no Council. The work of the Pre-Conciliar Commission of 1906 and the Pre-Conciliar Consultation of 1911–12 was set aside. Only with the end of the Orthodox monarchy did the Church gain some opportunity to compensate for the preceding centuries of Synodal rule. But the moment came late and it was far too brief.

The office of Chief Procurator was abolished at the request of its last incumbent A. V. Kartashev (1875–1960) in the summer of 1917. That same summer the first Council of the Russian Orthodox Church for two and a half centuries began its sessions. The first session (15 August 1917) took place at the very heart of the old Third Rome, in the Cathedral of the Assumption in the Moscow Kremlin. The Council's sessions continued until the following summer. Not least of its acts was to re-establish the patriarchate. It also elected three candidates for the post of patriarch. The final choice was by lot: this fell on Tikhon, newly elected metropolitan of Moscow (1865–1925).

Separation of Church and State

The Church which he was called upon to lead was faced with unprecedented problems. The new political situation rendered void or inapplicable the carefully elaborated legislation of the 1917–18 Council. The integrity of a Tikhon was therefore all the more needed in the regulation of Church affairs. With him began a new line of martyrs and confessors, for although the Church was suddenly separated from the State the new establishment was to subject it to every kind of indignity and constraint. With the old certainties swept aside, the Church was now to be proved by fire.

The Bolshevik* government's decree of 23 January 1918 on the separation of Church and State and of schooling from the Church affected all religious bodies, but none so obviously or so immediately as the formerly established Church of the Russian Empire. Under the Provisional Government* of 1917 there was still talk of the Orthodox Church preserving some kind of privileged position among the other confessions and religions. Now the Church found itself, like any other of these bodies, deprived even of the rights of a person at law.

The confiscation of Church property (legitimized by the same decree) soon led to confrontations. The newly elected patriarch's first encyclicals expressed a severity which bordered on militancy (19 January and 7 November 1918). But his insistence that the new leaders acted 'in a manner contrary to the conscience of the people' could only serve to confirm the Bolsheviks in their resolve to mould that conscience in accordance with their own ideology. For the Bolsheviks sought not only to undermine the Church economically: their intention was to displace it as the mentor of the people, and an intensive (generally crude) anti-religious propaganda campaign was put into operation as soon as the civil war was at an end (1922).

Reform movements in the 1920s

There was a more insidious device intended to diminish the authority of the Church. From 1922 the secular authorities gave support to a reform movement within the Orthodox Church: in effect, they fomented schism. The reform movement (usually termed Reno-vationist) was led by clergy who professed virtually unqualified loyalty to the new state and to its aspirations. Prominent among its leaders was Archpriest–subsequently Metropolitan–Alexander Vvedensky (1889–1946).

The arrest of Patriarch Tikhon (1922) was used as an opportunity to usurp his authority and, eventually, to 'depose' him at the reformers' second Council (1923). However, their movement was not a united one, nor was it well supported. Despite the premises and facilities which were made available to it, the movement was to lose its impetus before the outbreak of war (1941) and it was to be disbanded before its end.

Similar reform movements surfaced briefly in the 1920s among the Lutherans,* the Armenian Orthodox,* the Jews,* the Muslims and the Buddhists* of the USSR.

Confiscation of valuables

The Patriarch's arrest was the result of another plan (Trotsky's)* to discredit the Church. The intention was to take possession of the Church's movable property under the guise of famine relief. The state would gain financially; the Church would be disgraced by any resistance which might be offered to the confiscation of sacred items. In the event, Tikhon (who was willing to donate unconsecrated objects) legitimized such resistance. There followed clashes, deaths and arrests. Among those to be tried and executed was the meek and popular metropolitan of Petrograd Veniamin Kazansky (1922).

Patriarch Tikhon's succession

The patriarch emerged from prison in 1923 with a declaration that he was 'no longer an enemy of the Soviet government'. The declaration was to be echoed in his final testament, signed on the day of his death (7 April 1925). However, neither declaration resulted in government recognition of the Orthodox Church or of its administration. On the contrary, fresh confusion resulted from the arrest and exile (1925) of the patriarch's *locum tenens* Metropolitan Petr Polyansky (1863–1936). Most of the remaining bishops who had been designated possible successors were also in prison or in exile.

Nor was the confusion dispelled by the release from prison of Metropolitan Sergy Stragorodsky, or by his successful application for legalization (1927). For many churchmen believed that Sergy's declaration of loyalty to the state, however well-intentioned, was too compliant. They refused to recognize his authority, and further schisms resulted, led by such figures as Metropolitan Iosif Petrovykh (1872–?1937).

New restrictions

Metropolitan Sergy (1861–1944) became the 'deputy *locum tenens*' of the patriarchal throne on the eve of Stalin's* first Five-year Plan,* and of all the consequent or associated regimentation of life. The new order in respect of religion found its legal expression in the decree of 8 April 1929, a decree which was to remain in force until revised (c.1962) and published in its revised form in 1975. Like the decree of 1918 it affected all religious bodies.

Among its stipulations was that each religious association should be registered as such by the competent secular authorities—who, in the process, could be expected to gain some control of the association's administration. No religious association was permitted to give material aid to its members, and this despite the fact that the clergy were already deprived of civil rights (even of ration cards), while yet subjected to punitive taxation. A memorandum (1930) from Metropolitan Sergy to the government official charged with religious questions protested against some of the new requirements, but to no avail.

Meanwhile the state Constitution* was amended. Whereas the text of 1918 permitted 'freedom of religion and anti-religion to every citizen', the revised formulation restricted the 'freedom of religion' permitted by the text of 1918 to 'freedom of worship'. Anti-religious propaganda was permitted as before, but the right to issue any sort of religious propaganda was tacitly withdrawn (16 May 1929). The 1936 Constitution was to restore civil rights to the clergy, but religious propaganda was to remain unconstitutional in the revised Constitution of 1977 as in that of 1936.

The 1930s saw a drastic reduction in the number of churches, the apparently final dissolution of the monasteries, and the imprisonment of countless clergy. At the outbreak of war, hardly four bishops were at liberty to exercise their pastoral role within the narrow limits permitted by the authorities. And yet within and despite these limits—and even in the most appalling conditions—there were church members in their tens of millions who adhered heroically to their faith.

The impact of the Second World War

The war created an entirely new situation. On Soviet territory the government was brought to see the patriotic potential of the Orthodox Church. The first to point in this direction was Metropolitan Sergy, who made a dignified, immediate and apparently independent appeal for the defence of the homeland (22 June 1941). Stalin granted him an audience (4 September 1943) and permitted the convocation of a Council (8 September 1943). This Council proceeded to the election of Sergy as patriarch of Moscow and all Rus'. His death early in the next year was followed by another Council (1945) and the election of Metropolitan Aleksy Simansky (1877–1970) as his successor.

All this symbolized the revival of public life for the Church. Throughout the war churches were reopened and clergy restored to diocesan and parochial duties. By 1944 an Orthodox theological college was inaugurated in Moscow (the first since the 1920s): within a few years there were nine others.

The German invaders, for their part, had permitted the revival of church life in the occupied regions. The revival outlived the liberation. The many monasteries which had sprung to life in the western regions (as well as those which had survived the 1930s on non-Soviet territory) thus came to enrich the life of the post-war Church in the USSR. Sixty-nine monastic houses were to remain open until the early 1960s.

The patriotic role played by the Church was noted: new opportunities were to be found for it in the diplomatic field after the war. Its steadfast support for the state's foreign policy was the condition of the concordat achieved under Stalin. Such support was offered in the World Peace Council (from 1949), in the Christian Peace Conference (from 1958) and in the World Council of Churches (from 1961). In this respect the Orthodox Church did not differ from other religious bodies in the USSR, most of which were expected to engage in similar activities. The most prominent Orthodox leaders concerned with foreign affairs were (successively) two brilliant metropolitans, Nikolay Yarushevich (1892–1961) and Nikodim Rotov (1929–78).

The Khrushchev programme

But the state was not always to keep its side of the unwritten (or at least unpublished) concordat. At the end of the 1950s the concessions won by the Church in wartime came into question; the period of Khrushchev's* ascendancy saw the launching of a relentless campaign against religion (1958–64). Something like two-thirds of the Orthodox churches, seven out of the ten theological schools and the great majority of the monasteries were abruptly closed under one pretext or another. Anti-religious propaganda was once more intensified. There was a rash of well-publicized apostasies and, in response to them, several (in the circumstances courageous) excommunications (1959). Apart from a dignified speech in protest (1960) the aged Patriarch Aleksy maintained a sorrowful silence on the subject of the persecution. Khrushchev's fall (1964) brought an end to the worst excesses. But there was not to be any significant restoration of the Church's facilities. However, the death of Aleksy after a quarter of a century as patriarch was at least followed by another Council (1971) at which Metropolitan Pimen Izvekov (b.1910) was elected as his successor.

The persistence of religion

Since the Revolution of 1917 religious bodies in the USSR have been subjected to every conceivable strain, and the proportion of the population which overtly practises a religion has significantly declined. By the end of the Khrushchev period, however, there were church members who manifested a new vigour in pressing for an improvement in the situation. At the very least they urged that the Soviet authorities abide by the legal and constitutional standards which they themselves had established. Prominent among those who adopted a 'dissident'* position in respect of the establishment were Archbishop Ermogen Golubev (1896–1978) and the priests Nikolay Eshliman, Gleb Yakunin and Dimitry Dudko. In 1977 Yakunin was one of those who established a 'Christian Committee for the Defence of Believers' Rights' in Moscow.

Below: pre-war anti-religious placards on the wall of a Moscow monastery. Bottom: Christian and Buddhist dignitaries (Patriarch Pimen fourth from left)

Below: Orthodox clergy outside Zagorsk Theological Academy. Bottom: Believers in a Moscow cathedral wait for Easter eggs and cakes to be blessed

As to the numbers of believers, it is difficult to offer reliable statistics. The Orthodox alone still number several tens of millions. Administrative, social and intellectual pressures have been exerted by the ruling Party: industrialization, urbanization and secularization have all taken their toll. Yet religion remains a potent, albeit suppressed force. And while each of the officially recognized religious bodies has been required to accommodate itself externally to the demands of the state, it is not this which ultimately determines the quality of its inner life. *S.H.*

The Georgian Orthodox Church

The Georgian Church traces its history back to the 4th century. It was already subjected to various pressures by the imperial Russian government in the 19th century; indeed, from 1811 it was incorporated into the Russian Church. It regained its independence at the time of the Revolution (an independence which the Moscow patriarchate was to recognize only in 1943), but was to suffer depredations under the rule of Stalin,* at one time its seminarist (Tbilisi, 1894). At its head is the Catholicos-Patriarch of all Georgia, Archbishop of Mtsekheta and Tbilisi. Under the present incumbent, Iliya II (Shiolashvili), a long-awaited revitalization of church life is in progress. There is a small seminary at Mtsckheta (opened 1964). *S.H.*

The Armenian Church

The Republic of Armenia also possesses its own Church, which was established no less than 16 centuries ago. Unlike the Georgian Church, it is not of the same communion as the Russian Orthodox Church,* belonging as it does to the family of Churches–formerly (and misleadingly) designated 'monophysite'–which refused to accept the formulations of the Council of Chalcedon (451). The experience of the Armenian Church in the USSR until 1941 was an unhappy one. By the end of the 1930s most of its churches, if not all, were closed. But Stalin's* gesture in giving an audience to the future Catholicos, Kevork Cheorekchian, in April 1945 indicated that improvements were to be expected. Under the cautious Catholicos Kevork (1867–1954) the holy city of Echmiadzin was allowed to recover some of its dignity and facilities (including a seminary). Among other things it was given every opportunity to become a religious centre for the international Armenian community. It has continued to act as such in the reign of Kevork's successor Vazgen I (Palchian; b.1908). *S.H.*

Armenian Christians after a baptism at Gueghard Monastery

The Old Believers

Though formerly an integral part of the Russian Orthodox Church,* the Old Believers (or Old Ritualists) separated from it in the mid-17th century because of Patriarch Nikon's* reforms of the 1650s. However, they have long ceased to form one body or even to adhere to a common set of beliefs. They differ most obviously on the question of church order. No bishops adhered to the Old Believer schism in the early days. Many Old Believers thus felt bound to remain without ordained clergy. Others subsequently restored their orders through a former Orthodox bishop at Belo-Krinitsa in the Austro-Hungarian Empire (1846). But it is not simply a question of belonging to the 'priestly' or the 'priestless' category. There are numerous subdivisions (*tolki*) under each heading, particularly the latter. Among the most important may be mentioned the Archiepiscopate of Moscow and all Rus' (the Church of the Belo-Krinitsa Concord) which—as its name implies—possesses ordained clergy; and the Transfiguration Community of Old Believers (Staropomorsk Concord), which is priestless. The Old Believers were subjected to persecution by the tsarist authorities; the antagonism of the Soviet state therefore did not find them unprepared. Their profound conservatism, as well as their tendency to settle on the periphery of the realm, have always helped to preserve their way of life. They number several millions. *S.H.*

Russian sects

There are sects whose origins may be traced to the Old Believer⋆ movement. Others have their separate history. Some, like the Molokans or the Dukhobors, can look back to the 18th century, but several are of recent origin. Among these may be noted the True Orthodox Christians, who see Patriarch Tikhon⋆ as the last legitimate head of Russian Orthodoxy⋆ and who have taken a critical stance towards the official Church as well as to the government since 1925.   *S.H.*

Baptist-Evangelical Christians

Unlike the True Orthodox⋆ Christians, the Baptists and Evangelical Christians are recognized by the state. In the first decade after the Revolution they even had the state's approval, and in this respect their history was utterly unlike that of most other religious bodies. They earned this approval as formerly disadvantaged, oppressed and largely working-class denominations. Furthermore, their ability to proceed with socially productive labour in the new circumstances, particularly in the sphere of collective⋆ farming, brought them respect and admiration. In the late 1920s there was even talk of a utopian-communist/Evangelical Christian township, to be built according to the plans of I. S. Prokhanov (1869–1935). These were sanguine days, incongruous against the background of religious intolerance and persecution to which other denominations were simultaneously subjected. They were not to last. The period from 1929 was to see a reversal of Baptist and Evangelical fortunes and the 1930s were no more propitious for them than for others. Only towards the end of the war did they regain some of their standing. In 1944 the two bodies were united in an All-Union Council of Evangelical Christians-Baptists.

The Council's vigour in propagating the Gospel was necessarily tempered by the necessity to abide by the Soviet legislation and administrative requirements in respect of religion. By the 1960s a sizeable minority was no longer willing to accede to the state's demands. An 'Action Group' seceded from the Council and established its own Council of the Evangelical Christian-Baptist Churches (1965), members of which resolutely demanded reform of the law. Their campaign led to the imprisonment of many supporters. The rival Council has not been granted recognition as a body by the state. Even so, its endeavours have had a positive influence on the statutes and life of the official Union. The latter is governed by an elected council, of which the general secretary is A. M. Bychkov (b.1928). Perhaps the most prominent member of the secessionist body is G. P. Vins (b.1928), exiled and living in the United States since 1979.   *S.H.*

The Catholic Church

The Catholic Church on Russian soil was not strong at the end of the empire, and the Soviet authorities were to reduce its public life to the barest minimum by 1939. However, the incorporation of the Baltic

Communion service of Baptist-Evangelical Christians, (Ukraine)

Interment of a Catholic priest in Lithuania

republics*–particularly Lithuania–into the USSR (1940–4), together with certain other western territories, radically altered the situation. In Stalin's* time the Catholic Church was particularly suspect as a 'rival' international organization. In recent years the Soviet state has fostered a positive relationship with Rome. This policy has brought some benefit to the Western-rite Catholics of the USSR.

But Eastern-rite Catholics (Uniats, the heirs of the Council of Brest, 1596) have yet to gain anything from it. In previous centuries–and until the Second World War–there were several million of them in those western regions which became part of the USSR after 1944–5. In the dark years 1946–9 the Eastern Catholic Church was dissolved. Its members were required to join the Russian Orthodox Church.* Clergy who refused to do so were imprisoned (chief among them Metropolitan Iosif Slipyj). During the 1960s and 1970s the Church has once more come to life in its homelands, albeit surreptitiously. It is not accorded any official recognition, nor is there any indication that this state of affairs is likely to change.   *S.H.*

The Lutheran Church

In numerical terms, the Lutheran Church in the USSR has gained some importance only since the Soviet incorporation of the Baltic republics,* particularly Estonia and Latvia (1940–4). At least 600 000 Lutherans remain faithful to their Church, despite the considerable pressures to which its members have been subjected during the past four decades.   *S.H.*

Lutherans celebrate the opening of a church in Estonia

Judaism

The religious Jews* of the USSR have had to contend with adverse and destructive forces of many different kinds. The anti-religious policies of the 1920s and 1930s seriously disrupted the institutional life of the Jewish communities. The Nazi occupation* (which brought incidental and unexpected benefits to some religious bodies) brought them only death and devastation. The anti-semitism of Stalin's* last years inhibited any revival in the post-war years. Since the foundation of the State of Israel, it has been possible to use accusations of 'Zionism' as a cudgel against Jewish believers. Such accusations could, in their turn, serve to stimulate and 'justify' anti-semitism. It is perhaps no wonder that barely 60 synagogues have survived into the 1980s (of which the hospitable Republic of Georgia provides more

The last remaining synagogue in Moscow

than half). It is estimated that the Jewish religion has several hundred thousand adherents in the USSR, but it has no centralized organization. A religious academy (*yeshivah*) was opened in Moscow in 1956, and it has continued its modest existence more or less continuously since that date.   *S.H.*

Islam

The USSR contains a large Islamic population, particularly in Central Asia. Although it is difficult to ascertain how many count themselves Muslim* as the result of their ethnic/historical background and how many are Muslim by faith, several tens of millions are involved. Most are Sunnites (perhaps 90 per cent), the remainder are Shiites. After a tentative (diplomatic) toleration of the Muslim way of life in the early 1920s, the Soviet authorities began to persist ever more firmly with anti-religious and anti-traditionalist policies (1928–41). The Muslims' situation improved markedly with the war (despite the deportation of several Muslim nationalities for alleged collaboration with the occupation* forces). After the war the Soviet Union's policies toward its Muslim neighbours made it important that it should give no cause for offence by its domestic treatment of Islam.

Such considerations provided Soviet Islam with some kind of safeguard. Even so, the number of mosques and mullas has been drastically reduced over the years (notably during the period of Khrushchev's* 'offensive'). The Muslims of the USSR formerly had a single administrative centre at Ufa, and are now administered by four regional Boards at Ufa, Buinaksk, Baku and Tashkent (the foremost of the Boards). The present chairman of the latter is Mufti Ziiautnikhan ibn Ishan Babakhan (b.1908).   *S.H.*

Buddhism

There are probably several hundred thousand Buddhists in the USSR (principally in the areas bordering on Mongolia). The very strength of their institutions (datsans) and spiritual leaders (lamas) has provoked Soviet countermeasures from about 1929. The number of lamas was reduced from many thousands to a few hundred; the datsans were closed and only two (Aga and Ivolga) were reopened after the Second World War. The administration of the Buddhists in the USSR is entrusted to the Buddhist Religious Central Board, with the Bandido Hambo Lama at its head. The present incumbent, who resides at Ivolga, is Gomboev Zhambal-Dorji.   *S.H.*

Mufti Ziiautnikhan with Muslim seminarists, Tashkent

The 1977 Congress of Soviet Buddhists, Ivolginsk, Buryat ASSR

ART AND ARCHITECTURE

Church of St Nicholas,
Komsomolsky Prospekt,
Moscow: 17th-century guild
church of the linenweavers,
built in traditional Russian
style of a cube with five
cupolas

Scythian art

The Scythians,* warlike nomads who dominated the steppes north of the Black Sea during the 7th to the 4th centuries BC, are famous for their art, mostly practical or decorative objects of use such as jewellery, weapons, cups and bowls, often made from or adorned with gold. Like most nomads, they carried their wealth with them, so that their trappings and equipment had to be valuable as well as useful and easily portable. Since these warriors were buried with their earthly possessions, Scythian art is found in graves. The richest examples have been discovered in princely kurgans or burial-mounds – Kelermes in the north-west Caucasus (6th century BC), Chertomlyk on the river Dnieper (4th century BC) and Kul′ Oba in the eastern Crimea (4th century BC). Here chieftains were buried in elaborately furnished underground tombs where they were some-times accompanied by slain horses and human attendants.

The origins of Scythian art are yet to be completely known, but it is possible that some elements can be traced back to tribes who lived in Siberia and Central Asia during the third millennium BC. An early version of Scythian or steppe art has been discovered in the Golden Kurgans, in the Chiliktin Valley of Kazakhstan. These finds, dated in the 7th century BC, include small gold-foil feline animals in coiled form, stags, boars and abbreviated vultures (to be seen in the Hermitage Museum, Leningrad). Perhaps a little later in the 7th century BC, gold objects said to come from the site of Ziwiyeh in north-west Iran may reflect the Scythians' westward migration (Archaeological Museum, Tehran, and Metropolitan Museum of Art, New York).

The stylistic affinities in this early art demonstrate the wide-ranging connections of these nomads through trade, migration or warfare. At Chiliktin, contact with China is suggested by the coiled feline decorations, a motif which persists throughout the history of Scythian art. The Ziwiyeh gold work shows associations with Near Eastern art, an influence which continues in the objects from early steppe kurgans like Kelermes. During the 6th to the 4th centuries BC, while the Scythians ruled the steppes and traded with the Greek cities on the Black Sea, Scythian art took on a noticeable Greek hue. The Kul′ Oba tomb includes some pieces made for a nomadic chief by Greek craftsmen, as well as purely Greek objects which apparently pleased the taste of the wealthy barbarian.

Scythian art is commonly described as 'animal style' art, because the subject matter is often animals, typically single figures in curled-up or dangling-leg poses. Certain motifs (stags, birds of prey, felines) were used throughout the entire course of Scythian art, and may well have had totemic or magical significance. However, with the passage of time, Greek influence increased and the original simplicity was often lost; this transformation is very obvious in representations of stags. In early examples, like an early-6th-century BC large gold plaque shaped like a stag from Kostroma Kurgan in the north-west Caucasus (in the Hermitage), the animals are clearly reindeer, native to the regions of eastern Asia where the Scythians probably origi-nated. By the 4th century BC, the memory of reindeer seems to have become faint. The famous Kul′ Oba gold stag in the Hermitage was obviously made by a Greek craftsman who slavishly followed a model which he scarcely understood. Nevertheless, while the richness and splendour of late nomadic art testify to the exotic tastes cultivated by these once-primitive steppe-dwellers, the persistence of animal designs like the stag suggests the power and importance of such tradi-tional imagery throughout the history of Scythian art. *A.E.R.F.*

Scythian gold plaques for sewing on to garments

Scythian gold pectoral found at Tolstoe, southern Ukraine

The art and architecture of Western Turkestan

There have been two periods when the arts flourished in Western Turkestan. The first, as revealed by recent excavations, extends from about the first century AD to c.720, by which time the Arabs had consolidated their hold over the region and killed its figural arts. The second period was launched in the 9th century by Ismail the Samanid, who abandoned Zoroastrianism in favour of Islam* and established his capital in Bukhara. It reached its peak under Timur (1336–1405) and his grandson, the astronomer-poet Ulugh Beg (1394–1449), lingering on well into the 17th century.

Even in Bactrian times (fifth to sixth centuries BC) urbanism, and thus architecture, had flourished in Soghdia unimpeded by the nomads.* By the 4th to 5th centuries of the Christian era cities such as Afrosiab (ancient Marakanda/Samarkand), princely domains such as Varaksha, citadels such as Mug or Balalyk Tepe contained a variety of weapons, tools, domestic utensils and decorative and precious objects. The artistic styles and town plans are well represented at Pendzhikent, a walled 5th- to 6th-century town containing the chieftain's castle, the residential area, suburbs and cemetery. Its buildings of unbaked brick were often two-storied, with porticos or eiwans (three-walled vaulted chambers with tall, inverted-V-shaped entries) and vaulted or domed roofs, occasionally supported by wooden columns, even by caryatides. Some buildings contained 150 rooms. Rectangular reception halls had a continuous bench inserted into the three walls with paintings extending above it to the ceiling or to a frieze formed of stucco statues, many of them portraits. The vast mural compositions are outstanding; their subjects range over ceremonial scenes, battle, genre and religious themes, hunting subjects and illustrations of epics resembling those immortalized by the poet Firdausi (c.935–1020). The men are wasp-waisted, the women elegant. The style is monumental, accomplished, colourful; Sassanian influences prevail but the impact of Hellenism, as transmitted by Parthia, is evident, alongside that of Buddhism.* The costumes are made of expensive contemporary materials, some obvious imports from Persia, others indubitably of local make, recent research having revealed the existence in Soghdia, following the establishment of the silk-route and the end of China's monopoly in making silk, of a silk production and weaving industry there. The cut of the caftans is similar to that found in contemporary paintings in Eastern Turkestan. Throughout this period figurines, decorated ossuaries and painted vessels were made in unglazed pottery. In Samanid times Samarkand's potters discovered a slip which prevented their painted designs from running. They were able to decorate their glazed wares with superb script and abstract, geometric or floral designs executed in black (often on a white ground), brown and green. By the 10th century their creations were widely admired and their influence was felt in Persia. In the 14th and

WESTERN TURKESTAN

Details from 8th-century wooden shield, Zeravshan, and 5th- to 7th-century tempera mural painting, Varaksha

15th centuries they provided the glazed tesserae and tiles which enhance the excellence of this period's buildings.

From Samanid times onwards figural representations were replaced by decorations which, stimulated by advances in mathematics* and astronomy,* were chiefly geometric in character although often accompanied by plant arabesques. In architecture the introduction of baked bricks enabled many designs to be produced by varying the disposition of the bricks, as in the 9th- to 10th-century domed and cube-shaped Samanid mausoleum at Bukhara, the earliest example of a style which spread to Persia. In the 47m high Kalyan minaret (1127–9) at Bukhara the designs are disposed in 13 bands with, at its summit, the oldest recorded glazed blue tiles with relief designs which were to become so important in Timurid times. In the 12th to 13th centuries decorations were incised on terracotta and alabaster slabs, as, for example, on the 12th-century Magok Attari Mosque at Bukhara and, at Usgen, on the 11th-century mausolea of Nasr ben' Ali, Jalal-al-din al-Husein (1152) and another dated to 1186. Later script became a superb decoration.

In towns the walled citadel– the Ark–was surrounded by the walled residential area–the shahristan–its main roads, lined with open water-channels, connecting the registan (main square) to the gates. The garden suburbs lay outside the walls. Sections of some walls survive, as at Bukhara. Architecture is represented by mosques, Madrasahs (Muslim* establishments of higher education), round and slightly tapered minarets, and mausolea. Timur's ruined palace in his birthplace, Shahr-i-Sabz (ancient Kesh) provides the only extant example of domestic architecture, Ulugh Beg's sextant at Samarkand the only scientific relic. Domes, eiwans and porticos are the style's main features, the mosques being roofed. Only the 12th-century Kalyan Mosque at Bukhara and the Bibi Hanum (1399–1404), built by Timur in Samarkand in honour of his Chinese wife, recall in their ground plans the open-court layout of Arab mosques. Stalactite vaulting is customary while glazed-tile panels and majolica mosaics adorn the porticoes, eiwans and drums, sometimes overflowing on to the walls. Bukhara's chief monuments include the 14th-century mud-brick Chashma Ayub mausoleum and the Madrasah of Mir-i-Arab (1535/6), Kukeldash (1568–9), Abdulla Khan (1588–90), and Char Bakr (16th-century). Turcoman Tekke rugs are often miscalled Bukharas, probably because many were sold there.

Samarkand contains two of Islam's finest architectural creations. The earlier, the 14th- to 15th-century Shah-i-Zinda, is a street of mausolea; entrance to its steep flight of stairs–made, as in India, of

(1)

(1) Decorative panel from the Abd-al-Aziz Madrasah (1652), Bukhara. (2) Ismail the Samanid's cube-shaped mausoleum, Bukhara (9th to 10th century). (3) Kalyan minaret (1127), Bukhara. (4) Upper flight of steps in the Shah-i-Zinda (Street of Tombs). (5) The Islamic cemetery on southern slopes of Afrosiab, ancient Samarkand, late 14th/15th century

(2)

(3)

(4)

(5)

marble – is through Ulugh Beg's portico. The earliest tomb, situated at its summit, belongs to Kasim; those bordering the street include two belonging to Timur's ladies and are distinguished by the ridged, melon-shaped domes associated with Timur. All the mausolea are sumptuously decorated with glazed ceramics, but the isolated Gur Emir (1403–4) is the most glorious. Built by Timur to serve as the mausoleum of a favourite son, it became his own burial-place Samarkand's registan is bordered on three sides by the fine Madrasahs of Ulugh Beg (1417), Shere-Dor (1619–36) and Tilla Kari (1646–59) but many of the smaller mosques are scarcely less beautiful. *T.T.R.*

Below: the Ulugh Beg Madrasah, Bukhara. Bottom: the Shere-Dor (of the tiger) Madrasah, Samarkand

The architecture and arts of Transcaucasia

During much of their history the buffer kingdoms of Armenia and Georgia were coveted by Persia, which competed for them first with Rome, then with Byzantium and, finally, with Russia. In addition Arabs and Ottoman Turks attempted to annex them and convert them to Islam.* However, their trials were to some extent offset in the artistic field, where their talents and skills enabled them to benefit from their enemies' attainments.

On adopting Christianity* (Armenia in 303, Georgia by 330) the attention of both countries veered towards Byzantium, yet they met their need for churches by adopting the basilical type in use at the time in Palestine and Asia Minor. Stone – sandstone, tufa, basalt and granite – became their customary building material. They cut it into blocks dressed on the inside and out, and set them in fine mortar. In both countries architecture developed along parallel though quite distinct lines so that, at much the same time as the Georgians were building the fine, three-aisled basilica at Bolnisi, dated by their earliest stone-cut inscription to 478–91, the Armenians were doing so at Yereruk (c.600). Both kingdoms must have realized simultaneously that their ritual required churches with an internal cruciform plan rather than a basilical, preferably roofed with a dome at the intersection of the aisles. Although by the 3rd century AD the Romans were attempting to place a dome above a square by experimenting with the pendentive (or coved corner), the Sassanians, possibly even the Assyrians, had already done so by evolving the squinch arch. The Transcaucasians must surely have acquired

Church of the Cross at Dzhvari, Georgia, 6th to 7th century

the technique from their eastern neighbours since, between 586 and 604, the Georgians used the squinch at Dzhvari, near Mtskheta, and, c.600, the Armenians did so at Avan. The church at Dzhvari is shaped on the inside as a tetraconch (four semicircular apses), each bow of which is linked to the central area by niches aligned to frame a square which was roofed by a dome resting on squinches. After that, all that was needed to increase the size of the central area in buildings of that type was the introduction of four free-standing piers or columns to serve as supplementary supports for the dome, an experiment which was tried out in Georgia at Tzromi between 626 and 634. Where buttresses were required barrel-vaults were used to bind them to round or octagonal drums surmounted by domes which, in both kingdoms, were always pyramid-shaped.

The Golden Age

In the 7th century the Arab conquest of Transcaucasia checked all activities even in Armenia, where domestic architecture had become established in Urartian times (9th to 6th centuries BC) and had flourished under the Arsacid dynasty (AD 53–428)–as, for example, at Garni. However, the Muslims who established themselves in the region (particularly Azerbaijan) erected some interesting mosques, mausolea, baths and other purely Islamic monuments during the succeeding centuries. Conditions improved in the 9th century for the region's Christian inhabitants, towns became more prosperous, architecture revived. Palaces were built for notables and bishops, castles were enlarged and modernized, bridges were steeply arched to carry flood water, monasteries expanded and, in Georgia's Upper Svanetia, from 1096 at any rate, stone look-out towers replaced the wooden ones incorporated in the larger houses. Church-building

Cathedral at Ani, Armenia's 10th-century capital, now in Turkey

became more ambitious. In 964, at Kumurdo in Georgia, the architect Sacotsari built a domed cathedral with a cruciform exterior into which he inserted a sixth aisle, setting it at right angles to the five-aisled nave. When Ashot III of Armenia (952–77) chose Ani as his capital he embellished it with splendid palaces, cathedrals and fortifications and when Georgia was unified under King David IV (1089–1129) both kingdoms entered upon a Golden Age.

In architecture the style of these regions is distinguished by the sophistication of its facades and by the height and spaciousness of its churches. By blending features belonging to the basilical and domed cruciform types, church interiors came to resemble double basilicas. Their roofs acquired several levels, porches were added, transepts were emphasized, choirs were included and pillars, often grouped in clusters as later in western Gothic, marked the divisions of the aisles. At Ani some were already joined by slightly pointed arches but at Mtskheta those in Sveti-Tskhoveli (1010–29) were still rounded. Its architect, Arsukidze, broke the exterior of the cathedral's east wall into five tall sections, adding two niches for the preacher's use, and split its north and south fronts into three divisions. Often churches were paved with marble slabs, inlay or glazed tiles; in Georgia alone a low marble or stone screen formed of carved panels set between pilasters, never an iconostasis,* separated the nave from the sanctuary. Gradually, thicker mortar was used and brick courses were inserted in the masonry. In the 13th century further development was arrested by the Mongol* invasion yet much solid building continued to be done between the 16th and 18th centuries, although bricks were increasingly used and decoration often became excessive.

Sculpture and murals

Transcaucasian stone is excellent sculptor's material. In Armenia single slabs reaching the enormous in size were carved with elaborate, often foliated crosses (khachkars). Set up in the open, they symbolize the Christian faith and date from all periods. In Georgia (for example at 6th-century Khandisi) carved stellae (small columns) surmounted by crosses, recalling Saxon counterparts, gradually fell out of use while tall, slender wooden crosses encased in embossed gold leaf, often accompanied by a small, pyramid-shaped gold cap, were placed inside some cathedrals and were probably also carried in processions. Already at Dzhvari sculptures of a distinctive character embellished the church's exterior. With the years they became more numerous, appearing on the tympana, architraves, vaults, cornices, arches and capitals, framing windows and entrances, decorating the wooden shutters and doors. Certain scholars discern Romanesque features in some of them, others perceive eastern elements in the animal forms and interlaced and geometric designs, but it is the Byzantine style which prevails. Subjects range from the religious, animal and vegetal, with the vine given prominence, to symbolic crosses, rosettes, bosses and, as already at Dzhvari, royal donor and related portraits (for example, in Armenia, King Gagik at Aghtamar and a master mason at Zvartnotz). Portraits were also included among the interior mural paintings (in Georgia, George III and Queen Tamara in the 12th-century church in the rock-cut townlet of Vardzia).

In both kingdoms the mural paintings adhered to the Byzantine tradition but Constantinople's influence is stronger in the rare wall mosaics (such as the 12th-century Virgin and Child at Gelati, Georgia) while the Syrian tends to prevail in the paintings. In Armenia, where mural painting was done in Urartian times, the finest Christian examples are perhaps to be found at Ani and Aghtamar, the most elegant Georgian at Ateni and Ubisi. Few artists signed their paintings but a notable exception occurs in Upper Svanetia where an artist called Tevdore (Theodore) worked between 1096 and 1112.

The applied arts
In architecture the Georgians and Armenians must be ranked equally but whereas the Armenians may have produced the finer artists the

Below: illumination in the Echmiadzin Gospel, Matenadaran Library, Yerevan. Right: St John, detail from embossed and chased silver cover of the Bertsk Gospel by Beshken Opizari (*c.* 1184–93)

Georgians should perhaps count as the better jewellers. Manuscripts were illuminated in both kingdoms, but the Armenians appear as the more individualistic and wider-ranging in their choice of subjects, showing a more marked bent for elaborate interlaced designs. Artists in both countries worked in the Byzantine style, although Syrian influences are often to the fore in the religious scenes, while the Persian tend to dominate in the secular, especially in battle pieces (such as the 15th-century Georgian Jruichi Psalter). The earliest Armenian miniatures to survive adorn the Lazarev Gospel of 887 and some are bound up with the Echmiadzin Gospel of 989; the oldest Georgian illustrate the Ardishi Gospel of 897 and the Jruichi Gospel of 936–40, where the draperies are rendered with particular skill.

Georgia's love of the sumptuous and elegant is clearly evident in metal work, a craft which flourished there in the second millennium BC. In Christian times Georgia alone, with the exception of Kiev, was able to produce cloisonné enamels of the Byzantine type. Mastering that most difficult technique the Georgians achieved brighter, clearer and more varied colours than the Kievans. In the 12th century the enameller Asan of Tchkondidi may have had a workshop at Martvili. The earliest enamels (those adorning the Virgin of Kobi associated with Leo III of Abkhazia (957–67) and the earlier ones on the Khakhuli triptych) have a green background. The delicacy of Georgian filigree, wire and granule decorations has seldom been equalled. Those techniques are seen at their best on the exquisitely wrought gold triptych known as the Khakhuli, once the property of Gelati Monastery, where they provide a setting for delicate chased and repoussé designs, cabochon jewels and over 100 cloisonné enamels, 32 of them Georgian. The latter include a Virgin's head which cedes little in humanism to the near-contemporary Byzantine panel painting known as the icon* of the Virgin of Vladimir (*Vladimirskaya*, now in the Tret'yakov Gallery, Moscow). The Georgians' talent for embossing and chasing very thin sheets of metal—gold, silver, silver-gilt, copper and copper-gilt—led them to substitute such plaques for painted icons, as well as using them as book-covers. The earliest plaques to survive are a 5th-century silver-gilt representation of St Gregory the Illuminator and a 6th- or 7th-century silver-gilt disk of St Mamas. The monasteries of Opiza, Tbeti and Gelati became important centres of production. Only two jewellers are known by name, the more individualistic Beka who, in 1193, worked the cover of the Tselkendili Gospel and his near-contemporary, Beshken of Opiza, who signed one of his gospel-covers. That the Armenians were almost equally skilled is evident from the silver Skevra reliquary which the Catholicos Constantine presented to King Hetun in 1293. There was a large demand for jewellery in both countries, but more fine pieces of medieval date survive in Georgia. Later, excellent silver niello work was done, once again especially in Georgia.   *T.T.R.*

Folk art of Russia

Russian folk art is, of course, as old as the people themselves, but the material available for its study before the middle of the 19th century is scanty. With advancing prosperity, its products increased greatly, becoming more widely known, and although now influenced by competing mass-produced goods, they retain enough of their previous character to enable us to fill in the gaps in the earlier material and to form a picture of the whole tradition.

The main characteristics of Russian folk art – imaginative use of the available raw materials and rich decoration – are attributable to the conditions of peasant life. The geographical isolation of the villages, caused by the lack of roads, made it necessary for people to be almost entirely self-sufficient, and the long winters, when no work might be done in the fields, gave them ample time to perfect elaborate ornamentation. The decorative motifs they used naturally often illustrate ancient folk beliefs. The State Historical Museum in Moscow and the State Russian Museum in Leningrad contain rich collections of domestic and craft products, such as embroidery,

Chest with painting of a *sirin*, late 17th to early 18th century

wooden distaffs, gingerbread moulds and printing blocks. Not surprisingly embroidery, which requires only a background of woven material and a needle and thread, provides a fair proportion of the exhibits; much is no older than the 18th century, but two 15th- or 16th-century pieces have recently been discovered. The embroidered figures include fantastic buildings, animals (deer, unicorns), birds (peacocks, two-headed eagles), birds with human faces (the legendary *sirin* and *alkonost*) and a woman flanked either by two horses, which she holds by their bridles, or by two birds standing on her hands, and thought to represent a pagan mother-goddess with fertility connotations. Some of these designs continue to the present day, and are also found painted and carved on distaffs and carved on wooden door-lintels. The carved horse or cock often adorning the end of the main roof-beam in northern houses is also a pre-Christian symbol, bringing good and warding off evil. The birds on wedding-towels signify love, and the flowering bush frequently seen on gingerbread moulds is a symbol of rebirth.

19th-century gingerbread moulds with peacock (left) and shooting and domestic scenes (above)

It was customary for gingerbread to be given at the village festivals held on church holidays, and at weddings and funerals. The earliest moulds found date from the 12th and 13th centuries. The designs vary with the occasion: on St George's day the gingerbread was in the shape of birds, cows and sheep. The carvers knew all the traditional shapes by heart, and adhered to them until the beginning of the 19th century, when they began to look for new patterns in *lubki* (chapbooks or single printed sheets – 'broadsides' – with text and pictures prepared from wooden blocks).

In every household the women were engaged for much of the time in spinning, and distaffs were often given by men as presents to their wives, daughters and sweethearts. Datable specimens in the Russian collections go back to 1783, although of course the instrument is as old as spinning itself. Russian distaffs are larger than those of any other country, and are held upright in a base provided with a hole for that purpose and serving also as a seat for the spinner. Both the blade at the upper end which holds the wool and the base often display carved or painted designs, geometric and representational.

The production of wooden blocks for the printing of designs on dress-materials, table-cloths, church banners, book-covers, and so on is supposed to have originated with the icon*-painters, who worked in towns; but by the end of the 18th century this had become village work. In the 1830s mechanization was introduced, but shawls and kerchiefs continued to be hand-printed from wooden blocks; by the end of the 19th century whole districts were supported by this industry. The earliest designs were geometric, but in the 19th century representational designs appear, for example gallants and ladies in traditional costumes. These, like the designs on 19th-century gingerbread moulds, were copied from *lubki*. The earliest surviving *lubok* (1619–24) represents the Dormition of the Mother of God; the early subject-matter was always religious and *lubki* were hawked outside monasteries, but later they also conveyed political opinions expressed in religious symbols – at the time of Peter the Great* broadsides appeared for and against the tsar.

The emancipation of the serfs* in 1861, along with growing industrialization and economic expansion, influenced folk art through the style of factory-produced goods and the contact of peasants with urban life. For instance, one home-made distaff bears a picture of a fashionable tea-party with a lady standing by a samovar, welcoming guests. Rich townsfolk began to take notice of peasant art and concerned themselves to investigate, conserve and reproduce it. The beginning of this tendency is marked by the appearance in 1872 of V. V. Stasov's (1824–1906) book *Russian Folk Decoration*. An important patron was S. I. Mamontov (1841–1918), a leading figure in the Moscow-centred movement known as the Wanderers.* On his estate at Abramtsevo near Moscow he assembled in the 1870s gifted enthusiasts who not only conducted research into popular art but also set up craft schools where traditional designs were embodied in

Folk art of Caucasia

Caucasian★ folk art differs widely from Russian, its products reflecting the strong local and ancient traditions of fiercely independent non-Slav peoples. Their artefacts include the well-known knotted carpets and rugs, of which one unusual feature is quilting when a thin layer of wool is inserted between the rug and the lining. Knitted work, especially socks of wool or silk, sometimes incorporating gold threads, shows decoration in a contrasting colour, using figures of birds, the tree of life, the *buta* (a curved motif familiar from Paisley shawls), and other geometric shapes. The earliest example of bead work is a hookah stem of the 14th century; tambour work may be seen on the Azerbaijan national costume and resembles some kinds of Bukharan and Indian embroidery, the *buta* motif also being employed. Georgian embroidery is characterized by the free use of metal threads, and is based on traditions established in the 17th and 18th centuries in workshops supplying church vestments and icons.★ The pottery of Dagestan includes glazed ware with impressed designs and unglazed ware with painted designs, in either case geometric. Jewellery, daggers, drinking horns and other domestic articles are decorated with damascening or niello work.   *A.M.C.*

Folk art of Central Asia

This region is the home of peoples mainly of Turkic★ origin and tongue and traditionally of nomadic habits; important cities such as Bukhara and Samarkand established themselves on the great trade-route between East and West and encouraged the production of goods of high quality. The nomadic Kazakhs,★ like other peoples of this area, made woven and knotted rugs, but are specially remarkable for the felt matting (made from sheep's wool) with which they covered the floors and walls of the *yurts* (movable pavilions) in which they lived. Bold simple shapes were cut out of two superimposed squares of felt of different colours, often the black and white of the undyed wool. The cut-outs were then interchanged and the resulting patterned squares were joined in chequer-board fashion, the joins being covered with braid, and the whole mat sometimes surrounded with a fringe of dyed horsehair. Such mats were expected to last 50 years. Bukhara has given its name not only to carpets and rugs but also to embroidered wall-hangings and bed-covers of the 19th century, though these were often in fact made in Nurata, Fergana, Tashkent or Samarkand. The floral designs are usually embroidered in silk on cotton, sometimes with the tambour stitch used by Uzbeks,★ Tadzhiks,★ Kirgiz★ and Turkmens.★ Embossed leather was used to make flagons for koumiss (fermented mares' milk), milking pails, cases for drinking vessels and other domestic articles.   *A.M.C.*

Woodcut (*lubok*) 'The Cat of Kazan', late 17th century

articles for contemporary use. With their own hands they built the church, traditional in form, which is still there. V. D. Polenov (1844–1927), a painter and archaeologist, added a museum of national peasant art which also survives; its first exhibit was a carved lintel which he found in a near-by house.

Other estate colonies of craftsmen basing their designs on peasant work were organized, notably that founded by Princess Tenisheva at Talashkino near Smolensk. She not only helped to design the products, but also made a major collection of village articles in everyday use. Other important collections were those of P. I. Shchukin (now in the State Historical Museum in Moscow) and of Princess Aleksandra Sidamon-Eristov and N. de Chabelskoy. By the 1880s interest in Russian folk art, especially embroidery, had spread to other European countries: the Broderie Russe Company opened shops in London, Paris and other capitals, as outlets for work made or collected in Russia. Later (1911–20), the continuing interest in Britain was catered for by Madame Pogorsky's Russian Peasant Industries shop in London, stocking books of translated Russian folk-tales★ illustrated by I. Ya. Bilibin (1876–1942) in a style based on designs collected in Siberia, and still in print.   *A.M.C.*

The meaning of the icon

The word 'icon' (Greek: 'image', 'likeness') is applied to mosaics, frescoes, wooden panels, embroidery, sculpture and metal depicting subject-matter essentially relevant to worship in the Orthodox Church.* When Russia officially accepted Christianity from Byzantium in 988 it was a conscious choice resting on an experience of liturgical* beauty and meaning, combining word, song, architecture and image: an interrelated theological and artistic reality. The Russians inherited a mature tradition, consisting of a coherent and theocentric world-view.

Almost without exception, icons are unsigned: the name inscribed on the icon is that of the saint depicted. The universal creative principle underlying this culture is the fact of the Gospel message and the doctrine of the Incarnation of Christ: God has become visible and therefore depictable, and remains adored. His image – and that of each of the saints – is scrupulously and authentically personal, historical, opening an insight into the invisible and divine reality of

Mother of God of Tenderness (*Vladimirskaya* type), 17th century, Stroganov school

the holy in the context of eternity. Because the nature of any image is to make present the person depicted, the iconic reality derives from the indwelling of the holy one in his image, which both the painter and the beholder approach with awe. They venerate the image, but worship God. The particular Byzantine Christ representation that the Russians knew is that of the severe Pantocrator, the Heavenly King, the Almighty and Judge. Through their continual perusal of the Gospel Russian painters also developed the type of the humiliated 'kenotic' Christ, gentle yet strong, the God of Mercy. An example of this transformation may be seen in icons of Christ by Rublev compared with the earlier Pantocrator of St Sophia Cathedral in Kiev (15th and 11th centuries respectively).

With the icons of the Mother of God a similar transformation took place: the *Vladimirskaya* icon, now in the Tret'yakov Gallery, Moscow, depicts the rare Byzantine type of the *Umilenie* or 'Tenderness', which the Russians adopted more than any other type. Among the other most frequently venerated icons of the Mother with Child are: the Mother of God of the Sign, the *Tikhvinskaya* and the *Kazanskaya*, all derived from the favourite Byzantine type of the *Hodigitria* or 'Guide to Christ'. Other icons depict the Mother of God in various forms of intercession and veneration by the faithful; she is always, in some way, related to Christ in her icons, having assumed him entirely and is never depicted as showing one isolated virtue of her nature – she is always the Theotokos, the one who 'bore Christ'.

M.M.F.

The iconostasis

The God-centred attitude is further exemplified in the interior of a Russian church: the iconographic programme, also inherited from Byzantium, includes the iconostasis, as well as four specific areas of wall-painting within the architecture of the building. The iconostasis is an 'icon of the Church' in its growth, depicting in its various tiers the history of salvation from Adam to the Last Judgement. It delineates the borderline and manifests the unity between two worlds, the eternal and the temporal; the sanctuary representing the Kingdom of God, and the nave where the people stand in active vigilance and worship. The doors through which the celebrants proceed during the liturgy make this visually apparent. In its complete form it incorporates five tiers, a counterpart of what is proclaimed in word and song in the liturgy.* The upper tier, of the Forefathers, represents the Old Testament from Adam to Moses; the centre holds the icon of the Holy Trinity (the Three Angels appearing to Abraham). Below this is the row of the Prophets, from Moses to Christ; they hold scrolls prophesying the Incarnation. In the centre is the icon of the Mother of God of the Sign, a depiction of Isaiah's prophecy about the child Emmanuel. Below is the tier of Festivals, representing the New Testament. These icons depict the life of the Mother of God and Christ, as they are celebrated in the Church year. They include, among others, the Presentation of the Mother of God in the Temple, the Nativity of Christ, the Transfiguration. The next tier is called Deesis, 'prayer'. Here, angels and saints are set in relation to the central triptych – the kernel of the ancient sanctuary screen – where Christ is approached by his Mother and St John the Baptist in an attitude of intercession. Below is the 'local' tier: icons of locally-venerated saints or events, and two large icons of Christ and the Mother of God on either side of the Holy Doors which show the Annunciation and the Four Evangelists, symbolizing the advent of the Kingdom.

The outlining iconographic arrangement on the walls, in the dome, in the apse and on the west wall is given as a graphic narrative of Christ's ministry and of the world of the saints. The early use of mosaics was soon replaced by fresco painting. As a symbol of Heaven, the central dome contains Christ Pantocrator surrounded by angels and prophets, and in the drum the twelve apostles, while the four evangelists are in the four pendentives (coved corners). The apse contains a row of hierarchs of the early Church. Above this is represented the Communion of the Apostles, echoing the Eucharistic action by the clergy in the sanctuary. Higher still is a large icon of the Mother of God interceding for the world. The rest of the walls, pillars, vaults and arches are covered with the saints and with scenes from the life of Christ. This iconography reproduces what the faithful hear there in hymns and lessons. The comprehensive mural programme and the structure of the iconostasis is a logical, conscious development within the theocentric Church. The maturity of the Byzantine synthesis was the result of a living process, however turbulent, in which tradition is understood as a dynamic and creative presence in the world, a culture nurtured on worship (cult) and the Gospel.   *M.M.F.*

The painting of icons

The icon painter is, first of all, a theologian – not in the academic sense, but as a man or woman who worships God and venerates the saints. He is the first to venerate what he has created on behalf of and for the Church, and hence does not consider the icons as his exclusive achievement, glory or property.

The only iconographic canon is the *Podlinnik*, the painter's handbook, an anthology of outlines for every saint and sacred event, with indications of symbols and conventions aimed at preserving the identity, the likeness of the saint. The style of the icon derives from the same iconographic and theological tradition of the Church, in a language of lines and colour which the Russians have unhesitatingly

adopted. Significantly, the Greek and Russian words for icon painting are 'icon writing'. The lines and contours follow a logical structure, they are never arbitrary, neither do they ignore the shape of the body. The order is cosmic, not chaotic. The drapery follows the movement of the natural body it envelops without being naturalistic. The structure is architectural, the contours are strong, emphatic, the principal lines direct, unhesitating, uninterrupted, directing the lesser lines and supporting the over-all structure.

Paint is applied in superimposed transparent layers and fusion, from an all-enveloping dark gradually to smaller areas of lighter shades on top, ending in minute concentrations of light which achieve the characteristic luminosity of the icon. The only source of light is from within the saint depicted. There is no limit to this light which by its very nature casts no shadows: the Uncreated Light of God. Indicating divinity, the 'mandorla', an all-embracing halo, and 'assist', a fine network of gold lines, are reserved for Christ alone, and only in icons recording events where he had revealed his Godhead, depicting him outside his mission on Earth – with the exception of his Childhood and the icon of the Transfiguration. We see him in the Ascension, the Dormition, the Last Judgement and in icons of individual saints blessing them from Heaven, arrayed in white and gold, or gold ochre. 'Assist' sometimes spills over from Christ by contact into the very people or objects he touches: his Mother, the Book, the Throne.

Biographical icon of St George, 14th century, Novgorod

In the field of perspective the arrangement of space and the geometry of volumes are, in principle, distorted when depicted on the flat surface of an icon panel. The medieval painter reduced the field of depth by using undistorted parallel lines (furniture, buildings, books) and simultaneously endeavoured to enhance the visual amplitude of forms through direct (linear) or inverted perspective, instinctively alternating them freely in order to bring important features of the painting to the fore. Thus, the complexities of perspective are subordinated to the overriding artistic composition of the icon.

The over-all stylistic diversity is mild, and one cannot speak of independent 'schools' in the sense of Renaissance schools, but of strands of the same tradition. Painters travelled, and the icons travelled; this makes it often difficult to date and place an icon.

From the time of Russia's official conversion in 988 under Prince Vladimir I* of Kiev local artists collaborated with their Byzantine masters. But soon the Russians worked on their own, from time to time inspired by Byzantine work or by visiting masters. In the decoration of churches such as St Sophia Cathedral enough mosaic and fresco work remains as examples of iconic work of that period. No panel icons can be attributed to Kiev with any certainty. The earliest panel icons are from Novgorod, strongly influenced in the 11th and 12th centuries by Byzantine icons. The Annunciation Cathedral in the Moscow Kremlin has a magnificent St George with the large dominating eyes typical of the 12th century, the face finely modelled by the fusion technique and the features brought to life by direct, firm, expressive lines. The Saviour 'made without hands' in the Tret'yakov Gallery, Moscow (based on the traditional King Abgar Mandylion) is another Byzantine-based icon executed with the most economical, direct means to make the highest impact. Other icons in this early category characterized by very large expressive eyes, strong lines and painterly modelling by fusion are the head of the Archangel with golden hair in the Russian Museum, the so-called Yaroslavl' Mother of God of the Sign and the Ustyug Annunciation, both in the Tret'yakov Gallery.

The Saviour 'made without hands', Novgorod, 12th to 13th century

Yaroslavl' Mother of God of the Sign, 1220

The Ustyug Annunciation from Yur'ev Monastery, Novgorod, 12th century

Areas such as Rostov-Suzdal' with Vladimir as its capital, Yaroslavl' and Pskov are all famous for their early icons. The famous *Vladimirskaya* Mother of God, in Vladimir after 1155 (originally a gift by Constantinople to Kiev), must have made a great impact there, on the faithful and artists alike, as indeed must other such documented gifts of Byzantine masterpieces. Two Deesis panels also in the Tret'-yakov Gallery, one of Christ Emmanuel between two Angels, the other the adult Christ between the Mother of God and St John the Baptist, both from Vladimir-Suzdal', are reminiscent of this, as is the St Dmitry icon, also in the Tret'yakov Gallery, dated 12th or 13th century.

The Tatar* (or Mongol) inroads in the 13th and 14th centuries destroyed much of Russian works of art; they put a brake on further work and impeded contacts with Byzantium and the Balkans. Novgorod and Pskov remained free to continue creating, local characteristics coming more and more to the fore as Byzantine influence receded. The 14th and 15th centuries are considered the greatest in Novgorod. The themes were to the point, the means remained economic, direct, the colours were pure, bright, with flaming red predominating; white was used lavishly. Often the figures were short with biggish heads, the attitudes frontal in icons of Novgorod's favourite saints such as Paraskeva, Anastasia, George, Elijah, Nicholas and Blaise as well as Florus and Laurus. A small Mother of God of the Sign is often inserted as a semi-spherical icon below the upper frame of such groups of saints, as the documented Protectress of the town of Novgorod. Often red, the nearest colour to gold in the solar spectrum, was used for the background colour. Such icons as the Prophet Elijah in the Tret'yakov Gallery, St George in the Russian Museum and SS Varlaam Khutynsky, John the Almsgiver, Paraskeva and Anastasia, also in the Russian Museum, are good examples of this period in Novgorod.

In the 15th century the figures became elongated and the heads small; the impact of the colours remained strong and unmixed but superimposed. Painterly means became more sophisticated: examples include, in the Tret'yakov Gallery: Holy Women at the Sepulchre (*c*.1475), SS Florus and Laurus; in the Russian Museum, Leningrad: the Quadripartite Icon; and in the Museum of History in Novgorod: the icons on canvas, such as Christ among the Doctors.

Pskov icons are characterized by a strong dark green and bright orange, often dotted and decorated with white. The modelling of the faces with their important luminosity is often achieved by short thick white strokes or patches and parallel lines. A typical example is the Mother of God's Assembly in the Tret'yakov Gallery (*c*.1350–1400). The 14th-century icon of SS Paraskeva, Gregory the Theologian, John Chrysostom and Basil the Great in the Tret'yakov Gallery is a superb example of the scrupulous care which the painter took to be true to the saints' personal, authentic features. A famous icon from Tver', the Blue Dormition, 15th century, may also be found in the Tret'yakov Gallery.

Left: icon of the Pskov school showing (left to right) SS Paraskeva Pyatnitsa, Gregory the Theologian, John Chrysostom, and Basil the Great 14th century. Right: detail of Christ Pantocrator from a Deesis from Chernokulovo village, Vladimir, 15th century

Andrey Rublev:
Old Testament
Trinity, *c.* 1410–20

When Moscow* became the centralizing power in the 14th and 15th centuries much that had been created in Vladimir-Suzdal' was absorbed in the new rising culture and continued there. Moscow iconography also came under Paleologue influence. Feofan the Greek, after working in Novgorod, painted in the Kremlin in Moscow together with the young Andrey Rublev in the Annunciation Cathedral in 1405. They developed the iconostasis* to unprecedented heights. Rublev's most famous icon painted for the Trinity Monastery of St Sergy is the Holy Trinity icon in the Tret'yakov Gallery – perfect in expressing consent and assent by the Three Persons to the Sacrifice symbolized in the Chalice on the Table. He achieved the ultimate in luminosity and transparency in paint, his lines are delicate and direct; compassion, gentleness, dignity in humility are what he expresses. Among others the St Michael from Zvenigorod in the Tret'yakov Gallery is a good example. His influence was enormous in Russian icon painting.

Dionisy is the last name of known great icon painters (c.1440–1508) coming within this same tradition. His figures are elegant, refined, with light colours superbly blended and harmonious. Detail becomes important and that whole era of icon painting, with the refinement, aesthetic values, preciousness and ornamental detail characterizing the 16th and 17th centuries is already hinted at here.

The elongated figures of the so-called Stroganov school, perfect in technique to the point of virtuosity, and the 'verbosity' and fussiness in the narrative icons tell of a time in Russian icon painting where to simple statements of faith was added philosophical speculation. The Court and the mighty of the more regulated secular world have also left their impact here. From being an art founded in a spiritual reality developing out of an unfragmented world view and faith, iconic painting absorbed more and more secular matter while retaining the exterior shell. Introduction to Western naturalistic painting based on the Renaissance (which was partly pagan in inspiration) proved an irresistible temptation to the Russians. Simon Ushakov (1626–86) attempted a fusion of both worlds – the naturalistic and the transfigured – but instead of a 'spiritual body' (St Paul) he painted glistening flesh. The vision had become distorted and psychological states were mistaken for spiritual ones. However, side by side with this decadent phase in the Church and its art went another current which continued in the tradition of asceticism and spiritual life, producing sacred art. This is why, in the 20th century, icons are still being created from within the Church, true to its tradition and experience, alive in the spirit which perpetuated it. *M.M.F.*

Pokrov icon, 17th century, Stroganov school

Mother of God icon, 18th/19th century

Churches and monasteries

The natural and most ubiquitous building material in Russia was wood, but owing to its inflammable nature only isolated examples survive from before the 17th century. Masonry came into use with the introduction of Christianity. The earliest and one of the finest monuments is the Church of Holy Wisdom (Sophia) in Kiev, begun in 1037 – a five-aisled vaulted structure, surmounted by 13 domes and adorned with magnificent mosaics at the east end. The exterior was remodelled in the 18th century.

From the mid-12th-century the principal centre of building activity was the Vladimir area, where a good quality of white limestone was available. The traditional form for a church was usually a cube surmounted by a dome (symbolizing the earth with heaven above) with one or more apses at the east end. In larger churches massive rectangular piers supported the vaults and galleries. Externally blind arcading often girdled the building. Although officially the Orthodox Church★ did not encourage the use of sculpture, some churches in this area were adorned with low-relief carving representing figures, birds, animals and stylized plants. The principal monuments in date order are the church at Pereyaslavl' Zalessky (1152), the Cathedral of the Assumption (1158, enlarged after 1183) and the princes' church of St Dmitry (1195) in Vladimir; a fragment of the palace at Bogolyubovo and the nearby small Church of Pokrov (Protection of the Virgin's Veil) on the Nerl' (1165) and the latest in date, St George at Yur'ev Pol'sky (1234). This and St Dmitry are both richly adorned with sculpture, though probably not in its original order. The cathedral at Suzdal', begun in the 13th century and largely rebuilt during the 15th to 17th centuries, has retained its 13th-century doors with biblical scenes designed in gold on copper. On account of its many monasteries, bishop's palace and a quantity of small churches, Suzdal' has been declared a museum city.

In the 14th century building flourished mainly in the prosperous, independent city states of Novgorod and Pskov. The cathedral of Novgorod, a smaller version of that in Kiev and built only a few years later, was less lavishly adorned with frescoes instead of mosaics, and was badly damaged in 1941. One of its treasures is the pair of bronze doors from Magdeburg, reassembled by the Russian smith Abram in 1187. Two large monasteries and a number of small churches have survived, their walls usually divided into three sections by flat pilaster-like bands, sometimes ending in arches above, known as *zakomary*, and separate curved roofs. Many of these were later covered with flat roofs and are now being restored. In Pskov the

Top: the 14th-century church of St Theodore Stratilates, Novgorod. Right: interior of Fioravanti's Assumption (*Uspenskiy sobor*) Cathedral, Moscow Kremlin

original cathedral was rebuilt in the late 17th century. Two monasteries, the Monastery of the Saviour on the Mirozha river and the Monastery of St John survive, and a number of small churches, some with belfries over the porch. A few 17th-century houses built of masonry for rich merchants still stand, but originally they had wooden living-quarters above.

By the mid-15th-century Moscow* was in a position to erect its most splendid and still surviving buildings. The Kremlin, or citadel, had been a wooden fort originally. Stone walls were built in the late 14th century and were now replaced by the present brick walls and towers, which continued to be embellished in later centuries. But Russian architects had lost their former skill and the Cathedral of the Assumption they began collapsed. Ivan III* then invited a number of Italian architects to Moscow. The first to come, Rodolfo Fioravanti, was sent to Vladimir to learn the requirements of Russian ritual and the cathedral he built so astonished the Russians that he was named Aristotle. Its size, spaciousness, acoustics and beauty were due to deeper foundations, slender round piers and iron tie-beams to support the thin vaults. The interior was later covered with murals and served as the coronation church for all subsequent monarchs. The square in front was planned as the ceremonial centre of the city and remains its most impressive sight.

Builders from Pskov, who were famous for their skill, erected the Church of the Annunciation, adjoining the palace, in 1484–9. It is smaller, but sumptuously adorned with finely carved doorways, a floor of jasper and nine gilded domes. In 1505 Alevisio Novo designed the Church of St Michael the Archangel as a burial-place for the princely families. This has many Renaissance features of ornament, although basically Russian in plan. The Faceted Hall, outwardly Italian, also follows the Russian plan of a single massive central pier supporting the vaults. The tall Belfry opposite completes the varied yet harmonious design.

The fortified monasteries on the south-east of Moscow and the Trinity Monastery at Zagorsk contain a remarkable range of buildings dating from the 15th to the 18th centuries. At Kolomenskoe the high steeple or tent shape was first used (1532) to replace the cupola and became widespread till forbidden by Patriarch Nikon.* It is the central feature of the Church of St Basil in Moscow (1555–60), a conglomoration of nine separate churches, all differently treated and covered with exuberant ornament, though the colour was added only in the 17th century. It was then, too, that the metropolitan of Rostov, Iona, built himself a residence to rival the Kremlin and a remarkable number of fine churches were built in Yaroslavl', where rich merchants vied with each other in the lavishness of their designs. Often adorned with coloured tiles on the outside and fine murals within, they are a very Russian expression of the Baroque spirit before the fashion for neo-classical severity and uniformity led to the replanning of many cities and conformity in church and house

building. Meanwhile Moscow produced a change of plan in church design towards the end of the 17th century, when the New Cathedral in the Donskoy Monastery was built and the still more elaborate church at Fili. Both are quatrefoil in plan with the four domes placed over the apses at the cardinal points, instead of diagonally round the central rectangle. The Church of the Intercession at Fili was built by Lev Naryshkin and the new style came to be known as Naryshkin Baroque.   *M.C.*

Wooden architecture

Throughout the Middle Ages all over Russia and especially in the north, churches as well as private houses continued to be built of wood, mainly pine, with no other tools but the axe. Beams were laid horizontally, interlocking at the corners, and the size of the building was determined by the length of the logs. The earliest surviving church is St Lazarus originally at Murom, *c.*1390, now in the Museum of Wooden Architecture on the island of Kizhi on Lake Onega. It consists of three rectangular blocks, the central cube, a porch at one end and the sanctuary at the other. The porch is lower but wider than the centre. In some buildings the floor level was raised on stilts or foundations to avoid damp and an outside covered stair led into the building. The octagonal plan allowed a larger area to be enclosed and was often used for churches. The ceiling was low to ensure warmth, but the outer walls were often extended upwards in diminishing width to produce the tent shape, later used in masonry,

Log church, 1766, from Glotovo; now at Suzdal'

as at Kolomenskoe. Domes were added, single or in clusters, and covered with shingle, producing a silvery effect.

The highest complexity achieved by any carpenter was the Church of the Transfiguration built in 1714 at Kizhi, a combination of a cruciform plan round an octagonal centre and crowned with 22 domes, some resting on gabled barrel-shaped roofs (*bochki*) one behind another, forming a huge pyramid. Other wooden buildings, easily dismantled and re-erected, have been brought to the island for preservation and similar museums of wooden architecture have been created at Kolomenskoe, Suzdal', Novgorod and Kostroma.

In the 17th century wooden houses could be bought in the markets to be re-erected wherever required. Private houses continued to be built of wood throughout the 19th century with ever-increasing complexity of ornament in lace-like fretwork, and carvings of birds and animals, reflecting folk art.* Particularly good examples are still preserved in Tomsk, Siberia.   *M.C.*

St Petersburg (now Leningrad)

Founded in 1703, the new capital was grandly planned with wide streets and splendid river frontages. European as well as Russian architects helped to make it a city of noble buildings amid outstanding spaciousness. Domenico Tressini (1670–1734) erected the Fortress Church with its tall gilt spire and Peter I's* palace in the Summer Gardens. Jean Baptiste Le Blond (1679–1719) designed the parks and Great Palace at Peterhof (Petrodvorets). The palace was extended and completed by Count Bartolomeo Francesco Rastrelli (1700–71), who also built the final Winter Palace in the capital and the even more ornate Catherine Palace at Tsarskoe Selo (Pushkin), both with Baroque exuberance of sculpture and gilding. In the absence of stone, brick and plaster lent themselves to bold relief and delicate colour.

Catherine II* introduced a taste for more restrained neo-classicism and the principal architects working for her were Antonio Rinaldi (1709–94) who built a number of pavilions in Oranienbaum (Lomonosov) and the Marble Palace in the capital; Giacomo Quarenghi (1744–1817) added the theatre to the Winter Palace, built the Academy of Science,* the State Bank and the Smol'ny Institute. Charles Cameron (1743–1817) redecorated rooms in the palace at Tsarskoe Selo, built the Agate Pavilion and Gallery adjoining it, and the palace at Pavlovsk. Among the Russian architects, Savva Chevakinsky (1713–83) built the naval Church and Belfry of St Nicholas in the Baroque style and Ivan Starov (1743–1808) built the palace for Prince Potemkin with a columned portico in the severe classical style, which became the model for innumerable town and country houses during the next half-century. The immensely long

Admiralty, which originally enclosed a shipbuilding yard, was rebuilt by Andreyan Zakharov (1761–1811) in the neo-classical style and Andrey Voronikhin (1760–1814) used the severe Doric order for his Institute of Mines. He also designed the Kazan' Cathedral (1801–11), with a semicircular colonnade facing the Nevsky Prospekt. The most prolific neo-classical architect was Carlo Rossi (1775–1849), who not only designed many of the most famous buildings but laid out whole areas round them, such as the triumphal arch and semicircle of ministries facing the Winter Palace, the Mikhaylovsky Palace (now the Russian Museum) and surrounding streets and square, the Alexandrinsky (now Pushkin Drama) Theatre, the Public Library and area round them, and finally the Senate and Synod buildings, also with a triumphal arch between them and a wide open space along the river up to the Admiralty, with the monument to Peter I by Étienne Falconet (1761–91) in the centre. Another masterly piece of planning is the Stock Exchange by Thomas de Thomon (1760–1813), with rostral (beaked) columns, on the point of the Vasil'evksy Island opposite the Winter Palace. Further back along the same embankment is the Imperial Academy of Arts by J.-B. Vallin de la Mothe (1729–1800), who also designed the shopping centre, Gostiny

Arch by Carlo Rossi, General Staff building, 1819, Palace Square, Leningrad

The Hermitage Museum, Leningrad, 1764

Dvor, and the small Hermitage Museum for Catherine I's* ever-growing art collection. The German Yury Velten (1730–1801) added a further wing along the river and by 1852, when the collection was opened to the public, Leo von Klenze (1784–1864) completed the building with a heavy entrance portico. *M.C.*

Neo-classical Moscow

After 1760 the nobility began to rebuild their Moscow houses in the classical style, often using their own serf builders, as at Kuskovo and Ostankino. The two outstanding Russian architects trained abroad were Vasily Bazhenov (1732–99) who made the grandiose design for a new Kremlin palace, which was never carried out, and began a palatial retreat for Catherine II* at Tsaritsyno in the neo-Gothic style, which remained unfinished; and Matvey Kazakov (1733–1812), who built the Petrovsky Palace for her with a blend of neo-Gothic and Slavic elements, the Assembly Room for the nobility, now the Trade Union Hall, and the Senate building in the Kremlin, a masterly combination of a circular hall surrounded by a triangular office block. The handsome Pashkov house (now part of the Lenin Library) has been variously ascribed to Bazhenov or Kazakov. Many of their followers distinguished themselves in the extensive rebuilding of Moscow after the fire of 1812, when the city had to be largely replanned. Tree-lined boulevards replaced the old encircling walls; private houses, handsome hospitals and even warehouses reflect the prevailing neo-classical tradition. *M.C.*

The Romantic revival

Exotic elements began to appear in the latter part of the 18th century. Rinaldi* had introduced Chinoiserie in the interior decoration of his so-called Chinese Pavilion at Oranienbaum and he designed the Chinese village at Tsarskoe Selo, where there was also a Chinese pavilion by Velten* and a Caprice by Vasily Neelov (1722–82), who had been sent to England with his son in order to study landscape gardening before replanning the park according to Catherine II's* taste.

At Pavlovsk a circular colonnade was struck down by lightning in 1817 and the result was found to be so romantic that it was left in its ruined condition. Private gardens were adorned with ruined castles; a Gothic church, since destroyed, was erected in the Kremlin in 1817, and Nikolay Benua (1813–98) built the Imperial Stables in Peterhof in the English Tudor style. A mixed form of revivalism is seen in the Kremlin palace built by Konstantin Ton (1794–1881) in a pseudo-Renaissance style with Russian window-surrounds. In the second half of the 19th century the Slavic revival asserted itself all over the country. In Moscow the Museum of History built in 1878–83 and the state department store GUM (1888) are typical products, while in St Petersburg A. A. Parland's (1842–1920) Church of the Saviour, built on the spot where Alexander II* was assassinated, is an unfortunate intrusion of this style, completely out of line with the rest of the city.

When state control over building was relaxed in 1840, private enterprise added shops and offices, but this could not spoil the general layout of Leningrad. Since the siege of 1941–4 all new building there is confined to the suburbs in order to preserve the architectural character of the centre. *M.C.*

GUM department store, Red Square, Moscow

Architecture: Medieval Times to the Present

The Smol'ny Institute, Leningrad

The classical heritage

Patronized by Catherine II* and Alexander I* during the 18th and 19th centuries, Russian classicism had spread widely, and its revival at the beginning of the 20th century could be seen as a revival of Russia's own heritage rather than as a new wave of Westernization. This neo-classical style was applied not only to private residences and apartment buildings but with even greater enthusiasm to public buildings. The stronghold of the style was in St Petersburg. Among the leading architects there were Ivan Fomin (1872–1936) and Vladimir Shchuko (1878–1939), both of whom continued to play an important role in the post-revolutionary years. Ivan Fomin's Polovtsev mansion (now the sanatorium of the All-Union Central Council of Trade Unions) of 1911–13 demonstrates his commitment to neo-classicism. In the same stylistic vocabulary he designed the Workers' Palace for the Peterhof district in 1919 (unexecuted), used as a simplified version for the Mossovet (Moscow Soviet of Workers', Peasants' and Soldiers' Deputies) building (1928–30), and reverted to ornate neo-classicism in his competition project for the Academy of Sciences* of the USSR (1934, unexecuted). Shchuko built several apartment buildings in St Petersburg in the neo-classical style, used classic colonnades for the propylaea or entrance of the Smol'ny Institute (1923), a classic version for the Lenin Library in Moscow (1928–39 with Vladimir Gel'freykh, 1885–1967) and gained fame

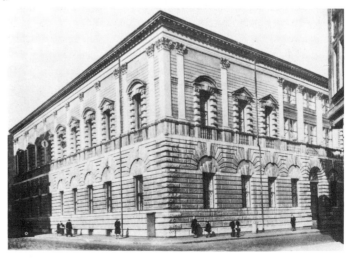

Top: the Lenin Library, Moscow. Centre: the facade of Kiev railway station, Moscow, 1913–26. Bottom: the Tarasov house, Moscow, by Ivan Zholtovsky, 1910

with his winning project for the Palace of the Soviets in Moscow in collaboration with Boris Iofan (1891–1976) and Gel'freykh.

Although neo-classicism was less popular in Moscow than in St Petersburg, it was applied to such diverse edifices as the Bryansk (today's Kiev) railway station of 1912–17 (by Ivan Rerberg, 1869–1932, and V. K. Oltarzhevsky), the Alexander III (today's Pushkin) Museum of 1912 (by Roman Kleyn, 1858–1924), the commercial building of the Treugol'nik Association of 1916 (by M. S. Lyalevich), as well as to apartment buildings and private houses. The most ardent and influential promoter of neo-classicism was Ivan Zholtovsky (1867–1959), who after the Revolution was appointed head of the architectural section of the Department of Visual Arts (IZO) of the Ministry of Enlightenment as well as of the architectural office of the Mossovet. He was the planner of the Russian Agricultural Exhibition in Moscow of 1923 and designed many of the exhibition pavilions, though the most innovative and best-known pavilion of this exhibition was the Makhorka pavilion by Konstantin Mel'nikov (1890–1974).   *M.B.*

Art Nouveau and the neo-Russian style

Two other styles were more important to Moscow's architectural scene at the beginning of the 20th century than neo-classicism. One was imported from France and accepted in Russia with its French name, the *style moderne* (or Art Nouveau, as it is known in English-speaking countries). The other was the outcome of a renewed interest in the Russian national tradition and medieval heritage, known as the neo-Russian style. While churches often followed historical precedents with utmost fidelity, as, for example, the Church of the Intercession of the Virgin for the Convent of Martha and Mary (1908–12), by Aleksey Shchusev (1873–1949), the neo-Russian forms were also adapted in the 20th century to contemporary uses with unusual freedom. The most outstanding examples are Shchusev's Kazan' railway station (1913–26) and the Yaroslavl' railway station (1902–4) by Fedor Shekhtel' (1859–1926). Shchusev, in fact, is best known for his Lenin Mausoleum (1924–30), the Ministry of Agriculture (Narkomzem) building, 1928–33, where he reverted to contemporary architectural forms, and the hotels Moskva (1930–5) and Borodino (1947) in the official Socialist Realism* style. Shekhtel' was one of Moscow's leading exponents of a clearly international Art Nouveau, as demonstrated by his Ryabushinsky house (1900–2, now the Maksim Gor'ky Memorial Museum) and the Derozhinsky house (1901). Art Nouveau was also applied in a more austere form for commercial buildings, as, for example, in the Utro Rossii printing-house (1907).   *M.B.*

Top: the exterior of Kazan' railway station, Moscow. Above: the Ryabushinsky house, Moscow, by Fedor Shekhtel'

Architecture and the avant-garde

The years of the First World War, the Revolution and the civil war brought architectural activities to a virtual standstill and gave architects the time for conscious re-examination of their professional roles, ideological commitments, social obligations and environmental contributions. Immediately after the Revolution, avant-garde circles consisting of architects, painters and sculptors began to search for ways to achieve the eternal ideal of fusing art with life. They envisaged a world where all man-made objects contributed to a continuous harmony of experiences and where life was nothing less than a total work of art. The first step toward the creation of such a world was the eradication of the differences between architecture, the arts, the crafts and the design of utilitarian objects.

This attitude was promptly adopted by artists such as Kazimir Malevich* (1878–1935) with his '*arkhitektony*', Vladimir Tatlin* (1885–1953) with his constructions and the Monument to the Third International (Comintern), the brothers Naum Gabo (1890–1978) and Anton Pevsner (1886–1962) with their constructions, and by architects such as the Vesnin brothers (A. A. Vesnin, 1883–1959 and V. A. Vesnin, 1882–1950) with their stage designs, L. M. Lisitsky (pseud. El' Lissitzky)* (1890–1941) with his '*Prouns*' ('projects for the assertion of the new') and Ladovsky and Krinsky with their experimental projects for a communal house. In May, 1919, Nikolay Ladovsky (1881–1941), Vladimir Krinsky (1890–1971) and the sculptor Boris Korolev (1884–1963) initiated the so-called Commission for Sculpture-Architecture Synthesis (*Sinskul'ptarkh*). While at the beginning the group was dominated by architects, by the end of 1919 this circle was joined by painters such as Aleksandr Rodchenko* (1891–1956) and Aleksandr Shevchenko* (1882–1968) and renamed Zhivskul'ptarkh (Painting-Sculpture-Architecture Synthesis). The group provided the initial membership to the Institute of Artistic Culture (INKhUK) when it was founded in May 1920 as well as the leading faculty of the Higher State Art-Technical Studios (Vkhutemas) when they were organized that summer. INKhUK and Vkhutemas became the common forum for both artists' and architects' research and exchange of ideas. *M.B.*

Constructivist architects

Although architecture was hailed as the leader of the arts and the culmination of the Constructivists' search, theoretical differences quickly divided architects into factions. One group, led by Ladovsky,* with El' Lissitzky,* Vladimir Krinsky* and Nikolay Dokuchaev (1891–1944), formed Asnova (the Association of New Architects) in 1923. The second group, with Moisey Ginzburg (1892–1946), the Vesnin brothers* and Andrey Burov (1900–57) among its leaders, formed OSA (the Society of Contemporary Architects) in 1925. Asnova's members devoted most of their energy to developing a rational, scientific method for the education and development of artistic creativity that was pertinent to all art forms and to any artistic endeavour (hence their name–the 'rationalists'). Since there were few possibilities of actual construction owing to the economic crisis, most of the new architectural ideas were expressed only in drawings and competition projects.

However, Lenin's New Economic Policy (NEP)* began to present some opportunities for building. Ladovsky, deeply interested in the

spatial perception of the pedestrian, had few executed projects (the pavilion of the Lermontov underground railway station in Moscow of 1935 is one example). He expanded his research in 1928 to include urban design and new town planning and in the same year founded ARU (the Union of Architects-Urbanists). Konstantin Mel'nikov* is the best-known member of Asnova probably because he was least involved in the theoretical and educational activities of the group, devoting his time during the 1920s and 1930s to competitions and to design for a wide variety of buildings. He gained international recognition with his Soviet Pavilion at the Paris International Exhibition of Decorative Arts (1924–5) and fame at home with five workers' clubs (Rusakov, Kauchuk and Frunze of 1927, all in Moscow; Pravda of 1928 in Duleva; Burevestnik of 1929 in Moscow), all of which are still functioning). Mel'nikov's own house on Krivoarbatsky Pereulok in Moscow (1927–9) is one of the most unusual and exciting examples of contemporary architecture in Moscow.

Konstantin Mel'nikov's highly original house in Moscow

The Rusakov Club, Moscow, by Konstantin Mel'nikov

Top: the Constructivist style of Panteleymon Golosov– *Pravda* building. Above: the Zuev Club by Il'ya Golosov

For the most part, OSA united practising architects, although Ginzburg was as much a theoretician and educator as practitioner. His theoretical works were published in the Society's own magazine *Modern Architecture* (*Sovremennaya arkhitektura*, SA), as well as in several books (such as *Ritm v arkhitekture* (*Rhythm in Architecture*), 1923). His deep concern with multi-family housing is demonstrated by his Sovnarkom (Council of People's Commissars) housing complex on Novinsky boulevard in Moscow (1928–30); his contributions to public buildings could be seen as far as Kazakhstan (namely, in the Alma-Ata Party headquarters of 1927–31); and his ability to design and coordinate large complexes was demonstrated in a sanatorium complex for the Ministry of Heavy Industry in Kislovodsk (1933–7).

The Vesnin brothers have been called leaders of Russian Constructivist architecture. They established a joint practice in Moscow in 1911 and, apart from private residences, designed three chemical factories and two industrial plants with workers' settlements before 1917. The best example of their work before the Revolution is the post office on Myasnitsky Street of the 1910s. Their project for the Palace of Labour competition, the first national architectural competition after the Revolution, received only third prize but was widely publicized as marking the beginning of modern architecture in the Soviet Union. During the 1920s the Vesnin brothers won many competitions and built numerous structures, all demonstrating the translation of Constructivist theory into actual forms and materials. Still standing in Moscow, for example, are their Palace of Culture at the Likhachev Automobile Works (1930–7) in the former grounds of the Simonov Monastery, and the House of Cinema Actors (1931–4), originally built for the Society of Political Prisoners. The architectural scene of the 1920s would be incom-

plete, however, without mention of the Golosov brothers (Panteleymon, 1882–1945; and Il'ya, 1883–1945) both active members of OSA and accomplished architects—as demonstrated by Panteleymon's *Pravda* newspaper building (1929–34) and Il'ya's Zuev Club (1925–9). Grigory Barkhin's (1880–1969) *Izvestiya* newspaper building (1925–7), likewise in Moscow, is also an important Constructivist achievement.   *M.B.*

State intervention in architecture

All experiments ceased by the end of 1932 due to three crucial governmental actions. First, in that year all architectural organizations were abolished and architects were forced into a single Union of

Soviet Architects. Private practice was banned and architects could work only in governmental planning and design studios organized in 1933. Secondly, the state demonstrated its desired direction for architectural development through its choice of the winning project in the competition for the Palace of the Soviets (1931–3). Finally, a controlling organization – Arplan – was established in 1933 to review and approve every project before its construction began. The aesthetic canon of the state was thus easily enforced and the results were clearly reflected in Soviet buildings of the subsequent decades. *M.B.*

Architecture since the 1930s

Soviet architecture and town-planning of the 50 years since 1930 can be seen as the interaction of two areas of concern, which were themselves shifting and evolving over the period in relation to wider political and economic circumstances. One concern has been quantitative, the other qualitative.

The First Five-year Plan★ was the only one until the Khrushchev★ period to promise a housing construction programme commensurate with the acute housing★ need. But its fate was to typify the constant vulnerability of the whole Soviet building★ effort, and of civic (as opposed to industrial or military) construction within it, to pressures of the national and international situation.

The main qualitative, or stylistic, concern over the period has been the achievement of an ideologically correct balance between 'national' and 'international'. Since the inauguration of 'Socialism in One Country' in the mid-1920s, architecture and town-planning,★ like other fields, have felt varying degrees of 'anti-cosmopolitan' pressure. It was greatest in the late 1920s and early 1930s, and in the cold war★ years after the Second World War. Within the constant over-all determination to create an architecture and a settlement★ structure reflecting the 'national' characteristics of the Soviet Union, there has likewise waxed and waned a concern to reflect republican nationhood in both its aesthetic and social dimensions. There has also been an attempt to reflect those regional differences conditional upon climate and geology which more mechanically determine both spatial organization and constructional methods in the built environment. All these dimensions of nationalism★ and regionalism remain live themes in Soviet professional and public debate. Their convergence with many concerns of the so-called post-Modernism now rampant in the West will perhaps increase Western sympathy towards stylistic shifts in Soviet architecture and town-planning which have historically been regarded here as incomprehensible abnegations of 'modernity'.

The illustrations summarize stylistic trends in Soviet architecture

during the 50-year period since 1930. As the turning-point in formulation of a Soviet socialist approach, the architectural equivalent of the Urbanist-Disurbanist planning debate was the Palace of Soviets competition of 1931–3. This enormous symbolic building for central Moscow represented a testbed of the adequacy of 'modernist' modes of composition and stylistic treatment to the propagandist role of public building, in the conditions of mass aesthetic taste of that time. Official competition commentaries spoke of the need for achieving 'a critical assimilation of the architectural heritage'; for 'utilizing the best of both modern and historical architecture, combining them with the highest technical achievements of today to create a distinctive architecture of the socialist age'. This general formulation was canonized as 'socialist realism'★ by the First Congress of Soviet Architects in 1937. Some of its most mature achievements were to be erected in the post-war period, when the prevailing 'anti-cosmopolitanism' produced greater incorporation of

Central tower of the Hotel Leningrad (1949–53), Moscow, by L. M. Polyakov (1906–65) and A. B. Boretsky

Government House (1955), Yerevan, Armenia, by S. A. Safarayan (1902–69)

republican and regional decorative themes than had been usual in the 1930s. The Hotel Leningrad in Moscow is an example. Having attracted a Stalin Prize for Architecture in 1948, this building was criticized by Khrushchev in his 1954 speech, which took an anti-decorative stance as part of a redirection of Soviet architecture on to a line recognized in the West as 'modern'. His emphasis on technical preconditions for quantity production gave rise to a broader anti-aestheticism which is still blamed by architects for a lowering of their status in relation to other professions. This, in turn, has had a serious impact on recruitment.

Among factors now helping to revive concern for regional and local expression in architecture is the increasing attention to community buildings in recent construction Plans. Such buildings are natural vehicles for experimentation in the richer handling of local micro-climatic problems; for reviving regionally characteristic decorative and spatial languages and palettes of colour and light; in short, for continuing the synthesis of the new with the 'popular' (narodnyy), which is seen as the basis of socialist 'assimilation' in these fields of public creative work. A highly regarded republican example of this trend is the Karl Marx Public Library in Ashkhabad by Abdulla Akhmedov, built in the middle 1970s.   C.C.

Town-planning since the 1930s

The massive nationwide new-towns building* programme of the First Five-year Plan* provoked a far-reaching discussion of principles: the so-called Urbanist-Disurbanist debate. This con-cerned the proper nature of that 'new settlement of mankind' which Marx,* Engels and Lenin* had predicted would emerge when socialist economic relationships were combined with transmissible energy and mass-production technologies; it brought together two well-known economists (Yu. Larin, real name M. Z. Luré, 1882–1932, and L. M. Sabsovich) on the former side, and the Constructivist* architects (led by Moisey Ginzburg* and sociologist M. A. Okhitovich) on the latter, all united against the uncontrolled growth of urban development threatening the USSR in the later 1920s, which was seen as inherently capitalist. Intimately involved with issues of collectivization* in agriculture and urban daily life, this debate was a major turning-point in identifying the range of factors determining form in this field, and in deciding the proper shape of Soviet settlement patterns during the era of 'transition to socialism'.

Various Communist Party* decisions (1930–2) canonized grad-ualism in collectivization of the urban way of life (byt). Preference was given to cluster patterns of limited-sized industrial and agricultural settlements and to heavy masonry (kapital'nye) construction systems rather than to the rapid erection of temporary stock. Principles governing the internal planning of Soviet towns derived from these decisions. The smallest planning unit, the kvartal, was seen as that unit within which the socialist state (or local government) would provide those daily-use services (public catering, laundry and infant care) which the individual bourgeois housewife hitherto performed within her private 'domestic economy'. The exact sizes of kvartaly varied with conditions. They were grouped into housing rayony, or districts, offering the next level of educational, recreational and retail facilities. Groups of these comprised urban rayony, certain of whose more specialized facilities might serve the town as a whole.

This simple hierarchical structure was premised upon such pervading features of the Soviet Union as the non-existence of a normal market in goods, services or land. It could also be accommodated within the Party's hierarchical agitational* and supervisory structure. The very uniformity of rayon structure and building type over the whole urban area was itself seen as a direct reflection of politics. It was the 'elimination of the difference between centre and periphery'–a division very marked in Russia's pre-revolutionary cities. Residential and productive zones would ideally be located to minimize both journeys to work and industrial pollution. With climatic and productive conditions varying greatly across the continent there were many 'model' new towns. Perhaps the most complicated problem facing town-planners in this period, however, was the 'socialist reconstruction' of existing towns and cities on to a similar pattern. Surgery was also applied to the dense inherited urban fabric so as to provide for public transport* arteries, green space, sunlight and fresher air; for basic public utilities such as running water, sewerage, gas, electricity (generally for the first time), and for rationalizing locations of certain important factories in relation to industrial needs. Moscow's 1935 Plan was the model for this process. Prepared under the direction of the pioneer of pre-revolutionary garden cities, Vladimir Semenov (1874–1960), it was among the world's first integrated city plans on this scale.

Regional planning was regarded as particularly demonstrating the benefits of socialism over capitalism. Here too the 1930s saw the need for theory and practice to develop virtually from first principles, both in over-all resource planning and in tailoring the agreed cluster and satellite forms of settlement* planning to local conditions. For practical reasons as much as ideological ones, the various planning and architectural design networks were by then rather more centralized than during the 1920s. In the extreme shortage of expertise, any competent professional–save those regarded as irredeemably determined to pursue 'abstract scheming' (*prozhekter-stvo*)–was usefully employed within them.

Stringent pressures of the 1930s naturally distorted both intended allocations and intended planning patterns. The most acute setback, however, was that caused by German destruction in the Second World War,* given by Soviet figures as 1700 towns and cities and 70000 urban settlements and villages 'completely or almost completely destroyed' (many of course newly built in the 1930s), and a total loss of six million buildings that left 25 million people homeless. One dimension of the post-war 'anti-cosmopolitanism' in architecture and planning was thus a passionate nationalism that, understandably, existed within the profession itself before it was reinforced by the wider campaigns. Meticulous reconstruction of architectural monuments was one expression of this; another was greatly increased emphasis upon that preservation of historic urban

plan-forms which had been a central, and at the time controversial, tenet of the 1935 Moscow Plan.

The need to re-establish complete urban infrastructures sucked resources from residential construction once more, and in the early 1950s the living space* per head in the urban housing* stock was again down around 4 sq m, below half the agreed 'sanitary minimum' of 9 sq m. First steps towards commensurate action were launched by Khrushchev's* speech to the All-Union Conference of Builders, Architects and Workers of 7 December 1954 'On the widespread introduction of industrial methods, improvement of quality and lowering of costs in construction'. By 1959 new building* techniques had been sufficiently developed for the Seven-year Plan to promise a doubling of the total Soviet urban housing stock. About 85 per cent of the promised 15 million new apartments were constructed, and they form much of the inner area of Soviet cities.

The mixing of two-storied facilities with higher residential buildings and the generally open, green site-planning are typical of all Soviet housing. Construction in the 1930s was lower, limited to four or five storeys by lack of lifts/elevators but was generally of this parallel-block form. Districts built in the post-war Stalin years were commonly of more enclosed form, around extensive park-like courtyards. In the first large-panel construction systems of the later 1960s and early 1970s, craning constraints produced rather open layouts and simple building geometry, but technical developments are now permitting more varied composition and the use of more interesting sites. Greater diversity of elevational treatment and apartment type is also becoming possible through dimensional and technical integration of the former multiplicity of 'closed' construc-

Institutes and housing for scientists in the new Siberian town of Akademgorodok

tional systems into a 'unified catalogue' for each region. In the virgin outskirts of cities such as Moscow, Leningrad, Tbilisi and the Siberian centres, the late-1970s house-building programme averaged one finished apartment per minute, and much of this housing is around 15 storeys, often of linear curving 'wall' form rather than in isolated tower blocks. When transport and services are adequate, these areas are generally much appreciated for their quietness, their immediate access to the countryside, and the modern living standards which their apartments provide.

Urban developments in the extreme north have long been the subject of special studies and employ climatically suitable building types. The appropriateness of the temperate-zone housing models to southern, Central Asian climates (and life-styles) is currently under research and debate, as are all matters of improving service and facilities distribution. The future model town structure embodied in the Moscow Plan of 1971 focuses upon relief of centre-periphery travel by creation of secondary retail and civic centres between these outer housing areas.   *C.C.*

Part of a holiday complex at Voronovo, completed 1977 (the design uses many elements from the Moscow region's 'unified catalogue' of house-building components)

The Academy of Arts and its influence

The 18th century was a time of dramatic changes in all walks of Russian life. The policy of rapid Westernization, initiated by Peter the Great,★ had an immediate and destructive effect on the patriarchal traditions of Russian culture. However, a direct result of this development was the formation of an important school of secular Russian painting that gained in momentum after the middle of the 18th century, a school that differed radically from the long tradition of icon-painting.★ The centre of this new movement came to be the Imperial Academy of Arts founded in 1757, and its influence on Russian art was considerable. Russia's first professional easel painters, such as Vladimir Borovikovsky (1757–1825), Dmitry Levitsky (1735–1822) and Fedor Rokotov (c.1736–1808), were closely associated with the Academy.

The principal style favoured by the Academy during the last decades of the 18th century and during the 19th was a Western, classical one supported and propagated by its teaching-staff who were mainly French, German and Italian. Levitsky's *Portrait of E. I. Nelidova* (1773) embodies the aesthetic principles of the early Academy: the very genre of the portrait, the virtuoso technique, the idealization of subject, the emphasis on pose and dress, the neglect of background and landscape – such elements are also identifiable with the Western European mainstream of the 18th century and bring to mind the portraits of Gainsborough and Reynolds.

Borovikovsky,
M.I. Lopukhina,
1797

During the 1800s and 1810s the influence of the classical canon of beauty was maintained at the Academy, affecting the important Russian painters of the time such as Orest Kiprensky (1782–1836), Karl Bryullov (1799–1852) and Aleksandr Ivanov (1806–58). Moreover, these artists were among the many Russian intellectuals who lived in Italy for short or long periods between 1810 and 1840 and who moved in the same circles as Gros, Ingres and the Nazarenes (a group of German artists living in Rome in the early 19th century).

Levitsky, *Portrait of E. I. Nelidova*

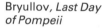

Bryullov, *Last Day of Pompeii*

Although it would be misleading to call Kiprensky, firmly rooted in the classical tradition, a Romantic, he was acquainted with the philosophies of Novalis, Schelling and Schlegel as well as with German and French Romantic painters. For example, in his portraits Kiprensky concentrated on the individual psychology, on the spontaneous and natural gesture of the sitter as is demonstrated by his famous *Portrait of the Poet Aleksandr Pushkin* of 1827. Kiprensky's vigorous portraits reflect his endeavour to overcome the limitations of the strict academic system by choosing a freer, more energetic style.

Kiprensky always complained that material circumstances forced him to paint portraits and that his patrons denied him the opportunity to use historical subjects. No doubt, he envied the fate of Russia's most successful son of the Academy – Bryullov. Bryullov's painting also relied on the classical ideals of the Academy, and the artist attained prestige at home and abroad as an excellent portrait painter, to which works such as the *Portrait of Princess Samoylova Leaving the Ball* (1838–42) testify. But unlike Kiprensky, Bryullov worked in various genres and media, including historical and mythological painting, and his celebrated *Last Day of Pompeii* (1830–3) is one of the grand flourishes of the 19th century. Together with other rhapsodical compositions of that time, *Last Day of Pompeii* owes much to Raphael (cf. *The Fire in the Borgo*) and Poussin (cf. *The Plague of Ashdod*). Bryullov's masterpiece interprets a popular theme, repeating Giovanni Pacini's opera of the same name and foreshadowing Bulwer Lytton's novel *The Last Days of Pompeii* of 1834. Some observers, such as Alexander Herzen (1812–70), saw a prophetic meaning in the painting, identifying the eruption and imminent destruction of the noble Pompeians with the contemporary predicament of aristocratic Russia, threatened also, so it was maintained, by an inevitable cataclysm. In this respect, it is relevant to recall that Bryullov's

Kiprensky, *Portrait of the Poet Aleksandr Pushkin*

picture was painted in the same decade that Gogol'* began his epic novel *Dead Souls*, the description of a Russia tired and sick at heart.

The pathos and melodrama of *Last Day of Pompeii* link it with the concurrent achievements of Western European artists such as Delacroix, Delaroche and Géricault. The work is very different from the painting of Bryullov's fellow-countryman and contemporary, Ivanov. This fanatical and fervent artist considered art to be the expression of a profound religious and moral experience, and he attempted to communicate this idea in his major work *The Appearance of Christ to the People* (1837–57). As in the case of Bryullov's canvas, the prototypes of *The Appearance of Christ to the People*, a huge painting measuring 540 × 750 cm, were entirely Western, ranging from Raphael's *Transfiguration* to the paintings of the Nazarenes. Still, the intent of Ivanov's picture was of particular relevance to Russia, for the artist regarded Moscow as the Third Rome and the Russian people as the future witness of the Second Coming. It is not surprising, therefore, that Ivanov should have included the deeply religious and patriotic Gogol' as well as a self-portrait among the observers of Christ's appearance. Of course, this interpretaton does not alter the fact that *The Appearance of Christ to the People* depends on academic or at least Western artistic principles. On the other hand, Ivanov's water-colours of scenes from the Bible from the 1840s and 1850s depart radically from traditional concepts. The musical, prismatic quality of these renditions distinguishes them from the heavy narrative style of most 19th-century historical painting, and these curiously refractive images have been compared to the work of William Blake and to the Symbolist* visions of Mikhail Vrubel' (1856–1910).   *J.E.B.*

The Russian school of painting

Ivanov* marked the culmination of the Western academic style in Russian art. Beginning in the 1850s Russian art became increasingly 'Russian', favouring scenes from everyday Russian life instead of aristocratic portraits and mythological episodes. Pavel Fedotov (1815–52) and the Realists* of the 1860s–80s developed this trend, producing their visual commentaries on the 'accursed questions' of Russian contemporaneity. Fedotov, for example, used Hogarth-like satires of Russian mores in order to focus critical attention on topical issues such as the inequality of women* (*The Major's Betrothal*, 1848) and the impoverishment of the aristocracy (*The Unexpected Guest*, 1849–50). However, it is important to remember that even before Fedotov and parallel to the achievements of Kiprensky, Bryullov and Ivanov, a number of artists were supporting an indigenous, more primitive style of painting based on commonplace themes from Russian life. In particular, there were Vasily Tropinin (1776–1857), a liberated serf* who brought a homeliness and simplicity to his portraits and genre scenes, and, above all, Aleksey Venetsianov (1780–1847).

In their establishment of an artistic code alternative to the Western academic tradition, Tropinin, Venetsianov and their pupils maintained the patriotic mood of the 1812 epoch when caricaturists such as Ivan Terebenev (1780–1815) ridiculed Gallic civilization and glorified the qualities of the ordinary Russian people. While appreciating some elements of the academic system, Venetsianov also turned to the theme of Mother Russia, finding artistic inspiration in the ingenuous activities of the Russian peasant. His paintings such as *Spring Ploughing* (1830s) influenced a whole generation of

Ivanov, *The Appearance of Christ to the People*

Fedotov, *The Major's Betrothal*

provincial painters in Russia, not least Grigory Soroka (1823–64). In turn, Soroka's distinctive luminist style, exemplified by the painting *The Fishermen* (1840s), bears a curious resemblance to American rural painting of the same period (cf. George Bingham's *Boatmen on the Missouri*, 1846). In America and Russia this kind of painting heralded the emergence of a new and powerful movement: Realism.★   *J.E.B.*

The birth of Realism

Realism, the dominant trend in the second half of the 19th century, gave Russian art its modern, national idiom. What Pavel Fedotov★ had been searching for – new subject matter, an appropriate pictorial language, and ethnic identity – found full expression in the works of the Realist painters. Hardly known and not highly valued in the West, they have played as important and continuing a role in Russian culture as have the great writers Turgenev,★ Tolstoy★ and Dostoevsky.★

Although Realism passed through different phases during the more than three decades of its pre-eminence, it had one distinct, over-all characteristic: an intense commitment to Russian subjects and scenes, which was grounded on the conviction that art should serve a social function – conveying civic, moral or national values – rather than concentrate on aesthetic expression and stylistic refinement. Realism was born in the 1860s, a decade of reforms that began with the emancipation of the serfs.★ Although the long-overdue changes were instituted from above, the intellectuals were swept up with national renovation. But in the absence of a free press, painters, like writers, had to comment covertly on current political and social issues in their works. The foremost critic of the day, Nikolay Chernyshevsky (1828–89), aptly expressed the prevailing spirit of civic motivation at the outset of the movement when he wrote: 'The goals of art are to understand reality, and then to apply its findings for the use of humanity.' Because of these historical circumstances, both dedication and 'literariness' characterized Russia's first modern art style.

The Wanderers

Vasily Perov (1833–82) best exemplified the initial political motivation. His *Village Procession* (1861) is not merely a meticulous depiction of drunken priests and peasants setting out to celebrate Easter. It is more than an indictment of clerical laxity, for in the eyes of the articulate public the Orthodox Church★ was a principal mainstay of autocracy. The censor's removal of the canvas from an exhibition confirmed for the politically alert intellectuals that art was actively enlisted in agitation against the regime. Other first-

generation Realists tended to be less outspokenly political. Their small-size narrative pictures were critical exposés of such social problems as rural poverty, drunkenness,★ child labour, or women's rights.

During the 1870s Realism attained maturity. The episodic and critical commentary of the opening phase gave way to more general statements on Russian themes; the range of subjects was enlarged; and the painters' technique improved. This art – produced outside the patronage of the Imperial Academy of Arts★ and in defiance of the neo-classical standards of 'high art' it upheld – was popularized by the first professional society of independent painters. Founded in 1870, it was named the Association of Travelling Art Exhibitions and was headed by Ivan Kramskoy (1837–87), who had organized a secession of graduating students from the Imperial Academy in 1863. For the next 20 years the Association counted the most talented and innovative painters among its members, and in annual exhibitions introduced their work in the two capitals, St Petersburg and Moscow, and in the major provincial towns. So successful was this educational and cultural mission that Realism and *Peredvizhnichestvo* ('the art of the travelling exhibitions') became synonymous.

The fortunes of contemporary art were also buoyed by the appearance of middle-class patrons. Foremost among them was the textile manufacturer, P. M. Tret'yakov (1832–98), who bought the best works at each Travelling Exhibition and in 1892 bequeathed to the city of Moscow an art gallery with his collection of some 800 works of the new national school.

Genres favoured by the Realists

Landscape was among the most popular themes introduced by the Peredvizhniki, or 'Wanderers', as members of the Association were called. The unassuming beauty of the Russian countryside had been celebrated in literature since Pushkin,★ but it was the Realists who undertook to picture their native land with lyrical insight. Among the prominent landscape painters were Aleksey Savrasov (1832–97), Ivan Shishkin (1832–98), Fedor Vasil'ev (1850–73), Arkhip Kuindzhi (1842–1910), and Vasily Polenov (1844–1927). Their manner varied greatly, from Shishkin excelling in an almost photographic rendition of forest and trees to Kuindzhi experimenting with the bold use of unusual colour schemes in depicting the Ukrainian countryside.

The Wanderers also created a national portrait gallery. These likenesses are so forceful that to this day they are *the* mental images Russians have of their great writers, composers and scholars. The explanation, in part, is that the portraitist sought to create an inspiring image, to convey his subject's commitment and resolve. Thus, Perov represented Dostoevsky as a writer racked by the problems of the times, and Kramskoy showed the civic-minded poet N. A. Nekrasov (1821–77) composing even on his death-bed.

Top: Kuindzhi, *The Birch Grove*, 1897. Above: Surikov, *Boyarina Morozova*. Right: Repin, *They Did Not Expect Him*

Historical paintings were, at first, oblique commentary on current issues. Nikolay Ge's canvas of Peter the Great* confronting his sullenly resistant son (1871) spoke to viewers of the diminishing tempo of the reform movement; the picture (1885) of Ivan the Terrible* cradling the blood-stained body of the son he had just struck with mortal blows (Il'ya Repin, 1844–1930) was a reminder that all too often in Russia brute force alone decided matters of state or an individual fate. Similarly, the pictures of Vasily Vereshchagin (1842–1904) denounced war at a time when Russia was conquering Turkestan. But a change occurred in the 1880s with the surge of nationalism, and Russian history found a panegyric chronicler in Vasily Surikov (1848–1916). He started by extolling in rich and colourful detail the defenders of old Russian traditions who opposed Peter the Great's Westernization programme (*The Morning of the Strel'tsy Execution*, 1881; *Boyarinya Morozova*, 1887), and went on to glorify Russian military exploits (*Yermak's Conquest of Siberia*, 1895; *Suvorov Crossing the Alps*, 1899).

Repin was the most talented and versatile painter of the Russian Realist school. One of his themes was the peasantry, and the large-scale *Boat Haulers* (1873) won him immediate acclaim with its sympathetic commentary on the lot of the people and its bold diagonal composition and striking colour. The individual portraiture in that multi-figure canvas typified one treatment of the peasant theme: giving the lowly the same respectful attention hitherto reserved for those much higher in the social scale; and Perov, Repin and Kramskoy produced a varied gallery of peasant types. Others, like Vasily Maksimov (1844–1911), objectively documented peasant customs or, like Sergey Ivanov (1864–1910), concentrated on the peasants' squalor and misery.

The revolutionary movement figured prominently in the work of the Realists. It is not that the painters openly supported the radicals; rather, the theme reflects the dilemma which the selflessness and persistence of the movement posed to men of principle. Repin painted the most memorable and artistically valuable canvases on the subject: *Under Conveyance* (1876); *The Propagandist's Arrest* (1878–92); *Refusal of Confession* (1879–85); and *They Did Not Expect Him* (1883–8), in which a returning prisoner facing his family suggests the theme of sacrifice and suffering in the symbolic references to Golgotha. Portraits of idealized revolutionary types were produced by Nikolay Yaroshenko (1846–98).

In these several themes the Realists were relating much of the story of Russia during the decades of their ascendancy. Other social genres documented the changes brought on by industrialization:* Konstantin Savitsky (1844–1905) depicted peasants working on the railroad; Nikolay Kasatkin (1859–1930) and Abram Arkhipov (1862–1930) chronicle the emergence of the proletariat; while Vladimir Makovsky (1846–1920) concentrated on the tribulations of the urban poor and the mores of the upper classes. *E.K.V.*

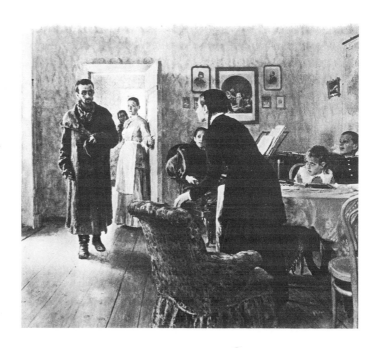

The move towards decorativism

The vigour of the Realist movement declined towards the end of the 1880s as artists achieved popular and personal success. The former positivist and utilitarian ethos began to lose its claim on younger artists, and reaction set in. The new generation was frankly interested in art *per se*, and more and more sought their training in the West. The Vasnetsov brothers, Viktor (1848–1926) and Apollonary (1856–1938), introduced fancy and the purely decorative in their paintings of mythical knights and medieval Moscow; Mikhail Nesterov (1862–1942) tried to capture the unique spirituality of the Russian Orthodox* religion; Isaak Levitan (1861–1900) turned to painting landscape outdoors; Valentin Serov (1865–1911) and Konstantin Korovin (1861–1939) made use of the colour discoveries of the Impressionists; while Vrubel'* experimented with Symbolist* decorative forms.

By the 1890s Russian Realism, having dominated the scene much longer than was the case elsewhere in Europe, was on the wane and the stage was ready for a new revolution in painting.   *E.K.V.*

Serov, *Ol'ga Orlova*, 1911

Modernism

Between the last decade of the 19th century and the October Revolution the arts in Russia manifested one of the foremost expositions of Modernism in the Western world. In addition to a generation of brilliant modern writers, such artists as Vrubel',* Vasily Kandinsky (1866–1944), Kazimir Malevich* (1878–1935) and Vladimir Tatlin* (1885–1953) achieved artistic maturity during this time. In addition, these were crucial years of growth and learning for a 'second generation' of the avant-garde, El' Lissitzky (L. M. Lisitsky, 1890–1941), Aleksandr Rodchenko (1891–1956) and the many Constructivists* of the 1920s. The multiplicity of centres available in Russia for artistic training, renewed and vigorous contact with Western European centres of art and the growth of a wide audience among the middle class, all contributed to the vitality of modern art. A time of change, germination and blossoming, this period of about 30 years has come to be known as the Silver Age of Russian culture.   *C.D.*

The World of Art association

In the late 1880s and early 1890s a group of students—the future World of Art association—including Konstantin Somov (1869–1939), Leon Bakst (1866–1924), Alexandre Benois (1870–1960) and Sergey Diaghilev (1872–1929) set themselves to study a wide range of topics, particulary 18th- and early 19th-century Russian art and 18th-century and contemporary French culture. Under the organizational

Benois, *Parade under Paul I,* 1907

leadership of Diaghilev (later well known in the West for his productions of Russian opera★ and ballet★) the World of Art in the late 1890s brought to the Russian public exhibitions of Scandinavian and European art and, through the lavish *World of Art (Mir iskusstva)* journal, published from 1898 to 1904, gave wide distribution to the art and ideas of such Western painters as Degas, Monet and Whistler, as well as to the group's own artistic endeavours. The World of Art turned attention away from the large historical and social canvases of the Academy★ and the Wanderers★ to a smaller, more intimate genre, for the most part works done on paper in water-colour, gouache, ink and similar 'secondary' media. The artists of the World of Art emphasized aesthetic quality and images of the 'beautiful' in its many connotations. Instead of the commonplace everyday subjects of their predecessors, they painted retrospective landscapes – Benois' *Feeding the Fish* (1897) and *The Pyramid at Versailles* (1906) – and morbid and erotic scenes – Somov's *Harlequin and Death* (1907). Bakst and Somov drew portraits of themselves and their friends in a sensitive precise late-academic style – Bakst's *Portrait of Andrey Bely* (1906) – and Benois and Bakst produced many stage and costume designs.   *C.D.*

Somov, *Harlequin and Death*

The Symbolists

The most significant theoretical and philosophical ideas for the development of modern styles in art derived from the Symbolist movement. The belief in a higher realm of existence, of which this world is only a reflection, and in the importance of art to the creation of a higher psychological and aesthetic consciousness in society, was shared by many artists at the turn of the century. In trying to express simultaneously both this world and another, they developed a variety of innovations in painting style. Favourite Symbolist motifs included women idealized as incarnations of grace and eternity, divine and demonic subjects, and archetypal events. Above all, Symbolist artists made it difficult for the viewer clearly to see and understand what was depicted. By making his work 'difficult' the artist hoped to induce in the viewer a subjective or intuitive perception of both worlds.

Although not officially associated with any Symbolist group, Mikhail Vrubel'★ painted in a uniquely expressive style which appealed to artists of Symbolist and other artistic persuasions. His famous *Demon Seated* (1890) and *Demon Cast Down* (1902), two of more than a dozen of Vrubel''s depictions of the protagonist of Lermontov's★ poem *Demon* (1839), were admired by World of Art artists for their precise, although complex, linearity and the romantic literary subject matter; by the Blue Rose Symbolists for their dominant blue and lavender colours – especially 'mystical' and 'ethereal' according to Symbolist tenets – and for the portrayal of an unearthly being; and, later, by avant-garde groups, who considered his work a direct stylistic predecessor of Cubism. A major artist of the modern era who worked in many media, Vrubel''s talent went unrewarded in his lifetime.

Viktor Borisov-Musatov (1870–1905), a Symbolist painter of women in landscapes of indeterminate time and place – *At the Pool* (1902), *Phantoms* (1903), *Slumber Divine* (1904–5) – was towards the end of his life associated with the outstanding group of Moscow

Vrubel', *Demon Seated*

Kuznetsov, *Blue Fountain*

literary Symbolists. He was also, for a time, the teacher of Pavel Kuznetsov (1878–1968) who from 1904 to 1907 followed an expressly Symbolist programme. During this time Kuznetsov produced beautiful but melancholy blue and grey paintings of scarcely discernible fountains and mysterious foetal creatures – *Blue Fountain* (1905), *Birth* (1906–7). In 1907 Kuznetsov organized the major Blue Rose exhibition, devoted almost entirely to Symbolist work.

Kuznetsov and other Symbolist painters were allied with the progressive *Golden Fleece* (*Zolotoe runo*) journal (1906–10) which sponsored Symbolist, post-Impressionist and Fauvist ideas and artists, both Russian and Western European. In its 'Salon' exhibitions of 1908 and 1909 the *Golden Fleece* presented the most advanced art of the time, including Gauguin, Matisse and Van Gogh, to the Russian public.

Vasily Kandinsky,★ who earlier had shared the contemporary Russian interest in folk★ art and Symbolist painting, from about 1909 displayed in his work the dominant Symbolist concern for the depiction of higher, archetypal events. Kandinsky, like other Russian Symbolists, made his pictures 'difficult', relying on colour and barely discernible Biblical subjects to affect the viewer subliminally – *Small Pleasures* (1913).   *C.D.*

The avant-garde

In 1910 Mikhail Larionov (1881–1964) and others organized an exhibition society called the Knave of Diamonds. The name was chosen for its lack of Symbolist associations and in opposition to the 'pretty' names – Blue Rose, World of Art★ – of earlier societies. The work of the Knave of Diamonds artists also contrasted sharply with that of its predecessors. Like the Symbolists,★ the fledgling avant-garde used colour for its own sake rather than naturalistically, but they preferred the clear, bright colours of the French Fauves and the German Expressionists to the misty and formless blues of the Blue Rose Symbolists. Among the artists exhibited at the first Knave of Diamonds exhibition (December 1910) were Aristarkh Lentulov (1878–1943), Aleksandra A. Ekster (1884–1949), Robert Fal'k (1886–1958), Petr Konchalovsky (1876–1956), Il'ya Mashkov (1884–1944), David Burlyuk (1882–1967), Kazimir Malevich,★ Vasily Kandinsky,★ Natal'ya Goncharova (1881–1962) and Mikhail Larionov. Current French and German work was also shown. Typical of the Knave of Diamonds interests at this time were bright colours, strong patterning and simplified forms, such as may be seen in Goncharova's *Washing Linen* (1910).

Larionov, Goncharova, Malevich and others soon left the Knave of Diamonds to organize their own exhibition in 1912, 'The Donkey's Tail'. The group advocated more primitive forms, even brighter colour and peasant subjects to make their work strong and vital. Malevich, for example, exhibited at The Donkey's Tail his *On the Boulevard* (1910) and *Man With a Sack* (1911), which show large bright figures with oversized, childishly drawn hands and feet. Their 'Target' exhibition (March 1913) was the first to show Larionov's and Goncharova's rayonnist style.

Slightly earlier than the Knave of Diamonds in Moscow, the Union of Youth was organized in St Petersburg. Initiated by Mikhail Matyushin (1861–1934) and Yelena Guro (1877–1913), the organization exhibited many of the painters associated with Moscow groups as well as their own members. Early in 1913 a group of poets and painters which adopted the name 'Cubo-Futurists' became formally allied with the Union of Youth. Headed by David Burlyuk, it had earlier been allied with the Knave of Diamonds. The decision to change affiliations coincided with the departure of Malevich and Tatlin★ from Larionov's organization, and they, too, associated themselves with the Union of Youth. During 1913 Malevich worked closely with Burlyuk's group, especially the poet Aleksey Kruchenykh (1886–1970), and with some members of the Union of Youth, most notably the painter and composer Matyushin and Ol'ga Rozanova (1886–1918).

The Cubo-Futurists had a strong theoretical and analytical orientation derived from both French Cubism and Italian Futurism as well as native literary and philosophical sources. They fractured their subjects into abstracted planes and volumes and sometimes reduced the illusionistic sense of space, as can be seen in Rozanova's *Man in the Street* (1913). The Cubo-Futurists also were attracted to the irrational, the accidental and the absurd. Malevich's *Englishman in Moscow* (1914) shows objects apparently unrelated to each other in size and narrative meaning combined on the canvas with words and parts of words without obvious significance. Malevich, Matyushin

Malevich, *Eight Red Rectangles*

The Cubo-Futurists and Suprematists felt their art to be more faithful in its rendering of things physically real than the art of previous times. They were especially aware of history and of scientific advances in physics, psychology and physiology, and sought radically innovative styles in their art in order to express these new interpretations of the world. Thus, from the beginning of the Symbolist movement at the end of the 19th century until the Revolution in 1917, the primary motivation of many Russian artists was the depiction of some non-visible reality. After the Revolution the world was to seem much more visible and concrete. *C.D.*

Post-revolutionary organization of art

The Revolution of October 1917 exerted an immediate and transformative effect on Russian art. Artists such as Malevich* and Tatlin* who, before 1917, had occupied an uncertain position in bourgeois society, now assumed administrative and pedagogical duties. Within the Department of Visual Arts (IZO) of the Ministry of Enlightenment (NKP) headed by Lunacharsky,* many radical artists played influential roles in Soviet artistic life, propagating their innovative ideas on an unprecedented scale thanks to the new state exhibitions, publications, art schools and research institutions. The ranks of the avant-garde* were filled by the return of artists from abroad such as Marc Chagall (b.1887), Naum Gabo (1890–1977), Kandinsky* and David Shterenberg (1881–1948), and IZO NKP acquired many works for metropolitan and provincial museums.

Under the auspices of IZO NKP artists prepared an ambitious programme of reconstruction. For example, new art schools known as 'Svomas' (Free State Art Studios) were opened in Moscow, Petrograd and other centres, enabling artists such as Ivan Klyun (1870–1942), Malevich, Rodchenko* and Tatlin to disseminate their ideas. Similarly, 1920 saw the foundation of the Institute of Artistic Culture (INKhUK) in Moscow, which sought to conduct researches into the psychological and physical properties of art. Kandinsky compiled an intricate programme for INKhUK, although it was rejected by his colleagues who favoured a more straightforward, more rational approach. Indeed, some artists and critics associated with INKhUK such as Boris Arvatov (1896–1940), Lyubov' Popova (1889–1924) and Rodchenko felt that studio art was incapable of further development and advocated a move to industrial design, contributing to the emergence of Constructivism* in 1921. The Petrograd affiliation of INKhUK, organized in 1922, retained a more intimate, more aesthetic stance, experimenting in form and colour theory under Malevich and Matyushin* and their students–Il'ya Chashnik (1902–29) and Boris Ender (1893–1960). *J.E.B.*

and Kruchenykh also produced an opera, *Victory Over the Sun*, which was performed in St Petersburg early in December 1913. A landmark in the history of theatrical performances, the opera features songs in Kruchenykh's language of the future set to Matyushin's quarter-tone music. Malevich's geometricized costumes and scenery, depicting partial objects and individual letters and musical notes, produced an impression of ambiguity and absurdity.

Tatlin in the second half of 1913 began to construct his assemblages of various materials, including glass, wood and metal, to form abstract three-dimensional works. These 'reliefs' were first shown publicly at 'The V Trolley' exhibition (March 1915).

The '0.10' exhibition (December 1915) was one of the most advanced of its time. There Malevich and a group of followers showed abstract Suprematist paintings for the first time. The new canvases, which depicted bright rectangles of colour against a white background–*Eight Red Rectangles* (1915)–did not suggest objects or forms abstracted from nature. Some conveyed a sense of weightlessness or flight; one consisted of a single large black square. At the same exhibition Tatlin displayed his 'corner reliefs', three-dimensional constructions suspended across the corners of a room–*Corner Relief* (1915).

Constructivism

Indicative of the sudden transference of allegiance from the studio to the street was the exhibition called '5 × 5 = 25' held in Moscow in 1921 at which five artists–Aleksandra Ekster,★ Lyubov' Popova (1889–1924), Rodchenko,★ Varvara Stepanova (1894–1958) and Aleksandr Vesnin (1883–1959)–each with five works, presented their latest and last investigations into abstract art. For example, Rodchenko's contribution included three canvases painted red, yellow and blue, a gesture that demonstrated the apparent impasse into which modern art had fallen. In 1922, therefore, the theoretician and apologist of Constructivism Aleksey Gan (1893–1942) felt justified in calling for 'Labour, technology, organization!' instead of the traditional media.

The Constructivists of the early 1920s attempted to remove the individualistic, 'bourgeois' impetus from art and to concentrate on a mechanical or scientific approach, resorting to the use of industrial materials such as aluminium and glass. The constructions of Rodchenko, especially his remarkable *Suspended Construction* of 1921, reflect this tendency, although, in fact, these works were no less idiosyncratic, and subjective than pre-revolutionary works. Even Tatlin★ moved from the pure art of his reliefs to utilitarian design, as demonstrated by his model for the 1919–20 Monument to the Third International (Comintern). Commissioned by the Soviet government, Tatlin designed a fantastic project incorporating four levels rotating at different speeds and encased within a single metal thermos. Tatlin's Monument was to have been taller than the Eiffel Tower and, while never built, signalled the advance of Soviet Constructivist architecture★ and interior design.   *J.E.B.*

Rodchenko, *Suspended Construction*

Popova's design for *The Magnanimous Cuckold*, 1922

Return to Realism*

Many young Soviet artists worked on functional projects during the 1920s, experimenting in many fields such as stage design (Aleksandr Ekster,★ Popova★), porcelain and book design (Natan Al'tman, 1889–1970; El Lissitzky★) posters and textiles (Dmitry Moor, 1883–1946; Varvara Stepanova, 1894–1958). However, many artists also continued to paint and to sculpt not necessarily in an experimental manner but rather in a more realist, more 'readable' vein. Symptomatic of this counter-movement was the establishment in 1922 of the Association of Artists of Revolutionary Russia (AKhRR) with its intention to 'depict the present day: the life of the Red Army, the workers, the peasants, the revolutionaries and the heroes of

May Day poster by Moor: the soldier bears the watchword of the 1848 Communist Manifesto 'Workers of all countries unite!' and the marchers carry Trotsky's slogan 'Hail to the world revolution!'

Deyneka, *Broad Vistas*, 1944 (below) and *The Defence of Petrograd*, 1927 (bottom)

labour'. The theoretical premise of AKhRR and the reportorial style of its key members such as Isaak Brodsky (1884–1939) and Yevgeny Katzman (1890–1976) came to serve as a departure-point for the Socialist Realist* programme in 1934 onwards. While AKhRR quickly emerged as a powerful artistic force, it did not completely overshadow the cultural arena, and alternative styles were followed at least until the early 1930s.

With the inauguration of Lenin's New Economic Policy (NEP)* in 1921, the private art market was re-established and a new bourgeois patron appeared, encouraging the development of an artistic style that was neither abstract, nor documentary, but reminiscent of Symbolism,* Expressionism and even Surrealism. This representational but still subjective movement was closely identifiable with the group known as the Society of Easel Artists (OST) led by Shterenberg,* Aleksandr Deyneka (1899–1969), Yury Pimenov (1903–78) and Aleksandr Tyshler (1898–1980). These artists painted scenes from contemporary Soviet life–factory workers, athletes, construction sites–emphasizing the expressive qualities of line and using anatomical distortion to bring the image of man closer to his mechanical, technological environment. Pictures such as Pimenov's *Give to Heavy Industry* (1927) exemplify this trend. *J.E.B.*

Government control of the arts

The coexistence of Constructivism,* the Association of Artists of Revolutionary Russia (AKhRR) and the Society of Easel Artists (OST) was indicative of the artistic diversity of the Soviet 1920s. Of course, thanks to the consolidation of the Party apparatus after 1922, the government came increasingly to dictate its will in cultural matters, and it was clear ever since Lenin's* 'plan for monument propaganda' of 1918 (when Lenin had commissioned monuments to socialist and revolutionary heroes) that art and politics were to be linked indissolubly under the Soviet regime. But even in the late 1920s artists were still free to experiment with industrial design and abstraction, although they were no longer encouraged to do so and the leftists were removed from positions of power. In 1929 Malevich* was granted his last Soviet one-man show, but in 1930 the long-awaited one-man show of Pavel Filonov (1883–1941) was cancelled after pressure from AKhRR members. In the same year the group known as 'October' opened its single exhibition, presenting examples of industrial design, photography and architectural* projects by Gustav Klucis (1895–1944), El' Lissitzky,* Rodchenko* and others, but by 1932 the artistic and political climate had so changed that October was criticized for committing 'vulgar mistakes' and 'abolishing art'.

Such accusations were made by those artists, critics and

Gerasimov, *Collective Farm Festivities*, 1937

administrators who sought to impose Realism★ as the correct and exclusive style on all Soviet artists. In practical terms, they achieved their goal by means of two important procedures. The first of these was the Party decree *On the Reconstruction of Literary and Artistic Organizations* of 1932 whereby existing cultural groups were suppressed, and writers, artists, musicians and architects were urged to join respective, exclusive unions (the Union of Artists of the USSR was formally set up only in 1939). This prepared the way for the establishment of Socialist Realism★ as the single, legitimate artistic and literary style in 1934 at the First All-Union Congress of Soviet Writers. Dicta such as 'we must depict reality in its revolutionary development' and 'create works with a high level of craftsmanship, with high ideological and artistic content' endorsed by the delegates to the Congress constituted the basis of the Soviet cultural policy for at least the next 20 years. Artists such as Aleksandr Gerasimov (1881–1963) and Boris Ioganson (1893–1973), proponents of Socialist Realism, attained national renown and political favour as 'court painters' to the Stalin regime.   *J.E.B.*

Socialist Realism

Monolithic Socialist Realism replaced the search for new forms of artistic expression during the two decades which followed the dissolution of art organizations in 1932. The term Socialist Realism evolved out of a literary debate as a description of the basic creative method of socialist society. In the visual arts it became synonymous with a style which earned itself the following ironic anonymous definition: 'Socialist Realism is a method of portraying our leaders in a way they will understand.' The imposition of this style upon Soviet

art was largely due to the influence of a group of artists who subscribed to the aesthetic principles first enunciated by the Wanderers★ (Association of Travelling Art Exhibitions) in the 1860s. They considered that art could be evaluated only in terms of its effectiveness as a social weapon, and that the aim of art should be the depiction of 'the plain truth'. In a socialist Russia, these neo-Wanderers argued, the truth lay in 'the heroic and optimistic reality of Soviet life'. It was the duty of the artist to capture this truth by means of an art which was 'national in form and socialist in content'.

In 1932 a new All-Russian Academy of Arts was established, and in 1934 the government appointed Brodsky★ as its director. A pupil and disciple of Repin,★ Brodsky had already established a reputation as an accomplished painter before the October Revolution with such works as *The Demonstration of the Tsar's Faithful Servants in Gratitude for the Saving of their Fatherland* (1914), and portraits of Kerensky and other members of the Provisional Government.★ After the Revolution Brodsky devoted his talents as a portraitist primarily to the depiction of Lenin:★ *Lenin against the Background of the Kremlin* (1924); *Lenin against the Background of Smol'ny* (1925); *Lenin against the Background of a Demonstration* (1927); and so on. His portrait of *Lenin at the Smol'ny* (1930), became particularly well known, especially as over five million reproductions of this work were printed between 1934 and 1937.

In 1928 artists of the 'left' had accused Brodsky of attitudes characteristic of a member of the 'reactionary bourgeoisie'. But after becoming director of the Academy of Arts in 1934, he ensured that artist of the 'left' (Constructivists, Suprematists, Analytical Expressionists) were replaced in art education by those committed to representational art. Artists of the 'left' also ceased to exhibit officially, except as theatre, book or textile designers. Thereafter they were to have little room for manoeuvre – they could turn to design as did Tatlin,★ they could renounce their 'formalist mistakes' and try to

Brodsky, *Lenin at the Smol'ny*

adapt to Socialist Realism, like Vladimir Lebedev (1891–1967), or face hardship, obscurity and even active persecution, as did Filonov★ and Malevich.★ Nevertheless, at first it seemed as if the work of representational artists with varying stylistic approaches could comply with the vague definition of Socialist Realism. Former members of the World of Art,★ Blue Rose, Knave of Diamonds, OST (the Society of Easel Artists) and other groupings exhibited and taught alongside the neo-Wanderers. Indeed the 'positive', 'life-assertive' portraits and still-lifes by former Knave of Diamonds artists such as Aleksandr Kuprin (1880–1960), Mashkov,★ Fal'k★ and Konchalovsky★ were at first singled out for praise, as was the 'social consciousness' of Kuz'ma Petrov-Vodkin (1878–1939).

But by 1939 the increasing isolation of the Soviet Union and growing xenophobia gave rise to the demand that true Soviet art dissociate itself from any form of expression developed during the years of free exchange of artistic ideas between Russia and Western Europe. As a result, all artists departing from the static, idealized canon of style introduced by the neo-Wanderers were accused of 'formalism' and 'decadence'. Even the OST painters Deyneka,★ Pimenov,★ and Petr Vil'yams (1902–47) and Yevgeniya Zernova (b.1900) came under attack: '[they] have not yet shaken the dust of formalism from their feet. They like machines and know them. Indeed too well. In Zernova's *Transfer of the Tank* the latter takes up half the canvas. Meanwhile the tank crew remain without facial expression. There is no new man here' (attributed to a contemporary Soviet critic by the historian G. Loukomski).

Brodsky died in 1939 and the leadership of Socialist Realism in art was taken over by Aleksandr Gerasimov,★ who started his career with a portrait of K. Ye. Voroshilov (Chairman of the Presidium,★ 1953–60) and devoted his life's work to the faithful portrayal of the great leader: *Stalin at the XVIth Congress of the Communist Party* (1933),

Gerasimov, *Stalin and Voroshilov at the Kremlin*

Stalin and Voroshilov at the Kremlin (1938) and so on. His portraits and other works earned him four Stalin Prizes, the Chairmanship of the Organizing Committee of the Union of Soviet Artists (founded in 1939), and in 1947, presidency of the USSR Academy of Arts.

'Stalin and the Soviet Peoples', an exhibition held in 1939 in the Tret'yakov Gallery, Moscow, further defined the official attitude towards art as a 'literary' form. The works exhibited were divided according to subject: Revolutionary and Historical Themes; Portraits of Distinguished Soviet Citizens; Man Transformed by Labour – the Image of our Motherland; and Soviet Industry. The neo-Wanderers were predominant. The painters exhibiting included Aleksandr Gerasimov, Sergey Gerasimov (1885–1964), Yevgeny Katzman,★ Brodsky, Georgy Ryazhsky (1895–1952), Vasily Yefanov (b.1900), Ioganson,★ Moisey Toidze (1871–1953). Sculpture was represented by the works of Nikolay Tomsky (b.1900), Matvey Manizer (1891–1966), Ivan Shadr (1887–1941) and Vera Mukhina (1889–1953), whose *Worker and Collective Farm Woman*, designed for the 1937 Paris International Exhibition, now stands outside the Exhibition of Economic Achievements in Moscow.

The official art of the Second World War and of the early post-war years was primarily devoted to Russia's heroic past – as in *Morning on Kulikovo Field* (1943–6), by Aleksandr Bubnov (1908–64), depicting Dmitry Donskoy's victory over the Tatars★ in 1380 – and to its tragic but 'heroic' present, for example, works by the Kukryniksy collective, the painters Mikhail Kupriyanov (b.1903), Porfiry Krylov (b.1902) and Nikolay Sokolov (b.1903). The latter were as well known for their political cartoons as for their easel paintings, such as *The Fascist Retreat from Novgorod* (1944–6).

Until the late 1950s the neo-Wanderers' naturalistic representation of an idealized reality was the sole form of official artistic

Yefanov, *An Unforgettable Encounter*, 1936

expression permitted. Art other than Soviet art, except for the Social Realism of artists such as Courbet and Millet, was criticized as bourgeois and was not on view.

The three decades following 1939 were barren and joyless; even the gentle sensuality which characterized the portraits of women workers in the 1930s was replaced by the ungainly massiveness of the female ideal of the wartime years. Nevertheless a few official artists were able to maintain a distinctive identity. Since Socialist Realism was 'national in form', artists of the non-Russian republics* such as the Armenian Martiros Sar'yan (1880–1972) and the Georgian Lado Gudiashvili (b.1896) could produce and exhibit paintings which, had they been the work of Russians, would have been dismissed as 'formalist'.

Graphic artists, many of them 'exiles' from easel art, also continued to produce varied and original work. The illustrations and engravings of such artists as Vladimir Favorsky (1886–1964), Aleksey Pakhomov (1900–73), Tyshler,* Lebedev, Andrey Goncharov (1903–79), Petr Miturich (1887–1956) and Dmitry Mitrokhin (1883–1973) are of enduring quality.   *J.H.*

Art after the thaw

In 1957 the republican Artists' Unions were finally united into the Union of Soviet Artists. The election of Konstantin Yuon (1875–1958) as the first chairman of the Union demonstrated that the 'thaw' had reached the visual arts. Yuon had never been closely associated with the Wanderers.* A member, before 1932, of World of Art,* the Union of Russian Artists and the Association of Artists of Revolutionary Russia, he had renounced the symbolism of his early work (for example, *The New Planet*, 1921) for the 'realism'* of the 1930s, but retained his inventive use of colour. Yuon died in 1958 and for the next decade the Union of Soviet Artists was headed by Sergey Gerasimov* and Ioganson.* In 1968 for the first time, the chairman was an artist whose career had begun after the Revolution, Yekaterina Belashova-Alekseeva (1906–71), a sculptor who first exhibited in 1934.

Since 1957 Soviet art has begun to show a real diversity. As the neo-Wanderers' version of Socialist Realism* shows signs of losing its pre-eminence, artists of the first three decades of this century are being reappraised. The early works of former members of World of Art, Blue Rose, Knave of Diamonds, the Union of Russian Artists and the Society of Easel Artists (OST) are again to be seen in the galleries, a number of books on art movements of the pre-1932 period have appeared, and Western art, both figurative and non-figurative, has become more accessible. This, together with the direct influence through art-school teaching of artists of the 1920s and early 1930s, has

played a great part in shaping contemporary Soviet art. In style, if not in spirit, the contemporary* art scene resembles that of the 1930s, and although official art remains exclusively representational, membership of the Union of Artists does not necessarily preclude experimentation with unofficial styles and tendencies.

The influence of the neo-Wanderers is, however, still apparent. There is little to distinguish *Motherhood* (1964) by Eduard Bragovsky (b.1923) or *The Parting* (1967) by Gely Korzhev-Chuvelev (b.1925) from the work of Ioganson. The works of Igor' Simonov (b.1927) and Boris Okorokov (b.1933) are faithful to the traditions of Socialist Realism in their 'heroic' portrayal of reality and their assumption that 'great ideas' require large canvases. The influence of OST can be seen in the spacious, almost monochromatic compositions of Tair Salakhov (b.1928). Mikhail Savitsky's (b.1922) *Partisan Madonna*, 1967, owes an obvious debt to Kuz'ma Petrov-Vodkin.* The post-Impressionism of the Knave of Diamonds survives in the works of Vyacheslav Stekol'shchikov (b.1938) and is to be discerned in the semi-abstract experiments with colour by Nikolay Gritsyuk (b.1922).

The work of Il'ya Glazunov (b. 1930), perhaps the only Soviet artist whose work has received official recognition at home and commercial success abroad, uses Russia's realist tradition in an interesting manner, exemplified by *The Return of the Prodigal Son*. This is full of references to Russia's past and present. Depictions of rulers, churchmen and writers closely modelled on well-known works by

Salakhov, *The Azeri Poet Rasul Rza*

Glazunov, *The Return of the Prodigal Son*, 1977

other artists, flank the central figure from *The Appearance of Christ to the People* by Ivanov,★ an artist from the Wanderers group. On the table lies a head from an icon★ of St John the Baptist and corpses in the snow from the Kukryniksy's★ *The Fascist Retreat from Novgorod*. The whole scene is observed from the right by one of Brodsky's portraits of Lenin.

An impressionistic simplicity distinguishes the work of artists from the Baltic republics,★ such as the Latvian Jemma Skulme (b.1925) and the Lithuanian Jonas Švažas (b.1925).

Soviet art has been adversely affected by the isolation which characterized the period 1934 to 1957. Sculpture, most dependent upon state patronage, has remained almost static. Size rather than concept seems to be the criterion. Graphic and easel art, however, show signs of recovery. Recent Soviet evaluations of Russia's artistic heritage, the growing influence of unofficial art and the increased exchange of ideas with other countries should enable art in the Soviet Union to follow new and interesting paths. *J.H.*

Twentieth-century arts in the non-Russian republics

Many of the artists associated in the West with modern Russian art – Mikalojus Čiurlionis (1875–1911), Klucis,★ Dmitry Nalbandyan (b.1906), Sar'yan,★ Salakhov,★ Niko Pirosmanashvili (1860/3–

1918), Aleksandr Volkov (1886–1957), Vrubel'★ – were not born in Russia. This impressive list of names indicates the substantial debt of Russian and Soviet art to the ethnic minorities comprising the non-Russian republics, especially of Georgia, Armenia, Azerbaijan, Uzbekistan and the Baltic states.

The art and architecture of 20th-century Georgia warrants primary attention. Before the Revolution Tiflis (now Tbilisi) enjoyed a vigorous cultural life and, for example, was exposed to the avant-garde★ through artists and writers such as Kirill Zdanevich (1892–1969), his brother Il'ya (Iliazd) (1894–1975) and the primitive Niko Pirosmanashvili. In 1918–19 Tiflis became a Futurist centre, witnessing the activities of the Dada group known as '41°' and the appearance of a whole series of unorthodox books and journals. After the incorporation of Georgia into the Soviet Union in 1921, its independent artistic life continued to flourish and to maintain international connections, especially with Paris, where Lado Gudiashvili★ and David Kakabadze (1889–1952), perhaps Georgia's most talented 20th-century artists, studied. While retaining the decorative quality of traditional Georgian art,★ Gudiashvili brought an Expressionist, sometimes apocalyptic force to his painting, as in *Fish* (1920) and *The Underprivileged* (1930). In contrast, Kakabadze created skilful abstract works during the 1920s, organized and restrained.

Inevitably, the move towards Socialist Realism,★ ratified in Moscow in the early 1930s, affected the development of Georgian art, producing its own 'protocolists' such as Ketevan Magolashvili (1894–1973) and Iraklii Toidze (b.1902), whose portraits of Stalin earned him a high position in Soviet cultural life. But because of Georgia's strong national traditions and comparative remoteness from the Kremlin, the doctrine of Socialist Realism did not gain the exclusive control of art it achieved in Russia. A number of Russian artists – Yevgeny Lancéray (E. E. Lansere, 1875–1946), Aleksandr Shevchenko (1882–1968), Vasily Shukhaev (1887–1973) – made their home in Georgia during the 1930s; this was symptomatic of a general drift from the main Russian cities to Central Asia of many artists and writers, including Aleksandr Drevin (1889–1938),

Pirosmanashvili, *Recumbent Woman*, 1905

179

Fal'k,* Kuz'ma Petrov-Vodkin,* Kuznetsov* and Nadezhda Udal'tsova (1885–1961).

Naturally, Georgian painting, architecture and design enjoyed substantial goverment patronage during the hegemony of Stalin* and the powerful G. K. Ordzhonikidze (1886–1937), often providing exotic combinations of Western European and indigenous motifs. Many buildings of the 1930s and 1940s in Tbilisi, multi-storey and constructed of ferro-concrete, have the appearance of ornamental rugs. Further, this oriental influence from Georgia (and from Armenia, Kazakhstan and Uzbekistan) manifested itself in the façades, mosaics and reliefs of the Stalin 'wedding-cakes' such as the Hotel Moskva in Moscow. After experiencing an Impressionist phase in the late 1950s and early 1960s, Georgian painting entered the so-called 'severe style' represented by Konstantin Makharadze (b.1929) and Radish Tordiia (b.1936). In turn, this movement contributed to the remarkable recent efflorescence of Georgian monumental art.

Armenia, annexed to the Soviet Union in 1920, strove to retain its cultural identity, although its most famous painter, Sar'yan, perhaps took his inspiration more from Gauguin and Matisse than from the traditions of the Armenian decorative arts and miniature. During the 1920s and 1930s a number of experimental artists came to the fore, including Georgy Grigorian (b.1897) and Akop Kodzhorian (1883–1959), whose dramatic *Shooting of the Communists* (1930) is a compelling example of Armenian Expressionism. From the mid-1930s onwards the exuberance and decorativeness of traditional Armenian art* yielded to the anonymous narrative style of Socialist Realism, of which Dmitry Nalbandyan, a last survivor from Stalin's 'court painters', is the most typical representative. The same process was evident in Azerbaijan and Uzbekistan, whose few avant-garde painters of the late 1920s and early 1930s – such as Gazanfar Khalykov (b.1898), Shmavon Mangasarov (b.1907), Ural Tansykbaev (b.1904) and Usto-Mumin (pseudonym of Aleksandr Nikolaev, 1897–1957) – were replaced by orthodox defenders of the Socialist Realist faith. Tair Salakhov,* First Secretary of the Union of Artists of the USSR, added some interest to this trend when he contributed to the 'severe style' of the 1960s, supported by Sarkis Muradyan (b.1927). Their colleague, Torgul Narimanbekov (b.1930) has succeeded in retaining the ornamental, colourful bias of his national culture.

While the Baltic states* (Lithuania, Latvia and Estonia) were incorporated into the Soviet bloc only in 1940, they had long maintained cultural ties with Russia. The Symbolist Čiurlionis lived in Lithuania before moving to St Petersburg in 1908; the etcher Vasily Masiutin (1884–1955), the critic and painter Waldemars Matvejs (Vladimir Markov, 1877–1914), the abstract painter and designer Klucis* and the sculptor Teodor Zalkaln (1876–1972) were all Latvian. Jemma Skulme,* the daughter of the celebrated painter and sculptor Oto Skulme (1889–1967), upholds the family's artistic

Muradyan, *Under Peaceful Skies*, 1972

tradition by heading the Latvian affiliation of the Union of Artists of the USSR. The painter Indulis Zarin (b.1929) is also worthy of mention. Tallinn in Estonia is the centre of a veritable renaissance of the graphic arts represented by Leonhard Lapin (b.1947), Malle Leis (b.1940), Raul Meel (b.1941), Mare and Tonis Vint (both b.1942), young artists who are the worthy successors to Eduard Wiiralt (1898–1954), one of the great visionaries of 20th-century European art. Among the non-Russian cultures of the Soviet Union in the 1970s, Baltic art shows the greatest vigour, independence and potential.

J.E.B.

Contemporary art: the alternative tradition

The early 1930s saw the stifling of Russia's revolutionary atmosphere, and the revolutionary avant-garde* suffocated in the cultural vacuum of Socialist Realism.* Yet some major figures of that avant-garde did remain inside Russia (among others, Malevich,* Tatlin,* El' Lissitzky,* Rodchenko,* Al'tman) and continued to work. Outcasts from official life, they applied themselves either to book and graphic design – mainly in propaganda journals published for foreign consumption (Lissitzky, Rodchenko) – or to design for the theatre (Natan Al'tman,* Tyshler,* and others). Malevich and Tatlin painted figurative portraits and still life, not because they had any desire to adapt to new demands, but because the collective structure of their creative activity had collapsed, and without it there was no point in avant-garde experimentation. The traditions of the avant-garde went underground, to be continued in private. Rodchenko, in 1943–4, painted a vast canvas entitled *Expressive Rhythm* which anticipated the spontaneous methods of what was to become *tachisme*. Sterligov continued to develop the theories of his master, Malevich. El' Lissitzky was, to the end of his life, producing projects for towns of the future. In such conditions, however, these activities were merely isolated episodes, with no direct consequences. Anything outside the realm of Socialist Realism remained in the studios, confined to a close circle of the artists' friends, and thus played no part whatsoever in the public aesthetic life of society. This alternative tradition became a broad movement only after the death of Stalin.*

Open opposition

From 1956 to 1963 cultural links with the West were more intense than at any other period of Soviet history. For the first time in a quarter of a century major exhibitions of French, English, Belgian and American art were held in Moscow and Leningrad. Articles on the subject began to be published; they may have been critical, but they did at least contain scraps of objective information. This first encounter with contemporary foreign art was decisive for Soviet art.

The opposition movement in art arose in the mid-1950s from two sources. Firstly, a 'left wing' appeared within the official Union of Soviet Artists. Without directly confronting the principles of Socialist Realism, young artists (many of whom entered art school straight from the front, wounded and decorated) sought to extend the notion of 'truth to life', and in order to express that truth, to master the entire range of modern methods. They painted portraits and landscapes, scenes of war and of work, and they made memorials to the dead; but all this was done not in the pompous style of official Socialist Realism but in an attempt to reflect life's dramatic, and sometimes tragic, confrontations. This line of Soviet art of the late 1950s and early 1960s has come to be termed the 'severe style'. Boris Birger (b.1923), Vadim Sidur (b.1924), Ernst Neizvestny (b.1925), Vladimir Veysberg (b.1924), Nikolay Andronov (b.1929), Pavel Nikonov (b.1930) and others gained widespread popularity and were featured in the Soviet press as the most talented representatives of the younger generation of artists.

The other and main source of this movement flowed from those who from the very beginning had not accepted the dogmas of official ideology. The older among them were of various backgrounds and followed various paths to non-conformism: some arrived at it via the prison camps* (Boris Sveshnikov, b.1927; Lev Kropivnitsky, b.1922), and others thanks to their teachers, or as a result of particular circumstances (for example, Oscar Rabin, b.1928; Vladimir Nemukhin, b.1925). The majority, however, were students (Dmitry Plavinsky, b.1937; Anatoly Zverev, b.1931; Oleg Tselkov, 1934; Vladimir Yankilevsky, b. 1938, and others). Like the artists of the 'severe style', they viewed their art, at that time, as 'forms of reflection of reality', but they filtered this reality through the prism of Surrealism, Expressionism, the grotesque, fantastic realism, as they tried to penetrate the social, spiritual and existential bases of life. A far smaller proportion of them embraced abstractionism (Lidiya Masterkova, b.1929; Mikhail Kulakov, b.1933, and others) or pure form-creation. At the start of the 1960s, however, the 'Movement' group (Lev Nusberg, b.1937 and others) was formed – the only body proclaiming direct descent from the traditions of the revolutionary avant-garde. At present, this line is continued in the 'Author Working Group', led by Francisco Infante (b.1943).

Political reaction

The existence of an artistic opposition successfully competing with Socialist Realism posed a serious threat to official Soviet ideology. In December 1962 the main guardians of this ideology – the members of the USSR Academy of Arts – were able to convince the Party leader, Khrushchev,* that this was indeed the case. At a major exhibition of the Union of Soviet Artists at the Manège (Moscow's most important exhibition hall), they pointed out to him the new trends, and branded them as ideological deviations threatening the very foundations of the Soviet state. That was the start of a nationwide campaign against 'liberal tendencies' in culture, which were seen as stemming from the influence of 'hostile Western ideology'. Harsh criticism was aimed not only at the outsiders, but also at the members of the Union of Soviet Artists who had created the 'severe style'. Some of them were forced to compromise, but the most talented were gradually shunted out of official life and were, in effect, transformed into 'unofficial' artists (Birger, Veysberg, Sidur, Neizvestny and others).

Nevertheless, throughout the 1960s the opposition movement expanded; fresh followers joined it in their hundreds; it spread to Leningrad and to the towns of the Union Republics. Its stylistic range became broader, and it developed with a more intense dynamism. In an amazingly brief period individual artists and groups of artists made the transition from Surrealism and Russian Constructivism to Western pop-art, photo-realism, happenings and conceptualism. The opposition movement had, in fact, joined the mainstream of European art. It had mastered the basic rules, and had created its own national variations on fundamental European themes, such as the 'soc-art' of Vladimir Komar (b.1943) and Aleksandr Melomid (b.1945) which openly parodied the values of the official ideology, or the *grob*-art ('grave-art') of Sidur.

From the inception of the opposition movement, the only channels of communication between the artists and the public were exhibitions arranged semi-legally in workers' clubs, research institutes and

Sidur, *Coffin Woman*, 1978

Zelenin, *Self-portrait*, c.1975

private apartments. Although such exhibitions were few, and although their duration was brief – for they were usually closed by the authorities as soon as discovered – they did create the impression of a living unofficial art, and inspired hope for the future. Through them information about the opposition movement in the USSR leaked abroad. From the mid-1960s the exhibitions were strictly prohibited; all mention (even critical) of the unofficial artists disappeared from the Soviet press; it was as if their art had been silently declared non-existent. It was death for the artists' work.

On 15 September 1974 a group of artists went out to a patch of waste ground in Moscow to display their work. This first free open-air exhibition was smashed by the authorities with the aid of bulldozers, fire-hoses and plainclothes militia. A number of pictures were burned on the spot. Some of the foreign correspondents present were subjected to physical harassment, with the result that the artistic opposition movement in the USSR received the full attention of the Western media. At the same time, members of the movement continued doggedly to press for their right to show their works. These are the factors which have largely determined the current situation in Soviet art.

Relationship to Socialist Realism

On the one hand, the authorities have been forced into making certain concessions. They have permitted a number of brief exhibitions of unofficial art (passed over in total silence by the press); in 1976 an organization which admitted nonconformist artists (the Graphic Artists Section of the city committee of soviets*) was set up in Moscow as a buffer between the Union of Soviet Artists and the flood

of unregulated unofficial art. On the other hand, pressure on the most active participants in the movement has been increased, and many have been compelled by threats to leave the country. The early 1970s saw the start of the second stream of emigration of artists from the country, the first having taken place in the 1920s. Mikhail Shemyakin (b.1943), Neizvestny, Nusberg, Rabin, Tselkov, Masterkova, Eduard Zelenin (b.1938) and many others have left. The authorities' aim is to eradicate the artistic opposition; yet it remains undiminished. It continues to absorb and rework in its own terms the latest ideas emanating from the West, and to rediscover elements of the forcibly broken Soviet tradition in avant-garde* art. In recent years it has paid particular attention to the theme of religion, with its roots in icon-painting* and in the work of certain early 20th-century Russian artists (Vitaly Linitsky, b.1934, and others).

Socialist Realism* has not, even now, renounced a single one of its dogmas; it is dominated by the same people and by the same ideas as in the 1930s and 1940s. However, the existence of an alternative does influence the character of official art. The possibility of choice for artists, and the danger of young talent switching from official commissions to unofficial, uncontrolled work, have somewhat broadened the notion of Realism: what was forbidden only yesterday becomes commonplace today. Soviet art is now a complex stylistic cocktail of old ideological clichés and 'new' formal devices drawn, for the most part, from the artistic arsenal of the late 1920s. The guardians of Socialist Realism close their eyes to these 'formal innovations', so as to preserve intact the essence of Socialist Realism itself – namely, its propagandist character and its social optimism. *I.G.(trans.S.F.)*

LANGUAGE AND LITERATURE

Chekhov (with Stanislavsky, director of the Moscow Arts Theatre, looking on) reads *The Seagull* to the cast for the first time, 1898

Russian, Ukrainian and Belorussian languages

Russian (R), Ukrainian (UK) and Belorussian (BR) together form the East Slavonic (ES) group of the Slavonic branch of the Indo-European family of languages, the other groups being West Slavonic (WS) (Czech (CZ), Slovak, Polish (POL) and Lusatian) and South Slavonic (SS) (Slovene (SN), Serbo-Croat (SCT), Bulgarian, Macedonian and Old Church Slavonic (OCS)). The accompanying tabulation of dates summarizes linguistic development. Long before their earliest recorded history the East Slavonic dialects had developed some of the main characteristics which distinguish them from West and South Slavonic. The acquisition of literacy came with the conversion to Christianity★ in 988; early literature confined to religious themes was written in Old Church Slavonic, with an admixture of East Slavonic dialectal features. Secular documents made use of the local vernaculars, which, up to the 14th century, were close enough to be dubbed either simply East Slavonic or Old Russian (OR), in the wide sense of ancestors of the three modern languages, containing in embryo their divergent characteristics, with the exception of accretions, chiefly lexical, from outside sources. Among the most important dialects were those of the Ilmen' Slovenes and Krivichi (North Great Russian), the Radimichi, Vyatichi and Severyane

(South Great Russian), the Polyanians and Volynians (Ukrainian) and the Dregovichi (Belorussian). From the 10th century until its sack by the Tatars★ in 1240 Kiev was the chief East Slavonic cultural centre; after that date there was a westward shift of power and influence to Galicia and Volynia which heralded the emergence of Old Ukrainian (14th to 16th centuries). From the 13th century divergent tendencies may be observed in Great Russian (for example, confusion of hiss and hush sibilants–*ts/ch* in Novgorod; *ts/ch*, *s/sh*, *z/zh* in Pskov) but disintegration was forestalled by the growth of Moscow,★ through the annexation of minor principalities and the suppression of the independent republics of Novgorod and Pskov, to become the undisputed political and cultural centre of Great Russia. The language which took shape in Moscow admitted elements from both North and South Great Russian, a happy blend which is reflected in the modern standard pronunciation with plosive *g* from the former and reduction of unstressed vowels (*akan'e*) from the latter.

Polish and Lithuanian domination of western areas encouraged the development of Old Belorussian and Old Ukrainian, at this stage (14th to 16th centuries) so close to each other as to be given the common name of Ruthenian by some scholars. First confined to legal documents, by the 16th century these dialects had become an adequate medium for contemporary literary genres such as Orthodox religious polemical★ tracts, vivid personal reminiscence and syllabic verse on the Polish and Latin pattern. The most striking feature of the

THE RELATIONSHIP OF RUSSIAN, BELORUSSIAN AND UKRAINIAN TO OTHER INDO-EUROPEAN LANGUAGES

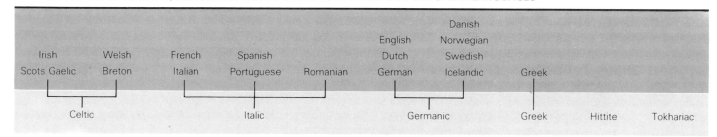

'Centum' dialects

INDO-EUROPEAN LANGUAGES

'Satəm' dialects

SYNOPSIS OF IMPORTANT DATES IN LINGUISTIC HISTORY

BC

2nd millennium	Split of Indo-European into 'satəm' and 'centum' dialects (so designated on the basis of the term used for 'one hundred')
1st millennium	Formation of Common Slavonic; in the second half, close association of Baltic and Slavonic

AD

c.500–800	Disintegration of Common Slavonic into East, West and South dialect groups
863	Mission of Cyril and Methodius to Slavs of Moravia and Pannonia; Slavs acquire an alphabet and a written language (Old Church Slavonic)
988	Conversion of Eastern Slavs to Christianity; introduction of alphabet and written language
1056–7	The oldest dated manuscript book written by a Russian scribe: Prince Ostromir's gospel-book
1130	The earliest dated secular document: the deed of Prince Mstislav Volodomirovich and his son Vsevolod
1491	Earliest Church Slavonic books for Eastern Slavs printed by Fiol in Cracow
1517	Dr Francis Skaryna commences publication of the Belorussian translation of the Bible: 1517–19 in Prague; 1522–5 in Vilnius
c.1553	First printing in Moscow
1596	The first Church Slavonic grammar and dictionary by the Belorussian monk, Lavrenty Zizany, printed in Vilnius
1627	The first Church Slavonic-Ukrainian dictionary by the Ukrainian Pamvo Berynda, Kiev; 2nd edition, Kuteina, 1657
1755	Publication of Lomonosov's* Russian grammar; founding of Moscow University
1798	I. P. Kotlyarevs'ky's parody of the Aeneid marks the rebirth of the Ukrainian literary language
1820–37	Pushkin's* mature work: the perfecting of the Russian literary language
1840	T. G. Shevchenko's collection of poems in Ukrainian, Kobzar (The Minstrel)

KEY

▢ Modern languages

▢ Ancient dialects and languages

Design by H. Leeming

Ruthenian literary language was its use of Polish and not Old Church Slavonic as a source of neologisms. The growth of Russian power under Peter the Great★ and Catherine II★ and the transfer of Ukrainian and Belorussian territories to the Russian state interrupted the further development of Ukrainian and Belorussian. The publication of I. P. Kotlyarevs'ky's parody of the *Aeneid* (*Eneyida*, 1798) and the first collection of poems (*Kobzar, 'The Minstrel'*, 1840) by T. G. Shevchenko (1814–61), national poet of the Ukraine, mark the re-emergence and consolidation of modern Ukrainian as a literary language. During the second half of the 19th century, when publication in Ukrainian was severely restricted by the tsarist authorities, the Austrian government encouraged the development of Ukrainian in Galicia. Since Galicia admitted a much stronger Polish element than the language of the other cultural centres, Kiev and Kharkov, the upshot was a legacy of strains and contradictions which are still being resolved.

The renaissance of Belorussian (or White Russian) as a literary medium and official language of the Belorussian SSR began rather later and was eventually confirmed by the writings of the poets Yanka Kupala (1882–1942) and Yakub Kolas (1882–1956). Both Ukrainian and Belorussian are now firmly established as literary, official, commercial and scientific media, with internationally recognized Academies. Some of their distinguishing characteristics from Russian are shown in the accompanying chart, but it is in the vocabulary, above all, that they differ, because of the relative infrequency of Church Slavonic and the richness of Polish elements in Ukrainian and Belorussian. For example, Russian has *obeschat'* = 'to promise' and *sokrovishche* = 'treasure' from Church Slavonic, whereas the equivalent words in the two other languages—BR *abyatsats'*, *skarb* and UK *obitsyaty*, *skarb*—are from Polish. *H.L.*

Russian literary language

The Russian literary language is the direct heir of Old Church Slavonic, the first written language of the Slavs,★ which came into being to answer the needs of a people newly converted to Christianity. Its roots are firmly set in the confident Graeco-Slavonic bilingualism of Cyril and Methodius (the 9th-century missionaries of the Slavs) and their followers, who transplanted a whole vocabulary of spiritual and moral concepts from Christian Hellenic ground into a new idiom in which it still lives and serves the purposes not only of the Slavonic branches of the Orthodox Church★ but also, in its Russian context, the secular state. In spite of an attempt by Lomonosov★ to codify the functions within Russian of the Church Slavonic elements it was not until the 19th century that a complete integration was achieved in the work of Pushkin.★ Russian continues to draw neologisms and

SOME DISTINGUISHING CHARACTERISTICS OF RUSSIAN, BELORUSSIAN AND UKRAINIAN

Belorussian	Russian	
soft consonants *ts'*, *dz'* example: *khadzits'*	*t'*, *d'* *khodit'*	= 'to go'
reduction of unstressed *o* and *e* to *a* and *ya* (so-called *akan'e* and *yakan'e*) example: *malako*	*moloko*	= 'milk'
vjaliki	*velikiy*	= 'great'
no soft '*r*' example: *berah*	*bereg*	= 'bank, shore'
n does not appear between preposition and personal pronoun example: *da yaho*	*k **n**emu*	= 'to him'

Ukrainian	Russian	
pronunciation of certain vowels *i* as ee in 'sweet' example: *sino*	*e* or *o* *seno*	= 'hay'
nis	*nes*	= 'he was carrying'
nis	*nos*	= 'nose'
y as i in 'bit' example: *byty*	*i* or *y* *bit'*	= 'to beat'
consonants are pronounced hard before the vowels *y* and *e* example: *dyvo* (hard *d*)	*divo* (soft *d*)	= 'wonder'
den' (hard *d*)	*den'* (soft *d*)	= 'day'

Belorussian and Ukrainian	Russian	
fricative *h* example: BR *holas*, uk *holos*	*g* *golos*	= 'voice'
initial *vo*, *vu* in some words example: BR *voka*	*o* or *u* *oko*	= 'eye'
uk *vohon'*	*ogon'*	= 'fire'
BR *vulitsa*, uk *vulytsya*	*ulitsa*	= 'street'

KEY

WS distinct from SS and ES: (1) Pol. *kwiat*; R *tsvet*
(2) Pol. *szary*, *wsze*; R *seryy*, *vse*
(3) Pol. *mydło*; R *mylo*

SS distinct from WS and ES: (1) Pol. *łokieć*; R *lokot'*; SCt *lakat*
(2) Pol. *robota*; OR *robota*; OCS *rabota*

ES distinct from WS and SS: R *gorod*, *bereg*, *molod*, *moloko*
Sn *grad*, *breg*, *mlad*, *mleko*
Cz *hrad*, *břeh*, *mladý*, *mléko*
Pol. *gród*, *brzeg*, *młody*, *mleko*
(Note that Czech and Slovak here diverge from the other WS languages and follow the SS line.)

Design by H. Leeming, from statistics in *Wielka encyklopedja powszechna*, Warsaw, 1967

derivatives not only from its dialectal base but also from the Church Slavonic thesaurus, as great a treasure-house for Russian as is Latin for the languages of western Europe. Some evidence of its use as an inexhaustible source for neologisms and derivatives, especially those of a moral, didactic or scientific character, may be noted in the following examples (Church Slavonic words capitalized): *vsya VLAST' SOVETAM* = 'all power to the soviets' (a revolutionary slogan); Lenin*GRAD*, Volgo*GRAD*, as against the native Novgorod; *MLECHnyy put'* = 'Milky Way' as against the native *molochnye produkty* = 'dairy products'; *GLAVA* = 'chief, chapter' as against the native *golova* = 'head—part of the body'. The West European languages began to make a significant contribution to the Russian vocabulary first via Polish mediation between the 15th and 17th centuries and later directly: German and Dutch in Peter the Great's* time, French later in the 18th century, German, and in a minor way English, in the 19th and 20th centuries. Russian has also acquired many loan-words from the Turkic and Finno-Ugric peoples on the eastern borders. All these diverse elements have played their part in making Russian a language of immense power and beauty, rich in synonyms, capable of expressing the subtlest nuances of meaning, the worthy instrument of the great novelists of the 19th century.

H.L.

DISTRIBUTION OF SPEAKERS OF MODERN SLAVONIC LANGUAGES
(figures in millions)

WEST SLAVONIC
(Pomeranian)
Polish 31.6
(Polabian)
Lusatian 0.1
Czech 9.7
Slovak 4.1

EAST SLAVONIC
Belorussian 8.5
Ukrainian 39.5
Russian 120

(Old Church Slavonic)
Slovene 1.6
Serbo-Croat 15.1
Bulgarian 8.5
Macedonian 1

SOUTH SLAVONIC

Russian folk-lore

Folk-lore is the traditional culture of the Russians, passed down from generation to generation. Originally much of it was connected with East Slavonic paganism, but after the introduction of Christianity* in the 10th century, it increasingly became the sole form of secular popular entertainment. Ritual folk-lore, often given Christian overtones, accompanied every event of significance in daily life, while non-ritualistic folk-lore, particularly the more artistic forms, was brought to the people by travelling minstrels or mummers, called skomorokhi. The Church fulminated against them, but they were not suppressed till the mid-17th century. Then they disappeared into the countryside to pass on their skills to talented peasants. Thanks to Russia's economic and social backwardness, folk literature was a rich and vital tradition right up to the Revolution, and even now is not defunct.

One of the most ancient and prolific folk genres is the tale. The Russians possess variants of well-known fairy tales such as Snow White or Cinderella, as well as many original subjects, each in countless different versions. Folk tales are of three kinds: fairy tales, animal tales and tales of everyday life. Best known are the fairy tales, perhaps originally connected with the primitive shamanistic beliefs of the Ural-Altaic peoples, attributing power over good and evil to the tribal priest-doctor. Their hero is either a prince or a low-born fool, Ivanushka Durak, who ultimately marries the princess. Fairy tales all centre on a dangerous quest, during which the hero encounters the famous figures of peasant folk-lore, such as the witch Baba Yaga, who lives in a house on chicken legs, and the dragon Koshchey the Immortal who can only be killed if the egg that contains his death can be discovered. To enable him to combat evil, the hero receives help usually either from magical animals or from objects like the comb that can turn into a forest or the purse that never empties. Animal tales, probably connected once to animistic beliefs, describe comic encounters between animals, who, as in the Brer Rabbit stories, are given a distinguishing human characteristic. Thus the most popular character, the Fox Lizaveta or Lisa Patrikeevna (lisa means fox) specializes in sweet words and flattery. Fearsome animals are turned into figures of fun: Mishka or Mikhail Ivanych, the Bear, though known for his strength as 'the uprooter of trees', is slow and clumsy. Even more stupid is the 'grey fool', the Wolf, who is constantly outwitted. Full of lively dialogue, rhymes and snatches of song, animal tales are still popular with Russian children.* The tales of everyday life are generally of more recent origin. They are based on the motif of the triumph of the underdog: the fool over the clever man. Their comic and satiric touches (the priest and the landlord are figures of fun) and their lively colloquial style ensure their popularity.

Rich and varied though folk tales are, they are less striking than the epic songs of Russia, the byliny. Preserved in the far north of Russia until relatively recent years, byliny were sung – or rather intoned – by peasant skaziteli (singers), who were famed for their narrative skill, poetic sensibility and, not least, their memory. Most byliny were composed before the 16th century. A few with superhuman heroes such as Svyatogor the giant, or Volkh Vseslavich who can turn himself into an animal, probably go back to pre-Christian times. Most others were composed either during the period of Kievan greatness (11th and 12th centuries), or after the Tatar* invasion. It is hard to tell, for the heroes – the bogatyri Il'ya of Murom, Alesha Popovich, Dobrynya Nikitich – are the same, and precise historical details are few. Whatever the period of composition, events are related back to an idealized heroic Kievan age. Other byliny are set in Novgorod. Unlike the Kievan bylina cycle which is usually concerned with heroic battles or love, the Novgorod byliny are altogether more prosaic: Vasily Buslaevich, the 'hero' of some, is little more than a drunken braggart. Byliny depend for their effect upon the skill of the singer, who must compose his text from memory with the aid of stock poetic formulas and situations; thus the description of saddling a horse is always the same, hands are always white, a maiden always fair. Epic features include threefold epic retardation and hyperbole – a bogatyr' wields his weapon with such force that he clears a roadway through the ranks of the enemy.

With time, byliny gave way to historical songs and ballads. Sung in the same tonic (accentual) metre as byliny, but shorter and lacking the heroic tone and stock situations, historical songs present popular, sometimes spurious accounts of historical episodes or personages. Ballads, on the other hand, have no obvious connection with history. Mainly composed between the 13th and early 18th centuries in a slightly freer tonic verse than byliny, ballads are dramatic tales of the fates of individuals such as the wife who murders her husband, or the wife slandered by her mother-in-law and killed by her husband.

Folk-songs* are not all narrative. Large numbers of lyric songs exist which were, and are, sung not by special singers but by ordinary people, usually women. The majority of songs describe peasant life, mainly its sadder sides: perhaps the most persistent theme is that of unhappy love and marriage. Other groups of songs centre round soldiers, bandits or barge-hauliers. The poetics of lyric songs depend to a great extent on a range of beautiful traditional nature symbols. Apart from these songs expressing personal feeling, Russian folk-lore possesses a wide range of ritual songs connected with festivals and ceremonies such as weddings. Even now in the north the age-old tradition of funeral laments is not entirely defunct. Using folk poetic expressions, the singer expresses her own and the family's profound grief by improvising a lament, which reflects the character and occupation of the deceased. Christian themes are also found in the dukhovnye pesni, spiritual songs, which present popular versions of biblical and hagiographical stories.

Some forms of folk-lore such as drama were less well-developed than in Western Europe. Modern times have produced their own forms, notably the *chastushka*, a four-line verse, often comic, satiric or bawdy in character, in fact something like the limerick. But though most of the traditional forms are in decline, not all have yet disappeared. They and the pithy sayings and proverbs that are part of colloquial speech are reminders that the average Russian today is still in touch with the traditional oral culture of his people.   *F.C.M.K.*

Literary genres, 11th to 17th centuries

Russian literature developed as a consequence of the conversion of the people to Christianity by the prince of Kiev, Vladimir I,* in 988. In adopting the Eastern Orthodox* form of Christianity from Byzantium rather than from Rome, the Russians received a liturgy in a Slavonic language, Old Church Slavonic, which in spite of its Greek syntax and specialized vocabulary was readily comprehensible. This facilitated the appearance of a literature in a language close to the vernacular within a mere half-century of the introduction of writing. In western Europe where the lingua franca was Latin, vernacular literatures evolved more slowly. Ultimately, the Russians were the losers, for they were isolated from intellectual movements in western Europe. The Renaissance and Reformation scarcely affected them, and Russian literature continued along medieval lines until the 17th century – far later than in western Europe.

Since literature followed upon conversion, much of it was naturally of an ecclesiastical nature – sermons, lives of saints and edifying works of various kinds. Even where it was secular it was still didactic; chronicles recorded events of significance, satirical and polemical works attacked abuses or proposed change, military tales told of great victories or defeats. The early Russian writer, who until the 16th century was usually a monk, saw himself as a medium for the conveying of information. He therefore was not interested in making up fictitious plots or inventing new literary forms. Indeed, the more a work conformed to the conventions of a given genre, the more it would be worthy of respect. But though didactic and traditional, Russian literature did not lack entertainment value: vivid stories, dramatic scenes, even wit and humour are present, but are always subordinated to tendentious aims. Similar attitudes are evident in the use of source materials: anything that served the purpose of a work could be included, and information that conflicted might be omitted with impunity.

Because of the fairly low literacy rate, early Russian literature was generally intended for reading aloud, in church, monastery or court, and, later, in houses of the wealthy. Ecclesiastical literature which had to convey ethical concepts and abstract arguments took account of this fact by employing rhetoric; repetition and euphony of the most varied kinds helped to make the work more pleasing to the ear. By contrast, secular literature, which tended to be more narrative, at least until the 16th century inclined towards simple syntax which made it easy to follow.   *F.C.M.K.*

Kievan literature, 11th and 12th centuries

The literature of this period is usually termed Kievan though works may actually have been written in one of the lesser principalities. At this stage regional differences are minimal.

The chronicles

Perhaps the most impressive of the literary works of the period is the Russian Primary Chronicle,* or the *Tale of Bygone Years*, which covers the period up to 1118. As in Byzantine annals, material is placed under the heading of a given year. Since no annalist of the early 12th century could be expected to remember precise dates for more than a few years, it is obvious that the Chronicle is a compilation. It was mainly written by monks of the Kievan Monastery of the Caves, among them Nestor, its first redactor or editor. Aptly termed a literary mosaic, the Chronicle includes folk legends, accounts of battles, lives of saints and a will, each written in the style appropriate to the subject matter. Subsequently it was imitated all over Russia. Local chronicles reflect regional tastes and preoccupations, and those from rival towns often provide fascinatingly varied views of the same events. They also often incorporate complete literary works such as the *Instruction of Vladimir Monomakh** found in the *Tale of Bygone Years*. This unusual document, composed by one of Russia's most energetic and talented princes, consists of series of precepts for his sons followed by an amazingly long list of his campaigns. The advice contained in the first section, which is largely culled from Byzantine sources, is particularly valuable for its picture of the ideal Kievan prince.

Sermons

Through translation the Russians received many of the best examples of the Byzantine art of homily. That they were appreciated is evident from native Russian sermons, which, though not original in their theology, reveal remarkable skill with argument and its expression. The most impressive is Metropolitan Ilarion's *Sermon on Law and Grace* (1037–51) intended as a stimulus to the canonization of Vladimir I.* Ilarion opens with a succession of beautifully balanced antitheses between Grace, the gift of Christ, and the Law of the Old

Testament. Grace, he argues, is superior to Law not least in its availability to all peoples, the Russians included. And so he turns to the specific theme of the conversion* of Russia, and as he does, he skilfully raises the emotional tone of the work until it culminates in a superb lyrical eulogy of Vladimir and his son, the ruling prince of Kiev, Yaroslav.* By contrast, the sermons written by the 12th-century bishop from Turov, Kirill, lack both Ilarion's patriotic tone and his skill with logical argument. Instead Kirill employs an ornate style to paint charming symbolic pictures of nature in which each detail reflects an aspect of the Church festival on which the sermon was to be pronounced.

Hagiography

Lives of saints were very popular in Kievan times, perhaps partly because the Byzantine model for rhetorical biography had been imperfectly absorbed, thus permitting realistic character portrayal and episodes inconsistent with traditional concepts of sanctity. Thus, of the versions of the deaths of the young princes Boris and Gleb, cruelly butchered by their elder brother Svyatopolk in 1015, only *The Lection on the Blessed Martyrs Boris and Gleb* written c.1078 by Nestor, conforms to Byzantine canons. Logically structured and carefully written, it presents an idealized portrait of the young princes, but is much less enjoyable than the more popular *Tale of the Holy Martyrs Boris and Gleb*. Though the *Tale* is an awkward fusion of conflicting legends, it contains dramatic episodes and vivid portraits of the two brothers, especially of Gleb as he begs for mercy from his murderers. Even Nestor's *Life of St Feodosy of the Monastery of the Caves* ignores convention with its superb portrayal of Feodosy's possessive bullying mother, who goes to all ends to thwart her son's monastic calling. Kievan literature also boasts its own patericon, a collection of edifying stories about monks. The *Patericon of the Kievan Monastery of the Caves*, begun in the early 13th century, recounted episodes from the lives of former monks of the monastery. Simply told, and often fantastic in character, some, such as the tale of Moisey Ugrin who virtuously resisted the blandishments of a Polish beauty, are well-developed narratives.

The Tale of Igor''s Campaign

One of the most famous works in all Russian literature, the *Tale of Igor''s Campaign*, was apparently composed about 1187 by a court bard. It tells of the disastrous expedition led by Igor', Prince of Novgorod-Seversk against the nomadic Polovtsians. The work is such a unique combination of folk poetry and literary traditions that doubts have frequently been cast on its authenticity, especially as the sole manuscript was destroyed in the great fire of Moscow in 1812. Written in a highly poetic prose full of nature imagery and symbol, the *Tale* gives an impressionistic description of the battle and defeat. Then follows the grand prince of Kiev's ominous dream and an exhortation to the powerful princes of Rus' to unite against the common foe. In the last section of the work, Igor''s wife Yaroslavna laments the loss of her husband, but Nature responds to her grief by facilitating Igor''s escape and return home. The work ends on a note of muted happiness. Although the *Tale's* authenticity may never be established completely, it nonetheless remains a work of undisputed genius.

F.C.M.K.

The Tatar period

The main theme of the *Tale of Igor''s Campaign*, the need for unity in the face of danger, appears frequently from the 12th century on. It evidently was the subject of the tantalizing fragment, the *Tale of the Destruction of the Russian Land*, a poetic lament for past glory. After the crushing Tatar* invasion of 1237–40, princely strife no longer seemed an adequate explanation of the current state of affairs. As Serapion of Vladimir (d.1275) declared in his *Sermon on the Merciless Heathen*, the defeat of the Russians was Divine punishment for their sins. In a period of isolation and national decline, it is not surprising that literature draws little from Byzantium, concentrating rather on those familiar literary genres that reflected current preoccupations—the recording of events in the chronicles and particularly of battles, some in independent military tales. The *Tale of the Capture of Ryazan' by Baty* describes the first encounter between the main Tatar army and the Russians in 1237. It provides a good example of a compilatory work: a basic story to which dramatic episodes and emotional colouring have been added over a period of time, in this case up to the second half of the 15th century. The defeat of the Ryazan' army and the sack of Ryazan' by Baty are part of the original story, but into this framework touching or dramatic scenes, often of dubious veracity, have been placed. Thus Prince Oleg the Fair, who refuses to be converted to Baty's 'false faith' and is chopped into pieces with knives, actually did not die until 1258. This and other epic stories—such as the tale of Yevpaty Kolovrat, who dies a glorious death after valiantly attempting to avenge the Ryazan' army against hopeless odds—were drawn from epic folk-songs. The author's aim is to increase the sense of patriotic grief for Ryazan'.

A period which valued military prowess was not likely to appreciate so well saintly virtues. It is not surprising that hagiography languishes at the expense of a hybrid genre, the secular biography of princes, which combined hagiographical and annalistic motifs and techniques. The *Life of Alexander Nevsky*, for example, which was written in the early 1280s, paints an idealized portrait of Alexander as warrior, statesman and Defender of the Orthodox Faith. To do so, the author was obliged to alter or ignore his less noble exploits. Thus both his battles, against the Swedes at the mouth of the Neva and against the Teutonic Knights on the ice of Lake Peipus, are falsely depicted as epic conflicts. To assist the author's intention of promoting Alexander as a hero saint, he is even shown performing miracles.

Not all the extant works of this period are concerned with battles and the Tatar invasion: the *Supplication of Daniil the Exile* is a curious 12th-century work, which was greatly added to by later copyists. The author seems to have been one of the retinue of the prince of Pereyaslavl'. Feeling badly treated by his prince, he complains bitterly in a series of pungent aphorisms drawn from the Scriptures, translated Byzantine works and folk-lore.*   *F.C.M.K.*

Muscovite literature, 14th to 17th centuries

Ecclesiastical literature

About 1330 a religious revival started in Russia. Scores of men seeking a life of contemplation left the towns for the inhospitable countryside. As disciples joined them, monasteries grew up, which were to spearhead a renaissance of religious art and literature. The most important, the Trinity Monastery founded by St Sergy at Zagorsk sheltered icon* painters such as A. Rublev and the brilliant hagiographer Epifany the Most Wise (d.1420). Given this name on account of his elaborate prose style called 'word-weaving', Epifany is the author of two highly ornate biographies, the *Life of St Sergy* (1417–18) and, about 1396, the *Life of Stefan of Perm'*, his friend who had converted a Finnic tribe to Christianity. Epifany was so overcome with veneration towards his subjects that he was forced into ever more elaborate word patterns to express himself. Such efforts were essential if Stefan were to be considered a worthy candidate for canonization, for he had performed no miracles, the normal prerequisite for a saint.

With the fall of Bulgaria and Serbia to the Turks at the end of the 14th century, numbers of South Slav writers fled to Russia. They brought with them a more controlled form of 'word-weaving' and a similar interest in the exploits of the saintly individual. the many lives and eulogies of saints composed by the 15th-century Serbian hagiographer Pakhomy Logofet display a good grasp of rhetoric but lack the deep feeling of Epifany. And yet because Pakhomy's writings were controlled in style, they became the model for later Muscovite hagiography, and 'word-weaving', losing its spiritual intensity, descends into a florid rhetoric which is increasingly found in secular literature of an official character.

Secular literature

The cultural revival of the late 14th century coincided with the first signs that the Tatars were not invincible. The battle of Kulikovo Field (1380), though little more than a psychological victory, was celebrated in a variety of literary works, from the ornate biography of Dmitry Donskoy, prince of Moscow, to epic military tales. The most interesting of the latter is the *Zadonshchina*, composed in an epic style very similar to that of the *Tale of Igor''s Campaign*.

Secular literature in the second half of the 15th century is of two kinds: either ideological, attempting to bolster the political or religious claims of a principality or ruler, or non-didactic. The move to free literature from the shackles of tendentiousness was unfortunately suppressed in the 16th century, which was dominated by an oppressive intellectual atmosphere.

Sixteenth-century political and religious polemic

Moscow* was by now head of a centralized Russian state and bitter debate ensued over the question of autocratic power. For the first time, writers are drawn from varied social groups, and literature depicts their respective viewpoints and the burning issues of the day. Of particular interest is the correspondence (1564–79) between Tsar Ivan the Terrible* and a former close associate, Prince Kurbsky. In elegant prose, Kurbsky argues the case for the old aristocracy, the boyars, whom he feels Ivan has slighted, and asserts their ancient right to change their allegiance, as he himself has done by leaving Russia for Lithuania. Ivan's response, couched in a language alternately lofty and crude, is to name Kurbsky's action as that of a traitor, insisting that he, Ivan, is the sovereign chosen by God and that the boyars must submit to him. The views of another social group, the 'service gentry', are presented by Ivan Peresvetov. Ostensibly describing the last days of the Byzantine Empire and the first of Turkish rule in Istanbul, Peresvetov's works are thinly disguised allegories about the Russia of his day, permitting him to make bold criticisms and advocate a programme of reform. It is interesting that many of his less radical proposals were actually taken up by the tsar.

Probably more bitterness surrounded the religious controversies of the 16th century. The so-called Trans-Volga Elders, advocates of monastic poverty and a life of contemplation, clashed with the Josephans (followers of Iosif of Volokolamsk), who were in favour of monastic property, which enabled the Church* to fulfil an active charitable role. Both sides, Nil Sorsky (1433–1508) and Vassian Patrikeev for the Trans-Volga Elders, Iosif of Volokolamsk (c.1439–1515) for the Josephans, defended their views, and elaborated their teachings. The eventual defeat of the Trans-Volgans destroyed a vital spiritual spark in the life and literature of Muscovy. Free-thinking in the form of heresy was ruthlessly suppressed – a number of polemical anti-heretical tracts testify to their vigour. Even life was regulated; the *Domostroy*, a prosaic guide to everyday behaviour, was drawn up under the auspices of Metropolitan Makary (1481–1563), who also reorganized hagiographical literature, ensuring where necessary the writing and rewriting of saints' lives in florid rhetorical style. The heavy weight of officialdom, secular and ecclesiastical, hung over literature.

Seventeenth-century literature

The great social upheavals of the Time of Troubles* (1598–1613) did much to dissipate the oppressive social atmosphere, but it had little effect on literature. Works of the period still employ heavy Muscovite rhetoric, though a new interest in rhyme is evident. But as time went on, it was clear that the conventions that had held Russian literature together for so long were breaking down. The reading public had expanded, creating a market for entertaining stories. Most were still heavily didactic, like the *Tale of Savva Grudtsyn* in which a young man is seduced by a married woman, falls into the clutches of the Devil but eventually seeks salvation in a monastery. The exception is the *Tale of Frol Skobeev*, where lively narrative is not burdened by any kind of moral: Frol is a rogue, who seduces a rich man's daughter and by cunning succeeds eventually in gaining his father-in-law's blessing. A further innovation is the deliberate use of folk-lore as a literary source, as in the *Tale of Woe-Misfortune* about a Prodigal Son who comes to grief through drink. The tonic (accentual) verse and many of the motifs and expressions are drawn from folk poetry.

The masterpiece of the 17th century came not from the secularization of culture but from the religious reaction to it, the Schism in the Russian Church of the 1650s and 1660s. The leader of the Old Believers* (as the Schismatics came to be called), the Archpriest Avvakum (c.1620–82), composed his autobiography between 1672 and 1675 while in a subterranean prison in the cold Far North of Russia. Though termed a Life, this differs from others of the genre, being a detailed autobiography which presents a vivid picture of the indomitable Avvakum and his forbearing wife and children as they endure years of appalling privation in Siberia. Writing in a pithy crude style close to the vernacular, Avvakum heaps abuse on his enemies, portrays his friends and family with tender affection and himself emerges as the first rounded portrait in Russian literature.

Avvakum's desire for a return to old Russian piety was partly a reaction to the growth of Western influence in Russia. Those scholars who, after the annexation of the Ukraine in 1654, moved from Kiev to Moscow brought with them new literary forms, the poetry and drama of the Baroque. Though there had been various attempts at verse in the first half of the century, it was Simeon Polotsky (1629–80), a product of the Kievan Academy, who really established literary verse. Written in rhyming lines with a regular number of syllables, Simeon's verse is notable for its amazing verbal effects and lack of serious content. Western influence also accounted for the emergence of secular court drama in the 1660s. Though the plays of this period, including those by Simeon Polotsky, lack dramatic qualities, they

helped set Russian literature upon a Western path of development. After 1700, the old forms of literature either died away or disappeared from the forefront of literary development to form a sub-culture among the broad mass of the people. *F.C.M.K.*

Kantemir, Trediakovsky, Lomonosov, Sumarokov

The gulf separating Russian literature from the literatures of Western Europe at the beginning of the 18th century was wide. Verse-writing and drama had made only a scant first appearance in the last third of the 17th century, and in 1700 there were effectively no authors, no reading public, no secular press, no theatre. The reign of Peter the Great* produced no significant literature, but the Western cultural orientation provided by his reforms led to the emergence of a sophisticated, europeanized literature from the 1730s. The period 1730–1800 saw a rapid development of literary culture from the crude beginnings in the works of Kantemir and Trediakovsky to the compositions of N. M. Karamzin* and V. A. Zhukovsky*, who could stand comparison with their Western contemporaries.

This rapid progress owed much to the fact that Russia began its literary apprenticeship in the age of classicism, which provided a comprehensive genre system and a wealth of models to follow. Two other important factors in the development of a modern literature were the creation of a balanced literary language,* which exploited the resources of Russian and Church Slavonic, and the adoption of the syllabo-tonic (or syllabic-accentual) system of versification in place of the purely syllabic system inherited from the 17th century.

The first 'modern' Russian writer was A. D. Kantemir (1708–44), a product of the Petrine age and a man of broad European culture. He is known principally for his nine verse satires (1729–39), unpublished in his lifetime, which were written in defence of enlightenment and contain many lively portraits of its enemies. He was the last author of note to use syllabic verse, on which he wrote a treatise.

Three authors dominated Russian literature until 1760: Trediakovsky, Lomonosov, and Sumarokov. All occupied positions in institutions of the state, which reflected the restricted, 'official' scope of literary activity at the time. In the theory and practice of literature, however, they achieved much and laid solid foundations for its further development.

V. K. Trediakovsky (1703–69), after studying in Holland and France, was employed in the Academy of Sciences.* More a scholar than an artist, he wrote on literary history and theory, on prosody (notably, his pioneering treatise on the syllabo-tonic system, 1735) and on language.* His original compositions were lifeless and cumbrously written, and his principal achievements were in the field of translation (Tallemant's *Voyage à l'île d'amour*, 1730; Fénelon's *Télémaque*, 1766).

M. V. Lomonosov (1711–65) has been called the 'Peter the Great of Russian literature'. Of humble family, he had a phenomenal career, achieving distinction as scientist, philologist and man of letters. A professor at the Academy of Sciences, he was the author of scientific works, a Russian grammar and a manual of rhetoric; in his *Letter on the Rules for Russian Verse*, 1737, he extended the prosodic reforms of Trediakovsky; and in his essay 'On the usefulness of church books', 1757–8, he prescribed the 'three styles' of language appropriate to the main divisions of literary genres. He embodied the civic tradition of classical literature and is, above all, famed for his 20 'solemn' odes (1737–64) celebrating events of state, victories, royal anniversaries and so on. The constant theme of the odes is the need to continue the policies of Peter the Great for enlightenment and the scientific and economic advance of Russia. These celebratory odes, which are heavily ornate in style, show great skill in form and language. Lomonosov also wrote religious and philosophical odes, sparser and more natural in style, of which the two 'Reflections ('Morning' and 'Evening') on the greatness of God' are outstanding.

A. P. Sumarokov (1717–77) was of gentry stock. He served in the army and, until 1761, occupied positions at court. He was the first Director of the Russian Theatre* (1756–61) and the most wide-ranging writer of his day. Following Boileau's *L'Art poétique*, he set out the canons of classicism in two verse epistles (on language and on poetry, 1747) and exemplified all the main genres in his own prolific writings. He is best known for his introduction of the classical tragedy into Russia (*Khorev*, 1747, and eight others) and his cultivation of the lighter genres of verse (songs, fables), in which he moved towards more natural forms of expression, both in language and verse structure. Though less talented than Lomonosov, he was more immediately influential in broadening the scope of literature and stimulating the growth of personal, as distinct from civic, themes. He favoured clarity in style and was critical of the embellished odes of Lomonosov. *I.P.F.*

Drama

From the 1760s literary development accelerated. There were more writers and more readers, and literature became more closely concerned with the problems of contemporary life. Western literature also became increasingly accessible through translations.

The drama flourished. The classical tragedy was continued in the works of M. M. Kheraskov (1733–1807), Ya. B. Knyazhnin (1740–91), N. P. Nikolev (1758–1815), V. A. Ozerov (1769–1816) and others. Comedy became a popular genre, especially satire, which,

with its attack on social follies and vices, provided both entertainment and moral improvement. In comedy, Sumarokov* played a pioneering role in the 1750s. The comic repertoire expanded rapidly in the following decades, with translations and adaptations of French plays, for example, those of V. I. Lukin (1739–94), as well as many original comedies by Knyazhnin, Nikolev, A. O. Ablesimov (1742–83), P. A. Plavil'shchikov (1760–1812) and others. The best verse comedy of the period is *Chicanery* by V. V. Kapnist (1758–1823), which, as well as being skilfully written, went beyond the satire of 'general' social vices and had political overtones.

The outstanding comedy-writer of the century was D. I. Fonvizin (1744–92). He wrote two celebrated plays in prose: *The Brigadier*, 1766–9, and *The Minor*, 1782. The first is a salon comedy, close to life in its humorous attack on corrupt morals, ignorance, and gallomania (attachment to things French). *The Minor* is an indictment of domestic tyranny and false education, and it touches also on larger social questions, such as serfdom.* While written in accordance with the classical 'unities' and, in the case of *The Minor*, slowed down by *raisonneur* moralizings, both these plays by Fonvizin are lively and entertaining, and merit their lasting place in the Russian theatrical repertoire. *I.P.F.*

The novel and the literary journal

The novel and the literary journal, which were unknown in the classical canon and reflected the broadening scope and function of literature, appeared in Russia in the 1760s. The first Russian novels were those of F. A. Emin (1735–70), a Hungarian or Pole by origin, who between 1761 and 1770 produced over 25 books, some original, some translations. The best known of these is *The Letters of Ernest and Doravra*, 1766, an epistolary novel influenced by Rousseau's *La nouvelle Héloïse*. M. D. Chulkov (c.1743–92) was the author of entertaining novels written in popular style – *The Mocker*, 1766–8, and *The Comely Cook*, 1770. Both these authors also engaged in journalism. Sumarokov had published the first Russian journal, *The Industrious Bee* (*Trudolyubivaya pchela*), in 1759, and from the late 1760s journals had a regular place in Russian literary activity, partly through the stimulus of Catherine the Great,* who had literary interests and herself published a journal – *All Sorts* (*Vsyakaya vsyachina*), 1769. The English *Spectator* was the prime model for the early Russian journals. The outstanding figure in the journalistic movement in the 1770s and 1780s was N. I. Novikov (1744–1818), who published a succession of satirical journals – *The Drone* (*Truten'*) 1769–70, *The Tatler* (*Pustomelya*) 1770, *The Painter* (*Zhivopisets*) 1772, and others. *I.P.F.*

Derzhavin

Novels and journals appealed to a wide public by their entertainment value and interest in mundane affairs, but they made little immediate impact on the established literary tradition. There, the revolution came from within, from a poet who began writing in the tradition of Lomonosov,★ but then abandoned its restrictions: G. R. Derzhavin (1743–1816), the most original Russian writer of the 18th century.

Derzhavin had a career as soldier (ten years in the ranks) and official (his last post was Minister of Justice). His major literary achievement was to move away from the rigid genre system and to bring life into Russian poetry. He abandoned the impersonality of classical authorship and gave the imprint of his own character to most of what he wrote. His best works are experience-based and noted for the accuracy and realism of their descriptions, particularly of nature. Derzhavin adopted a new approach to odic themes in his epoch-making *Felitsa*, 1782, a poem about Catherine the Great,★ which, unlike the traditional monarchic ode, is light in tone, human in scale, and breaks the genre code by combining panegyric with satiric themes. Derzhavin maintained the solemn odic tradition in poems on national themes, but these too are more down-to-earth and more natural in expression than the odes of his predecessors. His many outstanding works include robust civic poems (*To Rulers and Judges, The Grandee*), philosophical poems (*God, The Waterfall*), and domestic poems containing memorable, colourful descriptions of everyday life (*Invitation to Dinner, Life at Zvanka*). His style, sometimes rough, was rich and original and broke with many of the clichés of classical verse.   *I.P.F.*

Light genres; the fable

By the 1770s the balance was shifting from the more solemn genres to lighter forms of literature. The decade which saw the completion of Russia's first epic poem – M. M. Kheraskov's *Rossiada* – saw also the appearance of the mock-epic *Elisey* of V. I. Maykov (1728–78) and of *Dushen'ka*, the light-hearted narrative poem of I. F. Bogdanovich (1744–1803). Lighter genres, however, could still be serious in purpose – a characteristic exemplified by the fable, which enjoyed great popularity. Sumarokov★ had led the way with over 350 fables, written in vigorous, earthy *vers libres*. Later, more formal, writers in the genre included I. I. Khemnitser (1745–84) and I. I. Dmitriev (1760–1837). The greatest Russian fabulist, who ranks with the best of any country or age, was I. A. Krylov (1769–1844). He began his literary career as dramatist and journalist in the 1780s; later he turned to fable-writing (200 fables, 1807–34). The distinction of Krylov's fables lies in the originality of their themes, the harmony of their content and form, and the richness of their language.   *I.P.F.*

Sentimentalism

In the last quarter of the century classicism was ceasing to be the dominant literary mode. The European movement of Sentimentalism exerted its influence in Russia from the 1760s (the novels of F. A. Emin, the poems of M. N. Murav'ev, 1757–1807). The central figure in Russian Sentimentalism was N. M. Karamzin (1766–1826), who had a lasting influence on the development of Russian literature and the literary language.★ Prose was his chief medium, and he was the first author to write readable, elegant Russian, which he based on the ordinary language of educated society. After travelling in Europe, he published *Letters of a Russian Traveller*, 1791–2, which followed the tradition of sentimental travel literature with its casually intimate observations of life. The emphasis on the emotional and psychological aspects of human experience is reflected in Karamzin's stories of 1792–1803, the most famous of which is *Poor Liza*, 1792, a tale of a peasant girl abandoned by her noble lover. Certain of his stories, such as *The Island of Bornholm*, 1794, and *Sierra Morena*, 1795, are more romantic in theme and mood. Karamzin was also a journalist, and his *European Herald* (*Vestnik Evropy*) 1802 established the pattern for the 'thick' monthly literary-political journal which has flourished in Russia ever since. From 1803 Karamzin abandoned literature to write his capital work, *The History of the Russian State*.

Throughout the 18th century, directly or indirectly, the state exercised control over literature by censorship,★ and Russia's first literary martyrs date from this time. The best known is A. N. Radishchev (1749–1802), author of *Journey from St Petersburg to Moscow*, 1790. Radishchev's book, which contained radical criticism of Russian institutions (in particular, serfdom★), was banned as seditious and the author was exiled to Siberia.   *I.P.F.*

Early Romanticism: Zhukovsky

The century ended with the appearance of the first poems of V. A. Zhukovsky (1783–1852), the major Russian representative of early Romanticism. Zhukovsky's verse was reflective, elegiac, the direct expression of experience and feeling. He wrote original verse, but most of his works were translations, chiefly from German and English poets, whose works harmonized with his own mood. He introduced the narrative ballad into Russia with translations from G. A. Bürger, Sir Walter Scott, Robert Southey and others and with original compositions, such as *Svetlana*. The outstanding feature of Zhukovsky's verse is his command of form and language, which provided a norm of poetic expression for the following generation of poets. Zhukovsky became the friend and adviser of both Pushkin★ and Gogol′★ and thus provided a direct link between the traditions of two centuries.

A comparison of the work of Zhukovsky with that of Kantemir★ indicates how much Russian literature had progressed in a mere 70 years. In this time Russia had assimilated the experience of European literature, mastered existing techniques, created the formal and linguistic base on which the great writers of the 19th century were to build, and, in Lomonosov,★ Derzhavin, ★ Karamzin★ and Zhukovsky, had shown signs of its own original genius.   *I.P.F.*

Griboedov

The term 19th-century Russian literature refers to the period 1820 to 1917, which has a recognizable wholeness, a discreteness, surpassing that of most conventional eras in any national literature. It is marked at the beginning by the first major published work of Pushkin,★ and at the end by the Bolshevik Revolution.★

The early years of Pushkin's fame coincide with the tragically brief career of A. S. Griboedov (1795–1829). Both writers were steeped in the Russian and European literature which preceded them: but both subjected existing literary tradition to critical review, thus establishing styles and intellectual preoccupations which set the pattern for their successors. Griboedov was a man of precocious and diverse talents. Born into the Moscow gentry, he took degrees in science and law, privately studied history and literature, and was known as a musician, an amateur of philosophy and a wit. Though intimately associated with Masonic and revolutionary circles, he enjoyed a brilliant career in the diplomatic service. Cleared of all suspicion that he had been indirectly involved in the Decembrist★ revolt, he was promoted, and after Russia's victory in the war with Persia (1828) led a mission to Tehran to enforce the peace treaty. An enraged mob stormed the Russian legation, and Griboedov was killed.

Griboedov wrote only one genuinely original work, the play *Woe from Wit* (no translation does justice to the multiple implications of the Russian *Gore ot uma*). Superficially a satire after the manner of Molière and D. I. Fonvizin★ (1744–92), it is at core a work of portentous philosophical purpose. The focus of the drama is its central figure, Chatsky, the size of whose role relative to the whole text is rivalled only by that of Hamlet. Chatsky is a Russian type, yet also a model of modern European man, as that man will be seen through 19th-century Russian eyes. A natural product of cultural evolution through the Renaissance, the Enlightenment and the incipient scientific-industrial age, Chatsky is characterized above all by *um*–intellectual idealism, a conviction that man can and will achieve, through the exercise of intellect, a perfect individual and social life. Griboedov charts the tragic destiny of this human type, from the initial sacrifice of his emotional world (expressed in Chatsky by his futile adoration of the heroine Sofia) to alienation from human society, madness and oblivion. The tragic consequences of a Promethean arrogance based on the power of human intellect were to be more fully explored by Lermontov,★ Tolstoy★ and Dostoevsky.★ A second important theme is touched upon, if lightly. Though the plight of Chatsky is not seen to be of specifically Western origin, much satirical play is made upon the pernicious mimicry of Western manners in Muscovite society; and Sofia falls victim to a sentimental idealism born of European literary fashion.

Woe from Wit is richly innovatory in other ways. Cutting a swathe through the rigid neo-classical concept of genre, it blends its central tragedy with high satirical comedy, though Griboedov's 'gallery of types' are always more absurd than vicious. In addition, the playwright moulds the disorderly rhythms of contemporary speech into a strict iambic metre. Thus, in its partial rejection of the rigid canons of neo-classicism, its absorption into literature of the currency of everyday speech, its exploration of the theme of intellectual man, and its study of a question of *bytie* (human destiny) within a context of *byt* (ordinary human life), it did much to trigger off the sustained literary explosion of the next century. None the less, Griboedov's achievements are overshadowed by those of his contemporary, A. S. Pushkin.★   *M.H.S.*

Pushkin

Born into the landowning gentry, Aleksandr Pushkin (1799–1837) was educated at the Lyceum at Tsarskoe Selo and by the age of 20 had already acquired a considerable reputation as poet, rebel and rake. He was exiled in 1820 for his revolutionary and often blasphemous verse and epigrams, and thus preserved from direct involvement in the Decembrist★ revolt. In 1826 Tsar Nicholas I★ appointed himself Pushkin's 'patron', thus effectively putting the writer's movements, finances and the publication of his literature under official control. In 1834 Pushkin was appointed a 'gentleman of the chamber', a calculated slight devised by the tsar also as a means of ensuring the presence at court of Pushkin's beautiful but vacuous wife, Natal′ya. In 1837 Pushkin was lured into a duel in defence of his wife's honour and killed.

After a frivolous but witty exercise in mock-heroic (*Ruslan and Lyudmila*, 1820) Pushkin captured the attention of the Russian literary world with a series of narrative-descriptive poems on ostensibly Byronic themes. In *The Robber Brothers* (1821), *The Captive in the Caucasus* (1821) and *The Fountain of Bakhchisaray* (1822) he emulated perfectly the rich exoticism of Byron's Eastern poems: in mood and theme, however, Pushkin's poems constitute a deliberate rebuttal of Byronic Romanticism. Pushkin's quasi-Byronic figures embody not human freedom and unfettered individuality but their antithesis; they illustrate the internal and external factors (habit, passion, environment, history, nature) which limit the individual pursuit of freedom. *The Gipsies* (1824) summarizes Pushkin's scepticism: no man in any setting, wild or urban, is less un-free than the next, except he recognize that this is so, and thus find tranquillity. It also marks a final break with the Byronic manner. Its structure is a complex of narrative, description, song, dramatic dialogue and authorial observation. Its style is taut, stripped of ornamentation and packed with subtle parallels and ironies – clear indications of Pushkin's own mature voice.

Pushkin's novel in verse, *Yevgeny Onegin* (1823–30), is his most famous and influential work. Written over the whole central period of his literary career, it records and reflects in style, content and theme the process of maturation in Pushkin's art and outlook during those years. The heady effervescence of the first of its eight cantos (or chapters) gradually gives way to a more sombre and reflective manner. Its plot is slender: the novel is a complex experimental web of narrative, description and digression – a sustained discussion of the art of literature and a brilliant display of various poetic modes. While on one level *Yevgeny Onegin* can be seen as a metaphor of Pushkin's

Signed self-portrait of A.S. Pushkin

life as man and artist, of the tensions and processes at work within him, it treats also of vital Russian themes, notably the tension between East and West in Russian culture and the Russian psyche. The hero Yevgeny's essential Russian character is obscured by the assumed masks of an alien Western culture, absorbed in a second-hand form from the fashionable life of Petersburg. He is reduced ultimately to a pathetic wraith, knowing neither who he is nor what he feels. In counterpoint the heroine Tat'yana survives the transitory influence of European Sentimentalism, from which springs a youthful infatuation with Yevgeny; nourished by the good earth of rural Russia, she emerges as dignity and morality incarnate, the integrated personality at peace with itself and with the world.

Pushkin's only full-length play, *Boris Godunov** (1825), was modelled in broad approach, and also extensively in detail, upon Shakespeare. Combining elements of tragedy and history play, it has proved too concentrated and experimental an amalgam to function effectively on the stage. It is a study primarily of the ironies inherent in the movement of history, and of the illusoriness of freedom through power.

The so-called 'Little Tragedies' of 1830 (*Mozart and Salieri, The Feast at the Time of the Plague, The Covetous Knight, The Stone Guest*) and the unfinished *The Water Nymph* (1824–32) and *Scenes from the Days of Chivalry* (1831) are Pushkin's only other ventures into drama. The 'Little Tragedies' are concentrated experiments in the exposure of character and psychology through dialogue and soliloquy. They are replete with irony, and typical of Pushkin's art of saturating the text with meaning.

The narrative poem *The Bronze Horseman* (1833) is Pushkin's most perfect and mature display of poetic artistry; it also summarizes his complex view of the destiny of Russia and of individual man. The poem opens with a triumphant eulogy on the godlike figure of Peter the Great,* who in his divine wisdom and in defiance of nature, built St Petersburg* – a 'window into Europe', a fortress, and a city of beauty and delight. Petersburg is destiny: the triumphal prologue concludes with an exhortation to nature to reconcile itself with Peter's visionary creation. In the narrative section of the poem both nature – in the form of the river Neva – and man – in the form of a petty clerk – rebel. The river retreats: the petty clerk is driven to hallucination, madness and extinction. The poetry of *The Bronze Horseman* is rich in euphony, image, delicate epithet and hidden symmetry, and displays Pushkin's total mastery of a range of poetic styles. It is characteristic of Pushkin's self-assurance and sense of mischief that he slips in a passing jibe at a contemporary poetaster.

In the late 1820s Pushkin recorded, in *Yevgeny Onegin* and elsewhere, his intention to shift from poetry to prose. Poetry was 'the language of feeling', associated with youth and romanticism: prose he called 'the language of thought' – of maturity and realism. Between 1830 and his death he wrote mostly in prose, and developed a uniquely laconic and expressive prose style. His *Tales of Belkin* (1830) mocked the ornate cliché-ridden language and stereotyped characters of Romanticism and Sentimentalism, suggesting their total inappropriateness to Russian life, manners and literature. *The Queen of Spades* (1834) is a complex and intricate work whose central figure, Germann, in his obsessive pursuit of power through wealth and demonic egocentricity, foreshadows characters in Dostoevsky.★ *The Captain's Daughter* (1836), an historical romance after the manner of Walter Scott, is a masterpiece of stylistic economy.

Of all Pushkin's works his lyrics lend themselves least to translation. The dominant themes are love, friendship, poetry, the poetic vocation, reminiscence and the pursuit of tranquillity. His lyrics are noted above all for their precise laconic delineation of complex feeling, their absolute mastery of poetic euphony, their delicately interlocking imagery and their ability to elevate Pushkin's personal experience to one of general relevance and appeal.

Pushkin's writing also includes reworking of traditional Russian folk★ literature, notably *The Tale of the Priest and his Workman Balda* (1830) and *Tsar Saltan* (1824–31); other genres of narrative verse – the heroic *Poltava* (1828), the anecdotal *Count Nulin* (1825) and the comic-realistic *The Little House in Kolomna* (1830); reviews, critiques and travel notes such as *A Journey to Arzrum* (1836) and historical studies. Pushkin is recognized, in Russia at least, as the outstanding genius of Russian letters. His genius expressed itself in the range of styles and genres in which he experimented, and his remarkable

Still from the 1916 Russian film *The Queen of Spades*, directed by Yakov Protazanov (1881–1945)

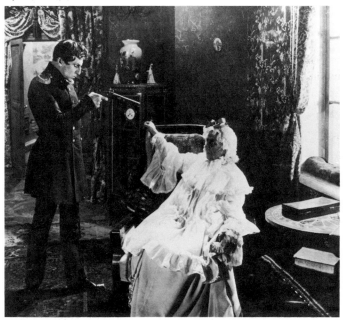

achievements in all of them; in his moulding of a rich expressive language for both verse and prose; in his establishment of motifs and themes which his successors would develop; and above all in his endowing Russian literature with a genuine and unique national identity.

M.H.S.

The Pushkin Pleiad

So dominant was the figure of Pushkin★ that a group of not inconsiderable poets of the same period have become known collectively as the 'Pushkin Pleiad' – a term which does less than justice to their individual talents. Baron A. A. Del'vig (1798–1831) is noted for the paucity of his output and the cold, formal brilliance of his verse. D. V. Davydov (1784–1839) wrote spirited verse predominantly on themes of warfare and debauch. Prince Petr Andreevich Vyazemsky (1792–1878), endowed with a superb gift for word-play, penned elegant rhymes on universal themes. K. F. Ryleev (1795–1826), executed as a ringleader in the Decembrist★ revolt, is known for his rousing and rebellious civic verse. Undoubtedly the brightest star in the Pleiad was Ye. A. Baratynsky (or Boratynsky) (1800–44). Much influenced by Pushkin, Baratynsky none the less developed a uniquely sonorous and compact poetic style, and achieved the difficult feat, rarely essayed by Pushkin, of converting the contemplation of abstract intellectual questions into pure poetry.

M.H.S.

Lermontov

The tragedy of Pushkin's★ death sparked into life another remarkable literary talent – that of M. Yu. Lermontov (1814–41). The descendant of a 17th-century Scottish migrant, George Learmont, he was intellectual, vain and introspective by nature. He entered Moscow University at the age of 16 but quickly abandoned formal study and joined the Guards, dissipating his energy in debauchery, and his intellect largely in the compiling of obscene verse for the amusement of his comrades. Enraged by the death of Pushkin, he wrote a poem (*Death of a Poet*, 1837) inveighing against those corrupt forces in and around the court who had conspired in Pushkin's destruction. For this rhetoric Lermontov paid with a year's exile to the Caucasus. The episode was his salvation as a writer.

Before 1837 Lermontov's poetry (excluding the unprintable) was immature, imitatively Byronic and packed with the jumbled imagery and sentiments of conventional melancholic Romanticism. Only a few isolated pieces hinted at his potential as a major lyricist. Among them are *The Cup of Life* (1831), *Desire* (1831), *The Sail* (1832), *The Angel* (1832) and *As the Flame of a Falling Star at Night* (1832). His romantic melodrama *Masquerade* (1835) is important only in that its central figure foreshadowed Pechorin, the protagonist of his greatest work, *A Hero of our Time* (1840).

In the remaining four years of his life, Lermontov developed and displayed a startlingly original literary talent. Two narrative poems, dating back in early draft to 1829–30, were revised and completed (*The Demon*, 1839; *Mtsyri*, 1839). Purely Romantic in spirit, they are remarkable for the sustained richness of their style and for a strain of genuine feeling which contrasts brightly with the simplistic poses of the early lyrics. Lermontov's lyric poetry of the period 1837–41 is distinct from the earliest immature work in two fundamental ways: firstly, in its rapprochement with the real world – if the lyric hero is still persecuted and oppressed, it is now by identified forces in reality; secondly, in its rapprochement in style with the Pushkinian virtues of terseness, expressiveness and shape. Some outstanding examples are: *When the Yellow Cornfield Ripples* (1837), *I Do Not Wish the World to Know* (1837), *Meditation* (1838), *The Poet* (1838), *Trust Not Yourself* (1839), *The Cliff* (1841). He also experimented in other poetic genres, notably the martial ballad (*Borodino*, 1837) and the epic folk★ poem, such as *The Story of the Merchant Kalashnikov* (1837).

Lermontov's novel *A Hero of our Time*, generally regarded as his greatest work, continues the Pushkinian tradition of experimentation in the novel form, though the nature of Lermontov's experiment

M. Yu. Lermontov as a young officer in the Guards

is unique. It is composed of five parts, all ostensibly modelled on such conventional prose genres as the Caucasian travel memoir and the diary: the chronology of events is shuffled and rearranged and the hub of the work, its hero Pechorin, is observed from various angles of view. This sophisticated structure is perfectly geared and subordinated to the book's main dynamic – a gradually sharpening focus on the character and psychology of the hero. The prose has all the clarity and delicacy of the mature lyrics, and Lermontov catches perfectly the respective 'voices' of his various narrators, from a simple army captain to his own introspective hero. The psychological make-up – and plight – of Pechorin marks a natural progression from Griboedov's★ Chatsky and Pushkin's Germann. Pechorin is a further model of modern man, whose inner life is so dominated by the power of analytical intellect that emotion is stifled, and human relationships are reduced to a deadly, one-sided game, conceived of and controlled by the mind. In Pechorin the tragic consequences of the tyranny of intellect over emotion and instinct are fully mapped. Acceptance of no external authority, moral, social, or divine, leads to ennui and the yearning for death. Pechorin admirably illustrates modern man's loss of wholeness, of oneness with the world. The proud Byronic hero is reduced, under realistic scrutiny, to a psychological cripple. *M.H.S.*

Gogol'

Lermontov's★ death brought the Golden Age of Russian poetry to its end. For 60 years Russian literature was to be dominated by prose, especially the novel, while poetry and drama became secondary genres. The first great prose-writer to follow Lermontov was N. V. Gogol' (1809–52), who was born in the Ukraine and moved to St Petersburg at the age of 19. Meditative, but profoundly ambitious, he was initially stunned by his failure to achieve instant success in either literature or the public service. Early collections of short stories, however, soon established him among the literary élite, and, apart from a short-lived and generally disastrous spell as Professor of History at St Petersburg University in 1834–5, Gogol' thereafter devoted himself to literature. Encouraged by Pushkin,★ and lauded by, amongst others, the critic Belinsky★ and the emerging Slavophils,★ he became obsessed not only by his art, but also by the sense of a divine vocation to purge Russia of its 'sins' and, through his works, lead it to salvation and the realization of its messianic destiny. Between 1836 and 1848 he resided in Rome, returning only periodically to Russia. Lapsing gradually into religious mysticism, he died, a melancholic semi-recluse, in 1852.

Gogol''s fiction falls into three categories: short stories, the novel *Dead Souls* and drama. His short stories comprise three cycles. *Evenings on a Farm near Dikan'ka* (1829–32), *Mirgorod* (1833–5) and

N. V. Gogol' in 1841

the cycle conventionally titled 'Petersburg Tales' (1831–41). The *Dikan'ka* stories, based on Ukrainian folklore, are romantic in spirit and conjure up a world of rustic harmony, shared by men, nature and the forces of the supernatural. Outrageous fun and Gothic horror merge in this version of a Slavic Arcady. In *Mirgorod* to Arcady is added – in the story *Taras Bul'ba* – Gogol''s rose-tinted notion of an heroic Slavic past, when Cossack heroes of Homeric stature rode out in defence of Orthodoxy* against the infidel Pole. But this idyll of rural and historic Russia is already tainted by the destructive forces which characterize modernity. In *The Old-World Landowners* the harmonious existence in nature of two old people is based on mere gluttony. Later, their rustic paradise is swiftly reduced to ruin by the incursion of alien urban forces, in the form of a wastrel heir and lackadaisical trustees. Even the spiritual and familial unity of the Cossacks in *Taras Bul'ba* is undermined by the forces of materialistic greed and sexuality. The magnificently mock-heroic *The Tale of How Ivan Ivanovich Quarrelled with Ivan Nikiforovich (The Two Ivans)* is in perfect counterpoint to *Taras Bul'ba*, revealing in already finished form Gogol''s nightmare vision of the degeneracy of modern man. Where the Cossacks rode shoulder to shoulder against the common foe, the two Ivans quarrel even unto death over some knick-knack or trifling insult and pursue their feud through petty litigation. It is a drab, disheartening world – but for Gogol' a rich source of comic invention. The grotesquely comic mock-epic manner of *The Two Ivans* clearly foreshadows his prose masterpiece *Dead Souls*.

The 'Petersburg Tales' expose the full nightmare of modern urban life which so terrified the mystic and prophet in Gogol' yet, paradoxically, so richly nourished his fertile artistic imagination. Wit, fantasy, absurdity and the grotesque flourish in such tales as *The Nose* and *The Notes of a Madman*, while in *Nevsky Prospekt* and *The Portrait* art and the artist are shown as specific and vulnerable targets of the demonic forces of corruption. *The Overcoat* describes an hilariously squalid petty clerk, who is lured to destruction by the dream of a new coat – this dream being rich in Freudian undertones. The wretched hero returns in phantom shape after death to take his vengeance on the city. The 'Petersburg Tales' are replete with a surrealistic fantasy which not only expresses Gogol''s view of a demon-ridden urban world but simultaneously allows him to take his vengeance upon it.

A recurrent theme in Gogol''s stories is the conflict between noble dream (of man or artist) and base reality. The motif of dream is modified and redeployed in his theatrical masterpiece *The Government Inspector* (1836). Khlestakov, a rascally nonentity, while passing through a symbolically anonymous provincial town, is taken by the town officials to be a government inspector incognito. Both Khlestakov and the mayor are dreamers, but their dreams are of power, rank and wealth – the ignoble dreams of vulgar men. The mayor's dream is compounded by nightmare visions of retribution for the sins of corruption. Gogol' creates a situation where the dreams of the various parties collide to complement and foster each other. The bubble finally bursts: Khlestakov melts away to perform his mischief elsewhere. To the discomfiture of the mayor is added that of the audience, whose sense of well-being, induced by their privileged knowledge, is shattered in the last act by a series of devices which turn the stage into a mirror. Gogol''s play has no equal in Russian for the sustained brilliance of its comic inventiveness.

In *The Two Ivans* and *The Government Inspector* the didactic and artistic impulses in Gogol' are perfectly in tune; the inevitable rift between them occurred in his greatest literary project – the novel *Dead Souls*. His intention was to write a three-part novel akin to Dante's *Divine Comedy*. Part I ('Inferno') is complete. Only fragments of Part II remain, Gogol' having burned the original completed draft in 1846. Part III was never written.

If the original project was based on Dante, it is the influence of Homer which pervades Part I – the novel as we now have it. As in *The Two Ivans* the essential manner is mock-epic: indeed, in broad structure Gogol''s *poema* is a splendidly ironic replica of *The Odyssey*. His anti-hero Chichikov roams the world of provincial Russia, driven by the single force of greed. He encounters all manner of half-monsters half-men – Russian landowners, from whom he would buy dead serfs. His notion is to pawn them before the next census officially registers their death. The style is a travesty of the epic manner. The trivial, the base, the vulgar become objects for detailed and fantastical description; the utterly banal is treated as though it were the infinitely noble. Meanwhile, in a series of lyrical digressions, in which the figure of Gogol' himself, prophet and teacher, looms large, a vision of the 'real' Russia is evoked, a land bright with colour, enriched by a tongue superior to all others and endowed with a messianic destiny among the nations of the world. Gogol''s voice is rarely absent from the work. Like Sterne and Pushkin, Gogol' for ever intrudes upon the text, manipulating, commenting, even merging here and there, in a sort of masochistic glee, with the wretched Chichikov himself. The all-pervasive theme of sin, purgation, salvation and the realization of a divinely ordained destiny pertain always as much to the writer as to his native land. There is no cause to lament the absence of the second and third parts of the novel. Part I of *Dead Souls* is a perfect expression of the whole, integrated Gogol'. His mischievous artistic imagination is wonderfully excited by the 'Inferno' of reality, which the teacher in him abhors. Part II, one senses, was written predominantly by the teacher and committed to the fire by the artist.

As though to replace Part III, Gogol' wrote *Selections from a Correspondence with Friends* (1847), a publicistic work in epistolary form. Seemingly in a last effort to discover within contemporary Russia the seeds of his imagined Slavic Utopia, Gogol' here heaps praise on (among other things) Russian Orthodoxy, literature, women and the paternalistic autocratic-feudal society. The tone of the piece is at once coyly self-castigatory and unrelentingly didactic. This melancholy victory of teacher over artist offers interesting parallels with the later part of Tolstoy's* career.   *M.H.S.*

Belinsky

The 1840s can be seen as a transitional period in the evolution of Russian literature. It is marked, first, by the emergence of four writers–Goncharov,* Turgenev,* Dostoevsky* and Tolstoy*– whose mature work would compose the great age of the Russian realistic novel; second, by the full flowering of the dispute between Slavophils and Westernists on the future cultural and historical evolution of Russia; and third, by the career of the critic V. G. Belinsky (1811–48). A *raznochinets* (an educated man of the 'middle', non-gentry, class), he had a vital and enduring effect upon Russian literary attitudes, largely through his critical reviews published in the journals *Notes of the Fatherland (Otechestvennye zapiski)* and *The Contemporary (Sovremennik)* during the 1840s. Acknowledged as the leader of progressive Westernist thought, he asserted that literature must be realistic in manner, relevant to the problems of real life and inspired by progressive socio-political ideas. Having mistakenly assumed that Gogol''s* work was motivated above all by an abhorrence of Russia's social and political institutions, he reacted to *Selections from a Correspondence with Friends* with the famous *Letter to*

V.G. Belinsky

Gogol' (1847) in which he scathingly rebuked his former idol for ostensibly betraying their shared ideals. Belinsky's conception of literature as primarily a vehicle for the expression of 'civic' ideas became deeply embedded in intellectual attitudes towards literature for the remainder of the 19th century and found further, more radical, expression in the works of N. G. Chernyshevsky (1828–89) and N. A. Dobrolyubov (1836–61). It was Belinsky too who through his critical columns welcomed into literature the great prose writers of the future–Turgenev, Goncharov and Dostoevsky.   *M.H.S.*

Turgenev

I. S. Turgenev (1818–83) was born of impoverished gentry stock. Educated in Moscow, St Petersburg and Berlin, he travelled extensively in Europe and was a lifelong admirer of European art and culture. His first literary success came with the publication of *A Hunter's Notes* (1847–52). This collection of sketches of peasant life, manners and character, superficially dispassionate, yet profoundly compassionate, was impressive not just for its lyricism of style, elegance of composition and delicate characterization, but also for its treatment of the peasantry as human beings in their own right. Turgenev was lionized by the progressive Westernist faction, who quite overlooked the work's underlying mood of romantic pessimism. This fatalistic philosophy, which saw man as the hapless and impotent plaything of nature, was the dominant force shaping the lives of men throughout Turgenev's literature: it is explicitly expounded in such diverse pieces as *A Journey to Poles'e* (1857) and the *Senilia* (or *Poems in Prose*, 1879–83).

Turgenev subsequently worked almost exclusively in the genres of *povest'* (novella) and novel. In both his central preoccupation is always the delineation of human character. The love story, upon which the Turgenev plot is most commonly built, is never an end in itself, but only an instrument by means of which the characters of the individuals concerned may be more penetratingly explored. Turgenev's prose is carefully wrought, yet remarkably at ease, striking a mean between the stark economy of Pushkin★ and the uninhibited effusiveness of Gogol'.★ It has measure, clarity and balance; it is the most natural of all Russian styles.

Outstanding among the *povesti* are *A Quiet Spot* (1854), *Asya* (1858), *First Love* (1860), *The Torrents of Spring* (1872) and *A King Lear of the Steppe* (1870).

In his novels, Turgenev sets his study of human fate and human types within the context of contemporary Russian affairs. Having suggested, in the essay *Hamlet and Don Quixote* (1860), a polarity in human type between 'Hamlets'–introspective, inactive egoists–and 'Don Quixotes'–extrovert altruists–he set out in the novels to measure figures from the contemporary Russian landscape against these two archetypes. The result is curious. The essentially Quixotic type, whom Turgenev lauded in his essay as a force for progress, is revealed in *On the Eve* (1860) as humourless, wooden and damned;

I. S. Turgenev, by I. Repin

the arrogant assumption of the hero, Insarov, that he can change the world is punished by nature through death from disease. The predominantly Hamlet types (Rudin in the novel of the same name, 1856, and Lavretsky in *A Nest of Gentlefolk*, 1859) talk and dream, but risk no active challenge to the fates. Rudin's 'heroic' death upon the 1848 Paris barricades is in fact no more than a final act of submission. If the Hamlets, by and large, survive, it is because they instinctively know what Turgenev knows–that any human challenge to that order and equilibrium established by nature, be it in the form of political commitment or the pursuit of a great love, will bring certain retribution.

Turgenev's greatest novel, *Fathers and Sons* (1862), is notable above all for its superbly tragic hero, Bazarov. Modelled upon the scientifically minded and materialistic 'nihilists' of the 1860s, Bazarov utters a Promethean challenge to nature, but discovering within himself natural forces of instinct and emotion which defy intellectual analysis and control, is reduced to woeful contemplation of his own triviality and to an acceptance of death as an act of reconciliation. *Fathers and Sons* surpasses Turgenev's other novels not only in its hero, but also in its finely worked narrative structure and its freedom from a 'Turgenevan heroine'–that insipidly Victorian epitome of integrity and morality which, introduced to throw his male figures into darker relief, mars the earlier works.

Harassed by critics of all political persuasions who could not, or would not, see that his novels were studies in human character, not political doctrine, the novelist himself finally succumbed. His last novels *Smoke* (1867) and *Virgin Soil* (1877) sank beneath a burden of talk on contemporary issues, and blatant authorial prejudice.

Apart from such pieces as *The Torrents of Spring* and *A King Lear of the Steppe* the last 20 years of his life were a period of decline. Turgenev died in France in 1883. *M.H.S.*

Goncharov

I. A. Goncharov (1812–91) was the son of a provincial merchant, and followed a career in government service, much of it as an official censor. Apart from the travel memoir *The Frigate Pallada*, written after an uncomfortable trip to Japan in 1854, and a few minor prose pieces, his work was limited to three novels, upon which he worked in desultory fashion for a total of nearly thirty years.

The first, *An Ordinary Story* (1847), returns to the Griboedovan theme of the conflict between ideals and reality, and traces in its hero the inevitable transition from youthful idealism to the sober and practical attitudes of later life. The third novel, *The Precipice* (1869), is marred by the intrusion of crotchety authorial attitudes, a schematic story line and wooden treatment of character. Like

I. A. Goncharov

Turgenev's* late novels, it is the work of a writer in decline.

Goncharov's fame rests almost exclusively on his second novel, *Oblomov* (1849–59), the eponymous hero of which has achieved almost mythic status. Oblomov is the eternal dreamer, adrift in a real world which does not answer to his dream. Ensconced in his flat within the dizzy modern world of Petersburg, Oblomov nurtures his half-remembered, half-imagined dream of a provincial Russian Arcady. Totally transcending its immediate context, Oblomov's dream represents the eternal yearning of man for the Golden Age, and of the adult for the innocent and secure world of childhood – both refuges from a threatening world. Resisting the efforts of Shtol'ts (Stolz), a symbolically half-German man of affairs, who attempts fruitlessly to stir Oblomov from his contemplative torpor, and the attentions of Ol'ga, a girl who loves in him not what he is, but what she can make of him, Oblomov finally discovers a surrogate for his dream in the undemanding love and care offered him by the plump widow Pshenitsyna. His tranquil death is likened to the running-down of a clock, which someone has forgotten to wind.

The central theme of *Oblomov* has a long literary pedigree. What distinguishes Goncharov's treatment of it is above all the delicate and sustained irony with which the author treats his hero, and his hero's dream. If Goncharov recognizes the undying appeal of the dream, he also recognizes its hopelessness. Yet the over-all rhythm of the novel reinforces that concept of time which lies at the basis of Oblomov's vision of existence: time is the rhythm of the seasons and of the geological evolution of the planet, not the dash of modern man to change the world before he dies. The emblematic quality of Oblomov is unrivalled even by the great characters of Dostoevsky.* *M.H.S.*

Dostoevsky

The son of a Moscow doctor, F. M. Dostoevsky (1821–81) achieved instant fame in 1845 with his first novel *Poor Folk*. In the next four years he completed *The Double* (1846), *The Landlady* (1847), *White Nights* (1848) and a considerable volume of shorter pieces. Throughout the 1840s Dostoevsky dabbled in radical politics. In 1849 he was arrested for his association with the socialist group known as the Petrashevsky circle (from its founder, the political dissident M. V. Butashevich-Petrashevsky), and sentenced to eight years' imprisonment and exile – though not before having been subjected to a traumatic mock execution, staged by the tsarist authorities. He returned to St Petersburg only in 1859.

Of his early pieces, *Poor Folk* is notable primarily for its sentimentally sympathetic treatment of the downtrodden and its grotesquely naturalistic manner; *The Double*, for its introduction of the theme of the divided personality; and the unfinished *Netochka Nezvanova* (1849), for the first appearance of another notable Dostoevskyan type – the demonically wilful 'infernal' woman.

After Siberia Dostoevsky quickly re-established his literary reputation with *The Humiliated and the Insulted* (1861), a novel highly reminiscent of his 'philanthropic' works of the 1840s, and *Notes from the House of the Dead* (1861–2), an account of his period of penal servitude, which, apart from its vivid descriptions of criminal types, gave first expression to two ideas which were to find an important

F. M. Dostoevsky

place in his later thought: firstly, that sin can be punished and expiated only by conscience; secondly, that the intelligentsia must re-establish their bond with the people and with the 'soil' of Russia.

Dostoevsky's outlook had, indeed, undergone a fundamental change. Abandoning his previous Westernist and progressive sympathies, he now propounded a mystic and conservative Slavophilism.* A visit to Europe in 1862–3 strengthened his conviction that Russia must resist the insidious influence of European culture and civilization, based on atheism and materialism. From 1860 to 1864 was a period of personal crises. His first marriage, contracted in Siberia, had broken down. A passionate affair with Apollinaria Suslova in 1862–3 and heavy losses in her company at the roulette tables of Europe were followed in 1864 by the deaths of his wife and his beloved brother Mikhail (with whom he had co-edited the ill-fated journals *Time* (*Vremya*) and *The Epoch* (*Epokha*), and finally by bankruptcy.

During the remaining 17 years of his life Dostoevsky proceeded to write a series of works which have made a unique contribution to the world's literature of ideas. Their starting point was the extraordinary *Notes from Underground* (1864).

Written in first-person 'confessional' form, *Notes from Underground* is ostensibly an attack, in the name of individual liberty and freedom of the will, upon all scientific, rational and materialistic theories of man. The result is paradox. The anonymous 'Underground Man' argues his case against reason *by* reason. Perversely he asserts that man's best interest lies in demonstrating his inalienable freedom by going against his best interests. The result is total unfreedom, symbolized by the wretched bolt-hole from which he speaks, inertia, alienation and the certainty that all he can believe is that he does not know what he believes. The key to his plight, never overtly stated, is hinted at in the figure of a prostitute, Liza, who responds to his malicious taunting with a display of selfless, unthinking humility.

Dostoevsky's first classic novel *Crime and Punishment* (1865–6) expands the themes of *Notes from Underground*. Its hero, Raskol'nikov, commits a murder apparently in the name of rational altruism. Subsequently, a deeper motive is revealed–demonic self-will, based not upon love, but upon absolute contempt for his fellow men. These apparently contradictory impulses within a single man are explained by Dostoevsky in terms of a sinister interconnection. Socialistic theory, based on 'enlightened self-interest' or 'rational utilitarianism' is no more than a mask for tyranny. As for the Underground Man, so for Raskol'nikov, redemption is promised through the agency of a prostitute, Sonya, representing the force of faith, humility and self-abnegation.

In 1867 Dostoevsky married his secretary, Anna Snitkina; under her stabilizing influence he gradually rid himself of gambling fever and debt. Driven abroad by dunning creditors in 1867, he was able to return to Russia in 1871. Meanwhile, under intense financial pressure, he had produced two more great novels, *The Idiot* (1868) and *The Devils* (1871).

In Prince Myshkin, the hero of *The Idiot*, Dostoevsky attempted to incarnate those Christian virtues of humility, selflessness and altruistic love previously outlined in the figures of Liza and Sonya. Myshkin, introduced into a corrupt Petersburg world dominated by the evil forces of materialism and lust, proves neither sufficiently human nor sufficiently divine to affect the hearts and minds of those whom he would save. As Myshkin finally lapses into insanity, Dostoevsky, playing the devil's advocate as always with disturbing ease, traces unerringly the inevitable victory of darkness over light.

In *The Idiot* Dostoevsky more clearly than ever before defined the opposing forces battling for the soul of Russia. At the devil's elbow stood the forces of West European culture and civilization–atheism, urbanism, materialism, rationalism, rampant individualism, and the twin systems of political tyranny–socialism and Roman Catholicism.* On the side of Holy Russia were faith ('the Russian Christ'), *narodnost'* (a spirit of oneness with the simple masses) and *sobornost'* (the innate, instinctive and religiously-based communistic spirit of the Russian people). Russia, he believed, must pass through suffering to salvation and thence to the fulfilment of its messianic destiny among the nations of the world.

In *The Devils* Dostoevsky considers the battle primarily on its political front. The devils of the title are nihilists who threaten to infect Russia with the virus of materialistic socialism. The novel is rich in exotic and terrifying characters, embodying various aspects of Dostoevsky's nightmare vision of the fate of modern man, who, rejecting faith, would arrogantly elevate himself to Man-God status.

Dostoevsky's last great novel, *The Brothers Karamazov* (1880), concludes and summarizes the cycle. In the various members of the Karamazov family the writer presents a composite picture of the body, mind and soul of contemporary Russia and of the forces at work within it. Their common heritage–'Karamazovism'–represents a phenomenal energy, which can find its expression equally in insatiable lust, demonic amoralism, intellectual scepticism, or in faith, humility and love.

The four great novels are all intensely dramatic in form. The narrative itself is rich in the stuff of melodrama–passion, murder, suicide–but the essential drama lies elsewhere, either in the conflict between different characters embodying opposing ideas, or in the internal conflict raging within the divided individual. This drama of ideas is enacted primarily through talk: dialogue between characters or within a single character, or the direct exposition of idea or theory. Melodramatic incident and dramatic dialogue, combined with elements of outrageous humour, move the novels along at a frenetic pace against a background of seamy contemporary life. There are no easy resolutions; the Dostoevskian novel concludes in uncertainty.

Other important works of the later period are *The Eternal Husband* (1870), *The Adolescent* (1875) and *A Writer's Diary* which, published in serial form from 1876, was a primarily publicistic work devoted to the promulgation of the writer's increasingly conservative views.

A career begun in debt and despair ended in domestic happiness, financial stability and fame. Having achieved a new pinnacle of public acclaim with his famous address on the occasion of the unveiling of a statue to Pushkin* in Moscow in 1880, Dostoevsky died in 1881. His funeral procession was followed by thousands.   *M.H.S.*

Tolstoy

The 'wholeness' of 19th-century Russian literature is in no way better illustrated than by the remarkable similarities in basic outlook between Dostoevsky* and his great contemporary Tolstoy – two men who, astonishingly, never met, and who in social origin, temperament, life-style and attitudes towards literature could barely have had less in common.

L. N. Tolstoy (1828–1910) was an aristocrat by nature as he was by origin. Orphaned by the age of seven, he none the less enjoyed a secure and contented childhood. He entered university at the age of 16; at 19 he dropped out, and returned to the family estate of Yasnaya Polyana to conduct an abortive experiment in rural reform. Four years in Moscow and St Petersburg pursuing the pleasures of the flesh

L.N. Tolstoy as a volunteer officer in the Caucasus, 1854

were followed by military service as a volunteer in the Caucasus.

His first work of fiction was experimentative and ambitious. In *The Diary of Yesterday* (1851), which survives as an unfinished fragment, Tolstoy set out to record every single thought, feeling, word and action in one day of its narrator-hero's life. The personal diary which Tolstoy kept intermittently from 1847 also offers many clues to his subsequent personal and literary development. In terms of its sustained and penetrative analysis of (his own) character, interspersed with passages of philosophical rumination, it is a characteristic piece.

In 1852 Tolstoy dispatched from the Caucasus to N. A. Nekrasov, editor of the journal *The Contemporary* (*Sovremennik*) a semi-fictional memoir of childhood. Its success was instantaneous. *Childhood*, together with its two sequels *Adolescence* (1854) and *Youth* (1857), is a seminal work for the understanding of Tolstoy's literature; here in embryonic form is the essence of his thought and literary art. It is first a fiction based upon, and tied to, personal experience; but above all it is a work dominated by the image of the child and the child's view. In *Childhood* Tolstoy sings the innocence of childhood, its instinctive moral virtue, emotional spontaneity, blissful security from intellectual introspection (and thus from the 'accursed questions' of existence) and the sexual instinct. All later theories of 'simplification' stem from this. At the same time the child's view, translated into literary art, becomes the very basis of Tolstoy's method in his fictional and non-fictional works alike. It is the simple, direct and innocent view, untouched by prejudice or conventional attitude, uninhibited by delicacy or deference, untainted by manners: its moral basis is that of instinct and conscience alone. It is experimental in that it recognizes no constraints of convention on form: it simply says what it wants to say in the way it feels it can best be said.

Adolescence and *Youth* mark the fall from innocence. Contact with the world of men, the awakening of intellect and sexuality, the competitive urge, all conspire to erode and destroy that perfect image of man embodied in the child. Tolstoy's subsequent career would be largely devoted to a pursuit of the means by which the grown man may rediscover the perfect goodness and innocence of the child, and thus be liberated from the spectres of evil and of death.

The many short prose works which Tolstoy wrote in the following ten years are consistently experimental and informed by an irreverent and iconoclastic attitude towards the form and topics of conventional literature. At the same time they amply illustrate a central Tolstoyan paradox. Tolstoy attempts to reduce man and human experience to a series of intellectually conceived and perceived rules, principles and categories, doing so through the profoundly intellectual medium of art. Simultaneously, however, he identifies intellect – man's consciousness of himself and the world – as the very bane of existence, debarring man from assimilation into life, moral virtue, and the acceptance of death. Not for nothing did Tolstoy wear a medallion of

Rousseau round his neck.

In *The Raid* (1853), *The Wood Felling* (1855) and the '*Sevastopol' Sketches*' (1855–6) Tolstoy subjects to scathing scrutiny conventional attitudes towards war, courage and the Caucasus, glorifying the unconscious and unsung bravery of the peasant soldier at the expense of the sham heroics of the educated officer class. In such blatantly 'moral' tales as *Notes of a Billiard Marker* (1853–5), *Two Hussars* (1856), *Lucerne* (1857), *Albert* (1858), *Three Deaths* (1858), *Polikushka* (1862) and *Kholstomer* (1863, published 1885) he consistently contrasts the vanity and immorality of civilized, intellectual–and frequently Western–man with the instinctive nobility and morality of 'simple' man, or (in a typically Tolstoyan *reductio ad absurdum*) of a horse or a tree. Simultaneously, the 18th-century technique of discovering truth by exposing reality to the unprejudiced and innocent eye is developed by Tolstoy to sometimes extraordinary lengths. Thus *Sevastopol' in December* is conducted in the second-person mode (Tolstoy tells you not what *he* sees, but what *you* see), while in *Kholstomer* human behaviour is observed by a horse.

Family Happiness (1859), written partly as an apology for Tolstoy's sterile flirtation with one Valeria Arsen'eva, is an analysis of the slow but ineluctable transformation of a marriage relationship between a young girl and an older man. Seen entirely from the point of view of the girl, it is a fine example of Tolstoy's ability to 'transfer' himself into a fictional character.

The Cossacks (1862), ostensibly another critical examination of the back-to-nature theme, sets its introspective hero Olenin amidst a Cossack tribe who live by purest instinct. The central embodiment of 'simple' virtue, the old hunter Yeroshka embraces a view of man and nature which transcends conventional morality. Lust and murder, in so far as they are part of a natural 'instinctive' existence, are not to be condemned. Olenin expresses a fundamental Tolstoyan dilemma. Striving consciously to emulate the natural virtue of the Cossacks, he is forced ultimately to recognize that no man can think himself into a state of virtue.

Having twice travelled to Western Europe, in 1857 and 1860–1, and seen nothing to please him, Tolstoy determined never to go again. In 1862 he married, and, blissfully ensconced at Yasnaya Polyana, set to writing *War and Peace*.

This work traces the interlocking fates of individuals and Russia itself during the turbulent years of the Napoleonic wars.* Its central heroes, Andrey Bolkonsky and Pierre Bezukhov, are largely projections of Tolstoy himself and of his struggle to understand the meaning and purpose of his existence, while the heroine Natasha Rostov is Tolstoy's most perfect incarnation of his ideal of innocent simplicity. *War and Peace* brought to full fruition all the promise of Tolstoy's early works, and pushed forward the frontiers of the novel form to a degree matched only perhaps by Sterne's *Tristram Shandy*. Combining elements of the family chronicle, the historical epic, the

novel of ideas and the fictionalized autobiography, it is a superb expression of the whole Tolstoy, both man and artist, and of the paradoxes within him. Describing life and historical event with the apparently beguiling objectivity of an innocent, it does so constantly in order to persuade. Proclaiming the primacy of the simple and uncultured over the civilized and the intellectual, it draws its characters almost exclusively from the upper echelons of Russian society. It denounces art, while superbly displaying Tolstoy's total command of literary artifice. Debunking conventional interpretations of history, it finds no better explanation for history than blind determinism, and tampers with historical fact as suits its purpose. It is the crystalline accuracy with which Tolstoy creates his illusion of human experience which makes the book so persuasive. Absorbed by its detail, we are induced to overlook the fallibility of its broad assertions. And when it is overtly polemical, it is brilliantly so: Tolstoy tears down with arrogant ease the idols of received ideas.

In *War and Peace* Tolstoy came as close as he ever did to persuading himself that the key to life's mystery was within his, and our, grasp. It lay in the absorption of the individual, and of human consciousness, into the stuff of 'simple' life–birth, marriage, procreation, the domestic round, tilling the earth. But like all of his 'solutions', it represented not so much an answer to the 'accursed questions', as a means of attaining that blissful state (akin to early childhood) when the questions never arise.

Anna Karenina (1873–7) demonstrates clearly the fragility of the solutions suggested in *War and Peace*. Tolstoy's second great novel is his most honest work and, therefore, his least conclusive. The optimism of *War and Peace* gives way to despondency. Death–an event of mystic grandeur in *War and Peace*–is now seen as ugly and bewildering.

Conceived originally as a tale of sin and expiation, the novel expanded to take a broader, balanced view of its adulterous heroine, Anna, and to incorporate a contrapuntal story–that of Levin, a Russian landowner, whose search for happiness and the meaning of life has (like that of Andrey and Pierre) its base in Tolstoy's own experience. Like *War and Peace*, *Anna Karenina* is a superbly organized novel, built upon the interlocking stories of Anna and Levin, two fundamentally different, yet in some ways curiously similar, characters, each dedicated to the pursuit of individual fulfilment. The novel is rich too in its treatment of a host of contemporary social and political issues, the discussion of which is more closely integrated into the text than were the philosophical digressions in *War and Peace*.

In certain ways *Anna Karenina* foreshadows two of the major works of Tolstoy's later years–*A Confession* (1882) and *What is Art?* (1897). The years during which he was working on the novel were a period of personal crisis too. The steady deterioration of his relationship with his wife made family life a less reliable refuge from the 'accursed questions'. Several deaths in his family reminded him forcibly of his own mortality. More convinced than ever of the futility of a rational approach to life's mystery, Tolstoy took the leap into faith: characteristically, however, the faith he now proclaimed was rebellious, intensely personal and, for all its intuitive base, developed and pursued with a dogged rationalism. *A Confession* is the dramatic account of Tolstoy's 'conversion' to a Christianity stripped of ritual and dogma, founded upon, and perceived through, the dictates of conscience.

What is Art?, worked on by Tolstoy over a long period before publication, represents the writer's final view of the nature and function of art. It is a typically Tolstoyan treatise–perverse, mischievous, iconoclastic, brilliantly destructive, numbering Shakespeare, Pushkin★ and Homer among its many victims. Its central thesis is that art must be simple, accessible to all men, and must infect those who experience it with good and moral feelings.

The major part of Tolstoy's work during the last 30 years of his life consists of efforts to fulfil, through fiction and treatise, the dictates of *A Confession* and *What is Art?*. Outstanding among the fiction of the period are *The Death of Ivan Il'ich* (1886), *Master and Man* (1895), *Hadzhi Murat* (1896–1904), and two treatments of the theme of sexuality, *The Kreutzer Sonata* (1889) and *The Devil* (1889). Tolstoy also experimented in drama, notably in *The Power of Darkness* (1887) and *The Fruits of Enlightenment* (1889).

As Tolstoy's fame and following spread throughout the world, his home became a place of pilgrimage. Although he was excommuni-

L.N. Tolstoy at work shortly before his death in 1910

cated by the Orthodox Church★ for his 'heresies' in 1901, Tolstoy's reputation saved him from governmental persecution. His domestic life, however, was reduced to endless series of quarrels and recriminations. In autumn of 1910 he fled his home, and shortly afterwards died at the wayside railway station of Astapovo. *M.H.S.*

Poetry and drama

For half a century or so the thunder of the great novelists almost completely obliterated the gentler sounds of poetry. Yet two fine lyric poets, Tyutchev and Fet, were at work throughout this period; and it is not surprising that they owe their present high reputation not to their contemporaries, but to their 're-discovery' by the poets and critics of the early 20th century.

F. I. Tyutchev (1803–73) came of noble stock and spent most of his adult life as a diplomat abroad. His early poetry is predominantly of a philosophical nature, grandiloquent, elegant, replete with archaisms and expressing a metaphysical system based largely on ideas of the German Romantics. In later life he wrote political verse expressing his increasingly reactionary Slavophil★ views. His finest achievement is his love poetry, and in particular the darkly passionate verses inspired by his liaison with E. A. Denis'eva, his children's governess.

A. A. Fet (real name Shenshin: 1820–92) is very much a 'poet's poet'. The range and depth of feeling, the sensitivity to nature and human emotion achieved in his poetry totally belied the staid, straitlaced exterior which he presented to the world. Richly metaphorical, saturated in feeling, exquisitely euphonic, his verse is sometimes philosophical, more commonly a pure celebration of love, nature or the poetic muse.

Neither Tyutchev nor Fet found much favour among the critics of their day, who saw literature's function as no more than the propagation of progressive ideas. The only civic themes in Tyutchev's poetry were mystic and reactionary. Fet, himself a political conservative, totally eschewed such unpoetic themes. The third major poet of the period, N. A. Nekrasov (1821–77), combined an ambitious, self-indulgent and snobbish character with a radical political credo, which found consistent expression in his verse. Though frequently lapsing into sentimentality or rhetoric, his verses on the Russian people, the poverty of their lives and the richness of their spirit, are sincerely felt and expressed with often formidable power. His finest works, *Red-Nosed Frost* (1863) and the unfinished *Who Can Live Happily in Russia?* (1863–77) draw widely on the motifs and the manner of folk★ poetry, and are among the finest celebrations of the 'simple people' in Russian literature.

Drama in the mid-century succumbed almost entirely to the dominance of the novel. Only two native dramatists made any

Top: (left) F. I. Tyutchev; (right) A. A. Fet, by I. Repin. Above: (left) N. A. Nekrasov; (right) A. N. Ostrovsky

significant contribution to the repertory of the Russian stage – A. V. Sukhovo-Kobylin (1817–1903) and A. N. Ostrovsky (1823–86). Both were primarily satirists, and interest in their work has diminished with time. Of Sukhovo-Kobylin's three plays, *Krechinsky's Wedding* (1855) has survived on the strength of a superbly contrived comic plot. Ostrovsky wrote some 50 plays: a handful are still staged, notably *The Thunderstorm* (1859) and *The Forest* (1871). These two plays owe their survival to the playwright's success in grafting such 'eternal' themes as the conflict between moral and sexual instinct on to a satirical treatment of purely contemporary types. *M.H.S.*

Lesser prose writers

M. Ye. Saltykov (pseudonym Shchedrin: 1826–89) wrote mainly in a genre falling midway between fiction and pamphlet. His *History of a Certain Town* (1869–70) is a microcosmic parody of Russian history, disguised as the chronicle of a small town. *Provincial Sketches* (1856–7), *Gentlemen of Tashkent* (1869–72) and similar pieces suffer from an excess of topical allusions and an 'Aesopic' language, devised to foil the censorship,★ which reduce their accessibility to the modern reader. Saltykov's outstanding work is *The Golovlev Family* (1872–6), which traces the decay of a family of provincial landowners, ultimately destroyed by their own greed, bestiality and hypocrisy. It is a powerful but unrelievedly depressing study in human decadence.

N. S. Leskov (1831–95) is an original talent who has found little honour in his own land. A *raznochinets* (educated man of the non-gentry class) by birth, he acquired a profound first-hand knowledge of the manners, culture and language of the provincial masses. His career in literature began badly with two long novels, *No Way Forward* (1864) and *At Daggers Drawn* (1870–1), which alienated the critics by their overtly hostile treatment of the young radicals.

Cathedral Folk (1872) is one of his finest works. A 'chronicle' centred upon a study of the provincial clergy, it is a marvellous compendium of the poignant and the hilarious, and establishes a fundamental theme in Leskov – that of the 'righteous man'. This *pravednik* is a uniquely Russian type, simple, selfless and submissive, yet endowed with many qualities of the *bogatyr'*, the epic folk-hero.★ Non-conformist and antagonistic to authority. Leskov's 'righteous men' are moved by conscience, instinct and a zest for life which takes no heed of conventional morality.

Outstanding among Leskov's other longer works are *The Enchanted Wanderer* (1874), *The Sealed Angel* (1874) and *The Hare Park* (1894, pub. 1917), while the most famous of his shorter pieces are *The Lady Macbeth of the Mtsensk District* (1865), *On the Edge of the World* (1876), *The Left-Handed Craftsman* (1882) and *The Sentry* (1887).

Though working within a prose tradition which at the best of times took little heed of formal convention, Leskov is by far the most daring and innovatory stylist of his age. Favouring the first-person narrative

M. Ye. Saltykov

N. S. Leskov, about 1883

mode, particularly that vernacular variety known in Russian as *skaz*, Leskov's narratives are characterized by a defiant disorder – a formal expression of his belief in the primacy of the natural and the instinctive. Nor has any other writer made such effective use of the rich expressive resources of Russian provincial dialects.   *M.H.S.*

Chekhov

With the death of Dostoevsky★ and the decline in Tolstoy's★ imaginative art after *Anna Karenina*, the 1880s were a relatively barren interlude; by the early 1890s, however, two new talents had emerged – A. P. Chekhov (1860–1904) and Gor'ky.★ Anton Chekhov's literary career was born of necessity. His father, a provincial shopkeeper, was reduced to bankruptcy in 1876. Chekhov was thus obliged in the early 1880s to combine his medical studies with the production of sketches and anecdotes for a variety of comic papers in order to support himself and the family. Itself of little intrinsic literary merit, this work afforded Chekhov valuable experience in the observation of human foibles and in the art of artistic compression. The writer's superficially comic but essentially gloomy view of a world of scoundrels, hypocrites and fools is occasionally enlivened by a sympathetic glance at children or some of society's hapless victims.

Gradually the focus of Chekhov's stories shifted from anecdotal incident to the inner world of his characters: at the same time he developed an impressionistic technique for psychological description which became fundamental to his mature manner. In such pieces as *The Kiss* (1887), *Happiness* (1887) and *The Steppe* (1888) narrative, description and image are transmitted largely via the perception of the central characters: herein lay the key to that particular Chekhovian phenomenon known as 'mood'.

Chekhov's first works for the stage were a series of superb short farces – *The Bear* (1888), *The Proposal* (1888), *The Wedding* (1889) and *The Anniversary* (1891) – together with two longer pieces – *Ivanov* (1887) and *The Wood Demon* (1889) – which gave some indication of his subsequent evolution as a major dramatist. By 1890 – in which year he made an arduous journey to the penal colony on Sakhalin Island to conduct a single-handed census – Chekhov had come to see himself as a 'serious' writer and to give precedence to his literary, over his medical, vocation.

The body of short stories written during the remainder of his short life offers a comprehensive picture of Russian life and manners of the period; yet it is the individual psychological experience with which Chekhov is always chiefly preoccupied. Such tales as *A Dreary Story* (1889), *Ward No. 6* (1892), *My Life* (1896) and *The Peasants* (1896) take a largely critical view of Tolstoyism and its psychological

implications. In *A Woman's Kingdom* (1894), *A Doctor's Visit* (1898) and *In the Ravine* (1900) he examines the impact of industrial capitalism. In others the baneful influence upon the human psyche of religion (*Three Years*, 1895) or the contemporary cult of pessimism (*The Wife*, 1892) is delicately observed. Stories on a love theme – *About Love* (1898), *Lady with a Little Dog* (1899) – take a sceptical view of conventional morality; while a host of others trace the pernicious afflictions of greed, complacency, ambition and self-indulgence. Chekhov observes the world with detachment and irony, content to let his readers be the judges. Though his characters are seen predominantly in spiritual or moral decline, pessimism is often averted by the implication that man can and will live better than he does.

Chekhov's fame in the West rests largely upon the four plays *The Seagull* (1895–6), *Uncle Vanya* (1897), *Three Sisters* (1900) and *The Cherry Orchard* (1903). All four are studies of the moribund provincial gentry class of Chekhov's day, but have transcended their

A.P. Chekhov

age to become classic studies of human hope, frustration and despair. As in his stories, Chekhov concentrates upon the internal world of his characters: drama consists in the emotional interplay between characters or in the struggle of the individual to preserve hope and integrity in a hostile world. Meanwhile, within dialogue and action he develops a system of symbols, clues and allusions which illuminate the inner world of thought and emotion. Not that Chekhov rid his plays entirely of the artifices of conventional theatre. Though such climactic events as suicides in *The Seagull* and *Three Sisters* or the crucial auction in *The Cherry Orchard* are shifted off stage, they, together with the framing device of arrival and departure, remain as vestigial traces of the traditional 'plot'. Moreover, the superficially naturalistic Chekhovian dialogue is so replete with implied meanings as to seem ultimately at least as contrived as the more overtly dramatic dialogue of conventional theatre.

Perhaps Chekhov's greatest contribution to literature as a means by which man may understand himself lies in his pervasive irony, suggesting, as it does, that what we do or say is at best a very indirect way of expressing what we actually mean or feel; and that the narrow pursuit of individual happiness is perhaps a betrayal of man's true calling. It is to be concluded from Chekhov's writing that whereas in success the human spirit dies, through misfortune it is tempered and regenerated. The unique blend of ironic scepticism and dogged idealism above all gives Chekhov's work its distinctive flavour.

M.H.S.

Gor'ky

Maksim Gor'ky (1868–1936) (whose real name was Aleksey Maksimovich Peshkov) was the son of a Nizhny Novgorod carpenter. His finest work, the trilogy *Childhood* (1913), *Amongst People* (1916) and *My Universities* (1923) is a vivid record of the forging of Gor'ky's extraordinary personality in a world of poverty and brutality, alleviated only by such rare examples of human warmth as his maternal grandmother, and by books and the pursuit of knowledge. His first published writing, and the adoption of the pseudonym Gor'ky (meaning 'bitter'), date from 1892. In romantic rebellion against the prevailing atmosphere of political oppression and intellectual stagnation, his early stories evinced a burning faith in human freedom. In *Makar Chudra* (1892) and *The Old Woman Izergil'* (1894) figures drawn from gipsy myth and folk-lore★ are set in a richly romantic landscape of forest and steppe. In *Emel'yan Pilyay* (1893) and *Chelkash* (1894) there emerged a new hero, the *bosyak*, loosely modelled on the itinerant labourers he had encountered on his travels about Russia, and embodying–in Gor'ky's romanticized version–the very essence of freedom, independence and will. As reality, in the form of wharves, slums and dosshouses, began to

impinge upon the earlier mythical settings, so too the psychology of his characters was treated with greater verisimilitude. In *Chelkash* Gor'ky's awareness of the psychological fragility of the self-isolated individual is already discernible. By *Konovalov* (1896) and *Boles* (1897) he had come to acknowledge the destructive potential of his earlier proclaimed ideal–the escape from an ugly world into a beautiful lie. His novel *Foma Gordeev* (1889) convincingly describes the inevitable crushing of the individual and inarticulate rebel by superior hostile forces in society.

By the turn of the century Gor'ky's fame as a writer was matched in Russia only by Tolstoy's:★ with fame came some measure of protection from police persecution. Drawn increasingly into political affairs, Gor'ky became associated with the Bolsheviks,★ for whom he was a valuable source of funds; thus began a long and tortuous relationship both with the Bolshevik Party and, more particularly, with Lenin.★ Forced to flee after the 1905 revolution, Gor'ky eventually settled on Capri, to return after the general amnesty of 1913.

His literary output, meanwhile, was prodigious. To the novels *Three of Them* (1901), *Mother* (1907), *A Confession* (1908), *Okurov Town* (1909) and *Matvey Kozhemyakin* (1910) were added his first attempts at the drama, notably *The Petty Bourgeois* (1901), *The Lower Depths* (1902), *Summer Folk* (1904) and *Enemies* (1906). Of the novels, *Mother* was lauded by Soviet criticism as a forerunner of the 'Socialist Realism'★ school. It is crude, tendentious and unconvincing–yet enlivened for all that by the curious religious-political philosophy of 'God-building' which underpins it. This contempor-

A. M. Gor'ky in 1899, by I. Repin

ary crackpot synthesis of Marxism-Leninism* and Christianity, to which Gor'ky (to Lenin's dismay) strongly adhered at the time, found even more eloquent and overt expression in *A Confession*. Gor'ky's plays are marred by a crude aping of modernist techniques and an immoderate tendentiousness–with the exception of *The Lower Depths*, whose dosshouse setting, vivid dialogue, colourful characters and delicately ambiguous treatment of the theme of 'ugly truth and beautiful lie' ensured it an initial *succès de scandale* and subsequent survival on the world's stage.

Of Gor'ky's writing after 1910 only such non-fictional pieces as the autobiographical trilogy, his *Recollections* (notably of Tolstoy, Chekhov* and Leonid Andreev) and *Notes from a Diary* (1924) are truly memorable. The novels *The Artamonov Business* (1925) and the unfinished *The Life of Klim Samgin* (1927–36) are monumental accounts of the evolution of the merchant class and the intelligentsia respectively. One late play, *Yegor Bulichev and Others* (1932), still enjoys some popularity.

After publishing a series of virulently anti-Bolshevik articles in 1917–18 and making heroic efforts in the aftermath of revolution to save starving members of the old intelligentsia, Gor'ky left the USSR again in 1921. Lured back in 1928, he died, in mysterious circumstances, in 1936. *M.H.S.*

Literary revolution

The years 1890 to 1910 were marked in Russia by a profound cultural and aesthetic upheaval on several interconnected fronts–art and art criticism, religion, philosophy and literature. It involved not only a rediscovery and reinterpretation of the ideas of the past, but also the promotion of new approaches. At its heart lay a rejection of those principles of social and moral utilitarianism which had so preoccupied the Russian mind for a half-century or more. The old gods of progress, reform and moral improvement were replaced by those of beauty, mysticism and unfettered individualism. In the field of art the leading spirits of the movement were Sergey Diaghilev* (1872–1929), founder of the influential journal *World of Art*★ and Alexandre Benois (Benua) (1870–1960), the painter and art critic. The outstanding religious-philosophical thinkers of the period were N. A. Berdyaev (1874–1948), V. V. Rozanov (1856–1919) and L. I. Shestov (real name Shvartsman: 1866–1938). A fundamental reappraisal of the work of Tolstoy,★ Dostoevsky★ and Gogol'★ was effected by the critical studies of D. S. Merezhkovsky (1865–1941).

The crowning expression of this 'revolution' in literature itself is the Symbolist★ school of poetry. The major poets associated with this school are Blok, Bely, V. Ya. Bryusov (1873–1924), Bal'mont and Fedor Sologub (real name F. K. Teternikov: 1863–1927).

K. D. Bal'mont (1867–1942) is known mainly for six books of original verse written between 1894 and 1904, in which he experimented in rhythm, euphony and pure sound. Bryusov, an early admirer of the French Symbolists, and an expert in the history and techniques of poetry, is now better remembered for his promotion of poetry through translation and commentary than for his own–often fine–original verse. Sologub's poetry is overshadowed by his extraordinary novel *The Petty Demon* (1892–1902), in which a provincial Russian town and its inhabitants are elevated to symbols illustrating the author's curious metaphysical system and morbid sensuality. Yet his poetry is often exquisite, matching in its delicate structures and meanings the finest poetry of Tyutchev.★

Andrey Bely (real name B. N. Bugaev: 1880–1934), a prolific writer of both verse and prose, was certainly in terms of personality–and, at the time, notoriety–the most influential member of the movement. Falling at various times under the influence of such religious-political mystics as V. S. Solov'ev (1853–1900), Rudolf Steiner and R. V. Ivanov-Razumnik (1878–1946), his poetry was marked always by metaphysical mysticism and formal experimentation. His finest prose work, the novel *Petersburg* (1910–16), is packed with vivid incident and character and written in an elaborately ornamental prose style. Yet its central theme, the mystic conflict in Russia between forces of East and West, now seems trite. For all its brilliant craftsmanship, Bely's work always lacked the spontaneity and intensity of feeling which was the hallmark of the poetry of Blok.★ *M.H.S.*

Blok

A. A. Blok (1880–1921) is the one outstanding genius of the Russian Symbolist★ movement. Two early cycles of verse, *Ante Lucem* (1898–1900) and *Verses about the Beautiful Lady* (1904), are the finest examples in Russian of pure Symbolist poetry, trapping elusive visions from beyond reality in a gossamer net of symbol, image and poetic music. The dimly perceived object, here as in much of Blok's verse, takes female form: it is associated with V. S. Solov'ev's mystic concept 'Sophia, Goddess of Wisdom'–and to some degree with the poet's wife. Reality subsequently encroached increasingly upon Blok's poetic vision. In *The Stranger* and *The Puppet Show* (1906) the early mood of reverent anticipation is replaced by ironic disillusion. From an ethereal world, Blok's verse descends into a landscape of brothels, pot-houses and dimly-lit streets. *The Snow Mask* (1907), a cycle of verse inspired by a stormy love affair, is dominated by the image of swirling blizzards, while *The City* (1904–8) and *The Terrible World* (1909–16) record Blok's visionary response to such contemporary phenomena as factories, aviation and modern warfare.

A. A. Blok

In the cycle *Homeland* Blok first gave clear voice to a mystic Slavophilism* latent in much of his verse, and expounded also in articles such as *The People and the Intelligentsia* (1908) and *The Intelligentsia and the Revolution* (1918). These works hark back clearly to mainstream literary ideas of the 19th century, particularly those of Dostoevsky.* The Russian intelligentsia, Blok suggests, had, by fostering the alien rational-scientific culture of the West, lost touch with Russia, its people, its mystic spirit and its messianic destiny. Further boosted by Blok's association in 1916–17 with R. V. Ivanov-Razumnik, this mystic-religious nationalism found its finest expression in two major poems of the revolutionary period – *The Twelve* (1917–18) and *The Scythians* (1917–18).

The Scythians is an impassioned plea to the West to reconcile itself to the Revolution and its mystic import, or suffer the consequences. The nature of this mystic import is eloquently suggested by *The Twelve*. This culminating masterpiece of Blok's literary career shocked and enthralled the reading public. Incorporating the imagery of storm, movement and colour of his early work with popular song, revolutionary slogan and the rough language of the streets, Blok created in *The Twelve* a rich texture of harmony and dissonance, of sacred and profane. Twelve Red Guards who patrol revolutionary Petrograd, brutally sweeping away all remnants of the past, are led – though they do not know it – by Christ: thus is the Revolution revealed as an apocalyptic cataclysm, heralding the Second Coming, and the fulfilment of Russia's messianic destiny. As revolutionary rapture gave way to the harsh realities of civil war,

famine and reconstruction, Blok was rapidly overtaken by a sense of disillusion, which contributed to his early death in 1921.

Blok was not alone in viewing the Revolution through a rose-tinted lens of mystical idealism. Other writers – notably Bely,* Yesenin,* Mayakovsky* and Pil'nyak,* and even Gor'ky* in his time – had awaited or welcomed the Revolution as a prelude to the establishment of a new 'Christian' era in Russia. All of them with the possible exception of Gor'ky, were to suffer in their individual ways the same disillusionment.   *M.H.S.*

The new regime and literature

The impact of the October Revolution on the established literary world was inescapable, although its reception varied considerably according to the political attitude and artistic inclinations of individual writers. Unlike their 19th-century predecessors, they were forced to declare their allegiance in an atmosphere where even the composition of lyric poetry, with its disregard for the surrounding turmoil, seemed to betoken a political stance. Immediately after the Revolution and during the early years of NEP (the New Economic Policy, 1921–8) state interference was minimal and subordination to Party* dictates was voluntary. More tangible attempts at external control followed quickly and the history of this period is that of greater or lesser pressure by the Party, through organized literary channels, to influence both the subject and its presentation in literature. The freedom and independence of the individual in his artistic as well as his personal life became the central preoccupation of those who resisted this regimentation; the assimilation of the individual into the collective was that of those who submitted, willingly or after a struggle.

Many groups, by virtue of their dubious claims to be the spokesmen of the masses, unsuccessfully sought the literary 'hegemony' only to discover A. V. Lunacharsky's (1875–1933) determination to resist any attempt to monopolize the direction of art. These included Mayakovsky* and the Futurists,* Yesenin* and the Imaginists,* and Proletkul't, the association of proletarian* writers founded in 1918.   *J.B.*

Mayakovsky and the Futurists

An instinctive revolutionary, V. V. Mayakovsky (1893–1930) joined the Bolshevik Party at the age of 15, was arrested three times in consequence and spent 11 months in prison for underground propaganda activity. A founder of the Russian Futurists, who

V. V. Mayakovsky

denounced writers of the past while praising technological innovation and revolutionary ideas in their poetry, Mayakovsky never went as far as V. V. Khlebnikov (1885–1922), whose 'trans-sense' language was intended to liberate the word totally from its meaning. But he did use a deliberately coarse and unpoetic diction, set in a declamatory, highly rhythmical form, to stifle the lyricism he had displayed in pre-revolutionary works (*Vladimir Mayakovsky*, 1913; *A Cloud in Trousers*, 1915), and tried to curb his egocentricity by hyperbolic eulogies of the Revolution and the people–*Mystery Bouffe* (1918), a dramatic poem for the the theatre; *150 000 000* (1920), a heavy-handed satire against the capitalist West, personified in Woodrow Wilson, to whom he opposes the heroic Russian peasant Ivan with his 150 million heads. However, in spite of his enthusiastic writing of agit-poetry (propaganda verse) and jingles for state advertising and his longer political works (*Vladimir Il'ich Lenin*, 1924; *It's Good*, 1927), the suppressed lyricism breaks through in *I Love* (1922) and *About This* (1923), a tragic poem with personal motifs, culminating in the beautifully written *At the Top of my Voice* (1930), where despair in his unhappy private life and disillusion in his commitment to a revolution which had allowed bourgeois values to reassert themselves are painfully revealed. This despair and petty harassment by the bureaucratic Russian Association of Proletarian Writers contributed to his unexpected suicide, a severe blow to the prestige of officially-approved literature. He is, with Yesenin,★ the most popular poet after Pushkin★ in the Soviet Union. *J.B.*

Yesenin and the Imaginists

Born in a village in provincial Ryazan', S. A. Yesenin (1895–1925) was a genuine peasant in origin. The emotional, lyrical poetry he brought to Petrograd (Leningrad) in 1915, with its colourful rustic imagery and religious symbolism, made him immediately famous as the voice of peasant 'wooden' Russia. Like Blok,★ he welcomed the Revolution as a force for spiritual renewal and foresaw in his anti-urban, anti-Western poem *Inoniya* (1918) the imminent arrival of a peasant paradise. In 1919 he moved to Moscow and joined the Imaginists, who were claiming the succession to the then 'defunct' Futurism as the leaders of poetic taste. They took to extremes the coarse language, the crude imagery and the public rowdyism of their predecessors, but replaced Futurist optimism with a morbid pessimism. Yesenin's *Confession of a Hooligan* (1920) and *Tavern Moscow* (1923–4), however, show true unhappiness: disillusionment with the anti-peasant, proletarian course of the Revolution and a despair exacerbated by his brief and disastrous marriage to Isadora Duncan and the drunken scandals which characterized the public image he had adopted. He attempted without success to adjust to the changes in village life under the soviets★ (*Soviet Rus'*, 1924), but the source of his sweet, melodious lyrics had altered beyond recognition; nor could he reconcile himself with Russia's rapid industrialization. His dramatic suicide–he wrote a farewell poem in his own blood– symbolized for many the fate of rural Russia. His popular appeal remains close to that of Mayakovsky.★ *J.B.*

Proletarian groups

The Proletkul't, led by A. A. Bogdanov (real name Malinovsky: 1873–1928), aimed to produce a specifically proletarian literature and to this end organized studios where an incongruous selection of pre-revolutionary writers, such as V. Ya. Bryusov, Andrey Bely, N. S. Gumilev (1886–1921) and Ye. I. Zamyatin (1884–1937) taught. Emphatically anti-individualist and anti-Modernist groups claiming proletarian origin, such as the Smithy and Cosmos organizations, wrote hymns to the proletarian collective, with no individual heroic figures; these productions often degenerated into the catchy propaganda jingles masquerading as poetry churned out by such as Dem'yan Bedny (real name E. A. Pridvorov: 1883–1945). In prose Serafimovich (real name A. S. Popov: 1863–1949), in his realistic novel *The Iron Flood* (1924), described the mass movement of an army, while D. A. Furmanov (1891–1926), in *Chapaev* (1923), recorded peasant guerrilla operations under a leader whose job was merely to direct the heroic peasant mass. Others do feature individual communists, as did Yu. N. Libedinsky in *A Week* (1922)–its subject a peasant revolt against communist rule–with an emphasis on individual psychology which lesser talents such as A. A. Fadeev (1901–56) or S. A. Semenov were to continue. By far the best known is M. A. Sholokhov (b.1905), with his epic *The Quiet Don* (1928–40), a complex and realistic panorama of the revolutionary period, with its clash of ideologies and parties. His hero, Grigory Melekhov, is an individualist who belongs to no party, and a fierce Cossack chauvinism imbues the whole narrative. Since publication Sholokhov has, probably correctly, been suspected of plagiarism from an author killed during the civil war,★ whose diary manuscript he adapted.   *J.B.*

The fellow-travellers

Between 1921 and 1932 the prevailing liberalism, made official in a decree of 1925, resulted in a wide variety of sophisticated and high-quality literature, mostly from the pens of the 'fellow-travellers' (Trotsky's★ term) who, while not with the regime, were either generally sympathetic to its aims or at least not its active opponents.

The Serapion Brothers
One such group, the Serapion Brothers (after a character in E. T. A. Hoffman's *Tales*), exemplify the extreme individualism persisting into the 1920s, their one common principle being freedom of thought and action in literature as in politics. Inevitably the Revolution, the civil war★ and its aftermath became their main subjects, frequently treated with a certain romanticism by those, such as V. V. Ivanov (1895–1963) (*Armoured Train No. 14–69*, 1922), more favourably inclined to the Bolsheviks;★ but all these authors concentrated on realistic description with often gruesome details of the fighting, and, most importantly, on the intellectual's task of defining his position in the new, generally alien world. K. A. Fedin's (1892–1977) *Cities and Years* (1924) was the first novel attempting to analyse rather than describe or eulogize the Revolution, through its weak, sentimental hero–a modern version of the 19th-century superfluous man, who is

M.M. Zoshchenko

willing but unable to subordinate the values of an intellectual and his own self-interest to those of the new society. The novel's construction, with the closing scene transposed to the opening pages and other time-shifts, was hailed as unusual and inventive. V. A. Kaverin (real name V. A. Zil'berg: b.1902) was one of many to develop the theme of freedom as a prerequisite for the work of the artist (*Artist Unknown*, 1931). M. M. Zoshchenko's (1895–1958) short sketches paint with the humour of cynical despair the sometimes cruel, sometimes absurd behaviour of Soviet citizens in mundane life.

Zamyatin
The most prominent and influential Serapion was Ye. I. Zamyatin (1884–1937). His reputation, which grew from his satirical tales of English life, written from personal experience (*The Islanders*, 1918; *The Fisher of Men*, 1922), was firmly established by stories of more immediate topicality, such as his moving account of the cold, hunger and human misery of War Communism★ in Petrograd (Leningrad) in *The Cave*, where the city is in the grip of a new ice age, mammoths stalk abroad and humans retreat to their cave-flats and god-stoves, their morality becoming ever closer to that of their primeval ancestors. The use of a central metaphor and the careful interweaving of related imagery transform the factual material of this logically narrated tale into something distinctly surrealistic. Zamyatin's independent viewpoint and aggressive individualism brought him continuous trouble with the Party,★ culminating in the publication abroad (1927) of his futuristic fantasy *We* (written 1920–1). Loss of

human dignity as a result of ideological fanaticism put into practice concerns him deeply in this consciously Dostoevskian★ polemic against the utopian socialist dogma, adopted by the Bolsheviks, that material well-being should have primacy over the individual's free will. In *We* its logical extreme, happiness without freedom for the many under the benevolent tyranny of a few, is realized in the One State, ruled by its Benefactor (with a sinister *ante diem* resemblance to Stalin) and the Guardians who save its citizens, identified only as numbers, from the consequences of their irrational instincts in a regimented society based on purely rational principles, where unity is all, rebellion is easily suppressed and total stasis is the ideal, soon to become the norm. Only when Zamyatin was permitted to leave for France in 1931 did the persecution provoked by *We* cease.

Other fellow-travellers

Those outside the Serapion group, but holding similar views, included Yu. K. Olesha (1899–1960) and V. P. Kataev (b.1897). Olesha's *Envy* (1927) presents the conflict between a fanciful poet doomed to failure and a solid, successful bureaucrat of the new order. Kataev in *The Embezzlers* (1927) relates the somewhat unsavoury scenes glimpsed through a drunken haze by two absconding officials travelling through Russia. He also provided the idea for his younger brother and a co-author which became the hugely popular satirical novel *The Twelve Chairs* (1928) by Il'f and Petrov (real names I. A. Fainzil'berg: 1897–1937 and Ye. P. Kataev: 1903–42), with its memorable crook Ostap Bender pursuing diamonds hidden in a set of chairs dispersed round Russia during the NEP★ (New Economic Policy, 1921–8) period. L. M. Leonov's (b.1899) works treat the outcasts of the new society with a sympathy reminiscent of Dostoevsky:★ *The Badgers* (1925) revolves around a group of peasant rebels who reject the Revolution as the old conflict between town and village takes on a new slant: *The Thief* (1927), set in the NEP period, has as its hero the leader of a gang of thieves disillusioned with life under Soviet rule. Leonov's concern for the variety and multiplicity of life, threatened by the sinister myth of equality–in practice conformity with a colourless norm–and his (then uncommon) interest in ethical questions–the sanctity of human life, the hypothetical right to kill–are similarly Dostoevskian in feeling. Among those loosely connected with the fellow-travellers it was the greatest talents, Pil'nyak,★ Babel'★ and Bulgakov,★ who later attracted the fiercest denunciations.

Pil'nyak

The novel *The Naked Year* (1922) by B. Pil'nyak (real name B. A. Vogau: 1894–1937) was the first to treat the Revolution and its effects on Russian life. Like others of his so-called novels (such as *Machines and Wolves*, 1925), it is a collection of episodes without a unifying plot, depending for its unity on devices such as repetition or verbal refrains. The influence of Andrey Bely's★ *Petersburg* and *The Silver Dove* can be seen in the many lyrical or historico-philosophical digressions, rhetorical questions and exclamations, the highly involved syntax and the time-shifts, which set a style for many aspiring writers. Russia's historical destiny as part-East, part-West fascinated both Pil'nyak and Bely. Pil'nyak interpreted the Revolution as a cleansing blizzard which preceded a renewal of social morality and justice for the downtrodden. He became disillusioned and began to incur displeasure, notably with his *Tale of the Unextinguished Moon* (1926), which was taken as an allusion to the suspicious death on the operating table of the civil war general M. V. Frunze. It was *Mahogany* (1929), published in Berlin before the Soviet censor had time to reject it, which caused the furore leading to his expulsion from the Russian Association of Proletarian Writers (RAPP). It treats with sympathy the romantic revolutionaries who mourn the passing of genuine communism, and its attitude to Soviet administrative personnel is distinctly critical. The same themes recur in *The Volga Flows into the Caspian Sea* (1930), Pil'nyak's hopelessly unsuccessful attempt at reparation for the crimes of *Mahogany*, which was his contribution to Five-year Plan literature and dealt ostensibly with plans to reverse the flow of the Volga. Only humiliating public recantations ensured his survival during the 1930s.

Babel'

An orthodox Jewish upbringing and an early love of French literature produced in I. E. Babel' (1894–1941) a distinctive writer at his finest in short, impressionistic sketches, usually founded on one incident and remarkable for their extraordinary style, highly concentrated, yet exotic in its ornamentalism. His masterpiece is the collection *Red Cavalry* (1926), tales from his own experiences in Marshal S. M. Budenny's First Cavalry Army in the Soviet-Polish war. Contrast and paradox abound–the weak Jewish intellectual leading a band of crude and brutish Cossack troops (traditionally viciously anti-Semitic), the blind cruelty of the Revolution and the humanity of its ideals, the almost sadistic details of the bloodshed and the poetic nature descriptions. Babel''s *Odessa Tales* (1931) are a unique literary record of the misery of a persecuted minority: childhood recollections of pogroms and the heavy seriousness of Judaism★ are, however, alleviated by the panache and exuberance of Jewish gangsterism in the archetypal figure of Benya Krik, the 'king' of Odessa's criminal life. Odessa Jews also feature in his play *Sunset* (1928); the poor reception of his detached ironic style made him decide to cultivate the 'genre of silence', only to be harassed for some years before disappearing to his death in a prison camp.★

Bulgakov

The short stories of M. A. Bulgakov (1891–1940) in his collection *Devilry* (1925), and in particular the science fantasies *Heart of a Dog* and *The Fatal Eggs* (1924), use humour and satire in their trenchant criticism of Soviet society, especially of the ignorant and uncultured ex-peasants and workers who reached positions of influence. His major novel, *The White Guard* (1924), later adapted into a successful play under the title *Days of the Turbins*, describes Kiev in the worst years of the civil war. The close family life and cultural heritage of the upper classes are defended to the death from a fundamentally hostile Revolution. That the play was staged at all is surprising: in *A Theatrical Novel* (1937) Bulgakov describes the difficulties of staging any of his works, and his love-hate relationship with the Moscow Arts Theatre (MKhAT). His masterpiece, *The Master and Margarita* (1938), is probably the outstanding novel of post-revolution Russia. Its main concern, which permeates all Bulgakov's work, is the conflict of the spiritual with the mundane, materialist world, here at its most acute in the confrontation of Christ, a figure of impressive dignity and simplicity, with Pontius Pilate in ancient Jerusalem, paralleled by that of the Devil (under his traditional name of Woland) and his motley attendants with the inhabitants of Moscow in the 1930s. Hilarious slapstick comedy in the antics of Woland's hangers-on, as they relentlessly expose the human weaknesses of the Muscovites, does not mask the conclusions he reaches during his visitation – namely that cowardice and avarice (inevitably accentuated by the conditions under Stalin*) are as much the ruling passions as during the time of Pilate, but are here frequently mitigated by a saving compassion and faith in the power of art and the spiritual world.

M. A. Bulgakov

Journals

The principal organ for fellow-travellers, the journal *Red Virgin Soil* (*Krasnaya nov'*) edited by A. K. Voronsky (who supported their right to a platform in spite of their ideological instability) was the victim of a prolonged campaign by the proletarian writers' organizations, particularly from their magazine *On Guard* (*Na postu*) which demanded a unified Party line in literature. In 1927 Voronsky and 'The Pass' group which shared his ideas and included writers of some talent such as V. P. Kataev (b.1897) or A. P. Platonov (real name Klimentov: 1899–1951) and well-known critics such as D. A. Gorbov (b.1894) and I. Lezhnev (real name I. G. Al'tshuler: 1891–1955), were attacked, and Voronskyism became a term of abuse as a synonym for nonconformity.

The Formalists

The same fate awaited the Formalist critical group Opoyaz (Society for the Study of Poetic Language), led by V. B. Shklovsky (b.1893) and featuring critics of stature such as R. O. Jakobson (b.1896), Yu. N. Tynyanov (1894–1943), V. M. Zhirmunsky (1891–1971) and O. M. Brik (1888–1945). The extreme Formalists reduced the study of a work of art to the 'sum of its stylistic devices'. Words, not images or emotions, are the real material of poetry, and the normal perception of the subject is distorted and deliberately 'made strange' by undue emphasis on one specific factor, such as metre or syntax; any connection between the work and the author's individuality is strenuously denied. Although the group's views moderated in the late 1920s, study of form as opposed to socially useful content became anathema. Even Marxist critics such as Trotsky,* A. V. Lunacharsky (1875–1933) and N. I. Bukharin (1888–1938), who advocated tolerance of variety, were losing their influence.   *J.B.*

The poets

The four major poets of the Soviet period were all well known before the Revolution: none, however, preserved the freedom to write as they chose and the consequence in their personal lives was as tragic as for their 19th-century precursors.

Pasternak

Before he became famous with *My Sister Life*, a collection of poems written in 1917 in direct response to the excitement and upheavals of that year, B. L. Pasternak (1890–1960) had studied philosophy and music, belonged briefly to a Futurist sub-group, and produced two well-received volumes of verse. The startling freshness and originality of his poems result equally from his astonishing metaphors, the novelty of his perception, his musical, yet taut, forms and his juxtaposition of the poetic with the highly prosaic. His theme is almost exclusively man and nature and their interaction. Attempts at longer poems more in tune with the predominant novel form in the 1920s (*The Year 1905*, 1927; *Spektorsky*, 1931) were unsatisfactory, and a new volume of lyric verse (*Second Birth*, 1932) signalled a return to his natural idiom. In 1936 he was censured for the personal and aesthetic aspects of his work and thereafter published nothing but translations, especially from Shakespeare, until *On Early Trains* (1943), half of whose poems reflected wartime experiences, as did the collection *The Terrestrial Expanse* (1945), in a more direct, less sophisticated style. The publication in Italy of his idiosyncratic and highly poetic novel *Dr Zhivago* (1958), and the subsequent scandal in the Soviet Union which forced him to refuse the Nobel Prize, shattered his life; persecution over it continued until his death.

Mandel'shtam

The early work of O. E. Mandel'shtam (1891–1938) is filled with a sober gratitude for this world, with man as its centre, which he shared with his fellow-Acmeists Akhmatova* and Gumilev, and which

Below: (left) B. L. Pasternak; (right) O.E. Mandel'shtam. Bottom: (left) Anna Akhmatova; (right) Marina Tsvetaeva

remained his major poetic theme throughout his life. His collection *Tristia* is resonant with the majestic tones of the classical world in its elegy for the culture symbolized in the city of St Petersburg, which he saw rapidly being transmuted into Hades. His reassessment in his 1921–5 poems (collected under that title) of the changed and apparently hostile world around him brought about a loss of confidence in the right to be a lyric poet. He filled the poetic silence with prose, the incisive semi-autobiographical *Noise of Time* (written 1923) and *The Egyptian Stamp* (1928), a longish surrealistic novella of some brilliance, set in the Kerensky summer of 1917. Poetry returned in 1930, after a systematic campaign to erase him from literature had restored his will to fight, and in 1934 he was arrested for a superbly vicious anti-Stalin epigram and exiled to Voronezh, where he composed the poems of his three *Voronezh Notebooks*, none of which was published in his lifetime. Like Pasternak,* the other truly great poet of the period, Mandel'shtam was highly sophisticated, European in his modes of thought and purely Russian in his loyalties, with the further dimension of a Jewish background. Mandel'shtam's work is wider-ranging than Pasternak's and relies on intellect rather than on instinct; there is the same command of metaphor, coupled with great vigour and *élan* within the austerely traditional forms from which he rarely departed. Mandel'shtam's arrests, the second leading to his disappearance and death in a transit camp,* form the subject of the impressive memoirs of his widow, Nadezhda Mandel'shtam (1899–1980), published in the West (*Hope against Hope*, 1970 and *Hope Abandoned*, 1972).

Akhmatova

The pre-revolutionary poetry of Anna Akhmatova (real name Gorenko: 1889–1966) is imbued with the despair of unrequited love, repentance for sensual pleasures and a religious sense of being justly punished for them. The restraint of her terse, classical form contrasts sharply with the depth of passion in her stanzas. In the 1920s these qualities in her verse and the fact of her earlier marriage to N. S. Gumilev (shot as a White conspirator in 1921) led to her being called an 'inner émigré' and forced her to stop publishing her intensely private, self-analytical poems. Maturity and later suffering – the 14 years spent in labour camps by her son and the arrest of close friends such as Mandel'shtam – gave her work a new, broader dimension to the point where, in her magnificent *Requiem* (1935–61), she became the voice of all those Russian women whose menfolk had been shot or imprisoned during the purges. Thus when A. A. Zhdanov's* infamous 'half-nun, half-harlot' accusation of 1946 ushered in a new period of disgrace for her, her personal dignity and poetic reputation remained undiminished. Her *Poem Without a Hero* (1940–56) is a brilliant, impressionistic masquerade based on her Petersburg literary friends, with their often tragic relationships, who make surrealistic, ghostly appearances from the mists of the year 1913, the last before the 'true 20th century' of war and mass destruction arrived. Finally rehabilitated, she was permitted to travel abroad to receive honorary degrees in 1965.

Tsvetaeva

The early collections of Marina Tsvetaeva (1892–1941) show a romantic and idealistic personality obsessed with the exceptional and the heroic, epitomized in the figure of Napoleon, whereas *Juvenilia* (1916) is more austere and decidedly pacifist in the wake of real warfare. *Versts I* (1916), a lyrical diary of her personal life in her native Moscow in that year, presents a calm historical perspective impossible thereafter: her later comparisons of the Revolution and civil war with the destruction of culture by the Tatar hordes show her firmly committed to the White cause espoused by her husband. In 1921 she left Russia to join him, living in near-destitution in Paris from 1926 onwards; her unconventional personality made it impossible for her to conform with the rigid attitudes of the émigré group★ there and her finest collection, *After Russia* (1928), with its disparate elements of Russian Futurism, folk★ lament, *byliny* (epic songs) and even the Bible, was poorly received. She returned to the Soviet Union in 1939 to discover that her husband, who had become a double agent in France, had already been shot, and after a period of hopeless misery she committed suicide. Immense energy and verbal force characterize her work – the reactions of a vivid and impulsive personality expressed in a direct, exclamatory style, often hectoring, rarely contemplative and never matched by its imitators.   *J.B.*

Socialist Realism in literature

Various groups from the Proletkul′t, the ex-Futurist LEF (Left Front of Art), the Constructivists,★ with their emphasis on scientific and technical vocabulary, and RAPP (Russian Association of Proletarian Writers) in its various mutations, which claimed to speak for the Party★ itself, flourished until the adoption of the first Five-year Plan in 1928, when *Pravda* (*Truth*) and other official organs attacked their lack of commitment to social tasks, and campaigns against individuals such as Zamyatin★ and Pil′nyak★ were launched. The Stalinist period, when writers were used for education and propaganda purposes only, was established with the liquidation of all groups and enforced membership in a Union of Soviet Writers under the control of the Party, at whose first Congress in 1934 Socialist Realism★ was adopted as (and remains) the union's literary policy. Stalinists (L. M. Kaganovich, P. F. Yudin and L. Z. Mekhlis) controlled the channelling of production and hence the livelihood of all writers, and during the Terror★ the union secretary, Stavsky (real name V. P. Kirpichnikov), was responsible for the imprisonment

and often the death of numerous authors.

The phrase 'socialist realism' was in itself a contradiction; 'realistic' description of actual life had simultaneously to depict the ideal 'socialist' reality, with its communist heroes and their inspiring deeds, while any criticism of substance was strictly forbidden. Since the term had no meaning other than obedience to Party directives, the period up to and immediately after the Second World War is one of almost total literary sterility. The majority of novels have but one plot: sentimentally idealized communists struggle, in hackneyed political clichés, against the unscrupulous class enemies or saboteurs whom they invariably defeat. Novels such as N. A. Ostrovsky's (1904–36) *How the Steel was Tempered* (1935), in which a poor boy joins the underground and, in spite of poverty, wounds and lack of education, becomes a militantly communist writer, or the *Story of a Real Man* (1946), by Boris Polevoy (real name B. N. Kampov: b.1908), where a Soviet pilot is shot down by the Germans, losing both feet, but returns to fight in the air, were written to inspire communist ideals in the young. 'Shock workers' feature in *The Second Day* (1935) by I. G. Erenburg (1891–1967) or *Time, Forward!* (1932) by V. P. Kataev (b.1897); directors of gigantic industrial projects are the protagonists in Leonov's *Road to the Ocean* (1935) and F. V. Gladkov's (1883–1958) *Energy* (1939); P. A. Pavlenko wrote of progress in the Soviet Far East (*In the East*, 1937); Yu. P German described a woman's regeneration through learning and work (*Our Friends*, 1936). In drama Nikolay Pogodin's (real name N. F. Stukalov) *Tempo, Poem about an Axe* and *Snow* (all 1930) are typical Five-year Plan plays, like his *Aristocrats* (1934), whose heroes are three Cheka-men (political police) against the background of the White Sea Canal. A. N. Afinogenov's play *Fear* (1931) has an old scientist repenting of his anti-Soviet actions. In poetry A. A. Prokof′ev, E. A. Dolmatovsky and A. A. Surkov delivered the requisite socially responsible works.

Although Erenburg and A. N. Tolstoy (1883–1945) became apologists for the regime, Tolstoy's *Road to Calvary* (1920–41) or *Peter the First* (1925–45) and Erenburg's *The Extraordinary Adventures of Julio Jurenito and his Disciples* (1922) or *Out of Chaos* (1933) are not without quality. M. M. Prishvin (1873–1954) and K. G. Paustovsky (1892–1968) with their works on nature and A. S. Grin (real name Grinevsky: 1880–1932), with his fantastic and romantic tales, chose uncontroversial subject-matter and remained relatively unaffected. But most gifted writers fell silent or were silenced. *J.B.*

War literature

A brief period of relative freedom came with the Second World War. K. M. Simonov's (1915–79) *Days and Nights* (1944) and V. P.

Nekrasov's (b.1911) *In the Trenches of Stalingrad* (1945) convey the immediacy of the siege of Stalingrad in a natural, unforced manner impossible a few years previously. Most established authors contributed to the war effort as both journalists and writers, thus working from experience. A. A. Fadeev's (1901–56) *The Young Guard* (1945) centres on an underground group of Komsomol members in the German occupation; L. M. Leonov's (b.1899) play *Invasion* (1942), which won one of the Stalin Prizes instituted in 1939, and Simonov's *Russian People* (1942) are self-explanatory. Simonov, A. A. Surkov, N. S. Tikhonov (b.1896) and two women poets Margarita Aliger (b.1915) and Ol'ga Berggol'ts (1910–75), all wrote lyrical and hortatory verse about the war. The immensely popular Vasily Terkin of A. T. Tvardovsky (1910–71) is a 'typical' folksy Russian soldier who, in the course of the eponymous long poem (1941–5), demonstrates–not without humour–his specifically Soviet courage at the front. His creation is perhaps the most memorable work of the war. *J.B.*

Zhdanovism

A sudden but predictable end to the relaxation of the war came with a Central Committee★ resolution of August 1946 in which the works of M. M. Zoshchenko (1895–1958) were denounced as bourgeois, apolitical and vulgar, and those of Anna Akhmatova★ as aesthetic, pessimistic and amoral, and journals were censured for publishing them. This signalled the tightening of controls and the opening of a virulent campaign master-minded by Stalin's son-in-law, A. A. Zhdanov, against the literary world. Enthusiastic optimism, glorification of the system and its successes (real or desired), extreme chauvinism associated with an open encouragement of anti-Semitism, and idolization of Stalin★ make the literature of the years 1946–53 a wilderness. Although K. A. Fedin, V. A. Kaverin, V. S. Grossman (1905–64) and F. I. Panferov (1896–1960) obliged with novels adhering strictly to requirements and N. Ye. Virta (1906–76), S. V. Mikhalkov and V. M. Kozhevnikov produced suitably anti-Western and anti-'cosmopolitan' plays, many writers had to wait for the death of Stalin to publish their true work. *J.B.*

The thaw

Concern over the stifling cultural legacy of Zhdanov★ had been publicly voiced before 1953, but with the death of Stalin★ criticism became more concrete and comprehensive. Symptoms of inauthenticity and insincerity in recent Soviet literature were discussed in 1953–4 by Fedor Abramov (b.1920) and Vladimir Pomerantsev (b.1907), while Ol'ga Berggol'ts (1910–75) appealed for the rehabilitation of genuine lyric poetry. If the mood of the 'Thaw' was captured in the short novel of that name (1954) by Il'ya Erenburg (1891–1967), then opposition to it was epitomized in the dismissal of Aleksandr Tvardovsky (1910–71) from the editorship of the literary journal *New World* (*Novy mir*) in 1954 and certain speeches at the Second Congress of the Soviet Writers' Union the same year. Thematic novelty was the outstanding feature of Erenburg's *The Thaw* and of such characteristic works of 1956 as the novel *Not by Bread Alone* by Vladimir Dudintsev (b.1918), the short story *The Levers* by Aleksandr Yashin (1913–68) and the drama *Petrarch's Sonnet* by Nikolay Pogodin (real name Stukalov: 1900–62). In these works the Stalinist model of leadership is exposed as dogmatic, corrupting and sterile. The intuition and conscience of individuals emerge as beneficial to the collective, while private life, including marital infidelity, is shown as unamenable to intervention on ideological grounds. This preliminary assertion of the right to treat complex human issues had a declarative, programmatic ring, entirely in the spirit of Khrushchev's★ condemnation of Stalin at the XX Party Congress in 1956. Its mirror image may be found in the 'anti-thaw' novel *The Yershov Brothers* (1958) by Vsevolod Kochetov (1912–73), part of the backlash prompted by the Hungarian uprising of December 1956. Such oscillations were a feature of the 1950s. The rehabilitation of liquidated or incarcerated writers and increased access to foreign literature were leavening ingredients, but in 1958 a Writers' Union of the RSFSR, of orthodox complexion, was established to counter free-thinking tendencies in existing literary organizations. Direct political intervention in literary affairs, though sporadic, could be harsh. The rejection for publication in his own country of the novel *Dr Zhivago* by Boris Pasternak★ (1890–1960) was followed by a foreign edition (1957), the award of a Nobel Prize and a scandal at home culminating in his expulsion from the Writers' Union and threats of deportation. *M.A.N.*

'Young' writing

After 1956 the younger generation, grown wary of authority, found new cult figures and filled sports stadia to hear recitals by its heroes. This audience responded not only to the pugnacious, declamatory verses of Yevgeny Yevtushenko (b.1933), but also to the technical virtuosity of Andrey Voznesensky (b.1933) and the robust lyricism of Bella Akhmadulina (b.1937). The enthusiasm of the young poets, which was by no means without support from older colleagues, stimulated the appearance of typewritten verse anthologies in the late 1950s, foreshadowing that upsurge in uncensored literary and publicistic expression known from the mid-1960s as *samizdat* ('self-publishing'). It was with officially published stories of disorientated and disaffected youngsters that Anatoly Gladilin (b.1935) and Vasily Aksenov (b. 1932, exiled 1980) made their names. Characteristic of their works (Aksenov's *Starry Ticket* (1961) is best known) is a rejection of epic continuity and narrative omniscience in favour of fragmentary structure and shifting point of view reflecting the preoccupations and jargon of the central figures. J. D. Salinger and Ernest Hemmingway are often cited as influences.   *M.A.N.*

The legacy of the past

A powerful, if short-lived stimulus to literary ferment was the XXII Party★ Congress of 1961 and the symbolic removal of Stalin's★ remains from the Lenin Mausoleum. From the mid-1950s onwards returning political prisoners had begun to appear as minor characters in literary works and allusions to the atmosphere of the purges had been permitted. However, the November 1962 issue of *New World* (*Novy mir*) carried a work which remains the most forceful treatment of the labour camp (GULag)★ theme to be published in the Soviet Union. *One Day in the Life of Ivan Denisovich* by Alexander Solzhenitsyn (b. 1918) meticulously recreates the point of view of a non-intellectual prisoner in conditions of average severity. It achieves more through understatement than did Boris D'yakov (b.1902) with his *Experiences Recounted* (1964), an attempt to preserve the image of the Party unsullied amidst the horrors of the camps. Upon Khrushchev's removal from office in 1964 his successors declared the labour camp theme exhaustively ventilated, leaving to *samizdat* and foreign publishers the accomplished and harrowing *Kolyma Stories* of Varlam Shalamov (b.1907), the novel *Faculty of Unneeded Things* (1964–75) by Yury Dombrovsky (1909–78) and Solzhenitsyn's remaining works on the subject. These include two 'polyphonically' constructed novels: *The First Circle* (1968) explores the contrasts and affinities between the closed world of a prison research institute and other circles of Stalin's inferno; in *Cancer Ward* (1968) it is not only the patients who are compelled to reconsider the meaning of their lives, but the diseased body politic and Soviet society as a whole. Solzhenitsyn's *The Gulag Archipelago* (1973–5), which spans many volumes and several genres, caused a sensation unmatched by any previously published account of the labour camp world. Although this is the theme with which the Nobel Prize-winning writer is chiefly identified, he himself regards it as a necessary distraction from his main literary task–the creation of a vast epic cycle devoted to the Revolution. *August 1914* (1971) represents the first fruits of this project and *Lenin in Zurich* (1975) is essentially a fragement of it. Neither could be published in the USSR.

In contrast, the Second World War remains a living theme in official literature. Its manifestations range from routine tales of heroism and pathos to such documentary reconstructions as *Brest Fortress* (1964) by Sergey Smirnov (1915–76) and *Blockade* (1968–73) by Aleksandr Chakovsky (b.1913). One of the first to combine motifs of de-Stalinization with the war theme was Konstantin Simonov (1915–79). His novel *The Living and the Dead* (1959), with its depiction of the culpably misdirected defence of the Soviet Union in the opening stages of the war, won a Lenin Prize. Other works stand out for their rejection of formulistic jingoism in favour of an unidealized examination of the psychological and moral stresses of life in the trenches: such are the stories of Vasily Bykov (b.1924), the poems of Boris Slutsky (b.1919), and the novels *The Battalions Request Fire Support* (1957) by Yury Bondarev (b.1924) and *An Inch of Ground* (1959) by Grigory Baklanov (b.1923). De-heroization could not be practised with impunity. In *Good Luck, Schoolboy* (1961) Bulat Okudzhava (b.1924) introduced a lovable but decidedly non-bellicose adolescent hero, only to be accused in some quarters of slandering a whole generation of Soviet youth. An outrageous satirical novel, *The Life and Extraordinary Adventures of Private Ivan Chonkin* (1963–70), by Vladimir Voynovich (b.1932, exiled 1980) could not be published at all and circulated in *samizdat*.   *M.A.N.*

'Village' prose

This category is sufficiently loose to embrace many of the most vigorous tendencies of post-Stalin Soviet literature–the quest for spiritual values, the reappraisal of the past, the rejection of formal and thematic determinateness. A precursor was Valentin Ovechkin (1904–68), whose cycle of sketches, *Weekdays in the District* (1952–56) cast an unprecedentedly critical eye upon *kolkhoz* life. No less influential have been the sketches and diaries of Yefim Dorosh (1908–72) and Vladimir Soloukhin (b.1924). Soloukhin's *Vladimir Country Roads* (1957) and subsequent works are marked by that lyrical, religiously tinged sense of national identity which, during the 1960s, found frequent expression in the journal *Young Guard* (*Molodaya gvardiya*). In his novel trilogy *The Pryaslins* (1958–73) Fedor Abramov chronicles the hard life of a North Russian peasant family since the war. Sergey Zalygin (b.1913) sets his short novel *On the Irtysh* (1964) in a Siberian village during the collectivization★ of agriculture, a process which he depicts without euphemism. Memorable among the gallery of Russian peasant types are the heroine of Solzhenitsyn's★ *Matrena's Home* (1963), Ivan Afrikanovich, the patient, perplexed and endearing creation of Vasily Belov (b.1932) in his *Same Old Story* (1966), and the tougher eponymous hero of *From the Life of Fedor Kuz'kin* (1966) by Boris

Mozhaev (b.1923). Vasily Shukshin (1929–74) devotes some of the best of his deceptively simple short stories to the social and moral disorientation of uprooted peasants. Salutary for Soviet literature as a whole has been the village-writers' rediscovery of the richness of authentic non-literary speech.   M.A.N.

Official versus unofficial literature

The years since the fall of Khrushchev★ have seen the reimposition of thematic taboos and the stabilization of literary-political relations, with periodic reprisals against recalcitrant writers. These extend from the conviction of Andrey Sinyavsky (b.1925, pseud. Terts), and Yuly Daniel' (b.1925, pseud. Arzhak), in 1966 for publishing 'defamatory' works abroad to the deportation of Solzhenitsyn★ in 1974 and extra-judicial measures taken in 1979 against the organizers of the uncensored anthology *Metropolis*. Throughout the 1960s *New World* (*Novy mir*), under the renewed editorship of Aleksandr Tvardovsky (1910–71) had served as first refuge of the liberal-minded writer and direct opposite of Vsevolod Kochetov's (1912–73) orthodox journal *October* (*Oktyabr'*). The dispersal of the *New World* editorial board in 1970 appeared to mark a watershed. At the same time, readers of *samizdat* had precarious access to a substantial alternative literature, which included the major novels of Solzhenitsyn, the verses of such officially neglected poets as Vladimir Uflyand (b.1937) and Iosif Brodsky (b.1940), and the tape-recorded ballads of Vladimir Vysotsky (1938–80) and Aleksandr Galich (1919–77). By the 1970s the boundaries between official and unofficial channels of

expression became more difficult to draw. The poems of Andrey Voznesensky (b.1933) and Bulat Okudzhava (b.1924), and the prose of Andrey Bitov (b.1937), Georgy Vladimov (real name Volosevich: b.1931) and Fazil' Iskander (b.1929) became known in the Soviet Union either through the official press or through *samizdat*; but with an increasing number of writers leaving the country, either voluntarily or under constraint, the picture grew more complicated. New works were written in emigration and earlier censored★ works were restored. Some émigré★ writings then found their way back into the Soviet Union. Among the better-known expatriate writers are the poets Brodsky, Galich and Naum Korzhavin (b.1925) and the prose-writers Solzhenitsyn, Sinyavsky, Anatoly Gladilin (b.1935), Viktor Nekrasov (b.1911) and Vladimir Maksimov (b.1932). At the same time, the official literature since 1964 may not be dismissed out of hand. For example, the vitality and integrity of the Siberian village-writer★ Valentin Rasputin (b.1937), as seen in his short novel *Live and Remember* (1975), and the incisive exploration of urban morality undertaken in the stories of Yury Trifonov (1925–81) do not become worthless simply because they are officially tolerated. Again, the fine play *The Joker* (1966) by Viktor Rozov (b.1913) and the consistently high achievement of his fellow playwright Aleksandr Vampilov (1937–72) are as much a part of Soviet theatre★ as are the embattled experiments of Yury Lyubimov, director of Moscow's Taganka theatre. The selective republication in the 1970s of such suppressed 20th-century classics as those by Boris Pil'nyak,★ Osip Mandel'-shtam,★ Mikhail Bulgakov,★ and Aleksey Remizov (1877–1957) is welcome even though it is principally intended for export.   M.A.N.

Émigré and dissident Russian literature

A scholarly bibliography listing works of émigré literature published between 1918 and 1968 includes some 17000 entries, yet this rich chapter in the history of Russian literature is largely inaccessible to the English-speaking reader. Although any uprooted culture tends to wither away, this process has been retarded in the literary life of the expatriate Russian communities by new waves of Soviet emigration,★ bringing widely different experiences and attitudes.

The First Emigration: 1918 onwards

As a result of the Bolshevik★ assumption of power, the collapse and evacuation of the White armies, the famine of 1921 and the selective expulsion of intellectuals, approximately one million Russians had left their homeland by the early 1920s. They were widely dispersed from the Far East to Western Europe and included an impressive number of established literary figures. Paris became the political, and

Alexander Solzhenitsyn taking leave of the deceased editor of *Novy mir*, A.T. Tvardovsky

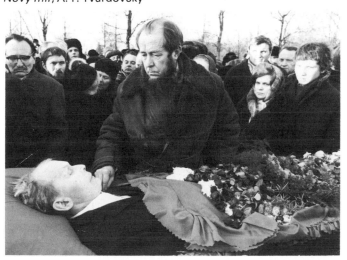

eventually literary, capital of the Russian Emigration, but in the first half of the 1920s it was Berlin which saw the most feverish literary and publishing activity. The Berlin publishing house of Z. I. Grzhebin, largest of many, catered for both the émigré and Soviet markets. It was in the Berlin newspaper *The Helm (Rul')* that Vladimir Nabokov (real name Sirin: 1899–1977) regularly published his early verse. But of some 600 émigré literary journals, almanacs and anthologies which have appeared since 1918 pride of place must go to the Paris-based *Contemporary Notes (Sovremennye zapiski)*. Published from 1920 up to the very fall of France, it became the literary embodiment of, and monument to, the First Emigration.

A number of writers now regarded as 'Soviet' spent periods abroad in the years after the Revolution. Il'ya Erenburg (1891–1967) took an active part in émigré literary life, whereas Maksim Gor'ky* held himself aloof. Aleksey Tolstoy (1883–1945) was not alone among emigrants in coming to terms with the Revolution in the spirit of the 'Change of Landmarks' movement of 1921 onward and eventually returning to the Soviet Union. Unrivalled, however, was the agility with which Tolstoy effected the transition from ardent propagandist of the White cause to Stalin Prize-winning classic of Socialist Realism.* Some writers of the older generation adjusted to the stresses of emigration better than others. Aleksandr Kuprin (1870–1938) failed to repeat his pre-revolutionary successes as a creator of realistic prose fiction and returned, already ill, to the Soviet Union a year before his death. In sharp contrast, Aleksey Remizov (1877–1957) maintained his extraordinary output of fiction, fantasy and documentary throughout a long career in emigration. It was in emigration too that Ivan Bunin (1870–1953) attained the height of his powers as a lyrical and psychological realist with the strongly autobiographical *Life of Arsen'ev* (1927–39) and the collections of stories *Mitya's Love* (1925) and *Dark Alleys* (1943). His Nobel Prize of 1933 lifted the morale of the émigré literary world. Boris Zaytsev (1881–1972), whose best prose is marked by an exquisite lyrical and impressionistic manner (*Pattern of Gold*, 1926; *House in Passy*, 1935) exemplifies a widespread reversion to religious themes and intonations. Other celebrated prose-writers were Ivan Shmelev (1873–1950), Dmitry Merezhkovsky (1865–1941) and Aldanov (Mark Landau, 1889–1957). Aldanov's historical novels of the 1920s and 1930s brought him world-wide recognition.

Outstanding among a generation of poets which included Zinaida Gippius (1869–1945) and Georgy Ivanov (1894–1954) were Vladislav Khodasevich (1886–1939) and Marina Tsvetaeva* (1892–1941). Tsvetaeva achieved some of her finest work in the collections *Craft* (1923) and *After Russia* (1928) but was unhappy in emigration and returned to the Soviet Union in 1939, there to die by her own hand. Khodasevich published sparingly, but the mature lyrics contained in the collections *The Heavy Lyre* (1923) and *European Night* (1927) are among the supreme achievements of émigré literature. Khodasevich's influence among younger émigré poets was at least equalled by that of Georgy Adamovich (1894–1972), a poet and a brilliant if impressionistic critic whose judgement was highly valued by such representatives of the younger generation of Paris poets as Lidiya Chervinskaya (b. 1907) and Anatoly Shteyger (1908–44).

The Second Emigration: 1945 onward

The war dealt a heavy blow to émigré culture as a whole. Several writers perished in concentration camps or in the ranks of the French Resistance. Some were affected by a damaging polarization towards 'Soviet patriotism' on the one hand and fascism on the other. With the dispersal of existing cultural centres many émigrés, including Vladimir Nabokov, moved to the United States, and the Russian-language literary journal *New Review (Novy zhurnal)*, founded in New York in 1942, grew quickly to prominence. The end of the war brought an influx of Soviet citizens via the displaced-persons camps of Europe, and the new literary voices among them were generally well received by the older emigration. Of the prose writers none could match the success of Sergey Maksimov (1917–67) with his widely translated novel *Denis Bushuev* (1949). Notable among the poets were Dmitry Klenovsky (b. 1892), Ivan Yelagin (b. 1918) and Vladimir Markov (b. 1920). The establishment of a new literary and socio-political journal *Facets (Grani)* in Germany in 1946 was an initiative of the Second Emigration. The literary aspirations of both emigrations were greatly furthered by the founding of the Chekhov Publishing House (New York) in 1951 and the appearance of the almanacs *Bridges* and *Aerial Ways* in the late 1950s and 1960s. There was no significant new emigration in those years.

The 'Third Wave': 1970 onward

Between 1970 and 1979 there were some 200 000 legal emigrants from the Soviet Union, the majority travelling on Israeli visas. During this period a number of well-known 'dissidents'* and unamenable writers, both Jews and non-Jews, chose, or were compelled to go abroad. Apart from Israel, the main centres of settlement have been Paris, New York and Rome. The longest-running journals of the Third Emigration are *Time and Ourselves (Vremya i my)*, Tel-Aviv, and *Continent*, which is edited in Paris by the novelist Vladimir Maksimov. The absence of a sense of political and cultural identity has led to internecine strife as well as to friction with the established émigré community. This fact, coupled with the closeness of some of the new emigrants to the literary life of the Soviet Union, has opened up a fascinating perspective on the whole complex of Russian literature – official, unofficial and émigré. *M.A.N.*

MUSIC, THEATRE, DANCE AND FILM

Alexandre Benois' décor (the Throne Room) for Stravinsky's opera 'The Nightingale', 1914

Russian music: development

Russian music is notable for its directness, colour, melodic richness, rhythmic vitality and strong emotional appeal. Symphonic works sound well, since Russian composers are excellent orchestrators. Orchestral music tends to cover a wide range of timbres and dynamics. Instrumental music is often characterized by brilliant idiomatic writing, though this is less evident in vocal★ music, where long-flowing cantabile lines are often preferred. The distinctive plaintive quality frequently discernible in Russian music may partly be explained by the presence of the folk idiom (for much Russian music contains certain intervals and melodic shapes characteristic of Russian folk★ music) and by employment of certain chords, especially those of the augmented fifth and the augmented sixth.

The development of Russian music can best be understood if it is viewed in the historical perspective of the development of Russia itself. During the first millennium of the Christian era the various Slav★ races were in a state of continual movement although by the end of the 9th century the Eastern Slavs had established themselves in towns such as Kiev, and subsequently Novgorod and Moscow. The adoption of Christianity★ in 988 linked Kiev with the Byzantine Empire and culture; the arts (including sacred chant★) flourished. When the Mongols★ overran Russia in the early 13th century, Kiev was captured and devastated but Novgorod escaped and the maintenance of its trading links with western Europe brought economic and artistic benefit. Folk music particularly developed: both Kiev and Novgorod are notable for their cycles of *byliny* (heroic ballads). Tatar domination until the mid-15th century left lasting traces on folk culture. During this time Moscow gradually established itself as the capital of the Russian state. First steps at conscious emulation of West European music were taken in the mid-17th century, when linear (five-line) notation was introduced and attempts were made at polyphonic composition and the writing of secular music. Still closer ties with western Europe were fostered by Peter the Great,★ whose policy was continued through the 18th century by the Empress Anna,★ Elizabeth★ and Catherine the Great;★ Catherine's magnificent palace, the Hermitage, became a centre of musical and theatrical activity. Prominent foreign composers (Cimarosa, Paisiello, Traetta, Galuppi) were invited to Russia, where they did much to stimulate musical education, and young performers of talent were sent to study in Italy. Russia's first acquaintance with foreign opera took place in 1731 with the visit of two foreign opera companies, after which there followed a steady stream of Italian, French and German opera companies. By 1780 operas★ were being written and performed by Russian musicians, vocal and instrumental music (mainly taking the form of keyboard sonatas and variations on Russian songs) was being composed,

instruments were being manufactured, and musical scores printed. The violin compositions of Khandoshkin show good understanding of violin technique. The nobility established their own theatres★ on their estates, with performers drawn from their own serfs,★ but it was only after the turmoil of the Napoleonic★ wars that professional theatres (as opposed to the popular street theatres) became accessible to a broader section of the community. Orchestral music in Russia dates back to this period, when orchestras in the Italian fashion were established at Court and in the houses of the nobility. A curiosity of the second half of the 18th century was the Russian horn band, in which each serf musician played only a single note on instruments varying from 95 mm to 2.25 m. Such bands, comprising some 40 players, had an extensive repertoire, including symphonies and overtures, and were extremely disciplined. The horn band persisted until the 1830s. The guitar and the harp remained popular domestic instruments for many decades, both as solo instruments and for accompanying sentimental songs.

Nineteenth-century Russia fell under the influence of Western Romanticism, manifested particularly by the operas of Spontini, Cherubini, Weber and Meyerbeer – talents against which no Russian composer could at first compete. With the coming of Glinka, however, a strong creative personality emerged to change completely the face of Russian music; his distinctive treatment of folk materials both in orchestral music and in his operas provided models for succeeding generations. Whereas *A Life for the Tsar* (1836) is concerned with the theme of patriotism in the person of the sturdy peasant, Ivan Susanin (an alternative title to the opera), *Ruslan and Lyudmila* (1842), based on the poem by Pushkin,★ is more innovative from the harmonic and orchestral points of view, and employs Georgian, Turkish, Arabian and Finnish elements and the whole-

An imperial horn band in the uniform of Catherine II

tone scale. Though foreign influences may be discerned in his work, Glinka's achievement was a remarkable one and may be compared with the role of Pushkin in formulating a Russian literary language.★

Though national elements may be found in the music of Dargomyzhsky and Serov, Glinka's real successor was Balakirev, who further developed orchestral music on national lines, both in his symphonies and his symphonic poems and orchestral overtures utilizing Russian themes. His chief piano work, the oriental fantasy 'Islamey', inspired by Liszt, is important in its imaginative treatment of exotic material and may be said to have had some effect on subsequent piano composers both in Russia and in Western Europe. It was Balakirev who gathered round him the group of five known as the *Moguchaya Kuchka* (literally the 'Mighty Handful' – the name given to the group by the critic V. V. Stasov in 1867) comprising Balakirev himself, Borodin, Cui, Musorgsky and Rimsky-Korsakov, all of whom were amateur musicians. Stasov was their literary spokesman and ideologist. Despite the disparity of their styles and personalities, each composer (influenced to some extent by the theories of the Slavophil★ and Populist movements) shared the common credo expressed by the composer Serov: 'Music, like any other human language, must be inseparable from the people, from the soil of the people, from its historical development . . . In repeating the ancient Hellenic myth of Antaeus, who remained invincible so long as he rested firmly on the earth, Russian art can draw inexhaustible forces from the folk element.' Nowhere is the desire for identification with the Russian people better seen than in the songs of Musorgsky (many of which use natural speech inflections and peasant expressions) and in his masterpiece the opera *Boris Godunov*. Drawing inspiration from Dargomyzhsky's experiments in musical realism, as well as from innovative elements in the music of Rubinstein and Serov, Musorgsky succeeded in creating a nationally-coloured melodic and harmonic language of striking originality; indeed, one so original that it was largely misunderstood by his contemporaries.

The compositions of Borodin, though not large in number, are notable for their emotional warmth and lyricism (in which effective use is made of chromaticism), rhythm, clear formal structure and skilful treatment of the thematic material. This is seen particularly in his heroic opera *Prince Igor* with its colourful orchestration and vivid characterization, and in his songs, chamber and orchestral works.

Rimsky-Korsakov's music, while lacking the dramatic intensity of that of Musorgsky and the heroic lyricism of that of Borodin, is nevertheless outstanding in its coruscating orchestration and striking and sonorous harmonies. Though his operas are uneven in quality, at their best (as in *The Snow-Maiden* and *The Golden Cockerel*) they make most effective theatre. Especially successful are the folk scenes and picturesque orchestral episodes reflecting Rimsky-Korsakov's interest in Russia's pantheistic past. His orchestral suite

Schéhérazade shows his creative talents at their best. He is also of importance as a teacher, among his pupils being Glazunov, Lyadov, Myaskovsky, Stravinsky and many others.

Apart from their work as composers, Musorgsky, Borodin, Rimsky-Korsakov and Cui (whose music lacks the strength and originality of the others) were all active at various times as letter-writers and critics. Examination of Cui's letters and writings alone, however (he contributed regularly to the *St Petersburg Gazette* from 1864 to 1917), are sufficient to demonstrate that the Five were far from united in their outlook and that their work was not received by their contemporaries in their native land with anything like the enthusiasm which it is accorded today.

A unique place in Russian 19th-century music is occupied by Anton Rubinstein, one of the few Russian musicians whose work was at all known outside the frontiers of his native country. A brilliant pianist, a talented and prolific composer, it was Rubinstein who succeeded in establishing the first Russian Conservatory (that of St Petersburg in 1862), thus placing music on a more professional basis. The Moscow Conservatory was founded by his brother Nicholas in 1866. Despite Rubinstein's immense contribution to Russian music (for he did much to popularize music by Russian composers in his concerts throughout Europe and to promote Russian-born performers), at present Rubinstein's efforts are largely ignored – a strange quirk of fate since in 19th-century Europe Rubinstein was regarded as the outstanding representative of Russian music, Tchaikovsky's music becoming popular only at the end of the century.

If the musical activities of the 'Mighty Handful' were centred primarily in St Petersburg, those of Tchaikovsky were based largely in Moscow. Tchaikovsky enjoys the distinction of being the first professionally trained Russian musician, a graduate of the St Petersburg Conservatory. While a patriot in outlook (for folk elements feature prominently in his work), he was an admirer of West European music, particularly that of Mozart and French opera (Gounod, Thomas and Bizet). His vast output of vocal, orchestral, chamber, ballet★ and operatic music, however, is notable for its excellent craftsmanship and his chief compositions have subsequently achieved international acclaim.

The 19th century saw the real flourishing of orchestral music, the St Petersburg Philharmonic Society being founded in 1802 and the Russian Musical Society in 1859. Branches of that Society were subsequently established in all main centres. Concerts were also given at the Free Music School, an organization set up in opposition to the St Petersburg Conservatory in 1862. The St Petersburg Court Orchestra was established in 1882, the Moscow Philharmonic Society in 1883, and Belyaev's Russian Symphony Concerts in 1885 which he founded expressly for the performance of Russian music. Outlets for the work of Russian composers were provided by the publishing houses of Bessel, Jurgenson and Belyaev.

Russian orchestral music from the start found itself in a unique position, having come into being almost entirely in the 19th century. With no symphonic tradition to fall back upon, Russian composers modelled their first orchestral compositions on West European Romantic prototypes. It was not from classical composers that they drew their inspiration but rather from certain works of Beethoven, Berlioz, Schumann and (at a slightly later date) Liszt. In all this music may be detected an unconventional attitude towards musical form, a particular penchant towards cyclic structure – that is, unification of a work by means of a recurring theme, often melodically and rhythmically metamorphosed – and (following the formal structures of Berlioz and Liszt) less concern with counterpoint and development but with greater emphasis on harmony, colour and rhythm.

Characteristic of the Russian Nationalist composers (the music of Anton Rubinstein is more classical in structure, although it still contains Romantic features) is a tendency towards programme composition and the employment of folk elements which have been consistently utilized from the time of Glinka onwards. One of the difficulties in using a folk-tune lies in its development, since it is already a highly developed entity. Glinka's solution was to repeat a folk-tune almost verbatim, but to introduce changes in orchestration and harmonization – a technique employed in his orchestral fantasy 'Kamarinskaya' (1848) and frequently used by his successors. Rimsky-Korsakov in his suite *Schéhérazade* (1888) utilizes a mosaic-like structure in which basic musical motifs, incessantly varied, succeed one another in a dazzling display of orchestral and harmonic colour, though the work is also unified by a number of orchestral motto-themes.

Apart from the existence of a small number of pieces for organ (mostly written by Glazunov), by far the greatest proportion of Russian keyboard music is for the piano. Since the piano was a much-favoured instrument in Russia during the 19th century, nearly all composers wrote extensively for it, in consequence of which there exists a large repertoire for piano solo, piano duet, or two pianos, ranging from the simplest children's pieces, mazurkas, impromptus, berceuses, preludes, bagatelles, polonaises, to studies, sonatas and operatic paraphrases, in many of which the influence of Chopin and Liszt is apparent. Among outstanding Russian piano works are Balakirev's oriental fantasy 'Islamey', Musorgsky's *Pictures from an Exhibition*, and works by Rubinstein, Tchaikovsky, Scriabin and Rakhmaninov.

Russian chamber music mostly takes the form of string quartets, occasional larger ensembles, and works for piano and strings. Though some pieces for wind do exist (for example Rimsky-Korsakov's Piano Quintet), combinations for wind alone are a rare phenomenon. Apart from its colour and vitality and emphasis on melody, Russian chamber music is characterized by brilliant writing for the individual instruments. Among the outstanding Russian chamber works are Glinka's 'Trio Pathétique' for piano, clarinet and bassoon, the String Quartets of Borodin, Tchaikovsky and Glazunov, Tchaikovsky's String Sextet ('Souvenir de Florence'), Arensky's Piano Trio and the collective composition 'Les Vendredis'. During the 19th century the Russian Musical Society organized in its branches chamber music concerts in which foreign virtuosi participated. The Petersburg Chamber Music Society was established in 1872 and the Belyaev Quartet Evenings in 1891.

In the years preceding the Revolution* diverse tendencies were apparent. While some composers such as Glazunov, Lyadov and Rakhmaninov continued to compose along traditional lines, others sought new means of expression; Scriabin explored the world of symbolism and mysticism; Prokofiev developed a highly personal language, full of astringent dissonances; commissioned by the impresario Diaghilev,* Stravinsky startled the Western world with his ballets *The Firebird* (1910), *Petrushka* (1911) and *The Rite of Spring* (1913); the composer Roslavets experimented with serial (atonal) music. Of these composers Stravinsky may be regarded as one of the most influential and innovative figures of the 20th century. Despite the heterogeneous nature of his style, however, Russian elements are to be found in the majority of his works. While revealing to West European audiences a vigour and colour perhaps hitherto unknown, his ballets mark the culmination of the music of the Russian Nationalist school.   *G.S.*

Soviet music

After the Revolution of 1917 the majority of Russian composers continued either to follow their former style of composition or to write music in accordance with the new communist ideals. Some left Russia permanently; Prokofiev departed in 1918 to return again in 1932. The first few years after the Revolution were essentially a period of consolidation; nevertheless, a number of organizations gradually came into being that were to play an important part in the country's musical development. Such were the Association of Proletarian Musicians (founded 1923 and renamed the Russian Association of Proletarian Musicians in 1929) and the Association of Contemporary Music (1925). As with the literary and pictorial arts, a notable factor in the musical life of this period was the element of experiment, manifest in the work of such composers as Shostakovich, Mosolov and others. To the innovators, modernism was the order of the day and close attention was paid to developments in avant-garde West European music. Concert programmes included music by advanced contemporary Western composers such as Paul Hindemith, Ernst Křenek and Franz Schreker, while Alban Berg attended in person the Leningrad première of his expressionistic opera* *Wozzek* in 1927. Experiments in electronic musical instruments* were carried out by Termen, whose Théréminvox was subsequently demonstrated in Europe and America. Having made a striking début with his First Symphony in 1925, Shostakovich was officially commissioned in 1927 to write a symphony to celebrate the 10th anniversary of the October Revolution, and incorporated the sound of a factory whistle in the score, while into his Third Symphony, sub-titled 'First of May', he introduced a chorus singing a contemporary text.

In 1932, however, the Russian Association of Proletarian Musicians, together with other writers' associations, was dissolved by the Communist Party* and replaced by the Union of Soviet Composers, branches of which were established in the principal cities. Its journal *Soviet Music* (*Sovetskaya muzyka*), which superseded existing music periodicals,* was founded in 1933 and runs to this day. To this period belongs the commencement of the official doctrine of 'Socialist Realism'* which is defined as 'truthful, historically concrete presentation of reality in its revolutionary development'. This marks the true beginning of Soviet music, of which Dzerzhinsky's opera *Quiet Flows the Don*, written in 1934, is regarded as a classic example.

The establishment of new artistic criteria had far-reaching consequences. Shostakovich's opera *The Lady Macbeth of the Mtsensk District*, which had played to packed houses in Leningrad since 1934, was, two years later, severely criticized in the press and was subsequently withdrawn; the première of his Fourth Symphony was cancelled. It was not until the end of 1937 that Shostakovich reappeared with his Fifth Symphony, sub-titled 'A Soviet Artist's Reply to Just Criticism', a work which won general acclaim. To this period belong Prokofiev's ballet* *Romeo and Juliet*, the First Symphony by the Armenian-born composer Khachaturyan and the mass songs of Dunaevsky; immediately before the outbreak of war Prokofiev wrote *Alexander Nevsky*–originally incidental music to a film* by S. M. Eisenstein (1898–1948)–and Shaporin his *On the Field of Kulikovo* (1939). Shostakovich's Seventh Symphony was completed during the siege of Leningrad and its score was microfilmed and flown to the West, where its frequent performance helped to foster support for the Soviet war effort. Other orchestral works of this period were Shostakovich's Eighth Symphony (1943), Prokofiev's Fifth Symphony (1944) and Khachaturyan's Violin Concerto (1940). Shostakovich's Piano Quintet (1940) and Piano Trio (1944), together with Prokofiev's Piano Sonatas nos. 7–9 and his Sonata for Flute and Piano (1943–4), are outstanding chamber works. Khachaturyan's ballet *Gayane*, from which comes the well-known 'Sabre Dance', was written in 1942.

The post-war Party decree of 10 February 1948 accused a number of Soviet composers of 'formalism', singling out Muradeli's opera *The Great Friendship* for particular admonition (though this was mitigated by another decree 10 years later). Prokofiev died in the same year as Stalin,* 1953. Shostakovich continued to dominate the scene as a composer of orchestral music, although his Thirteenth Symphony, written in 1962 to verses by Yevgeny Yevtushenko (b.1933) on the subject of 'Baby Yar' (the scene of a massacre of Jews*) ran into ideological difficulties over the text and was slightly revised. His secular oratorios *Song of the Forests* (1949) and *The Execution of Stepan Razin* (1964) achieved success abroad. Solov'ev-Sedoy gained wide acclaim with his song 'Evenings in the Moscow Woodlands'. Sviridov's *Oratorio Pathétique* (1959), to words by Vladimir Mayakovsky (1893–1930), was much praised in the Soviet musical press and was awarded a Lenin Prize; other notable works of this period were Prokofiev's last opera *War and Peace* (première 1955), Shaporin's opera *The Decembrists* (1953) and Khachaturyan's ballet *Spartacus* (première 1956). Among women composers may be mentioned Galina Ustvol'skaya and Aleksandra Pakhmutova.

The period since 1965 has seen profound changes in the nature of Soviet musical life, including the loss of two leading composers– Shostakovich and Khachaturyan. By the time of his death in 1975 Shostakovich had completed 15 symphonies and 15 string quartets, the music of which virtually constitutes a history of Soviet music. His recently published memoirs (which have been dismissed as spurious in the Soviet Union and have evoked mixed responses in the West) suggest the presence of programmatic elements in a number of his symphonies, a fuller understanding of which may become apparent in the course of time. A complete edition of his works is proposed. Recent Soviet composition, however, has revealed an increasing familiarity on the part of young Soviet composers with West European contemporary techniques. Aleatoric and serial elements (though used with tonal implications) are found, for instance, in Slonimsky's *Concerto buffo*, written in 1966 for a combination of flute, trumpet, piano, percussion and strings, a work which has been recorded and published, though only in Leningrad, while the score of Shchedrin's 'Poetoriya' (published 1975) has a decidedly 'new look'. Recent piano composition reveals knowledge of contemporary West European keyboard music. However, such experiment is only peripheral and by far the greatest part of Soviet music is conservative in nature. There is relatively little concern with music composed before 1750. The Soviet composer must ensure that his music is ideologically sound: the symphony is usually programmatic; song, opera, secular cantata and oratorio should employ appropriate texts; chamber and keyboard compositions should contain folk* intonations. For, as Khrennikov, First Secretary of the Board of the USSR Composers' Union, himself has put it: 'The basis of genuine music has always been, is and will be melody...I think that of greatest importance to the composer are not the methods and systems but the lofty aims and tasks which he places before him...Music in the Soviet Union, in fact, is not for entertainment'.   *G.S.*

Music in the Soviet republics

Whereas some republics, such as the Ukraine, Armenia and Georgia, possessed well-developed musical cultures before the Revolution, elsewhere acquaintance with the forms and practices of West European music has been a comparatively recent phenomenon. Today, however, in virtually all the 15 republics will be found opera* and ballet* theatres, a state conservatory, music and choreographic schools, a Union of Soviet Composers, performing groups attached to radio* and television,* and a philharmonic organization embracing symphony orchestras,* orchestras of folk instruments,* and choral* and instrumental groups. While much is done to encourage local musical life and to maintain interest in national customs (ensuring at the same time development along correct ideological lines), composers and musicians are reminded that they form an integral part of the Soviet Union and share a common policy.

The Ukraine has a long musical tradition and it was from the Ukraine and Belorussia that polyphony based on that of the Catholic Church* was introduced into Russian sacred music* in the 17th century. Ukrainian singers and composers (notably Bortnyansky) were prominent at the Russian Court in the 18th century. Lisenko's operas are of national importance in the 19th century. Of the modern Ukrainian composers (some of whom are Jewish) Glière is probably the best known outside the USSR, other figures being the violinist David Oistrakh, the pianist Emil Gilel's, the conductor Rakhlin and the bass singer Boris Gmyrya. Odessa has been the home of many outstanding musicians.

Armenia is particularly rich in musical traditions. The Armenian Church* with its wealth of sacred chant, was established in the 4th century, and there is a strong idiosyncratic folk music.* Of the Armenian composers of the 19th century Komitas and Spendiarov are notable, while among more recent composers are Arutyunyan, Babadzhanyan and Mirzoyan. The outstanding composer is Khachaturyan, whose ballets, symphonies and concertos have achieved world renown. Prominent Armenian musicians are the conductor Melik-Pashaev and the singers Goar Gasparyan (coloratura soprano) and Zara Dolukhanova (mezzo-soprano).

There is evidence that music has existed in Georgia since pre-Christian times, notable being the folk music with its highly individual choral polyphony, and the sacred music (the Christian Church in Georgia was established in the 4th century). Georgia was annexed by Russia in 1801. During the 19th century an important part in the country's musical development was played by Ippolitov-Ivanov, other more recent composers being M. A. Balanchivadze, Muradeli, Taktakishvili (whose piano concerto has been performed in the West), Tsintsadze and Machavariani. Tbilisi has a fine opera house in which a prominent performer is the veteran dancer and ballet-master Chabukiani; the Georgian State Dance Company is well known.

The musical development of Azerbaijan and Uzbekistan has been influenced by the Muslim* religion; latterly a number of composers have arisen, among whom Kara Karaev and Melikov are outstanding in Azerbaijan.

In the Baltic area, Lithuania, Latvia and Estonia are all musically active, and each has a distinctive profile. But whereas a national music did not develop in Estonia and Latvia till the mid-19th-century because of foreign cultural domination, music in Lithuania has a much longer and more developed musical history extending back to at least the 14th century. In Estonia Lidiya Auster, A. Kapp, V. Kapp, Rääts and, especially, Pärt have all produced interesting compositions; an outstanding singer was Georg Ots. In Latvia Vītols, Grinblat and Ivanovs (a prolific composer of symphonies) have all made contributions, while in Lithuania there are the artist-composer Čiurlionis, and the contemporary symphonist Juzeliūnas.

There is also much musical activity in Belorussia and Moldavia and in Asiatic republics such as Kirghizia, Tadzhikistan, Kazakhstan and Turkmenia. So far no composer of major stature is known in the West and there appears to be resistance to Western and Russian musical concepts in the Asiatic republics.

Opportunities for Soviet musicians to assess developments in music of the Soviet republics are provided by the various annual gatherings and plenums held in Moscow or in regional capitals, where new works from the republics are performed and discussed.   *G.S.*

Sacred music

Historical survey

It is fairly certain that sacred chant was introduced into Russia from Byzantium after the adoption of Christianity* by Prince Vladimir, grand prince of Kiev, in 988. In the course of the following two centuries it underwent a gradual process of transformation. Like the Byzantine rite the Russian was purely unaccompanied, no instruments being permitted in its performance apart from the human voice. It also shared with Byzantium similar melodies, hymn texts (probably translated into Russian), and the system of eight 'modes', though these were not modes in the West European sense of the word but rather melodic formulae. Though at first no specific Russian notation existed, various systems gradually evolved, of which the *znamennyy* notation (from the word *znamya*, meaning a 'sign') is the most important. The *znamennyy* chant, which dates from about the 11th century, is the foundation of Russian sacred music. Like Gregorian chant in Western Europe, Russian chant had no fixed metre and followed the inflection of the words.

During the 16th century an attempt was made to rid the chant of corruptions which had crept into it over the preceding centuries and which had arisen through developments in the Russian language. Through the insertion of extra syllables in the chant, and the addition of excessive ornamentation by singers, the services had increased greatly in length. The ecclesiastical assembly (the *Stoglav* Council) convened by Ivan IV★ in 1551 introduced reforms, among which was the creation of special schools for the preparation of singers and precentors. Attempts were made to improve and simplify the *znamennyy* notation and two important choirs were formed belonging to the tsar and the patriarch respectively. Some rudimentary attempts were made at sacred polyphonic writing, at that time highly developed in Western Europe.

It was in the 17th century, however, that great changes occurred which affected sacred music. In order to offset the increasing influence of the Catholic Church★ (whose sacred polyphonic music had a strong emotional appeal) and to strengthen the power of the Russian Orthodox Church,★ from 1654 onwards Moscow was visited by Greek, Ukrainian and other scholars who introduced a kind of sacred polyphonic part-song, utilizing a five-line notation, a type never previously employed in Russia. The enforcing of polyphony and the new notation, with other radical changes in religious usage, were among the causes of the Great Schism, resulting in the flight of many Old Believers★ to remote parts of the country. The *Musical Grammar* by Nikolay Diletsky (c.1630–c.1690), written about 1680, is of importance in that it was the first work to introduce Russia to West European musical terminology and to explain some of the principles of polyphonic composition. Further attempts at correcting errors in the books of sacred chant were made by Aleksandr Mezenets in 1655 and 1668. The last part of the 17th and first part of the 18th centuries saw the rise of a number of composers of sacred music in Russia, among them Vasily Titov, though technically this music, comprising concertos, psalms and polyphonic chants, was inferior to West European counterparts.

During the second half of the 18th century, as with most other arts, Russian music fell under Italian influence, an important part being played by the Italian masters Galuppi and Sarti. Galuppi's most outstanding pupil during his residence in Russia (1765–8) was the Ukrainian Bortnyansky, who, having studied in Italy, was appointed to the Court Chapel, of which he eventually became director. Under his aegis the singing of the Imperial Chapel reached a high degree of technical perfection, while his own sacred music, though influenced by the Italian idiom, served as a model for future generations.

Notable during the 19th century was the work of L'vov, director of the Imperial Chapel, who not only raised the standard of singing to unprecedented heights but, having assembled a huge body of chants, undertook the immense task of publishing the complete cycle of liturgical chants for the church year – the *Obikhod*. Glinka also composed sacred music, in which he was influenced by the writings of Prince Vladimir Odoevsky (1804–69), a particularly well-informed man for his time and a connoisseur of sacred chant. Odoevsky appears to have been the first Russian scholar to draw attention to the existence of theoretical writings on Russian chant, and by discussing the manuscripts of Mezenets and others did much to provoke interest in the subject. Before the Revolution sacred music was written in St Petersburg by composers such as Rimsky-Korsakov, Lyadov, L'vovsky and especially Arkhangel'sky, who was one of the first to use women's voices in sacred Russian chant.

The chief centre of sacred composition in Moscow was the Moscow Synodal School, where much valuable work was undertaken by its director, Smolensky and the assistant choirmaster Kastal'sky. In his arrangements Kastal'sky strove to devise a homogeneous musical language in which the harmony and counterpoint arose spontaneously from the chant, particular attention being paid to the words. Fine choral works were also written by other members of the Moscow school – Chesnokov, Grechaninov, Kalinnikov, Taneev, Rakhmaninov and others. Rakhmaninov is remembered for his *Liturgy* in free style (1910) and for his *All-Night Vigil* (1915). Tchaikovsky composed a *Liturgy of St John Chrysostom* (1878) for unaccompanied choir, Op. 41, which is one of the few attempts at setting a complete service, and an *All-Night Vigil*, Op. 52 (1881). Mention should also be made of Anton Rubinstein's sacred operas and oratorios such as *Paradise Lost, The Tower of Babel, Moses, Sulamith* and *Christus*, which were performed outside Russia.

The mid-19th-century onwards saw an increasing interest in the study of Russian chant, important works being by D. V. Razumovsky, Yu. Arnol'd, and later I. Voznesensky, S. Smolensky, V. Metallov and A. Preobrazhensky. After the Revolution, researches into sacred music in Russia virtually ceased until the 1960s, when there was a revival of interest. Today little sacred music is published in the USSR and the liturgical compositions of Glinka, Tchaikovsky and Rimsky-Korsakov are not included in the state edition of their complete works. However, the whole question of Russian chant, its provenance and its relationship with other branches of Eastern chant, is currently being re-examined by scholars both in the Soviet Union and elsewhere. *G.S.*

The liturgical background

Mainly known in its choral form, Russian sacred music embraces a range of participants: being a function of the total worship of the Orthodox Church,★ this liturgical singing concerns as much the worshipping people who participate through their attention and, on occasion, their singing, and the officiating clergy, as it does the more specialized choir and individual singers and readers. Inherited from Byzantium, Christian worship in Russia has its particular vocal expression in the chanting and singing of the human voice, the only verbal and the most sensitive of all musical instruments. Psalmody, melody and harmony combine to make the music of the liturgy. Ordinary speech is never used: only when he delivers a sermon does the priest 'speak'. Bells summoning the people to attend the various services through their elaborate harmonies and sparkling rhythms hang outside the church building; being incapable of verbal expression, all other instruments have been barred from use in the liturgy.

The language used in the liturgy is Church-Slavonic, a linguistic relative of the native Russian* tongue, dating back to the 9th century and having its own history of development. Beloved by the believer for its beauty and depth of meaning, this near-vernacular, through its employment in the liturgical re-enactment of sacred events and festivals, considerably influences the making and interpretation of church melodies which, in turn, have a powerful didactic role. The essential experience of the collective liturgy is that of the personal divine presence in the Church, in which God – not only the people – is the prime 'listener'. Any noticeable departure from this basic liturgical attitude (such as theatrical or concert-like performances) must be deemed untypical and worldly.

The character of the singing varies according to the role of the participants: the deacon chants the litanies and the Holy Scripture and conducts the congregation in prayer; there are no pews and everybody stands in worship. The priest, a living image of Christ the High Priest as well as representing the people, voices the words of the sacraments, sings the Gospel and addresses God on behalf of all. Through the skill of their voices the choir-leaders with their choirs, the individual singers and the readers are able to express in the liturgy the mind and feeling of the Church (repentance, joy, praise) as well as to convey the continuity of its teaching in the festal, lenten and ordinary hymnographies. In monasteries the antiphonal form is in use: the alternative singing of two choirs and their coming together in prominent liturgical sequences such as the Evening Hymn at vespers or the Great Doxology at matins; the movements of the clergy (when they cense the icons* and the people, or carry the Gospel book in solemn procession to the ambo); and the iconographic layout in the church – all reveal the spatial, architectural purpose and shape of the sacred building. Similarly, in cathedrals and major parishes two choirs often share the choral programme of the liturgy: a senior choir on the right-hand side of the sanctuary is more skilled and technically ambitious; that on the left is simpler, and in many ordinary parishes a single choir suffices.

The liturgical forms of worship may be classified as follows.

The life-cycle of a person: in sacraments such as baptism, the Eucharist, marriage and unction, and services of prayer held on occasion of trials and joys (journeys, illness, new undertakings) and of death (funeral and memorial services) the Church sanctifies the entire existence of a Christian, emphasizing the many manifestations of joy, grief, hope, endurance, love, entreaty, trust, faith.

The yearly lenten and festal cycles: in the movable Easter cycle the seven weeks' lenten preparation gives rise to the liturgical climax of Good Friday, without which neither the peace of Saturday in Holy Week nor the festivities of Easter can be understood. The other fixed festal cycle centres on Christmas and embraces nine feasts of the Lord and his Mother, as well as numerous saints' days throughout the year.

The weekly cycle: this focuses on Sunday and culminates in the Divine Liturgy, the Eucharist, for which (due to its largely unchanging shape) many composers have written a variety of original settings reminiscent of the Western motet or anthem, as well as complete liturgies sung by the right-hand choir. A popular service of praise is the *akathist* sung by the priest and the congregation.

The daily cycle: this is best represented by its music in the Saturday night vigil where, apart from occasional anthems, considerable use is made of the eight-tone musical system, the *Oktoikh*, which gives the liturgy a definite stylistic consistency. M.F.

Folk music

Russian folk-song is remarkable for its wealth and diversity. In its oldest form it reaches back into the period before Russia's conversion to Christianity* in the 10th century and texts of the most ancient folk-songs contain references to worship of pagan deities and reverence for primeval forces. The early songs, such as the *khorovod* (round dance*) and calendar song (relating to the seasonal year) are of limited compass and of simple structure, often consisting of variations on a basic theme. A unique place in both literature* and music is occupied by the *byliny* (heroic ballads), which were written primarily in the towns of Kiev and Novgorod (centres of civilization before Moscow

Russian folk instruments illustrated in Istomin's *ABC* (1692)

achieved supremacy) and describe events occurring from about the 11th to the 16th centuries, in which typical subjects are heroes such as Il′ya of Murom, Dobrynya Nikitich, Sadko and others. Some of the tunes of the *byliny* show resemblance to sacred chant★ and apparently were sung in a solemn and dignified manner. *Byliny* of a humorous and faster nature, however, are also encountered. In the course of time the *byliny* were supplanted by the 'historical' songs, of which the subjects were more concerned with specific historical events. Their full flowering occurred between the 16th and 18th centuries. The *Dukhovnye stikhi* (spiritual verses) are melodically similar to the *byliny* and historical songs, but employ subject matter taken from the Bible and the lives of the saints. A special and substantial place in Russian folk music is occupied by the wedding songs. Collated over a long historical period (and thus showing diversity of structure) they formed an essential part of the traditional peasant wedding, a long and elaborate ritual accompanied by songs and laments. The performance of the comic or humorous songs depended upon the *skomorokhi* (the Russian clowns or buffoons, equivalent of the West European merrymen, Spielmänner or jongleurs). Unique in Russian folk-song is the so-called 'lyrical' song, which came to full fruition during the 16th and 17th centuries. Notable for its rich melodic content, rhythmic freedom and wide vocal range, the lyrical song may be said to express the poetic feelings of the performer; its language is often symbolic and metaphorical, in which the singer draws extravagant parallels between his own emotions and natural phenomena (the sun, the dew, rivers, birds and trees). The lyrical song is often performed in a special kind of folk polyphony, which is improvised in accordance with certain traditions; it may be regarded as the culmination of Russian folk-song composition, for with the advent of the 18th century, new song forms influenced by West European music began to appear particularly in the towns, among which may be mentioned the 'town song', the recruit song, and (at a later date) the *chastushka* (witty jingle). Other types of song include Christmas carols, soldiers' songs, sailors' songs, hauliers' songs, robbers' songs, prison songs, revolutionary songs, children's songs.

The first attempts at collecting the words and music of Russian folk-songs were made in the 18th century; Vasily Trutovsky, a Ukrainian, issued four volumes (1776–95), followed by that (1790) of Jan Práč (d.1818) and a collection (1818) by Kirsha Danilov. Important 19th-century collections, inspired by the Slavophil or Russian Nationalist movement, were those of Balakirev (1866), Tchaikovsky (1868–9) and Rimsky-Korsakov (1876), all of whom included folk-songs in their own compositions. It was not until the last part of the century, however, that musicians began to realize that many of the Russian folk-tunes were modal in nature (not written in the conventional major-minor system), that folk-songs were not sung each time in exactly the same manner but were melodically and rhythmically varied, and that certain types of folk-song and folk

Title-page of the first edition of Práč's folk-song collection published in St Petersburg, 1790

music could be sung and performed polyphonically – factors which may be seen in the collections (1879, 1885) of Yu. N. Mel′gunov (1846–93), and (1904, 1909) of Ye. E. Lineva (1853–1919) and others. Lineva was one of the first Russian folk-song collectors to record folk-songs on a phonograph.

During the Soviet period there has been intensive research into virtually all aspects of Slavic folk music. Following the pattern set by the Imperial Russian Geographical Society in the years preceding the Revolution, numerous expeditions have taken place to collect folk-songs in remote districts and the results have been analysed and some published. Collections of folk instruments★ have been established, substantial numbers of folk-songs have been recorded and new folk-song volumes are regularly being issued. There is by no means total agreement among scholars as to the precise structure of Russian folk-song, however, and existing scholarship is constantly being reassessed.   *G.S.*

Vocal and choral music

Of the many songs written by Russian composers during the 19th century, those of Musorgsky are outstanding in their melodic and harmonic originality, the melodies themselves often revealing folk influence. Not only is there a close link between words and music but many of the songs show psychological insight into the life and condition of the Russian peasant. Of Musorgsky's song cycles, that entitled 'The Nursery' vividly portrays events seen through the eyes of a child. The songs of Tchaikovsky and Rakhmaninov are also well known outside Russia. Among Soviet composers the songs of Prokofiev, Shostakovich, Kabalevsky and Sviridov deserve special mention.

If secular choral music in pre-revolutionary Russia tended to be overshadowed by sacred★ (one of the few outstanding secular choral works is Rakhmaninov's 'The Bells', written in 1913), the Soviet era has seen the appearance of a number of secular oratorios and cantatas, among which may be mentioned in particular Prokofiev's *Alexander Nevsky* (1938), Shaporin's *On the Field of Kulikovo* (1939), Koval''s *Yemel'yan Pugachev* (1942), Shostakovich's *Song of the Forests* (1949), Salmanov's *The Twelve* (1957), Sviridov's *Poem in Memory of Sergey Yesenin* (1955) and *Oratorio Pathétique* (1959). Petrov's *Peter the First* (sub-titled 'vocal-symphonic frescoes, utilizing original texts and historical documents and ancient folk-songs', published 1974) and Shchedrin's 'Poetoriya' to words of A. A. Voznesensky (b.1933) (a concerto for poet, accompanied by a woman's voice, mixed chorus and symphony orchestra, including a beam of light, published 1975) have both excited favourable comment and have been widely performed in the USSR.   *G.S.*

Opera

Russian opera differs from West European opera in its more extensive employment of folk★ material, its use of national subjects, its wide use of choral elements, its emphasis on male vocal roles and the relative absence of female coloratura. Though the first Russian operas were composed in the 18th century, it was in the hands of Glinka that the real foundations of national opera were established and in his two operas *A Life for the Tsar (Ivan Susanin)* (1836) and *Ruslan and Lyudmila* (1842) he ingeniously combined Italian arioso, Germanic counterpoint and heterogeneous folk materials to form a distinctive musical language. In style, however, his two operas are almost completely different. Whereas *A Life for the Tsar* is in the epic tradition with considerable emphasis on the peasant folk element, *Ruslan and Lyudmila* is harmonically and orchestrally more

adventurous, with oriental dances, richly ornamented arias, powerful choruses and brilliant orchestral numbers. Throughout the 19th century Russian composers were influenced by Glinka's operas; Musorgsky's *Boris Godunov* and Rimsky-Korsakov's *The Tsar's Bride* continuing the epic vein, while their *Khovanshchina* and *The Golden Cockerel* are both in the exotic tradition. Of Rimsky-Korsakov's other operas *May Night* utilizes a plot by Gogol',* while his *Sadko* employs *byliny* (heroic ballad) material from the Novgorod cycle. *The Golden Cockerel*, based on Pushkin's* poem, completed in 1907, encountered difficulties with censorship* and its performance was never permitted in the Imperial Theatres. Though Tchaikovsky was also a prolific opera composer, only his *Eugene Onegin* and *The Queen of Spades* (in which he exploited and sentimentalized Pushkin's plots) have achieved lasting success outside Russia. A unique place is occupied by Borodin's *Prince Igor* – perhaps the finest manifestation of the heroic element in Russian opera. While support for opera came primarily from the Imperial Theatres, a private opera company was founded by S. I. Mamontov (1841–1918) in Moscow in 1885, and was succeeded by S. I. Zimin's (1875–1942) opera theatre in 1904. The season of Russian opera given by the impresario Diaghilev* in Paris in 1908, which included Musorgsky's *Boris Godunov* with Chaliapine in the title role, made an unforgettable impact on Western Europe. Stravinsky's opera *The Nightingale* was written in 1914 and his *Mavra* in 1922.

Of the many operas composed since 1917 those of Prokofiev and Shostakovich are of special importance. Whereas Prokofiev's *The Love for Three Oranges* (1919) and *The Fiery Angel* (1927) were written during his absence from Russia, *Semyon Kotko* (1939), *The Duenna* (1940), *The Story of a Real Man* (1948) and *War and Peace* (1952) all show the influence of Socialist Realism.* Shostakovich's best-known operas are *The Nose* (1928) and *The Lady Macbeth of the Mtsensk District* (1932) – the latter now performed in a modified version under the title *Katerina Izmaylova*. The music and text of Glinka's *A Life for the Tsar* have likewise been altered, and it is entitled *Ivan Susanin*. While many operas by Soviet composers are highly rated in the USSR (for example, Shchedrin's *Not Love Alone*, 1961; Slonimsky's *Virineya*, 1967), only a few of these, through lack of recordings or other reasons, have become at all known outside the Soviet Union; Shaporin's opera *The Decembrists* (performed in 1953) is a rare example. Operetta also enjoys great popularity in the USSR and has attracted the attention of composers such as Shostakovich, Dunaevsky, Kabalevsky and Khrennikov. *G.S.*

Top: chorus in the execution scene in Musorgsky's opera, *Khovanshchina*. Centre: scene from the Bol'shoy Theatre production of Borodin's *Prince Igor*. Bottom: scene from Prokofiev's opera *War and Peace* at the Bol'shoy Theatre.

Russian and Soviet performers

Among the many outstanding Russian performers, mention may be made of Fedor Chaliapine the famous Russian bass, the pianists Anton Rubinstein, Vladimir de Pachmann, Sergey Rakhmaninov and Sergey Prokofiev. The violinists David Oistrakh, Igor' Oistrakh and Leonid Kogan, the cellist Mstislav Rostropovich, the pianists Svyatoslav Rikhter, Emil Gilel's and Lev Oborin, and the singers Mark Reyzen, Galina Vishnevskaya, Zara Dolukhanova and Yelena Obraztsova have achieved international recognition. *G.S.*

Soviet orchestras

A novel experiment in the early days of the Soviet period was the 'Persimfans' – an orchestra without a conductor, which existed in Moscow 1922–32. The most famous Soviet orchestra, however, is the Leningrad Philharmonic (1917), which developed from the former Court Orchestra, while in Moscow of chief importance are the State Symphony Orchestra of the USSR (1936), the Bol'shoy Symphony Orchestra of the All-Union Radio and Television (which acquired its present name in 1958), the Symphony Orchestra of the Moscow Philharmonic (1953), the Moscow State Symphony Orchestra (1955), and the Moscow Chamber Orchestra, directed by Rudol'f Barshay. The conductors Kondrashin, Melik-Pashaev, Mravinsky, Rozhdestvensky, Svetlanov and Zanderling are well known, and the Tchaikovsky Piano Competition annually excites international interest. *G.S.*

Music education

Until the middle of the 19th century music education in Russia was not organized on a systematic basis, though there is evidence of tuition being provided by sacred bodies, orphanages, theatre schools, universities and visiting foreign musicians. The Moscow Synodal School for the study of sacred chant* was opened in 1857, and was also the first educational establishment in Russia to introduce a scheme for the study of folk music.* With the inception of the Russian Musical Society in St Petersburg (1859), thanks to the efforts of Anton Rubinstein, music classes were opened; the Conservatory there was founded in 1862, and that of Moscow in 1866; other branches of the Society set up music classes during the course of the century. For lack of skilled teachers in Russia, Rubinstein drew many of his staff from western Europe, especially Germany, and the imprint of Germanic thought and method had far-reaching effects. Music education in Russia then relied largely on textbooks translated from foreign writers; however, Tchaikovsky's manual on harmony, Taneev's book on counterpoint and Rimsky-Korsakov's volumes on harmony and orchestration are all internationally known. Despite the fact that the Russian Musical Society and the Conservatories were founded for the benefit of Russian music, strong opposition was encountered from Slavophils* such as Balakirev, who (with

Below: an infant violin group performing at Podol'sk music school near Moscow. Bottom: six-year-old children of workers at Baku power station rehearsing Russian folk music

Lomakin) opened his own Free School of Music in 1862 as a rival establishment. In 1883 the Moscow Philharmonic Society started a School of Music and Drama. Around the turn of the 19th century there were several initiatives towards education for the masses, among which may be mentioned the People's Conservatory opened in Moscow in 1906. The Gnesin Music Institute, founded in Moscow in 1895, is still in existence.

In the Soviet period music education has been standardized. Detection of musical talent begins at kindergarten level; at about the age of six students of outstanding ability enter a 'ten-year school'* where children's normal academic studies are augmented by special musical instruction, often conducted by leading musicians. Children less musically gifted are sent to a 'seven-year school', then enter a secondary specialized school* after which successful pupils from both this and the 'ten-year school' may enter a state conservatory, the most prestigious being those of Moscow and Leningrad. Tuition at the conservatory (which may include musicology) lasts for five years, after which a further period of postgraduate study is possible. Employment is usually arranged by the Union of Soviet Composers, an organization which is not concerned with composition alone. Political training* plays an important part in the life of the Soviet musician and much emphasis is placed on correct ideological attitudes. To write music for children is a task expected of all Soviet composers.   *G.S.*

Popular touring ensembles

During the 19th century a number of Russian ensembles toured abroad, among which may be mentioned the peasant choir conducted by Prince Yury Golitsyn and that of Agrenev-Slavyansky whose group, formed in 1869, specialized in folk-song.* An unusual ensemble for the period was the Vladimir Hornplayers, formed by N. Kondrat'ev in the 1870s, whose music was played polyphonically on shepherds' horns (in no way connected with the single-note metal horns of the earlier Russian horn band). The first orchestra of folk instruments* was that of Andreev: his Great-Russian Folk Orchestra (founded 1886) toured extensively and notably included 'families' of balalaikas and domras, constructed to his own specifications. Pyatnitsky founded his folk chorus in 1910.

Since the Revolution great attention has been paid to popular ensembles. The Andreev ensemble, enlarged in size, instruments and repertoire, is now known as the Osipov Russian Folk Orchestra. The Pyatnitsky Russian Folk Chorus has retained its name, but since 1938 has been augmented by a dance group and folk orchestra. The All-Union Radio and Television Orchestra of Russian Folk Instruments formed in Moscow in 1945 is well known in Russia, while the Ensemble of Song and Dance of the Soviet Army (1928), the Moiseev Ensemble (1937), the Berezka Ensemble (1948) have achieved world renown. Other outstanding Soviet ensembles are the Voronezh Ensemble (1943), the Georgian State Dance Company (1945), and the Siberian Omsk Folk Chorus (1950).

Choral ensembles are also extremely popular. The oldest surviving choir in Russia today is that of the Academic Kapella in Leningrad, which traces its origins back to the Grand Ducal Singing Clerks established by Ivan III* in 1489 to participate in services in the Cathedral of the Assumption in the Kremlin. With the founding of St Petersburg,* the Singing Clerks were transferred to the new capital, and were named in 1763 the Imperial Court Chapel Choir – a title that was retained until 1917. The Choir of Patriarchal Singing Clerks came into being in 1589, being renamed the Moscow Synodal Choir in 1721; its tour of Europe in 1911 was a memorable event. The St Petersburg Philharmonic Society was founded in 1802, Beethoven's *Missa Solemnis* being given its first performance there in 1824. Mention should also be made of the Russian Choral Society founded in Moscow in 1878 and Aleksandr Arkhangel'sky's mixed choir, established in 1880, which performed sacred* and secular Russian works both in Russia and abroad. Outstanding among present-day choral ensembles are the Academic Russian Choir, founded 1936, the Republican Choir (1942), the Moscow State Chorus (1956) (all based in the capital), and the Academic Kapella and the Kapella Boys' Choir in Leningrad. Well-trained choral ensembles are also maintained by radio* and television.*   *G.S.*

Soviet jazz music

The first concert in the USSR of anything that might be called jazz took place in Moscow on 1 October 1922. Valentin Parnakh, minor poet, was the leader of the band. What had attracted him to jazz was its 'theatricality' and 'eccentricity'. Parnakh's second concert was attended, and its music discussed, by such theatrical luminaries as V. E. Meyerhold (1874–1940) and S. M. Eisenstein (1898–1948). Soviet audiences experienced the real sounds of this new, rude music in 1926 with the tours of the Frank Withers Quintet, featuring Sidney Bechet, and the *Chocolate Kiddies* revue, accompanied by the Sam Wooding Orchestra. The ubiquitous critic and politician A. V. Lunacharsky (1837–1933) attended one of the Withers Quintet's concerts. These tours by black American jazzmen are a reminder that the USSR in the 1920s was more receptive to outside artistic influences that it later became.

Two names are associated with the development of big bands that also played jazz. Aleksandr Tsfasman organized *amadzhaz* in Moscow in 1927, and in 1928 first recorded and broadcast. In that year in Leningrad Leonid Utesov, under the inspiration of such jazz-influenced entertainment orchestras as those of Paul Whiteman and Jack Hylton, organized the first of his many orchestras. Utesov, then as later, had his finger on the pulse of popular taste. He made the genre of *estradnaya muzyka* (stage music) his own. I. Dunaevsky composed and arranged for Utesov, together they brought into the repertoire popular songs of purely Russian and Soviet origin. This coming together of song and jazz is typical of the 1930s in all countries. The two also collaborated on the musical film *Happy Kiddies* of 1934. The line of development of the big band of the pre-

A Soviet jazz group

war years ended with the formation of the Jazz Orchestra of the All-Union Radio Committee in 1938.

The post-war years – as in the West – saw the emergence of small groups, with the orientation towards instrumental mastery, away from song and entertainment. The Zhdanov★ decrees did not leave jazz unscathed; in the early 1950s vicious and ignorant attacks on this music were published – even Gor'ky's★ antediluvian 'jazz is the music of the fat' was exhumed. Jazz began to pick up only in 1957, when the Sixth World Festival of Youth brought foreign jazz groups to Moscow. By the end of the decade the Komsomol★ was taking an active interest and helped to found jazz clubs in Leningrad (1958) and Moscow (1960). This was also the period of the first jazz festivals. There was a regular radio★ programme and the record firm★ Melodiya put out the first jazz records. Jazz, no less than the other arts, has been the victim or beneficiary of current Communist Party★ thinking. The year 1967 marked a turning-point, bringing a policy of official retrenchment. Some musicians have been able to emigrate; Valery Ponomarev, for example, in the 1970s occupied the trumpet chair in Art Blakey's Jazz Messengers. Jazz has always been a problem for the authorities. If it could simply be regarded as the urban folk music★ of an oppressed black minority, it would be less difficult to handle, but then its home is indisputably the USA, which means that it is 'the bearer of bourgeois ideology'. Soviet musicians have acquired the jazz spirit, admittedly under the most adverse conditions, only with difficulty; the art of improvisation has not been easy. The only original Soviet contribution to jazz, partially successful and having no effect on the mainstream of development, has been the incorporation of folk-tunes into the music. There has been a search for a Soviet 'own path' in jazz and for 'the creation of a Soviet jazz music', which is clearly a contradiction in terms. (These folkloristic attempts may also have had in them an element of self-protection on the musicians' part.) A. Ye. Tovmosyan's *Lord Novgorod the Great* (1962) and A. N. Zubov's *Byliny-stariny* ('*Ballads*') (1968) are the most successful compositions in this area. *C.A.J.*

Soviet rock music

During the 1960s and 1970s there has been a widespread awakening of interest in rock music, and although this is largely derivative, being imitative of Western groups, some talented Soviet performers have recently appeared. Among these may be mentioned the Armenian Stas Namin, the Belorussian group known as 'The Singers', the Ukrainian singer Sofia Rotaru and the Ukrainian group 'The Hollyhocks' founded by Alyosha Bordkevich. The Jewish composer David Tukhmanov writes particularly for the singer Valery Leontyev, while the vocalist Janna Bichevskaya has been described

Poster advertising a rock 'discothèque' in Fergana

as a Soviet Joan Baez and the most popular 'pop' star has been Alla Pugachova. In comparison with the hostile official attitude of former years towards 'pop' music, there appears to be greater tolerance, confirmed by the fact that albums of rock music have been issued (albeit in small numbers) by Melodiya, the state record company.★ *M.R.B.*

Music theatres

The principal Russian theatres★ are centred in Moscow and Leningrad. The best known in Russia is the Moscow Bol'shoy, which originated in 1776. A theatre was erected on its present site in 1821–4, but it suffered from a severe fire in 1853, being rebuilt with substantial alterations by Alberto Kavos (Cavos) in 1856. Opera★ and ballet★ by Russian composers have been given there since 1825 and since the 1930s it has attracted the finest performers. Since 1961 the Bol'shoy Company has also performed at the Palace of

Congresses, a huge hall seating 6000 people, located in the Kremlin. Operas and ballets are also staged at the Stanislavsky and Nemirovich-Danchenko Theatre, founded in 1941, whose repertoire tends to include lesser-known works, and at the Opera Studio of the Moscow Conservatory. Music plays an important part in the programme of the Moscow Gipsy★ Theatre and the Moscow Music Hall, and there is also an Operetta Theatre. Concerts are given in the many palaces of culture and halls, in particular the Palace of Congresses, the Concert Hall of the Moscow Conservatory and the Tchaikovsky Hall (both of which contain an organ), and the Gnesin Music Institute.

In Leningrad pride of place is occupied by the Kirov Theatre, which occupies the site of the former Imperial Mariynsky Theatre. After the founding of a Russian dramatic theatre by Catherine II★ in 1756, the Directorate of the Imperial Theatres was established in 1766. From 1783 performances were given in St Petersburg at the Kamenny (or 'Stone') Theatre (also known as the Bol'shoy). In 1855 the opera company moved to a new building, the Theatre-Circus, which was renamed the Mariynsky Theatre in 1860, to which the ballet company returned in 1886. The former Kamenny Theatre was rebuilt in 1889 by the Russian Musical Society and is now the home of the Leningrad Conservatory. Many notable first performances of works by Russian composers were given at the Kamenny and Mariynsky Theatres and it was also visited by celebrated foreign opera singers, such as Patti, Tamburini and Rubini. To this day operas and ballets are presented in a sumptuous, grandiose manner, abstract décor being eschewed in favour of realistic staging. Operas are also given at the Maly Theatre, founded in 1918, and at the Opera Studio of the Leningrad Conservatory. Operettas are performed at the Musical Comedy Theatre (founded 1929). Of the many concert halls in Leningrad, notable are those belonging to the Philharmonic (of which the larger was formerly the 'Hall of the Nobility') and the Concert Hall of the Leningrad Conservatory. Concerts are also given in the Hermitage and in the Hall of the Academic Kapella. Opera and ballet companies, operetta and music hall, are well established throughout the Soviet Union and each large city has its own theatres, symphony orchestras and concert halls.   *G.S.*

Music museums and libraries

Materials relating to the 18th-century serf theatre★ are to be found in the Sheremetev Palace at Ostankino. The Bol'shoy Theatre in Moscow and the Kirov Theatre in Leningrad both possess extensive libraries★ and archives of programmes, letters, model sets, costumes, décors and musical sketches. The Maly Opera and Ballet★ Theatre, Leningrad, also contains musical and theatrical materials such as

posters, photographs, letters, concert programmes, while music holdings and recordings★ are also found in the Leningrad Theatrical Institute. The Music Library of the Kirov is one of the richest of its kind and contains many sets of orchestral parts and a host of other materials relating largely (but by no means exclusively) to the history of the Russian opera.★ The largest music museum is the Glinka Museum, situated in the building of the Moscow Conservatory, which contains more than 20 000 original manuscripts of Russian and West European composers, including Glinka, Borodin, Rimsky-Korsakov, Tchaikovsky, Prokofiev, Shostakovich, as well as Wagner, Liszt, Grieg, Ravel, Saint-Saëns and others. It also contains a large library of recordings as well as materials on folk music★ and the music of the Soviet republics.★ The Lenin Library in Moscow possesses the largest collection of music bibliographical materials in the USSR, and mention should also be made of the Central State Archive of Literature and Arts. As regards music library holdings in general, those of the Leningrad Public Library and the Leningrad Conservatory are substantial and contain many bibliographical rarities. Much can also be found in the Library of the Institute of Theatre, Music and Cinematography (though this is currently being redistributed), in the library of the Leningrad Conservatory, the Leningrad Philharmonic, the Academic Kapella (the former Imperial Chapel), the Leningrad Radio, the University Library, the Central Historical Archive and the Academy of Sciences.★ The Leningrad Conservatory possesses a large collection of recordings, some of them unique, while the Phonogram Archive of Pushkin House contains a considerable collection of recorded folk music, both Russian and of the Soviet republics.

In Leningrad the Hermitage contains many iconographic materials relating to Russian and non-Russian music, taking the form of

Theatre built by Count P. B. Sheremetev (1713–88) at Ostankino (adjustable floor levels allowed seating for 300)

paintings, drawings, sketches and sculptures. There are House Museums devoted to specific composers such as the Tchaikovsky House in Klin (established 1894), the Tchaikovsky Museum in Votkinsk (established 1940), the Scriabin Museum in Moscow (established 1922), and the Rimsky-Korsakov Museum in Tikhvin (established 1944).

In the Alexander Nevsky necropolis in Leningrad lie the graves of many Russian composers, including those of Glinka, Balakirev, Musorgsky, Borodin, Rimsky-Korsakov, Tchaikovsky, Serov and Rubinstein.   *G.S.*

Music periodicals and criticism

The first music periodicals appeared in Russia in the late 18th century, although these were all short-lived. It was not until 1840 that a music journal was firmly established; this was the *Nouvelliste*, which survived in various forms until 1916. The major music periodicals were *Russkaya muzykal'naya gazeta* (*Russian Music Gazette*) (1894–1918), *Muzyka* (*Music*) (1910–16) and *Muzykal'nyy sovremennik* (*Musical Contemporary*) (1915–17), but substantial articles on music and related subjects are found in a host of other publications such as the *Yearbooks of the Imperial Theatres* (1892–1917). A number of periodicals, mostly of only a few years' duration, appeared in the 1920s and early 1930s. They included *Sovremennaya muzyka* (*Contemporary Music*) (1924–9), *Muzyka i revolyutsiya* (*Music and Revolution*) (1926–9) and *Proletarsky muzykant* (*Proletarian Musician*) (1929–32), but all these were superseded by the journal *Sovetskaya muzyka* (*Soviet Music*), which, with the exception of a few years during the Second World War, has appeared regularly since 1933. The journal *Muzykal'naya zhizn'* (*Musical Life*) founded in 1957, is lightweight in content.

The first Russian writer to have a regular music column in a newspaper appears to have been Kashkin in the 1860s in Moscow. Though critical articles on musical composition and concerts appeared in Russian journals during the 19th and early 20th centuries, however, it was only rarely that reviews followed concert performances the next day. Among notable Russian music critics may be mentioned Odoevsky, Serov, Stasov, Cui, Famintsyn, M. M. Ivanov, Larosh, Findeyzen and Asaf'ev. Discussion of international contemporary music and reportage of musical events was a feature of Russian journals during the 1920s but since the early 1930s, apart from occasional articles in leading newspapers and periodicals, musical criticism (primarily of musical life in the Soviet Union) is found mostly in the official journal *Sovetskaya muzyka*. There is available in the English language a large body of memoir literature relating to Russian composers, and works by Glinka, Rimsky-Korsakov, Musorgsky, Tchaikovsky, Chaliapine and Prokofiev.

Among the notable 19th-century music publishers mention should be made of the firms of Bessel, Jurgenson, Gutheil (Gutkheyl) and Belyaev. Kusevitsky's firm was founded in 1908. From 1918 music was published by MUZGIZ (State Publishing Company), and since 1964 by Muzyka.   *G.S.*

Instrument manufacture and collections

Russian folk* instrumental music is closely connected with vocal* music. Of the stringed instruments important are the *gusli*, the domra, the balalaika and the *gudok*. The *gusli*, counterpart of the West European psaltery, is one of the oldest Slavic instruments and is plucked with both hands, the instrument being placed on the player's lap. The *gudok* (equivalent of the West European rebec) was a three-stringed instrument, played with bow, dating back to about the 11th century. The domra was a three-stringed plucked instrument often employed by the *skomorokhi* (clowns, tumblers) in the 16th–17th centuries, while the triangular-shaped balalaika, which gradually replaced the domra, consists of two or three strings plucked with a plectrum. The balalaika became popular at the end of the 19th century, when other members of the family were constructed and popularized by folk orchestras. Among the wind instruments are the

Playing a cow-horn *zhaleyka*

rog (primitive horn), the *truba* (wooden trumpet), the *rozhok* (wooden horn with finger holes); there are the *dudka* or *sopel'* (types of flute), and the double end-blown flute – the *svirel'*; reed instruments include the *zhaleyka* and the *surna*, while the *volynka* is the equivalent of the Scottish bagpipe. The *garmon'* (concertina) came into popular use from the 19th century onwards. Of unusual interest is the *kuvikly* or *kuvichki*, consisting of a cluster of cane pipes held loosely in the hand. Percussion instruments include *bubny* (tambourines), *lozhki* (type of castanets), as well as rattles, jew's harp and different species of drum. A large collection of folk instruments of the world's peoples and other musical instruments is found in the Institute of Theatre, Music and Cinematography, Leningrad.

Of the musical instruments manufactured in Russia before 1917 mention may be made of the work of the violin-, cello-, and guitar-maker Batov and of the guitar-maker Arkhuzen. During the 19th century a piano-making industry was established in St Petersburg which accounted for 80 per cent of all keyboard instruments produced in Russia. This relied almost entirely on imported parts, however, which were then locally assembled. After the Revolution it was on the basis of the existing firms of Bekker (Becker) and Shreder (Schröder) that the Krasny Oktyabr' ('Red October') firm was established, now the largest piano-manufacturing firm in the USSR. The Zimmermann wind-instrument factory, opened in St Petersburg in 1876, was nationalized in 1917. Plucked instruments (balalaikas, harps, mandolins, guitars) have been produced at the Leningrad Lunarcharsky factory since 1926, while accordions (using either keys or buttons) are produced in large numbers. The experimental work of Termen in the early 1920s, resulting in the invention of the Théréminvox, followed in the 1930s by further work on electrical musical instruments by A. V. Rimsky-Korsakov and A. A. Ivanov in Leningrad, led to the invention of the Emeriton, various models of which have subsequently appeared. Instrument-making classes are held in the Leningrad and Moscow Conservatories.

Rare musical instruments, including music-boxes, violins and harps, are to be found at the Hermitage. The State Collection of Unique Musical Instruments, founded in Moscow in 1919, contains about 50 instruments by Italian, French, German and Russian craftsmen, including violins, cellos and violas by Stradivarius, Amati, Montagnana and Guarneri. These may be borrowed by musicians for occasions such as international competitions. *G.S.*

Modern instruments: 4-string alto domra; alto balalaika

The recording industry

The first factory to produce records within the Russian Empire* was established by the English Gramophone Company in Riga (now capital of the Latvian SSR) at the beginning of the 20th century. The first factory in Russia itself was opened by the firm of Pathé in 1907. By 1915 there were six factories in Russia producing 20 million discs per year. In 1913 Moscow alone had ten stores devoted to the sale of records. After the Revolution,* following the nationalization of all industry, record factories were set up on an extensive scale. In 1964 the national record firm of Melodiya was established under the direction of the Ministry of Culture and in 1975 produced nearly 200 million records, of which 13 million were purchased in Moscow, nearly two million of them at the Melodiya Store in Kalinin Prospekt (opened 1969). In 1975 Moscow city and oblast (some 14 million people) had two stores specializing in records, though some cities have none. Of the records produced, 31 per cent are said to be of 'serious' music (consisting primarily of works by Russian and Soviet composers and some Western composers); the remainder include light music, folk music, mass songs, children's records, verse and speech records. Though jazz* records are produced, these are often in short supply and the lack of liaison between producers and sellers (the Melodiya store in Moscow for instance – like most retail outlets – is under the control of the Ministry of Trade) is frequently criticized in the Soviet press. A new improved stereo record-player is now available, though cassette recorders and tapes are far less common than in the Western world. In 1975 all Shostakovich's symphonies were issued by Melodiya in conjunction with HMV. A notable event was the issuing of 'Band on the Run' by Paul McCartney's group Wings in 1976. *G.S.*

Musicians: biographical notes

Composers

ARAKISHVILI, Dimitry Ignat'evich (1873–1953). Georgian symphonic and operatic composer; his *Legend of Shota Rustaveli* (1914, prem. 1919) is one of the first Georgian operas.

ARENSKY, Anton Stepanovich (1861–1906). Russian composer and teacher; Director of the Imperial Chapel 1895–1901; chief works: opera *A Dream on the Volga* (prem. 1890), piano pieces.

ARKHANGEL'SKY, Aleksandr Andreevich (1846–1924). Russian sacred composer and conductor, member of the St Petersburg school of composition; his mixed choir also toured abroad.

ARUTYUNYAN, Aleksandr Grigor'evich (b.1920). Armenian composer; chief works: vocal symphonic poem *Tale of the Armenian People* (1961), Piano Concerto (1941).

ASAF'EV, Boris Vladimirovich (1884–1949). Russian composer and musicologist (literary pen-name Igor' Glebov); chief works (incl. 10 operas and 27 ballets): ballet *The Fountain of Bakhchisaray* (1934), opera-monodrama *The Bronze Horseman* (1942).

AUSTER, Lidiya Martinovna (b.1912). Estonian composer; chief works: opera *Tiyna* (prem. 1955), Piano Concerto (1952).

BABADZHANYAN, Arno Arutyunovich (b.1921). Armenian composer; chief works: Poem-Rhapsody for Symphony Orchestra (1954), Piano Trio (c.1955).

BALAKIREV, Mily Alekseevich (1836–1910). Russian composer, pianist, teacher and conductor, founder of the 'Mighty Handful' and of the 'Free School of Music'; Director of Imperial Chapel 1883–94; chief works: *Overture on Themes of Three Russian Folk-Songs* (1858), *Overture 1000 Years* (1862, rev. 1887), symphonic poem *Tamara* (1882), Oriental Fantasy for Piano 'Islamey' (1869), 2 symphonies (1898, 1908), folk-song collections (1866, 1900).

BALANCHIVADZE, Andrey Melitonovich (b.1905). Georgian composer and teacher; composer of first Georgian ballet *Heart of the Mountains* (1936, rev. 1938), ballet *Mtsyri* (1964).

BALANCHIVADZE, Meliton Antonovich (1863–1937). Georgian composer (father of preceding) and folk-song collector; chief works: songs.

BORODIN, Aleksandr Porfir'evich (1833–87). Russian composer and chemist, member of the 'Mighty Handful'; chief works: opera *Prince Igor* (1869–87–unfinished, completed Rimsky-Korsakov and Glazunov), 2 symphonies (1867, 1876), symphonic picture *In Central Asia* (1880), 2 string quartets (1879, 1881), songs, piano pieces.

BORTNYANSKY, Dmitry Stepanovich (1751–1825). Ukrainian composer of sacred and secular music; studied in Italy; Director of Imperial Chapel 1796–1825; chief works: sacred concertos, Liturgy, 6 operas, orchestral, vocal and chamber music.

CHESNOKOV, Pavel Grigor'evich (1877–1944). Russian sacred composer, choral conductor and teacher; member of the Moscow school of sacred composition; after the Revolution composed secular choral music.

ČIURLIONIS, Mikalojus (1875–1911). Latvian artist and composer of first Latvian symphonic poems: *In the Forest* (1900), *The Sea* (1907); his pictures are inspired by music: *Sea Sonata* (1908).

CUI, César Antonovich (1835–1918). Russian composer and critic, member of the 'Mighty Handful'; by profession a military engineer; chief works: operas *William Ratcliffe* (prem. 1869), *Angelo* (prem. 1876).

DARGOMYZHSKY, Aleksandr Sergeevich (1831–69). Russian composer, forerunner of the 'Mighty Handful'; chief works: operas *Rusalka* (1855), *The Stone Guest* (completed by Cui and Rimsky-Korsakov, prem. 1872); songs and orchestral works.

DUNAEVSKY, Isaak Osipovich (1900–55). Russian composer and conductor, renowned for his operettas, film music and songs; chief works: the song 'Song of our Native Land' (1936); music to films *Happy Kiddies* (1934), *Circus* (1936).

DZERZHINSKY, Ivan Ivanovich (1909–78). Russian composer; his opera *Quiet Flows the Don* (1934, prem. 1935) was held up as a model of Socialist Realism when Shostakovich's *The Lady Macbeth of the Mtsensk District* was castigated.

GLAZUNOV, Aleksandr Konstantinovich (1865–1936). Russian composer, conductor and teacher; Director of St Petersburg (Leningrad) Conservatory 1905–28; from 1928 lived in Paris; chief works: tone poem *Stenka Razin* (1885), ballet *The Seasons* (1899, prem. 1900), 8 symphonies.

GLIÈRE, Reyngol'd Moritsevich (1874–1956). Ukrainian-born composer and conductor; chief works: Programme Symphony *Il'ya Muromets* (1911); opera *Shakhsenem* (1925, rev. 1934); ballet *The Red Poppy* (prem. 1927).

GLINKA, Mikhail Ivanovich (1804–57). Russian composer, founder of the Russian Nationalist School; chief works: operas *A Life for the Tsar* (renamed *Ivan Susanin*) (1836), *Ruslan and Lyudmila* (1842); orchestral fantasy 'Kamarinskaya' (1848).

GRECHANINOV, Aleksandr Tikhonovich (1864–1956). Russian composer, especially of operas, children's pieces and sacred music; left Russia 1922; chief works: operas *Dobrynya Nikitich* (1901, prem. 1903), *Sister Beatrice* (1910, prem. 1912), 2 Liturgies.

GRINBLAT, Romuald Samuilovich (b.1930). Latvian composer; chief works: ballet *Rigonda* (1959); Piano Concerto (1963).

Below: Glazunov, by I. Ye. Repin. Bottom: Glinka (seated)

IPPOLITOV-IVANOV, Mikhail Mikhaylovich (1859–1935). Russian composer, conductor and teacher; Director of Moscow Conservatory 1906–22; chief work: *Caucasian Sketches* (1894).

IVANOVS, Janis Andreevich (b.1906). Latvian composer and prolific symphonist (Symphony no. 15, publ. 1975).

JUZELIUNAS, Julius Aleksandro (b. 1916). Latvian composer; chief works: ballet *On the Seashore* (prem. 1953), Concerto for Organ, Violin and String Orchestra (1965), symphonies.

KABALEVSKY, Dmitry Borisovich (b.1904). Russian composer, conductor and educator, concerned particularly with music education; World President of International Society for Music Education, 1974; chief works: opera *Colas Breugnon* (1938), Suite *The Comedians* (1940), Violin Concerto (1948).

KALINNIKOV, Vasily Sergeevich (1866–1901). Russian composer; chief work: Symphony no. 1 (1895).

KAPP, Artur Iosifovich (1878–1952). Estonian composer and teacher; chief work: Symphony no. 1 (1924).

KAPP, Villem Khansovich (1913–64). Estonian composer (nephew of preceding); chief works: vocal-symphonic poem *On the Northern Sea* (1958), opera *Lembitu* (prem. 1961).

KARAEV, Kara Abul'faz-ogly (b.1918). Azerbaijan composer and teacher; chief works: ballets *Seven Beauties* (prem. 1952), *Path of Thunder* (prem. 1958; Lenin Prize, 1968); symphonic poem *Leyli and Medzhun* (1947).

KASTAL'SKY, Aleksandr Dmitrievich (1856–1926). Russian sacred composer, conductor, teacher and specialist in folk-song, member of the Moscow school of composition.

KHACHATURYAN, Aram Il'ich (1903–78). Armenian composer, conductor and teacher; chief works: ballets *Gayane* (1942), *Spartacus* (1954, prem. 1956); Violin Concerto (1961); Piano Concerto (1965).

KHANDOSHKIN, Ivan Evstaf'evich (1747–1804). Russian composer and violinist, writer of sonatas, 'Russian Songs' with variations.

KHRENNIKOV, Tikhon Nikolaevich (b.1913). Russian composer and teacher; for many years First Secretary of Union of Soviet Composers; chief works: operas *Into the Storm* (1939, rev. 1952), *Frol Skobeev* (1950); ballet *By Love for Love* (1976); incidental music to film *Much Ado About Nothing* (prem. 1936).

KOMITAS (real name: SOGOMONYAN, Sogomon Gevorkovich) (1869–1935). Armenian composer, conductor and performer and folk-song specialist; after c.1910 resident abroad; chief works: folk-song arrangements.

KOVAL' (real name: KOVALEV), Marian Viktorovich (1907–71). Russian composer; chief work: opera *Yemel'yan Pugachev* (1942).

LISENKO, Nikolay Vital'evich (1842–1912). Ukrainian composer, pianist, conductor and folk music specialist, whose operas mark the beginning of national opera in the Ukraine; chief work: opera *Natalka Poltavka* (1889).

L'VOV, Aleksey Fedorovich (1798–1870). Russian composer, violinist, conductor; Director of the Imperial Chapel 1837–61; chief work: the Imperial Russian National Anthem 'God Save the Tsar' (1833); sacred music.

L'VOVSKY, Georgy (1830–94). Russian composer of sacred music of the St Petersburg school; chief works: liturgical compositions.

LYADOV, Anatoly Konstantinovich (1855–1914). Russian composer, conductor, teacher and folk-song arranger; chief works: symphonic pictures *Baba-Yaga* (1904), *The Enchanted Lake* (1909), *Kikimora* (1910), *From the Apocalypse* (1913), *Eight Russian Folk-songs* (1905); piano pieces, incl. *A Musical Snuff-box* (1893)

MACHAVARIANI, Aleksey Davidovich (b.1913). Georgian composer and teacher; President of Union of Composers of Georgian SSR; chief works: ballet *Otello* (1957); Violin Concerto (1950).

MELIKOV, Araf Dzhangirovich (b.1933). Azerbaijan composer; chief works: ballet *Legend of Love* (1961); Symphony no. 2 (1970).

MIRZOYAN, Edvard Mikhaylovich (b.1921). Armenian composer; chief work: Symphony for String Orchestra and Drums (1962).

MOSOLOV, Aleksandr Vasil'evich (b. 1900). Ukrainian composer, renowned for his experimental tendencies in the 1920s; chief work: symphonic episode *The Factory* (1926); opera *The Hero* (1927, prem. 1928, Frankfurt-am-Main).

MURADELI, Vano Il'ich (b.1908). Georgian composer, whose opera *The Great Friendship* was severely criticized in a Party decree of 1948; chief works: operas *The Great Friendship* (1947), *October* (1964); Second Symphony (1945); mass songs; operetta *Girl with Blue Eyes* (1966).

MUSORGSKY, Modest Petrovich (1839–81). Russian composer, member of the 'Mighty Handful'; chief works: operas *Boris Godunov* (1869, rev. 1872, prem. 1874), *Khovanshchina* (completed Rimsky-Korsakov, prem. 1886), *Sorochintsy Fair* (1874–81, uncompleted); piano suite *Pictures from an Exhibition* (1874); songs.

MYASKOVSKY, Nikolay Yakovlevich (1881–1950). Russian composer (born in Poland) and teacher; chief works: 27 symphonies; Violin Concerto (1938); Cello Concerto (1945); 13 string quartets; poem-cantata *Kirov is With Us* (1942); piano music; songs.

PAKHMUTOVA, Aleksandra Nikolaevna (b.1929). Russian composer, renowned for her songs.

PALIASHVILI, Zakhary Petrovich (1871–1933). Georgian composer, conductor, teacher and folk-song specialist; chief works: operas *Abesalom and Eteri* (1910–18, prem. 1919), *Daisi* (1923); *Georgian Suite* for symphony orchestra (1928); Georgian Liturgy.

Below: Musorgsky by I. Ye. Repin.
Bottom: Prokofiev, by P. P. Konchalovsky

PÄRT, Arvo (b.1935). Estonian composer; chief works: oratorio *Approach of Peace* (1961); Children's Cantata *Our Garden* (1959); *Collage on the Theme BACH* (1964); *Musica Sillabica* (1964); Polyphonic Symphony (1968).

PETROV, Andrey Pavlovich (b.1930). Russian composer; chief works: ballet *Shore of Hope* (1959); *Peter the First: Vocal-symphonic frescoes* for soloist, chorus and orchestra (publ. 1974).

PROKOFIEV, Sergey Sergeevich (1891–1953). Russian composer, pianist and conductor; chief works: 8 operas incl. *The Love for Three Oranges* (1919, prem. 1921), *The Fiery Angel* (1927), *War and Peace* (1943, rev. 1946 and 1952, prem. 1955); 7 ballets incl. *Chout* (1920, prem. 1921), *Le Pas d'Acier* (1925, prem. 1927), *Romeo and Juliet* (1936, prem. 1938), *Cinderella* (1941, prem. 1945); 7 symphonies, 2 violin concertos; 5 piano concertos; 2 cello concertos; Symphonic Tale *Peter and the Wolf* (1936); *Scythian Suite (Ala and Lolly)* (1915); secular cantata *Alexander Nevsky* (1938); Overture on Hebrew Themes for Sextet with Clarinet and Piano (1919); 9 piano sonatas.

RÄÄTS, Jaan Petrovich (b.1932). Estonian composer of symphonic and chamber music.

RAKHMANINOV, Sergey Vasil'evich (1873–1943). Russian composer, pianist and conductor; from 1917 resident abroad; chief works: opera *Aleko* (1892, prem. 1893); Poem for Orchestra, Chorus and Soloists–*The Bells* (1913); symphonic poem *Isle of the Dead* (1909); Three Russian Songs (1926); Symphonic Dances (1940); 3 symphonies; 4 concertos; Rhapsody on a Theme of Paganini (1934); songs; piano works.

RIMSKY-KORSAKOV, Nikolay Andreevich (1844–1908). Russian composer, conductor and teacher, member of the 'Mighty Handful'; Assistant Director of the Imperial Chapel (1883–94); chief works: 15 operas, incl. *May Night* (1878, prem. 1880), *The Snow-Maiden* (1881, prem. 1882), *Sadko* (1896, prem. 1897), *Tale of the Invisible City of Kitezh* (1904, prem. 1907), *The Golden Cockerel* (1907, prem. 1909); *Spanish Caprice* (1887); *Russian Easter Festival Overture* (1888); *Schéhérazade* (1888); choral, chamber, vocal and keyboard works.

ROSLAVETS, Nikolay Andreevish (1881–1944). Russian composer of atonal music, whose work is ignored by Soviet music historians; chief works: Violin Concerto (1927); orchestral, chamber, vocal and piano music.

RUBINSTEIN, Anton Grigor'evich (1829–94). Russian composer, pianist, conductor and teacher, founder of the Russian Musical Society (1859) and the St Petersburg Conservatory (1862); chief works: opera *Demon* (1871), prem. 1875); sacred operas and oratorios; 6 symphonies; 5 concertos; 10 string quartets; songs; piano music.

SALMANOV, Vadim Nikolaevich (1912–78). Russian composer and teacher; chief work: secular oratorio *The Twelve* (1957).

SCRIABIN, Aleksandr Nikolaevich (1872–1915). Russian composer, pianist and teacher, inclined towards mysticism; chief works: symphonic poems *The Poem of Ecstasy* (1907), *Prometheus: Poem of Fire* (1910); 3 symphonies; much piano music.

SEROV, Aleksandr Nikolaevich (1820–71). Russian composer, critic and writer on Russian folksong; chief works: operas *Judith* (1862, prem. 1863), *Rogneda* (1865), *The Hostile Power* (completed by V. Serova and N. Solov'ev, prem. 1871); sacred music.

SHAPORIN, Yury Aleksandrovich (1887–1966). Russian composer and teacher; chief works: opera *The Decembrists* (prem. 1953); symphony-cantata *On the Field of Kulikovo* (1939); oratorio *Tale of the Battle for the Russian Land* (1944).

SHCHEDRIN, Rodion Konstantinovich (b.1932). Russian composer; chief works: opera *Not Love Alone* (prem. 1961); ballet *The Little Humpbacked Horse* (prem. 1960); *Anna Karenina* (1971); 12 preludes and fugues (1963–64); Polyphonic Notebook for Piano (1972).

Rakhmaninov, by K. A. Somov

Rimsky-Korsakov

Shostakovich and Khachaturyan, 1970

SHOSTAKOVICH, Dmitry Dmitrievich (1906–75). Russian composer and pianist; twice censured (1936, 1948) but exculpated; chief works: operas *The Nose* (1928, prem. 1930), *The Lady Macbeth of the Mtsensk District* (1932, prem. 1934; rev. ed. named *Katerina Izmaylova*, prem. 1962); ballet *The Age of Gold* (1930); secular oratorios *Song of the Forests* (1949), *The Execution of Stepan Razin* (1964); 15 symphonies (no. 7: Lenin Prize, 1942; no. 11: Lenin Prize, 1958); 15 string quartets; Piano Quintet (1940); Piano Trio no. 2 (1944).

SLONIMSKY, Sergey Mikhaylovich (b.1932). Russian composer and teacher; chief works: opera *Virineya* (1967); ballet *Icarus* (pub. 1973); *Concerto buffo* (1966); Vocal Scene *Farewell to a Friend* (1970).

SOLOV'EV-SEDOY (real name: SOLOV'ÉV), Vasily Pavlovich (1907–79). Russian composer, renowned particularly for popular songs, notably 'Evenings in the Moscow Woodlands'· (1956, Lenin Prize, 1959).

SPENDIAROV (SPENDIARYAN), Aleksandr Afanas'-evich (1871–1928). Armenian composer and conductor; chief works: *Crimean Sketches* (2 suites, 1903, 1912); *Erevan Sketches* (1925); songs.

STRAVINSKY, Igor' Fedorovich (1882–1971). Russian composer, pianist and conductor; left Russia 1914; chief works up to 1914: ballets *The Firebird* (1910), *Petrushka* (1911, rev. 1946), *The Rite of Spring* (1913).

SVIRIDOV, Georgy Vasil'evich (b.1915). Russian composer; chief works: *Oratorio Pathétique* (1959, Lenin Prize, 1960); *Poem in Memory of Sergey*

Tchaikovsky

Yesenin (1955); *Songs of Kursk* (1962); *Spring Cantata* (1972); songs.

TAKTAKISHVILI, Otar Vasil'evich (b.1924). Georgian composer; chief work: Piano Concerto (1951).

TANEEV, Sergey Ivanovich (1856–1916). Russian composer, pianist, teacher and theorist; chief works: opera *Oresteia* (musical trilogy 1887–94, prem. 1895); sacred cantata *John of Damascus* (1884); *On the Reading of a Psalm* (1914–15); 4 symphonies

TCHAIKOVSKY, Petr Il'ich (1840–94). Russian composer, teacher and conductor; chief works: operas *Eugene Onegin* (1878, prem. 1879), *The Queen of Spades* (1890); ballets *Swan Lake* (1876, prem. 1877), *The Sleeping Beauty* (1889, prem. 1890), *The Nutcracker* (1892); 6 symphonies; Violin Concerto (1878); Piano Concerto no. 1 (1875); Fantasy-overture *Romeo and Juliet* (1869, rev. 1870, 1880); *Italian Caprice* (1880); *Overture 1812* (1880); *Liturgy of St John Chrysostom* (1878), Vesper Mass (1882).

TITOV, Vasily Polikarpovich (c.1650–c.1710). Russian composer of many-voice sacred concertos.

TSINTSADZE, Sulkhan Fedorovich (b.1925). Georgian composer; chief work: String Quartet no. 2 (1948).

USTVOL'SKAYA, Galina Ivanovna (b.1919). Russian composer and teacher; composer especially of orchestral music–*Song of Praise* for Boys' Chorus, Piano, 4 Trumpets and Drums (1961).

VĪTOLS, Jazeps (1863–1948). Latvian composer, teacher and critic; founder of the Riga Conservatory; chief work: symphonic poem *The Feast of Ligo* (1889).

Conductors

AGRENEV-SLAVYANSKY, Dmitry Aleksandrovich (1834–1908). Russian choral conductor, singer and folk-song collector, whose choir toured Russia and abroad from 1869.

ANDREEV, Vasily Vasil'evich (1861–1918). Russian conductor and balalaika virtuoso, founder of Great-Russian Folk Orchestra in 1886.

BARSHAY, Rudol'f Borisovich (b.1924). Russian conductor and viola player, founder (1956) of Moscow Chamber Orchestra.

GOLITSYN, Yury Nikolaevich (1823–72). Russian prince and conductor of a choir of serfs which toured Russia and abroad.

KONDRASHIN, Kirill Petrovich (b.1914). Russian conductor, originally of operatic but later mainly orchestral music.

LOMAKIN, Gavriil Yakimovich (1812–85). Russian choral conductor, both of Count D. Sheremetev's private chapel (1850–72) and of the Free School of Music (1862).

MELIK-PASHAEV, Aleksandr Shamil'evich (1905–64). Armenian conductor of the Bol'shoy Theatre from 1931; chief conductor 1953–62.

MRAVINSKY, Yevgeny Aleksandrovich (b. 1903). Russian conductor 1932–8 of Leningrad Kirov Theatre; from 1938 chief conductor of Leningrad Philharmonic; Lenin Prize, 1961.

PYATNITSKY, Mitrofan Yefimovich (1864–1927). Russian conductor and folk music specialist; founder in 1910 of the Pyatnitsky Russian Folk Chorus.

RAKHLIN, Natan Grigor'evich (b.1906). Ukrainian conductor, chief conductor of State Symphony Orchestra of the USSR from 1945.

ROZHDESTVENSKY, Gennady Nikolaevich (b.1931). Russian conductor 1951–60 of Bol'shoy Opera; 1961–4 chief conductor of Bol'shoy Symphony Orchestra of the All-Union Radio and Television; 1965 chief conductor of Bol'shoy Opera; left the USSR and in 1977 was appointed principal conductor of BBC Symphony Orchestra.

SVETLANOV, Yevgeny Fedorovich (b.1928). Russian conductor and composer; chief conductor of Bol'shoy Opera 1962–4; chief conductor of State Orchestra of the USSR from 1965.

TSFASMAN, Aleksandr Naumovich (1906–71). Russian composer, pianist and conductor of a jazz orchestra, 1942–6.

UTESOV, Leonid Osipovich (b.1895). Ukrainian-born composer and conductor of various light orchestras since 1928.

ZANDERLING (SANDERLING), Kurt (b.1912). German-born conductor, who settled in Russia in 1936.

Performers and impresarios

CHABUKIANI, Vakhtang (b.c.1900). Georgian ballet-dancer and choreographer.

CHALIAPINE (SHALYAPIN) Fedor Ivanovich (1873–1938). Russian singer (bass), renowned for his dramatic roles–Mephistopheles, Boris Godunov; from 1922 resident abroad.

Chaliapine, by K. A. Korovin

Diaghilev, by L. Bakst

DIAGHILEV, Sergey Pavlovich (1872–1929). Russian impresario and aesthete, founder of the journal *World of Art* (1897); organized seasons of Russian music in Paris (1907), of opera (1908), and ballet (1910–13); from *c.*1914 resident abroad.

DOLUKHANOVA, Zara (b.1918). Armenian singer (mezzo-soprano); Lenin Prize, 1966.

GASPARYAN, Goar Mikaelovna (b. 1922). Egyptian-born Armenian coloratura soprano, possessing a phenomenal vocal range.

GILEL'S, Emil Grigor'evich (b.1916). Ukrainian-born pianist; Lenin Prize, 1962.

GMYRYA, Boris Romanovich (b.1903). Ukrainian singer (bass).

KOGAN, Leonid Borisovich (b.1924). Russian violinist; Lenin Prize, 1965.

OBORIN, Lev Nikolaevich (1907–74). Russian pianist.

OBRAZTSOVA, Yelena (b.*c.*1940). Russian soprano.

OISTRAKH, David Fedorovich (1908–73). Ukrainian-born violinist; Lenin Prize, 1960.

OISTRAKH, Igor' Davidovich (b.1931). Ukrainian-born violinist and teacher, son of preceding.

OTS, Georg Karlovich (1920–75). Estonian singer (baritone).

PACHMANN, Vladimir de (1848–1933). Ukrainian-born pianist of international reputation and eccentric habits.

REYZEN, Mark Osipovich (b.1895). Russian singer (bass) and teacher.

RIKHTER (RICHTER), Svyatoslav Teofilovich (b.1915). Russian pianist; Lenin Prize, 1961.

ROSTROPOVICH, Mstislav Leopol'dovich (b.1927). Russian (b. Baku, Azerbaijan) cellist and teacher; Lenin Prize, 1963; from 1974 resident in West.

VISHNEVSKAYA, Galina Pavlovna (b.1926). Russian soprano, wife of Rostropovich; from 1974 resident in West.

Instrument-makers

ARKHUZEN, Johann (Iogann Fedorovich) (1795–1870). Copenhagen-born guitar-maker who settled in St Petersburg; his son Robert (1844–1920) was also a well-known maker.

BATOV, Ivan Andreevich (1767–1841). Russian instrument-maker of violins, cellos and guitars.

BEKKER, Yakov Davydovich (1851–1901). Also known as Becker, founded largest piano-manufacturing firm in 19th-century Russia, based St Petersburg and in 1924 transformed into the 'Red October' factory.

IVANOV, Aleksandr Antipovich (b.1907). Russian engineer, inventor (with A. V. Rimsky-Korsakov) of the electrical instrument the Emeriton.

RIMSKY-KORSAKOV, Andrey Vladimirovich (b.1910). Russian engineer, specialist in acoustics and electrical instruments, nephew of the composer; inventor (with A. A. Ivanov) of the Emeriton.

SHREDER, Karl Ivanovich (d.1889). Also known as Schröder, founded piano-making firm in St Petersburg in 1874, employing contemporary construction techniques; the firm acquired that of Bekker, but was nationalized in 1917.

TERMEN, Lev Sergeevich (b.1896). Russian engineer, inventor of the Théréminvox, an electrical musical instrument, which was demonstrated abroad in 1927 and for which works were written by Varese and Martinů.

ZIMMERMANN, Julius Heinrich (1851–1922). German-born music publisher and manufacturer of wind instruments; founded a publishing firm in St Petersburg (1876) with branches in Moscow (1882), Leipzig (1886), London (1897), and Riga (1903).

Writers on music, publishers

BELYAEV, Mitrofan Petrovich (1836–1904). Russian publisher and patron of Russian music; his Glinka Prizes (established 1884) awarded annually for outstanding compositions by Russian composers; his Russian Symphony Concerts established 1885; his publishing firm (Belyaev/Belaieff) set up in Leipzig to publicize Russian music in 1885; his Friday evenings of quartet music commenced in 1891.

BESSEL', Vasily Vasil'evich (1843?–1907). Russian music publisher, firm established 1869.

FAMINTSYN, Aleksandr Sergeevich (1841–96). Russian critic, composer and specialist on folk instruments and pre-19th-century Russian musical history.

FINDEYZEN, Nikolay Fedorovich (1868–1928). Outstanding Russian musicologist, founder of the periodicals *Russian Musical Gazette* (1894–1918) and *Musical Antiquity* (1903–11); writer of many books and monographs on Russian and Western music; his work is the foundation of Soviet musicology.

GUTKHEYL, Aleksandr Bogdanovich (1818–82). Russian music publisher (also known as Gutheil), active from 1859 in Moscow; in 1914 his firm was acquired by Sergey and Natal'ya Kusevitsky (Koussevitzky), whose own firm *Editions Russes de Musique* had been founded in 1909, the profits from which went to Russian composers.

JURGENSON, Petr Ivanovich (1836–1904). Russian (born in Tallinn) music publisher and writer, whose firm opened in Moscow (1861) and became the basis of the State Music Publishing Company established 1918.

KASHKIN, Nikolay Dmitrievich (1839–1920). Russian music critic and teacher.

LAROSH, German (Herman) Avgustovich (1854–1904). Russian music critic, author of works on Glinka and Tchaikovsky.

ODOEVSKY, Vladimir Fedorovich (1804–69). Prince Odoevsky did much to stimulate musical life as a critic of Russian and Western music and supporter of the St Petersburg Philharmonic Society, the Russian Musical Society, and the Petersburg and Moscow Conservatories.

SMOLENSKY, Stepan Vasil'evich (1848–1909). Russian writer on sacred music, choral conductor, teacher, and composer of sacred compositions; Director of the Imperial Chapel 1901–3.

STASOV, Vladimir Vasil'evich (1824–1906). Art critic, historian and music biographer.

USPENSKY, Viktor Aleksandrovich (1879–1949). Russian ethnomusicologist, teacher and composer, specialist in the music of Central Asia.

G.S.

The Russian theatre

The theatre came late to Russia; apart from crude fairground shows and performances at court by foreign actors, there was virtually no theatre in Russia until the Empress Elizabeth* established the first public theatre at St Petersburg in 1756, with an annual subsidy of 5000 roubles, under the direction of the poet and playwright A. P. Sumarokov.* Originally somewhat artificial, socially exclusive entertainments confined to the capitals and a few provincial cities, the first plays were translations or clumsy Russian imitations of foreign works. The theatre was, however, much fostered and popularized by Catherine the Great,* herself a playwright; she inaugurated the Imperial Theatre Administration (which for nearly 100 years monopolized control of all Russian theatres), founded the Imperial Theatre School in 1779 and authorized in 1780 the building in Moscow of the Petrovsky (now Bol'shoy) Theatre. The first truly original Russian playwright was D. I. Fonvizin (1744–92); his comedy *The Minor* (1782), a vigorous satire on contemporary manners, is still played today. Uniquely Russian was the serf theatre;* rich landowners built theatres and trained companies of actors from among their more talented serfs, many of whom achieved such fame that their owners were obliged to emancipate them.

Under Alexander I* and Nicholas I* the number of theatres increased, notable foundations of the period being the Maly Theatre in Moscow (1808)–where the great actor M. S. Shchepkin (1788–1863) established a distinctively Russian school of acting–and the Alexandrinsky (now Pushkin) Theatre (1832) in St Petersburg. A Theatre-Circus was built there (1847–9) for pantomime and circus shows and the first permanent circus was established in 1877. In 1839 Nicholas I gave the Imperial Theatres comprehensive statutes which remained in force, virtually unchanged, until 1917. Poets and novelists of genius (Pushkin,* Gogol,* Lermontov,* Turgenev*) began writing for the stage, although many of the best plays of that era were banned by censorship* for many years–as happened with the wittiest, most mordant social satire of them all, *Woe from Wit* by A. S. Griboedov.* Written in 1823, its full version was not staged until 1869. Even Aleksandr Pushkin, Russia's greatest poet, suffered under the theatre censorship: his great chronicle play *Boris Godunov* (1825) was not performed until 1870. Also unstaged until 1862 was M. Yu. Lermontov's* *Masquerade* (1835), a romantic drama of character. The best known of all Russian plays dates from this period–*The Government Inspector* (1836) by N. V. Gogol', a classic comedy of mistaken identity. To the comedy of social criticism inaugurated by Griboedov and Gogol', I. S. Turgenev* added a new element: a subtle but keen awareness of the psychological tensions that underlie conventional human relationships. Turgenev's masterpiece in this genre is the ever-popular *A Month in the Country* (1850;

first performed 1872). The following decades saw the rise of authors who were first and foremost playwrights; prominent among them was A. V. Sukhovo-Kobylin (1817–1903), whose own bizarre life-story (falsely accused of murder, he spent decades in the toils of the archaic Russian legal* system) provided much material for his grotesque satirical comedies, *Krechinsky's Wedding* (1855), *The Case* (1861; first performed in 1882) and *The Death of Tarelkin* (1869; first performed 1900), which prefigure Kafka in their nightmarish indictment of a vast, oppressive bureaucracy.

Alexander II's* more liberal reign relaxed theatrical censorship; it also nourished the career of Russia's most protean man of the theatre, A. N. Ostrovsky (1823–86), who in his 57 plays (7 written in collaboration) created many quintessentially Russian characters. His influence as director and teacher equalled his popularity as a playwright; best known is his tragedy *The Thunderstorm* (1859). A. K. Tolstoy (1817–75) and L. N. Tolstoy* added enduring plays to the repertoire: of A. K. Tolstoy's historical trilogy, *Tsar Fedor Ioannovich* is a moving verse drama; contemporary themes were treated naturalistically in L. N. Tolstoy's *The Power of Darkness* (1887; first performed 1895) and *The Living Corpse* (written 1900; published and first performed 1911), humorously in his comedy *The Fruits of Enlightenment* (first performed 1891).

At the turn of the century the Russian theatre experienced a creative renaissance, beginning in 1898, when K. S. Stanislavsky (real name Alekseev: 1863–1938) and V. I. Nemirovich-Danchenko (1858–1943) founded the Moscow Arts Theatre (MKhAT). Three principal elements underlay its worldwide influence: respect for the author's intention; rigorous training to analyse and express character truthfully; subordination of individual performances to ensemble. The MKhAT also 'discovered' A. P. Chekhov.* When *The Seagull*

The new building of the Moscow Arts Theatre

V. E. Meyerhold, 1938, by P. P. Konchalovsky

Yury Lyubimov, chief producer of the Taganka Theatre, Moscow

(1895–6) failed in St Petersburg, the MKhAT production (1898) made it triumphantly successful and thereafter it gave premières of *Uncle Vanya* (1899), *Three Sisters* (1901) and *The Cherry Orchard* (1904). Maksim Gor′ky's★ long career as a playwright (20 plays) also began with the MKhAT 1902 productions of *The Lower Depths* and *The Philistines*. Symbolist★ influence on the theatre culminated in the experimental, non-realistic productions by V. E. Meyerhold (1874–1940) at the St Petersburg theatre of actress and manager Vera Komissarzhevskaya (1864–1910), notably his 1906 production of Blok's★ *The Puppet Show.*   *M.V.G.*

The Soviet theatre

After the Revolution, the nationalized Soviet theatre expanded and appealed to wider audiences: in 1917 Russia had 250 theatres; by 1937 there were 560. In the 1920s it led the world in originality and innovation, thanks largely to three outstanding directors. Teacher of a whole generation of actors, Ye. B. Vakhtangov (1883–1922) used sparse but evocative staging. His 'fantastic realism' was epitomized in the 1922 production of Carlo Gozzi's *Princess Turandot.* A. Y. Tairov (real name Kornblit: 1885–1950) pioneered Constructivism★– multiple, visually neutral platforms giving flexibility and concentrating attention on the actor. In his 'synthetic' or total theatre, mime and acrobatics augmented conventional acting techniques. Meyerhold★ took Constructivism even further towards abstraction in searching

for the ultimate in non-realistic expressivity. Training actors to great responsiveness by his technique of 'bio-mechanics', he aimed at 'a simple, laconic stage idiom that evokes complex associations'.

Soviet plays have generally been undistinguished. Perhaps a dozen authors have written good plays, among them Nikolay Erdman (1902–70); Mikhail Bulgakov★ (1891–1940), who has survived the censors' attacks; the short-story writer Isaak Babel'★ (d. 1941 in a labour camp★); the satirist Yevgeny Shvarts (1896–1958); Aleksey Arbuzov (b. 1908), who limits his themes to personal relations; Viktor Rozov (b. 1913); and the young playwright Aleksandr Vampilov (1937–72). Since 1956 a new vitality has emerged in the work of adventurous directors such as Georgy Tovstonogov (b.1915), Oleg Yefremov (b.1927) and Yury Lyubimov (b.1917). The liveliest theatrical arts–mime, clowning and satire–have migrated to a more robust institution, the Soviet circus.   *M.V.G.*

Russian folk-dance

Russian folk-song and folk-dance are closely connected; indeed, from the earliest period of Russian history there is evidence to show that folk-dance played an important part in pagan (and subsequently Christian) ceremonies. The annual festival of Svyatovit was celebrated after the harvest with worship, songs and dances, ending with a general feast; the cult of Rok ('fate' or 'destiny') persisted up to the 16th century, likewise being accompanied by dancing, while the festivities on St John's Night, celebrated with dances and the leaping of people across the flames of a crumbling bonfire, persisted until recent times. The various events of the seasonal year were commemorated in song and dance, such being the singing game 'And we were sowing millet'. An important place in all these customs and rituals was played by the *khorovod*, a round dance performed originally only in the spring, accompanied by dramatic action and singing; it is widespread throughout the slavic* peoples, being known as the *kolo* (literally 'wheel') in Yugoslavia, and the *vesnyanki* in the Ukraine. *Khorovody* are found in the first collections of Russian folk-songs published in the 18th century and they have been widely studied by Soviet researchers.

Examples of dance-songs are also found in the first printed collections. With melodies in some cases clearly of great antiquity, the dance-songs are in rapid tempo and full of rhythmic vitality, the tunes often being constructed on a variation principle. Such dances must have formed part of the repertoire of the *skomorokhi* (clowns, buffoons or tumblers) who appeared not only on secular and sacred occasions but also at Court, certainly up to the time of Peter the Great.* Their dances must also have included the squatting dance and dances with bent knees.

The *trepak*, which comes from the old Russian verb *trepat'*, to stamp with the feet, is a dance in 2/4 time performed with verve at a lively tempo: the *trepak* in Tchaikovsky's* *Nutcracker* suite is well known. The *kazachok* and *gopak* are both Ukrainian dances.

All these dances form an essential part of the repertoire of Soviet companies such as the Ensemble of Song and Dance of the Soviet Army, the Moiseev Ensemble, the Berezka Ensemble, the Georgian State Dance Company and many others, for folk-dance music and folk instrumental music are closely interwoven.   *G.S.*

Dancing to the balalaika

The Russian ballet

Ballet in the Soviet Union today is the heir to almost 250 years of a continuous tradition, with a rapid expansion of activity since 1945 which has established permanent companies in each of the constituent republics. These form a pyramid of 34 companies in 32 cities, with Moscow and Leningrad (each having two companies) at the peak. They range in size from about 45 dancers in the smaller companies to over 150 in the largest, and most of their dancers join as graduates from 20 or so State Choreographic Schools, of which more than half provide a complete nine-year course in vocational and general education.* All companies and schools are state-financed and, continuing a practice established since the 18th century, the special nature of a dancer's career is recognized by the provision of a full pension* after 20 years' professional work.

Origins

The origins of theatrical dance in Russia are found in Court entertainments on one hand, and folk-dances* on the other, together with the groups of privately-owned serf-dancers maintained by rich estate owners at least until 1806, when the last large group of such entertainers was bought by the Imperial Theatres in Moscow. As early as 1624, Tsar Mikhail, first of the Romanov* dynasty, engaged a dancing-master, Ivan Lodygin, to teach children of humble origin who became Court entertainers, and on 8 February 1673 the first recorded ballet in Russia, *The Ballet of Orpheus and Euridice*, was performed for Tsar Aleksey at the then summer palace of Preobrazhenskoe, near Moscow. After the Court was moved to St Petersburg* by Peter the Great* (who had already set up a *Teatral'-naya khoromina*, or 'theatre room' in the Kremlin), with his encouragement of dancing as a social accomplishment, the French ballet-master Jean-Baptiste Landé was invited to St Petersburg in 1734. Four years later he received permission to open there the first Russian ballet school, where children of palace servants and orphans were taught the technique of the *danse de l'école* as it had originated in France. Their training took three years, the school becoming the basis for the ballet element in the state system of imperial theatres* initiated by Catherine II* in 1756. The Directorate of the Imperial Theatres was formally constituted in 1766, with the ballet division an integral part of the theatre school and state pensions for the artists.

From 1759 the Vienna-born dancer and choreographer, Franz Hilverding, was given charge of the ballets at St Petersburg and Moscow, where he developed the narrative *ballets d'action* on the principles formulated by Jean-Georges Noverre, as did Hilverding's pupil, the Milanese Gasparo Angiolini, and Noverre's pupil, Charles Le Picq. The first Russian ballet-master of renown was Ivan Val'-berkh (1766–1819), who studied under Angiolini, danced under Le

Picq and was appointed inspector (general manager) of the company at St Petersburg's Bol'shoy Theatre and director of the ballet school there in 1794.

Meanwhile, an Italian dancer at St Petersburg, Filippo Baccari, was engaged in 1773 to give dancing lessons to children at the Moscow Orphanage over a three-year period. At the end of that time he was to receive 250 roubles for each qualified solo dancer and 150 roubles for any other who attained an agreed standard. The results exceeded expectations, and from 1776 ballets began to be staged regularly for public entertainment in Moscow. They were first performed at the Znamensky Theatre until it was destroyed by fire in 1780, and then at the Petrovsky Theatre which opened in that year on the site where Moscow's Bol'shoy Theatre now stands. The Bol'shoy Ballet of today is the direct heir of the dancers who first appeared at the Znamensky, and the company therefore dates its origin from 1776, recently celebrating its bicentenary accordingly.

Val'berkh moved to Moscow in 1807, where he reorganized the ballet school and company, while St Petersburg came under the lasting influence of another Noverre disciple, Charles-Louis Didelot (1767–1837), first in 1801–11, when he revised the teaching system and laid the foundation for what became the renowned St Petersburg style of ballet, and again from 1816 until his death. During this time he staged a number of significant ballets, notably *Raoul de Créquis* (1819), *La Fille mal gardée* (1827) and the first Pushkin★ ballet, *The Prisoner of the Caucasus* (1823). Pushkin declared of Didelot: 'There is more poetry in his ballets than in all the French literature of his times', and it was Pushkin's reference (in *Yevgeny Onegin*) to 'the Russian Terpsichore's soul-inspired flight' that summarized in one sentence the entire spirit and character of the Russian school of ballet.

The nineteenth century

In their elements of human interest, local colour and greater bodily freedom, with even a rudimentary use of *pointe* dancing for the ballerinas at moments of emotional climax, Didelot's ballets were true precursors of the 19th-century Romantic ballet first embodied by Marie Taglioni (1804–84). This style, with its emphasis on lightness, grace and modesty, gave a fresh purpose to theatrical dance, enabling it to become more poetic and imaginative, an art of illusion rather than illustration. Taglioni brought the seeds of Romantic ballet to Russia with her début at St Petersburg in 1837 in her father's production of *La Sylphide* (1832), following its original success at Paris. She and her contemporaries from the West also performed other outstanding Romantic ballets such as *Giselle* (1841), which established Yelena Andreyanova (1819–57) as the first Russian Romantic ballerina at St Petersburg; her Moscow counterpart was Yekaterina Sankovskaya (1816–78).

Sankovskaya also choreographed her own version of *Le Diable à quatre* at Moscow four years before Taglioni's former partner, Jules

Perrot (1810–92), staged the ballet at St Petersburg during his tenure as ballet-master from 1848 to 1859. Perrot, one of the creators of *Giselle*, who first made London an important centre for ballet during the 1840s, mounted new versions of his London and Paris successes as well as creating other ballets which extended the prestige of the St Petersburg style. He was succeeded by another Frenchman, A. Saint-Léon (1821–70), whose ballets included *The Little Humpbacked Horse* (1864) based on a Russian fairy-tale, which contained national dances in a stylized form and was destined to be a classic of Russian ballet for several generations. Saint-Léon moulded Marfa Murav'eva (1838–79) as a ballerina of brilliant technique.

Ballet at this time continued along parallel lines in Moscow and St Petersburg, often sharing the same productions, sometimes pursuing independent ideas. St Petersburg reflected courtly taste and interests, while Moscow, the mercantile centre, drew its audiences from a wider public and tended to be more independent. The native Russian flavour in ballet was consolidated by *The Fern* (1867), with choreography by Sergey Sokolov, a student of Saint-Léon, and music by Yury Gel'ber, first violin and conductor of the Bol'shoy Theatre Orchestra at Moscow. Two years later the St Petersburg company came under the despotic control of Marius Petipa (1818–1910), whose 46 original ballets include some of the greatest glories of the Imperial Russian Ballet.

The Imperial Ballet

Petipa, born at Marseilles, first went to St Petersburg in 1847, having already toured in France, Spain and the USA, and was a leading dancer of the Imperial Russian Ballet until 1858, when he became second ballet-master under Saint-Léon. In this capacity he staged his first important ballet, *Pharaoh's Daughter* (1862), with music by Cesare Pugni, then staff ballet composer to the Imperial Theatres. Petipa's mixture of Perrot's dramatic principles with exotic divertissements, fantastic transformations and multiple apotheoses, not necessarily logical to the narrative, constituted the new *ballet à grand spectacle*, a type which dominated Russian ballet for the rest of the century. *The Sleeping Beauty* (1890), in which Petipa and Tchaikovsky★ first collaborated, remains the outstanding example, but scenes and *pas de deux* by Petipa have survived from such other ballets as *Don Quixote* (1869), *Bayaderka* (1877), *Paquita* (1881) and *The Corsair* (1899), as well as from his 1895 production of *Swan Lake*.

This, the best-known of all Russian ballets, had its origins in a domestic entertainment for Tchaikovsky's family, probably about 1871, but it was first staged professionally as a four-act ballet at Moscow's Bol'shoy Theatre in 1877, where the ballet-master Julius Reisinger was responsible for the first, not very successful choreography. It continued in the repertory through a new choreographic version by Joseph Hansen in 1880, but disappeared after 1883. It then remained unperformed until after Tchaikovsky's death, when the most famous version by Petipa and his assistant, Lev Ivanov (1834–1901), was originally mounted at St Petersburg in 1895, in the wake of the greater successes of *The Sleeping Beauty* and *The Nutcracker* (1892), for the second of which Ivanov was largely responsible.

Ivanov worked so much in the shadow of Petipa, mostly revising older ballets, that the transitory nature of unrecorded choreography has denied him much posthumous fame, but the known share of his contribution to *Swan Lake*, preserved in the familiar lakeside scene of Act 2, is evidence of his choreography's exceptional (and musical) distinction. Soviet historians also point to his original choreography for the Polovtsian Dances in the first production (1890) of Borodin's★ opera, *Prince Igor*, on which the better-known version by M. M. Fokin (1880–1942) 20 years later was to some extent based. At the end of his life, however, Ivanov had to petition the Imperial Theatres for financial assistance after 50 years' service, and he died in poverty.

During Petipa's ascendancy at St Petersburg, ballet in Moscow went into a relative decline for want of comparable artistic direction, although there was no lack of outstanding individual dancers for both centres. Many were trained by the Swedish-born Christian Johansson (1817-1903), regarded as one of the chief architects of the Russian school of ballet. His most celebrated pupils included Mathilda Kshesinskaya (1872–1971)–she and the Italian-born Pierina Legnani (1863–1923) were the only dancers ever to be officially awarded the title 'prima ballerina assoluta'; Ol'ga Preobrazhenskaya (1870–1962); Pavel Gerdt (1844–1917)–the most famous Russian male dancer of his time; and the brothers Nikolay and Sergey Legat.

Moscow ballet revived under A. A. Gorsky (1871–1924), who was born and trained at St Petersburg under Petipa, and went to Moscow as ballet-master in 1900. He adapted to ballet the principles of dramatic expression propounded by Konstantin Stanislavsky (1863-1938) at the Moscow Arts Theatre, and achieved a form of realistic drama in choreographic terms that revivified the art of dance. Gorsky began with his own revisions of Petipa's *Don Quixote* and *Raymonda*, made no less than five progressive versions of *Swan Lake* which became the basis of the Bol'shoy Ballet's subsequent presentations of that work, and was the first choreographer anywhere to set a classical ballet on a pre-composed symphony, using A. K. Glazunov's★ (1865-1936) Fifth Symphony in 1915. He also initiated the recording of ballets in 'Stepanov notation', a system devised by Vladimir Stepanov (1866–96) which was of crucial importance when the classic Russian ballets were first mounted on British companies in the 1930s.

After Petipa's retirement in 1903, new directions were sought at St Petersburg. Following unrest among the dancers, these crystallized around Fokin, whose approach to choreography may also have had some influence from the American free-style dancer Isadora Duncan when she first appeared in Russia in 1905. Fokin, whose distinguished career took wing with such ballets as *Les Sylphides*, *The Firebird* and *Petrushka*, and other dancers from St Petersburg including Anna Pavlova (1881–1931), Tamara Karsavina (1885–

Anna Pavlova

Tamara Karsavina

Vaclav Nijinsky in his ballet *Jeux*, 1913

1978) and Vaclav Nijinsky (1889–1950), together with Igor' Stravinsky* (1882–1971) as composer, became more widely known through Sergey Diaghilev* (1872–1929). Diaghilev's touch of genius changed the face and fortune of classical ballet within five years through the seasons of ballet he organized and presented in Paris and London from 1909 to 1914, with dancers from both St Petersburg and Moscow. Some then remained with him in exile, but Fokin returned to St Petersburg in 1912 and was made ballet-master; he added several more works before the Revolution of 1917, but thereafter he rejoined his fellow-exiles in the West.

Soviet ballet

Instead of being swept away by the October Revolution as a symbol of imperial decadence, as many activists wished, classical ballet survived through its defence by Lunacharsky,* the first People's Commissar for Education, as a national asset that deserved to be made worthy of the people. The traditions of the Russian ballet were accordingly preserved and nurtured by leading teachers, notably Agrippina Vaganova (1879–1951), whose methods remain an obligatory teaching foundation throughout the USSR. Gorsky's naturalistic style of dance-drama was found to accord closely with the new aims of Socialist Realism* in art, and these were furthered by new ballets like Fedor Lopukhov's The Red Whirlwind (1924), and especially The Red Poppy (1927) by Vasily Tikhomirov and Lev Lashchilin with music by Reyngol'd Glière* (1874–1956), which remained successfully in the repertoire.

Otherwise the new Soviet ballet passed swiftly through its phase of post-revolutionary experiment to cultivate a richer harvest in the classical tradition. Yelizaveta Gerdt (1891–1975), the daughter of Pavel Gerdt, successfully made the transition from old to new leading roles, and was appointed prima ballerina in 1919 (she later became a distinguished teacher of a new generation of leading ballerinas, including Maya Plisetskaya (b.1925), Raisa Struchkova (b.1925) and Yekaterina Maksimova (b.1939)). Vaganova meanwhile taught Marina Semenova (b.1908) as the first ballerina to be wholly schooled in the Soviet aesthetic of ballet: she was prima ballerina of the Bol'shoy Ballet, 1930-52. Her male counterpart was Aleksey Yermolaev (1910–75), who personified the virile, heroic manner of male dancing that is a hallmark of Soviet ballet, particularly in the emotional human drama set against a revolutionary political background which became a prominent theme in the balletic repertory.

This was virtually initiated by Vasily Vaynonen's (1901–64) The Flames of Paris (1932), to music by Boris Asaf'ev* (1884–1949), but naturalistic dance-drama reached a peak in the work of Leonid Lavrovsky (1905–57). He began choreography in the 1930s at Leningrad, where the state company from 1935 took its name from the renamed Kirov Theatre. Lavrovsky's major achievement was his Romeo and Juliet (1940) to Prokofiev's* (1891–1953) music. It

Galina Ulanova and Yury Zhdanov in *Romeo and Juliet*

opened the Bol'shoy Ballet's first visit to the West, in Britain, in 1956, when Juliet was danced by the most celebrated of Vaganova's pupils and the outstanding Soviet ballerina of the mid-20th century, Galina Ulanova (b.1910). She began her career in Leningrad, where her first major role was in Rostislav Zakharov's (b.1907) Pushkin-based The Fountain of Bakhchisaray (1934), and moved to the Bol'shoy Ballet from 1944; she gave her farewell performance in 1962 but remained active as a teacher and coach.

Ulanova's personification of a total commitment to a dramatic role, using musical phrasing to heighten emotional expression, and a technique of broader outline and more impassioned character than Western dancers attempted, brought about a new focus of style in classical ballet. Before going to Moscow, Ulanova was evacuated with the rest of the Kirov company during the Second World War to Perm' (then Molotov) in the Urals, where the school then established has brought about a resident company (since 1971 under Nikolay Boyarchikov) which has also toured in the West and is regarded by some observers as the Soviet Union's next best company after those of Moscow and Leningrad. Other important regional centres of ballet among the 30 other companies are located at Kiev, Novosibirsk, Saratov, Sverdlovsk and Tbilisi.

The Leningrad Kirov Ballet appears to be the chief repository of the classical tradition. Since 1977 it has been directed by Oleg Vinogradov (b. 1937), former choreographer of the Maly Theatre Ballet, where the city's second company has been active since 1933. However, the lack of innovative choreographic experiment is a prime reason why several leading Kirov dancers, notably Rudolf Nureyev (b.1938), Natal'ya Makarova (b.1940), Mikhail Baryshnikov (b.1948) and Valery and Galina Panov, have sought fresh careers in the West. In Moscow Yury Grigorovich (b. 1927), director of the

Top: Rudolf Nureyev, January 1962. Above: V. V. Vasil'ev and Yekaterina Maksimova in *Spartacus*

Bol'shoy Ballet since 1966, has also sought to reassert the supremacy of the classical style in ballet, but used with more freedom of imagination: his version of *Spartacus* (1968), with music by Aram Khachaturyan,★ epitomizes the company's forceful, spectacular style and attack. Moscow's second home for ballet is the Stanislavsky and Nemirovich-Danchenko Music Theatre (the company is generally known as the Stanislavsky Ballet), which had a notably fruitful period of naturalistic dance-drama under Vladimir Bourmeister, director from 1930 until his death in 1971. *N.G.*

Pre-revolutionary film-making

In Russia, as elsewhere, the cinema began life as a music-hall novelty and a fairground attraction. The first demonstration of the new machine took place in St Petersburg in May 1896 between two acts of an operetta called *Alfred Pasha in Paris*. The novelty spread like wildfire, proving very popular at the Nizhny Novgorod Fair, where Gor'ky★ first saw it in 1898, describing it as the 'kingdom of the shadows'. To the tsar, Nicholas II,★ it was and remained 'an empty, totally useless, and even harmful form of entertainment'. (Nevertheless he allowed a filmed record of his family to be kept which was later shown in cinemas and proved a rich source of material for documentary film-makers.) In the early years of the cinema films were very short and simple. They were shown by travelling projectionists who moved from town to town as their audiences and supply of films were exhausted. Initially, the monopoly of production and distribution for these films lay with French firms like Pathé and Gaumont, but in 1908 the first Russian films were produced. By the outbreak of the First World War the audience for the cinema exceeded that for all other forms of public entertainment in Russia's towns put together. Films were becoming longer and more complex but 90 per cent of them, and all film stock and equipment, were still imported. On the outbreak of the war the Russian cinema was thrown back on its own resources: by 1916 imported films were down to 20 per cent of those shown. Many films were made to stir the patriotic feelings of the audience, but even more were made to offer them escape from the realities of war. The government was on the point of taking the cinema under its control when the revolutions of 1917 swept it away. *R.T.*

The Soviet cinema

The Bolsheviks★ had always been acutely aware of the need for political agitation and propaganda and in this light Lenin★ remarked that 'Of all the arts, for us the cinema is the most important'. The cinema already had an enormous audience in the cities and one of the principal tasks of the 1920s was to spread this audience to the countryside: partly to this end agit-trains were sent all over the country during the civil war and the early years of Soviet power. They showed short films called *agitki* or 'living posters' which by their simplicity and essentially visual impact were ideal vehicles to communicate the basic principles of the new ideology to a backward, illiterate and multilingual population. As most peasants had never before seen a moving picture the impact upon them was all the greater: the Bolsheviks became associated in the popular mind with modern technology and, by implication, with progress.

The October Revolution caused most of the pre-revolutionary entrepreneurs to flee the country, taking their much-needed equipment, films and personnel with them. The disruptions of the civil war reduced the cinema to chaos. There was no stock with which to make the necessary films but students at the new State Film School perfected new techniques in so-called 'films without film'. These techniques were applied in practice as film stock became available. After several abortive deals, supplies of the necessary materials and equipment were restored through Willi Münzenberg's International Workers' Aid movement, a subsidiary of the Communist International,★ based in Germany and operating throughout Europe. The Soviet cinema was taken into state ownership in August 1919 and the first centralized state cinema enterprise, Goskino, was established in 1922. It failed to live up to rather exaggerated expectations and was reorganized in 1924 into Sovkino. This organization presided over what is known as the 'golden era of Soviet film', 1925–30, when in turn it was formed into Soyuzkino, with the task of bringing the cinema firmly under Communist Party★ control. After further changes the Soviet cinema was finally placed under a separate Ministry of Cinematography in 1946: the organization is subdivided into different studios for each Union Republic, with several, including Mosfilm and Lenfilm, serving the Russian Federation.

The Soviet cinema has always been regarded, by Party and film makers alike, as *the* art form of the Revolution. Since the late 1920s little has been left to chance and from 1930 cinema has been organized to ensure that it reflected the official view. Before then, in its 'golden era', it expressed the spontaneous enthusiasm of those active in the industry. This was the period when all the most famous Soviet silent films were made: S. M. Eisenstein's (1898–1948) *Strike* (1925), *Battleship Potemkin* (1926), *October* (1927), *The Old and the New* (formerly *The General Line*, 1929); V. I. Pudovkin's (1893–1953) *Mother* (1926), *The End of St Petersburg* (1927), *Storm Over Asia* (1929); Dziga Vertov's (1896–1954) *Forward, Soviet!* (1926), *A Sixth Part of the World* (1926), *The Eleventh Year* (1928) and *The Man with the Movie Camera* (1929); A. P. Dovzhenko's (1894–1956) *Earth* (1930), criticized officially for its 'defeatism'. Although all these film-makers were united in their enthusiastic support for the Revolution, they were divided in their method of expression. The 1920s and early 1930s were marked by increasingly bitter polemics between those who felt that the documentary film was the major revolutionary art form, that the newsreel was the most appropriate vehicle for revolutionary propaganda, or that the fictional feature film fulfilled this role more effectively. Within the latter category there were partisans of editing (montage), as opposed to acting, on the one hand, and of different schools of acting on the other. Some directors

(Eisenstein) portrayed the mass as collective hero while others (Pudovkin) chose individual stereotypes as representative of the mass. The avant-garde techniques developed at this time have exerted a profound influence on subsequent generations of film-makers throughout the world.

Despite the immense importance of this period from the standpoint of cultural history, there is ample evidence to suggest that the films from this era that are now famous were not at all popular with contemporary audiences, who were looking for entertainment and enjoyment rather than experimentation. *Battleship Potemkin* was taken off early in 1926 after two weeks because audiences preferred to see Douglas Fairbanks in *Robin Hood*. In fact it was not until ten years after the Revolution, when imports were deliberately reduced, that box-office receipts from Soviet films exceeded those from imports. Until then Soviet films continued to be more popular abroad than they were at home: *Potemkin* showed in more cinemas in Berlin alone that in the whole of the USSR. Soviet films gained access to the world market through subsidiary organizations of the Communist International such as Prometheus and Weltfilm in Germany. Soviet enterprises also co-produced films with such companies: because such films were made for export they were less polemical, more 'entertaining', and thus also more successful with Soviet audiences

Scene from Eisenstein's silent classic *Strike*

too. But the most popular Soviet films were the melodramas produced with the support, and often the active participation, of Lunacharsky,★ the People's Commissar for Education: these films – among them the serial *Miss Mend*, 1926 (F. Otsep, 1895–1949, and B. V. Barnet, 1902–65), *Salamander*, 1928 (G. L. Roshal, b.1899), *The Bear's Wedding*, 1926 (K. Eggert, 1883–1955) – were modelled on American productions. Many had little or no overt political content and were denounced as 'bourgeois' and 'counter-revolutionary'.

At the end of the 1920s, with the resignation of Lunacharsky, the end of the silent film and the advent of the First Five-year Plan,★ the 'golden era' of experimentation came to an end. Henceforth the cinema was to be harnessed directly by the Party to confront the enormous tasks of the 'cultural revolution' that was to accompany the social and economic transformation of the country's life. New levels of censorship★ were introduced, Party cells vetted films at all stages of their production, and before distribution all films were submitted to an audience of selected workers to ensure that they were 'intelligible to the millions'. This system survives more or less intact to the present day.

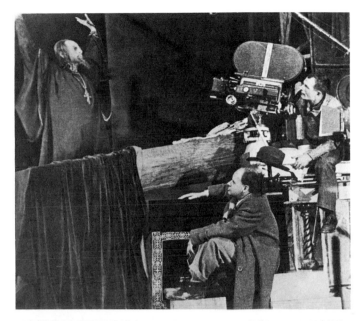

The films themselves began to reflect the official view much more closely. The collective or mass hero gave way to the individual leader-figure: the Gor'ky trilogy of Mark Donskoy (1901–81), *Chapaev*, 1934 (Vasil'ev brothers: G. N., 1899–1946 and S. D., 1900–59), *Peter the First*, 1939 (V. M. Petrov, 1896–1966, and S. I. Bartenev, b.1900), and *Alexander Nevsky*, 1938 (Eisenstein) are obvious examples, but it is even more instructive to compare *October*, 1927 (Eisenstein) or *The End of St Petersburg*, 1927 (Pudovkin) with *Lenin in October*, 1937 (M. I. Romm, b.1910) and *The Man with a Gun*, 1938 (S. I. Yutkevich, b.1904). Film makers were no longer able to portray reality as they perceived it, but had instead to portray reality as the Party perceived it. This enhanced reality was baptized 'Socialist Realism'.★ The cinema became what Trotsky★ would have described as a 'hammer' for social change, rather than a 'mirror' reflecting society and its problems.

During the Second World War the cinema, like other art forms, was fully mobilized for the war effort. Many leading film-makers went to the front bringing back some of the most remarkable war footage ever shot. Feature films, to boost morale, portrayed the great heroes of the past: *Suvorov* (Pudovkin and M. Doller, 1941), *Bogdan Khmel'nitsky*, 1941, (I. A. Savchenko, 1906–50), *Kutuzov*, 1944 (Petrov), and *Ivan the Terrible*, 1941–6 (Eisenstein), were all immortalized on film as examples for contemporary audiences; in 1946 Stalin★ himself appeared with a halo in M. E. Chiaureli's (1894–1974) *The Vow*. In the same year the Party's Central Committee★ signalled a further tightening of ideological controls in its resolution

Top: S. M. Eisenstein shooting *Ivan the Terrible* in 1945. Right: Nikolay Cherkasov as Ivan

denouncing *A Great Life*, 1946 (L. D. Lukov, 1909–63) and other films, including the second part of Eisenstein's *Ivan the Terrible*. This film was banned, its very existence denied, until after Khrushchev's* 1956 secret speech denouncing Stalin's 'personality cult'.

After the death of Stalin the Soviet cinema entered a new and much more fruitful period. Earlier technical problems have been overcome: the ravages of war have been made good and both stationary and mobile sound cinema installations cover the entire country. The industry is completely self-sufficient in the production of film-stock and equipment. Many films are still imported and these are often shown mainly to film-workers to keep them abreast of Western developments; much is also exported and an increasing number of films, such as I. Talankin's *Tchaikovsky* (1970) or A. Kurosawa's *Dersu Uzala* (1975), are co-produced with foreign organizations.

For some 20 years after the Second World War the Soviet cinema was known abroad principally for its re-creations of that war in films such as *The Cranes are Flying*, 1957 (M. K. Kalatozov, b.1903) or *Ballad of a Soldier*, 1959 (G. N. Chukhray, b.1921) and for its screen version classics of Russian literature – *The Lady with the Lapdog*, 1960 (I. Ye. Kheyfits, b.1905) *The Nest of Gentlefolk*, 1969 (A. Mikhalkov-Konchalovsky) or the 12-hour version of *War and Peace*, 1963–7 (S. F. Bondarchuk, b.1920). Since the 1960s this stereotyped view has become less and less applicable as the Soviet cinema has turned to grapple with contemporary problems. Sometimes this has been done indirectly through the historical epic (*Andrey Rublev*, 1966: A. Tarkovsky, b.1932), or the science-fiction epic (*Solaris*, 1972: Tarkovsky). On other occasions the problems are tackled more openly and directly as in *The Beginning* (G. Panfilov, 1970). In any case the Soviet cinema, although still operating within the over-all constraints of the principles of Socialist Realism, has become much more flexible in its interpretation and application of those principles. This can also be seen in the rapid increase in the number of films from the Union Republics with a distinctly national flavour, such as Mikhalkov-Konchalovsky's *The First Teacher* (Kirghizia, 1965), S. Paradzhanov's *Shadows of Our Forgotten Ancestors* (Ukraine, 1964) and G. Shengelaya's *Pirosmani* (Georgia, 1971).

In the 1920s the Soviet Union produced a cinema that has profoundly influenced all subsequent film-making; in the 1970s it had the highest per head audience figures in the world. It has clearly resisted the encroachment of radio* and television* and remained, if not (as Lenin prophesied) the most important, at least among the 'most important of all the arts'.   *R.T.*

Top: S. F. Bondarchuk filming *War and Peace*. The scene shows the execution of fire-raisers after the French capture of Moscow. Centre: Tarkovsky's *Andrey Rublev*, with A. Solonitsyn as Rublev, Irma Tarkovskaya as a Fool. Bottom: scene from Tarkovsky's *Solaris*

THE SCIENCES

Assembling the Soviet 6-metre telescope with the world's largest mirror, sited in the Caucasus, 1970

Scientific development from the 18th century to 1917

The foundations of modern science and technology in the USSR were laid during the reign of Peter I.* His conviction that the transformation of Russia into a powerful state required the effective use of a systematic knowledge of nature received no support from the Church,* and Peter proceeded to set up various institutions as focal points for spreading scientific knowledge. The School of Mathematics and Navigation, founded in 1701 (from 1715 the Naval Academy), was the forerunner of establishments for training artillery and engineering officers and military medical personnel; a public library (1714) and museum (1719) followed, and eventually the Academy of Sciences* was founded in 1725. European scientific societies were much concerned with the surveying of natural resources, to the benefit of industry and agriculture, and also of many branches of learning. The international fame of the St Petersburg Academy derived also from the results obtained by members of such academic expeditions–notably of P. S. Pallas (1741–1811) and I. I. Lepekhin (1740–1802)–sent out to survey the vast expanses of the Russian Empire.

The need for trained chemists to participate in these expeditions prompted M. V. Lomonosov* (1711–65)–in the same year (1736) as he enrolled at the Academy–to go to Germany, to Marburg to study physics and chemistry and to Freiberg for mining and metallurgy. On returning to St Petersburg, he set up in 1748 a chemical laboratory in which much attention was given to the common ground where physics and chemistry met. There is no doubt that after formulating the idea of the conservation of matter in a letter to the Swiss mathematician, L. Euler in 1748, Lomonosov in 1756 was experimenting on lines similar to those of A. L. Lavoisier, the French chemist, later. However, Lomonosov had clearly no knowledge of oxygen and its role in combustion;* he also explained physical and chemical changes in terms of corpuscular movement at a time when they tended to be interpreted on the basis of fluidal concepts. Perhaps for this reason his work, although by no means unknown to the scientific world outside Russia, had little effective influence. Nevertheless, with his encyclopedic interests (scientific, artistic and industrial pursuits, poetry and historical writing, and proposals for linguistic and educational reforms) in a country which had experienced neither the Renaissance nor the Reformation and had scarcely come to terms with the Enlightenment, Lomonosov personified the desire of intellectual Russia to break with the past and to develop its national cultural potential.

In spite of the founding of half a dozen universities and several learned societies, the perennial grip of government censorship* during the first half of the 19th century still affected all fields of intellectual endeavour, particularly the suppression of the Decembrist* rising (1825)–even the most moderate liberal ideas were suspect. A consequence was to bring Russian intellectuals working in different fields into closer contact; the links with non-scientists added another dimension to Russian scientific thought. An inclination towards broad generalization with considerable philosophical implications characterized much of the original thinking of leading Russian scientists of the pre-revolutionary period. The relative isolation of one of the founders of non-Euclidean geometry, N. I. Lobachevsky (1792–1856), who spent most of his life at the provincial university of Kazan', did not prevent him from familiarizing himself with basic philosophical questions about the nature of space and of mathematical knowledge; he was critical of the Kantian idea of absolute space, and also rejected the view that mathematical knowledge was a product of the pure mind unconnected with the external world. His advocacy of 'mathematization' of science in turn influenced his view of the role of science in education. Others such as M. V. Ostrogradsky (1801–61), Sofia Kovalevskaya (1850–91) and especially P. L. Chebyshev (1821–94) were better known to the outside world than was Lobachevsky, of whom it had been said by the English mathematician J. J. Sylvester that he performed for geometry what Copernicus did for astronomy. Another mathematician, N. N. Zinin (1812–80), founded an influential school of chemistry; his method of producing aniline, the mother compound of aniline dyes, was historically if not industrially significant (the manufacturing climate in Russia did not greatly favour the growth of chemistry). Zinin's pupil, A. M. Butlerov (1828–86), helped to develop the theory of chemical structure (1861).

The achievements, aims and frustrations of Russian scientific minds of this period are best symbolized by the life and work of D. I. Mendeleyev (1834–1907). His Periodic Law of elements (1869–71) did not merely introduce order into the classification of known elements, but boldly demonstrated that a scientific generalization had as much to cover existing knowledge as to lead the way to the unknown–to the prediction of properties of undiscovered elements. Mendeleyev often clashed with official opinion, was never elected to the membership of the Academy of Sciences and had to relinquish his St Petersburg Chair after he had transmitted a students' petition to the Ministry of Education. He eventually headed the Central Bureau of Weights and Measures, and–always interested in the role science and technology* could play in the economic development of Russia–he became especially concerned with the utilization of its coal, oil and ore reserves.

Mendeleyev brought the concept of evolution into chemistry.* At the same time, it was in connection with the contributions to embryology of Berlin-born C. F. Wolff (1733–94) and Baltic German K. E. Baer (1792–1876)–both members of the Academy of Sciences who had worked in Russia–that Russian biologists (K. F. Rulye,

1814–58) and others became familiar with evolutionary thinking. The writings of Charles Darwin, extensively read by the Russian intelligentsia, reinforced their widely held belief in the humanist and civilizing role of science; they eschewed social Darwinism and positivism. The ideas of organic evolution were carried over into biology by the embryologist A. O. Kovalevsky (1840–1901), his palaeontologist brother (and husband of Sofia) V. O. Kovalevsky (1842–83), the microbiologist I. I. Mechnikov (1845–1916) and the plant physiologist K. A. Timiryazev (1843–1920), among others. Evolutionary concepts also underlay the work of the physiologist I. M. Sechenov (1829–1905), who attacked the problem of the mind-body relation by developing and applying the reflex concept to brain activity. The view that consciousness could and should be investigated scientifically was further developed by I. P. Pavlov (1849–1936), who brilliantly extended his own experimental work on the physiology of digestion (for which he gained a Nobel Prize in 1904) into brain physiology and introduced the concept of the conditioned reflex. According to Pavlov himself in a letter to the Sechenov Physiological Society in Leningrad in 1934, the study of the central nervous system constituted 'the Russian contribution to world science and generally human thought'. Among other internationally-known scientists of pre-revolutionary Russia were P. N. Lebedev (1866–1912), who demonstrated the existence of pressure of light–a disclosure of far-reaching significance in the history of modern physics; A. S. Popov (1859–1905), whose claim to have achieved radio communication in 1895–6 independently and at the same time as Marconi can be substantiated; and V. I. Vernadsky (1863–1945) and his pupil A. E. Fersman (1883–1945) who helped to develop geochemistry, one of the early border sciences. Ever since the work of N. I. Kibalchich (1854–81)–his career was cut short by execution for participation in the assassination of Alexander II*– space fascinated Russian scientists; N. E. Zhukovsky (1847–1921) and K. E. Tsiolkovsky (1857–1935) were among those who made fundamental contributions to aerodynamics, preparing the way for their country's later pre-eminence in space research.*   M.T.

Science in the Soviet state

The Soviet government was immediately interested in gaining the support of the Russian scientific intelligentsia. Lenin* suggested that the Academy of Sciences* should be made responsible for the study of natural resources,* and set up committees to plan for the reorganization of industry and the economy, but in 1920 a State Commission for the Electrification of Russia (GOELRO), comprising 200 scientists and other experts, was established outside the Academy under the chairmanship of G. M. Krzhizhanovsky (1872–1959). This old political associate of Lenin had been trained as an electrical engineer and was much influenced by the writings of the English chemist F. Soddy. Soddy's perception that the nucleus was a potential source of electricity appealed to Krzhizhanovsky, who advised Lenin that Russia could not overcome its backwardness unless it was thoroughly electrified. During the civil war* the relations between government and scientists became somewhat strained; Maxim Gor'ky,* the writer, often acted as mediator and in 1921 Lenin signed a decree officially recognizing the significance of Pavlov's work and materially assuring its continuation. Pavlov's own swing from 1920s disaffection to 1930s appreciation of the state attitude to science was in many ways symptomatic of feeling among the remaining intelligentsia who had not emigrated.

As the country embarked on its Five-year Plans* the Academy became responsible for the application of planning to science, which despite many shortcomings proved of benefit. It was gradually realized that specific scientific discoveries could not be anticipated but that areas of scientific research could be defined and financial resources allocated according to their social importance. This policy aroused interest in Western scientific circles, and also doubt whether planning of science could accelerate scientific progress or increase its efficiency. It was only after the Second World War that planning of research* in one form or another became an accepted procedure everywhere.

Belief in the social function and conditioning of science, influenced by dialectical and historical materialism (the philosophy underlying Marxism-Leninism*), aroused expectations in the 1930s that science would permeate socialist society. However, the oppressive political

I. P. Pavlov conducting an operation at the Leningrad Institute of Experimental Medicine

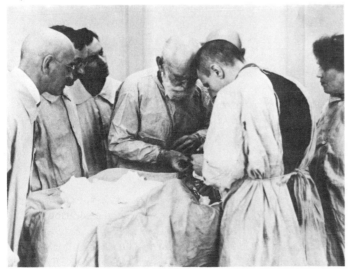

system operated by the Communist Party* leadership under Stalin* severely damaged scientific life in the USSR; travel abroad, a long-established practice under the tsarist regime, was increasingly restricted. Even the highly original physicist P. L. Kapitsa (b.1894), after a holiday in his homeland in 1934, was refused an exit visa to return to Cambridge (where he had been working with E. Rutherford since the early 1920s), while encouraged to continue his fundamental studies of the behaviour of matter at lowest possible temperatures. Many scientists were imprisoned; some continued their work in prison research institutes but some, such as N. I. Vavilov (1887–1943), were falsely accused of sabotage and perished in confinement. The traditional interest of Russian scientists in general philosophical questions persisted but free discussion, even of the role of Marxist philosophy in science, had progressively less chance to develop, and – paradoxically but significantly – stimulating work in this field began to be produced outside the USSR.

The rise of the USSR to super-power status could not have been achieved without government support for fundamental scientific research and its application to military* needs. It may well be that the development of space research* reinforced the position of the home critics of T. D. Lysenko (1898–1976) who, because of his dominating influence, has been justifiably blamed for the insufficient development of research in various biological areas. He certainly underestimated the significance of the study of radiation on living matter, the knowledge of which is of primary importance for the health of astronauts. After the first United Nations* Conference on the Peaceful Uses of Atomic Energy (1955), where discussion included the effects of radiation on organisms, contacts between Soviet scientists and their colleagues abroad began to be re-established on a broader basis. Thus, having suspended the publication of summaries in a Western language, certain Soviet journals resumed their provision.

Soviet progress in science and technology, spectacularly demonstrated in the penetration of space, was also reflected in the series of Nobel Prizes won for basic work on the chemical and physical properties of matter. The first, in 1956, was awarded to N. N. Semenov (b.1896) for work on the chemistry of chain reactions. In 1958 he was followed by a team, P. A. Cherenkov (b.1904), I. Ye. Tamm (1895–1971) and I. M. Frank (b.1908), who explained the nature of light emitted in liquids and solids exposed to radiation or particles travelling at a speed greater than light. In 1962 L. D. Landau (1908–68) gained a Prize for a wide range of theoretical work, especially on 'condensed matter' (solid and liquid states). In 1967 N. G. Basov (b.1922) and A. M. Prokhorov (b.1916) were awarded a Prize for their studies on the interaction of radiation and atoms, which led to the development of masers and lasers. In 1978 Kapitsa was given a Prize in recognition of his lifelong contributions to low temperature physics.*   *M. T.*

The development of medicine and health care

Early medicine

Before the reign of Peter the Great* medical care in Russia was provided by a few, chiefly foreign, doctors recruited by the Apothecaries' Chamber established in 1581 and renamed in 1620 the Apothecaries' Office. A significant event in preventive medicine was the establishment of the first quarantine posts in 1592. Peter's programme of Westernization after his tours of western Europe required a greatly expanded medical service, primarily for the army* and navy* but also for the new industrial communities and growing cities. Physicians were recruited abroad, mainly in England, Scotland, Holland, Germany and Sweden. The Medical Chancellery legislated on such matters as burial of the dead and the wholesomeness of food. The whole medical organization was presided over by the Imperial Physician: the first occupant of this post was a Scot, Dr Robert Erskine (d.1718). To train Russian doctors a 'Gofshpital' with a medical school was founded in Moscow in 1706; others followed in St Petersburg and Kronstadt (1733). Peter's Admiralty Regulations (1722) defined the medical service for the navy and dockyard workers and served as the basis for General Regulations on Hospitals (1735) and for later health legislation in industry. The first factory hospital, staffed by a surgeon, was set up at Sestroretsk naval ordnance factory in 1724 and more ambitious arrangements were made at the new Urals industrial centre of Yekaterinburg in 1734.

In 1739 public health boards were appointed in Moscow and St Petersburg, chaired by a Town Physician, for medico-legal duties and to organize the urban medical services. In 1775 Russia was divided into provinces (*gubernii*) and these into counties (*uezdy*), each with its medical officer. Provincial medical boards were established in 1797 by Paul I* to ensure local observance of central governmental regulations and to organize measures against epidemics, which were becoming a major problem. Inoculation against smallpox, introduced by Dr Thomas Dimsdale at Catherine the Great's* invitation (1768), was vigorously pursued.

These administrative measures were generally unsuccessful, largely because of the shortage of doctors, and steps were taken to improve the supply. The first university faculty of medicine opened in Moscow in 1775. The 'Gofshpital' schools were replaced by medico-surgical academies, with a more scientific but less practical curriculum, in St Petersburg and Moscow (1799). The St Petersburg Academy, reorganized in 1805 by a Viennese physician Dr Peter Frank, and later enlarged, became the Imperial Medico-Surgical Academy in 1809, with the Scot Sir James Wylie as its first president. It trained doctors mainly for the army, and in 1881 was renamed the Military Medical Academy.

Private medical practice existed only in the towns, where there were sufficient people wealthy enough to afford it. Charitable hospitals were built, many of them on a magnificent scale, to meet the needs of the poorer citizens. Outside the large towns, however, medical aid was virtually non-existent; the only time a peasant might see a doctor was when being medically examined for military service. Rural hospitals, staffed mainly by German or Polish doctors who rarely spoke Russian, were in a deplorable state and most of the work was done by nominally supervised medical auxiliaries (feldshers).

Legislative provision for local medical care

The introduction of the *zemstvo* system of local government under Alexander II* was a major milestone in pre-revolutionary Russian health care: the 1864 laws made the *zemstva* responsible, 'within legal and economic limitations', for the health of the community, and aimed at a uniform availability of medical care throughout the country, free to all who paid their contributions. Each county was divided into four or more districts (*uchastki*), each to have a central hospital (on average one per 20 000 population in central Russia and one per 60 000 population in eastern Russia). Various types of staffing were tried, with one or more physicians per county, assisted by feldshers. The medical departments of the provincial *zemstva* managed their own hospitals (which served the whole province for psychiatric cases) and funded hospital construction in the counties. They organized feldsher training schools, convened congresses of *zemstvo* doctors (the first in 1871) and published some remarkably erudite statistical and medico-topographical surveys. The control of epidemics was, nevertheless, their most important function and some established herds of calves for vaccine preparation, and bacteriological laboratories for making antisera against rabies and diphtheria. By 1890 *zemstva* were functioning in 34 out of the 50 provinces of European Russia excluding Poland and the Caucasus; in those provinces of European Russia (other than Poland and the Caucasus) without *zemstva* the central government was gradually establishing a medical service, but far inferior in staffing ratio.

Laws of 1870 and 1892 required the urban authorities to provide a public health service and some personal health care, but the general situation left much to be desired, especially outside the main cities. In 1884–7, 40 per cent of persons dying in the better-off districts of Odessa and 94 per cent of those dying in the poorer quarters had not sought medical advice. In 1882 a free universal medical service was established for the poor of St Petersburg through government doctors (nearly half of them women). It was intended originally to deal with epidemics of diphtheria and scarlet fever, but in 1883 it

became permanent, and in 1885 provided 215 000 consultations and 49 000 domiciliary visits.

A law of 1866 required factories to have a hospital with beds at the rate of one per 100 workers, but at most factories the medical service existed only on paper (in the 1880s only 67 000 of a total work-force of 150 000 in Moscow province enjoyed an actual medical service). By 1890 there were 9892 doctors in civilian posts (four times as many as in military practice) and of these the number employed in industry was rising steadily; the first All-Russian Congress of Factory Doctors was held in Moscow in 1909. By that year, of a total of 19 866 civilian doctors (1328 women), 14 398 lived in towns and 5468 in rural districts, making one doctor to 7800 inhabitants. On average in the towns there was one doctor to 1500 inhabitants and in rural districts, one to 24 600. The situation was aggravated by their irregular distribution: even the better-served area of European Russia compared unfavourably with other countries of Europe both in the absolute level of infant mortality* and in the rate of its decline during the three decades before the First World War. Under the Soviet health service,* the use of the place of employment was maintained as the focus for primary medical care but local provision was also much expanded; by 1979 there was one doctor to 275 inhabitants.

INTERNATIONAL COMPARISON OF INFANTILE MORTALITY

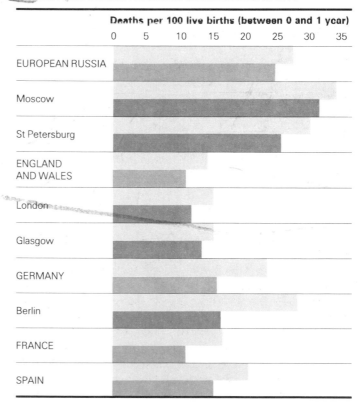

KEY

 1881–5   1906–10   1912–4

Medical education and research

From an early date the right to practise medicine in Russia was limited to those who had passed official examinations, and the University Code of 1844 accepted only candidates who had completed 10 half-year terms. In 1896 there were ten medical schools: the Military Medical Academy and the Universities of Moscow, Kiev, Khar'kov, Warsaw, Kazan', Yur'ev, Dorpat (now Tartu), Helsingfors (now Helsinki) and Tomsk; Odessa University opened a medical school in 1900. Russia was the first country to organize postgraduate medical specialization, at the Medico-Surgical Academy in 1841. The Grand Duchess Yelena Pavlovna Clinical Postgraduate Medical Institute, the first such establishment in the world, was founded in 1885. In the 32 years until 1917 it trained 9906 doctors. After the Revolution medical education★ was radically reorganized (1930): a shortening of the course was made possible by early separation into specialities. Research was fostered by the creation of an Academy of Medical Sciences in 1944.

It was not until the mid-19th century that Russian medical research began (although on the territory of what is now the Uzbek SSR an important medical school had flourished in Samarkand a millennium previously: the *Canon of Medicine* of the Arab physician Ibn Sina or Avicenna (980–1037) served as a textbook in East and West for some five centuries). The most notable of the pre-revolutionary Russian medical scientists were N. I. Pirogov (1810–81) in military and orthopaedic surgery, anaesthesia and anatomy; I. I. Mechnikov (1845–1916) in the pathology of inflammation and the discovery of phagocytosis; S. S. Korsakov (1853–1900) in psychiatry;★ V. M. Bekhterev (1857–1927) and N. I. Vvedensky (1852–1922) in neurology; I. M. Sechenov (1829–1905) and I. P. Pavlov (1849–1936) in neurophysiology (particularly the discovery of conditioned reflexes); F. F. Erismann (1842–1915) in preventive medicine, and D. I. Ivanovsky (1864–1920), who has a sound claim to be regarded as the founder of virology. Russian doctors and scientists also made important additions to knowledge of the epidemiology and pathology of plague, cholera and typhus fever.

After the Revolution the emphasis on the prophylactic approach to medicine and medical research continued, although in some fields (such as human genetics★) research has been retarded by political interference. Valuable research has been and is being pursued in the aetiology (Ye. N. Pavlovsky, 1884–1965) and prevention (V. M. Zhdanov) of infectious diseases; in cancer research (L. M. Shabad); in neuropsychology★ (A. R. Luriya, 1902–77), neurology (V. M. Bekhterev, 1857–1927, and, more recently, N. P. Bekhtereva) and neurosurgery (N. N. Burdenko, 1876–1946); in oesophageal surgery (S. S. Yudin, 1891–1954); in cardiac surgery (P. A. Kupriyanov, 1893–1963, and, more recently, B. V. Petrovsky, b.1908–Minister of Health from 1965); and in resuscitation (S. S. Bryukhonenko, 1890–1960, and, more recently, V. A. Negovsky). *B.H.*

Science policy

From the earliest days of the Soviet regime the development of science has been considered a matter of the highest priority. In the difficult years immediately after the Revolution measures were taken to retain the services of scientists, many of whom were unsympathetic to the new order, and to expand the network of research organizations, in particular by creating institutes able to assist in the country's industrial development. Although at some periods priority for pure science has been greater than that for applied research and development (R and D), in the 1970s there was more emphasis on the need to accelerate the practical application of fundamental research findings. Efforts have been directed to strengthening the links between academic institutes and industry and to creating R and D facilities, either within the Academy system or in close proximity to its institutes. The Siberian Division of the USSR Academy of Sciences★ and the Ukrainian Academy of Sciences have been in the forefront of these developments. The Academy system represents a powerful concentration of scientific forces and enjoys considerable prestige in Soviet society.

The formulation of science policy and the planning and management of R and D involve the Communist Party★ at all levels; its Central Committee★ has a department of science and educational establishments headed, since 1965, by a historian, S. P. Trapeznikov. It is notable that many of the members of the Politburo, including Brezhnev,★ have engineering and technical backgrounds.

At the highest level of government the Supreme Soviet★ approves new legislation, including laws relating to the development of science. Its two chambers both have standing commissions for science and technology★ which participate in the preparation of legislation and the examination of the relevant sections of state Plans, and also monitor the functioning of government agencies involved. General leadership in developing science and technology is the responsibility of the USSR Council of Ministers,★ but direct coordination of R and D is exercised by a number of subordinate specialized government bodies, notably the State Committee for Science and Technology (GKNT), the State Planning Committee (Gosplan★) and the USSR Academy of Sciences.

The GKNT is responsible for securing a unified national science policy in accordance with Party and government directives; its brief does not extend to military★ R and D. It was established in 1965, replacing the previous State Committee for the Coordination of Scientific Research. Functional departments are concerned with such questions as planning, finance, scientific and technical information and external relations, while branch departments are organized according to particular sectors of the economy★ or branches of industry. There are also scientific councils for the main inter-branch problems of science and technology; staffed by leading scientists and representatives of industry, these analyse the state of research in particular fields, plan future work and coordinate the activities of the R and D organizations concerned. The chief functions of the GKNT include the determination of the main directions of development and the preparation of forecasts; the elaboration, with the Academy of Sciences and Gosplan, of draft plans of research work; and the presentation, jointly with the Academy, of proposals to the government and Gosplan for the use of new research findings in the economy. The GKNT approves and oversees the fulfilment of complex programmes for solving the main inter-branch R and D problems included in the Five-year Plan.* In the 1976–80 Plan there were 200 such programmes, accounting for approximately one-quarter of all R and D expenditure. The Committee has a small reserve fund, but is not otherwise involved in the financing* of research.

The State Planning Committee draws up the five-year and annual plans of the economy which include sections devoted to the development of science and technology, elaborated with the participation of the Academy of Sciences, the GKNT and branch ministries* and departments. Gosplan has responsibility for planning the introduction of scientific and technical achievements into the economy and, jointly with the Ministry of Finance, plans the financing of science.

Under the leadership of a special council of the Academy of Sciences and the GKNT, many organizations have participated in the elaboration of a Complex Programme of Scientific and Technical Progress and its Social and Economic Consequences, extending to the year 2000. This ambitious forecasting exercise is intended to provide a framework for preparing Five-year Plans and for selecting priorities among specific scientific and technical programmes. *J.C.*

Science manpower and finance

The growth of scientific potential can be judged from the number of those recorded as 'scientists' (all persons with a higher degree or academic title and others employed as professionals in scientific, academic and industrial-research work regardless of their formal qualification): 12 000 in 1913, 98 300 in 1940, 163 500 in 1950 and 1 340 600 in 1979; expenditure from the state budget rose from 1000 million roubles in 1950 to 19 300 million in 1978 in current prices and represented an approximately 14-fold increase in constant prices.

Those with higher degrees in 1979 comprised 383 600 candidates of science (equivalent to a Western Ph.D.) and 37 100 were doctors of science (D.Sc.). By international standards the USSR has a high proportion of women scientists: in 1975 40 per cent of all scientists were women, but their proportion in the most highly qualified

categories is somewhat lower – 14 per cent of doctors of science and 10 per cent of academicians* and professors. Representatives of the technical sciences account for almost 45 per cent of the total scientific labour force. Russians and Ukrainians* predominate, but a notable feature of the Soviet period has been the development of science in republics whose economies were formerly extremely backward.

In recent years the proportion of scientific research financed from the state budget has steadily declined, from approximately 60 per cent in 1965 to 45 per cent in 1978. Most of the fundamental research of the USSR and republican Academies and of the higher education* institutions (VUZY) is financed from this source, as is much of the work on the most important inter-branch research and development (R and D) problems. Other research is financed from the internal resources of ministries* and departments. Since the end of the 1960s industrial ministries have been transferring to a new system according to which R and D is financed from a single 'unified fund for the development of science and technology' formed from profits. Much R and D is undertaken to contracts between client organizations and R and D establishments, and such contract research plays a large role in the higher educational sector and, increasingly, in the Academy system. *J.C.*

The Academy of Sciences system

The leading centre of Soviet science is the USSR Academy of Sciences, which is responsible for most of the country's fundamental research and for general scientific leadership of all research in the natural and social sciences. It is subordinated to the USSR Council of Ministers.* The Academy was founded by a decree of 1724 and officially began its activities in St Petersburg in the following year. By the end of the 19th century the Imperial Academy of Sciences, as it was then known, had become the main scientific centre of the country, although its contribution to Russia's economic and technical development was meagre. After the 1917 February revolution it was renamed the Russian Academy of Sciences. In the 1920s a new charter was adopted and other steps were taken to increase the relevance of the Academy's work to the country's development and also to enhance the influence within it of the Communist Party.* The present name was adopted in 1925 and in 1934 its headquarters moved from Leningrad to Moscow. Concern with practical problems increased sharply during the Second World War, but in the early 1960s many of the Academy's technically-oriented institutes were transferred to the industrial research network.

In 1976 the Academy had 733 full members (academicians) and corresponding members and 91 honorary foreign members. Research is carried out at 244 institutes, observatories and other scientific establishments employing a total of over 150 000 people, including 43 000 scientists. The supreme body of the Academy is the General Assembly of all academicians and corresponding members, which meets at least twice a year to discuss the development of science in the USSR, to resolve important organizational problems and to select members. The leading executive body is the Presidium, elected every four years by the General Assembly, and headed by the President of the Academy. All Academy elections are by secret ballot. The Presidents have been A. P. Karpinsky (May 1917–36), a geologist; V. L. Komarov (1936–45), a botanist; S. I. Vavilov (1945–51), a physicist; A. N. Nesmeyanov (1951–61), an organic chemist; M. V. Keldysh (1961–75), a mathematician; and A. P. Aleksandrov (b.1903; elected 1975), a nuclear physicist.

The Presidium has four sections which control the work of departments and research establishments: physical, technical and mathematical sciences; chemico-technological and biological sciences; earth sciences; and social sciences. Each section consists of a number of departments organized on the basis of disciplines and headed by academic secretaries.

Academician A.P. Karpinsky. Below: the headquarters of the USSR Academy of Sciences, Moscow

In 1957 the Siberian Division of the USSR Academy was created under the direction of the Presidium and the RSFSR Council of Ministers. Approximately 50 research establishments of Siberia are controlled by the Division, including the well-known Akademgorodok, a powerful complex of research and development (R and D) organizations located near Novosibirsk. The USSR Academy also embraces scientific centres in the Urals and the Far East and branches in a number of autonomous republics (ASSR) and regions (AR) of the RSFSR. The Siberian Division and the regional centres and branches undertake fundamental research of national importance, but also investigations relating directly to the development of their regions.

The Academy has over 200 scientific advisory councils, an extensive network of libraries,* including a Central Library in Leningrad, and responsibility for one of the oldest and largest scientific publishers* in the world (founded in 1727), Nauka, which annually issues over 2000 books and 150 journals.

Each of the Union Republics, with the exception of the RSFSR, has its own Academy of Sciences. At the end of 1976 the 14 republican Academies employed a total of approximately 45500 scientists working in almost 370 establishments. The largest and oldest republican Academy is that of the Ukraine, founded in 1919; the youngest that of Moldavia, founded in 1961. Many of the institutes of this republican system occupy leading positions in Soviet science and make a substantial contribution to the economic and cultural development of their respective republics. There are also four branch Academies, the All-Union Lenin Academy of Agricultural Sciences, founded in 1929 and employing over 11000 scientists in 1978, the USSR Academy of Medical Sciences (founded 1944), the USSR Academy of Arts (1947) and the USSR Academy of Pedagogical Sciences (1966). *J.C.*

Below: the 'science city' of the Siberian Division of the Academy of Sciences–Akademgorodok, near Novosibirsk. Bottom: solar observatory at a Siberian institute in the Sayan Mountains

Research bases

Research in the higher education* system

Whereas the USSR and republican Academies of Sciences* employed only 7 per cent of all Soviet scientists in the mid-1970s, 36 per cent were employed in the higher education system. However, the primary concern of these scientists working in higher education establishments (VUZY) is teaching; the research institutes and laboratories of the VUZY account for only 5 per cent of total research in terms of expenditure. Most VUZY are under the Ministry of Higher and Secondary Specialized Education, either directly or through corresponding Union-Republican ministries. Research in the VUZY is undertaken in academic departments, in research institutes and design offices, and in departmental laboratories classed either as 'problem-oriented' (engaged primarily in fundamental research financed through the state budget), or 'branch' (applied R and D contracted with ministries and enterprises).

Branch R and D organizations

The largest component of the Soviet science potential is the network of R and D organizations under the branch ministries and departments, in particular those of industry, agriculture and other sectors of the economy. Branch research organizations employ approximately 48 per cent of all scientists. A feature of Soviet industry is the fact that its R and D establishments tend to be concentrated at the level of the ministries (or their intermediate administrative bodies) rather than at the level of the production enterprises. Very few scientists work in enterprise R and D subdivisions, but recent measures taken to overcome this organizational separation of research and production include the creation of 'science-production associations' – amalgamations of R and D organizations and enterprises. By 1979 there were approximately 200 such associations, the majority headed by research institutes. Some R and D organizations have also been incorporated within the ordinary production associations now becoming the primary organizational unit of Soviet industry.

Inventions and discoveries

Responsibility for questions relating to inventions is vested with the USSR State Committee* for Inventions and Discoveries under the USSR Council of Ministers.* The Committee exercises general leadership of all activity in this field, provides expertise for the confirmation of inventions, maintains a register of them and promotes their use in the economy. An inventor receives a 'certificate of authorship' for a confirmed invention, which then becomes the property of the state, plus a payment on a scale determined by the economic return derived from the use of the invention in the economy. Patents are usually granted only to foreigners. The scale of inventive activity can be gauged from 1975 figures: 152 464 claims for inventions were submitted and 41 826 certificates of authorship and 2295 patents were granted; 48 011 inventions were used in the economy, including 14 856 used for the first time. A register of new scientific discoveries is also maintained: those responsible for confirmed discoveries receive diplomas and financial rewards. Between 1959, when the system was introduced, and 1975 over 160 discoveries were registered.

The Committee is also concerned with the promotion of rationalization measures, such as improvements in the design of products and technology, that raise quality, reduce costs or save materials. If a rationalization proposal is new to a particular enterprise or branch of industry, authorship is acknowledged and rewarded by a payment related to the size of the savings achieved from its use.

Voluntary scientific activity

A notable feature of Soviet science is the promotion of mass voluntary participation in R and D activities. The All-Union Society of Inventors and Rationalizers (VOIR), formed in 1958, works under the leadership of the trade unions* and has the aim of involving workers and specialists in creative technical activity. In 1976 it had a total membership of more than eight million (two million in 1960), with over 78 000 primary organizations; over half the members are shopfloor workers. The Society's monthly journal *Izobretatel' i ratsionalizator* (*Inventor and Rationalizer*, founded 1929), has a print of approximately half a million copies.

There is a long tradition of participation of scientists and engineers in voluntary activities for the promotion and popularization of science and technology. The present-day Scientific and Technical

Societies (NTO), which originated in the Russian Technical Society founded in 1866, are also under trade union sponsorship and have a total membership of eight million scientists, engineers, technicians and workers. The 23 societies are organized by branch of production and are united by an all-Union council. They participate in measures for the creation of new technology, the rationalization of production and the general promotion of scientific and technical progress. They are also involved in the planning and management of R and D: half the primary organizations also serve as enterprise production-technical councils. The VOIR and NTO both create and lead a range of voluntary organizations, including research institutes and laboratories, and offices for design, technical information and economic analysis.

The NTO are also involved in the popularization of science, an activity which is the central concern of the All-Union Znanie ('Knowledge') Society, founded in 1947. This Society organizes lectures and publishes a wide range of literature on scientific and political themes, including the popular monthly journal *Nauka i zhizn'* (*Science and Life*), with a print of over three million copies. All the republics also have Societies for the Protection of Nature, which promote rational use of natural resources* and care of the environment.*   *J. C.*

Scientific and technical information

The leading centres of the elaborate network of organizations concerned with scientific and technical information are the long-established All-Union Institute of Scientific and Technical Information (VINITI) – subordinated jointly to the State Committee* for Science and Technology (GKNT) and the USSR Academy of Sciences* – and the Central Institute of Scientific Information for the Social Sciences (INION) of the USSR Academy, founded in 1969. Both institutes are engaged in the collection, processing and publishing* of scientific information from all over the world and produce a large range of reference and abstracting journals. Information on current research being undertaken in the USSR is analysed and disseminated by the All-Union Scientific and Technical Information Centre of the GKNT. In 1975 this network of information organizations employed approximately 166 000 people working in 10 all-Union institutes, 86 central organizations specialized by branch, 93 territorial information centres and over 11 000 information offices and departments of research institutes and enterprises. This system is supplemented by a national network of scientific and technical libraries,* headed by the State Public Scientific and Technical Library in Moscow.

Scientific and technical literature is published not only by Nauka, but also by a number of universities and a range of specialized publishing houses concerned with particular technologies or branches of industry—for example, Khimiya, Mashinostroenie, Energiya and Atomizdat. In 1975 approximately 20 000 scientific books and brochures were published, together with 220 journals devoted to the natural sciences and mathematics. *J.C.*

International scientific relations

Under Stalin* Soviet science became increasingly isolated from the rest of the international scientific community. Relations gradually revived during the 1950s and 1960s, and developed vigorously during the next decade. In 1976 the USSR Academy of Sciences* maintained links with scientists and organizations of 108 countries. There is extensive collaboration within the framework of Comecon,* growing coordination of five-year plans for scientific and technical development and participation in bilateral and multilateral projects. Two notable examples of such cooperation are the Interkosmos space research* programme and the joint development and production of computers. Scientific relations with capitalist and developing countries expanded rapidly during the 1970s: the number of countries with which the USSR had such links grew from 49 in 1970 to 97 in 1975. In many cases these relations are often based on intergovernmental scientific and technical cooperation agreements. Participation of Soviet scientists in international projects and exchanges of personnel has greatly increased, dramatically instanced in the joint Soyuz-Apollo space flight in 1975. Besides space research and astronomy,* areas of strong interest for international collaboration include medical* research, energy* (including the physics* of controlled nuclear fusion based on the Soviet Tokamak installations) and environmental protection.* Scientists from Western as well as Eastern countries participate in the work of the Joint Nuclear Research Institute at Dubna near Moscow.

The USSR Academy of Sciences is the organization primarily responsible for international links in the field of fundamental research, but the coordination and planning of scientific and technical relations of Soviet ministries* with foreign organizations, including individual Western firms, is the concern of the GKNT. From 1965 the USSR has adhered to the Paris Convention for the protection of international property, since when Soviet participation in the international trade in patents and licences has greatly increased, although still extremely small relative to the magnitude of the country's scientific potential. *J.C.*

The 1976 Tokamak-10 reactor at the Institute of Atomic Energy, Moscow, named after I. V. Kurchatov (1903–60)

Exploration

In many people's minds the Russians are less closely associated with exploration than the English, Spanish and Dutch, yet Russia has a long history of expeditions into little known territories of the globe. In 1500 the Russian state was confined to the forests west of the Ural mountains but during the following century expansion* took place into Siberia, to which early expeditions usually were financed by merchants, led by Cossack fortune-hunters and motivated by the quest for furs. The economic motive for exploration remained dominant until the reign of Peter the Great* when the search for scientific knowledge became a driving force, with the state providing encouragement and backing for many expeditions of discovery, and the leaders of such expeditions being of the 'gentleman explorer' category familiar in the West. The tradition of scientific exploration has remained with the Russians to the present day.

The breakthrough into Siberia was made in 1581 by a band of Cossacks led by the outlaw Yermak (d.1584) and within 60 years the first Russian reached the Pacific coast. The so-called 'conquest of Siberia' opened a new world for exploration. Moving up the Siberian rivers Russians reached the northern coast and, taking to their flat-bottomed boats (*kotchi*), they entered the Arctic seas and explored the northern coast, although little was made of the discoveries there until the 18th century, when the Great Northern Expedition was launched. During the course of several shipping seasons exploratory parties, under constant threat from ice and scurvy, mapped the northern coastline, and the charts produced remained in use for two centuries.

Interest in the area was inspired partly by the desire to discover whether a north-east passage to the Orient existed. Discovery of the passage is credited to another Cossack, S. I. Dezhnev (*c.*1605–72/3), who supposedly set sail in 1648 from the Kolyma river in his *kotch*, rounded the easternmost cape of Asia (now Cape Dezhnev) and endured shipwreck to arrive, after a long overland trek, on the river Anadyr which flows into the Pacific. Expeditions in the centuries following confirmed the existence of the passage and made further discoveries in the north-west Pacific. V. I. Bering (1681–1741), a Dane serving in the Imperial Navy,* and A. I. Chirikov (1703–48) between 1725 and 1743 sailed from Okhotsk through the Bering Strait to the eastern cape and later discovered Alaska and the Aleutian Islands. In 1820–4 F. P. Vrangel (1797–1870), travelling by dog-sledge over the frozen sea, charted the coast west of the cape and discovered the island which now bears his name.

Exploration was not confined to the cold lands of Siberia: from the 17th century Russians explored as far afield as Mongolia, China, India, Africa and Brazil; they also carried out detailed investigations of Middle Asia and the Caspian Sea basin. In the first half of the 19th

ARCTIC EXPEDITIONS BY DRIFTING STATIONS AND BY AIR LANDINGS, 1937–8 AND 1948–57

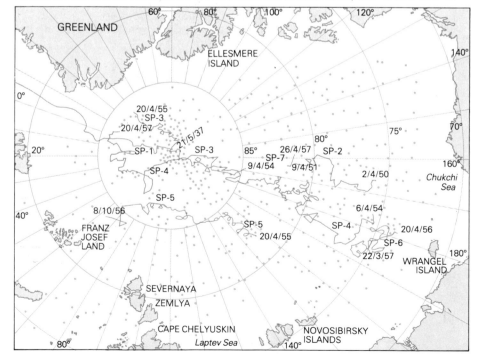

KEY

〰 Course of drifting stations

· Aircraft landings

Source: T. Armstrong, *The Russians in the Arctic: Aspects of Soviet Exploration and Exploitation of the Far North, 1937–57*, London, 1960

Right: observing ice-floe drift from North Pole 13 drifting station

century Russian ships for the first time circumnavigated the globe, while 1819–21 saw the voyage of F. F. Bellingshausen (1779–1852) and M. P. Lazarev (1788–1851) to the Antarctic ice barrier and the discovery of Peter I and Alexander Land.

In Siberia and the other places they visited, Russians gave to Europe often the first detailed knowledge of places hitherto poorly represented on maps. For the 17th and 18th centuries the most celebrated traveller scientists include F. I. Soymonov (1682–1780), V. V. Atlasov (d.1711) and S. P. Krasheninnikov (1711–55) and for the 19th and 20th centuries, V. A. Obruchev (1863–1956), P. P. Semenov-Tyan-Shansky (1827–1914) and P. K. Kozlov (1863–1935).

Soon after the 1917 Revolution the frontier of exploration shifted to the Arctic Ocean and here the new Soviet government pioneered the use of aircraft in polar research. The first Russian flight in the Arctic was made in 1914 but it was not repeated until the 1920s. Since that time aircraft have increasingly been used in the Arctic and in the early days some spectacular flights were made, such as V. P. Chkalov's (1904–38) transpolar flight to America in 1937. In 1941 I. I. Cherevichny (1909–71) made a return flight to the northern 'pole of inaccessibility', stopping *en route* at a number of points on the ice for scientific observations. The expedition lasted 68 days and covered 15 000 miles, and firmly established the principle of using aircraft for reconnaissance work and to service surface expeditions.

Drifting ice stations have also been used in polar exploration – the first in 1937 when a team led by I. D. Papanin (b.1894) was set down on a North Pole ice-floe to observe sea-ice drift. They remained on the ice for nine months before being taken off, having drifted to the Greenland coast. This drift was followed by others in the post-war years and, together with air exploration, they have helped to establish Soviet research workers as undisputed experts on the central Arctic region.   *J.P.*

Geography

Geography in pre-revolutionary Russia had a long, varied and distinguished history, still inadequately recognized in the rest of the world. Moreover its progress and emphases have been unusually responsive to the distinctive developments and needs of the country and its people. Notable geographical work in Russia dates from the time of Peter the Great,★ whose vigorous interest in map-making, geographical expeditions, and the discovery and appraisal of natural resources★ resulted in the first national atlas, edited by I. K. Kirilov (d.1737). All in all, the achievements of geography probably outshone those of other sciences during his modernizing reign. A large number of original studies were published in the 18th and 19th centuries, combining in a distinctively Russian way exploration★ and scientific analysis with a reforming zeal for the betterment of the life of the peasant and, to this end, searching for the most appropriate regional systems. P. P. Semenov-Tyan-Shansky (1827–1914), for instance, who directed the Russian Geographical Society for several of its most vigorous decades, was a member of the Committee for the Emancipation of the Peasants from the Bonds of Serfdom at the same time as he was organizing his expeditions to the Tyan-Shan mountains, and also assembling his comprehensive statistical survey of the Russian Empire.

Map of the Middle Volga from an atlas of Russia published in St Petersburg in 1745 by the Imperial Academy of Sciences 'in conformity with the rules of geography and with the latest observations'

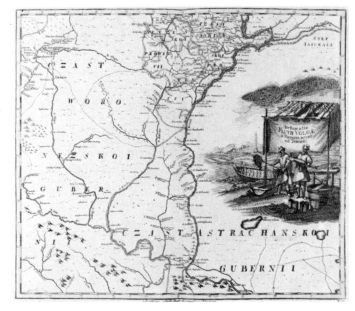

The Imperial Russian Geographical Society, founded in 1845, was generally recognized as the most successful of the many learned societies before the Revolution, in tune with contemporary national aspirations, crises, needs and ways of thought. Regional branches were set up in Siberia and Caucasia, as well as in Russia proper, with their own publications and lectures, and the Society assumed initial responsibility for geology, meteorology, anthropology and archaeology as well.

Russian geography, in its Golden Age from about 1880 to the First World War, compares well with that of any other country of the period. Its major figures, notably A. I. Voeykov (1842–1916), V. V. Dokuchaev (1846–1903) and D. N. Anuchin (1843–1923), as well as Semenov-Tyan-Shansky, were both scientists and humanists. The overwhelmingly rural cast of the society, landscape and national problems may account for the distinctive content of Russian geography at this time. Dokuchaev's theory of soil★ formation and natural zonation and Voeykov's theory of heat and moisture balance clearly derived from their experience with the dominant natural zones, such as the 'black-earth' steppe and the podzol *taiga* (coniferous forest) and eventually had a considerable influence on world science. Voeykov's monumental *Climates of the World* (1884) established his reputation as a world pioneer of climatology. He taught at St Petersburg University, but the major figure in university geography as such was Anuchin, who taught it also (with anthropology) at Moscow University from 1884 until his death in 1923. During this period Prince Peter Kropotkin (1842–1921), who had early made his mark as a geographer in Russia, and kept up this scientific interest throughout his life, was in exile in Britain. Other famous Russian scientists, such as the chemist D. I. Mendeleyev (1834–1907), the geochemist V. I. Vernadsky (1863–1945) and the plant geneticist N. I. Vavilov (1887–1942), were also active contributors to geography and to the Geographical Society.

Thus there was a vigorous body of geographical scholarship and tradition in Russia by the time of the Bolshevik Revolution, combining natural scientific and humanist approaches, and focusing on human environmental and regional studies. While this tradition carried over into the 1920s, it was – as were most aspects of life and thought in Russia – severely disrupted in the Stalinist★ period (1928–54); one extreme example of isolationism was a secret regulation of 1948 that meridians and parallels should be incorrectly plotted on published maps to deceive airborne attackers. Geography's humane and international cast was submerged by the formation and mobilization of large bodies of specialists who were directed towards practical tasks. Since much of the urgent work was of a primary nature and human-oriented studies tended to be politically vulnerable, geography had changed overwhelmingly into a physical science by the mid-1950s; it had also become heavily fragmented, since official doctrine discouraged those integrated studies of man and his

environment that had been central to the subject before 1930. However, in spite of the difficulties, elements of the broken heritage were kept alive, notably through the 'landscape school' of L. S. Berg (1876–1950) and the 'regional school' of N. N. Baransky (1881–1963).

The post-Stalin decade (under Khrushchev★) was characterized by a ferment of vigorous disputation about the nature and direction of geographical studies, in which the most prominent and successful advocate of a more integrated and humanized geography was V. A. Anuchin (b.1913), whose catalytic book, *Theoretical Problems of Geography*, appeared in 1960. After this relatively relaxed period, a decision was again taken to distort the correct locations of some Soviet towns and other geographical features in the 1967 second edition of the Soviet World Atlas.

Since the mid-1960s, the restructuring of geography around a set of integrated, 'constructive' studies of specific problems and regions, with a strengthened economic component, has proceeded steadily. Multipurpose regional projects, environmental protection,★ population distribution, appraisal of natural resources★ and urbanization are some of the recurring themes in this rejuvenated Soviet geography which, although still somewhat nation-bound, is much more balanced and purposeful than at the death of Stalin, and firmly back in contact with its pre-revolutionary roots.   *D.H.*

Geology

Mineral exploration

There may be as many as 250000 earth scientists and technicians currently working in the USSR, where the geologist is lauded as a pioneer in the struggle to develop an enormous Motherland. The role of geology here is unequivocal – to search for and discover new mineral wealth – and primary geological exploration and mapping, particularly east of the Urals, has always been a principal preoccupation. Pre-revolutionary Russian geology had a strong mining tradition dominated by the famous Mining Institute in St Petersburg, founded in 1773; coal and metal mining were concentrated largely in European Russia, although the construction of the Trans-Siberian Railway in the 1890s gave considerable impetus to the investigation of Siberia's natural resources.★ The gigantic prospecting operations conducted in Soviet Central Asia, Siberia and the Soviet Far East since the Revolution have resulted in a greatly increased level of economic mining activity: for coal, iron and precious metals from southern West Siberia, the Kuznetsk basin and the Altay; for copper and nickel from Noril'sk, inside the Arctic circle; for tin and gold from the Soviet Far East.

The Baku oil-fields were first developed in the late 18th century, and are still productive although reserves are low. The search for new petroleum deposits involves a high degree of geological input, and the discovery under I. M. Gubkin (1871–1939) of major reserves in the Volga-Urals petroleum zone (the 'second Baku') is regarded as a major achievement of Soviet petroleum geology. This was followed by massive discoveries in the West Siberian basin (the 'third Baku') during the 1960s; several other major sedimentary basins in Siberia and the Far East are being explored. Appropriate technology still lags behind the West (some say by 15 years) but active steps have been taken to improve the situation, partly through cooperation with Western companies. In particular, the Soviet oil industry is keen to acquire the offshore drilling technology that will enable it to step up exploration of the huge Pacific and Arctic continental shelves.

Geological sonar survey down to 10km in the West Siberian basin where oil exists in the high-pressure rock

Mapping

The history of systematic geological mapping in Russia began in 1881 with the establishment of the Geological Committee which undertook to map Russia on a scale of 1:420 000 (the *desyativerstka* maps—ten versts to an inch). This ambitious project was never achieved, although about 10 per cent of maps and a number of more detailed surveys of mining districts had appeared by the end of the century, and a small-scale map (1:2 500 000) of European Russia was produced before the 1897 International Geological Congress in St Petersburg. A. P. Karpinsky (1847–1936), widely regarded as the father of Soviet geology, headed the Geological Committee from 1885 to 1903, before going on to help establish, and for many years lead, the post-revolutionary Academy of Sciences.★ The Committee survived the Revolution virtually intact, and was expanded considerably in the 1920s when particular emphasis was placed on mapping east of the Urals. Priority was naturally given to regions of known economic potential (such as the Kuznetsk and Tungus coal basins, the Kolyma gold-fields) but extensive reconnaissance surveys using air, boat, horse or even reindeer transport were made and by the 1937 International Geological Congress in Moscow it was possible to produce the first geological map of the entire Soviet Union, albeit on a small scale (1:5 000 000). Much of the detail of regional geological surveying, particularly that accomplished since the 1940s, is contained in the series *Geologiya SSSR*. This massive work, published in 48 parts, gives in a fairly standard format the detailed stratigraphy, igneous and metamorphic history, tectonics, geomorphology and a synthesis of geological development of each region. The volumes are accompanied by geological maps, on scales of 1:1 000 000, 1:1 500 000, or 1:2 000 000, along with correlation charts, cross section and so on. The first volumes appeared in the 1940s, but most have been published since 1963 under the general editorship of A. V. Sidorenko (b.1917); the series (very nearly complete in 1980) occupies about 2m of library shelf.

Stratigraphy and palaeontology

One of the strengths of Soviet geology has been its ability to direct large numbers of specialists on to specific tasks, such as the palaeontological description and correlation of sequences. The aim has been, through exhaustive palaeontological study, to extend standard stage terminology and correlate biostratigraphic horizons throughout the USSR, often at the expense of the original lithostratigraphic terminology. A number of interdepartmental committees were set up in the 1950s to supervise this 'unification' and the main results are set out in another major book series, *Stratigrafiya SSSR* (14 volumes, edited by D. V. Nalivkin, b.1889).

Tectonics

A Russian school of tectonics, which emphasized vertical oscillations during geological time, had developed during the 19th and early 20th centuries, and is particularly associated with the work of Karpinsky. Working primarily on the Russian platform, Karpinsky and his followers recognized a close dependence of palaeogeography on oscillatory vertical movements controlled by fundamental tectonic structures ('Karpinsky lines'), and this tradition has continued to dominate Soviet tectonic thinking.

The first tectonic maps covering the whole country were compiled under N. S. Shatsky (1895–1960) during the 1950s. An atlas of 'lithologo-palaeogeographic' and palaeotectonic maps was published during 1967–9, edited by A. P. Vinogradov (b.1895). This massive work is in four volumes with over 70 stage-by-stage palaeogeographic and 20 palaeotectonic maps at 1:7 500 000 scale as well as 50 larger-scale regional maps. A new series of palaeotectonic compilation maps, with even more detail (1:5 000 000) and accompanying text, began publication in 1977, editor T. N. Spizharsky. These works are a major achievement in the Karpinsky tradition and represent an enormous task in compilation and cartography; nothing quite like them exists outside the USSR. While following this tradition, Soviet tectonic geologists have remained aloof from developments in the West, from Alfred Wegener's first proposal of continental drift in the late 1920s to the 'plate tectonic' scientific revolution of the late 1960s. These global theories emphasizing large-scale horizontal movements were anathema to leading scientists such as V. V. Beloussov (b.1907), and only recently have some Soviet geologists begun to examine the possible application of, and evidence for, this 'new global tectonics' in the USSR. This may lead to a fascinating re-evaluation of the geology

of this vast country, only possible now that the preliminary exploration and mapping has been accomplished. Major revisions of some traditional concepts are likely (for example, the recent debate on the status of the 'Kolyma Block'), and the 1980s may see many new interpretations of Soviet, and therefore world, geological history.

N.J.R.W.

Ecology

Ecological science in the Soviet Union is vested in the Academy of Sciences★ of the USSR and is dominated by V. Ye. Sokolov (b.1928), head of the Institute of Evolutionary Animal Morphology and Ecology in Moscow. The All-Union Academy of Sciences, usually in association with republican academies, has established ecological training and research institutes and organizes expeditions to many remote regions of the USSR, the scale of cooperation being exemplified in an interdisciplinary Soviet-Mongolian Expedition comprising over 20 Soviet institutes and universities (including Moscow and Irkutsk) which made notable advances in ecological and agricultural science. The interdisciplinary nature of such expeditions is indicated by their inclusion of specialists in ecosystems, community ecology and phytosociology and their work in extending the inventory of flora and fauna★ and in obtaining specimens.

The all-Union and republican Academies advise the republican Ministries of Agriculture in the setting-up and running of a large number of nature reserves distributed throughout the country,

NATURE RESERVES

KEY	• Nature reserve

Designated Biosphere Reserves	Date established	Present area
		ha
1 Berezina (Belorussian SSR)	1925	76 500
2 Caucasus (Krasnodar kray)	1924	262 500
3 Tsentral'nochernozemny [Central Black Earth] (Kursk oblast)	1935	4 200
4 Prioksko-Terrasny [Oka Terrace] (Moscow oblast)	1945	4 800
5 Repetek (Turkmen SSR)	1928[1]	34 600
6 Sary-Chelek (Kirgiz SSR)	1959	20 700
7 Sikhote-Alin' (Primorsk kray)	1935	310 100

[1]On the basis of a station set up in 1912

Source: *Bol'shaya sovetskaya entsiklopediya*, 3rd edn, Moscow, Vol. 9, Vol. 22

within some of which research field stations are situated. The Repetek State Reserve in the Karakum Desert in the Turkmen SSR (administered by the Institute of Arid Lands of the Turkmen Academy) possesses a modest residential field station at which up to 20 staff and research students investigate the arid zone ecosystem. The range of work which has been carried out there is typical of the outstanding opportunities for research in all aspects of arid zone ecology and desert management as part of a worldwide effort. The Soviet authorities are clearly aware of a need for environmental protection,* conservation of nature and land management sensitive to ecological principles. In accord with the Unesco programme of Man and the Biosphere, seven reserves, managed jointly by the

Below: the Repetek Biosphere Reserve, Turkmenia. Bottom: European bison (*Bison bonasus*) on a reservation in the Panevezhis oak forest, Lithuania–a 1970 count registered only some 350

Academy of Sciences and the Ministry of Agriculture, have been declared Biosphere Reserves. These, regarded as world monitoring stations on the state of the natural environment, are Berezina, Sary-Chelek, the Caucasus Reserve, Prioksko-Terrasny and Sikhote-Alin', all of which are forest and watercourse reserves, the Central Black Earth Reserve, which is forest and steppe, and Repetek, which is a desert reserve. On some forest reserves such as those at Prioksko-Terrasny and Voronezh which have natural forest, there are experimental plots of up to 50 years' standing; batteries of meteorological instruments and traps for leaf litter and animals have been set up to measure change, and breeding stations for captive bison and beaver have been established. It was announced in 1980 that a new wildlife reserve was to be set up in the Lake Ladoga region, covering 40 000 ha and bringing the total area of nature reserves to 12 million ha.

The achievements in ecological science are in some respects less than in the West. For example, the organization of research on waterfowl shows that the status, ecology and migratory behaviour of wildfowl wintering in western Europe have been followed in much greater detail by Western observers than for the same birds during their breeding period in the Soviet Union. However, the exchanges of information facilitated by various technical and cultural agreements with Western states should enable both sides to keep abreast of each other's advances in many areas of ecological science, including chemical communication in animals, the effects of pesticides on wildlife, migration and protection of birds and methods of monitoring the environment.   *J.M.B.*

Systematic botany

For more than 250 years scientific botany has been continuously studied in what is now the Komarov Botanical Institute of the Academy of Sciences of the USSR. Founded in 1714 as the Apothecaries' Garden by Peter the Great* on a large island to the north of St Petersburg* (now Leningrad), the Institute is still in the Botanic Garden on the same site. This tradition of systematic and floristic botany produced the monumental 30-volume *Flora of the USSR* (1934–64), under the guidance of its editor-in-chief, V. L. Komarov (1869–1945), and after his death under B. K. Shishkin. By any standards, this scientific reference work to the flowering plants and ferns wild over an area approximately one-fifth of the land surface of the earth is a remarkable cooperative achievement. Both in its reference collections (an estimated six million herbarium specimens makes Leningrad equal in importance to Kew) and in its large, well-trained staff, the Komarov Institute continues to be one of the leading centres for the study of the floras of the world. In recent years more attention is being paid to tropical floras of Asia and Africa, although the study of the vast flora of the USSR continues to have some priority. Cooperation between Soviet systematic botanists and those in the West has always been good, as witnessed in the completion of the five-volume *Flora Europaea* in 1979, for which A. A. Fedorov (b. 1908) of the Komarov Institute is an advisory editor.

In systematic botany (especially the writing of Floras or works of identification) linguistic barriers are minimal, because of the operation of the International Code of Botanical Nomenclature by which a Latin binomial is the legally-agreed name for every wild plant. An English translation of *Flora of the USSR* is available, however, rendering it even more accessible to Western botanists. A second edition may be undertaken, but of special interest to European workers is the continuing project to write a new *Flora of the European part of the USSR*, of which the fourth volume appeared in 1979, taking into account (while not necessarily confirming) relevant work published in *Flora Europaea*.   *S. M. W.*

The final illustration in the thirtieth volume of *Flora of the USSR* depicts two species of Hawkweed (*Hieracium*)

Genetics

The science of genetics has had a unique history of official support (1917–35), condemnation (1936–64), and renewed support (1965 onwards). The condemnation of genetics has been ascribed to a supposed Marxist★ fondness for Lamarckism (the doctrine that acquired characteristics are inherited) because of an imagined affinity between Lamarckism and meliorism–the faith in human self-improvement that Marxists share with many other people. This widespread explanation is without basis in logic or in history: Lamarckism can just as readily subvert faith in progress on the assumption that centuries of deprivation and oppression have bred inferiority into the lower classes and the darker races. In any case, Marxists do not have a special record of unusual fondness for Lamarckism, and Soviet support for genetics was originally based on meliorist dreams. N. I. Vavilov (1887–1943), an eminent plant scientist who studied in England with William Bateson before the Revolution, argued that genetics would show breeders how to 'sculpt organic forms at will'. In the 1920s he won support for a great network of research institutions under VASKhNIL (the All-Union Academy of Agricultural Sciences named after Lenin★) and fostered pure research in such institutions as the Institute of Genetics of the USSR Academy of Sciences★. By the end of the 1920s geneticists of Marxist persuasion, such as A. S. Serebrovsky (1892–1948), won ascendancy for the belief that genetics is the realization of dialectical materialism★ in biology.

Collectivization precipitated the crisis of Bolshevik★ faith in genetics. Soviet leaders expected that their new agrarian system would facilitate rapid adoption of the most advanced techniques, such as the replacement of scraggy peasant varieties of plants and animals by high-yielding–and highly demanding–improved varieties. Such expectations were cruelly disappointed: the new agrarian system generated such massive disincentives that even the simplest old techniques declined in efficiency. Central agricultural authorities were drawn to admiration of T. D. Lysenko (1898–1976), an agronomist of peasant extraction who had a flair for public relations and fanatical faith in his intuition for agronomic panaceas. The first and most famous was 'vernalization,' originally a word he coined for moistening and chilling seed before planting, and ultimately his catch-all term for almost any kind of seed treatment, and for an imaginary period in plant development. His claim of great practical benefits to agriculture was based on crude, brief tests of his recipes; careful statistical testing was in official disfavour as the 'bourgeois' specialists' way of subverting revolutionary enthusiasm. Scientists who criticized Lysenko's theoretical justifications of his agronomic schemes exposed themselves to accusations of separating theory from practice.

By the mid-1930s the central authorities were persuaded that Lysenko had created a distinctive Soviet science, called agrobiology or Michurinism (after the plant-breeder I. V. Michurin, 1855–1935), in advance of 'bourgeois' plant physiology and genetics. Research and teaching in genetics were sharply curtailed and subjected to waves of harsh criticism, which culminated in utter condemnation of the science at a highly publicized meeting of VASKhNIL in 1948. Within a few years, however, the disappointing practical results of Lysenko's concepts began to disturb the agricultural authorities. Starting in the last year of Stalin's★ life and accelerating after his death, there was a revival of the contest for official favour between genetics and Lysenkoism. In 1965, after the ousting of Khrushchev★, the appropriate statistical study of some Lysenkoite proposals, such as training cows to improve their heredity, destroyed his claim to practicality for good and all. The government gave its complete support to the restoration of research and education in genetics.

There are still many specialists, especially in plant breeding, who were trained to Lysenkoism and retain some sympathy with it. Geneticists proper feel the weight of the past in other ways, for they may not rekindle enthusiasm by a thorough discussion of the 30-year war against genetics, nor call attention to their most remarkable accomplishment, which was simply keeping their science alive during that bitter era which destroyed the leading position in world science their predecessors were winning in the 1920s and early 1930s. The great names of Soviet genetics are still those of an abortive past: S. S. Chetverikov (1880–1959), who pioneered the mathematical theory of natural selection before he was arrested; N. V. Timofeev-Resovsky (b.1901) and Theodosius Dobzhansky (1900–75), who made their major contributions to the science in Germany and in the USA; and N. K. Kol'tsov (1872–1940), who might have led the race to analyse the molecule of heredity, if his research institute had not been taken from him and ruined. *D.J.*

Psychology and psychiatry

The main task of Soviet psychology according to A. R. Luriya (1902–77) is 'the scientific (materialistic) investigation of the highest forms of human psychic (mental) activity, of their evolution in the process of socio-historical development, and of the fundamental laws of their operation'. In pre-revolutionary Russia, psychology developed as in the West from philosophy but with a cultural-historical approach. This led to problems after the Revolution in reconciling the subject with Marxist-Leninist★ theory. The search for the correct approach proved difficult, especially as Lenin★ had specifically formulated a philosophical basis of psychology, namely, that the mind, the product of highly organized matter, is an active, not merely a passive, reflection of external reality. The reconstruction of pre-revolutionary

T.D. Lysenko lecturing Khrushchev, Mikoyan and Suslov on his theories in 1962

psychology into a Marxist image severely restricted its growth as late as the 1950s. For example, no psychology journal existed.

Two main influences permeated the topic. First, the physiological approach based on the reflex patterns described by I. M. Sechenov (1829–1905), I. P. Pavlov (1849–1936) and V. M. Bekhterev (1857–1927) became important, especially when later workers such as P. K. Anokhin (b.1898), G. V. Gershuni (b.1905) and M. V. Sokolov pointed out that reflex cycles provided active adaptation and not just rigid responses to the environment, thus harmonizing reflexology with Leninist doctrine. By the 1950s, the physiological approach had received so much official approval that it tended to swamp psychology.

The other influence was sociological/developmental: the organism comprised complex functional systems in which the highest mental processes were determined environmentally by social factors and education. Principles evolved in accord with this approach were very influential in determining education* policies. After Stalin's* death insistence on crude materialistic concepts became muted and psychology began to develop again. International recognition was evidenced by the choice of Moscow for the 18th International Congress of Psychology in 1966.

In the late 1970s, the chief topics pursued in a variety of university departments and research institutes were general experimental psychology, medical (clinical) psychology and industrial psychology. A journal is devoted to psychology and numerous research publications and monographs appear. Nevertheless, the approach of Soviet psychologists has been greatly conditioned by the physiological and socio-historical aspects just mentioned: experimental studies are often interpreted in terms of either neurophysiology or dialectical materialism (the philosophical foundation of Marxism-Leninism), sometimes in ways difficult for Western psychologists to appreciate.

Psychiatry in Russia followed the development of the subject in Western countries but often with a delay of decades or centuries. As elsewhere in Europe, medieval Russia left the care of the insane to the monks. Ivan the Terrible* laid a therapeutic responsibility on the Orthodox Church* to cure the mentally afflicted through religious and moral correction. Peter the Great* decreed the institution of special hospitals for the insane but it was not until the early 19th century that any real psychiatric facilities came into being. As in the West, funding, staff, buildings and treatment were quite inadequate. Local government councils (*zemstva*) took over responsibility for these institutions, and by 1892 financed and adminstered 34 mental hospitals with 9000 beds and 90 psychiatrists.

Academic psychiatry was instituted by the appointment of I. M. Balinsky (1827–1902) to the first chair of psychiatry in the Medico-Surgical Academy of St Petersburg in 1860; S. S. Korsakov (1854–1900) was the most celebrated Russian psychiatrist of the century. The social consciousness of the psychiatrists was much in evidence at their meetings and the Psychiatric Society (formed in 1862) was among the first medical institutions to offer to assist the Bolsheviks* after the October 1917 Revolution.

The subsequent reorganization of medical facilities* including psychiatry led to an emphasis on the prevention of illness and on the setting-up of district services within the community. Thus, the initial medical consultation is arranged in the health clinic. If a specialist opinion is needed, the mentally ill patient is referred to the nearest psychiatric clinic. Admission to hospital is avoided wherever possible, and out-patient or day-hospital attendance is encouraged. Social problems are sought out and corrected. Understanding the illness is often attempted along Pavlovian lines – that is, in terms of conditioning processes to external events and influences.

An important aspect of treatment is industrial training and rehabilitation. The work ethos is important in the day clinics, as it is in other aspects of Soviet life. Rehabilitation after severe mental illness is carefully organized and sheltered work is routinely provided. Contracts are established between industry and the clinic workshop for the manufacture, or more commonly assembly, of components and goods. As in the West, more seriously ill patients need admission to mental hospital. Treatment is by staff different from the out-patient clinics and mainly comprises drug therapy. Insulin coma and sleep therapy (in which the patient is kept heavily sedated for days or weeks) are still favoured, despite their obsolescence in Western opinion. Electroconvulsive therapy is used as in the West. Psychosurgery (leucotomy) is banned. Psychoanalysis, Freudian or otherwise, is not encouraged but simple supportive psychotherapy is provided. The patient is encouraged to come to terms with his problems and his positive qualities are emphasized.

The main research institute, the Institute of Psychiatry of the Academy of Medical Sciences, is in Moscow, as is the Forensic Psychiatry Institute; several research facilities exist in other centres. The All-Union Society of Psychiatrists has over 20 000 members. Psychiatric research in the Soviet Union tends to concentrate on a few topics, of which schizophrenia is the most popular. The Soviet concepts of schizophrenia are much wider than those of the West: many patients are labelled schizophrenic who would be regarded as manic, depressed or merely odd in the West. Political dissent* has attracted attention from the forensic psychiatric services in numerous well-publicized instances: after arrest for a political offence, dissidents have been diagnosed as schizophrenics, lost their legal rights and been consigned for an indefinite period to a prison mental hospital, where they received powerful tranquillizers; some were released only when they renounced their 'deviant' views. The international psychiatric community became increasingly concerned at this abuse of psychiatry and at the World Congress of Psychiatry in 1977 in Hawaii a motion of censure criticizing the practices of some Soviet psychiatrists was narrowly passed. *M.H.L.*

Chemistry

The origins of chemistry in Russia and of the Russian chemical and general scientific language* are usually traced to the polymath M. V. Lomonosov (1711–65). He recorded his chemical work in Latin and subsequently translated it into Russian. His device for rendering 'international' (Greek/Latin) scientific terms was stem-by-stem translation (hydrogen = *vodorod*). Although this natural mechanism is still productive (supersonic = *sverkhzvukovoy*), it is now at least matched in importance by the direct adoption of international terms, to which are added Russian terminations (physical chemistry = *fizicheskaya khimiya*). This shift has slightly eased scientific communication with non-Russians and easily survived Stalin's attempt to Russify science. The scale of effort in chemistry in the USSR today is comparable with that in the USA. It is tempting to speculate that the readiness of the two languages Russian and English to adopt foreign words, with their extensive mechanisms for word formation, have contributed to their pre-eminence, in weight of publication at least, in a realm which lives by its novel concepts.

Russian contributions to chemistry have assumed large proportions only in this century. However, the 19th century saw the publication of that supreme synthesis of chemical knowledge, D. I. Mendeleyev's (1834–1907) periodic classification of the elements (1869–71)–a codifying of family resemblances and trends in the properties of scores of diverse chemical elements, which has since become a cornerstone of chemical thinking. K. K. Klaus (1796–1864) discovered ruthenium, F. F. Beilstein (1838–1906), with others, systematized the documentation of organic chemistry; other distinguished names of this period are G. I. Hess (1802–50), V. N. Ipat'ev (1867–1952), N. A. Menshutkin (1842–1907), P. Walden (1863–1957) and L. A. Chugaev (1873–1922). After the Revolution Russian chemistry significantly increased its pace; its organization and development has paralleled that of physics.* Between the wars many research institutes were established which produced notable work in physical chemistry, inorganic chemistry, electrochemistry* and radiochemistry; organic chemists such as N. D. Zelinsky (1861–1953), S. V. Lebedev (1874–1934), A. Ye. Arbuzov (1877–1968), A. N. Nesmeyanov (1899–1980) and N. A. Preobrazhensky (b.1896) were particularly recognized for work on hydrocarbon transformations, organo-metallic compounds, organophosphorus chemistry and natural products.

Chemistry and science generally have had to survive the major political-philosophical intrusions of Stalin's* era; one example of such intrusion was the proscription of the valence bond method, a valuable theoretical tool in the description of chemical bonding, reputedly because it invoked an abstract concept (that of a resonance 'end-form') deemed incompatible with socialist philosophy. Since Stalin's death a freer climate has prevailed, yet the partial isolation of Russian chemistry before 1953 led to some interesting examples of independent and simultaneous discovery in both chemistry and physics. Chemistry research facilities both within the Academy of Sciences* network and in universities have been still further expanded since the 1950s and useful industrial applications have been developed; significant achievements have been mainly in electrochemistry* and combustion science.* *T. B. & P. G.*

Combustion science

Soviet research in the field of combustion, flame and explosion is pursued by a very large number of workers, mainly in research institutes, and particularly in those of the Academies of Sciences.* The volume of fundamental work published (nearly all in Soviet journals) is very substantial. Much applied work is also done; its volume can only be guessed at.

On the fundamental side, one man's influence has been continuing and unsurpassed: N. N. Semenov (b.1896). A physicist by training, his own earliest work was done in the A. F. Ioffe Institute in Leningrad. Since 1931 he has headed the Institute of Chemical Physics there (which moved to Moscow in 1941), and attracted and led other scientists of immense distinction and varied background, pre-eminent among them V. N. Kondrat'ev (1902–79), D. A. Frank-Kamenetsky (1910–70) and Ya. B. Zel'dovich (b.1914). With its daughter institutes at Chernogolovka near Moscow and at Novosibirsk it remains a focal point of activity.

A less personal tradition, probably of equal significance, is the support afforded by Russian and Soviet traditions of excellence in applied mathematics,* on which combustion scientists have been able to draw; the relative ease with which distinctly uncommercial books could be published may also have helped here.

Chemical pathways in combustion

The complexity of organic oxidations was recognized by A. N. Bach (1857–1946), who at the same time (1897) as Engler advanced the 'peroxide theory' of slow oxidation. The next distinctively Russian contribution in this field was the application by Semenov of branched-chain ideas: degenerate branching or secondary initiation was proposed to interpret slow oxidation reactions. Contemporaneously, Kondrat'ev (1930) identified the species emitting light in cool flames, and soon after inaugurated Soviet mass-spectrometric studies of related reactions, a line expanded by V. L. Tal'rose (b.1922). General work on cool flames was begun by M. B. Neimann and others from 1932. These themes have continued, and electron-spin-resonance techniques have subsequently been applied by A.

Nalbandyan (b.1918) and V. V. Voevodsky (1917–67). The monumental book (1960) by V. Ya. Shtern is still of importance; much very detailed work is in progress, and many liquid-phase oxidations in biological as well as in chemical systems are now studied by N. M. Emanuel and others.

Thermal explosion and chain-branching theory

Soviet workers from Semenov onwards have made fundamental and continuing contributions in the areas of thermal explosion and branched-chain explosion (which overlap with each other) as well as with related problems of flame propagation and detonation.

The idea of chain reactions is due to Bodenstein and Nernst. The most extreme form is afforded by branching chains, in which one free radical is replaced by more than one. This idea was put forward by Semenov in 1927 to explain features of the oxidation of phosphorus vapour, long known but not understood, and soon applied by him (and by Sir Cyril Hinshelwood in England) to the hydrogen-oxygen reaction, for which work they were awarded a Nobel Prize. The next development was the idea, also due to Semenov, of degenerate branching, or secondary initiation, in hydrocarbon oxidation.

The branching-chain reactions most familiar today are those of nuclear fission, nuclear fusion and astrophysics; after pioneering contributions in chemical fields both Frank-Kamenetsky and Zel'-dovich moved to these fields of physics.*

Semenov perceived (1928) common ground between the problems of dielectric breakdown and those of thermal explosion; he rediscovered and made famous the geometrical representation of criticality and was the first to give an algebraic analysis. He established the small degree of self-heating necessary to cross the brink of instability and found the relationships between critical conditions and temperature.

In the 1930s O. M. Todes and P. V. Melent'ev opened up the investigation of induction periods and non-steady states and also discussed exothermic, autocatalytic reactions. In 1938–9, the conductive theory of thermal explosion was inaugurated by Frank-Kamenetsky. Forty years of study have not displaced this more general starting point, and the Institute (especially its section at Chernogolovka) continues to house the largest group of workers in the world on these themes, to which more recently many significant contributions have been made by A. G. Merzhanov, F. I. Dubovitsky and S. I. Khudyaev.

Heterogeneous combustion and catalysis

In 1938–9 Frank-Kamenetsky put forward the unifying thermo-kinetic theory of ignition and extinction in exothermic heterogeneous reactions, first exemplified by the combustion of coal and later (1946) by a catalytic oxidation. In translation (1955) his book became known to Western combustion scientists if not chemical engineers.

Reactor stability in open systems

In 1941 Zel'dovich and Yu. A. Zysin published their original and authoritative work on the theory of exothermic, first-order reaction in a well-stirred reactor, predicting multistability and explaining ignition and extinction. In 1948 another contribution of striking originality was made by I. E. Salnikov in the systematic application of stability-of-motion studies to chemical reactions. The early stationary-state work was codified by L. A. Vulis and modern experimental and theoretical reactor studies are pursued at the Institute of Catalysis and Kinetics under G. K. Boreskov (b.1907).

Flame propagation

Soviet workers have made significant experimental and theoretical advances in all types of flame propagation. Pioneering descriptions in the 19th century were inadequate, though V. A. Mikhel'son (1860–1927) gave an early (1890) and correct description of the pre-heating zone. A proper solution of the appropriate eigenvalue problem was reached in the West in the 1930s. Subsequent Soviet work promptly gave an adequate approximate solution (Zel'dovich and Frank-Kamenetsky, 1938). It might be said that much of Soviet theoretical research is characterized by this striving for intelligible and adequate models capable of lending physical insight, whether or not solutions or more complete models are to hand.

Important contributions to combustion studies have been made by K. K. Andreev, A. A. Shidlovsky, Merzhanov and A. F. Belyaev (burning of solid mixtures; propellants, pyrotechnics and explosives), by I. M. Gel'fand, L. D. Landau, K. P. Stanyukhovich and Zel'dovich (theories of complex heat transfer and fluid flow), by A. Ya. Apin, Belyaev, Ya. B. Khariton, R. I. Soloukhin, K. I. Shchelkin (study of the steps from small stimulus to flame to detonation) and by Zel'dovich, Voevodsky, Kondrat'ev, Semenov, L. N. Khitrin, Nalbandyan and A. S. Sokolik (ignition in the gas phase).

Detonation

The phenomenon of stable detonation (supersonic combustion) was clearly identified in Paris in 1881. The motion was correctly associated with shock waves, and an expression for detonation velocity was derived in 1895 (Chapman, Jouguet). In Russia, Mikhel'son made some early studies of detonation and shock, and the simple course of the variation of pressure with density in a steady detonation is known in the USSR as the Mikhel'son line. In the 1930s and 1940s significant theoretical and experimental progress was reported, much of it from the Institute of Chemical Physics.

Wide-ranging studies of the build-up to, and propagation of, detonation especially in solids and liquids were made by Khariton, Belyaev, Apin, Andreev, S. D. Roginsky and V. K. Bobolev. In the early 1940s came the first solution of the structure of the steady one-dimensional detonation wave in the absence of dissipative processes. It was independently found by J. von Neumann (USA), by W. Döring (Germany) and by Zel'dovich (USSR). Further Russian work shows close correspondence in content and timing with that in the West, usually with American studies in the van. Significant progress has been made in the realms of instabilities in the growth and propagation of detonation (A. N. Dremin, Soloukhin, Shchelkin) and in theoretical descriptions of important but complex configurations and effects (Zel'dovich, Stanyukhovich). *T.B. & P.G.*

Electrochemistry

Research in electrochemistry in the USSR is probably on a larger scale than anywhere else in the world. This development from a relatively small effort at the beginning of the 20th century has been largely due to the outstanding contribution and influence of A. N. Frumkin (1895–1976). Born in Moldavia, he received his early education in Odessa and began research in Strasbourg and Bern. During the First World War he carried out the work for his thesis 'On electrocapillary phenomena and electrode potentials', which was published in Odessa in 1917. This laid the basis for much of his subsequent work, which was concerned with the structure of charges interfaces and the kinetics of electrochemical reactions. He provided a clear explanation of the source of the electromotive force of a galvanic cell which was the subject of a long controversy between 19th-century physicists and chemists, as well as developing a clear understanding of the properties of the charged layer at the junction between two phases.

In 1922 Frumkin moved to Moscow, where he founded a department in the Karpov Institute. During the Second World War, he was director of the Colloido-Electrochemical Institute (later the Institute of Physical Chemistry) of the Academy of Sciences.* In 1958 he formed a new Institute of Electrochemistry and remained its director until 1976. V. E. Kazarinov succeeded him and in the 1970s the Institute numbered several hundred people working in a variety of groups on themes such as theoretical electrochemistry, photo-electrochemistry, bioelectrochemistry and optical techniques.

Of many other institutes working on electrochemical problems, often with senior members trained in Frumkin's laboratory, probably the most important are the Karpov Institute, Moscow, under Ya. M. Kolotyrkin (b.1910) studying fundamental problems of corrosion; the Institute of Power Sources under N. S. Lidorenko (b.1916) studying new batteries and fuel cells; the Institute of Organic Catalysis and Electrochemistry, Alma-Ata, under D. V. Sokol'sky studying the relation between electrochemical and heterogeneous catalysis; the Institute of General and Inorganic Chemistry, Kiev, under A. V. Gorodysky (previously under Yu. K.

Delimarsky) studying mainly the electrochemical properties of molten salts; the Institute of Metallurgy (attached to the Sverdlovsk Polytechnic Institute) formerly under O. A. Yesin, studying the electrochemical properties of slags and other industrially-important ionic melts, as well as groups in Moscow State University, the Georgian Academy of Sciences in Tbilisi and Tartu State University.

The strength of Soviet electrochemistry lies in its contributions to the fundamental problems of the subject, although there are undoubtedly many applications in technology. These contributions include the development of the concept of the potential of zero charge as a characteristic property of an electrode; detailed analysis of the structure of the interfacial layer and adsorption properties of a wide variety of electrodes in many solvents; the development of methods for the study and control of electrode reactions, notably the alternating current method and the rotating-disk electrode and the ring-disk electrode; the understanding of semiconductor electrodes; the laws of photoemission from electrodes; the development of the quantum theory of charge transfer between metal and electrolyte; and the effect of the structure of the interface on the kinetics of electrode reactions. The electrochemical nature of corrosion processes was first explained in terms of conjugated charge transfer reactions by Frumkin and many electrochemical problems in physico-chemical hydrodynamics were solved by V. G. Levich. *R.P.*

Biochemistry and molecular biology

Biochemistry shared in the general development of Soviet science in the 1920s, and V. A. Engel'gardt's (b.1894) work demonstrating that the oxidation of foodstuffs in various tissues was accompanied by the synthesis of organic phosphates appeared in 1930. In 1939 V. A. Belitser (b.1906) and E. T. Tsybakova more directly established the existence of oxidative phosphorylation – the use of the energy of respiration to synthesize adenosine triphosphate (ATP). Engel'-gardt's demonstration (with his wife, M. N. Lyubimova), also in the 1930s, that myosin, a major component of muscle fibrils, was the enzyme that broke down ATP was the first step towards the understanding of the mechanism by which chemical energy is converted into the mechanical work done by muscle. A further important advance was the discovery by A. Ye. Braunstein (b.1902) of transamination, the process by which nitrogen can be exchanged from one amino acid to another, with the result that several of the amino acids needed for protein synthesis can be made in the body and are thus not essential components of the diet of animals.

The harsher political conditions of 1930–53 and the Second World War hit biochemistry even more than many other sciences. This was because of the imposition of T. D. Lysenko's (1898–1976) views in place of the firmly established findings of genetics,★ with disastrous consequences in biological education. *Biokhimiya* (the biochemistry journal first published in 1936) became filled with much routine work on agricultural products, virtually excluding fundamental science.

The expansion of biochemistry after Stalin's★ death was marked by the foundation of many institutes in Moscow or its environs (Pushchino), and throughout the country (Akademgorodok near Novosibirsk); the Institute of Molecular Biology in Moscow opened in 1959, although it was called the Institute of Physico-Chemical and Radiation Biology until 1965, Lysenko's views having some official backing until 1964. Many scientists who had earlier avoided the biological label came to the subject from physical and chemical institutes. A journal of molecular biology, *Molekulyarnaya biologiya*, started publication in 1967. In the 1970s Soviet biochemical work diversified greatly, studies spreading to genetic engineering, to the arrangement of DNA (deoxyribonucleic acid) in chromosomes, to the mechanisms of photosynthesis and oxidative phosphorylation, and to the structure of ribosomes, organelles involved in protein synthesis. Enzyme mechanisms had long been studied, and x-ray crystallography★ joined the methods used. Well-established work on peptides, steroids, antibiotics and other natural products was recognized, after M. M. Shemyakin (1908–70) died, by the renaming of the institute he had directed (till then the Institute of the Chemistry of Natural Products) as the Shemyakin Institute of Bio-organic Chemistry. Many institutes joined in a project (1974–8) on reverse transcriptase, an enzyme produced in animal cells by tumour-causing viruses, which had been discovered in the USA. The project included isolation of the enzyme and its direct scientific study, as well as many applications especially (as in other parts of the world) the programming of bacteria to make plant or animal products by making DNA for incorporation into the bacterial genome from plant or animal messengers. Approaches ranged from the purely chemical (building on the great Russian tradition of organophosphorus chemistry to synthesize RNA primers needed for the start of transcription) through use of the enzyme for determining RNA sequences, to those of applied biology. Most biochemical work, however, is less centrally co-ordinated and planned.

The standard and ingenuity of supporting physics★ and engineering★ are among the assets of Soviet biochemistry and molecular biology, but the difficulties and delays in obtaining what Western scientists regard as generally available apparatus, materials and reagents, together with the limitations on foreign travel, handicap these subjects as they do many others. By the mid-1970s much of the work in these fields was being published in Western journals, and although still modest in comparison with that of other developed countries it was already making a major contribution to world science–a great change from 25 years earlier. *H.B.F.D.*

Physics

Physics in the USSR has advanced from a relatively modest level at the turn of the century into a major influence on the worldwide development of the subject. Although it was generously supported financially from the 1920s, progress in the 1930s was considerably slowed by restrictions on international communication and by Stalin's purges.★ Even so, major advances were made in the pre-war years by outstanding individual scientists such as L. D. Landau (1908–68), I. Ye. Tamm (1895–1971), P. A. Cherenkov (b. 1904), V. A. Fock (1898–1974), Ya. I. Frenkel' (1894–1952) and P. L. Kapitsa (b. 1894). However, the isolation of Soviet physics, which lasted until the mid-1950s, led to many instances of parallel and independent discoveries of which the Russian part is often little known outside the USSR.

Since the Second World War there has been a great expansion in the resources devoted to physics research, mainly in specialized research institutes of the Academy of Sciences.★ In contrast to the European and United States pattern, most of the universities have primarily a teaching role. The over-all scale of physics in the USSR is now comparable with that in the USA, and there are a number of fields in which Soviet physicists play a leading role. Russia has long had a strong mathematical★ tradition which has been maintained in theoretical physics, where the Soviet style has been characterized as attempting to predict new phenomena rather than concentrating on the explanation of previous experimental results. This has encouraged a notable creative imagination in the leading Soviet theoretical physicists. For many years it seemed that experimental work was somewhat hindered by the lack of an advanced industrial base and by the much slower development of electronics but this factor is now

L. D. Landau receiving the Nobel Prize for Physics, 1962

becoming less important as international contacts become much more frequent.

The most important achievements in Soviet physics have been in four main areas: the physics of condensed matter, plasma physics, quantum electronics and high-energy physics. The primary aim of the physics of condensed matter is to understand the properties of solids and liquids, which being characterized by strong inter-atomic interactions are best studied at low temperatures: hence the description and prediction of the low-temperature properties of metals, semiconductors and the quantum fluids such as liquid helium have been central problems, for which Landau's almost unique physical intuition developed a new and very fruitful approach. In 1937 he predicted a remarkable spectrum for the excited states of liquid helium (this included quantized rotations, which were not observed directly for a further 20 years). His theory explained the superfluidity of liquid helium (its ability to flow without resistance through even very narrow channels), which had just been discovered by another Soviet physicist, Kapitsa, and predicted other unusual new properties that were also later observed. Subsequent development of the theory by N. N. Bogolyubov (b.1909) and by Landau in collaboration with I. M. Khalatnikov (b.1919) led to a fairly complete description of liquid helium.

In 1956 Landau provided a conceptual framework (quasiparticles) both for the theory of liquid helium three, which for quantum reasons behaves very differently from the common isotope, and for the modern theory of electrons in metals. Present knowledge of the dynamical properties of the mobile electrons that make metals electrically conducting also owes a great deal to the theoretical work of I. M. Lifshits (b.1917) and the Moscow school. The phenomenon of superconductivity, in which some metals suddenly lose all their electrical resistance below a certain low temperature, was for over 40 years one of the most intractable problems of physics. Although the basis of the effect was eventually explained by the American physicists J. Bardeen, L. N. Cooper and J. R. Schrieffer in 1957, a complete microscopic theory was only later developed by Bogolyubov and L. P. Gor'kov (b.1929). The widespread present use of superconducting alloys to produce very high magnetic fields is based on the elegant theories of V. L. Ginzburg (b.1916), Landau and A. A. Abrikosov (b.1928) on how a magnetic field can penetrate some superconductors without destroying the superconducting state.

The accepted equations for the microscopic behaviour of plasmas owe much to the pioneering work of Landau and A. A. Vlasov (b.1908). The theoretical possibility of using controlled nuclear fusion in thermo-nuclear plasmas has led to major research efforts, (in which notably Tamm and A. D. Sakharov (b.1921) collaborated), and the large programme in the USSR has been one of the most successful in elucidating the basic physics. The most important product of this work is the doughnut-shaped Tokamak, in which a low-density hydrogen plasma is confined in a vacuum by a magnetic field and heated by a current induced around the ring of plasma. Workers with Kurchatov and L. A. Artsimovich (1909–73) took a leading part in both experimental and theoretical attempts to understand and circumvent the many instabilities of these inherently unstable plasmas and thus increase the containment time, but a device that produces more energy than it consumes is not yet in sight.

The field of quantum electronics was essentially founded in 1954 by the simultaneous, but independent, proposals of N. G. Basov (b.1922) and A. M. Prokhorov (b.1916) in the USSR and C. H. Townes in the USA, of a molecular oscillator which could be used as a coherent oscillator or amplifier at microwave frequencies. Basov and Prokhorov's later proposal of a three-level pumping scheme solved one of the severe problems in adapting these ideas to the construction of a similar oscillator for light—a laser. The group headed by Basov has since made major contributions to the development and use of semiconductor, chemical and other lasers and has been one of the world leaders in the use of pulses of intense laser radiation for thermonuclear fusion.

In 1934 Cherenkov discovered that fast electrons passing through matter emit light. I. M. Frank (b.1908) and Tamm later explained this puzzling effect in terms of the electron velocity being higher than that of light in the medium; in fact the mechanism is somewhat analogous to the shock-wave produced by a supersonic aircraft. A

The proton synchroton at Serpukhov, RSFSR

detailed quantum mechanical theory was later given by Ginzburg. This is now universally known as Cherenkov radiation, and detectors based on it are important in high-energy physics.

A decisive advance in the design of high-energy particle accelerators was made in 1944 by V. I. Veksler (1907–66) who proposed the phase-focusing principle used in the synchrotron. This discovery, made independently in the USA by E. M. MacMillan, enabled designers to overcome the relativistic limitations on final energy. The Soviet Union has since had a major programme in high-energy physics. Important results in the theory of strong interactions were derived by Bogolyubov and by I. Ya. Pomeranchuk (1913–66). Large resources have been devoted to the construction of particle accelerators, culminating in the 70-GeV proton synchrotron at Serpukhov, which was for a time the world's most powerful. Some very ingenious techniques were developed, in particular the use by the Dubna group of a low-density hydrogen-jet target inside the accelerator beam chamber and G. I. Budker's (b. 1918) proposal of electron cooling for a planned antiproton storage ring. The trend to more and more complex experiments has recently led to increasing international cooperation.*   M.G.P.

Crystallography

Crystallography is much studied in the USSR, as elsewhere, both for the specific scientific interest in crystals and substances that crystallize (including biological macromolecules) and for the application to crystalline mineral resources,* in which the country is particularly rich. Research in this field being pursued in many Soviet universities and institutes has important applications in industry and in a wide range of uses for the armed forces,* from satellites to submarine detection.

Although the name crystallography suggests the mere drawing of crystals, the subject embraces their study in many ways, all based on the recognition of a crystal as a lattice-like repeating structure. An outstanding Russian contribution to theories of three-dimensional repeating patterns involving considerations of symmetry was Ye. S. Fedorov's (1853–1919) derivation (the first, 1890) of the 230 'space groups' which represent all the possible ways in which a basic structural component (atom or complex set of atoms) may repeat to form a crystal (assumed, for this purpose, to be perfect). Several methods, the most widely-practised being diffraction of x-rays by the crystal, are now available for determining the dimensions of the repeating pattern directly and the details of the basic component less directly: Soviet research has played a leading role in developing the use of electron diffraction for these purposes. In Moscow the Institute of Crystallography, first director A. V. Shubnikov, grew

from a laboratory of the Academy of Sciences;* it now numbers its personnel in hundreds and is particularly well equipped. The subjects of theoretical studies there include antisymmetry, colour symmetry and imperfections; the crystal chemistry of silicates and the structures of very large biologically important molecules are among the objects of crystal structure determinations. Also investigated are the mechanical, optical, thermo-optical and electrical properties of crystals. The Institute's fundamental work on the growth of crystals has resulted in a national industry for the production of monocrystals, which are indispensable for the development of radio, quantum and semiconductor electronics and of optical and acoustic precision apparatus.   H.M.P.

Physical metallurgy

The post-war developments in the field of physical metallurgy took a somewhat different course in the USSR than in Western Europe and the USA. In the non-communist world, the seeds of the dislocation theory of the plastic properties of metals which had been sown in the immediate pre-war years began to germinate after the war and their growth dominated metallurgical thought for the next decade. The belief that many of the properties of metals and alloys were controlled by 'imperfections' in the metallic lattice may have proved a difficult ideological concept for those who believed that if 'imperfections' were removed a better society would result. Research on physical metallurgy in Russia during the period 1945-55 was hence influenced almost entirely by techniques that depended upon lattice perfection such as x-ray and electron diffraction.

Welding equipment with its developer Academician B. Ye. Paton, son of the noted metallurgist, Ye. O. Paton (1870–1953)

By 1957 the experimental evidence in support of the role of dislocations in the plastic flow of metals had become incontrovertible with the first direct observation in the electron microscope of dislocations and their movement in thin metal foils. These observations led to a general acceptance by Soviet metallurgists of the implications of lattice imperfections and from then the patterns of research followed closely those in other countries; electron optical methods for the study of metallurgical structures assumed a dominant role in Russia, as elsewhere.

The application of metals and alloys in gas turbines made it necessary to examine their behaviour at high temperature, and a significant Soviet development has been in the field of high-temperature metallography, where special optical microscopes, linked with stage straining devices, have become widely available to research laboratories.

In an attempt to produce unusual properties in a wide variety of materials there was a flurry of Soviet investigations during the 1960s of the influence of strong magnetic fields applied during the time a metal or alloy was undergoing a thermally-induced structural change. The results reported were treated with some scepticism in the West and it would now appear that interest in the topic has subsided. But with the development of high field superconducting magnets, the topic is one that could be due for revival.

The formulation of new alloys is a direct consequence of the general understanding and quantification of structure-property relationships that have been the pervading theme of physical metallurgy in the USSR and the rest of the world for the past 20 years. However, alloy development is also influenced by national needs: the high cost of extracting nickel in the remote North has led to much study of manganese in a wide variety of steels in which the nickel is replaced by manganese, an element abundant in the Caucasus; the ready availability of titanium has led to Soviet metallurgists becoming the leading authorities in the extraction of this metal from its ores and its subsequent alloying and fabrication. From this work a titanium alloy hull for a nuclear submarine was developed. As in the West, older heat-treated low-alloy steels are still in use.

While Soviet metallurgy is of a high standard, reports of metallurgical failures in supersonic aircraft suggest persisting problems of producing critically-stressed metallic components of a uniformly high quality.   *J.N.*

Mathematics

Medieval Samarkand and Khorezm were the birthplaces of major mathematical advances: the first word of the 9th-century treatise on quadratic equations, *Al-jebr wa'lmuqābala*, gave the term 'algebra'
and the author's name, Al-Khorezmi, the term 'algorithm'. Ibn Sina (known in the West as Avicenna) was an original mathematician as well as compiler of all existing knowledge of medical* science, while Al-Biruni (known also as Beruni) was mathematician as well as historian. The territory that is now the USSR did not lose mathematicians as the intellectual glory of Samarkand faded in the 17th century, for the first of Peter the Great's* scientific institutions in Russia was a School of Mathematics and Navigation just as the 18th century began. The great names of Russian mathematics are of the ensuing century, however – N. I. Lobachevsky (1792–1856) and P. L. Chebyshev (1821-94) in geometry and the latter, A. M. Lyapunov (1857–1918) and A. A. Markov the elder (1856–1922) in probability theory.

Many of the modern centres of research in mathematics in the USSR were set up in the first few years after the October Revolution. Although research was influenced by established mathematicians such as V. V. Stepanov (1889–1950) (trigonometrical series), and N. N. Luzin (1883–1950) and M. Ya. Suslin (1894–1919) (operations on sets), the 1920s saw the inauguration and development of important trends. In topology, P. S. Aleksandrov (b.1896) and P. S. Uryson (1898–1924) jointly or separately made significant contributions to the theory of compact and locally compact topological spaces, the homology theory of general topological spaces and dimension theory. A. N. Tikhonov's (b. 1906) now classical result on the topological product of an arbitrary set of compact topological spaces dates from this period. L. A. Lyusternik (b.1899) and L. G. Shnirel'-man (1905–38) developed a topological apparatus that was used to estimate the number of solutions of variational problems. In probability theory, S. N. Bernshtein (1880–1968) investigated limit theorems for Markov series and sums of stochastically independent random variables, and contributed to the theory of heterogeneous Markov chains. Pre-revolutionary research on the law of large numbers was completed by A. N. Kolmogorov (b.1903), who with A. Ya. Khinchin (1894–1959) generalized the law of iterated logarithm to sums of independent variables. In analysis, D. Ye. Men'shov (b.1892) obtained results on the representation of functions by trigonometric series and the monogeneity of functions of a complex variable. Variational-geometric methods were developed to solve extremal problems arising in hydrodynamics and later in oscillating wing theory. The contributions to the theory of quasi-conformal mappings initiated by M. A. Lavrent'ev (1900–80), and work on approximation of functions and applications to the problems of plane elasticity theory are noteworthy. The Russian group-theoretical school was founded by O. Yu. Shmidt (1891–1956) in the late 1920s.

All these directions continued in the 1930s. Kolmogorov's work on analytic methods in probability theory laid the foundation for the theory of Markov processes; developments in stationary random processes and related work on the geometry of Hilbert spaces led to contributions to the theory of isotropic turbulent flow. Urgent and complicated mathematical problems arising in aircraft construction resulted in the contributions of M. V. Keldysh (1911–80) to the theory of oscillations and self-oscillations of aircraft structures, and unstable flow; studies on the oscillation of systems with a dissipation of mechanical energy later led to work on non-selfadjoint operators in functional analysis. In the 1930s the latter was emerging as an independent branch of mathematics, and significant contributions were made by L. V. Kantorovich (b.1912) and M. G. Krein (vector lattices), and by I. M. Gel'fand (b.1913) (Banach algebras). Important contributions to the theory of systems of partial differential equations were initiated by I. G. Petrovsky (1901–73), and links between Markov processes and solutions of certain problems in this field were investigated. Results and methods of partial differential equations had important applications in the theory of elastic shells.

The 1930s saw a creative contribution to a new branch of group theory (the theory of soluble and nilpotent infinite groups) by A. G. Kurosh (b.1907) and co-workers, while significant developments on topological groups were made by L. S. Pontryagin (b.1908). By 1950 numerical methods had been developed to handle a wide range of problems involving infinite systems, integral and partial differential equations; fundamental results on the approximation of functions by polynomials are due to Lavrent'ev and Keldysh.

These directions of research were developed and extended in the post-war years and the 1950s. Substantial contributions were made to the qualitative theory of systems of partial differential equations, ergodic theory and the classification of dynamical systems. Men'shov obtained fundamental results on the representation of functions by trigonometric series. In non-linear analysis Yu. A. Mitropol'sky (b. 1917) investigated oscillation processes in non-linear systems, while M. A. Krasnosel'sky and others used functional methods to study problems involving non-linear integral equations. The introduction of generalized functions of any class by Gel'fand and G. Ye. Shilov (b. 1917) stimulated investigations into the behaviour of solutions of general systems of partial differential equations. In computational mathematics algorithms were devised to improve the effectiveness of difference methods for the solution of multi-dimensional non-stationary problems in gas dynamics and elsewhere. The studies of Gel'fand, M. A. Naimark and others on infinite-dimensional representations of groups were applied to problems in elementary particle physics★ and the quantum theory of fields.

The 1960s and 1970s saw extensions of research to the factorization of groups and locally finite groups, to global analysis, to non-linear differential equations with variable coefficients, quasi-periodic systems and pseudo-differential operators. Regularization methods have been developed to solve a wide class of ill-posed problems and

for integral and operator equations and inverse problems. Advances have been made in reliability theory, Markov processes and the solubility of partial differential equations with infinitely many variables, singular integral equations, and in the mathematical simulation of biophysical and other processes. *L.L.*

Automation

Until the 1930s developments in automatic control theory originated from classical methods of E. Routh in England, A. Hurwitz in Germany and I. A. Vyshnegradsky (1831/2–95) and A. M. Lyapunov (1857–1918) in Russia for the stability analysis of linear systems. The importance to science, industry and agriculture of the subject was recognized by the formation in 1939 of the Institute of Automation and Remote Control in Moscow. The late 1930s and the 1940s saw significant developments in several directions: the introduction of frequency methods; the extension of the Nyquist stability criteria for linear feedback systems to closed loop systems, distributed parameter systems, and those with a lag; the structural stability of control systems; and the autonomy of multivariate systems and its application to the control of power systems. The work of L. V. Kantorovich (b.1912) on mathematical★ methods for the organization and planning of production (1939) (which merited a Nobel Prize for Economics in 1975) was the starting point for the subsequent construction of a theory of the optimal planning★ of the

The first Soviet automated irrigation system, Kirgizia

national economy. The stimulus provided by A. A. Andronov (1901–52) (with his collaborators) and the leading schools in non-linear oscillation theory led to the development of a theory of non-linear systems with piecewise linear components and its application to servo-mechanism design. The harmonic balance method of N. M. Krylov (1879–1955) and N. N. Bogolyubov (b.1909) led to the development of methods for analysing self-oscillations in certain non-linear systems; these methods and others resulted in a comprehensive transient analysis of non-linear systems.

The mathematical theory of optimal control began to develop in the early 1950s; a significant contribution to this is due to L. S. Pontryagin (b.1908) and co-workers who developed a maximum principle permitting the solution of a very extensive class of problems with an arbitrary performance index and equality and inequality constraints. The principle has been proved for linear pulse systems, extended to distributed parameter systems and formulated in an abstract framework to investigate extremum problems in linear topological spaces.

Investigations in stochastic optimal control theory based on the work of A. N. Kolmogorov (b.1903) in the USSR and N. Wiener in the USA resulted in the creation of broad methods of synthesizing linear and non-linear optimal control systems with any statistical performance index. The ideas of Wiener and other Western cyberneticists had been denounced in 1953 in the principal Soviet philosophical journal as a pseudo-science serving capitalist interests. Recognition of the industrial significance of cybernetics and increasing pressure from Soviet scientists themselves (including Kolmogorov, who withdrew his earlier opposition) soon reversed this view. In 1958 an Academy of Sciences Scientific Council on Cybernetics under A. I. Berg pioneered development, a periodical was founded and in 1963 an Institute of Cybernetics was set up at Kiev under V. M. Glushkov (b. 1923). Subsequent research found widespread applications in the economy.

In the early 1970s, N. N. Krasovsky (b.1924) and co-workers produced methods of estimating from given observations the state of a controlled system subject to random perturbations.   *L.L.*

Technology

Policy

The Communist Party* of the Soviet Union attaches great importance to the improvement of the technology of production processes as a factor in economic growth; in an advanced industrial economy the raising of productivity depends increasingly on such technical progress. The Party fosters scientific research to accelerate such progress, but not to the exclusion of a certain continuity of production processes, as exemplified in the emphasis laid on a basic production of iron and steel, and on preservation – unchanged as far as possible – of the specifications of final products. Especially in the first post-revolutionary years the popular presentation of technological policy was in terms of electrification and mechanization, but electrification has been a real and continuing influence in the Soviet development strategy as well as being a slogan: Lenin,* when defining communism* as equalling soviet power plus the electrification of the whole country, envisaged this as a universal force for modernizing and transforming economy and society. In 1931, during Stalin's* First Five-year Plan,* mechanization was formulated as an objective wherever manual work was laborious (this spirit did not, of course, infuse the widespread construction carried out by forced labour which simultaneously began to be used). In many directions mechanization has since become extensive, although frequently – as in coal-mining, agriculture, or factory handling of materials – markedly uneven; for instance, agricultural field work was mechanized much more than livestock rearing. Automation has jumped into official favour even where economically hardly justified, yet nationwide it is not particularly advanced. Until fairly recently (the 1960s as regards industrial design) refined aspects of person-machine relationships – as affected, for example, by differences in skill or in the organization of the workplace, or other ergonomic influences – received slighter attention.

The bias in favour of scientific progress may have distracted attention away from solving problems in production technology, but probably has favoured military-scientific purposes; in the late 1950s twice as much was spent on pure science as on technology whereas in the USA more was spent on the latter than on the former. Both military* and institutional considerations have apparently had the result of promoting a special emphasis on welding, research into which is headed by the Paton Institute of the Ukrainian Academy of Sciences. A second bias was the denial until 1956 of obsolescence as possible under socialism; machinery once installed had to be run until physically worn out. Correspondingly, and because also (up to 1965) equipment was not resold to enterprises, the practice became engrained of ordering only the latest and best equipment, normally that embodying the largest scientific contribution. Far from being always economically justified, this practice left no scope for introducing 'intermediate' (low capital-intensive) technology. Among negative effects of the technological profile of Soviet industrialization may be mentioned substantial environmental problems,* polluting water more than air; the ecological results of dam- and canal-building have not been entirely satisfactory.

Much heed has been paid to standardization, especially as expressed in state standards. Characteristic of the Soviet space* programme, and conferring significant advantages in the production and deployment of defence supplies, standardization is also widely (and usually beneficially) diffused in Soviet consumers' goods.★ Large-scale processes are favoured, which matches both the economy's needs for large-volume output and the abundance of most natural resources.★ Where the technique had originally been imported, the creation of larger versions ('scaling-up') has been common. Miniaturization has correspondingly tended to be backward. The problem of discovering appropriate criteria of plan-fulfilment has reacted upon design: reckoning machinery by weight has not surprisingly led to the production of unduly heavy machines. While the main emphasis in Soviet development has been on quantity, much more attention was paid in the 1970s to bettering quality; for instance, to improving operational reliability (where absolutely necessary there may be recourse to duplication of equipment), or to achieving production without defects.

Imported technology

Russian pre-revolutionary economic development was founded overwhelmingly on imported technologies and this has remained almost equally true of Soviet economic development, despite the creation of a greatly diversified capability for scientific and technical research with a more than one-hundredfold multiplication over 60 years in the number of people qualified in these spheres. Among the exceptions before the Revolution★ was oil refining, where the technology applied in Russia (though partly based on foreign inventions) was relatively advanced, having outgrown an earlier hindrance imposed by the Excise. The creation of new techniques in Soviet laboratories, followed by their industrial application, has been of comparatively minor importance, although exemplified in the manufacture of synthetic rubber. By contrast, imported technology or 'know-how' has been identified in all major sectors. Foreign prototypes also have been imported and reverse-engineered (often, naturally, with their faults as well as their virtues) and then assimilated into production cycles. Where equipment has been imported, the indigenous contribution has sometimes been restricted to providing a building and its appurtenances. Certain adaptations to conform with local conditions or national standards have little more than modified this over-all picture.

Technologies, somewhat more than designs, often seem to have been selected; thus, such items as caterpillar tractors or cameras were in the 1960s produced in quantities surpassing (relative to other needs) domestic requirements. In a number of cases, however–including those just mentioned–choices appear to have been influenced by the feasibility of employing either the manufacturing technique or the final product for military as well as civilian purposes. Whereas in the earliest stages of Soviet industrialization equipment was imported primarily for the extractive and basic materials branches, there has since been a shift towards imports embodying very advanced technology with a high scientific content. Soviet reliance upon such imports from Western countries increased markedly between 1966 and 1979, but was checked at the beginning of 1980 by the US embargo as a response to the Soviet invasion of Afghanistan.★ Obversely, the years 1961–5 represented a peak in the number of new types of equipment–machinery, apparatus and instruments–created first in the USSR.

Technological imports have had a most important economic effect, although (because of organizational or other circumstances) it may not be possible to raise the productivity of imported equipment to that achieved in its country of origin, at least immediately. The impact of Western technology in the Soviet economy is nevertheless estimated for the 1970s at three to four times that of the same volume of investment in technology of home origin. Soviet exports of machinery have also increased, but those to Western countries in the late 1970s were below 10 per cent of imports from those countries.

Eastern Europe, especially the GDR and Czechoslovakia, is also an important technological supplier: about three-quarters of total Soviet equipment imports come from other socialist countries. The import of technology other than that embodied in equipment is achieved through licensing and industrial cooperation agreements, and particularly with Eastern Europe, through intergovernmental arrangements. A huge organization, the All-Union Institute of Scientific and Technical Information★ (VINITI), peruses and translates extracts from some 30 000 publications received from over 100

Production line supplied by Fiat of Turin for the Volga Automobile Plant, Tol'yatti (Togliatti), RSFSR

countries; industrial espionage too has played a part. The 'technological gap' between the USSR and the most advanced countries was nevertheless not being narrowed, even when reliance on importing highly advanced technologies was at its peak in the 1970s.

Technological level

The extremely wide range of technology in the USSR needs to be borne in mind when its level is assessed. On the whole, while the level is below that of other advanced countries, the gap tends to be smaller in industry than in other sectors, and also within a given branch is highly variable as between factories. Defence industries probably are on average more efficient than the civilian sector, although not to the extent that was suggested by Western evaluations in the 1960s. Heavy industry tends to be more efficient than light industry, and production of capital goods than that of consumers' goods. Service branches, and ancillary branches such as factory handling, are especially backward.

The USSR is fairly advanced – and indeed in some subdivisions may be considered advanced – in applications of materials science, such as metallurgy★ (notably chemical inhibition of corrosion), ceramics, chemical composites and fibres, and welding (a long tradition, culminating in the application of lasers), in many branches of engineering★ – notably machine tools (although metal-cutting, as distinct from forging and pressing, has been over-emphasized, and numerically-controlled technology has lagged for some years) and electronics (including microchips), energy★ transmission-systems for electricity at very high voltage and for coal as slurry, although compressors for gas-pipelines had to be bought in the West. Techniques in building,★ building materials (glass-making technology has been imported) and the extractive industries are in the main on a somewhat lower level; the USSR adopted prefabrication in construction on a large scale from 1957 onwards (in sharp contrast to the traditional means still used in individual house-building) and produces very large items of machinery for open-cast mining, construction and civil engineering, a group of sectors which as a result have had a low priority in imports. The chemical industry, especially 'small chemistry' (as distinct from large-volume output used in industrial processes, such as the production of sulphuric acid) and synthetic fibres, has heavily depended on foreign purchases of high technology. The same may be said of the motor vehicle industry, which has been backward in almost all respects (excluding some go-anywhere vehicles). Textiles and clothing, timber, pulp and paper, and the food industries (except processing on board ship) are also behind, having benefited relatively little from imported technology since 1932.

Computers have been slow to develop, for reasons which include their organizationally disruptive effects and the lack of incentives on the part of management (as distinct from military and scientific-

A computer operator examines punched tape carrying information supplied by oil rigs in the Tyumen' region

engineering circles). Hardware has been evolved faster than software, where systems have been adopted and copied from the USA: as a consequence of the 'Ryad' programme in Comecon,★ software has been improved, though problems remain in diffusion, in maintenance and in the range and distribution of peripherals. The lag behind the USA in the development of computers is estimated to be 8–10 years.

Civil engineering has to its credit immense hydroelectric constructions, such as the damming of the Volga and Angara rivers and canal-building (the present century being the country's great canal age). Railway★ construction too, facilitated by the spacious and generally flat terrain, has continued on a fairly substantial scale. On the other hand, road-building★ has been backward and has not yet provided an adequate network of highways. The programme of military construction (of missile silos, for example) has been very large, but technical details are not published.

The Soviet fishing fleet is modern; the relatively unspecialized composition of the mercantile marine permits more flexible utilization, including military. The aircraft industry is advanced in producing large helicopters, and in 1980 completed tests on a wide-bodied airbus (IL-86); it has assimilated the design of aircraft with variable geometry and vertical take-off. Much Soviet military equipment appears fairly advanced, yet easy to maintain and service. Tanks are given good nuclear-biological-chemical protection; the AK-47 assault rifle is the guerrillas' favourite; the latest generation of warships has shown remarkable originality, especially in the development of long-range ship-to-ship missiles. Gradual improvement, rather than dramatic innovation, is characteristic of most types of Soviet military designs, which as a rule are probably more novel than the technologies employed in arms manufacture.   *R.H.*

Astronomy and astrophysics

Astronomers in the USSR have made many notable contributions to the science. Historically the dominant person is Ulugh Beg (1394–1449), an eminent Uzbek astronomer, who at the age of 15 became governor of Samarkand and towards the end of his life ruler of an immense territory in Western Turkestan.* Here he gained an international reputation, compiling a catalogue of 1018 stars, mainly based on observations made at his observatory. Archaeological investigations have shown that the main instrument was a sextant of 40-m radius made of polished marble set in a rock-hewn trench on the meridian. This would have been used for measuring the altitude of

Left: the remains of Ulugh Beg's 15th-century sextant, Samarkand. Below: the Ratan 600 radio-telescope at Mt Simirodriki

the Sun; trigonometrical tables correct to the ninth decimal place were computed at the observatory to allow important astronomical constants to be determined to high accuracy. Ulugh Beg's results first became available to Europeans in 1643, when John Greaves (1602–53), Professor of Astronomy at Oxford University, compiled astronomical tables based on Beg's observations. When these were first published in Europe catalogues requiring extended observation and exacting reductions were rare. They had considerable practical value because methods of determining terrestrial longitudes, a pressing problem as navigation developed, depended on precise star positions.

The 19th century saw the establishment by Nicholas I* in 1839 of a major observatory at Pulkovo, which remains one of the centres of Soviet astronomy, having both optical and radio telescopes. The famous Struve dynasty practised astronomy there for almost a century. V. Ya. Struve (1793–1864), of German birth, was appointed director of the Dorpat observatory; in 1824 he perfected the first clock-driven telescope and commenced classic work on double stars, which he continued after his move to Pulkovo in 1839. His son Otto (1819–1905) followed his father and became director in 1861; in turn, Otto's sons Karl (1854–1920) and Gustav (1858–1920) became directors of the Berlin (1904) and Kharkov (1894) observatories. Gustav's son Otto (1897–1963), born at Kharkov, fought with the White Army in the Revolution and eventually reached the USA in 1921, where he was director successively of the Yerkes, McDonald, and National Radio Astronomy Observatories. Four of the Struves (Karl excepted) each received the Gold Medal of the Royal Astronomical Society.

Between the mid-20th century and 1980 Soviet astronomers have steadily built up their observational facilities to the point where they have several instruments of world class. The 6-m reflector (1976) at Mt Simirodriki in the Caucasus is the world's largest optical telescope. At the same site is a major radio telescope (1978) some

600m in diameter. The Crimean observatory possesses a 2.64-m reflector and in Armenia the Byurakan observatory has a 2.6-m instrument. Radio astronomy is vigorously pursued at the Crimea and Pulkovo observatories. With such fine instruments Soviet astronomers can for the first time compete with European and American observers.

The greatest achievements in this century have unquestionably been made by theoretical astronomers, and Western scientists have gone to considerable lengths to visit them in Moscow and invite them to international symposia. The Copernicus Astronomical Institute (1978) in Warsaw is the major meeting point, and was specifically funded by the USA to improve the exchange of ideas.

I. S. Shklovsky (b.1916) has made numerous contributions to the theory of radiation; he gave the first correct account (1952) of the production of radio waves in objects such as radio galaxies and the remnants of exploded stars. In particular he predicted from his theory that the visible light from such an object would be polarized; this was confirmed in 1953 by V. M. Dombrovsky, working at Byurakan. After a brilliant start the Moscow school has continued a distinguished tradition, V. L. Ginzburg (b.1916) and S. P. Syrovatsky having written the standard works on the subject. Another important area has been cosmology and gravitation, particularly the development of knowledge of the early universe, to which Ya. B. Zel'dovich (b.1914) and the Moscow school have made significant contributions concerning the behaviour of elementary particles in the first second in the life of the universe.

In space astronomy the main achievement apart from selenology* is the landing of Venera 9 and 10 on the surface of Venus (October 1975). These craft functioned at high temperature (485°C) and pressure (90 atmospheres) for about one hour, long enough to transmit the first photographs ever obtained on the surface of another planet.   S.M.

Selenology and selenography

Soviet astronomy covers all branches of the subject, but although lunar research was no exception, it is fair to say that before space-flight became feasible studies of the Moon were confined to a relatively few enthusiasts. Many theoretical papers were, however, published in the immediate post-war period, notably by N. P. Barabashov (b.1894) and A. V. Markov, who put forward theories of the nature of the Moon's surface which proved very close to the truth.

In the USA most authorities regard the major formations on the Moon's surface to be of impact origin. Opinion in the USSR (and in much of Europe) is more divided, and it is felt that both internal and external processes have played major roles in the moulding of the

surface. An important contribution was made on 3 November 1958 by N. A. Kozyrev, using the large refractor at the Crimean Astrophysical Observatory: he recorded a red event in the crater Alphonsus, and obtained spectrographic confirmation. Though his interpretations have been questioned, there seems little doubt that an event did occur, proving that the Moon is not completely inert. Other 'transient phenomena' have been recorded both before and since, but Kozyrev's observation is probably the most significant of its kind.

The main Soviet contribution to lunar study has been in the field of space research.* The first successful lunar probes were launched in 1959: Luna 1 (January) passed within 5955km of the Moon, Luna 2 (September) made an uncontrolled landing, and Luna 3 (October) made a circumlunar trip, sending back the first photographs of the Moon's far side – never visible from Earth because (allowing for some oscillation) 41 per cent of the total surface is permanently averted. From the Luna 3 results the Soviet authorities were able to publish the first maps of the far side, and named some of the features, notably the Mare Moscoviense (a dark plain) and the important, dark-floored crater Tsiolkovsky. These designations have been officially adopted, though some errors were also made; thus the so-called 'Soviet Mountains' proved to be non-existent.

The next few Luna probes were not successful, and meanwhile the US Orbiter programme (succeeding the Ranger series of crash-landing vehicles) enabled American astronomers to compile much improved maps of the entire lunar surface. However, an important advance was made on 31 January 1966 with the automatic Soviet probe Luna 9, which made a controlled landing in the grey plain named the Oceanus Procellarum, conclusively disproving the theory that the lunar maria were covered with deep layers of soft dust.

Of the two dozen Soviet lunar probes of the 20 years after 1959 three (nos. 16, 20 and 24) have been returned to Earth, carrying samples of moon material, and two set down mobile vehicles, termed Lunokhods. The first Lunokhod was carried to the Moon in Luna 17

A lunar globe showing the far side of the Moon, composed from photographs taken by the Luna 3 probe, 1959

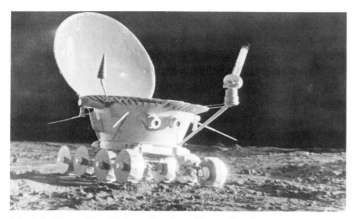

Model of Lunokhod 1 in a simulated lunar landscape

(November 1970), and operated for 11 months; the area photographed exceeded 80 000 sq m involving 200 panoramic pictures and 20 000 photographs; a distance of over 10km was travelled before its power failed. It also made soil analyses and transmitted back the results. Lunokhod 2, carried in Luna 21 (January 1973), had a shorter active life of four months, but was able to travel a distance of 37km: whereas Lunokhod 1 had descended in the Mare Imbrium, well away from the site of any Apollo landing, Lunokhod 2 operated in the Le Monnier area, only 180km from the landing-point of the US astronauts Cernan and Schmitt in the previous December.

Results from the Soviet probes are in good accord with those of the manned and unmanned American vehicles. The samples obtained from the automatic Soviet recovery vehicles are of great value because they involve entirely new areas of the Moon, despite the fact that the amount of material brought back is relatively small. There has been a pleasingly free exchange of Soviet and American lunar samples, and so far as lunar research is concerned there continues to be full cooperation between the various national teams.

Lunar satellites have also been dispatched from the Soviet Union; for instance, Luna 19 (launched 28 September 1971) remained in contact for over 4000 lunar orbits. Among the features studied were the enigmatical mascons (a convenient acronym for *mass con*centrations below some of the maria and large walled plains) which had been discovered in 1968 by the American astronomers P. Muller and W. L. Sjögren, from studies of the movements of Orbiter 5. Here again the Soviet and American results are in good accord.

It would be idle to claim that the Soviet photographs obtained from probes are equal to those of the US Orbiters and Apollos, though there is still one region, near the Moon's south pole, which has been covered only by the Luna pictures. So far as earth-based research is concerned, papers continue to appear in all the main Soviet astronomical periodicals; most are purely theoretical, though a new lunar atlas has been issued.   *P. M.*

Space research

Sputnik

On 4 October 1957 the Soviet Union astonished the world by launching the first artificial satellite from a secret base in Central Asia. Called Sputnik 1, it was little more than a radio transmitter encased in an aluminium sphere from which long 'whip' aerials extended, but the regular 'bleep-bleep' of its transmitter picked up all around the world signalled the dawn of a new age. That it was the USSR which had achieved this breakthrough from a less advanced technological base than the USA was the major shock, and its political and military impact was deeply felt in the Western world.

Two men were primarily responsible for this 'golden day' in Soviet history: the brilliant spacecraft designers S. P. Korolev (1906–66), who headed the rocket teams, and V. P. Glushko (b.1908), who designed the engines. Both had played pioneer roles in Soviet rocketry before the Second World War.

Their crowning achievement would not have been possible, however, without the political support given from the time of Stalin* to the development, in the military* programme, of an intercontinental ballistic missile (ICBM) bigger than anything conceived in the West. The plan to use this rocket to launch satellites is said to have sprung from a recommendation by Korolev himself. The ICBM was to become the mainstay of the Soviet space programme, which for some time continued to outpace that of the USA.

Sputnik 2 carried a dog, Laika, into orbit and Sputnik 3 took the form of a 1327-kg geophysical observatory. Modifications to the basic launch vehicle, including the addition of another rocket stage, soon produced even more spectacular results. Selenological* research proceeded with unmanned Luna space probes, which in 1959 passed, hit and circumnavigated the Moon; Luna 3 sent back the first pictures of the Moon's far side by television. The Soviet leadership under N. S. Khrushchev* was quick to realize the political importance of space achievement for enlarging Soviet prestige and influence, and continually pushed the rocket teams to greater effort. Before the USA could launch the first Americans into space, Yu. A. Gagarin (1934–68) was making his single orbit of the earth in a Vostok spacecraft. His epic flight on 12 April 1961 lasted 108 minutes and was the final act that set America on course for the Moon in Project Apollo, announced by President J. F. Kennedy to a joint session of Congress on 25 May 1961.

The Soviet teams maintained their pace: the cosmonauts who followed Gagarin included the first space woman, Valentina Tereshkova (b.1937), who circled the earth 48 times in Vostok 6, in a journey lasting 70 hours 50 minutes. On 18 March 1965 A. A. Leonov (b.1934), clad in a pressure suit and wearing life-support equipment on his back, became the first man to walk in space from the orbiting

N. S. Khrushchev receiving three cosmonauts: Valentina Tereshkova, her husband A. G. Nikolaev and Yu. A. Gagarin

Voskhod 2. To make this possible, Korolev modified a Vostok by fitting an extensible airlock. The first successful landing of an instrument capsule, Luna 9, on the Moon followed on 3 February 1966: pictures were transmitted from the Ocean of Storms, west of the craters Reiner and Marius.

In the mean time, the first Russian space probes had been sent to Venus and Mars in a determined effort to roll back new frontiers. Instruments landed on Venus in the early 1970s endured atmospheric pressures 90–100 times greater than on earth and temperatures exceeding 470°C; and yet in 1975, despite these hostile conditions, the first television pictures were obtained directly from the surface. However, success with Mars was to be denied in 1971 when an instrument capsule made a heavy landing in a dust storm between the regions of Electris and Phaethontis. The transmitter started to send a television picture but stopped after only 20 seconds.

Kosmos

An ambitious new project, Kosmos, began in 1962 initially at Kapustin Yar (east of Volgograd) but later at the original Sputnik base of Tyuratam-Baykonur (in the Karaganda region of Kazakhstan) and at Plesetsk (south of Archangel). The first objective was to extend investigation of the earth's atmosphere and cloud cover, ionosphere, magnetic field, radiation belts and the influence of solar radiation and cosmic rays upon the general environment. Satellites for this purpose were generally of a standardized construction using many common components; the scientific investigation was later expanded to include experiments from other countries within the Interkosmos programme. A second range of Kosmos activity included the testing of satellites which later emerged as fully-fledged operational systems, of which early examples were the Meteor weather and Molnya communications satellites. Projected manned space systems are also tested under the Kosmos label. The third category concerned the testing of military* space systems. A large family of reconnaissance and surveillance satellites also operates within the Kosmos programme.

Soyuz and Salyut

Further success in developing manned spacecraft after Vostok and Voskhod was not achieved without mishap. After experiencing difficulty with the control of Soyuz 1, cosmonaut V. V. Komarov (1927–67) was killed when the parachute lines of his capsule became entangled as he tried to land. The tragedy delayed the Soyuz programme for a year and a half but eventually cosmonauts were able to fly extended missions in earth orbit drawing electrical power from solar 'wings' which opened out in space. It was also possible to use craft of this type to obtain experience in the art of space docking, as a step towards the Salyut space station.

Soyuz was later modified for ferrying cosmonauts to Salyut stations but after the Soyuz 11 incident in June 1971, when three men died in a depressurization accident while returning to earth, the spacecraft was made into a two-seater and was given extra safety equipment. The cumbersome solar 'wings' were removed and the craft depended on chemical batteries which could be recharged from the solar panels on the space station after the craft had docked.

One of the major achievements of the Soviet space programme has been the ability to dock unmanned Progress cargo ships with Salyut which bring fuel, equipment, food, water and other supplies. If necessary they can act as 'space tugs' using their engines to push the station into a different orbit. These versatile craft, developed from Soyuz, are later filled with waste materials, separated from the station and made to burn up harmlessly over the Pacific Ocean. Cosmonauts have thus been able to use the Salyut workshop for extended periods of research. In 1978 two Russians, V. V. Kovalenok (b.1942) and A. S. Ivanchenkov (b.1940), were aloft for a record 139 days 14 hours

The manned Salyut spacecraft

48 minutes, far exceeding the maximum stay of 84 days by Americans aboard the Skylab space station. In 1979 came another record-breaking flight in which two Salyut 6 cosmonauts V. A. Lyakhov (b.1941) and V. V. Ryumin (b. 1939) spent 175 days in earth-orbit–not far short of the flight time for a journey to Mars. In 1978 and 1979 cosmonauts of other socialist countries (Czechoslovakia, Poland and the GDR) made week-long visits to Salyut stations in conjunction with Soviet colleagues. More joint flights followed, including cosmonauts from Hungary, Bulgaria, Vietnam, Cuba and Mongolia; and Ryumin, making another flight with a Soviet commander, set a new duration record of 184 days 20 hours 12 minutes.

Work performed aboard Salyut includes astronomical observations, study of the earth's natural resources, pollution monitoring and researches in medicine and biology. There have also been 'space-factory' experiments in which materials have been melted in electric furnaces to discover how they behave under micro-gravity conditions prevailing in space. This research has included the testing of new metal alloys free of the distortions caused by gravitational pull; the formation of ultra-pure semiconductor materials such as gallium arsenide, of great potential for the electronics industry; and efforts to produce glasses of high purity which could find wide application in fibre-optics and optical instruments (telescopes, cameras). Cosmonaut V. V. Gorbatko (b.1934) who flew in Soyuz 7, anticipates 'the production of homogeneous alloys from components that are immiscible on earth . . . under orbital conditions it should be possible to alloy metal and glass, and metal and ceramics. Consider the possibilities of ultra-lightweight foam steel. The designers and builders of space vehicles are keen to have such materials.'

Zond

Soviet ambitions at the time of the United States manned landing on the Moon remain unclear, for Zond spacecraft were being flown unmanned around the Moon and back to earth. They resembled the Soyuz spacecraft except that they omitted the orbital module used for experiments in earth orbit.

In September 1968 Zond 5, carrying tortoises and other biological specimens, looped the Moon and returned to splash down in the Indian Ocean. Similar spacecraft–Zond 6 (November 1968) and Zond 7 (August 1969)–made an aerodynamic 'skip' when they encountered the earth's atmosphere which enabled them to land back on Soviet territory. Zond 8 (October 1970), the last of the series, splashed down in the Indian Ocean. Whether or not these were meant to be trial runs for a man-around-the-Moon spectacular the Soviet authorities have never stated. If they were, it was a very small craft in which to make the attempt; in the event no manned flight occurred, although ingenious robot devices were landed which drilled into the Moon's soil and flew home with small samples, and roving vehicles performed soil tests.

The super-booster

A huge Soviet multi-stage rocket, bigger than America's Saturn V moon rocket, was reportedly destroyed at the Tyuratam-Baykonur cosmodrome in the summer of 1969. The rocket, known in the West as type G-1, is believed to have caught fire during a pre-flight fuelling exercise on the launch pad, causing much damage. If this was the vehicle envisaged for landing cosmonauts on the Moon, it did not get very far: two more of the super-boosters are said to have been destroyed after being launched on test in 1971 and 1972 respectively. Unofficial reports in 1971 stated the the G-1 was intended to launch modular components of a large space station, but it could have had an early connection with the Soviet moon programme.

Space policy

What seemed to be a breakthrough in bilateral collaboration reached its climax in July 1975 when an Apollo spacecraft carrying a special docking attachment linked with a Soyuz above the earth; while the craft were together their crews exchanged visits and conducted simple experiments. Not only did this symbolic meeting between East and West involve astronauts and cosmonauts visiting each others' countries for training but Soviet and United States research teams collaborated to render compatible the docking facilities of the two dissimilar ships. The joint mission was a complete success and it was planned that spacecraft of both countries would have common docking facilities allowing them to take part in cooperative programmes of space research. Preliminary discussions of a possible link-up between a future Salyut space station and an American space shuttle took place.

B. N. Petrov (1913–80), vice-president of the USSR Academy of Sciences and chairman of the Interkosmos Council (of socialist countries) stated that the USSR would 'continue the exploration of outer space, expand investigation of space facilities for the study of earth's natural resources–for meteorology, oceanography, navigation, communications and other needs of the national economy. The Soyuz-Salyut scientific complex is an excellent base for multipurpose research activities and for remote observation of our planet.'

Soviet designers have been suggesting the possibility of assembling larger space stations from 'plug-in' modules, using 'space tugs' to push the components together, and of a Soviet Kosmolyot (space plane) to ferry cosmonauts regularly between the Tyuratam-Baykonur cosmodrome and space stations. Apart from the utility of orbital stations as scientific outposts and 'space factories', Petrov expected them to become launch pads for flights to other planets. 'At these stations final adjustments can be made to spaceship systems; there will be training sessions and cosmonauts will be able to acclimatize to space conditions and participate in the assembly and inspection of interplanetary ships.'   *K.W.G.*

THE POLITICAL SYSTEM

Political ritual at the opening of the XXV Party Congress, 1976: Pioneers greet the CPSU leadership, delegates and foreign guests

The evolution of Marxism-Leninism

As defined in official Soviet theory, Marxism-Leninism is a comprehensive and scientific system of philosophical, social and political views constituting the world outlook of the working class and the Communist Party,★ and thus the ruling ideology of the USSR and all socialist states. Marxism-Leninism comprises a philosophical method (dialectical materialism), a theory of historical development (historical materialism), a critique of the political economy of capitalism, and a theory of the development of socialism and communism★ (scientific communism). Departing from the official terminology, Marxism-Leninism may be seen as consisting of three parts: a philosophical method, a set of doctrines laying down laws of social development, and an action programme derived from the above and continually modified in the light of changing political realities.

The materialist interpretation of the world and its historical development formulated by Heinrich Karl Marx (1818–83)–a German national of Jewish extraction–still constitutes the basis of the philosophical and doctrinal foundations of Marxism-Leninism. According to Marx, just as man's material situation determines his social, spiritual and political life, so the forces of production condition his relationship to his work as well as the class relations within society as a whole. Together these economic and social factors and relations (the base) largely condition the legal, religious, institutional and political superstructure. Historical development is generated by technological change rendering production relations outdated and thereby undermining the whole social and political edifice that perpetuates the power of the ruling exploitative class. The focus of Marxian analysis is on the process of change from capitalism to communism in which the conflict between the old and the emerging order is embodied in the class conflict between the bourgeoisie and the proletariat. As mounting endemic crises plague the capitalist economy and de-stabilize its political superstructure, so the proletariat grows in numbers, misery and revolutionary consciousness to become the prime force in the social revolution that ushers in the transition to communism. As the post-revolutionary system develops towards full communism, exploitation and all class antagonisms cease and their political counterpart, the State,★ rapidly gives way to self-administration. Marx stressed throughout his writings that no new system comes into existence without first ripening within the fully developed, and therefore conflict-ridden, framework of the preceding mode of production. Thus the proletarian revolution would not occur until capitalism had reached its highest stage of development.

As a Russian revolutionary Lenin★ was concerned primarily with the prospects for revolution not in developed capitalism but in a largely agrarian economy with a small capitalist sector and proletariat and with embryonic rather than fully mature bourgeois democratic institutions. Essentially, Lenin's contribution to the ideology consists of modifications in Marxian doctrine and the addition of an action programme designed to facilitate a Marxist revolution in

A granite statue of Karl Marx in central Moscow

Title-page of the first edition of the Russian translation of Karl Marx's *Das Kapital*, published in 1872

conditions of backwardness. Lenin invested social and economic backwardness with a new revolutionary potential by contending that the uneven development of capitalism meant that conflicts were often most exacerbated where advanced capitalism penetrated largely pre-capitalist social and political orders. Thus the 'weak links' in the capitalist chain could be the first to break. While retaining Marx's distinction between the bourgeois democratic and proletarian revolutions, Lenin greatly telescoped development between these two stages, insisting that the proletariat, allied with the peasantry, could hasten the end of the bourgeois phase and ensure an uninterrupted transition to the socialist revolution. The key to this whole process was the revolutionary party. Experience of the revolutionary movement in Russia and analysis of its lack of progress in Western Europe made Lenin highly sceptical about the proletariat's inherent revolutionary consciousness – in which Marx

had so much confidence. Left to themselves, workers under capitalism would develop a 'trade-union consciousness' that would restrict their demands to narrow economic bounds. Such 'spontaneous' development had to be avoided by means of a consciousness-building exercise mounted by a party of revolutionaries who alone could lead the workers to proletarian revolution. Lenin accordingly called for a small, highly-disciplined party of professional revolutionaries organized along democratic centralist* lines. All this had important repercussions for Lenin's elaboration of post-revolutionary development. Whereas Marx had only once distinguished between an initial and a higher stage of communism, Lenin drew a clear line between what he called socialism and communism. Communism broadly corresponded to Marx's definition: a classless, harmonious and self-governing society. The concept of socialism transformed what Marx had envisaged as a short transitional phase,

One of four million posters printed for the 50th anniversary of the October Revolution

in which social, economic and political inequalities and a state machine would continue to exist, into a fully-fledged stage of post-revolutionary development. Having to contend with the prospect of considerable opposition after the Revolution, Lenin made the proletarian state – the dictatorship of the proletariat – a central feature of the post-revolutionary order. His dictatorship of the proletariat emerged as a powerful, one-party-dominated state using all available means of coercion for a considerable time and persisting *qua* state for decades rather than the years or even months envisaged by Marx. The one factor that could shorten this long-drawn-out post-revolutionary development was world revolution, the prospects for which, Lenin argued, were altered by the expansion of imperialism. Colonialism prolonged the life of capitalism in imperialist countries but it harnessed the struggle for national liberation to the revolutionary cause.

The diminishing prospects of international revolution by the mid-1920s prompted Lenin's successor Stalin* to formulate the doctrine of 'socialism in one country' which declared that the Soviet Union could build socialism without external help. To justify his centralized and bureaucratic system of rule, Stalin extracted from Lenin's writings an official Leninism which emphasized their most authoritarian features and transformed many revolutionary expedients into dogmatic law. In so doing, Stalin changed Marx's and Lenin's varied revolutionary doctrine and strategy into the monolithic ruling ideology of Marxism-Leninism. This ideology centred on a militarized Communist Party which held a monopoly of political power reducing all other organizations to transmission belts for its policies and using bureaucratic and coercive methods to engineer rapid social and economic transformation. Egalitarianism* was

The changing of the guard at the Lenin Mausoleum

denounced and communism was reduced to the attainment of high levels of economic growth and material prosperity. In 1936 Stalin declared that the Soviet Union had achieved socialism 'in the main'; the paradoxical growth of coercive state power was justified by two purportedly dialectical insights. Stalin contended that the elimination of classes involved the intensification of class struggle and that the State would die away only by becoming stronger. Furthermore, it was declared that the State would continue to exist even under communism if the Soviet Union were still confronted with hostile capitalist governments. While the main body of Marxism-Leninism as codified under Stalin was left unchanged, these two additions were rescinded as part of the de-Stalinization* process. The replacement of 'capitalist encirclement' by 'peaceful coexistence' not only shifted relations with the West from out-and-out confrontation to ideological and economic competition, but also removed the major doctrinal justification for the persistence under socialism of coercive state power. According to the 1961 Party Programme, social unity had become sufficient for the dictatorship of the proletariat to be superseded by an 'all-people's state'. The Programme was itself the high spot of a general shift under Khrushchev* to a more dynamic and forward-looking ideology which minimized the importance of centralized bureaucratic control and emphasized the role of mass consciousness and participation in building a communist society based on material abundance, equality and self-government. A time-table was even established for this task which stipulated that the material and technical basis of communism would be created by 1970 and a communist society would have been built 'in the main' by 1980.

Khrushchev's specific undertakings about the timing of progress towards communism have been quietly forgotten by his more cautious successors. Since 1964 ideological innovation has been more sober and moderate than that of the Khrushchev period. Many of the concepts introduced by the 1961 Party Programme – notably the all-people's state – have been institutionalized by inclusion in the 1977 Constitution.* By far the most important ideological development since 1964 has been the adoption of the term 'developed socialism'* to define the current state of Soviet development. Advancement towards communism is now seen largely in terms of harnessing the power of the scientific and technological revolution to the cause of socialist progress by developing increasingly sophisticated and complex methods of management, administration and control. The Khrushchevian emphasis on the boundless potential of mass consciousness and participation has been replaced by the aim of steady progress under the leadership and management of the governmental and Party machines. Developed socialism typifies the conservative element in the current interpretation of Marxism-Leninism which has elevated institutional continuity and policy incrementalism to the level of ideological orthodoxy. *A.P.*

The role of ideology

According to Soviet commentators, Marxism-Leninism determines all aspects of Soviet development; guided by its principles the Communist Party* leads the USSR to its pre-ordained destination of communism.* However important the ideology may have been to Bolshevik* policies in the early post-revolutionary years, its influence has declined markedly since Stalin* made Marxism-Leninism into an instrument for justifying and extending his power at home and abroad. The action programme and parts of the doctrine have long been modified to close the frequent gap between Soviet theory and practice. Yet the salience of the ideology as the rationalization of policy should not be allowed to obscure its general role within the society. Marxism-Leninism is the language of political communication between the central authorities on the one hand and their hierarchical subordinates and the public on the other; the ideology provides the rationale and content for the effort to create a 'new Soviet man'.* Though it is difficult to evaluate the exact effect of official political socialization on leaders and masses, it is reasonable to assume that Marxist-Leninist doctrine has some impact on their values and outlook. In general policy, ideological doctrine can favour the pursuit of certain alternatives, such as the drive for atheism or the subordination of agricultural to industrial expansion. It can also disfavour the adoption of others – extension of private agriculture is a case in point – and can blinker politicians to the full significance of certain problems as well as to the most effective solutions. When, however, the requirements of political power loom large, apparent ideological constraints seem easily overcome. Overwhelmingly, inconsistencies between policy and Marxist-Leninist principles have been countered by an adjustment of the ideology – so much so that frequently political action seems to have been a guide to theory rather than vice versa. Yet the very fact that Marxism-Leninism is continually adjusted to fit policy betokens its operation as an authenticating and legitimating factor at several levels. Individual leaders strive to associate themselves with some notable 'advance' in Marxism-Leninism in order to enhance their standing. Incumbent leaderships make great efforts to present their achievements within the framework of progress towards ideologically set goals. Most importantly, Marxism-Leninism legitimizes the regime and the system in at least three ways: it perpetuates the political myths and symbols that underpin the revolutionary and progressive nature of the political system; it validates the Communist Party's claim to embody the interests of the working class and thereby of the whole of Soviet society; and lastly, the purportedly scientific nature of Marxism-Leninism lends the imprimatur of guaranteed success to the entire enterprise of building a communist society. *A.P.*

The concept of the State

Lenin* follows Marx* and Friedrich Engels (1820–95) in defining the State as an instrument of class oppression which withers away with the disappearance of class conflict and the growth of public self-administration. The fact that the dictatorship of the proletariat strengthened the power of the regime in the Soviet Union even after the declared advent of socialism in 1936 is explained in terms of the persistence of class conflict and an external capitalist threat. By the early 1960s both sources of tension had declined sufficiently to permit the supersession of the dictatorship of the proletariat by an 'all-people's state' – a concept making little sense in Marxist terms – which embodies the new organic unity of Soviet society under developed socialism.* No longer an instrument of class oppression, the all-people's state retains sufficient coercive capability to uphold the law and defend the USSR, the international socialist cause and world peace. Overwhelmingly, however, its functions now lie in education,* management* and administration. Far from this functional shift denoting a decline in state power and a commensurate increase in public self-administration, the growing scale, complexity and interdependence of economic, social and political affairs under developed socialism mean a strengthening and extension of the regime's managerial, administrative and coordinating powers. Even if the State is still scheduled to 'wither away' with the advent of communism in the Soviet Union and of socialism throughout the world, the current emphasis on its growing social and economic regulatory role makes this a distant and unlikely eventuality. *A.P.*

Democratic centralism

Originally formulated by Lenin* as the principle of Communist Party* organization, democratic centralism has long been applied throughout the political (and economic*) system. As defined in Article 3 of the 1977 Constitution,* the term comprises two democratic elements – the electivity of all bodies of state authority and their accountability to the people; and one centralist element – the obligation of lower bodies to obey the directives of higher ones. The Party rules (Article 19) and Soviet theorists add another centralist element – the strict subordination of the minority to the majority. Once a decision has been taken, no minority insubordination is permissible. It is claimed that democratic centralism makes possible the symbiosis of its constituent components which are seen as complementary rather than incompatible. The concept thus allows for the simultaneous strengthening of democracy and centralism while avoiding 'bureaucratic centralism' on the one hand and 'anarchistic lack of discipline' on the other. The logic of these claims rests on an assumption of pre-existing unity of objectives, outlook and method within the organizations involved and within society at large. In practice democratic centralism seems to ensure centralism in decision-making and to allow a measure of popular initiative and 'feedback' in implementation.   *A.P.*

Socialist democracy

Democracy is apprehended in terms of class content rather than abstract rights or political process. The claimed superiority of socialist democracy over its bourgeois counterpart is based on the absence of exploitation and class conflict and the provision, under these conditions, of social and economic rights that underpin civil and political liberties; the embodiment of workers', and thereby the public, interest in Communist Party* policy; effective, accountable and recallable representatives; and direct participation of the masses in social and state administration. The organic social unity of mature socialism supposedly marks a new and higher stage of socialist democracy, the further development of which is to be gauged (among other results) by increased popular sensibility of political involvement and efficacy as well as by higher levels of public participation in social and state bodies, particularly the soviets.*   *A.P.*

Developed socialism

The concept of developed socialism (*razvitoy sotsializm*) – mature socialism (*zrelyi sotsializm*) is a less-frequently used synonym – first appeared in official pronouncements in the late 1960s. Used by Brezhnev* at the XXIV Party Congress in 1971 to define the current stage of Soviet progress, developed socialism was established in this key role in the preamble to the 1977 Constitution.* The evolution of the Soviet system is now seen as falling into four phases: the transitional period (1917–36) when the material and technical basis for socialism was laid down; the building of a developed socialist society, completed in the early 1960s; the stage of development of mature socialism, during which the material and technical basis for a communist society is to be created (there is no official time-table for this but indications are that it may take more than 50 years); finally, the consummatory stage of communism.* Developed socialism can be seen as a convenient and useful way of registering and affirming the progress made since the proclaimed achievement of 'basic' socialism in 1936 without arousing undue expectation of the proximity of communism – hence the stress on the current stage as advanced

socialism rather than undeveloped communism. Just as the major reason for the introduction of the concept is supposedly the enormous headway made by the Soviet economy* since the late 1930s, so economic growth and modernization appear as the dominant characteristics of developed socialist society and the major factors of its further maturation. Central to this stage of Soviet growth is the scientific-technological* revolution. The successful development of mature socialism hinges on the effective harnessing of the modernizing forces of technology – to reinforce social unity and to help create the prerequisites for communism. Under developed socialism economic growth must be balanced, giving full weight to improving the standard of living and the general quality of life of the Soviet population. A similar emphasis on the social dimension of economic development emerges in discussions of planning* and management* which are considered key areas for improvement along lines indicated by 'systems theory'. Integrated social, economic and political management and control are seen as a major objective under developed socialism. Attainment of such integration is supposedly facilitated by the high levels of social, moral and political unity that characterize the 'new' community of the Soviet people. Such, it is argued, is the harmony of Soviet society at this stage that the Party* has become the vanguard not just of the working class but of the entire people and the dictatorship of the proletariat has been succeeded by the 'all-people's state'. The present concept of all-people's state (unlike Khrushchev's*) does not signal any diminution in state power. On the contrary, while developed socialism is associated with increasing public participation and growing socialist democracy,* the technical complexity and interdependence of mature socialist society mean increased guidance, organization and management by Party and government.   *A.P.*

Communism

Communism is the consummatory value of Marxism-Leninism and the culminating stage of society's development. Whereas socialism is based on the principle 'From each according to his ability, to each according to his work', communist society is founded on distribution according to need. This pre-supposes: an abundance of material wealth generated by extremely high levels of technology and organization; the elimination of differences of ownership, class and type of work (language and nationality difference will persist well into the communist period); and universal altruism, industry, devotion to the common weal. For the first time in history the individual is to be able to realize his full potential through his work and other community activity. Given social harmony and the inner-directed-ness of 'Communist man', the State and law are to become redundant and the whole system is to be administered by self-governing public bodies based on social organizations, notably the Communist Party. *A.P.*

The composition of the Party

Though the Communist Party of the Soviet Union (CPSU) is a very large organization in absolute numbers (17 480 000 on 1 January 1981), only a minority of Soviet citizens belong to it (just over 6 per cent of the total population and almost 10 per cent of adults. The largest category of members is that of 'white-collar' employees and professional people (*sluzhashchiye*) (43.8 per cent), while manual workers make up 43.4 and peasants on collective farms 12.8 per cent (1981 figures). These official Soviet figures are based on occupation at the time of joining the Party, and since membership is often followed by job promotion, considerably fewer members are currently manual workers and peasants than the percentages indicate. Serious efforts have been made to increase the number of manual workers in the post-Stalin years and their proportion has, indeed, gone up–mainly at the expense of the peasants (whose share in the population is also declining) and of those 'white-collar' workers performing the more routine tasks.

Virtually all posts of political responsibility in the country are held by Party members, and the same is true, to only a slightly lesser degree, of positions of influence in the economy, education and the mass media. In general, the greater the social and political significance of a job, the more certain it is to be held by a Party member. Something depends, though, upon the ideological significance of the profession–it is easier for a doctor, actor or natural scientist to make a mark in his profession without joining the Party (though even there Party membership is likely to help him in his career) than it is for an economist or historian. In general, the more education people have, and the higher their social position, the more likely they are to be Party members. In 1973, whereas only 7 per cent of those aged over 25 with no education beyond the eighth school class were Party members, this compared with 18 per cent of those with a completed secondary education, 31 per cent of those who had completed higher education, and 46 per cent of those with a higher degree.

Men greatly outnumber women within the Party, but the gap between them has been narrowing. By 1980 just over a quarter of members were women, whereas in 1966 they constituted just over a fifth of the membership. So far as national composition is concerned, of the 15 nationalities enjoying Union Republican status, only three– the Russians, the Georgians and the Armenians–have a proportion of members in the Party higher than their percentage of the population. Thus, in 1976, though Russians made up a little over half of the total Soviet population, they constituted over 60 per cent of the Party membership. The most 'over-represented' ethnic group is, however, that of the Jews* (who are classified as a nationality* in the Soviet Union). Though their territorial unit is no higher than an autonomous region (AR) (in which most Soviet Jews do not even live), there are more than twice as many Jews in the CPSU as their proportion of the population would warrant. This merely underlines the extent to which the Party recruits disproportionately from urban areas and from among well-educated specialists; it reflects the high level of urbanization and educational attainment of the Soviet Jewish population.

CPSU MEMBERSHIP IN THE FIFTEEN UNION REPUBLICS (1979)

Union Republic	Population		Party membership	
	thousand	*percentage*	*thousand*	*percentage*
Russian Republic (RSFSR)	137 552	52.41	10 339	61.83
Ukraine	49 757	18.95	2 808	16.79
Belorussia	9 559	3.64	561	3.35
Uzbekistan	15 391	5.86	534	3.19
Kazakhstan	14 685	5.59	702	4.19
Georgia	5 016	1.91	338	2.02
Azerbaijan	6 028	2.29	314	1.87
Lithuania	3 399	1.29	161	0.96
Moldavia	3 948	1.50	153	0.91
Latvia	2 521	0.96	154	0.92
Kirgizia	3 529	1.34	118	0.70
Tadzhikistan	3 801	1.44	104	0.62
Armenia	3 031	1.15	156	0.93
Turkmenia	2 759	1.05	87	0.52
Estonia	1 466	0.55	93	0.55

Source: Based on information in *Ezhegodnik Bol'shoy sovetskoy entsiklopedii 1979*, Moscow, 1979

The incidence of Party membership varies considerably from one Union Republic to another. Only the RSFSR and Georgia are over-represented among Union Republics, while Estonia breaks even (but not Estonians, for Russians in the Estonian republic contribute disproportionately to CPSU membership there). Many factors influence the varying proportions of Party membership between republics, including levels of urbanization and industrialization, the numbers of qualified professional people and the age structure. Thus, the higher proportion of children in the Central Asian republics helps to account for the low incidence of Party membership there. *A.H.B.*

The structure of the Party

The Party rules state that the guiding principle of the Party's organizational structure is democratic centralism.* Sometimes described by Party theorists as 'centralism of a new type', this doctrine is, in principle, open to more than one interpretation but in practice has generally been used to justify a high degree of centralization within the Party.

The formal Party structure set out in the rules places the Congress at the top of the hierarchy as the supreme organ of the CPSU. Party Congresses are indeed generally important events. They require long and careful preparation, are frequently the occasion of major policy pronouncements and guidelines, and the Congress delegates formally elect a new Central Committee and Central Auditing Commission. Congresses usually last for approximately ten days but are convened only once in five years. This infrequency of meeting –

quite apart from the degree to which Congress agendas and decisions are controlled from above by the Party leadership – means that the Congress, by definition, cannot act as the supreme policy-making body within the Party on a day-to-day basis. Those tasks fall to the Central Committee and especially to its inner bodies, the Politburo and the Secretariat of the Central Committee.

At all levels of the Party hierarchy except the lowest, the organization follows the territorial structure of the country. Thus there are Union Republican Party organizations, with their own five-yearly Congresses, their Central Committees and Secretariats and their inner (directing) bodies, the bureaux – these being functionally equivalent at that level to the Politburo at the all-Union level. The one exception is the Russian republic, which is so large in population and territory that it does not elect a separate Congress and Central Committee, but is simply the predominant part of the all-Union Party organization and a disproportionately large supplier of members of the Politburo, Secretariat and apparatus of the Central Committee.

POWER STRUCTURE WITHIN THE COMMUNIST PARTY OF THE SOVIET UNION

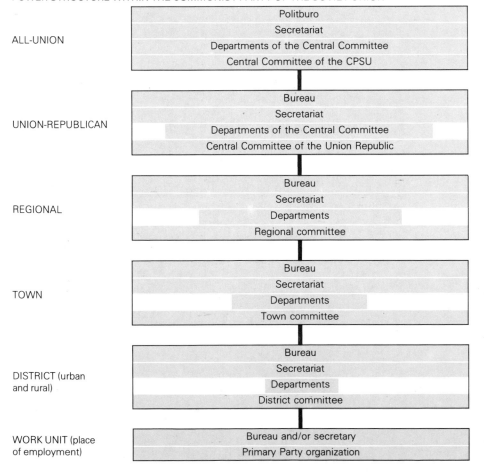

ALL-UNION	Politburo
	Secretariat
	Departments of the Central Committee
	Central Committee of the CPSU
UNION-REPUBLICAN	Bureau
	Secretariat
	Departments of the Central Committee
	Central Committee of the Union Republic
REGIONAL	Bureau
	Secretariat
	Departments
	Regional committee
TOWN	Bureau
	Secretariat
	Departments
	Town committee
DISTRICT (urban and rural)	Bureau
	Secretariat
	Departments
	District committee
WORK UNIT (place of employment)	Bureau and/or secretary
	Primary Party organization

This chart naturally simplifies reality. It deliberately omits the Party Congress since it portrays the real power structure rather than the formal hierarchy of Party institutions. It perforce leaves out a number of Party institutions, such as, for example, the Committee of Party Control* and the Central Auditing Commission* as well as the Party organizations in Autonomous Republics and autonomous areas (AA) (the latter to be found within the RSFSR) and the autonomous regions (AR) which exist within only four out of 15 Union Republics. Town Party organizations are shown as subordinate to the regional Party organization. That is the general pattern, but some cities are so important that they come under direct Union-Republican Party subordination, while Moscow is responsible to the Central Committee at all-Union level. The indentation of 'departments' in the chart indicates their greater number at all-Union Central Committee level and their declining number down the Party hierarchy

Regions, cities, towns and districts each have their committees, the leading members of whom compose the bureaux, and the power of the Party organization reflects the importance of the territorial unit. At the lowest level come the primary Party organizations which are based upon workplace rather than residence.

The Politburo
The Party is not simply one political institution but an entire complex of institutions, the most powerful of which is the Political Bureau of the Central Committee (or Politburo), a body charged in the Party rules with the direction of the work of the Party between plenary sessions of the Central Committee. Since the Central Committee normally meets only twice a year – for a day or two each time – and the Politburo meets once, and sometimes twice, weekly (most Thursdays and some Tuesdays), it is clear that it is intended to be a more effective policy-making organ than the larger body, the Central Committee,

A Soviet poster of the Politburo, showing full members followed by candidate members, early 1980

which nominally elects it. Recruitment to the Politburo is in reality a process of collective cooption, whereby the Central Committee is called upon to ratify changes within its inner body which have already been agreed by a majority of existing Politburo members. The compact size of the Politburo–14 full members and eight candidate, or non-voting, members (in 1981)–is also suited to its role of principal policy-making organ within the Party. It devotes much attention to foreign policy and current international affairs, but is also the ultimate court of appeal for all matters of domestic policy– including economic ones–which cannot be settled by the Presidium of the Council of Ministers★ or within the apparatus of the Central Committee. Soviet posters portraying the Party leadership put full Politburo members in the first place, followed by candidate members of the Politburo and then by Secretaries of the Central Committee who lack Politburo membership; powerful though the Secretariat is, a move from that body to the Politburo is recognized as promotion.

The Secretariat of the Central Committee
The Secretaries of the Central Committee are in over-all charge of the

ПОЛИТБЮРО ЦК КПСС

M. A. Suslov, veteran Politburo member and CPSU Secretary

Party apparatus, acting as overlords to the various departments of the Central Committee, and having themselves considerable powers of appointment and in execution of policy. There is a substantial overlap between membership of the Politburo and that of the Secretariat. The Secretariat is the smaller of the two bodies; it had ten members in 1981, of whom five were full members of the Politburo and one was a candidate member. It is the practice, however, even for those Secretaries of the Central Committee who are not Politburo members to attend Politburo meetings in addition to the weekly Wednesday meetings of the Secretariat. Within the Politburo only those Secretaries who are also full Politburo members have a vote and it is this possession of a vote and a powerful voice within both of these inner bodies of the Central Committee which makes them, along with their Politburo colleague who is Chairman of the Council of Ministers, the most important members of the 26-man Party leadership. (Taking full and candidate members of the Politburo and Secretaries of the Central Committee together, they numbered 26 in 1981 and were all men. Only one woman has ever attained Politburo membership, Ye. A. Furtseva (1910–74) from 1957 to 1961.) A long-standing member of both Politburo and Secretariat acquires great power within the system: a notable example is M.A. Suslov (b.1902) who joined both bodies in the 1950s and was still a leading figure within them in 1981.

The General Secretary

Among the Secretaries of the Central Committee who enjoy Politburo status, the most powerful single figure, who has the advantage of chairing both Politburo and Secretariat, is the General Secretary of the Central Committee. Stalin,* after Lenin's* death, used the General Secretaryship to acquire a dictatorial position by the 1930s and for at least the last 15 years of his life he was more powerful than the rest of the Politburo put together. Khrushchev,* who held this office (designated the First Secretaryship from 1953 to 1966) from 1953 until 1964, and Brezhnev* (1964 onwards) never attained or aspired to the power of a Stalin, but the fact that they wielded a greater power than any other individual within the leadership is demonstrated by the number of personal protégés they were able to place within the Secretariat and Politburo and (at least in Khrushchev's case) by success in pushing through policies which were viewed with scepticism or alarm by colleagues. The General Secretary's wide power of appointment in relation to the Secretariat, and the fact that his voice counts for more than any other on promotions to the Politburo, set him apart from his colleagues, even though the modern General Secretary is far from being a personal dictator of the Stalin type.

Departments of the Central Committee

The apparatus of the Central Committee–party functionaries responsible to the Secretariat and Politburo–is divided among more than 20 departments. Some of these are peculiar to the Party and have no counterpart in the ministerial network. Thus, for example, the Department for Party Organizational Work monitors lower Party organs and selects candidates for Party offices, while the General Department acts as a secretariat to the Politburo and to the General Secretary in particular. Other departments act as Party watchdogs and overlords of a number of state institutions. Thus, the Department for Science and Education has within its purview such important ministries and quasi-ministerial bodies as the Ministry of Education, the Ministry of Higher and Secondary Specialized Education, the State Committee for Science and Technology and the Academy of Sciences, while the important Department for Administrative Organs supervises such sensitive state institutions as the KGB,* the Ministry of Internal Affairs (MVD), the Ministry of Defence, the Procuracy* and the Supreme Court. Heads of departments of the Central Committee are less well-known figures within the Soviet Union than ministers, but they exercise a power at least as great as that of the average minister. Even though a minister is more often a full member of the Central Committee than is the Committee's departmental head, a ministry will seldom contemplate taking a policy initiative without first consulting its corresponding Central Committee department. The departments themselves are sub-divided into sections and though the number of employees in these various sections is not officially made known, the best estimates suggest that the Central Committee apparatus comprises some 1500 responsible officials (excluding clerks and others in routine work).

Since the Politburo and Secretariat at their regular meetings do not have the time to consider a wide range of policy issues in depth, officials in the apparatus who prepare the papers for these meetings have a very important influence on the policies adopted. Moreover, only a minority of matters requiring a decision can be passed upwards to the top Party leadership; many decisions are made by departmental officials acting in the name of the Central Committee.

The Central Committee
The Central Committee, which has gradually grown in size over the years, is elected at Party Congresses, but 'election' here means that the delegates merely approve a list of names prepared in advance by the Party leadership. At the XXVI Party Congress in 1981 319 full members and 151 candidate members were thus elected to the Central Committee. Since the latter attend Central Committee sessions (though they may not vote), these become large gatherings of over 400 people. The proceedings of the Central Committee are not published in full–often only the broad subject of discussion and the names of the speakers are made public. It would appear, though, that fairly frank speeches are made and some criticism is voiced at these meetings. The infrequency of the sessions (twice a year and seldom lasting longer than a day at a time) suggests, however, that the advantages Central Committee membership bestows upon a prominent Party member do not lie primarily in the opportunity to attend plenary sessions but rather in a greater authority within the system (whether the member is, for instance, a minister or regional Party secretary) and a greater access to high-level political information (between, as well as at, Central Committee meetings).

The Party rules accord the Central Committee a place in the political system second only to that of the Congress. Article 34 states that 'between Congresses, the Central Committee ... directs the entire activity of the Party and its local bodies, selects and appoints leading functionaries, directs the work of central government bodies and public organizations of working people through the Party groups in them, sets up various Party organs, institutions and enterprises and directs their activities, appoints the editors of the central newspapers and journals operating under its control, and distributes the funds of the Party budget and controls its execution.' This is a formidable array of powers, but in practice they are exercised mainly by the Politburo, the Secretariat and the various departments of the Central Committee apparatus. The elected members of the Central Committee are, however, the people who have the greatest responsibility for implementing Party policy throughout the length and breadth of the Soviet Union. Many important posts automatically entail Central Committee membership. This is true, for instance, of the First Secretaries of Union Republics and of the heads of the major ministries and state committees. There are also always some leading representatives of the military, the security forces, science

and the cultural establishment. The largest single category of Central Committee members is, however, that of the regional party secretaries and one of the best indications of the political and economic importance of a region (as perceived by the Party leadership) is whether its regional first secretary is a full member, candidate member or non-member of the Central Committee. Once a Party secretary or minister has been elected to the Central Committee, this strengthens his political standing and influence in his everyday dealings, though it by no means gives him a completely free hand. Even Central Committee members are subject to Party discipline and must keep their criticisms within the bounds permitted by Party convention.

Though, for the most part, the Central Committee as a whole accepts the guidance and policy initiatives of its 'inner' leadership, the Politburo and Secretariat, its formal superiority to the latter bodies–according to the CPSU rules–is not always a mere formality. In two leadership crises (1957 and 1964) the Central Committee in plenary session determined the fate of Khrushchev. On the first occasion they supported him against a Politburo majority (the so-called anti-Party group* crisis) and on the second they concurred with the overwhelming majority of the Politburo who had decided that the time was ripe to remove Khrushchev. These demonstrations of the latent power of the Central Committee evidently encouraged Khrushchev's successors–both Brezhnev and his Politburo colleagues–to take into account the known views or likely reactions of Central Committee members when formulating policy.

The Central Auditing Commission
The Central Auditing Commission is elected at Party Congresses at the same time as the Central Committee. This conveys a somewhat inflated idea of its importance. It is charged with supervising Party finances and auditing accounts–not inconsequential functions, but not to be compared with the political significance of Central Committee membership. Election to the Commission is a kind of consolation prize for Party worthies who have not quite attained Central Committee status.

The Committee of Party Control
This body is charged with ensuring that Party discipline is observed and with taking action against members who deviate from the Party line. One of the most important functions of the Control Committee is to consider appeals against decisions to expel, or in other ways discipline, Party members made by the Central Committees of Union Republican Party organizations or by regional committees. The Committee of Party Control is not independent of the will of the Party leadership and will automatically align itself against any member who has incurred their wrath. It can, however, act more judicially in cases of high-handed action by lower Party committees.

Republican and local Party organs

Union Republican Party organs–the bureau and secretariat, the Central Committee and its departments–are in duty bound to implement the broad lines of policy laid down by the all-Union Party leadership, in accordance with the principle of democratic centralism. In the post-Stalin years, however, they have paid increasing heed to the sensibilities of the major nationalities* within each republic. Thus, more than in Stalin's day, it is now usual for the First Secretary of a Union Republic to belong to the major indigenous nationality of that republic, though the Second Secretary is generally a Russian. The republican Party leadership has to steer a careful course in attempting to satisfy its superiors in Moscow and at the same time defend the distinctive interests of the republic. Any republican leader held to be insufficiently firm in combating local nationalism– as distinct from fostering an all-Soviet patriotism–finds himself in trouble. Thus, for instance, one of the main charges against P.E. Shelest (b.1908), when he was replaced as First Secretary in the Ukraine by V.V. Shcherbitsky (b.1918) in 1972, was that he had been indulgent to Ukrainian nationalism.

In addition to 14 Union Republican Central Committees, there were within the Party (in 1980) 165 Party committees of regional or higher status. The first secretary of an *obkom* (regional committee) is one of the key figures in the Party hierarchy. The regions are very large–about the size of states in the USA–and the *obkom* secretary exercises great power within his area. He is, in a sense, the successor to the pre-revolutionary provincial governor. Plenary sessions of the regional committee have to be held at least three times a year, but as usual most of the work is done by the bureau, the regional secretariat and the apparatus in the departments of the regional Party organization. Regional Party conferences are held every two or three years.

Below the regions come 862 town Party committees and 616 urban district and 2868 rural district committees (1980 figures). Town and district committees meet at least four times a year and convene a conference every two or three years. Again the decisive inner bodies are the bureaux of the Party committees and their secretariats with their staff of full-time functionaries.

Primary Party organizations

The primary Party organizations are described in the Party rules as 'the basis of the Party' and though they are the lowest rung of its hierarchy, they play a decisive role in making the Party 'the leading and guiding force of Soviet society and the nucleus of its political system' (Article 6 of the 1977 Soviet Constitution*). The 414 000 primary Party organizations (in 1981) are formed at the workplaces of Party members–factories, state and collective farms, army units, educational institutions, offices. Wherever there are not fewer than three Party members, a primary organization may be formed. (A few

are organized on the residential principle in villages and housing settlements.) It is the task of members to ensure that Party policy is enacted in their workplace; as the primary organization almost invariably includes within its membership the leading personnel of the establishment in question (who are thereby bound by Party discipline), this greatly reduces the risk of its adopting an independent line, one contradictory to the wishes of the Party leadership. The significance of this is especially apparent in the case of units of the armed forces* and of the security* police who, given the coercive force at their command, could threaten the Soviet leadership and the nature of the system if they were not kept under Party control by the primary organizations and by other means, such as the *nomenklatura*.*

Party meetings of members of the primary organization must, according to the Party rules, be convened at least once a month. In the larger organizations (generally those with over 300 members) a Party committee is formed; the smaller have only a bureau as their inner body; the smallest (with fewer than 15 members) do not elect even a bureau, but only a secretary and deputy secretary. The secretary of the larger primary organizations is usually a full-time, salaried Party functionary, but those with fewer than 150 members generally have a part-time secretary rather than a salaried official released from other work within the institution. Among the major functions of the primary organizations listed by the Party rules are: admission of new members to the CPSU; education of members in a spirit of loyalty to the Party cause; organization of the study of Marxist-Leninist* theory; the enhancement of the vanguard role of the Party within the enterprise; organizing 'the working people in the performance of the current tasks of communist construction'; conducting agitational and propaganda* work among the people; and combating bureaucratism, parochialism and violations of state discipline.

The apparatus

A much greater power is wielded within the Party by its full-time employees–its secretaries and the staff of the departments at various levels of the hierarchy–than by the Party member who combines membership with another job. The term, apparatus (*apparat*) is applied to these full-time Party functionaries. Soviet sources do not give precise information on the size of the professional apparatus, but out of a Party membership of over 17 million it seems likely that this is somewhere between 100 000 and 150 000.   *A.H.B.*

The individual Party member

The primary Party organization* has no more important task than that of recruiting individuals to Party membership. Citizens are eligible to be considered for this from the age of 18. Applicants must submit recommendations from three Party members of at least five years' standing who have worked with the applicant, professionally or socially, for at least one year. The vast majority of contemporary recruits come via the Komsomol* and in their case a recommendation from the district or city committee of the Komsomol is required and is regarded as equivalent to the recommendation of one Party member. Once a membership proposal has been accepted by the general meeting of the primary organization, it requires the endorsement also of the district Party committee (or of the town committee in towns not large enough to be divided into districts). This is followed by a probationary year as a candidate member of the Party, during which the applicant must demonstrate the necessary personal qualities and political reliability. In its selection the primary organization must bear in mind the current priorities that the Party leadership have laid down in their membership policy. At various times, there have been drives to change the membership ratio among social groups, between the sexes, or to alter the age structure. In recent years, for example, there has been an emphasis on increasing the proportion of working-class members and of women.

Party members have to pay monthly membership dues. These range from a nominal 10 kopecks a month for those with very low earnings (less than 50 roubles a month) to 3 per cent of the income of those earning over 300 roubles a month. Motives for wishing to join vary. Some are prompted partly by an idealistic desire to serve the community and motherland through the Party. For those of orthodox social and political views, Party membership is, moreover, an honour and a privilege. For anyone with political ambitions, it is a necessary first step; the aspiring political decision-maker considers that he will have no influence outside the Party. Membership also opens the way to further privileges,* such as easier access to foreign travel. Probably most significant for a majority of would-be joiners, membership helps the individual in his own career, even if it is not overtly a political one; the Party member is more likely to get promotion to responsible posts.

Since the Party has allotted to itself a vanguard role in Soviet society, by no means all who wish to join its ranks are given the opportunity to do so. But it is worth noting that not all citizens desire Party membership. There are those holding critical political views – by no means confined to the active dissidents* – who do not wish to associate themselves with Party policy. Of greater numerical significance, however, are those governed by political apathy; while most such non-joiners regard themselves as loyal Soviet citizens, they have other uses for their spare time than attendance at Party meetings or propaganda work. For Party membership does make demands upon time (as well as money). The Party is also more interested in the views and life-style of its members; a person may thus feel less of a free agent within the Party than outside it. *A.H.B.*

The *nomenklatura*

One of the principal ways in which the Party exercises its 'leading role' and keeps other institutions, as well as individuals, in order is through its control over careers. There is a general sense in which every Soviet citizen's career prospects are furthered or damaged, depending upon whether or not he is in good or poor standing with his proximate Party organs. More specifically, however, there is the institution of *nomenklatura*, which consists both of a list of people who are regarded as competent and politically reliable – and suitable, therefore, for appointment to one of a number of responsible posts – and a list of posts considered to be of such political or social importance that they come under the supervision of a particular Party committee – whether the Central Committee* of the CPSU or a Party committee at local level. The posts concerned, ranging from ministerial office and newspaper editorships to factory managerships and headships of institutes and schools, can be filled only with the confirmation of a specific Party organ. Such approval is often a formality, but it is yet another available power in the Party's hands which helps to ensure that the institutions which make up the CPSU maintain their dominant position in relation to other institutions within the Soviet system. *A.H.B.*

The Young Octobrists

The Young Octobrists (*Oktyabryata*) came into existence in 1923–4 to cater for children aged between 7, when formal schooling commences, and 9 years. The organization essentially prepares them for admission into the Pioneers* at the age of 10; based upon groups of five each under the direction of a Pioneer or younger Komsomol* member, it has its own set of rules which enjoin members to study well, be honest and truthful, and live happily together. Young Octobrists wear a five-pointed lapel badge showing Lenin* as a boy. Two national publications, *Veselye kartinki* (*Merry Pictures*) and *Murzilka*, are produced for this age-group, as are comparable republican journals in the major Soviet languages. *S.W.*

The Pioneers

Immediately senior to the Young Octobrists,* the Pioneers caters for young people aged 10–14/15 years. It was founded in 1922 as an auxiliary to the Komsomol* and also to displace the pre-revolutionary scouting organizations; its central council comes under the over-

all direction of the Komsomol. All schoolchildren of the appropriate age may join if accepted by their local Pioneer organization (based upon school or place of residence), and virtually all who are eligible do so. Entrants must take the Pioneer oath, respect the Pioneer Laws in such matters as truth, courtesy and patriotism, and may wear the red Pioneer neckerchief, its three corners representing the unity of Pioneers, Komosomol and Communists. According to the Komsomol statute, and jointly with the school, the organization must bring up its members as 'convinced fighters for the Communist Party cause, inculcate in them a love of labour and of knowledge, [and] assist the formation of the younger generation in the spirit of communist consciousness and morality'. Pioneers hold regular meetings to discuss both organizational matters and recent films, books or other subjects; they also parade on important occasions, arrange visits to local places with revolutionary or military associations, and hold summer camps. The national twice-weekly Pioneer paper, *Pionerskaya pravda* (*Pioneer Truth*), produced an average of 8.9 mllion copies per issue during 1978; 27 other republican and regional newspapers cater for this age-group as well as a comparable number of periodicals. The orgaization had about 25 million members in 1979.   *S.W.*

Above: a depiction of Lenin as a child on the wall of a youth camp in Belorussia. Below: a parade of young Pioneers in a provincial town

The Komsomol

The Komsomol (All-Union Leninist Communist Union of Youth–VLKSM), the youth organization senior to the Pioneers,* is the most important, catering for those aged 14–28 years. It was founded in 1918 as an auxiliary to the Communist Party (CPSU)* itself, and throughout its history it has been closely controlled by the Party and subordinated to its purposes. Komsomol members, for instance, took part in the civil war* and in the industrialization and collectivization* drives of the late 1920s and 1930s, and many members were prominent in the armed forces and partisan resistance during the Second World War (when the organization won the first of its Orders of Lenin). Total membership has grown regularly over this whole period and is steadily increasing – 21 000 in 1918, 10.5 million in 1950, over 38 million in 1979 (about 70 per cent of the population within the relevant age-group). More than 150 million people have at some time been members.

The structure of the Komsomol closely parallels that of the CPSU. Members are admitted by one of the primary Komsomol organizations, of which there were 433 500 at various places of work and study in 1979, and have the right to elect representatives to successive levels of the hierarchy above them, at each of which a committee or bureau is elected to run day-to-day activities. At the apex is the Congress of the Komsomol, meeting once every five years, which elects a central committee that is supposed to meet not less often than once every six months. This in turn elects a bureau and a secretariat to guide the work of the organization between its meetings, and also a First Secretary (B. N. Pastukhov was elected in 1978). Like the CPSU, the Komsomol functions on the basis of democratic centralism,* a principle which ensures that there is little effective opposition to firm and even authoritarian central leadership.

According to its statute, the Komsomol 'helps the Party to educate youth in the communist spirit, to draw it into the work of building a new society [and] to train a rising generation of harmoniously developed people who will live and work and administer public affairs under communism'. Komsomol members are encouraged to further their political education and to take an active part in socio-political life. More than 46 million in this age-group, for instance, were reported to have participated in the discussion of the draft Soviet Constitution* in 1977, and young people aged under 30 made up 32.4 per cent of the deputies elected to local soviets* in 1977 and 21.1 per cent of those elected to the USSR Supreme Soviet* in 1979. Komsomol members also assist in major industrial projects and in harvesting; meetings are held with Revolution and war veterans; tourist groups are dispatched abroad and received into the USSR through the organization's travel agency 'Sputnik'; and regular sporting* events are sponsored. Komsomol members enjoy some preference in admissions into the CPSU (more than 70 per cent of Party recruits in recent years have come through the Komsomol, although this represents only a small proportion of all Komsomol members); Komsomol membership and service are factors considered relevant to employment and higher educational admission and awards. The organization owns three publishing houses in Moscow (Molodaya Gvardiya), Kiev and Tashkent; it publishes the daily newspaper *Komsomol'skaya pravda* (*Komsomol Truth*) and 233 other newspapers and journals in 26 different languages of the USSR.   *S.W.*

The evolution of Soviet federalism

The USSR is the world's largest and most heterogenous multinational state, comprising over 100 nationalities grouped in 15 Union Republics and 38 subordinate autonomous units, and claims officially to be the first state to have solved the problems of multinationalism; despite such claims, the whole nationalities question remains one of the most serious problems facing the Soviet leadership. The universal difficulties of integrating nationalities with such different cultures and traditions are compounded by the somewhat contradictory institutional and policy framework within which Soviet nation-building takes place. Official policy legitimizes the existence of distinct national groups and the federal structure provides an institutional base for their development. At the same time, the legacy of imperial Russia,* the centralism of the Soviet state and the Russians' numerical, economic and political hegemony within the USSR make it difficult to separate Soviet integration from assimilationist Russification.

Lenin* supported national self-determination as a force which undermined the tsarist empire, but he adopted federalism very late in the day and then only as a temporary solution to accommodate buoyant nationalist movements. If the Bolsheviks'* declaration of December 1917 on national self-determination aroused hopes of national autonomy under socialist rule, the civil war* brought back the harsh realities of Russian domination. In 1918 all the nationalities within Russia were bound together in a highly centralized Russian Socialist Federative Soviet Republic (RSFSR), which corresponded to Stalin's* concept of regional federalism envisaged as a brief stage along the road to a unitary state. Ukrainian and Georgian attempts to diverge from this course and establish truly independent Soviet republics were crushed by the Red Army* in 1920–1. Troubled by such use of force and the attendant dangers of Great Russian chauvinism, Lenin pressed for a federation of sovereign republics. His ideas were reflected in the Union of Soviet Socialist Republics (USSR) established by treaty in December 1922 and confirmed in the 1924 Constitution.* Given the economic and political supremacy of the RSFSR, the other republics—the Ukraine, Belorussia and the Transcaucasian Soviet Federative Republic which united Georgia, Armenia and Azerbaijan until 1936—were equals in name only.

The 1920s saw some genuine attempts to implement the 'national in form, socialist in content' approach and to encourage the development of national identities and cultures under local leaderships. Stalin's social and economic revolution engulfed such policies while the purges of 1934–8 destroyed local élites. The elaboration of a fully-fledged federal system in the 1936 Constitution struck a discordant note in a chorus of mounting Russification reinforced by the Second World War: Soviet patriotism became indistinguishable from Great Russian nationalism, an identification that persisted until Stalin's death.

De-Stalinization* brought condemnation of the worst excesses of forced assimilation, including the deportation in 1943–6 of seven small nationalities from their homelands on grounds of their doubtful loyalty in wartime. The more tolerant political climate and economic decentralization of the early Khrushchev* period encouraged pressures for greater republican autonomy, which in turn prompted a reassertion of central controls. Khrushchev's fall in 1964 was followed by a wide-ranging debate on federalism in which two major schools of thought emerged, each claiming to expound 'true' Leninist policies. The federalist school advocated the recognition of the federal system as the framework for a gradual drawing together of nationalities while the assimilationists pressed for the phasing-out of federal structures and the accelerated fusion of all groups into one

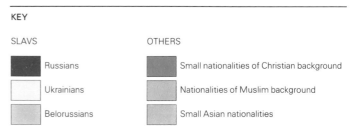

KEY

SLAVS

■ Russians

□ Ukrainians

▨ Belorussians

OTHERS

■ Small nationalities of Christian background

□ Nationalities of Muslim background

▨ Small Asian nationalities

Crossbars indicate heavy intermixture of two or more nationalities without clear predominance of either.
Source: J. A. Armstrong, *Ideology, Politics and Government in the Soviet Union*, London, 1974

PROXIMITY OF NATIONALITIES IN THE USSR

Soviet nation. The persistence of such differences of opinion within academic and political circles greatly prolonged the gestation period of the 1977 Constitution,★ which came down between the two positions. While the federal structure of the 1936 Constitution emerged almost unscathed, the new Constitutional recognition of the existence of 'the Soviet people' (*sovetskiy narod*) was a gain for the assimilationists. In nationality policy, the Brezhnev★ leadership has pursued a pragmatic course, combining flexible if firm central control over the republics with a tough response to any signs of nationalist insubordination.   *A.P.*

The federal structure

Soviet federalism is nationality-based, its major administrative divisions corresponding to the territories occupied by national groups united by ethnicity, language, culture and tradition. These divisions fall into three groups–Union Republics, Autonomous Republics (ASSR) and autonomous regions (AR) and areas (AA)–which constitute the upper tiers of the territorial-administrative structure. By far the most important group is that of the 15 Union Republics, each covering the homeland of a major historical nationality which thereby enjoys nation status. With the exception of the Kirgiz★ and Kazakhs,★ the titular nationalities constitute a large majority of each republic's population.★ All Union Republics are, in principle, sovereign states, complete with their own constitutions, Supreme Soviets, Councils of Ministers and Supreme Courts. Located as they all are on the borders of the USSR, the republics have a constitutional right to secede from the Union, a right which is unique to Soviet federalism. The secession right has never been more than a symbol of the supposed voluntary nature of the Union.

Twenty of the smaller nationalities inhabiting areas within Union Republics enjoy ASSR status, while a further 18 are accorded the lower level of AR or AA. Thirty-one of the 38 divisions below Union Republic level are situated within the RSFSR, which covers two-thirds of the area and includes over half the population of the Soviet Union. ASSRs are not sovereign states but otherwise are smaller versions of the Union Republics. The AR and AA are distinguished from the ordinary administrative region (oblast) or territory (kray) by the official standing of their local language and their right to elect deputies to the Soviet of Nationalities, which comprises deputies from the various levels within the federation (32 per Union Republic, 11 per ASSR, 5 per AR and one per AA).

An examination of the constitutional division of powers between the national (all-Union) and republican level indicates the highly centralized nature of Soviet federalism. Predictably, defence, state security, foreign trade and national foreign policy come exclusively under all-Union jurisdiction. All-Union bodies also possess all-embracing powers over the country's social, economic and political development as well as the dangerously vague right to 'resolve . . . other questions of all-Union importance' (Article 73 of the Constitution★). Perhaps most important is the fact that the whole federal structure is set within a system based on democratic centralism★ and ruled by a highly centralized unitary Communist Party.★ Given this context, it comes as no surprise to find that all-Union laws prevail constitutionally over republican legislation and that the all-Union government is empowered to countermand and override actions taken by its republican counterparts.

On paper, the Union Republics have the right to enter into relations with foreign states, but none of them has anything resembling a foreign policy distinct from that of the USSR. In all major domestic sectors the republics' main role is to ensure that all-Union policies are effectively implemented. Republics do, however, have some say in the use of capital investments in the sectors over which their governments exercise jurisdiction. They also formulate republican economic plans and can exercise some influence over

TERRITORIAL ADMINISTRATIVE STRUCTURE OF THE USSR

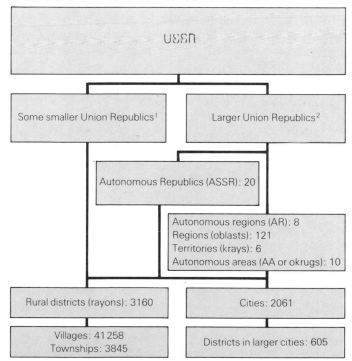

¹Lithuania, Moldavia, Latvia, Armenia, Estonia
²RSFSR, Ukraine, Belorussia, Uzbekistan, Kazakhstan, Turkmenia, plus the smaller Georgia, Azerbaijan, Kirgizia, Tadzhikistan
Source: based on information in D. Zlatopolsky, *State System of the USSR*, Moscow, n.d. and *Ezhegodnik Bol'shoy Sovetskoy Entsiklopedii*, Moscow, 1979

their planning committees convey to the centre. Republican governments have the right to be consulted on any economic policies that affect their area and reportedly use these rights to some effect. Financially, the republics are heavily dependent on the centre. Since 1960 the proportion of republican as against all-Union expenditure has risen, and republics have more control over how the money is spent; nonetheless, their budgets remain constrained by all-Union budgetary directives and their revenues continue to be tightly controlled by Moscow.

Perhaps the clearest picture of all-Union and republican powers is provided by the division of ministerial responsibilities. Two kinds of ministries* exist at the centre: the all-Union and the Union-Republican. The all-Union ministries and state committees* exercise direct and sole control from Moscow over the most strategically important sectors of the economy.* Union-Republican ministries operate at central and republican levels, with a head office in Moscow and branches in all republican capitals which come under 'dual subordination', being responsible to the republican Council of Ministers which appoints them, and obliged to implement all directives issued by their direct administrative superiors in Moscow.

The downward exercise of power is reinforced by the subordination of all republican Councils of Ministers to their all-Union counterpart and by the direct administration from Moscow of some key enterprises and institutions. Union-Republican ministries operate in sectors where jurisdiction is shared between all-Union and republican levels. The areas concerned include agriculture, finance, light industry, trade and nearly all the non-economic spheres of governmental activity: such as justice, the police, health, culture, and secondary, specialized and higher education. Similarly, the great majority of state committees are of the Union-Republic type

KEY

Autonomous Republic (ASSR)

Autonomous region (AR)

Autonomous area (AA)

Source: after P.E. Lydolph, *Geography of the USSR*, Elkhart Lake, 1979

NATIONALITY-BASED TERRITORIAL ADMINISTRATIVE DIVISIONS OF THE USSR

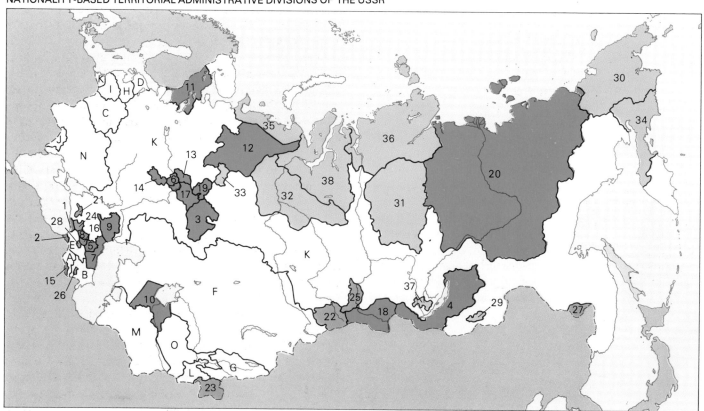

and cover areas such as economic planning, material and technical supply and labour.

Last and least, there are republican ministries and state committees which exist only at republic level and are responsible solely to the republican Council of Ministers. Each republic has five or six such ministries–compared with over 20 Union-Republican ministries–covering areas such as road construction, retail trade, local industry, housing and social services all of which fall within exclusive republican jurisdiction and correspond broadly to local government responsibilities in Western states. *A.P.*

The 15 Union Republics and the 38 autonomous units within them

UNION REPUBLICS (SSR)

A Armenia	F Kazakhstan	K Russian Federation (RSFSR)
B Azerbaijan	G Kirgizia	L Tadzhikistan
C Belorussia	H Latvia	M Turkmenistan
D Estonia	I Lithuania	N Ukraine
E Georgia	J Moldavia	O Uzbekistan

AUTONOMOUS REPUBLICS (ASSR)

1 Abkhaz (Georgia)
2 Adzhar (Georgia)
3 Bashkir (Russian Federation)
4 Buryat (Russian Federation)
5 Chechen-Ingush (Russian Federation)
6 Chuvash (Russian Federation)
7 Dagestan (Russian Federation)
8 Karbardino-Balkar (Russian Federation)
9 Kalmyk (Russian Federation)
10 Karakalpak (Uzbekistan)
11 Karelian (Russian Federation)
12 Komi (Russian Federation)
13 Mari (Russian Federation)
14 Mordvin (Russian Federation)
15 Nakhichevan (Azerbaijan)
16 North Osetin (Russian Federation)
17 Tatar (Russian Federation)
18 Tuva (Russian Federation)
19 Udmurt (Russian Federation)
20 Yakut (Russian Federation)

AUTONOMOUS REGIONS (AR)
21 Adyge (Russian Federation)
22 Gorno-Altay (Russian Federation)
23 Gorno-Badakhshan (Tadzhikistan)
24 Karachay-Cherkess (Russian Federation)
25 Khakass (Russian Federation)
26 Nagorno-Karabakh (Azerbaijan)
27 Jewish (Russian Federation)
28 South Osetin (Georgia)

AUTONOMOUS AREAS (AA)
29 Aginsky-Buryat (Russian Federation)
30 Chukot (Russian Federation)
31 Evenki (Russian Federation)
32 Khanty-Mansi (Russian Federation)
33 Komi-Permyak (Russian Federation)
34 Koryak (Russian Federation)
35 Nenets (Russian Federation)
36 Taymyr (Russian Federation)
37 Ust'ordinsky Buryat (Russian Federation)
38 Yamalo-Nenets (Russian Federation)

Political integration and control

The various federal institutions, together with the Communist Party,★ serve both as channels of integration and as agencies of political mobilization and control. According to official claims, the political equality and harmony of all nationalities is demonstrated and secured by their proportionate representation in bodies such as the Supreme Soviet★–the parliament of the USSR. Great care is taken to ensure the representation of the smaller nationalities in the Supreme Soviet, so much so that the non-Slav groups are over-represented among its deputies. This is of little consequence in view of the weakness of the Supreme Soviet.

There seems to be little discrimination on nationality grounds in recruitment to the Communist Party.★ The domination of Russians is, however, apparent in the composition of central executive bodies. *Ex officio* membership of chairmen of republican Supreme Soviets and Councils of Ministers in the Presidia of the all-Union bodies does not offset the over-representation of Russians in the upper ranks of the Party and state apparatus. Even if some of this imbalance can be explained in terms of education, it appears that non-Slavs are at a disadvantage. Top *nomenklatura*★ posts in other key institutions, such as the armed forces,★ also seem to be Russian- and Slav-dominated–over 90 per cent of army generals appointed since the 1940s have been of Slav origin.

At republican level greater care is taken to secure control without destroying the semblance of political equality. The highest political offices–First Secretary of the republican Communist Party, Chairman of the Council of Ministers and Chairman of the Supreme Soviet–are almost invariably held by local nationals. However, in order to ensure central control over personnel and Party organization, it has long been general practice to appoint a Russian (or Ukrainian) to the post of Second Secretary of the republican Communist Party. Slavs also figure disproportionately as chairmen of republican Committees of State Security (KGB),★ particularly in Central Asia. Titular nationalities are strongly represented in the leading executive positions as a whole. Only in Moldavia and Kazakhstan do Russians dominate; in Belorussia and most of the Central Asian republics non-Russians hold between half and three-quarters of leading posts and this proportion rises to 90 per cent in Uzbekistan, the Ukraine and the Baltic republics. Armenians, Georgians and Azeris★ appear to administer themselves. How can these variations be explained? Political trustworthiness does not seem to be the criterion, as Belorussia and Moldavia are not reputedly insubordinate, nor are the Caucasians★ renowned for their loyalty to Moscow. The strong presence of Russians in the populations of Moldavia, Belorussia and Kazakhstan provides part of the answer, yet the most important factor appears to be the level of higher education. Moscow seems to encourage self-administration where local nationalities are sufficiently well qualified. While this policy may further the cause of political equality and mobilization, it also tends to foster republican political identity among the native élites and to strengthen their capacity to evade central control. It is interesting that the most serious instances of republican insubordination and nationalism have occurred in republics largely or almost wholly administered by local nationals (Armenia, 1960, 1973–4; Azerbaidjan, 1959, 1969; Georgia, 1956, 1972–3; the Ukraine, 1972).

The relative ease with which Moscow has replaced insubordinate local leaders testifies to its ultimate power. Yet the invariable recourse to purges underlines the shortcomings of institutional controls. More importantly, the regularity with which such local political crises have occurred since Stalin's* death points to the failure of existing institutions to satisfy republican interests and incorporate local political élites. *A.P.*

Economic integration

Soviet leaders tend to view economic inequalities as fundamental to nationalist discontent and even to the very existence of nationalism. It has therefore been official policy since Lenin's day to eliminate all economic inequalities between nationalities by creating a highly integrated and prosperous Soviet economy. Given the large disparities in levels of economic development among the republics, it has proved difficult to reconcile the political need for equalization with Soviet economic growth. Until the late 1950s, large investment in Central Asia narrowed the gap between rich and poor republics even if it did not succeed in altering their rank order. With the end of the period of extensive economic development, investments were shifted to the higher-yielding areas of Siberia and the Far East. This shift, plus the rapid population* increases in Central Asia, has resulted in a widening of the economic gap between republics. Since 1972 considerations of all-Union economic interest have been placed above those of equalization between republics as, according to Brezhnev,* such inequalities have been largely overcome.

All nationalities of the USSR have obviously derived great material benefits from the processes of modernization and economic integration involved in what may be called Sovietization. Yet Sovietization has not necessarily undermined nationalism; in some respects, it has aggravated the problem. Not only are there the basic difficulties of rural populations adjusting to urban conditions; Sovietization has become associated with the influx of large numbers of Russians who occupy many of the best-paid jobs, particularly in the Ukraine and the Baltic and Central Asian republics. Centrally-directed planning* has led to the one-sided development of many republican economies, and while local populations may appreciate the increases in living standards, the better educated among them tend to resent Moscow's opposition to economic diversification. With heavy investment in the eastern regions of the RSFSR, the poorer republics have had to fight much harder for resources – national solidarity and economic nationalism thrive on such competition. Sovietization has perhaps done more to engender economic nationalism among the wealthier national groups. In the Baltic republics, the Ukraine and, to a certain extent, in European parts of the RSFSR, there has long been a feeling that they have contributed more to the Union than they have received in return. *A.P.*

Cultural integration

Cultural and psychological differences present the most formidable barriers to Soviet integration policy. The difficulties of building a new 'Soviet' identity are compounded by the commitment to maintain existing languages and cultures rather than fuse them in the melting-pot fashion of the USA. Another problem lies in the close identification of Soviet with Russian, which is constantly reinforced by the prominent role accorded to Russian language* and Russian education as vehicles of cultural integration. It is not surprising that non-Russians see cultural integration as Russification. Official policy promotes bilingualism by developing Russian alongside the local language. The education* system therefore has schools teaching in 45 different languages and the great majority of non-Russian schoolchildren are taught in their native tongue. Underlying the policy of bilingualism is the ultimate goal of making Russian the first language of all nationalities, thus transforming their cultural and (it is hoped) psychological identity; Russian schools exist throughout the USSR and the teaching of Russian in indigenous schools is vigorously promoted.

According to the 1979 census, 49 per cent of all non-Russians speak Russian. Predictably, the highest proportions of Russian speakers are to be found among the other Slav* groups and the lowest among Central Asian nationalities. To take the extremes, while more than one in two Belorussians* speak Russian, only one in seven Uzbeks* does so. If the promotion of bilingualism has been relatively successful, the attempt to dilute nationality through linguistic assimilation has proved more difficult. The number of non-Russians giving Russian as their first language rose from 10 million in 1959 to over 16 million in 1979, but the assimilated come from a narrow band of nationalities: Belorussians, Ukrainians* and dispersed groups such as Jews* and Poles. More importantly, linguistic assimilation does not necessarily mean cultural and psychological integration.

Eighty-two per cent of Jews regard Russian as their mother tongue yet Jewish identity remains strong. The very successes of linguistic assimilation in the Ukraine have provoked nationalist demands for an expansion of Ukrainian education and culture to resist Russification; and even where, as in the Caucasian and Baltic republics, Russian has made no great headway, the cultural threat felt has been sufficient to generate nationalist protest.

The pattern of linguistic assimilation is repeated in intermarriage; this ultimate form of integration has made limited headway, but only among Slav groups. The millions of Russian and Ukrainian settlers in Central Asia remained separate from the indigenous population. This failure to intermingle is largely accounted for by the survival of strong cultural barriers, the most important of which are sustained by the persistence of Islam.* Sovietization and the attempts at cultural integration have failed to undermine Central Asians' strong sense of cultural identity. It is highly unlikely that national identity will be weakened by more education as the new Russian-speaking élites tend to be more nationalist-minded than their backward rural compatriots. Furthermore, given present population* trends, these unintegrated groups will continue to grow far faster than the Russians and the more easily integrated Slavs. *A.P.*

Varieties of nationalism

Nationalism is a sponge-like phenomenon, capable of soaking up a wide range of sentiments and grievances. In the USSR traditional ethnic attachments, newer nationalist loyalties and fears of Russification have combined with economic and political centre-periphery conflicts to produce three broad types of nationalist movement. The first involves the efforts of small diaspora groups to settle in their chosen homeland. Since 1957 the 300 000-strong community of Crimean Tatars* have pressed the authorities to allow them to return to the Crimea from where they were deported during the Second World War,* but so far have not secured resettlement. Greater successes have been achieved by the Germans* and, especially, the Jewish* minority.

Nationalism within the Union Republics has far wider implications; it is expressed largely in the form of protests against the denationalizing effects of Soviet policies. Since the 1950s demands have been voiced by Balts, Georgians, Armenians and Ukrainians* for greater linguistic, cultural and economic autonomy to roll back Russification, which they all condemn as a violation of their constitutional rights. To some extent such protests are the result of a nationality programme which purports to support national cultures while working in practice to undermine them. The ambivalence of Soviet nationality policy has drawn a different kind of criticism from

Russian nationalists (a considerable force since the late 1960s commanding both popular support and sympathy in political circles), who complain that the federal system diminishes the stature of Russia and betrays her natural imperial rights.

The strongest and most activist nationalism has developed among the Georgians, a cohesive nation with a long historical tradition, and the Ukrainians, second to the Russians in size and economic strength, who feel threatened by Russification. In both cases Moscow has taken such nationalist dissent* extremely seriously and has responded harshly to its more radical manifestations: such dissenters have been the only political dissidents executed in the post-Stalin period. None the less, with the exception of a few groups, such as the Armenian United National Party, nationalists have not called for political separation nor for the destruction of the existing system. For the most part, they have expressed support for the Soviet system and only demanded reforms which would give them greater cultural autonomy and allow republican paper rights to be translated into practice.

By the standards of Western federalism, Soviet federalism appears as a way of devolving administrative responsibility within a unitary system. Neither Lenin's* objectives nor current Soviet claims about nation-building are reflected in practice. Yet judged by the more neutral yardsticks of steadily furthering integration and maintaining political stability in such a large and heterogeneous multinational state, Soviet performance has been impressive. *A.P.*

Evolution of the ministerial system

When the Bolsheviks* came to power in 1917 they created a government which was given a 'revolutionary' name, the Council of People's Commissars; Lenin* was its first Chairman. The commissariats included, among others, foreign affairs, education, labour, in some cases simply taking over an old ministry. However, even in the early days, the locus of major policy-making was the Politburo* and Central Committee of the Communist Party.* In the 1930s, against the background of the industrialization* programme, the Council became more and more heavily involved in the planning and administration of industry. Gosplan, a State Planning Commission which had existed in the 1920s, became responsible for drawing up the national economic plans;* more and more industrial commissariats were created to run the different branches of industry. Most of the original commissariats continued to exist but they were now part of a growing economic apparatus and one moreover in which the People's Commissariat for Internal Affairs (the NKVD) had clawed out for itself a commanding role. From perhaps 1934 to 1953 the NKVD became one of the major institutions running the country. In 1946 the

Lenin (seated, top) presiding over a meeting of the People's Commissars, October 1922

Council of People's Commissars was renamed the Council of Ministers.★

The post-Stalin★ period has seen three important changes. First, as part of a drive to reduce the power of the security organs, the Ministry of State Security (successor to the NKVD) became a Committee for State Security (KGB)★ and not until 1973 did its chairman gain a seat on the Politburo. Second, under Khrushchev★ most of the industrial ministries were abolished and the task of running the economy devolved upon regional economic councils and central state committees; in 1965 the Brezhnev★-Kosygin leadership brought back the ministries but retained (and subsequently expanded) the system of state committees. Third, whereas both Stalin and Khrushchev took on the Chairmanship of the Council of Ministers as well as the First Secretaryship of the Party, since 1964 the posts have been kept separate. A. N. Kosygin (1904–80) was Chairman from then until October 1980 when he resigned (dying two months later) and was replaced by N. A. Tikhonov (b.1905).

With the adoption of the new Constitution★ in 1977, a new statute on the Council of Ministers was clearly desirable, and one was passed in July 1978 by the Supreme Soviet (the parliament of the USSR). In this law the Council of Ministers is described as 'the government of the USSR – the highest executive and administrative organ of state power', responsible to the Supreme Soviet, by whom it is appointed and to whom it reports. Its tasks include the issuing of 'decisions' (*postanovleniya*), preparing the national economic plans and budget, ensuring the maintenance of law and order in the country, working out social welfare and cultural programmes, administering foreign policy, and supervising the execution of decisions by individual ministries, republican and local agencies.   *M.M.*

The Council of Ministers

Method of appointment

At the first meeting after its election, the Supreme Soviet appoints the Chairman of the Council of Ministers, the first deputy and deputy chairmen, the ministers and chairmen of the state committees.★ The chairmen of the Councils of Ministers of the Union Republics also have places on the USSR Council of Ministers. In addition to this basic membership, the Chairman can request the inclusion of deputy ministers or deputy chairmen of individual ministries★ or committees, and the heads of other organs or institutions subordinate to the Council. This does not mean that every five years, with a new Supreme Soviet, there is a new Council of Ministers. Essentially the Supreme Soviet ratifies any new ministries that have been created, with their existing ministerial incumbents. It is for the Chairman of the Council of Ministers to recommend the 'appointments' to the Supreme Soviet. His own appointment, and probably those of the first deputy and deputy chairmen, will be a Politburo★ matter. When the Supreme Soviet is not in session, the Chairman of the Council turns to the Presidium★ of the Supreme Soviet with proposals for the creation of a new ministry, or a merger, or for ratification of resignations and new appointments. Thus ministers may come and go at any time during the year and many remain at their posts for 10–20 years. Formally it is for the Council of Ministers itself to appoint the deputy ministers of individual ministries and the deputy chairmen of state committees but this only amounts to ratification. Individual ministers are usually responsible for appointing their deputies – without doubt in consultation with the cadres department of the Party Central Committee.★ It has been suggested that when the ministries were brought back in 1965, a Party official from the Central Committee often appeared as a deputy minister, indicating the close links between Central Committee apparatus★ and Council of Ministers on personnel matters.

Those who became ministers under Stalin★ (and some returned in 1965) tended to come up through the individual ministry and consequently had considerable expertise in their particular branch. A different pattern now appears to be developing – that of the 'Party generalist' who moves to ministerial work at some stage in his career, or of 'specialist' posts (for the industrial ministries) and 'generalist' posts (Ministry of Justice, KGB,★ State Committee for Science and Technology).

Structure

From 1978 the Council has had approximately 100 members. Apart from the Chairman and his deputies who have responsibilities for either over-all or partial coordination of activities, and the coopted chairmen of the republican Councils of Ministers, almost all are either ministers or chairmen of state committees. Sometimes deputy ministers or deputy chairmen of state committees are included, or the head of an agency (such as the Central Statistical Administration). The ministries and state committees can be divided between the all-Union institutions with jurisdiction over enterprises or agencies throughout the USSR (Ministry of Foreign Trade, Ministry for the Gas Industry, Ministry of Defence, State Committee for Science and Technology), and the Union-Republican institutions which have ministries or agencies at both central and republican level (Ministry of Higher and Secondary Specialized Education, Ministry of Meat and Milk Industry, State Planning Committee (Gosplan), Committee for State Security (KGB), State Committee for Labour and Social Questions).

Its size and the range of its work reduces the feasibility of frequent meetings and decision-making by the whole Council, which meets four times a year; it is to an inner cabinet, the Presidium of the Council of Ministers, that much essential decision-making falls. The 1978 law merely states that the Presidium, acting as a 'permanent organ' of the Council of Ministers 'meets regularly' (perhaps weekly) and consists of the Chairman, first deputy chairmen and deputy chairmen. In the 1970s there were usually two first deputies and perhaps ten deputy chairmen – the latter almost always important ministers or chairmen of key state committees (agriculture, Gosplan). The Chairman himself is responsible for appointments, coordinates the work of his deputies, organizes the work of the Council as a whole and presides over meetings.

Functions

In all its activities the Council of Ministers is guided by Party policy decisions and the existing legislation; for example, it produces the economic plan and the budget but within the guidelines laid down by the Politburo. On issues of key importance which involve them, the Ministry of Foreign Affairs or the KGB will report direct to the Politburo (on which their representatives sit). The Council of Ministers is not a collective decision-making body determining the policies in all areas for which its ministries or agencies are responsible; rather, individual ministries participate in policy-making with other Party or state agencies in the areas in which they have special competence. The Presidium tries to coordinate the activities of the economic ministries and state committees with the aim of internally reconciling the requirements of branches of industry, regions, domestic versus foreign and military versus domestic demands; here it will proffer advice to the Politburo.

Although in these respects the Council of Ministers is less of a policy-maker than appears implicit in its statute, in another important respect it oversteps its statutory rights. Before the 1978 law, lawyers asked for clarification of the Council of Ministers' right to issue new legislation. According to law, any 'decisions' (postanov-

leniya) or 'ordinances' (rasporyazheniya) issued by the Council of Ministers should merely implement existing legislation; law-making was the prerogative of the Supreme Soviet. But in fact, as some lawyers recognized, postanovleniya (often issued jointly by the Council of Ministers and the Party Central Committee*) frequently do establish new rights or legal relationships. Some argued that it was necessary to confirm the sphere in which the Council of Ministers had the right to create new 'legal norms'. However, the law of 1978 left the situation unchanged, and practice remains the same.   *M.M.*

The ministries

The minister appoints (and dismisses) his deputy ministers, the heads of the chief administrations (glavki) and departments and other ministerial staff, aided by the personnel department, the Party committee and the trade union* in the ministry. The personnel department, in turn, appoints enterprise directors (in an all-Union industrial ministry) and participates in the appointment of republican personnel in a Union-Republican ministry. All such posts come under what may be called 'administrative procedures', whereby an individual can appeal against dismissal or demotion only to the organ above that which appointed him; he has no right to be present at the hearing; he cannot turn to the courts. The ministries have been criticized for having no established criteria for promotion, no qualifying tests for jobs, no open competition for vacant posts, and for overstaffing and inefficiency. Indeed, the growth of the administrative apparatus has been one factor prompting the policy-makers to argue for the abolition of some of the chief administrations and the creation of a simplified structure: ministry–industrial association–enterprise.

Within each ministry a 'cabinet' (kollegiya) is formed, composed of the minister, deputy ministers, and some other leading officials. This meets perhaps weekly for decision-making purposes; a decision is effected by the minister's prikaz (order): his is the ultimate responsibility and he can be held liable for ministerial acts. Internal kollegiya disagreements may be referred by either the minister or his subordinates to the Council of Ministers.* (Whether this often happens is another matter.) Since 1971 the Party committees within the ministries have been given the right of 'control' and indeed urged to make use of their authority to improve ministerial efficiency, but it is not clear whether this has made for any change.

Non-industrial ministries – the Ministries of Foreign Affairs, Justice, Health or Finance – are more like traditional Western ministries although sharing policy-making, even for their area, with a number of other institutions. The Ministry of Health is responsible for the health budget, for allocating resources to the republics, for laying down new policy directions in general terms, and for arguing the case for more resources; the republican ministries adapt their budget allocations to suit local needs. One of the most important ministries is the Ministry of Finance, responsible for the budget, and consulted on major policy questions; it is reputedly a conservative body which objects to proposals for change. The industrial ministries are responsible for all the enterprises in their branch, and for the performance of the branch as a whole. They issue the enterprise plans and provide the resources. Despite the attempt in 1965 to limit ministries' control over enterprise activity and to emphasize instead their role as creative innovators devising far-reaching plans for the future of their industries, the ministries have reasserted their sway, and all their old failings (late plans, inadequate supplies, neglect of innovation and hampering of progress) are the subject of steady press criticism.

The move to streamline the ministries and to group enterprises together in associations is probably intended to strengthen the position of the enterprise and to create a more efficient ministerial structure, but progress towards such reforms is slow. *M.M.*

The state committees

The state committees came of age in 1978 when they became members of the Council of Ministers,* no longer subordinate to it, so ratifying their actual position. It is clear that some (notably Gosplan, the KGB*) are among the most powerful institutions of either state or Party. They are headed by a chairman instead of a minister; they too have deputies; the staffing procedure and *kollegiya* principles are the same as for the ministries. Likewise, there are all-Union and Union-Republican state committees. Gosplan, as a Union-Republican committee, has agencies at republican level and below, responsible for drawing up the economic plans for the region or republic, and for sending them to the centre to be coordinated and changed in the light of new policy directives or requirements. It is for Gosplan at the centre to devise the Five-year Plans,* to break each down into one-year components and to break these down even further for republics and for individual ministries. The KGB too is a Union-Republican committee with agencies at republican and regional level. Its representatives are presumably influential participants in decision-making at all levels. A state committee which can serve as an example of the wide brief these bodies enjoy is the Committee on Labour and Social Questions. Created in 1955 as the State Committee on Labour and Wages, its tasks are as follows: to inspect ministerial performance in the sphere of labour and wages;* to work together with the trade unions* and Ministry of Finance to produce wage scales for different industries and regions; to check skill-handbooks and classify

enterprises; to check on labour regulations and produce projects for improvements. It has established itself as the leading institution on all questions of labour and wages. *M.M.*

The Committee for State Security (KGB)

The initials are the Russian abbreviation for Committee for State Security, since 1954 the main Soviet organization for national security at home and intelligence operations abroad. It is the successor of the Cheka (All-Russian Extraordinary Commission for Combating Counter-Revolution and Sabotage, 1917–22), the GPU (State Political Administration, 1922–3), the OGPU (United State Political Administration, 1923–34), the NKVD (People's Commissariat for Internal Affairs, 1934–43), the NKGB (People's Commissariat for State Security, 1943–6), the MGB (Ministry for State Security, 1946–53) and the MVD (Ministry of Internal Affairs, 1953–4).

In addition to its secret-police functions the Cheka was also in charge of corrective labour camps (later within the GULag* system), internal security troops,* and press censorship*. In 1922 most of these functions passed to the NKVD, to which the GPU was made subordinate. While the OGPU was then separated from the NKVD, this change was reversed in 1934. Although the relevant division of the NKVD was then called the Main Administration for State Security (GUGB), this name was not widely used, and common practice was to refer to the secret police simply as the NKVD. An analogous situation arose in 1953–4, until the KGB was created as a body with ministry status, again separated from the MVD. Although formally part of the USSR Council of Ministers,* and thus of the government, in practice the KGB reports primarily to the top Communist Party* organs.

The KGB and its predecessors have been headed by F. E. Dzerzhinsky (1917–26), V. R. Menzhinsky (1926–34), G. G. Yagoda (1934–6), N. I. Yezhov (1936–8), L. P. Beria (1938–43 and 1953), V. N. Merkulov (1943–6), V. S. Abakumov (1946–51), S. D. Ignat'ev (1951–3), I. A. Serov (1954–8), A. N. Shelepin (1958–61), V. Ye. Semichastny (1961–7) and Yu. V. Andropov (1967 onward).

For its internal security functions the Cheka, as the Bolsheviks' 'punitive arm', was given very wide powers to detect and suppress 'counter-revolutionary elements' of all sorts. The OGPU concentrated mainly on the Church,* 'socially alien' individuals, and former members of opposition parties; then, from 1928, on entrepreneurs and traders, members of the pre-1917 intelligentsia, and–in a series of vast operations–on the peasantry, whom it forcibly collectivized* and 'de-kulakized'. The NKVD carried out Stalin's* Great Terror* of 1934–8, becoming an economic empire on the strength of camp labour, deported numerous Poles, Ukrainians and Balts in 1939–40

Stalin with N. I. Yezhov, NKVD chief, 1937

and a million Soviet Germans in 1941, and ruthlessly enforced political control in the armed forces* and civilian life during the Second World War.* The NKGB and MGB, under Beria's protégés, deported to distant territories whole nationalities in 1943–6 for alleged collaboration with the Germans, simultaneously transferring suspected collaborators and 'alien elements' from all Soviet territories occupied by the Germans, and imprisoning civilians and prisoners of war returning from Germany. They also launched a new general terror in 1949, among the chief targets of which were 'rootless cosmopolitans' (mainly Jews) and former supporters of Zhdanov* in Leningrad. On Stalin's death in 1953 Beria used the MVD as his base in his bid for power. His arrest and subsequent execution led to the reduction of KGB powers and its subjection to tight bureaucratic administration to prevent any future escape from Party control or deployment in leadership power struggles. Mass terror had been ended in 1953, and torture, previously legalized, was banned. These setbacks were compounded by Khrushchev's* de-Stalinization* policy and his claims that the USSR no longer had any political prisoners. Under his successors the KGB's status was restored, and in

1973 its head, Andropov, entered the Politburo.* From its grass-roots offices in every workplace of any size the KGB tries to prevent or combat political crime* and dissent.* The rise since the late 1950s of many types of organized dissent has presented it with a serious challenge.

The KGB's role in foreign intelligence (much more central than that of the GRU, the military* intelligence organization) has been very important ever since the USSR came fully into international politics at the end of the Second World War. Agents operate around the world under cover of postings as diplomats, trade officials, journalists, and so on; a Soviet ambassador abroad may not know who the senior KGB officer (or *rezident*) in his embassy is, and has no control over him. Since 1945 an average of about 15 Soviet agents a year, most of them KGB officers, have been expelled for espionage or related activities, from a wide range of countries. The organization appears to have about half a million employees, of whom some 90 000 are officers, 220 000 are border and internal security troops, and the rest support staff.   *P.R.*

The electoral process

Elections figure prominently in the Soviet political calendar with all-Union and republican Supreme Soviet elections taking place every five years and those to local soviets* every two-and-a-half years. All Soviet citizens over the age of 18 may vote and extraordinarily large numbers of them do so with remarkable unanimity. While such near perfection is hailed by Soviet commentators as proof of political democracy, it confirms Western observers in their view of Soviet elections as highly manipulated plebiscites.

Nothing in Soviet election law precludes more than one candidate standing for any seat, yet voters are never presented with a choice. The absence of choice on polling day is justified on two grounds: the existence of fundamental consensus in Soviet society and the democratic nature of the selection process. All recognized public organizations as well as collectives of workers, employees, farmers and the military are entitled to put forward candidates for nomination. Nominations are supposed to be freely discussed and finally decided at voters' meetings. In practice, the whole selection process is closely controlled by the Communist Party.* Central Party guidelines laying down the composition of the candidate body in terms of social origin, occupation, organizational affiliation, sex and age (18 is the minimum age for local deputies and 21 for Supreme Soviet deputies) are applied by district Party officials. Individuals to fit the bill are selected by local Party, trade union,* youth league* and other organization officials. Any multiple candidacies or disagreements are resolved by these or by the district Party organization,

Yakut reindeer-breeders vote in the elections to the Supreme Soviet of the USSR

which vets all nominations before they go forward for endorsement by workplace collectives. After registration by the election commission, which is also under tight Party control, candidates are adopted at formal voters' meetings.

The three-week election campaign is organized by the district Party in collaboration with the local Soviet executive and election commission. Media promotion of national policies is intensified, and increased coverage is given to local issues which are taken up at electors' clubs and agitation centres (*agitpunkt*) and by canvassers, each of whom contacts 15–40 voters twice before polling day. There is no legal obligation to vote but the authorities make every effort to get the maximum turnout. Polling usually takes place on a Sunday and polling stations are established in every conceivable location. Electors may choose to vote for the candidate by placing an unmarked ballot paper in the box or may register their disapproval by crossing out the name. Screened polling booths are provided but are used only by an estimated 2–5 per cent of those voting. Since the late 1930s

turnout has exceeded 90 per cent and in recent years it has topped 99.9 per cent, though if absentee certificate-holders and proxy voters are deducted the real figure is nearer 75 per cent. All but a tiny handful of votes are cast for the official candidates. In Supreme Soviet elections, where the single-member election districts include up to three million electors, no candidates ever fail to get the simple majority required, and most of the hundred or so defeats in local elections – out of a total of over 2 million candidates – occur at village level where 20 votes can be decisive.

Soviet elections perform several important functions. The campaign period and the act of voting can further political education★ and socialization. Elections provide unique opportunities to test governmental capacity to mobilize the entire population, and local organizations are judged by their performance. More importantly, elections are ritualist public acclamations which reaffirm the legitimacy of the Party and the regime. In recent years some Soviet academics have called for an opening-up of the selection process and for the introduction of a choice between candidates at local level to raise the quality of deputies and to stimulate public interest in elections. So far, the loss of executive control such reforms might involve has prevented their adoption.

A.P.

'All power to the soviets'

The Soviets of People's Deputies are officially referred to as 'organs of state power', and are the product of a line of evolution that goes back to the revolutions★ of 1905 and 1917. At that time they were essentially strike committees, consisting of workers' and later soldiers' representatives, which sprang up to coordinate the revolutionary activity. Their significance was recognized by Lenin,★ who saw them as genuinely proletarian institutions, and campaigned at the head of the Bolshevik★ party in 1917 under the slogan 'All power to the soviets'. During the interval between the February and October revolutions, the Petrograd Soviet wielded real influence in competition with the Provisional Government,★ and it was the II All-Russian Congress of Soviets that endorsed the Revolution on 25 October 1917. The Congress of Soviets became in principle the supreme organ of state power in the new political system, and in the ensuing years soviets (councils) were established throughout the country as the basic institutions in the state to which they gave their name. The soviets thus have a highly symbolic function and importance in the USSR's political rhetoric, linking the present with the revolutionary tradition – even though the formal, highly structured and carefully controlled institutions of today bear little but the name in common with the spontaneous creations of the revolutionary workers.

R.J.H.

Selection of deputies to the soviets

The soviets exist at all levels in the administrative hierarchy. Headed by the USSR Supreme Soviet (the only two-chamber soviet in the country), there are Supreme Soviets in the Union and Autonomous Republics, and over 50 000 local soviets at regional (oblast), city, urban and rural district, settlement and village levels. They are elected by the adult population, in an electoral process* carefully guided by the Communist Party of the Soviet Union (CPSU).* They consist of representatives, the deputies, numbering perhaps 30 at village level, and 1500 in the USSR Supreme Soviet – 750 in each of the chambers: the Soviet of the Union, and the Soviet of Nationalities. There are considerably more than two million deputies at any one time and, in view of the high turnover rate, upwards of five million in a decade. This points to a further function of the soviets: they are a means of giving citizens the experience of involvement in political life, or, as Soviet writers express it, they are 'schools of communism', and are hence involved in developing the political culture.

They are intended to serve politically as representative institu-

tions, and with this in mind, candidates are carefully selected to achieve the appropriate social balance before the electors are invited to endorse the choice at the poll. This thorough vetting and balancing of different social categories is done by the political authorities (ultimately the local Party committee), and results in the broadly representative composition of the soviets. While reflecting the predominant economic complexion of the territorial unit – the balance of industry, agriculture, administration, the various public services – a given soviet will contain representatives of different age-groups, nationalities and occupations, and will retain a measure of continuity while bringing in fresh blood. Certain categories are fairly uniformly represented across the country: women* account for a little under 50 per cent, as do Party members (although there is a strong tendency for increased Party strength and decreased numbers of women at the higher levels). Nevertheless, representation is not proportional, as has been recognized inside and outside the Soviet Union. The Party is over-represented, women are under-represented, as are some of the nationalities and certain occupations, particularly in the service industries; religious* and dissent* groups have no 'representatives' among the deputies, all of whom are endorsed by the CPSU and are deemed to be members of the 'bloc of communists and non-Party people', carefully chosen as 'the best sons and daughters' of the nation.

An extraordinary session of the Supreme Soviet of the USSR adopting the 1977 Constitution

The soviets may, however, be representative in another sense: the deputies may reflect and voice the interests of their constituents, a theme that was given increasing emphasis during the 1970s. In order to retain direct contact with the thoughts, needs, demands and aspirations of their electors, Soviet deputies–even at Supreme Soviet level–are not full-time politicians: they maintain their regular employment, from which they are released without loss of pay to attend sessions of the soviet. Thus, in theory, they do not become preoccupied with their own status as public figures.   *R.J.H.*

Role and functions of the soviets

The formal meetings of soviets are held four or six times a year (twice for the Supreme Soviets), and it is in this forum that the deputies perform one of their most important functions: giving legal force to policies decided on by the Communist Party.* Soviet commentators emphasize that Party committees have no power, and that their decisions are not legally binding on citizens until given the force of law by a decision of the appropriate soviet. In practice, such are the political relations between Party and soviets that the latter have no option but to comply with the Party's wishes. Party bodies frequently draft the legislative documents and present them to the session, where the Party members among the the deputies are bound to argue and vote in favour of the resolution, which is then implemented, again under the supervision of Party members strategically positioned in the administrative apparatus. This circumstance leads many critics to dismiss the sessions as mere rubber-stamping occasions. In fact, the Party's own members form a majority of deputies in soviets at any level of importance (about 75 per cent in the USSR Supreme Soviet), and the voting, by show of hands, is always unanimous.

Even so, this formal stage of legally endorsing Party policy is accorded great significance in Soviet accounts of the political system

A deputy to the Supreme Soviet of the Armenian SSR meets his constituents

of developed socialism.★ The significance of the act is associated with a far-reaching attempt to develop the soviets, which had been permitted (or forced) to decline into a moribund state under Stalin.★ Since 1957 the Soviet political leadership has repeatedly turned its attention to the soviets, with lengthy statements and new legislation, aimed at revitalizing them and finding for them an appropriate role in a society that is becoming more complex, more diversified, better educated and less reliant on coercion. Since the 1950s Soviet scholars, and in their wake politicians, have come to recognize that in such a milieu citizens may hold a vast range of opinions and specific interests, in addition to the basic goal of building a communist society, and that it is the task of the political system to coordinate and aggregate these interests in the policy-making process. The soviets and their deputies are now called on to perform the role of interest articulation in the system.

This development is reflected in a greater exactingness towards deputies. Formerly, particularly under Stalin, the soviets consisted largely of local public figures and officials supplemented by outstanding workers such as Stakhanovites for whom membership was regarded as a reward for achievement in production, regardless of their political or administrative aptitudes or even inclinations. This may have been perfectly adequate when their main function was to rubber-stamp party policy, but with the development of the representative functions of the soviets, a more sophisticated type of deputy is required—educated, experienced, energetic and with an interest in political matters; moreover, to serve their constituents effectively they need to be trained. The modern soviet deputy is encouraged to take a more professional attitude towards his role, which itself is being extended so that although the official sessions still retain their formalistic character, the deputy's role as representing his constituents' interests is a continuous one. Informally, deputies see their electors in local office meetings, and intervene with the authorities to get matters moving over such questions as speeding up housing allocation, arranging for pensions, getting a roof fixed or a street-lamp bulb replaced. To strengthen the deputy's hand in dealings with officials, the government in 1972 introduced a Statute on the Status of Soviet Deputies, conferring a degree of authority formerly lacking, and the right to demand fair treatment and an efficient response to petitions.

On a more formal level, the majority of deputies are involved in the work of the permanent (or standing) commissions, whose ambit is to supervise the administration of health, social welfare, budgeting, industry, transport, agriculture and other specific areas. These bodies, formed by the deputies from among their own number, and often involving volunteer 'activists' as well, have substantial powers of inspection in checking the efficiency of management. The commission system has been much expanded since the 1960s, particularly at Supreme Soviet level, where a restructuring in 1967 significantly increased the chances for deputies to be involved in behind-the-scenes monitoring of policy-making and performance.

The soviets also serve as an adjunct to the planning mechanism, through the system of 'mandates'. During the election campaign, deputies are given specific requests agreed by their electors, which it is their duty to strive to have implemented by the soviet: opening a crèche, providing a bus service, laying a footpath. These are aggregated by the full soviet, and ultimately incorporated into the economic plan for the town or district; the plan thereby more closely reflects the needs of the population. This is particularly useful at local level, where the local soviet executive committees and their administrative departments are responsible for running affairs—transport, housing, shops, schools, hospitals, parks—in between sessions of the full soviet. Moreover, the significance of recent developments lies in their implications for the relationship between

STRUCTURE OF A LOCAL SOVIET

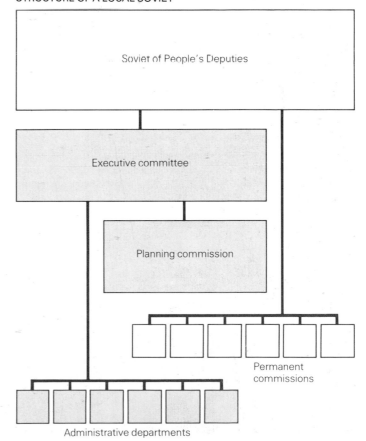

Administrative departments

Permanent commissions

KEY

Representative bodies

Administrative organs

the deputies (as representatives of the electors) and the administrative bodies. Although these are formally elected or appointed by the deputies at the first session of a new soviet, to which they are answerable, in practice the executive bodies dominate the institutions to which they are legally subordinated. They consist of the area's leading politicians, including (invariably) the Party committee's first secretary, who are inadequately balanced by a small number of 'ordinary' deputies. Since the soviets meet infrequently, much administration is carried out by the executive that cannot be effectively controlled by the soviet, so the permanent commissions can become quite important instruments for monitoring the administration.

The Presidium of the Supreme Soviet

At Supreme Soviet level the Party General Secretary Brezhnev★ had long been a member of the Presidium before his assumption of its chairmanship in 1977. Under the 1977 Constitution★ that body has vested in it a range of exclusive powers which in practice lend it far greater political importance than the Supreme Soviet itself. These include calling elections★ and convening Supreme Soviet sessions; coordinating the work of the permanent commissions; interpreting laws; ratifying and abrogating international treaties; appointing and dismissing the military high command; proclaiming martial law; ordering mobilization – a formidable list of powers in which the Presidium is not answerable even to the Supreme Soviet.

The Kremlin building where the Presidium of the Supreme Soviet holds its meetings

Party guidance

The whole of state administration is 'guided' by the Communist Party; indeed, the interlocking membership between Party bodies and those of the state ensures that all Party policy is loyally endorsed and implemented by the state institutions, and that these do not enjoy independent policy-making powers. Policy-making remains the prerogative of the Party. Reformist developments are aimed at ensuring a greater degree of information flowing upwards, and a higher level of public involvement in implementing policy. In that way, it is hoped, the effectiveness with which the Soviet Union's complex modern society is run will be improved, and in turn this will raise the prestige of the political system, in which the Party – not the state – occupies the central place.   *R.J.H.*

History of the Constitution

The 1918 RSFSR Constitution

The first RSFSR Constitution, adopted by the V All-Russian Congress of Soviets★ on 10 July 1918, consolidated the tactical victories of the Bolsheviks.★ Its first Part repeated previous decrees stating that all power was in the hands of the soviets★ (councils) of workers', peasants' and soldiers' deputies, and abolished the private ownership of land, natural resources, and so forth; the second Part listed basic freedoms (conscience, the press, association) and duties (labour and defence) and outlawed privileges which might be used to the detriment of the Revolution;★ the third Part dealt with the organization of the central authority. Supreme power was stated to be vested in the Congress of Soviets composed of representatives of local soviets. This elected the Central Executive Committee (CEC) with up to 200 members, with supreme legislative and administrative power and with authority to appoint the Council of People's Commissars (CPC) composed of 18 ministries. Local government was to be carried out by a hierarchy of councils, each with its executive committee for routine administration. Universal suffrage was introduced but was denied to those who employed labour for profit or lived on unearned income, and to 'middlemen' and the clergy. There was no express monopoly of the Bolshevik party, nor any head of state. From 1919 to 1922 similar constitutions were adopted in Belorussia, the Ukraine, Azerbaijan, Armenia and Georgia and (with variations) in Central Asia.

The 1924 Federal Constitution

The various republics united in a formal Federation of 30 December 1922, the Constitution of which was ratified on 13 January 1924. By this, power was (in theory) merely delegated to the Union and each republic retained the right to secede. The Union was given full capacity in international matters together with control of economic planning, the budget, the armed forces, transport, the judiciary and the basic principles of law in virtually all fields. Supreme authority was still said to be vested in the annual meeting of the indirectly elected Congress of Soviets. Its CEC, however, contained features which have persisted – a two-chamber system of the federal* Soviet (representing the population as a whole) and the Soviet of Nationalities (representing the major ethnic groups in the constituent republics). Its Presidium of (ultimately) 27 members formed a collective head of state with full legislative authority, but accountable to the CEC, and with power to appoint the CPC (that is, the government). No bill of rights was included, those of the republican constitutions remaining in force. During the 1920s there were certain structural changes in the Turkmen and Uzbek republics.

The 1936 Stalin Constitution

The Stalin Constitution of 5 December 1936 defined the USSR as 'a socialist state of workers and peasants' and – for the first time – described as their 'vanguard' the Communist Party of the Soviet Union (CPSU).* It reaffirmed the socialist ownership of the means of production and enacted a federal bill of rights and duties. Again, in theory, the federal power was delegated and limited, and the right of secession persisted; in practice federal authority was supreme and all-embracing. For the previous Congress of Soviets there was substituted a two-chamber Supreme Soviet with power to amend the Constitution by a two-thirds majority vote. In fact there is no record of any law having failed to secure unanimity. There was no provision for judicial review of the constitutionality of laws. The republican and local organs of power, appropriately adjusted, paralleled the federal structure.

The 1977 Constitution

The de-Stalinization* process of the 1950s and after provoked discussion of a new constitution. Formal preparation began in 1962 but no draft appeared until May 1977. After widespread public discussion (in which, according to Brezhnev,* four-fifths of the adult population took part) and some amendment, it was adopted in October 1977. It is not radically new, stressing in the Preamble the 'continuity of ideas and principles' with its three predecessors. The 1977 Constitution does, however, reflect post-war social and industrial changes, incorporate the effect of much post-Stalin legislation, and lay greater emphasis on individual rights.

The first Part describes the social and political principles of the system. The USSR is defined as 'a socialist state of all the people, expressing the will and interests of the workers, peasants and the intelligentsia and of the working people of all the country's nations and nationalities'. All power belongs to the people and is exercised through the Soviet of People's Deputies; the latter can, however,

decide to have a law enacted by nationwide referendum. The state and its agencies are to operate on the basis of socialist legality and to ensure the rights and liberties of citizens. The CPSU is now formally recognized as 'the leading and guiding force of Soviet society, the nucleus of its political system and of state and public organizations'. The economic system* is based on socialist ownership of the means of production; private property (called 'personal') is based on earned income and covers housing, personal effects and the like. No one may use socialist property for selfish purposes, nor his own belongings to acquire unearned income or to harm the interests of society. The earlier slogan 'he who does not work, neither shall he eat' has gone, to be replaced by: 'From each according to his ability, to each according to his work'. Thus a person's status in society is said to be determined by his socially useful labour. The provisions on the social system promise the industrialization of agriculture and the development of public services.

The theme of State and individual is developed in the second Part, thereby (unlike the Stalin Constitution) preceding the provisions on the state structure. This Part lays down the principle of complete equality and lists a bill of rights – work, health care, social security, housing, education, freedom to criticize, freedom from arrest, etc. Freedom of the press and of assembly is granted for the same aim as before: 'in conformity with the people's interests and for the purpose of strengthening and developing the socialist system'. All these rights and liberties are declared inseparable from the performance of civic duties: labour, safeguarding the interests of the state, military service, and so on.

The third Part (the state structure) reiterates the federal* nature of the Union of 15 Republics, confirming the right to secede and once again giving (by Article 73) virtually unlimited power to the USSR itself over its constituent parts. The Union Republics may be subdivided into Autonomous Republics and regions (oblasts); thus the RSFSR (the largest) has 16 of the former and 5 of the latter organized on ethnic bases. Within federal limits each republic has its own constitution (that of the RSFSR was adopted in April 1978), internal sovereignty and (in theory) the power to enter into international treaties.

The two-chamber Supreme Soviet of the USSR is the only body to enact federal statutes (the highest form of legal act). It meets for about a week twice a year and seems invariably to act with enthusiastic unanimity. It also 'elects' the Presidium* (a Chairman and 37 members) which acts by decree, amending statutes if necessary (subject to later ratification by the Supreme Soviet), supervises the constitutionality of laws (there is no judicial review), interprets them, ratifies treaties, and so forth. The government (Council of Ministers*) is appointed by, and accountable to, the Supreme Soviet; within its jurisdiction it makes binding regulations.

In the Union and Autonomous Republics their Supreme Soviets

exercise similar functions and appoint similar bodies. The local authorities operate, within their territory, through permanent executive committees.

In practice this whole machinery is controlled by the CPSU. *B.R.*

The legal system

The Judiciary

The Constitution* contains only the basic principles: that judges are elected and subject to recall (directly at the lowest level, and by the appropriate soviet at higher levels); that judges are independent; and that justice is open and impartial. Disputes between state enterprises fall within the jurisdiction of a distinct, specialized set of tribunals.

The court structure is governed by various all-Union and republican statutes and is extremely complex. The courts hear both civil and criminal cases. In first-instance hearings the judge sits with two elected lay assessors; appellate and review procedure comes before a bench of three judges. A legal training is not formally required but seems to have become the norm. There is no system of binding precedent, but the Supreme Courts at all-Union and republican level give 'guiding explanations' which are (and are meant to be) followed. Furthermore, the Communist Party* is frequently invoked. Thus the 1976 USSR Supreme Court Decree on the Administration of Justice, after reciting that the quality of judicial

activity had improved through the efforts of the Party, ordered the lower courts to 'bear in mind that all their activity must be carried out in accordance with the tasks assigned by the Party'. After a case has been disposed of at first instance, one appeal (in the sense of a decision on the merits) is open to the loser. Proceedings to review the law as stated by the lower court may be instituted by the courts or (and, in practice, usually) the Procuracy; thus a case may be considered many times and finally by the Plenum of the USSR Supreme Court. Military tribunals constitute a separate, federal, system under the Military Chamber of the USSR Supreme Court.

The Procuracy

In 1722 the Procurator was called 'the eye of the tsar'. The Soviet Procuracy is still a distinctively centralist and federal feature of the legal system. The Procurator-General, appointed by the USSR Supreme Soviet, controls his officials throughout the Union; they are not subject to the authority of their local soviet. To use rather inexact Western analogies, the office combines the functions of District Attorney, Inspector of Prisons, Attorney-General and Ombudsman. Thus it is the Procurator who supervises investigation in criminal cases, authorizes arrest, prosecutes offenders and supervises prisons; he refers judicial decisions to higher courts for review; and he exercises general supervision over the entire administration. This last function makes the Procuracy the channel through which citizens' complaints are considered and, for this, the Procurator may call for documents, explanations and so on. He does not, however, decide the

Counsel for the defence speaking at a People's Court in the Sverdlovsk district, Moscow

The Procurator addressing a People's Court in the Dzerzhinsky District, Moscow

case on its merits but refers the matter by way of 'protest' to the appropriate higher authority, sending—if he wishes—an account to the local Party organ.

The legal profession

Advocates are under the control of the Ministry of Justice at all-Union and republican level and, locally, of the justice department of the local executive committee. They must normally be law graduates and have completed a period of practical training. The local Bar admits recruits and administers and supervises the work of the profession; it appoints the head of local law offices, where work is distributed and fees, fixed by ministerial tariff, are collected. Advocates are to employ any lawful means to assist their client, whose communication with them is privileged. Representation by advocate in court is not mandatory, though it seems to be usual. In addition to this, advocates give legal advice and draft documents.

Jurisconsults are legal advisers to state enterprises, government agencies, and other institutions and must usually have a law degree. They draft internal rules, contracts and commercial documents and represent their employer in court. In so far as their functions are those of advocates they come under the Ministry of Justice.

Notaries are state officials organized under the Ministry of Justice and usually have either legal education or practical experience. They attest documents, draw up conveyances, mortgages, wills and the like but may not issue documents which violate the law or which, though apparently legal, have the aim of violating the interests of the socialist state.

Substantive law

The fundamental principles of the various branches of law are enacted at all-Union level and then expanded in the Codes of the republics. Although the system repudiates any formal division into public and private law, one category deals with essentially the public sector: land law, water resources, health, education and the like. A second category directly affects the individual as well as state enterprises. Thus the RSFSR Civil Code is, in appearance, not unlike that of other Western countries. It defines the legal capacity of both natural and juridical persons; and lays down the principles of the law of property, beginning with a sentence very similar to that in the Napoleonic Code: 'The owner shall have the powers of possession, use and disposal of property within the limits established by law.' The difference is, of course, functional rather than formal and lies in the limits imposed by the Constitution* and the criminal law. The Civil Code then deals with the law of contract as applied both to individuals and to state enterprises; with the law of tort, likewise; and with that of wills and inheritance. Family law and labour law are contained in separate Codes. A particular feature of all three is their reference to moral and ethical standards: for instance the Civil Code provides 'In

exercising their rights and performing their duties citizens must . . . respect the rules of socialist community life and the moral principles of a society that is building communism.'

Comrades' Courts

Although not part of the formal legal structure, Comrades' Courts illustrate community support of its ethical basis. They are bodies of neighbours or work-mates with power to call a hearing, to impose small sanctions and to express formal condemnation of bad behaviour. Thus, on the one hand they can institutionalize community attitudes (say, on dress, diet or belief) which are not the business of formal legislation; on the other hand they may be an efficient adjunct to the legal system. Conduct for which there exist legal sanctions both civil and criminal—such as deliberate failure of a parent to maintain infant children—may be referred instead to the more immediate reaction of the Comrades' Court. In this way the distinction between the pressures on individual decision imposed by the state through its laws and by society through its disapproval is quite deliberately blurred.   *B.R.*

The penal system

The Criminal Code lays down two prerequisites to criminal liability: the judgment of a court; and the infringement of an express provision of the criminal law. Thus the old rule under which conduct could be punished by 'analogy' with the nearest applicable statute has gone.

A suspect may be detained for up to three days without warrant. Thereafter he can be detained only by court decision or (most commonly) by order of the Procurator* until trial; but the maximum period of pre-trial detention is nine months. At the conclusion of the preliminary investigation and thereafter he is entitled to defence counsel. His trial should be public (save where state secrets are involved) and may be held in a factory, on private premises or in the normal courtroom. In addition to professional advocates, the court may permit representatives of the community (CPSU,* trade union,* Komsomol*) to appear as social accuser or defender.

The law provides that the court may not transfer the burden of proof to the accused; that he need not testify; that he may call evidence; that the verdict must be according to the evidence given; and that a confession alone is not sufficient evidence. The prosecution is conducted by the Procurator who may also recommend sentence; he is to be guided by the law and his 'inner conviction'. In common with European systems, the bench does not merely act as umpire; the judge is expected to question witnesses himself and indeed, if the Procurator drops the case during the hearing, the judge must continue it.   *B.R.*

Law enforcement agencies

The People's Militia

Militia is the name given to the police, the latter word being used only of the force in bourgeois countries. It is organized under the Ministry of Internal Affairs (MVD) whose structure has been often altered. The latest general regulation on the militia is a 1973 Decree (*Ukaz*) of the USSR Supreme Soviet Presidium.★ This lays down the basic duties and powers of the militia and emphasizes the principle of dual subordination, the force being subject both to its own superior agency and to the local soviet.★ Thus the appointment of recruits – who must be of proven political and practical competence – is made by the local militia chief and approved by the local soviet.

The militia's main tasks are: criminal investigation and prevention, for which they have powers to demand identification, to enter buildings and to arrest; the maintenance of public order which includes the detention of vagrants, beggars and drunken persons and the exposure of 'people declining socially useful work and leading an anti-social parasitic way of life'; enforcement of the passport system★ (internal and external) with powers of entry into dwellings; licensing the possession of firearms, explosives and photo-copiers; traffic control including the administration, licensing and inspection of motor vehicles. Militia departments are organized into branches: uniformed police, criminal detection, passport section, state automobile inspection (GAI), prosecuting section (when investigation is not undertaken by the Procuracy★ or the KGB★) and training and administration sections. There is a special transport militia subordi-

Traffic police (GAI) using a stereoscopic camera at the scene of an accident in an icebound Moscow street

nate both to the regular militia and the appropriate transport organization.

The Criminal Code imposes stricter penalties (including death) for crimes against the militia, and they may shoot if attacked or to prevent the escape from arrest of an adult male.

The People's Guards

The word here translated 'guards' (*druzhiny*) is an ancient term describing the close advisers and comrades-in-arms (the 'Household Guard') of the medieval Russian princes. In the late 1950s it was revived by RSFSR joint Party-government decrees (source of the quotations which follow) as part of a movement to 'enlist working people in the cause of protecting public order and the observance of legality', which also produced Comrades' Courts'.★ They are volunteers of 'professional, moral and political qualities' who organize detachments in factories, collective farms, institutions, apartment blocks and so on, directed by Party★ agencies, and with a hierarchical structure up to district or city level; their members are equipped with a guard certificate, badge and arm-band.

Their main function is to increase people's 'respect for the law and the rules of socialist community life' – in particular to help maintain public order and combat drunkenness, child neglect, road accidents and the like. They must also support the agencies of the Ministry of Internal Affairs, the Procuracy★ and the courts and report suspected crimes★ to the police. To carry out these tasks they may demand passports, driving licences and other documents, enter public gatherings (cinemas, sports stadia) detain malefactors for delivery to the police and, in emergencies, commandeer private transport. To assist them they have free travel on public transport (except taxis) and the free use of office and factory telephones. To protect them, the criminal law equates them with policemen in cases of resistance or violence. Although the activity is unpaid, disability incurred in connection therewith attracts preferential benefits. A good record may qualify the guards for extra paid holidays and preference in housing.

A USSR Party-government Decree of 1974, after describing shortcomings, urged the formation of more zealous detachments and enacted a model statute thereon – the main formal difference being to place them under the direction of the local soviets.★　　　*B.R.*

Dissent: its rise and diversification

The Democratic Movement and *samizdat*

While political opposition of any consequence has not existed in the USSR since the 1920s (except in the Ukraine and the Baltic republics 1944–53), open dissent from various Soviet norms and policies began to emerge soon after Stalin's★ death ended his system of mass terror in 1953. With important exceptions this dissent did not take on organized forms until 1965–8, years which saw the maturing of the Human Rights Movement. Initially this was primarily a defensive reaction by a few thousand well-educated urban people against the first moves by the post-Khrushchev★ leadership to reduce the area of conditional freedom opened up for the 'creative intelligentsia' by Khrushchev. By openly resisting political trials and campaigning for them to be conducted with full observance of the law, these people hoped to reverse what they saw as neo-Stalinist tendencies in policy. As the movement developed, however, it resisted injustices steadily in more areas of human rights, and sought reforms and dialogue with the authorities. When these declined to enter into any but occasional and usually indirect discussions, and launched countermeasures more readily than reforms, the dissenters increasingly called for support from their fellow-citizens and from organizations abroad.

Many dissenters have been concerned not only, or even mainly, with defending the human rights of others, but also with free self-expression–individually or in groups–in such areas as literature,★ the arts, politics, economics, trade unions, law and religion, determined to exercise a much greater freedom of expression and association than the authorities have usually been prepared to grant. This broad community–comprising a wide range of political views–has been more informally and loosely structured than the Human Rights Movement, which it incorporates, and is often known as the Democratic Movement. Such a community could develop only because of the ideological vacuum left in much of society by the mass terror, and because the dissenters managed to break down important taboos built up by a related product of the terror, social atomization. Thus dissidents have put loyalty to each other above obedience to the secret police (KGB★); have formed unofficial groups; interceded for persecuted individuals and groups; founded samizdat (privately circulated typescript) periodicals to publish independent writing and information on conflict situations involving human rights; spirited samizdat material out of the country to be published abroad and, more important, broadcast back into the USSR by foreign radio stations, thus circumventing the censorship★ which denies them access to Soviet media; given press conferences for foreign journalists; and each had appeared by the spring of 1980.

The 5000-odd samizdat items which reached the West between the early 1960s and 1980 vary in length from one-page protest documents to novels and anthologies of 800–900 pages. Among them are about 40 periodicals which have come out with some regularity for greater or lesser periods of time. The best known of these is the main organ of the Human Rights Movement, *Khronika tekushchikh sobytiy* (*Chronicle of Current Events*), of which 56 issues (of up to 200 pages each) had appeared by the spring of 1980.

Among the better known groups within the Human Rights

Patients exercising in partitioned compounds outside the Oryol Special Psychiatric Hospital

Movement have been the Initiative Group for the Defence of Human Rights in the USSR (founded in 1969), the Human Rights Committee (formed in 1970 by Andrey Sakharov★–born 1921, Nobel Peace Prize, 1975, exiled to Gor'ky in 1980–and others), the Groups to Assist the Implementation of the Helsinki Agreements★ in the USSR (set up in 1976–7 in Moscow, Ukraine, Lithuania, Georgia and Armenia), and the Working Commission to Investigate the Use of Psychiatry★ for Political Purposes (founded in 1977).

Among the better known samizdat authors writing in Russian have been Sakharov, Alexander Solzhenitsyn,★ Andrey Amalrik (1938–80), Vladimir Voinovich (b.1932), Anatoly Marchenko (b.1938), Pyotr Grigorenko (b. 1907), Alexander Zinoviev (b.1922), Roy Medvedev (b.1925), Zhores Medvedev (b.1925), Nadezhda Mandel'shtam (1899–1980), Natalya Gorbanevskaya (b. 1936), Vladimir Bukovsky (b.1942) and Valery Chalidze (b.1938). The best known leader of dissenting artists has been Oskar Rabin (b.1928).

Nationalist and religious protest

The Democratic Movement has developed links over time with a wide variety of dissenting national minority groups. Most of these object to the regime's declared goal that all the peoples of the USSR should eventually merge into a single Soviet people, and see this as a lightly disguised policy of Russification. One category of groups consists of those belonging to nations with their own Union Republics, who seek to assert their constitutional right to considerable autonomy in language, culture, the economy and politics. The most powerful such movement is in Lithuania, where the interlocking of national and religious values (as in Poland) gains for it the support of a majority of the population. The others, in descending order of strength of their open dissent, are in the Ukraine, Georgia, Armenia, Estonia and Latvia. Dissent among the Muslims* of Central Asia appears to be quite strong, but largely covert. The best known figure among dissenting Russian nationalists is Solzhenitsyn. These oppose the revolutionary internationalism of the regime, its non-Russian ideology, its suppression of important national traditions, its persecution of the Orthodox Church,* and its squandering of the national patrimony by foreign sales of raw materials. Most of them, however, enjoy a certain official tolerance, evidently due to the authorities' hope of more popular support.

A second category contains the emigration* movements among the USSR's three million Jews* and two million Germans,* who by their militancy forced the regime in 1971 to allow a significant scale of emigration; between 1968 and 1980 some 250 000 Jews had left for Israel and elsewhere, and over 60 000 Germans had emigrated to West and East Germany.

'We Germans want to go to Germany'. Ethnic Germans from Estonia demonstrate outside the West German embassy in Moscow

A final category comprises, first, the Crimean Tatar* movement which aims at return from the exile in Central Asia to which Stalin deported their people (with great loss of life) in 1944; and second, the analogous movement of the Meskhetians, natives of southern Georgia, whose situation differs only in that Stalin did not accuse them of mass collaboration with the German invaders. The Crimean Tatars were absolved of this charge in 1967, after the first stage of a massive lobbying campaign begun in the late 1950s.

The Democratic Movement has also developed strong links with dissenting religious groups. Some of these, like the dissenting sectors of the Baptists,* Pentecostalists and Adventists, are concerned almost exclusively to resist state control of their activity and achieve greater freedom for religion. Others, like Lithuanian and Ukrainian Catholics,* or Russian or Georgian Orthodox,* often support in addition the socio-political aims of their own nationalist movement. Organized dissent among most denominations began in the early 1960s, in response to Khrushchev's anti-religious campaigns. The Baptists gave a strong lead, quickly developing a high level of *samizdat* activity, which they have maintained ever since. The number of Baptists in prison at any one time decreased from about 250 in the late 1960s to about 40 in early 1979.

The balance of intolerance

The dissenting groups and movements have considerable achievements to record. Mainly because of the Human Rights Movement's capacity to cooperate with all groups, and act for them as both a sounding-board and a civil liberties organization, the outside world and the Soviet population have gained access to extensive and accurate information about their situation. This information and other writings by dissidents have contributed substantially to the tarnishing of the official Soviet image of the USSR as a liberalized and contented society ruled by a peace-loving and universally popular regime. The dissenters have also broken down the virtual ban on emigration and made the authorities more hesitant than before about staging political trials or committing well-known figures to psychiatric hospitals; they often prefer to push would-be defendants into exile abroad. On the other hand the dissenters have achieved very little liberalization of the law, and may indeed have unwittingly provoked many of the changes in the opposite direction, such as those in the 1977 Constitution* which, in effect, outlaw dissent. And while the official campaigns to portray dissidents as agents of imperialist powers, or, at best, as swayed by bourgeois propaganda, have broadly failed, the Democratic Movement has only slowly widened its support base.

The instinctive tendency of the authorities to treat dissent in a defensive, heavy-handed way has been partially countered by the dissenting groups' capacity to absorb punishment and still develop, slowly but steadily, in depth and breadth. A second powerful factor –

also largely a product of the dissenters' efforts–has been the USSR's discovery that access to Western technology, goods and credit may be limited unless it curbs somewhat its intolerance of dissent. Underlying this intolerance appear to be fears about the regime's legitimacy and about the long-term growth potential of dissent. These make the regime's policy toward dissent basically reactionary, and inhibit it from trying to alleviate the root causes.   *P.R.*

Creating the 'new man'

The Soviet authorities, consistent with the principles of Marxism,* regard the transition to full communism* in the USSR as dependent primarily upon changes in the material basis of society–increased labour productivity, material abundance and technological advance. Progress towards full communism, however, is held to depend also upon changes in the values, beliefs and social practices of Soviet citizens themselves, the ultimate aim being the creation of a 'new Soviet man' to inhabit the communist society of the future. As the present Communist Party of the Soviet Union* Programme, adopted in 1961, puts it: 'In the struggle for the victory of communism, ideological work becomes an increasingly powerful factor. The higher the social consciousness of the members of society, the more fully and broadly their creative activities come into play in the building of the material and technical basis of communism, in the development of communist forms of labour and new relations between people and, consequently, the more rapidly and successfully the building of communism proceeds. The Party considers that the paramount task in the ideological field in the present period is to educate all working people in a spirit of ideological integrity and devotion to communism, and to cultivate in them a communist attitude to labour and the social economy; to eliminate completely the survivals of bourgeois views and morals; to ensure the all-round harmonious development of the individual; [and] to create a truly rich spiritual culture. Particular importance is attached by the Party to the moulding of the rising generation.'

The elaboration of a programme of measures towards this end has been the object of considerable attention, virtually since the establishment of the regime itself in 1917. This programme extends very broadly indeed: literature* and the arts,* the educational system,* libraries* and museums, the mass media,* and the multiplicity of posters and slogans that adorn Soviet streets and workplaces, are all instruments of the 'ideological work of the Party'. The two most important agencies by which the Party's message is conveyed to the population, however, are the 'system of political and economic education', a network of schools and study circles intended primarily (but not exclusively) for party members; and 'mass-political work' (or *agitprop*–propaganda and agitation), a less formal system of political talks and lectures designed for the adult population as a whole. It is upon the effectiveness of these two systems that the creation of 'new Soviet man' primarily depends.

The system of political and economic education is organized at three main levels, primary (Elementary Political Schools), intermediate (Schools of the Fundamentals of Marxism-Leninism*) and advanced (Universities of Marxism-Leninism, Schools of the Party *Aktiv*–most active members–theoretical seminars and other forms).

THE SYSTEM OF POLITICAL AND ECONOMIC EDUCATION

Level	Form and period of study	Students in 1976–77 *million*	Subjects of study
Primary	Lectures and discussion; 5–6 years	2.4	Biography of Lenin, fundamentals of political and economic knowledge, current Party policy
Intermediate	Discussion and independent study; 6–8 years	8.0	History of the CPSU, political economy, Marxist-Leninist philosophy, fundamentals of scientific communism
Advanced	Mainly independent study and practical work; period of study depends upon form concerned	10.4	Various; depends upon form of advanced political education concerned
Komsomol	Lectures and discussion	7.0	Komsomol history, fundamentals of Marxism-Leninism, current Party policy
Economic	Lectures and discussion	35.0	Economic and production questions and current Party policy

Source: *Partiynaya zhizn'*, no. 21, 1977

THE MASS AGITATION SYSTEM

Personnel	Number in 1976 *million*	Typical method of work
Agitators	3.7	15- to 20-minute talk or discussion usually on production theme; normally conducted weekly
Political informers	1.8	20- to 30-minute lecture on economic, political, cultural or international theme; conducted three or four times a month
Lecturers (dokladchiki)	0.3	1- to 2-hour lecture on major questions of foreign or domestic policy; conducted on important occasions and anniversaries
Znanie Society lecturers	3.0	Lectures on philosophy, Party history, popular science; varying frequency

Source: *Partiynaya zhizn'*, no. 10, 1976

Classes are conducted by 'propagandists', of which in 1979 there were about 2.3 million. Together with the Komsomol* and economic education systems, which provide political and economic instruction at a less advanced level, about 70 million people are at present engaged in political and economic education.

The system of *agitprop* or mass-political work is intended to extend more widely; indeed virtually the entire adult population is supposed to be exposed to some form of political influence of this kind. Each level of the system comes under Party control at an appropriate level in the hierarchy; and together with less formal systems of agitation and propaganda, such as the Znanie (Knowledge) Society lectures, they constitute a system of political persuasion of formidable proportions. During 1978, for instance, the Znanie Society alone provided more than 25 million lectures to a total audience of over 1262 million people; and this figure excluded the Society's radio and television lectures.

The effects of this massive programme of indoctrination are not easy to determine. Party spokesmen certainly claim, as did Brezhnev at the XXV Party Congress in 1976, that the historical experience of

The director of a school museum lectures pupils on the youth of Karl Marx

Soviet rule has brought into being a man who 'overcoming all hardships, has changed himself beyond recognition, who combines in himself ideological conviction and tremendous vital energy, culture, knowledge and the skill to apply it', a man who 'while a fervent patriot, is and will always be a consistent internationalist'; a man who (in the words of a *Pravda* editorial) is 'in a word and in all things – a dedicated and active fighter for the Party's great cause, for the triumph of communist ideas'. A good deal of behavioural evidence tends to support such claims. Membership of political and social organizations, for instance, has steadily grown; electoral* turnout has risen continuously since the early years of Soviet rule; and levels of participation in socio-political life more generally have also increased, and become more evenly distributed between the sexes, generations and nationalities.

Political participation in the USSR, however, is not necessarily an entirely voluntary matter, and growth of this kind cannot therefore be taken in itself to indicate a corresponding change in political beliefs and values. Empirical investigations conducted within the country since the early 1970s have established that substantial proportions of those who attend political education classes and lectures do so only under Party or administrative pressure. Interest in subjects such as Marxist-Leninist philosophy and political economy lags consistently behind interest in current affairs and developments abroad; and the content of classes and lectures appears to leave a good deal to be desired, so far as both the Party and the audiences are concerned. Those who attend such sessions regularly are better informed than their colleagues about most areas of national and local life, but this appears to be largely because the better-informed are, in the first place, more likely to participate. Substantial proportions of the population, moreover – particularly younger people, housewives and pensioners – appear to lie outside the scope of the political propaganda system altogether.

Soviet citizens generally appear to be committed to many of the basic principles of the Soviet way of life, such as public ownership of most sectors of the economy, extensive state intervention in virtually all areas of life, and a welfare-oriented health and education system. The best efforts of the propaganda system, however, appear to have failed to secure overwhelming popular endorsement for the principles of Marxism-Leninism, or – perhaps more important – for authoritarian single-party rule; and as younger generations grow up with a more accurate appreciation of the real state of affairs in capitalist countries, and without personal involvement in the heroic achievements of the Soviet past, such an endorsement is likely to become no easier to secure. 'New Soviet man', in other words, has not yet been created; it seems likely, rather, that the basis of commitment to the Soviet political order will increasingly come to rest upon a relatively shrewd assessment of its social and economic performance in comparison with that of its major global competitors.   *S.W.*

THE ECONOMY

Open-cast mining in the Urals requires giant equipment: a mobile excavator with a 100-metre boom and 100 cu m shovel, 1978

Retardation under serfdom

During the millennium that elapsed between the emergence of Russia as a political entity in the ninth century and the abolition of serfdom in 1861 the country witnessed vast territorial expansion, a rise to imperial* status and fundamental changes outside its borders in the economies and societies of Western Europe under the impact of the Industrial Revolution. Throughout, Russia's economy remained backward compared to Western Europe, the bulk of its income and wealth deriving from traditional low-yielding agriculture* and artisan industry pursued to an overwhelming extent on a subsistence basis.

One period (roughly 9th-13th century) does not fully conform to this pattern. The basis of wealth creation in Kievan* Russia was not agriculture, which was largely primitive, but trade with Byzantium, western Europe and the Orient. Successive nomadic* invasions put an end to this trade, and the devastation following the Mongol* invasion of 1240 completed the displacement of the Russian people to the relative safety of the forests of the north-east, the cradle of future Muscovy.* The Mongol onslaught and the two and a half centuries of occupation constituted the first major crisis to affect the economy and society of Russia. The low-yielding agricultural economy allowed for little accumulation, while the tribute imposed by the Mongols and their repeated raids and punitive expeditions meant a continuous drain of resources. However, the Mongol fiscal organization based on censuses of households was to be a useful means of resource mobilization in the hands of Moscow rulers, although it is uncertain whether the peasant commune (*mir*), which was to be such a significant feature of Russia's agrarian structure at least until 1906, had its origins here. The *mir* periodically redistributed land among households and regulated agricultural use of common land.

The second major crisis occurred in the 16th and early 17th century and was associated with the despotic policies of Ivan IV,* the Livonian War, the civil war and foreign intervention following the extinction of the dynasty. Several consecutive famines depopulated central areas through flight or death, economic activity declined and serfdom began to be imposed. However, this period also saw positive developments: the exploration* of the White Sea route, the temporary gain of a foothold on the Baltic, the conquest of Siberia, the freeing of the Volga route from the Tatars*–all elements in the growth of trading potential.

The 17th century marked the beginnings of a business economy. English and, above all, Dutch merchants activated Russia's internal and foreign trade and turned increasingly to industrial activities with the encouragement of the Russian government. Native businessmen appeared less enterprising: they lacked the resources and experience of their foreign counterparts and were taxed more heavily than the latter. Russian and foreign merchants alike suffered from the ruler's right of pre-emption on the most lucrative goods.

The commercial and industrial advances of the 16th and 17th centuries were insufficient to meet fully the demands of Peter the Great's* military effort in prising open access to the Baltic. While Peter's economic achievements were largely a function of his military ambitions and involved massive state intervention in the provision of capital, markets and labour, in the long run private initiative and autonomous growth were released; the 17th century 'manufactory' was the transmitter of technology, skills and entrepreneurship. During the 18th century Russia became the single largest exporter of iron and had a virtual monopoly on exports of products such as flax, hemp and tar. The development of ports, canals and roads* quickened the pace of internal commerce, as did to some extent the abolition of internal tariffs, the beginning of organized banking, and initially the issue of paper money under Catherine II.*

Victory over the Turks gained for Russia access to the Black Sea, opening foreign markets to grain export. However, as price differentials suggest, the isolation of individual regions remained, probably because of transportation difficulties and inadequacies in commercial organization. Private industrial entrepreneurship, no longer foreign only, appeared among serfs, noblemen and merchants, and operated in areas of consumer rather than state demand. But whereas the Industrial Revolution had had its effect in most of Western Europe and above all in Britain by the end of the Napoleonic wars, relative retardation made Russia assume the role of supplier of foodstuffs and primary products to those industrializing and urbanizing countries. Russia's increased agricultural output (first the fortuitous outcome of Peter the Great's Poll Tax, and after 1775 consequent upon price rises) was due to area extension rather than to

Peter the Great's Admiralty iron-works and shipyards

improved yields. The internal market for grain was limited and exports were hampered by the British Corn Laws, distance and inadequate transport. Nevertheless, Russia was far from stagnant: the over-all value of manufacturing output grew 40 times between 1799 and 1858 – a fivefold increase per head – and made up about 15 per cent of the gross national product. However, though the factory labour force likewise grew about fivefold between 1804 and 1860 it represented only about one per cent of the population. Two-thirds of the value of industrial output came from artisan workshops and domestic industry which was scattered over the vast empire. Modern technology began to be employed on a significant scale in two industries working for an internal consumer market, sugar refining and cotton spinning; in the rest of industry handicraft methods prevailed. By the mid-century (1859) only about 7 per cent of the population lived in cities, compared with some 50 per cent in England and Wales and 25.5 per cent in France (1850).

This retardation has been ascribed to various causes. Serfdom, a means for securing not so much supply of labour as of taxes and recruits, was introduced by statute as late as 1649, though it had been evolving since at least the end of the 15th century. While it certainly stifled initiative and advance, induced apathy and kept demand low, it was not the only reason for Russia's long-standing backwardness. Another factor was an excess of government involvement in the economy which crowded out private enterprise and caused commercial decisions to be taken on non-economic grounds, although without state support in the early 18th century little economic progress could have been achieved. The physical environment* – poor quality soil, climate, distances and location of resources on the periphery – has been a factor both in Russia's poverty before the industrial age and in the high cost and effort involved in economic development since. To this must be added the cost of first attaining and then sustaining great-power status, which meant a continuous drain of resources away from domestic accumulation through the budget for military and strategic purposes. *O.C.*

The start to industrialization

The emancipation of the serfs by an Imperial Manifesto of 19 February 1861 under Alexander II* was the dividing line between old and modern Russia. Soviet historians see it as the symbol of the transition from feudalism to capitalism: they rightly insist that the reform was a precondition of industrialization on the capitalist model and of agricultural expansion, and consider that a 'revolutionary situation' existed in 1858–61. In political terms the tsar preferred that 'hostility between peasants and their owners' be dealt with 'from above rather than from below', but his government's economic

motivation was to foster industry after Russia's defeat – substantially due to inadequate armaments – in the Crimean War: the lifting of the yoke of serfdom would allow manpower to take jobs wherever offered.

The emancipation freed 22 million serfs (40 per cent of the nation), but failed to establish conditions for an independent and prosperous peasantry. Excluding Poland, the land allocated to peasants was on average 13 per cent less than that which they had previously tilled for their own use, and remained subject to redistribution by the *mir*, thereby perpetuating the serf's indifference to land improvement. The government financed the land allotment to former serfs against redemption dues payable over the ensuing 49 years. Reduction of burdens on the peasantry did not begin until 1881, with the abolition of the poll tax on landless peasants, the moderation of redemption dues, and the establishment of a Peasant Land Bank to finance the purchase of land. By the mid-1890s, however, tax arrears had reached equality with tax assessments; peasant (and worker) unrest increased under the impact of the depression of 1900–2 and continued sporadically until it culminated in the uprising of December 1905.

On the eve of emancipation, the industrial labour force included 1.2 million serfs, but despite the apparent mass availability of rural manpower after 1861 employers in mining and manufacturing tended to choose capital-intensive plant. Workshop and individual artisan industry often had a competitive edge over large-scale factory industry, with high fixed costs and overheads, and factories, particularly after the depression, concentrated into larger units or formed cartels. On the eve of the First World War Russia could be described as a 'dual economy' – big modern firms in industry, and small-scale activity in artisan trades and agriculture.* The 'dual economy' is a characteristic of many underdeveloped countries,

A blast furnace in central Russia, 1890s

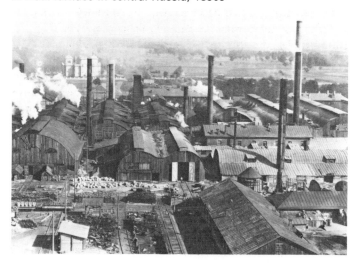

The Economy in a Time Perspective

LOCATION OF INDUSTRY, 1900

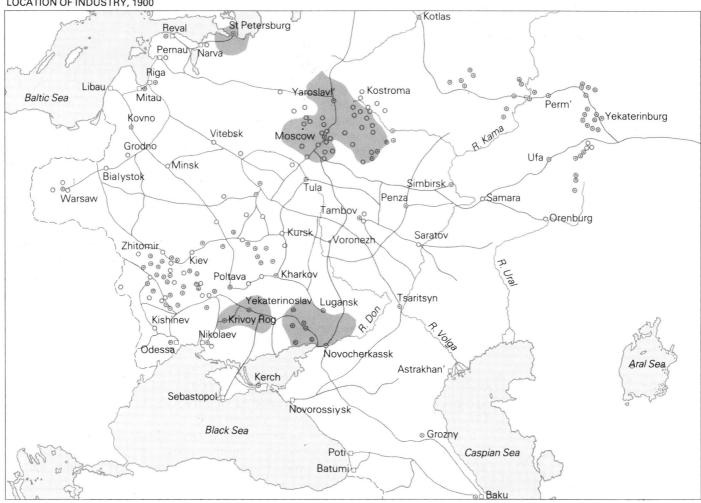

KEY

	Railways
	Areas with greatest influx of workers from other regions
⊙	Predominantly producers' goods
○	Predominantly consumers' goods
□	Principal ports

Source: M. Gilbert, *Russian History Atlas*, London, 1972

Opening of a new bridge on the Trans-Siberian Railway, December 1911

which are unable to rely on direct taxation because of the small share of income arising in money form in the peasant and handicrafts sector. Indirect taxation made the peasant bear much of the cost of the bureaucracy, state investment and subsidies to guarantee interest on foreign loans. The landowning classes neither saved nor were taxed in proportions that would generate substantial domestic investment and by spending much on travel abroad burdened the balance of payments. West European investment financed both the savings and the foreign-exchange gaps.

RUSSIAN ECONOMIC EXPANSION 1890–1913

	percentage increase
Population	37.3
of which urban	68.9
Per capita output of grain	35.3
Per capita industrial output	124.0
Employment in mining, manufacturing and railways	128.5
Length of railway network	132.0

Source: A. Kahan in *The Cambridge Economic History of Europe*, vol. vii, Part 2, Cambridge. 1978

Railways* especially attracted foreign capital for their construction and constituted material security for loans; they stimulated the growth of Russian industries to supply them (for example with rails, rolling stock and coal), provided training for entrepreneurship and management, and greatly widened the Russian market. The Trans-Siberian Railway (built 1891–1915) and other lines distributed peasants deeper into the steppe and the further these settlers were from towns, the more they committed their grain to the railway for cash disposal (freight-tariffs were geared to export sales).

The imposition of a customs tariff in 1885 further fostered industrial investment and, despite relative stagnation in and after the depression of 1900–2, impressive growth was achieved in both industry and agriculture. Farming was stimulated after the 1905 revolution by the Stolypin* reform, whereby redemption dues were liquidated from 1907. From October 1906 the peasant could receive an internal passport* without the consent of the commune; this gave him the right to settle elsewhere, but most stayed on the land to constitute what Stolypin hoped would be 'a class of small proprietors–this basic cell of the State and in its very nature an adversary of all destructive theories'.   *M.K.*

Revolution and 'War Communism'

It was one of the 'destructive theories' that Stolypin* feared–Marxism* as interpreted by Lenin*–which inspired the Bolshevik* victory of 1917, but it is questionable whether the Russian war economy was so grossly inefficient that the tsarist collapse was inevitable once hostilities began. The output of armaments (mainly due to increasing productivity in the munitions industry) expanded substantially in 1915 and 1916 and the civilian standard of living was not reduced before the end of 1916. The economic element in the 1917 revolutions was the withdrawal of labour from farming by conscription to the army and a food supply crisis in 1917. Although there is controversy over the weakness of government wartime industrial organization and whether it was effectively replaced by committees of private manufacturers, the Provisional Government* (February–October 1917) introduced a centralized control structure, headed by an Economic Council, with a Supreme Economic Committee as its executive agency. The Soviet authorities transformed that Committee into the Supreme Economic Council ('Vesenkha', from its Russian initials) and Lenin toyed with schemes of a mixed economy and of cooperatives until the emergence of direct worker management–such factory committees constituting a political threat to the local soviets*–compelled him to nationalize large-scale industry (28 June 1918). The rest of industry was expropriated on 29 November 1920 and the period to March 1921 is known in retrospect as 'War Communism'.

The exigencies of supply in the civil war* were a major factor in the new Soviet government's choice of complete nationalization, the administration by directive of industry and transport and the

Muscovites queue for food outside a bullet-scarred store, 1920

Citizens of Kerch (Crimea) set off for unpaid Saturday labour
– a feature of 'War Communism'

Payment of tax in kind at Yegor'evsk, near Moscow, 1922
– N. I. Bukharin's 'riding into socialism on a peasant nag'

compulsory procurement of foodstuffs from farmers. But there was an ideological motive in rejecting use of the market and of the money mechanism – antipathy to the 'spontaneity' of the market and preference for planning in terms of physical targets. The government tolerated, if not encouraged, inflation (in 1920 currency circulation rose from 225 to 1169 thousand million roubles), characterized by E. A. Preobrazhensky (1886–1937), Trotsky's principal economist ally, as 'the machine-gun of the Commissariat of Finance, attacking the bourgeois system in the rear and using the currency laws of that system to destroy it'. All banks were abolished and money itself was on the point of being replaced by 'labour units'. The state budget financed all nationalized production enterprises, which were thereby relieved of having to pay, and be paid by, one another (the practice became known as 'glavkism', after the name of the administering state agencies). Money wages being almost worthless, payment in kind and rationing predominated. A State Commission for the Electrification of Russia (GOELRO, 1920) drew up a plan on the basis of material balances – that is, of projected availabilities and requirements of energy and industrial material in physical, not money, quantities. To implement it a State Planning Commission (Gosplan) was established in February 1921.   M.K.

Lenin's 'New Economic Policy'

Peasant risings in late 1920 against compulsory procurement of farm produce and the Kronstadt mutiny in early 1921 warned the Party* leadership against the excesses of a 'command economy'. Lenin* secured a Central Committee* resolution criticizing Trotsky* for 'the

degeneration of centralism and militarized forms of work' in December 1920 and presented the X Party Congress in March 1921 with a formula for replacing requisitions in agriculture* by a tax related to level of income and numbers of dependents. For that and the following year the tax was levied in kind, but from 1923 it was payable partly (and from 1924 wholly) in cash. The peasant could market the rest of his surplus and a general return to a money economy was re-established under the 'New Economic Policy' (NEP).

Inflation was halted by a currency reform (1922–4), introducing a new, partly gold-backed* rouble and a banking system to control money supply (the State Bank in October 1921 and specialized, state-run investment banks during 1922). Decrees of August and December 1921 handed back so much property to private owners that only 8.5 per cent of industrial enterprises remained nationalized. These latter, however, occupied 84 per cent of the labour force, thereby retaining, as Lenin put it, the 'commanding heights' of the economy in the hands of the state. Even at the peak of NEP in 1925/6, private plants produced only 3.5 per cent and foreign concessions (permitted by a decree of March 1923, but withdrawn after September 1928) a mere 0.4 per cent of the output of large-scale industry. State entities were largely restricted to wholesale trade (thereby exercising some control over prices* and distribution); 76 per cent of retail turnover was in private hands by 1923.

Bias towards the independent peasantry – politically determined by Lenin's policy of their 'alliance' with the urban working class and economically by the importance of restoring food production – was demonstrated in the 'Scissors Crisis' of 1923/4. On an index 1913 = 100, the price of farm produce was 89 and of industrial goods 276; the symbolism was of a widening of the price 'handles' of the 'scissors' to cut the standard of living of the peasantry. The

'On steel horses to socialism' caps the 'peasant nag' at the 1930 opening of the Stalingrad tractor plant

Grain delivery by camel from a newly-formed collective farm near Stalingrad, 1931

government ordered state production trusts to reduce prices and until early 1927 continued to keep industrial prices artificially low. The right wing of the Party, as represented by N. I. Bukharin (1888–1938), advocated the maintenance of such preference for farming: sales of foodstuffs at home and for export would generate savings which could be taxed for industrialization. The left – notably Trotsky and E. A. Preobrazhensky (1886–1937) – urged 'unequal exchange' between country and town, that is a policy of direct exploitation of the agricultural surplus, for rapid industrialization. A temporary curtailment of grain marketed in 1927/8 – deliberately magnified by Stalin into a 'grain crisis' – helped the Party Central Committee* in July 1928 to adopt a 'high variant' of the draft Five-year Plan* and to demand a 'tribute' from the peasantry to furnish the necessary accumulation; in September the fight against the richer farmer (the *kulak*) was equated with that against external class enemies. *M.K.*

The pre-war Five-year Plans

The First Five-year Plan was inaugurated on 1 October 1928, and declared to have been completed in the four and a quarter years to 31 December 1932; it launched a programme of industrial investment on an unprecedented scale (mainly in the capital goods' industries). The Second Five-year Plan (1933–7) consolidated and broadened those projects, while the Third (1938–42) was interrupted by the German invasion of 22 June 1941. In 1928–37 industrial production* increased by 12–18 per cent a year, machine-building expanded particularly rapidly, and many new industries were established; tractors, trucks, iron and steel-making equipment and modern tanks

and aircraft, for example, were all produced for the first time on a mass scale. Industrial growth was achieved partly by a massive increase in the labour force: the number of persons employed in industry, including building,* increased from 4.3 million in 1928 to 11.6 million in 1937. But capital stock in industry increased much more rapidly than the labour force, so capital per worker rose substantially; consequently, after an initial decline in 1930–2, labour productivity (output per man-year) also increased rapidly. No clear evidence is available about the efficiency with which resources were utilized, though emphasis was placed throughout these years on growth rather than on care for costs and avoidance of waste. Attention was also devoted to the social services: employment increased at the same rate in education* as in industry, and employment in the health services* also expanded rapidly.

In contrast, personal consumption per head of population declined in 1928–32, and did not regain the 1928 level until well after the Second World War. The production of industrial consumers' goods* increased much more slowly than that of capital goods, and, even according to official figures, agricultural production per head of population was about 10 per cent lower in 1937–9 than in 1927–9. The decline in food production per head was even greater, particularly during the First Five-year Plan when there was a catastrophic fall in the number of livestock. In 1932–3 famine was widespread in the countryside.

While agricultural production did not increase in 1929–41, or increased very slowly, major changes occurred in the structure of agriculture. During enforced collectivization,* mainly carried out between the autumn of 1929 and the end of 1931, 20 million individual farms were amalgamated into 250 000 collectives. The boundaries between strips were removed, and arable land was

The Economy in a Time Perspective

worked in common, using, as they became available, tractors and other agricultural machinery from machine-tractor stations; these gradually replaced the individual's horse and plough. At the same time each collective-farm household also owned some livestock, and retained a personal plot for vegetables and fruit. A large part of collective production, particularly grain, was compulsorily supplied to the state at low prices;* but some collective and much personal production were sold on a free market (officially sanctioned in 1932). The collective farm was thus a compromise between social and private ownership; planned controls similar to those used in state industry were combined with a market mechanism, which together constituted an effective, if not an efficient, means for increasing the supply of grain to the state. The state in turn sold grain to the rapidly expanding urban population and also (in 1930–2, when machinery imports greatly increased) on the foreign market (annual deliveries were 30 million tonnes in 1938–40 as compared with 10 million tonnes in 1926–8, although the harvest was only 3–4 million tonnes higher). The system also facilitated the release of labour to the towns: the agricultural labour force is estimated to have fallen from 71 million in 1928 to 57 million in 1937 (in early stages in industrialization elsewhere in the world, the rural population* tended to rise). But the pressure on the collective farm to supply the state at low prices destroyed incentives, while the slaughter of livestock in 1930–3 greatly reduced capital, including draught power. Supplies to agriculture were nevertheless substantial: that of machinery increased, and peasants received high prices on the free market.

The net effect of the introduction of the collective-farm system on the process of industrialization is still disputed: although it provided a crucial, if costly, mechanism for the supply of agricultural products and labour to the state, a large amount of machinery and consumers'

goods was supplied by industry to agriculture in return for the supply of agricultural products to the towns. The mechanism of controls over industry was also by directive: materials and capital equipment were allocated to factories and construction sites. The central control of wages,* made possible by subordination (by 1929) of the trade unions,* restricted urban purchasing power and for several years reduced the standard of living of most of the urban population, in favour of expenditure on capital goods.

Neither the industrial nor the collective-farm system consisted simply of physical controls. Rationing of food and consumers' goods, introduced in the towns in 1928–9, was abolished in 1935, after which the authorities attempted to balance supply and demand on the retail market: consumer choice, if not consumer sovereignty, to some extent existed. At the same time, most industrial workers and other state employees (those outside the growing forced-labour of the prison camps*) remained free to change their jobs; an imperfect market for labour existed. Cost controls and profit-and-loss accounting*, major features of state industry in the 1920s, were resumed and strengthened from 1931 onwards. Thus a money economy, with recognized market elements, existed together with physical planning; and official planning* was supplemented and made to work more smoothly by a variety of unplanned black and 'grey' markets.

The achievements were immense: the USSR was transformed into a major industrial power and equipped for defence in the Second World War.* Mass unemployment was eliminated, and millions of illiterate or poorly-educated peasants were trained in industrial skills. But the costs and failures were also immense. Many people suffered and died. The planning system was crude; control of quality was difficult; innovation from below was inhibited. Economic and

---

Work in progress in 1929 on DneproGES, the biggest hydro-electric project of the First Five-year Plan

Car production at the AZLK plant, Moscow, in the 1930s

INDUSTRIAL OUTPUTS IN THE SOVIET PERIOD

Product	1913	1940	1965	1979
Electricity (*million MWh*)	2 W	49	507	1239
Oil (*million tonnes*)	10	31	243	586
Natural gas (*cu km*)	—	3	128	407
Coal (*million tonnes*)	29	166	578	719
Steel (*million tonnes*)	4	18	91	149
Mineral fertilizer (*million tonnes*)	0.1	3	31	95
Sulphuric acid (*million tonnes*)	0.1	2	9	22
Synthetic fibres (*thousand tonnes*)	—	11	407	1100
Metal-cutting machine tools (*thousands*)	2	58	186	231
Lorries (*thousands*)	—	136	380	780
Motor cars (*thousands*)	0.1	6	201	1314
Tractors (*thousands*)	—	32	355	557
Paper (*million tonnes*)	9990 3	1	3	5
Cement (*million tonnes*)	2	6	72	123
Textiles: cotton (*million sq m*)	1817	2715	5499	6974
wool (*million sq m*)	138	155	466	774
Leather footwear (*million pairs*)	68	211	486	739
Refrigerators (domestic) (*thousands*)	—	4	1675	5954
Sugar (*million tonnes*)	1	2	11	11

Source: *SSSR v tsifrakh v 1979 godu.* Moscow, 1980

social differentiation were far more extensive than any Soviet Marxist had envisaged before 1930. In 1929–41 a new political, economic and social order was created in the USSR, admired and hated in the West, envied but often misunderstood in countries which were not yet industrialized. R.W.D.

Planning in wartime and in reconstruction

In the five months following the German invasion (22 June 1941) 1500 industrial enterprises were dismantled for shipment east and ten million people were resettled. Mineral extraction and hydro-electricity generation cannot be transferred, and losses of ores and energy at first seriously hindered the war effort. Forced labour, which the Terror* of 1937–8 had made available in millions, was extensively used to extract non-ferrous ores in climatically harsh territories–notably at Karaganda in Central Asia, Noril'sk on the Arctic littoral and at Kolyma-Indigirka in the Far North-East. Some scientists among those arrested were placed in prison laboratories

where their research and development work was especially valuable in the production of military aircraft.

At its nadir in 1942 net material product was two-thirds of the 1940 level (agricultural output, due particularly to the German occupation of the Ukraine, was little more than one-third of pre-war), but no less than 55 per cent of it was devoted to military* purposes. That the USSR converted to armaments so extensively and so quickly under conditions of extreme shortage (and before lend-lease supplies became available from the USA) was undoubtedly due to central planning on material balances (a technique adopted by other belligerents) and to strict financial controls which inhibited wartime inflation (between 1940 and 1944 industrial wages rose 53 per cent and retail prices increased 120 per cent). The budget ran a significant deficit only in 1941 and 1942, taxation and bond sales matching the enlargement of public expenditure. Supply (chiefly by rail through Persia and by sea to Murmansk) from the Western Allies was crucial for opening bottle-necks (as in road transport), but it was the conversion of domestic industry to military needs that was quantitatively decisive for victory.

In conditions of peace the architect of the war economy, N. A. Voznesensky (1903–50), chairman of the USSR Gosplan, attempted to rationalize Stalin's* command system: he encouraged economics as a discipline (until 1943 Party* ideology had rejected any application of 'the law of value' to the public sector) and introduced a far-reaching reform of wholesale prices* (January 1949) which would have eliminated subsidies and fostered the profitable operation of state industry. For reasons which remain obscure (association with an opposition in Leningrad is one explanation), Voznesensky was dismissed in early 1949 and executed a year later. His reforms were annulled and improvements in price relations and in economic administration had to await the death of Stalin (March 1953).

By that time the reconstruction of a severely war-ravaged economy had been completed. The Fourth Five-year Plan (1946–50) had envisaged an increment of net material product, on an index 1940 = 100, from 83 in 1945 to 138 in 1950. The target was abundantly achieved at 173 by overfulfilment for producers' goods which more than offset a serious underfulfilment in farm output (and doubtless also in consumers' goods,* for which no goal had been published). Shortages of consumers' goods would have been worse if most of the cash in personal hands had not been confiscated simultaneously with the lifting of rationing in December 1947, but the real wage of 1928 was only regained in 1952.

Stalin's immediate successors–a 'collective leadership'* led by G. M. Malenkov (b.1902)–judged a stronger consumer orientation necessary and promulgated in October 1953 ambitious revisions of the Fifth Five-year Plan (1951–5). Though few of these were fulfilled, the output of consumers' goods significantly bettered the original goals. M.K.

Khrushchev's Seven-year Plan

Khrushchev* abandoned the Sixth Five-year Plan (1956–60) and the structure of economic administration which had formulated it, but his Seven-year Plan (1959–65) was much more than a revision of targets. It innovated by lengthening the period planned and by introducing rolling targets; broadened the group of priority sectors to include the chemicals* industry and private and cooperative housing;* accelerated railway* electrification and dieselization within a general programme of energy* shift from coal to oil and pursued the encouragement of agriculture.* Collective farming benefited in September 1953 by price increases for obligatory deliveries and in 1958 by the disbandment of machine-tractor stations, but Khrushchev alienated local Party officials in 1962 by dividing the CPSU* into agricultural and industrial sections. The objective was to make the Party more directly concerned with economic performance and, in its emphasis on local responsibility, to further the industrial reorganization, which was the issue on which he had defeated the 'anti-Party group'* in the Politburo.* In 1957 all the industrial ministries* save that dealing with nuclear engineering were abolished and their powers divided between the USSR Gosplan, the Union-Republican Gosplans and newly-established regional economic councils (*sovnarkhozy*). Since the boundaries of the 105 regional councils coincided with those of oblasts or groups thereof, the first secretary of the oblast Party committee had something like the authority of a minister, dealing, however, not with a single branch but with all his region's large-scale industry (smaller enterprises were subordinated to the Union Republic). The principal aim was to obliterate the ministerial demarcations, which under 'taut planning' induced ministries to produce materials and components for their own plants and often to deliver them across great distances while identical products crossed them within the supply system of another ministry. Unfortunately, the conditions which induced ministries to be self-sufficient obtained also for the regional authorities, and a recentralization began as early as 1962–3, when quasi-ministries returned in the form of state committees, and *sovnarkhozy* were merged into much bigger units.   *M.K.*

The economy under Brezhnev and Kosygin

Khrushchev's* reorganizations were castigated as 'harebrained schemes' by the revived 'collective leadership'* which replaced him in October 1964. He was also criticized for heavy imports of grain in 1963, because, despite his efforts to foster agriculture,* food supplies remained at the mercy of the weather. To pay for North American grain he had also depleted Soviet reserves of gold.*

The new administration, within which the Party General Secretary,* Brezhnev,* steadily gained precedence over the Chairman of the Council of Ministers,* A. N. Kosygin (1904–80), at first conformed in structuring the economy to Stalin's* injunction that the rate of growth of producers' goods exceed that of consumers' goods.* The Eighth Five-year Plan (1966–70) laid down a 51 per cent increment for the former and 45 per cent for the latter. In fulfilment, the rates of growth were almost identical (51 and 49 per cent respectively) and the government actually reversed the priorities for the Ninth Plan (1971–5)–a 46 per cent rise for consumers' goods and only 43 per cent for producers' goods. Two bad harvests within the period reduced supplies for the consumer-goods sector (and required purchases of North American grain) and the achieved growth rates were underfulfilments at 31 and 41 per cent respectively. Under the Tenth Plan (1976–80) investment resources were switched into farming and agriculture-supporting industries, and the over-all pace of industrial growth slackened to 24 per cent (against 36 per cent planned).

In re-establishing the Party and ministerial* structures which Khrushchev had broken up, the Brezhnev–Kosygin administration could, without divesting itself of central authority over the economy, have chosen among many proposals for 'automating' economic decisions. A school of mathematical* economics–repressed under Stalin and little regarded by Khrushchev–offered a variety of models whereby centrally-set plans could be formulated and implemented without the intervention of bureaucratic (and certainly non-optimizing) agencies. Although some use was made of electronic data-processing for plan construction and reporting, the most that was undertaken was an alleviation of the plan mechanism as it impinged on the basic production unit, the collective farm and the state industrial enterprise.

In March 1965 Brezhnev announced that procurement quotas would be fixed for five-year periods. Such stability would enable collective farms to gain a return from investment for themselves without danger of losing some of it to an increased quota. The government did not fully adhere to its undertaking because, through local and Party authorities, it pressed farms which increased output to deliver additional supplies, albeit at a premium of 50 per cent above the procurement price.

The reform of industrial administration of September 1965 implemented some of the proposals put forward in September 1962 by Ye. G. Liberman (b. 1897), a professor at Kharkov, for harnessing the profit motive to enterprise management and liberating contractual relations between enterprises from control by detailed allocations from above. The number of plan indicators required to be fulfilled by each enterprise was reduced to seven, chief among which ranked 'profitability'–profits as a rate of return on capital assets. Retained profits were divided between reinvestment, social facilities and bonuses to workers and management. Further liberalization was halted when the leadership convinced itself, for the invasion of Czechoslovakia,★ that economic devolution was associated with a loss of political control. Modest changes in procedures for managing state industry were made in April 1973 and July 1979, but wholesale and retail prices★ nevertheless remained both centrally determined and constant for long periods and there was no sense in which the state sector as it entered the 1980s could be seen as a market.   *M.K.*

KEY

Railways

o Predominantly producers' goods

◎ Predominantly consumers' goods

□ Principal ports

- - - Baykal–Amur Mainline (under construction)

Source: *Bol'shaya sovetskaya entsiklopediya*, 3rd edn, Vol. 24

Agriculture

Collectivization and state control

The small-peasant structure of Soviet agriculture was transformed during the 1930s into one of large socialized units–mostly nominally autonomous collectives, but also state farms. The change was brought about with ruthless force and cost millions of lives. Contrary to the intentions of the Party★ leadership, industrialization profited little, if at all, from the process because of the concomitant heavy economic losses; food production per head regained the 1928 level only 25 years later. By 1940 a collective farm (*kolkhoz*) worked on average 1400ha of agricultural land and was governed under a Model Statute centrally issued in 1935, which allowed for only small variations by regions or individual farms. In 1969, when the average area had by mergers and expansion reached 6100ha, a revision of the Statute brought only a little decontrol; the average was 6700ha in 1979. The state farm (*sovkhoz*), averaging 17 600ha in 1979 (12 200ha in 1940), and others run by public bodies held over half of arable and two-thirds of total agricultural land. Until 1958 machinery was

LOCATION OF INDUSTRY, 1976

exclusively owned by the state, either on its own farms or on machine-tractor stations having the dual role of servicing and supervising collective farms in their locality. Under Stalin★ collective and state farms were the main suppliers of food to the towns, while the rural population lived mainly on the output of collective-farmers' household plots (averaging 0.3ha) and livestock (state-farm workers were entitled to still smaller plots). This private sector also produced for the free market, as direct sales by producers (but not by intermediaries) were permitted on the 'collective farm market' from 1932; by 1940 such sales accounted for almost 50 per cent of total, and 27 per cent of marketed, output. Only with this private production, which – given the shortages in state shops – was much higher-priced than that originating in state deliveries, could the farm population survive.

The changes which have taken place since Stalin's death in 1953 have not substantially altered the agrarian system he imposed, but have nevertheless modified it in a dozen significant aspects: the prices of agricultural produce with respect to goods bought by farms were improved, enabling farms to increase investment and labour remuneration; procurement quotas were substituted for the former strict control over production; although with an interlude (1957–63) of efforts to the contrary, restrictions on private-plot production were relaxed; the sown area was enlarged by some 35 million ha of dry-farming land ('virgin lands campaign') during 1954–6; the machine-tractor stations were liquidated in 1958 and their machines were sold off to the collective farms; many collective farms were converted into, or amalgamated with state farms, mainly during 1958–61 but also subsequently; the state-farm wage★ system was reformed in 1961–2 and a guaranteed minimum wage was introduced into collective farms in 1967–70; industrial supplies for agriculture were increased, mainly since 1961; a new programme for expanding the irrigated areas was inaugurated in 1962 and accelerated in 1966; state farms were put on cost accounting★ in 1966–70, in replacement of budget funding, and requiring a revision of the prices paid to them (previously lower than those paid to collectives); pursuant to the Party Programme of 1961, some horizontal and vertical integration was undertaken from the late 1960s and more energetically promoted from 1973; finally, a long-term programme for rural infrastructure investment★ was launched in 1974 in the depressed agrarian areas of the west, central and north-east RSFSR (the 'non-black-earth zone').

Mechanized harvesting in the Kustanay steppe, Kazakhstan, a quarter-century after the 'virgin lands campaign'

The administrative centre of a state farm, Krasnodar kray

Agricultural investment

Probably the paramount single development since the death of Stalin was the increased supply of capital to agriculture after long neglect. Fixed assets (excluding livestock) in agriculture are officially shown to have increased by 130 per cent during 1950–8, by another 191 per cent during 1958–65 and (on a changed price basis) by 260 per cent during 1965–79. With assets increasing, more reinvestment was needed, and the net effect declined, but the volume of gross investment in absolute terms during 1965–76 was more than double the cumulative total of 1918–64.

Capital supplies in Soviet agriculture are below those in Western industrialized countries. Compared to Canada, where natural conditions are similar, there were in 1977 1.1 tractors per 100ha of arable and perennial-crop land against 1.4, six tractor hp per worker against 50, and one grain combine-harvester for each 187ha under grain against 120. The supply of fertilizer amounted to 80kg of effective nutrient equivalent per hectare of arable and perennial-crop land, about that of Canada, but much below European standards.

The climate* is another factor placing demands on capital investment, for such purposes as the conservation and distribution of water resources* or to enable crops to be harvested quickly in adverse weather or to be promptly dried and transported. Only 27 per cent of Soviet territory can be agriculturally utilized, and only 10 per cent is arable; more than one-third is north of 60° latitude. In those agricultural areas where precipitation is sufficient, average tempera-

COMPARATIVE AREA AND LATITUDE OF THE USSR AND THE USA

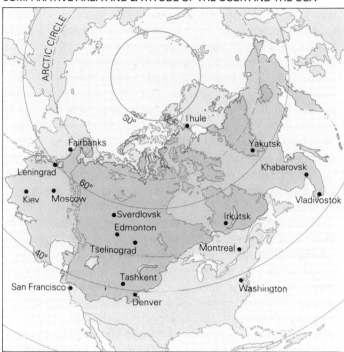

The USSR is almost 2.5 times as large as the USA; climatic conditions are generally analogous to areas in Canada and the north central Plains states
Source: *USSR Agricultural Atlas*, Washington D.C., 1974

PROBABILITY OF DROUGHT, MAY–JULY

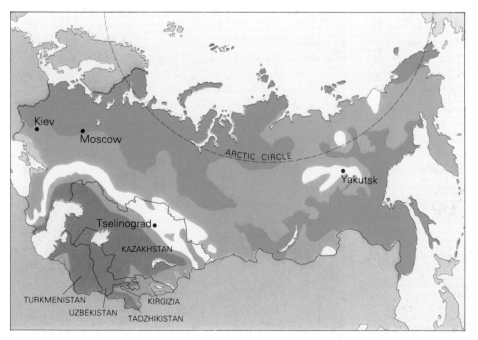

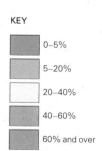

KEY

	0–5%
	5–20%
	20–40%
	40–60%
	60% and over

Source: *USSR Agricultural Atlas*, Washington D.C., 1974

tures are low and the soils* mostly poor (west, north-west and north-east of the European parts), regions with the excellent 'black soil' suffer from barely sufficient precipitation with recurrent years of drought, and the extensive dry-farming stretches of the south-eastern RSFSR, western Siberia and Kazakhstan, while endowed with good soils, are those with the highest risk of drought and wind erosion. Climatically favoured are the fruit-, wine- and vegetable-growing regions adjacent to the Black Sea and in Transcaucasia, the areas of intensive irrigation farming in Central Asia, and the small monsoon region in the southernmost part of the Far East. In the mountainous and subpolar regions, extensive range farming predominates. Only rarely (in Krasnodar and parts of the Ukraine) are the natural conditions comparable to those of the American Midwest. Yet in areas of the European part yields equal to those of northern West Germany and southern Scandinavia are possible. Thus, the arable land of 0.9ha per head of the population has great potential for output growth and for meeting likely food demand.

Farm production

Average agricultural production in 1976–9 was two and a half times greater than in 1940 and 1950. In quantitative terms, the nutritional standard has been satisfactory since the late 1950s (3000 calories per head), but the supply of animal protein and of the finer vegetables and fruit does not yet meet demand. In part such excess demand is due to the inadequate supply, at the retail prices determined by the state, of non-food consumer goods* and services*; household purchasing power is hence directed towards the higher-quality foods.

The output growth was earlier achieved by expanding the cultivated area, and later by increasing yields per hectare and per animal. Productivity per man, on the other hand, has risen very slowly and in 1979 was only four-fifths greater than in 1913, when farm manpower was more than double. Despite an outflow (of some 0.5 per cent annually since 1950) roughly nine workers are occupied (in full-time equivalent) per 100ha, and townsfolk, schoolchildren, students and troops are brought in large numbers to help with the harvest. The amount of land cultivated, but not the output, in state farms now exceeds that of the collectives, because most of it is in regions with extensive crop farming. The total number of cattle and pigs is greater in collectives, while state farms raise more sheep. In January 1981 when 30 per cent of all cows, and 20 per cent of pigs were privately owned, a decree obliged state and collective farms to help assure fodder for private livestock, authorized state farms to give young families livestock free of charge and introduced schemes to encourage state-farm workers and collective farmers to raise the productivity of their plots and livestock. Poor milk yields (2215kg per cow in 1979) are an unequivocal indicator of poor breeding and inefficient care of animals, representing low feed-conversion ratios (1.7 of oats-units per unit of milk, 9.1 for pork), whereas the modest

average grain yields (1.63 tonnes per hectare in 1976–9) can in part be attributed to climate and to the expansion of grain-growing into regions of marginal dry-farming. Russian and Soviet plant breeders have been long renowned for their research, but the dissemination of their achievements, including new cropping technology, leaves much to be desired.

In the early 1960s farms were allowed and encouraged to develop non-agricultural subsidiary production, and cooperate with other farms in specialized enterprises. Vertical linkages have, however, been largely limited to activities immediately connected with farming (machinery repair, local building, and the processing of perishables). The long-term objective is to merge collective and state farms into a uniform 'agro-industrial complex'. *K.-E.W.*

Energy

Although only 6 per cent of the world's population lives in the USSR, the country produces one-quarter of the world's coal and natural gas and one-fifth of the world's oil. In 1979 it was the world's biggest producer of oil (586 million tonnes) and coal (719 million tonnes) and second only to the USA in natural gas (407 cu km). Its deposits of energy-raising minerals* are more than those of any other industrialized country (3993 thousand million tonnes of hard coal, 1720 thousand million tonnes of brown coal, 8138 million tonnes of oil and 17 136 cu km of natural gas); its timber stand (79 cu km) is greater than that of North America or of Brazil (constituting one-third of the world total), and it has extensive resources of peat and hydroelectric potential. Save by errors of planning or of organization, the USSR should not in this century fall into deficit with respect to the domestic supply of energy, but it is insuring its future provision by diversification away from fossil fuels, such as by harnessing geothermal power in Kamchatka, and solar and wind power in Central Asia. Moreover, there being no organizations to lobby legislators or to mobilize public opinion against such an option, long-term reliance is placed on nuclear power. In 1980 there were 12 000 MW of nuclear-power capacity installed (generating 10 per cent of the electricity supply) and research on plasma physics* and nuclear fusion could bring feasibility by the end of the century.

Soviet primary energy production in 1979 in tonnes of coal equivalent (7 million kcal) comprised 837 million of oil (43 per cent), 484 million of coal (25 per cent) and 482 million of natural gas (25 per cent); nuclear power supplied 3 per cent and firewood, peat and shale-oil about one per cent apiece. Of the aggregate of 1926 million tonnes produced, 314 million were exported (nearly three-quarters in oil, most of the rest in natural gas and a little electricity); with imports 26 million, net exports constituted 15 per cent of

Oil-drilling rig at Samatlor, a 'super-giant' oil-field in West Siberia which produced 145 million tonnes in 1979. The rig is mounted on railway bogies to facilitate movement after a well is exhausted

KEY

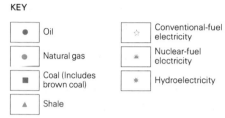

● Oil	☆ Conventional-fuel electricity
● Natural gas	⚙ Nuclear-fuel elcctricity
■ Coal (Includes brown coal)	✳ Hydroelectricity
▲ Shale	

Ihe map registers electricity generating stations (completed or under construction in 1976) with over 2 mn kW capacity
Source: *Bol'shaya sovetskaya entsiklopediya*, 3rd edn, Vol. 24

SOURCES OF ENERGY PRODUCTION

output. If energy consumption (6.2 tonnes per head in 1979) were at the average of Western Europe, Soviet exports could be doubled, but, as for minerals generally, Soviet utilization per unit of gross national product is higher than in the West. In 1975 industry consumed 54 per cent of all energy, transport 12 and households 20.

The system of central planning* has enabled consumption to be restrained – particularly by the low production of automobiles, the absence of any major road-building* (there is no east-west road at all across Siberia), the concentration of freight on to the railways,* and generally by the tight rationing of energy to industrial users. With little consequent scope for conservation (or, save at high cost, substitution between sources), the USSR is committed to heavy investment for oil and gas extraction in remote regions in Siberia, and in off-shore sources (Baltic, Barents, Caspian and Okhotsk seas). Operations in low temperatures and permafrost* make for high capital outlays. The USSR is seeking economic collaboration* with Western corporations, which would share in the investment cost with repayment in products for 20 years after output begins. Japanese firms are engaged in the joint extraction of coking coal in South Yakutia and of oil off Sakhalin, and trunk pipelines deliver oil to East Europe and gas to both East and West Europe. For the future the USSR is keenly interested in maintaining energy exports. In 1979 the USSR earned 57 per cent of its total hard-currency export receipts from oil alone and guaranteed delivery during 1981–5 of 80 million tonnes of oil to other members of Comecon (approximately half its oil exports at the 1979 rate. *M.K.*

Metals

In the second half of the 18th century Russia was the world's largest iron producer. This pre-eminence was lost in the 19th century and by 1917 the iron and steel industry was relatively weak in comparison with those of the major powers. The expansion of ferrous metallurgy was a high priority of the pre-war Five-year Plans* during which the foundations of modern Soviet industry were laid. The great Ural-Kuznetsk combine was built, leading to a substantial increase in output in the Urals and beyond. By 1979 output was 149 million tonnes, compared with 127 in the USA and 112 in Japan.

Apart from some small-scale production at engineering factories, the industry is administered by the USSR Ministry of Ferrous Metallurgy, which has responsibility for all stages from ore extraction to the finished product. In the early 1970s ferrous metallurgy employed approximately 4 per cent of the total industrial labour force and accounted for almost 10 per cent of the total industrial capital stock. Production is highly concentrated in very large combines, the major centres being the Ukraine, the Urals, Western Siberia and the

central industrial region of the RSFSR. By international standards the industry has a high technological level and a number of new Soviet processes are in use in other countries on a licence basis (technology* for continuous casting, electro-slag remelting and the evaporative cooling of blast furnaces). In recent years, however, the industry has been slow in adopting such progressive new processes as oxygen-converter and electric arc steel-making and continuous casting: in 1975 the traditional open-hearth process still accounted for almost two-thirds of steel production (20 per cent in the USA, 1 per cent in Japan). In the 1970s there was evidence of strain in meeting output plans and greater emphasis on the need for economy in the use of ferrous metals.

The non-ferrous metals industry is largely a product of the Soviet period. By 1941 the industrial production of aluminium, magnesium, nickel, wolfram and other metals had been organized for the first time. In the post-war years expansion has been rapid but difficult to measure in the absence of production statistics, an absence reflecting the strategic importance of the industry. The Ministry of Non-Ferrous Metallurgy has responsibility for the extraction and processing of ores, the production of metals and alloys and their

The 5000cu m blast furnace under construction at Krivoy Rog, Ukraine, 1974

conversion into finished metal products; important by-products include mineral fertilizers and sulphuric acid. The industry is highly concentrated: the 30 largest combines account for approximately half the total output. Major centres of non-ferrous metallurgy are located in Siberia, Kazakhstan and the Far East. The ore deposits are frequently located in remote, inhospitable and sparsely populated regions giving rise to high costs, although some activities benefit from the availability of cheap hydroelectric energy.* The USSR, unlike other major producing countries, is highly self-sufficient in all the important non-ferrous metal ores, and has large unexploited mineral* reserves; recent products have included titanium and zirconium used by the aero-space industry and semi-conductor materials used in electronics technology. The USSR is a major producer of gold* and diamonds, which play a vital role in the country's foreign economic relations.* There is a large favourable balance of trade in non-ferrous metals, but the range of Soviet imports indicates that the quality of domestically produced metals is not always of an adequate standard.

J.C.

KEY

■ Iron		● Copper	
◩ Manganese		▫ Tin	
▲ Nickel		○ Gold	
△ Bauxite		◐ Polymetallic ores	

Source: *Bol'shaya sovetskaya entsiklopediya*, 3rd edn, Vol. 24

Engineering

Engineering is by far the largest sector of Soviet industry, accounting for approximately 28 per cent of total output and employing almost 40 per cent of the industrial labour force. Before the Revolution* the industry was weakly developed; its products were technically backward and the few more advanced branches were dominated by foreign capital. During the 1930s the foundations of a modern

LOCATION OF METAL EXTRACTION

machine-building industry were laid with the setting-up of many large new enterprises for the manufacture of machine tools, motor vehicles, tractors, aircraft and heavy engineering products. At the same time a strong new production base was created to the east of the Urals, which during the years of the Second World War provided a secure location for military* production.

In 1980 20 ministries were responsible for the administration of Soviet engineering. Civilian machine-building was the concern of 11 ministries: those for electrical; chemical and oil; heavy and transport; and power engineering; and those producing motor vehicles; machine tools; instruments, means of automation and control systems; road and construction-industry machinery; tractors and agricultural machinery; machinery for the light and food industries and for consumer equipment; and machinery for stock-breeding and fodder production. Nine ministries had responsibility for what, in the USSR, are considered to be branches of the defence industry (official titles in parentheses); electronics, the radio industry, the communication equipment industry, aviation, shipbuilding, rockets and missiles ('general machine-building'), nuclear weapons ('medium machine-building'), ammunition ('machine-building') and armoured vehicles, artillery and small arms ('defence industry'). Engineering has consistently been the most dynamic branch of industry—a 68-fold growth between 1940 and 1979 against 20-fold for industry as a whole. Areas of particular strength include the production of aircraft, machine tools, heavy industrial machinery, tractors, and equipment for electric-power generation and transmission. Until recently engineering products dependent on semiconductor electronics were less developed: the serious lag in computer technology* has been tackled with some success in the 1970s within the framework of Comecon* cooperation. A high priority during the

Main assembly line of the Kama Automobile Works (KamAZ), with an annual capacity of 150 000 trucks and 250 000 engines

Tenth Five-year Plan has been nuclear engineering and the construction of a vast new specialized enterprise at Volgodonsk in the Rostov region of the RSFSR. The Soviet engineering industry has increasingly drawn on the technology of Western countries in order to pull up backward sectors: the rapid expansion of passenger car production (quadrupled in two decades) has owed much to cooperation with the Italian Fiat company in building the Volga factory in Togliatti, with an annual capacity of 660 000 vehicles. The USSR now exports 30 per cent of its passenger car output. Foreign equipment also figures prominently at the new heavy-truck-building complex, KamAZ, at Naberezhnye Chelny, one of the largest projects of the 1970s.

There is a substantial two-way trade in machinery between the USSR and the European members of Comecon, but problems have been encountered in expanding machinery exports to industrially advanced capitalist countries. For many years machinery and equipment has represented one-fifth or less of total Soviet exports, but in the 1970s this sector accounted for over 35 per cent of total imports. Considerable efforts have been made to raise the technical level and quality of engineering products, but many problems remain.   *J.C.*

Chemicals

Administrative responsibility for the manufacture and development of chemicals in the USSR is divided between ministries for the chemical industry, for fertilizers and for the oil-refining and petrochemical industry, though basic chemicals are produced in appreciable quantities by others. Assisted by generous resources* of oil, natural gas and minerals* (notably apatite and phosphorite) the USSR is the world's leading producer of mineral fertilizers (over 94 million tonnes were manufactured in 1979) and a very substantial producer of relatively simple inorganic and basic organic chemicals. Within each of these general categories, however, quality, variety and technological sophistication tend to be markedly inferior to advanced Western countries, particularly in synthetic materials (plastics, fibres and rubber). Almost alone among major industrial nations the USSR, while ranking in output value second only to the USA, is a net importer of chemical products. Exports are strongest in unprocessed minerals, fertilizers and inorganic acids, which rest upon relatively simple and well established technologies;* but these exports are far outweighed by substantial imports of plastics, man-made fibres, agricultural chemicals, pure reagents, additives and catalysts. The USSR obtains half its imports from Comecon partners but is still very dependent on Western countries for the supply of technologically advanced chemical goods in the quantities it requires.

Many of the industry's current problems stem from factors which lie in the past. The pre-revolutionary industry was markedly backward with respect to the diffusion of chemical technologies, despite Russian scientific advances in chemistry;* the infrastructure of the industry was negligible. Against this background the frantic attempts to develop the chemical industry during the 1930s could be only partially successful, and difficulties were exacerbated further by the dislocation and damage inflicted on chemical plants during the Second World War. However, Soviet technological backwardness is due also in some measure to a cumbersome research and development* system, to insufficient investment during key phases in the evolution of the industry and to conservative technological strategies. The decisive movement away from coal to oil and natural gas as the main sources of organic feedstocks began only in the late 1950s and early 1960s under Khrushchev*–long after a similar movement had occurred in the West. This policy entailed a re-location away from the traditional industrial centres of European Russia, thus consolidating a trend begun by the wartime evacuation of chemical plant to eastern regions.

From the early 1960s heavy imports of Western chemical plant have rendered this industry more dependent on foreign equipment than any other, while the huge scale of some of these deals and Soviet insistence that suppliers must be compensated by products ('buy-back') have provoked anxieties among Western manufacturers about dumping on international markets.   *R.A.*

Synthetic fibre plant, Mogilev, Belorussia, completed in 1970 with plant supplied by ICI, the UK chemicals group

Consumers' goods

Food processing has expanded substantially faster than agricultural* production; this was the case especially during the Second Five-year Plan* (1933–7), when canned fruit as a proportion of canned foods increased sharply at the expense of meat and fish. During 1940–75 while canned-food output grew 13-fold (the biggest proportionate increase being in natural juices and vegetables), most food-processing branches grew about 4–5 times (the largest proportionate increases being in dairy products and wines). By virtue of sales by peasants, total production of meat in 1975 was 52 per cent larger than the quantity processed; of butter, 7 per cent larger. The most recent trends, though still mainly upwards as in sea-foods, meat, sausage, dairy products, alcoholic drinks and salt, have been declining as regards sugar, frozen vegetables and dried fruits.

The more rapid growth of food processing than of food production largely reflects industrialization accompanied by urbanization and a shift away from individual food growing to purchasing. The trend permits also a more even seasonal availability of many foods and their more complete utilization. Yet, particularly recently, the processing branches have been hampered by shortages of raw materials. Where they have been available (for example an enlarged production of broiler chickens, or of sea-food in train with the growth of the fishing and whaling fleets) food processing has correspondingly rapidly expanded.

The outputs of the textiles, clothing and footwear industries have grown since 1940 by 3–4 times in the principal branches–that is, at a rate comparable to that of the food processing branches although a little more slowly, and more variably between sub-categories. Textiles and leather goods (including footwear) have grown at about equal rates, garments (a more seasonal branch) somewhat faster (including knitwear, faster still), whereas hose have merely kept pace with shoes. In quantity, the chief Soviet-produced textile is cotton with woollen, linen and silk textiles considerably behind. The output of cotton textiles rather more than doubled during 1940–75 (reaching in 1979 6977 million sq m), and that of the other fibres increased somewhat more. While production of artificial and synthetic fibres (except artificial silk) lagged behind that of basic chemicals, the production of synthetic fibres has been greatly enlarged and diversified through large infusions of foreign technology, although the proportion of synthetics among man-made fibres remains well below that in advanced countries. In terms of weight, Soviet production of artificial and synthetic fibres now exceeds one-third of the production of raw cotton. Production of 'leather' footwear, which contains a substantial proportion of artificial materials, has grown about as fast as that of rubber footwear; that of felt boots (traditionally worn in the countryside) has grown more slowly. Imports of footwear

Clothing for spring on display in a Moscow shop window

have recently significantly expanded. While there is little production of leather clothing apart from sheepskins, annual production of fur or part-fur hats–mostly from natural furs–exceeds 40 million.

As in the USSR new fashions are supposed to be introduced in an organized manner, styles of clothes and footwear have tended to lag behind foreign styles and to be rather immobile and lacking in variety. For instance, womens' slacks were slow to arrive, men's jackets long retained padded shoulders, and exotic fashions were unrepresented; model clothes were rarely obtainable in the main retail outlets. Clothing is excluded from the sphere of interest of the national industrial design organization. However, thanks partly to imports from Eastern Europe, differences between town and country have been reduced and standards of dress substantially raised. *R.H.*

The building industry

Within an over-all responsibility for building and architecture,★ the State Committee for Construction (Gosstroy) examines and coordinates research projects undertaken by state agencies engaged in construction, architecture and the manufacture of building materials, and promotes innovation and productivity. In 1963 a subordinate State Committee for Civil Construction and Architecture (Gosgrazhdanstroy) was established with, among other tasks, the coordination of research on the standardization and prefabrication of housing and civic buildings, since numerous organizations had been working independently of each other. Concomitant with this policy has been the rationalization of the building industry by concentrating construction and assembly work in the hands of trusts and combines under the control of specialized ministries: larger units

permit the reduction of costs (particularly high on repairs) by the introduction of new techniques, the mechanization of production and the more efficient use of building equipment.

As a result the application of standard designs in house building rose from 55 per cent in 1955 to 96 per cent in 1977. The proportion of all housing★ erected using large panels rose from 1.5 per cent in 1959 to 53 per cent in 1977, reaching 60–80 per cent of all accommodation built in the largest cities. Compared with traditional building methods using bricks, this form of construction cuts labour costs by 35–40 per cent and reduces the building time of a five- or six-storey block of flats from 2–3 years to 3–4 months. In 1959 the first house building combine was established in Leningrad; the scale 20 years later can be judged from the fact that 60 per cent of combines have an annual capacity of 50 000–200 000 sq m of living space and 12 per cent a capacity above this. Each combine manufactures the components, transports them to a building site, using its own custom-built vehicles, erects them and completes all the necessary interior finishing work. Such methods represent an attempt to raise labour productivity in an industry which absorbs more and more manpower–in 1979, the average number of employees in the building industry stood at 11.5 million (2.6 million in 1940; 9.2 million in 1970). Despite this growth, building organizations suffer from labour shortages, and the authorities hope to achieve a rise in labour productivity. High labour turnover has prompted them to

The USSR's first industrialized house-building plant, Leningrad: prefabricated panels await dispatch

raise wages★ so that in 1979 the average wage of a manual worker in building was 11 per cent higher than in industry.   *G.A.*

Housing

During the Second World War 1710 towns and settlements were destroyed with a loss of 70 million sq m of dwelling space, equivalent to one-sixth of the country's urban housing stock, and a further one-sixth was damaged. This exacerbated the already acute shortage of accommodation which investment priorities and urbanization had created, when during 1926–39 the urban population had increased by 113 per cent. Little relief was afforded until Khrushchev★ launched a house-building programme in 1957, substantially increasing state investment, and industrializing construction– thereby both accelerating construction and reducing cost. For a short time – at least until 1960 – greater scope was allowed for urban houses to be built by individuals, whose contribution peaked at 14.4 million sq m in 1960 but was down to 6.3 million in 1979 (from 24.4 per cent to 8.8 per cent of all urban house building). A strategy for urban development★ has been formulated under the State Committee for Civil Construction and Architecture.

Industrialization of construction has enabled the USSR to claim to have solved the problem of providing low-cost housing of an acceptable standard for the mass of the population. Although far from everyone is well housed, the fact that during 1960–79 8.2 million people annually moved into a new flat or private home and that a further 2.6 million improved their living conditions is a convincing achievement. Space standards are rising and by end-1979 the national average stood at 12.8 sq m of over-all living space★ (including kitchen, bathroom, corridor and hall) having risen from 8.8 sq m in 1960. Republican and city variations in accommodation standards remain considerable, ranging from 9.1 sq m in Uzbekistan to 16.1 in Estonia. Despite the increase, family living is still extremely cramped: over 75 per cent of the urban housing stock consists of one- and two-roomed flats even though the average size of an urban family is 3.5 persons with 74.8 per cent of all urban families consisting of three or more people.

The ownership of housing falls into two broad categories: the socialized (or state) sector and the private. The former is divided among local soviets,★ state enterprises, institutions and other bodies, and is also held to include houses belonging to house-building cooperatives, other cooperatives and trade unions.★ In Soviet terminology housing in the private sector belongs to individuals by virtue of the right to 'personal' property but not 'private' property, since the latter is seen as a source of unearned income. While most statistical handbooks employ this twofold division of the housing

stock, administrators operate with four categories. Accordingly, houses belong to: local soviets; enterprises, trade unions and other cooperative bodies (the 'departmental fund'); house-building (and dacha-building) cooperatives; and individuals. 'Departmental' housing as a form of tenure is clearly distinguished from housing belonging to local soviets,★ for whereas the latter allocate housing to individuals living within their administrative jurisdiction, irrespective of where they work, a 'department' provides for those with whom it has productive relationships. Local soviets wish to see all state housing in their hands, but this is resisted by 'departmental' owners, who use housing as a means of attracting and retaining labour.★

Although (on 1978 data) the state owned 76 per cent of the urban housing stock and was responsible for 84 per cent of all new building in towns, the private and cooperative sectors continue to fulfil important functions in meeting the demand for accommodation. In the countryside 85 per cent of the rural housing stock is privately owned and 65 per cent of new construction is by individual builders. In 1958 the size of new private houses was limited (with a few exceptions) to a maximum of 60 sq m of living space; the erection of individually-owned homes was prohibited from January 1964 in cities with populations exceeding 100 000. Private owners living in areas subject to renewal may be offered a choice of being rehoused in state-owned accommodation, or receiving compensation for the building and the loss of garden produce, or the physical transfer of the building to another plot. It is unlikely that the state will expand

New housing for a collective farm, Odessa region

private house construction for, like the private plot, it is regarded as a vestige of capitalism. Government aims to transfer a proportion of the cost of providing accommodation to the tenants themselves will be achieved by encouraging house-building cooperatives which, after their abolition in 1937, were resuscitated in 1962.

Because the basis on which rents are calculated has not changed since 1928, the annual state subsidy in the late 1970s was running at 5000 million roubles. Rent accounts for 3 per cent of the average family budget and with fuel costs the total expenditure amounts to no more than 10 per cent of the average budget. The house-building cooperative has not developed as rapidly as envisaged because the monthly repayment on a 10- to 20-year loan even at a rate of interest of 0.5 per cent is considerably higher than rents paid for state accommodation, and because cooperative members bear the responsibility for maintenance and other running expenses. Instead of the predicted 80 per cent rise in the amount of living space built in this sector during the Ninth Five-year Plan period, 3.5 per cent less living space was erected than in the Eighth Five-year Plan period. Since 1975 the official statistical yearbook has not distinguished cooperative from state housing. *G.A.*

Urban development strategy

The literal translation of the Russian word for town-planning–*gradostroitel'stvo*–is 'town-building': over 20 new towns a year are built in addition to 'populated places' never destined to become significantly large, and major construction programmes are under way to expand housing,★ improve urban services and increase personal mobility by the end of the century. With the focus increasingly upon management of the urban system as a whole, the Soviet town-planner's role will increasingly resemble that in the West: management procedures, modelling techniques and data-handling systems for this field have recently been the subject of research and experiment, and their dissemination throughout the profession, alongside traditional technical and aesthetic training, is being achieved via both regular and mid-career education.

Preparation and scrutiny of town-planning proposals for existing towns and cities is initiated through the professional and ministerial★ hierarchies, overseen by the State Committee for Civil Construction and Architecture (Gosgrazhdanstroy), of which the chairman is the

THE USSR GOSPLAN GENERAL SCHEME OF SETTLEMENT, 1975

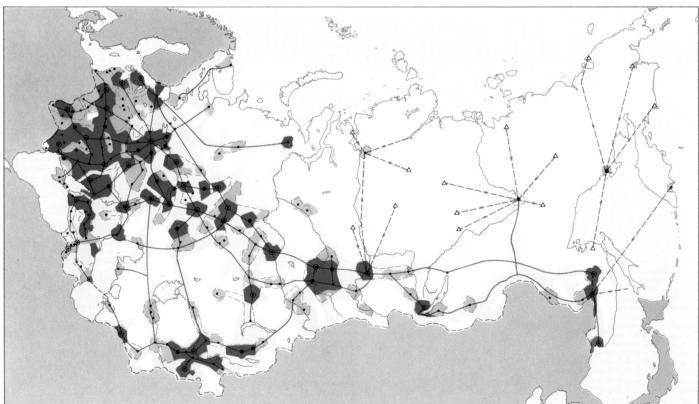

first deputy chairman of its parent body, the State Committee for Construction (Gosstroy). Unlike Gosstroy itself, this committee has no hierarchy at republican level, but a republican Gosstroy must accept its rules on spatial and planning norms, strategies and techniques. Of the 18 national institutes within its research network, most are concerned with specific building* types (housing, public facilities, transport structures), each of these pursuing an optimal solution of its own and hence requiring the coordinating role of the Central Scientific Research Institute of Town-Planning, Moscow. The latter seeks a 'best' solution from these often-competing demands in accordance with the principle of *kompleksnost'* enshrined in Soviet town-planning since the early 1930s – the objective being optimization of the middle way between such priorities as production efficiency and minimal journeys-to-work for the labour force, environmental amenity and access to services, and capital costs versus management costs. Certain regions with climatic or geological problems (such as Siberia, or the seismic area of Uzbekistan) have multi-disciplinary 'zonal' institutes, organized through the republican Gosstroy. An important concept is that of the 'group', a unit conceived as connecting the region and the settlement. It is a network of transport-linked cities, towns and villages, self-sufficient in all but the most specialized services and amenities. Each settlement type would remain appropriate in size and form to its employment base, and would offer its own characteristic physical environment, but would have relatively equal access to the facilities, employment and educational opportunities offered by the group (on the basis of certain maximum measures of time and distance across the transport* network). The General Scheme of Settlement on the Territory of the USSR, in the variant confirmed in 1975, shows the over-all strategy for the location and development of a national network of such groups, which is based upon the equally long-term General Plan for the Location of Productive Forces confirmed by the USSR Gosplan in 1971.   *G.C.*

Transport and communications

The Soviet Union is faced with immense difficulties in ensuring adequate transport and communications within its vast territory, not only because of the size of the land but because of its varied nature, including great deserts, high mountain ranges, huge swampy tracts and, above all, the climate.* To the length of the winter and the extent of the snow cover is added the effects of the spring thaw, known through history as the *rasputitsa* (the roadless season).

Roads
Russian roads have always had a bad reputation; before the railways, travelling great distances on the rutted or muddy tracks was exhausting and frequently hazardous. In spite of sub-zero temperatures, winter was looked upon as the season for travel because temporary 'winter roads' laid on snow and ice provided better conditions, and in spring widespread reconstruction of roads is still necessary. Such conditions have delayed development of extensive motor transport, but recent expansion of vehicle manufacture has resulted in a marked growth in the use of the private car as well as of trucks and buses. The official view is that road transport should generally be limited to short hauls. In terms of tonne-kilometres of traffic (including farm transport), the roads (on 1978 returns) carry only about 7 per cent of all freight movement, but because there are so many short journeys tonnage loaded on to road vehicles amounts to over 80 per cent of all goods loaded. On the more restricted definition of public service transport the percentages are respectively 2.5 and 57. In passenger movement the road contribution is higher because of urban movements, the roads carrying about 43 per cent of traffic in terms of passenger-kilometres and accounting for 91 per cent of passengers boarding public vehicles. The average length of journey is, however, only about 7.5km for passengers and 17km for freight.

KEY

POTENTIAL CENTRES OF:

⊙ Regional systems

• Large group systems

· Medium group systems

△ Nodal points for dispersed, very small-scale settlements lying outside the major systems

ZONES FOR THE FORMATION OF:

Large group systems

Medium group systems

Small-scale group systems

Areas of dispersed, very small-scale settlements lying outside the major group systems

Areas inhabited only on a seasonal or expeditional basis

Transport and planning axes linking the centres of systems

Air-transport links of regional significance

Boundaries of regional zones of concentrated settlement

Source: A.V. Kochetkov and F.M. Listengurt (eds), *General'maya skhema rasseleniya na territorii SSSR*, Moscow, 1977

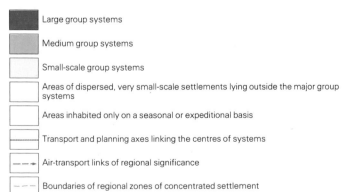

Railways

The first railway in Russia, from the tsar's palace at Tsarskoe Selo to St Petersburg (later Leningrad), was opened in 1837 but the main development of the network did not come until the 1850s and 1860s. The Great Siberian (Trans-Siberian) Railway was commenced in 1891, and was the most spectacular railway construction undertaking in the world for sheer length and the crossing of difficult terrain. At first built to rather low engineering standards and for a time running on track across the frozen Lake Baykal in winter and by ferry in summer (until a link was made round the southern shore), it is now one of the finest multi-tracked systems in the world. The USSR is one of the few countries still building new lines on a large scale, a major undertaking being the Baykal-Amur Mainline (BAM), which will provide an alternative, more northerly, route across eastern Siberia

FREIGHT FLOWS OF GRAIN BY RAIL

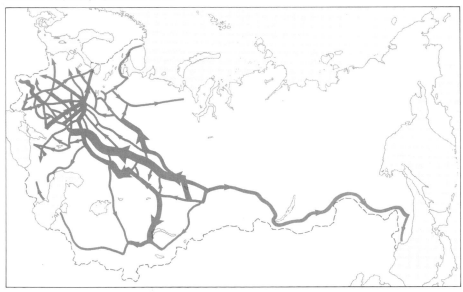

The thickness of the line is proportional to the freight carried c.1960
Source: R. E. H. Mellor in L. Symons and C. White (eds), *Russian Transport*, London, 1975

FREIGHT FLOWS OF TIMBER BY RAIL

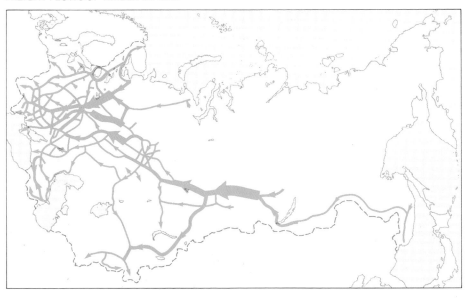

The thickness of the line is proportional to the freight carried c.1960
Source: R. E. H. Mellor in L. Symons and C. White (eds), *Russian Transport*, London, 1975

and will open up vast new tracts of territory and valuable deposits.

Soviet railways are among the most intensively used in the world. They are the main freight carriers and also take large numbers of passengers, both on long-distance and suburban services. The mean length of passenger journeys is 91km (27km for suburban services) and the average haul for freight is 861km, contrasting with the lower averages for road journeys, especially freight. Railways are con-structed to a gauge of 1524mm (5 feet) so through trains from eastern Europe need to have bogies changed at the frontiers, but the wider gauge permits more spacious coaches, particularly noticeable in sleeping cars. The route length is over 135 000km under the control of the Ministry of Railways, with industrial lines adding to the network. About one-fifth of the system is electrified, diesel locomotives having replaced steam on all other main routes.

INTERNAL AIR ROUTES OF MAJOR INTER-REGIONAL SIGNIFICANCE

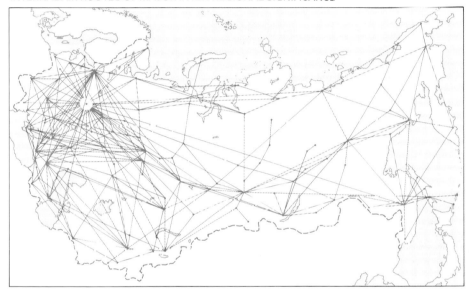

Source: L. Symons in L. Symons and C. White (eds), *Russian Transport*, London, 1975

THE UNIFIED TRANSPORT SYSTEM

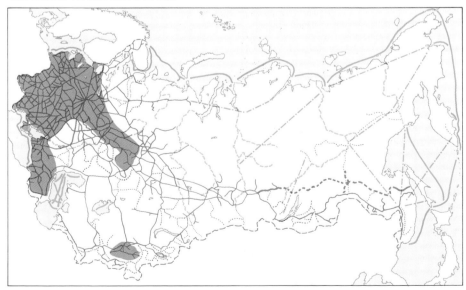

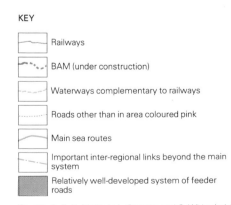

KEY

‾‾‾	Railways
·—·—·	BAM (under construction)
–·–·–	Waterways complementary to railways
········	Roads other than in area coloured pink
‾‾‾	Main sea routes
–·–·–	Important inter-regional links beyond the main system
▓▓▓	Relatively well-developed system of feeder roads

Source: R. E. H. Mellor in L. Symons and C. White (eds), *Russian Transport*, London, 1975

The railways' share of freight traffic (1978) is 59 per cent of the total in terms of tonne-kilometres, and about 17 per cent in terms of tonnage loaded (or 36 per cent of public-service transport). They account for about 40 per cent of passenger-kilometres covered and about 8 per cent of passenger journeys in terms of bookings. Their share in long-distance travel has been eroded by air transport and local journeys by buses but the railways will undoubtedly remain the core of the Soviet transport system.

Air transport

The great distances to be covered encourage the use of air transport and even winter conditions do not bear as heavily on aircraft as on surface transport, because of the clear skies typically associated with the winter high-pressure climatic conditions of the cold continental areas, and because turbine engines are less difficult to maintain and easier to start under cold conditions than the older piston engines. All civil aircraft are under the control of Aeroflot, which is responsible for both internal and overseas air services, agricultural, ambulance, survey, forest fire-fighting and other aerial operations. The airline routes exceed 800000km, of which about one-quarter is accounted for by international links serving 90+ countries. Over 100 million passengers are carried annually, internally and overseas. Within the

SOVIET PASSENGER TRANSPORT

	1928	1940	1955	1970	1979
	thousand million passenger-kilometres				
Rail	24.5	100.4	141.4	265.4	335.3
Sea	0.3	0.9	1.5	1.6	2.5
Inland waterway	2.1	3.8	3.6	5.4	5.8
Road	0.2	3.4	20.9	202.5	376.0
Air	—	0.2	2.8	78.2	151.0
Total	27.1	108.7	170.2	553.1	870.6

Source: *SSSR v tsifrakh v 1979 godu*, Moscow, 1980

SOVIET FREIGHT TRANSPORT

	1928	1940	1955	1970	1979
	thousand million tonne-kilometres				
Rail	93.4	420.7	970.9	2494.7	3350.0
Sea	9.3	24.9	68.9	656.1	842.3
Inland waterway	15.9	36.1	67.7	174.0	232.8
Pipeline	0.7	3.8	14.7	281.7	1140.7
Road	0.2	8.9	42.5	220.8	418.0
Air	—	0.02	0.25	1.9	2.9
Total	119.5	494.4	1165.0	3829.2	5986.7

Source: *SSSR v tsifrakh v 1979 godu*, Moscow, 1980

USSR the airways account (on 1978 data) for about 16 per cent of passenger-kilometres. In terms of numbers boarding, only about 0.2 per cent of all travellers depart by air but in some of the more remote regions aircraft provide virtually the sole communication, and it is official policy to encourage air travel over long distances by low fares. The average length of a journey is about 1000km, while the average freight consignment, which includes mail, newspaper plates and other items requiring high-speed transit, is carried for 1310km. At the other end of the scale, helicopters are extensively used for mainly short journeys but with special roles in lifting heavy items such as oil exploration and development equipment into remote areas.

Water transport

The rivers* provided a major means of communication in pre-industrial Russia and valuable routes for the exploration* of Siberia. The long period during which they are frozen is a drawback, but great rivers such as the Volga, Dnieper, Don, Ob' and Yenisey are still arteries for the movement of heavy goods and some passenger traffic, in which hydrofoils as well as conventional vessels are employed. Canals provided important links before the railways, and have continued to be developed to provide networks such as the Volga-Don Canal, completed in 1952. In all, inland waterways account for about 4 per cent of all freight movement (on 1978 statistics), with an average haul of nearly 500km. They include substantial sea transport on the Caspian Sea and other water bodies. In addition the Soviet merchant fleet operates many services to other countries; the Northern Sea Route, through arctic waters, assists in transport of bulky commodities such as timber and minerals for up to 18 weeks a year with the aid of ice-breakers, including some powered by nuclear reactors. Nearly all Soviet ports require the services of ice-breakers for some periods of the winter, the most favourable conditions being at Murmansk, which is ice-bound for about 50 days per year, and at Odessa in the Black Sea; Vladivostok suffers from ice for over three months and Leningrad for about six months of each year.

Pipelines

A rapid expansion of pipelines for oil and natural gas has been achieved since the Second World War (the first short pipeline was completed in 1879) and by 1980 the combined length exceeded 190000km. They carry over 5 per cent of total tonnage originating, or 19 per cent in terms of tonne-kilometres. Further development is taking place to link new sources of energy*—oil, gas and coal (as slurry)—with centres of industry and to add to existing capacity on established routes.

Top: the nuclear-powered icebreaker ship *Arktika*. Bottom: laying a pipeline at Surgut, West Siberia, to carry oil from the Samotlor deposits to the European part of the USSR

Kirovskaya Metro station, Moscow

Urban transit

Urban and suburban movement accounts for most of the road passenger transport and a substantial proportion of the road freight movement. Passenger bus services exist in all large and medium-sized towns, and tramways and trolley-bus services are also common in the larger cities. Suburban railways, mostly electrified, are heavily used; the Moscow Metro is one of the world's most efficient and extensive underground mass-transit systems with about 150km of routes. Underground railways exist in Leningrad, Kiev, Baku and Tbilisi, Kharkov and Tashkent. Taxis are also available and tariffs were very moderate until 1977. The demand for them remains so strong that private car owners and drivers of official cars provide an informal supplementary service.

Posts and telecommunications

Before the Revolution* post and telegraph services were thinly spread even in European Russia and mail was delivered only in towns. They have since been developed to give reasonable coverage everywhere although the network is still comparatively widely spaced. Rail, road, and, especially in recent times, air transport are all involved. Telecommunications are widely used in preference to the slower postal services and automatic exchanges are now general in urban areas; cable and radio-relay lines and increasingly sophisticated electronic links are improving services, and satellites are coming into use for long-distance communications.   *L.J.S.*

Consumer services

Personal services

Services have been the most backward area of Soviet consumption, which itself has been the least developed of the economy. This is attributable to the Marxian emphasis on production, and exclusion from the national income of services to consumers; greater opportunities for raising labour productivity in extractive and manufacturing industry; and ideological objections to private business, which, in most economies, provides a substantial proportion of personal services. Consumption per head of services, including housing, tripled during 1951–75, and in contrast to all other major categories of consumption rose faster in the 1960s and 1970s than in the 1950s, due to an enhanced priority which the government accorded repair and personal services after 1963. Soviet statistics for particular services provided by the state and cooperative network show the following indexes for 1975 (1965 = 1): shoe repairs and bespoke shoemaking, 2.6; clothes repair and dressmaking, 2.3; repair of radio, television, household equipment, vehicles and metal goods, 5.8; furniture-making and repair, 8.8; dry-cleaning and dyeing 3.5; repair and making of knitwear, 8.1; laundering, 3.4; public baths, 1.1; hairdressing, 2.0; hire of household equipment 6.3; photography, 3.1; building* and house repairs, 15.7. Even so, per head expenditure in 1979 reached only 28 roubles (varying as between republics from 16 in Azerbaijan to 43 in Estonia), or only 2.8 per cent of state and cooperative trade (including canteen and restaurant meals). In 1979 25 per cent of services consisted of clothes repair and dressmaking, 11 per cent repairs of household equipment and vehicles, and 8 per cent building and house repairs; following the improvement of housing conditions the proportionate importance of public baths has declined. Demand for some services, such as the hire of household equipment (2 per cent) and laundries (5 per cent), is being modified by the growing availability of equipment to install in the home (limited nevertheless by house-room as well as by the scarcity and unsatisfactory quality of such appliances). Private domestic service is permitted.

Retail trade

State trade and cooperative trade are differentiated organizationally and territorially (cooperative trade being chiefly in rural areas) but are similar in other respects, and comprise about 98 per cent of total trade, excluding collective farm trade in villages. Sales of non-food products in state and cooperative trade have fairly consistently grown almost twice as fast as sales of food products, which in turn have grown slightly faster than catering; this last appears anomalous given that living standards have been rising, and reflects (besides a shortage of restaurants) the fact that attendance at works canteens was previously already large.

Retail trade in the USSR is normally a sellers' market, and this has manifold repercussions upon availability and presentation. For instance, the customer normally pays the cashier before obtaining the goods, self-service being a recent innovation. Shops remain open late and are usually open on Sundays; their numbers, still insufficient to cope with demand, have grown only very slowly, although their average staffing size increased during 1965–75 by about half. While shops in central urban districts tend to be very crowded, more spacious conditions may sometimes be found in new suburbs. Retail outlets are only very slightly responsive to consumer pressures and the availability of goods (especially imports, including sugar) tends to be rather erratic; in the absence of advertising, to ascertain precisely what is on sale demands frequent visits. On the other hand, prices* (fixed by the State Committee on Prices) are very stable. A weekly 'fish-day' is common. Alcoholic drinks are usually in abundant supply. Trade is concentrated in towns and cities, where most shops are: the rural population buys less per head and in significant degree uses the better-supplied urban shops, which contain much more varied assortments. Over half the turnover is in foodstuffs and beverages; the proportion scarcely differs between town and country, which illustrates, in addition to lower rural living standards, how little such households are now self-sufficient in food.

Much the larger part of state trade comes under the Ministry of Trade, some is through the workers' supply departments run by enterprises, or in better-provided 'closed stores', access to which is a privilege.* There are in addition shops selling only against foreign currency or equivalent 'certificates'.

Collective-farm market trade (by 1979 comprising only 2.6 per cent of total sales) predominantly in foodstuffs remains important in higher quality foods to provide variety in a diet much affected by the seasons. Prices are usually well above corresponding prices in the state and cooperative shops but produce is more consistently available. This trade includes some simple handicrafts.

Retail trade is carried on mainly without advertising, store prices being uniform within a given zone (the USSR is divided into three such zones) and consumer pressure already being ample to clear most shelves, even though shoppers have recently become more discriminating. The latest estimate is that total promotional outlay in 1967 corresponded to a mere 0.07 per cent of household consumption. Against the savings from not advertising must be offset the waste of time and inconvenience caused to potential buyers.

Parallel markets

A 'second economy' of substantial dimensions exists in consumer services–especially in building, repairs and transport* using private or official cars and larger vehicles. Unofficial activities also include trading and manufacturing, but economic crime* such as 'specula-

Makeshift stalls of an informal 'parallel' market

Soft-drinks vending machines, Moscow

tion' (buying with an intent to sell, if by unauthorized individuals) are punishable by imprisonment and in aggravated cases even by the death penalty. Although no statistics are published, earnings from unofficial sources must fill what appears to be a sizeable gap between visible living standards and what would correspond to officially reported wages divided by shop prices.

Catering and tourism

Very little construction of hotels or restaurants was undertaken between the Revolution and the 1960s; priority being given to serve important Communist Party* or government officials and foreign guests and delegations, extremely few hotel places could be offered to others. In the capital some grandiose but uneconomic skyscrapers exemplified architecture* under Stalin, but substantial additions did not take place until the 1970s, especially for the Moscow Olympic Games.* Restaurants, most of which were attached to hotels or, in Moscow, were showpiece establishments of the various Soviet republics – offering traditional dishes ponderously served in imposing surroundings – have in the 1970s been supplemented by some brighter and more informal cafes, but pressure on space persists as more people can afford to eat out. In towns state-owned stalls sell such items as kvass (a drink based on rye), ice cream, and soft drinks (also available from vending machines). Outside the central urban zones the principal form of public catering is the *stolovaya* (translatable as 'diner') or, in Central Asia, the *chaykhana* (tea-room).

Whereas motels began to be developed only for the Olympic Games, adequately equipped camping grounds were put along officially accepted tourist routes when foreign tourists were allowed to come by car (and to hire cars) in the 1960s. Considerable areas remain closed to foreigners by whatever means of access. For Soviet citizens, tourism is envisaged as organized recreation,* often with physical cultural overtones, and is largely provided from 'tourist excursion bases' used by about 20 million people annually. Tourism to the West is limited to the politically reliable. *R.H.*

Central planning

Soviet authorities speak of their system as 'directive planning', meaning that the plans are obligatory, that they are orders which management must obey. It is distinguished from 'indicative' planning, sometimes practised in the West, whereby governments make forecasts and seek by indirect means to influence the decisions of firms, which themselves are free to act as they think fit in their own interests. In the Soviet system the object is not only to direct but to ensure that compliance with the directives is in the interests of management and labour alike: plan fulfilment should override all other considerations.

Except for collective farms* and the still-significant privately-owned livestock and household plots, virtually all economic activities are state-owned and state-operated. Thus there is – in a sense – one giant firm divided for administrative convenience into various industries, which are further divided within a planning-and-management hierarchy, to which the nearest Western parallel is the large industrial corporation, where too there is a hierarchy, which plans, manages and issues instructions to subordinate units, and where headquarters can dismiss managers who do not obey orders. Not only production★ but also distribution is in the hands of state organs. Legislation on economic crime★ forbids individuals to buy and sell for profit (although cabbages grown or dresses made by an individual may be sold by him), or to employ anyone to make goods for sale. Nearly all industrial producers' cooperatives were abolished in 1960–1, but there are signs that they may be revived.

The complexity of the planning task and the need for a multiplicity of planning organs to carry it out can only be appreciated on examination of the many different aspects of the plan. Since the role of the state in the economy combines planning with management, both the future shape of the economy and the short-term assurance of goals and supplies for each productive enterprise must be planned and integrated. Thus the current production plan is a multiplicity of interdependent instructions, not only relating supplies and outputs, but also the value of sales, labour productivity and other plan indicators.★ Because transactions are in money–enterprises sell their output and buy their supplies–there are also financial plans, including profit plans designed to safeguard economic use of resources. Serious problems arise out of the complexity of this plan-and-management system.

Nevertheless, not all activities are centralized; the USSR is a federation of 15 Union Republics, each with its own planning structure, and some industries are under republican control. There are also small-scale industries operated by local government bodies. However, the centre exercises a dominant role, because in a modern industrial economy most productive units send their output all over the country (and sometimes beyond its borders), while drawing supplies from many areas. Therefore regional planning organs, although they play some role in drafting development plans for their regions, have relatively modest powers. From the standpoint of planning, the republics are the wrong size: the Russian republic (RSFSR) is much bigger than all the rest put together, and contains half the population, while the smallest, Estonia, has below 2 million.

The top of the pyramid, in economics and politics alike, is the Politburo.★ The apparatus★ of the Central Committee of the Communist Party★ has economic departments which play an important role, and the Council of Ministers★ carries out Party policy. The State Planning Committee (Gosplan) headed by a deputy premier is the coordinating planning agency, responsible to the government. Its task is to ensure the coherence and balance of plans both in the long and in the short term; it is also responsible for allocating key materials and products to the principal users. In this it

ORGANIZATION OF ECONOMIC ACTIVITY

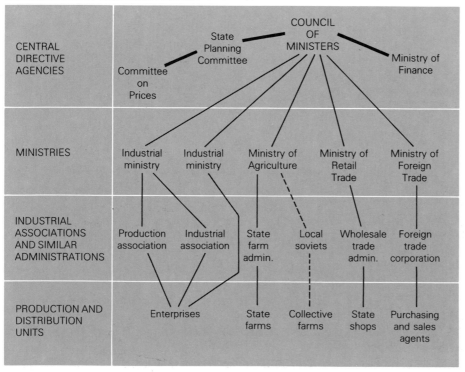

KEY

Lines of subordination in state sector

Coordination and planning

No legal subordination in collective sector but Ministry of Agriculture imposes procurement quotas and local authorities (soviets) have certain supervisory powers

Design by M. Kaser

is assisted by the State Committee on Material-Technical Supply (Gossnab), also headed by a deputy premier. By the method of material balances available supplies of the more important goods are related to estimated requirements (output with the needed inputs) thus identifying the need to increase supplies and/or to cut utilization. These and similar coordinating bodies do not themselves administer productive units, which are subordinate to 'industrial' ministries,★ of which in 1979 there were 31 classified as all-Union and 22 as Union-Republican. The latter will have counterparts at republic level and most administer their enterprises through an industrial association (*obyedineniye*). These latter agencies are categorized as 'industrial' (in which case they may be all-Union, or republican), or 'production' (anything from a merger of small local factories to a giant production complex such as the Noril'sk mines in northern Siberia). These associations group enterprises (*predipriyatiya*) all under the supreme authority of the appropriate ministry, which passes down the plan targets, appoints and dismisses managers (subject to control by Party organs) and collaborates with the plan-coordinating agencies to ensure that the plans for each ministry are consistent and coherent in relation to the rest of the economy.

On the one hand, the Politburo indicates to the planners the medium-term goals which it is desired to pursue, and on the other, there flows upwards to the planners information, proposals and

The headquarters of the State Planning Committee in Moscow

pressures–the ministries put up schemes for new investments in their branches; republican and local Party and state authorities urge the needs of their respective areas; the military★ planners make their claims, as do those responsible for health,★ education,★ housing,★ and so on. Affecting each flow are issues connected with foreign trade★ (export needs and opportunities, import requirements), and the coordination of investments with those of allies. The political leadership resolves the principal issues of long-term development – the Five-year Plan and 'perspective' plans–and operational priorities in the annual or quarterly plan. Gosplan, together with other coordinating agencies, should ensure that the plans that finally emerge are internally consistent. If the requirements originally determined by the Politburo add up to more than it is in fact possible to implement, the planners must so inform their political superiors. For it remains true that one cannot build today's factories with tomorrow's bricks.

Enterprise management

Management is not merely the passive recipient of orders which it must carry out. The proposals it makes and the information it provides affect the decisions of its association and ministry and, because the complexity of the task of planning, shared between a number of agencies, can lead to inconsistencies, management may have to choose between complying with certain instructions at the cost of disobeying others. Moreover, there are so many different products (12 million, according to a 1977 Soviet estimate) that it is quite impossible to tell management exactly what to produce and, with output instructions aggregated, management determines details of the product mix in negotiation with customers. The material supply system is not wholly reliable, and managers often have to use ingenuity (and sometimes semi-illegal methods) to obtain essential materials and components. These functions are additional to the everyday tasks of actually operating the plant and dealing with labour problems so that although the manager is under the command of the appropriate ministry, he holds in fact a key position, and many problems in the Soviet economy arise from the attitudes of management to the instructions of planning and ministerial officials.

Plan indicators

Management is financially rewarded for the fulfilment of plan indicators and penalized for underfulfilment. Even if attention is confined to the plans for output, the central planners face the problem of ensuring that the product mix accords with requirements: to collect information and issue orders about 12 million items is impossible. Plans are in fact made (at some administrative level) in respect of 48000 items, which means that on average each plan instruction subsumes 250 sub-items. Plan indicators for output have to be expressed in terms of some total–tonnes, square metres, pairs, roubles – opening management to the temptation to produce whatever best fits the chosen measure. Examples frequently encountered in the Soviet press are of a plan indicator expressed in weight, inducing management to prefer heavy products, and of clothing enterprises fulfilling plans in money by concentrating on the more expensive clothes. Numerous complaints are printed about construction enterprises, which select the work which is 'worth' more in terms of plan fulfilment, instead of what is needed to complete the building. Another frequently-criticized effect of plan indicators expressed in money for global output, labour productivity, value of sales or turnover is that the use of costly materials is encouraged, provided that these can be included in the price. A change of plan indicator from global output to 'normed net output' from 1980 was intended to counter such an effect in favour of producing the type or quality required by the user.

Profits might be a useful criterion in assessing enterprise performance but the price system is such that profitability can be a misleading measure. The reasons are that wholesale prices do not reflect need, demand nor the degree of shortage, and are based on estimated costs which frequently no longer correspond with actual costs; thus the price schedules established in 1955 were not systematically revised until 1967, and most prices are not to be revised until 1981. As there are several million prices which have to be fixed by state agencies, many anomalies arise: goods in urgent demand turn out to be unprofitable to produce.

For all these reasons, there are shortages of many goods, even while others turn out to be unsaleable. There is often excess demand both for industrial materials and for consumers' goods,* accompanied by the phenomena of a sellers' market: queues, hoarding, illegal transactions (the many cases of foreign visitors being asked to sell clothes at inflated prices). These problems are frequently the subject of press comment, and the authorities are aware that quality (of both producers' and consumers' goods) is often unsatisfactory, reflecting the fact that plans are predominantly quantitative. The Soviet system is capable of big achievements, and not only in weapons production – for example, the vast and successful investments in extracting oil and gas in north-west Siberia, in the face of formidable natural obstacles. The system seems to be at its best in large-scale planning of priority projects; the routine of current planning, despite the help of computers, is too overwhelmingly complex. *A.N.*

The economics of socialism

The Soviet leaders have claimed that the present system is one of 'developed socialism',* even while admitting, even stressing, the existence of many defects. In living standards and in technology the West (with all its problems) is still ahead. In seeking ways of overcoming the existing defects of the Soviet system, how can socialist economic theory help?

This is an area of controversy. Marx envisaged a full socialism, or communism, in which there would be no markets, no sales or purchases, no money, no wages, no need for material incentives, since there would be abundance; there would moreover be no state, officials, army nor police. The USSR is evidently not like that and could not be. Its economists are acutely aware that they are in a world of scarcity, in which material incentives and monetary calculation are essential. The practical questions are: what are the unavoidable limitations of centralized planning? What degree of decentralization is feasible which does not erode the advantages of central control, but which provides rational criteria for managerial decision? Is it possible to dispense with plan indicators adherence to which distorts the product mix? How can initiative and innovation be rewarded instead of obstructed? What sort of prices would stimulate efficiency, and how could they be determined? Marxian labour-value theory is of little help, because it relates values to human effort, while of course a planned economy should maximize not effort but result.

Some reformers advocate a move towards a market economy, with current output plans no longer laid down by central planners and ministries; the product mix would then result from orders from customers, and not instructions from superiors. It is urged that plans should be essentially long-term, relating to major investments and structural changes; current plan production, supply, sales, should be

The pennant awarded for productivity to a Communist Labour Brigade at a Moscow footwear factory

the responsibility of management, with profitability as a guide and with prices so fixed as to make what is needed conform to what is profitable. This was the principle underlying the Hungarian economic reform of 1968. Some wish also to introduce a greater degree of worker participation in management decisions.

Such proposals as these have been rejected so far. Everyone from Brezhnev* down agrees that production should be more closely geared to the requirements of the users, that waste and inefficiency should be eliminated, and that some plan indicators stimulate irrational and undesired responses. However, there is concern about the possible consequences of dismantling the production-and-material-allocation mechanism, especially under conditions of chronic excess demand. Priority sectors may suffer in consequence. Then there are ideological obstacles. Marxists tend to contrast the 'anarchy of the market' with the advantages of planning, and they see also that a market mechanism requires competition and the encouragement of profit-seeking acquisitiveness. On a lower plane, officials fear for their jobs, since many of them replace the 'invisible hand' of the market. The troubles of market economies in the West reinforce the Soviet leaders' sense of caution. At the same time partial or gradual reform is self-defeating: to remove a portion of the economy from the centralized planning system would create confusion, especially with regard to the planning of the material inputs of the unplanned sectors.

The debate continues, both at the theoretical and the practical level, since the government itself is acutely aware of the need to eliminate inefficiencies, especially at a time of shortage of labour and tight investment resources; ambitious growth plans can be fulfilled only if resources are used effectively. Consumer dissatisfaction is also of real concern to the leadership, and Brezhnev has several times drawn attention to this problem. New and determined efforts are being made to improve the functioning of the centralized system, by such means as reorganization, devising new and better plan indicators and making the payment of plan fulfilment bonuses conditional upon fulfilling delivery obligations to the customers. The ultimate question is: whether the efficiency which is being sincerely sought can be achieved without major reforms in the direction of decentralization and whether there can be decentralization without a bigger role for market forces.   *A.N.*

Accounting and enterprise finance

Lenin* declared that accounting and control were the main requirements for the proper working of socialist* society, but enterprise accounting disintegrated during War Communism* and had to be rebuilt slowly on traditional lines during the NEP* period.

Immediately following the introduction of the Five-year Plan the XVI Party Conference (1929) resolved that socialist accounting should be a unified system providing the indicators needed for monitoring the implementation of the national plan, and a brief attempt was made in 1931 to create a system for generating both accounting and statistical data. The two data processing systems have since been distinct but complementary, each containing the stages of recording, reporting and analysis: the statistical flow monitors the realization of the plan and accounting data are for the short-term surveillance of enterprise performance.

The standard system of accounting, implemented by all enterprises, is the joint responsibility of the Ministry of Finance and the Central Statistical Administration. The former issues the general rules, while more detailed instructions are issued to their subordinate enterprises by ministries. The main features of the system are the national plan of accounts, uniform accounting records and accounting returns, standard procedures for the classification and processing of transactions (such as common rules for asset valuation, treatment of depreciation or profit determination). Historical absorption costing is used for accumulating the cost of commodity output. Financial and cost accounting are integrated into a single system oriented to the requirements of external users. There is a comprehensive disclosure of accounting data to the supervising authorities but the final accounts of enterprises are not made public. A series of *ad hoc* accounting and operating data records service the needs of specific enterprise managers. Audits, or inspections, of the accounting records are made by the controlling industrial ministry, the Ministry of Finance and, if criminal activities are suspected, by the Ministry of Internal Affairs.

The Central Statistical Administration, Moscow, designed in 1928 for the consumer cooperatives by Le Corbusier

THE ACCOUNTING SYSTEM

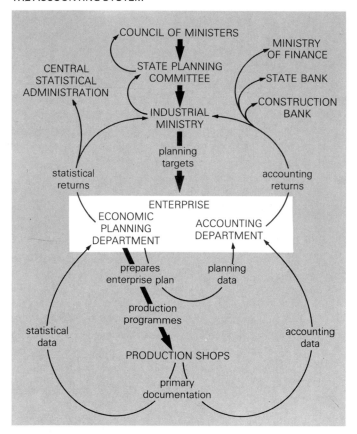

The standard system applies both to institutions funded from the budget* and to enterprises on profit and loss accountability (*khozraschet*); the enterprise's integrated plan (*tekhpromfinplan*) is a component of the national plan. Excluding capital expenditure, financed largely from the state budget, enterprises are required to recoup expenditures and generate a profit. The primary profit appropriations are bank interest, payment for the use of productive funds and a fixed payment (in respect of excess profits). From the assets remaining are made transfers to the economic incentive funds, the bulk of the residual being appropriated to the state budget. Short- and medium-term finance, if needed for the implementation of the corporate plan, is made available by the State Bank (Gosbank). Medium-term finance for capital expenditure is provided by the Construction Bank (Stroybank). *D.B.*

The central financial system

The Soviet financial system shares many of the features of that of a market economy–an annual budget forecasts revenues and expenditures; a banking system holds budgetary and other funds, and is a medium for payments; wages are paid; transactions are expressed in money and based on price-lists–but it is authoritarian in content. The budget is the financial dimension of the annual economic plan, the great majority of prices are fixed, and wage funds are rigidly controlled.

The budget
The most flexible instrument of financial management is the budget, but its analysis from elsewhere than its author, the Ministry of Finance, is very difficult: detailed breakdowns are not provided; 'defence' is not subdivided at all and appears improbably small; and entries frequently do not sum to totals. Most external observers consequently see the published figures as a dubious reflection of actual financial flows. The 'unified' budget comprises federal, Union-Republican and local-authority accounts (consolidating some 55 000 budgets).

Revenue is derived overwhelmingly from indirect taxation, the principal elements being 'turnover tax' (on sales) and 'payments from profits' (about one-third of which now comprise payments as a proportionate charge on capital assets); both are defined as from the 'socialist sector' but this only means that they are not direct taxes. Income tax–in 1961 scheduled for abolition by 1965–remains low (the maximum rate is 13 per cent and in 1979 it yielded only 8 per cent of total revenue). The federal budget invariably shows a small surplus of revenue over expenditure, which is stated to be used for credits or as a reserve.

'Maladministration–Misappropriation' Poster illustrating the role of the enterprise accountant as a watchdog over state property

Expenditure consists mainly of three large items: 'finance of the national economy', 'social and cultural measures', and 'defence' (in that ranking by magnitude); in 1979 these amounted to 95 per cent of spending, with 'state administration' another 1 per cent. 'Social and cultural measures' comprises education and science, health services and physical culture, social security and social insurance (including pensions, and children's and unmarried mothers' allowances), and since 1965 a contribution to the social security fund of collective farmers. By far the largest element is education* and science,* the latter amounting throughout the 1970s to about one-quarter of this sub-total, having expanded primarily at the expense of higher education. Space research,* and possibly some military* research outlays, are included under science. 'Defence' includes the pay of the armed forces, though probably not of troops under the Ministry of Internal Affairs or the Committee for State Security (KGB).* Soviet sources convey an impression that procurement of defence material is included, but their language is imprecise. 'Finance of the national economy' includes state-financed investment, certain subsidies (especially of agricultural products), state material reserves, provision for wage adjustments in abnormal years and compensation to foreign trade organizations for differences between internal and external prices.* These outlays appear to leave almost half the total

allocation unaccounted for under this head: one possibility is that part of the residual is defence procurement and another that it is offset by revenue.

Over time, the behaviour of these three main expenditure items has been substantially different. Expenditure on 'social and cultural measures' is affected by major policy changes (for instance, to increase pensions or scientific spending). By contrast, 'finance of the national economy' tends to rise especially at the start and towards the end of Five-year Plans while 'defence' adopts in some degree the opposite rhythm (apart from changes induced by the international situation). Although this behaviour suggests that these clauses conform to their titles at least in a general way, occasional quantitative leaps suggest transfers (although unreported) from one entry to another. Although in certain years 'finance of the national economy' can be broken down into expenditure on industry, agriculture and so on, with usually just under half devoted to industry, it is impossible to deduce how much within each sub-division is for investment.

The budget is presented to the Supreme Soviet* usually in December of the preceding year, but is not substantively debated and is quickly adopted by unanimous consent with only trivial amendments. Subsequent alterations are rarely revealed, but can sometimes be deduced. Relative to original projections, overfulfil-

OFFICIALLY REPORTED BUDGET EXPENDITURE (at current prices)

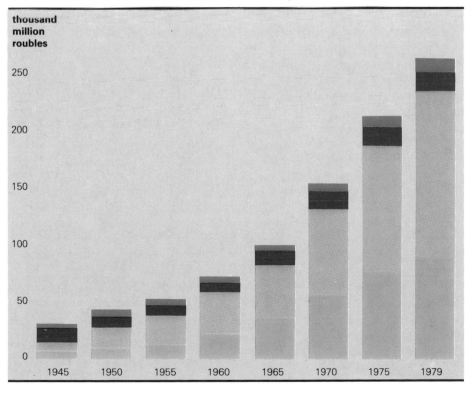

KEY

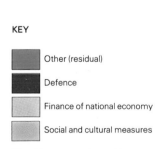

Other (residual)

Defence

Finance of national economy

Social and cultural measures

10 roubles were exchanged for one new rouble in 1961; expenditures before 1961 have been converted to new roubles

Source: *Narodnoe khozyaystvo SSSR* for relevant years

ment is much more common than underfulfilment. Among expenditures, this applies especially to economic outlay; usually socio-cultural is also overspent, but by a smaller margin. As for defence, since 1963 only a single annual total has been published to represent both planned and actual spending; this is so unlikely that deviations must presumably be accommodated elsewhere.

The republic budgets reflect the size of the individual republics of the USSR, that of the RSFSR comprising more than half their total. The federal budget may disburse subsidies to particular republics. The federal component tends to shrink if the share of defence declines or that of socio-cultural outlay increases, or if there is any trend of financial decentralization. When during 1957–65 most industry was placed under regional economic councils, the republican share in economic expenditure rose sharply, and that of localities much less so.

When the budget is made public, certain non-budget expenditures are forecast. Whereas all spending on defence is budgetary, other outlays are considerably augmented from other sources – in 1962 total spending on the economy was to be 74 per cent higher than budget spending alone. The distinction between budget and non-budget financing is, however, not fundamental in the Soviet system, either source presupposing levels of demand and of prices which, given the total economic environment, are – like the budget – alterable.

Money and banking

Primarily for use outside the state sector (apart from the payment of wages), both notes and coin (100 kopecks = 1 rouble) are in circulation. The rouble is not convertible, its export is prohibited and its rate of exchange* is at the discretion of the government. A few stores accept only precious metals or foreign currency.

The state savings banks pay a low interest rate. In 1965–79 the volume of deposits grew almost eightfold, which is evidence of both increasing wellbeing and repressed inflation. The overt inflationary spiral of rising wages and prices is absent by reason of the tight control of all wages* and most prices.* The savings bank system operates a giro, the expected transactions of which are taken into account in the quarterly cash plan of the State Bank (Gosbank), the bank of issue. The volume of cash in circulation is not published, however, partly because it might disclose the operation of parallel markets.* Every state enterprise is required to keep an account at the State Bank, whose duty it is to monitor the accounting system* and to report if amounts or prices diverge from those stipulated in plans or contracts. The Bank also extends short-term credit (at low rates of interest) to state organizations – credit from one such organization to another has not been permitted since 1930 – because they are intentionally supplied with less working capital of their own than they need. The sole investment bank, the Construction Bank (Stroybank) handles the bulk of investment funds in accordance with the plan. The Foreign Trade Bank (Vneshtorgbank) handles external transactions.

Investment

Investment is financed in conformity with plans, each project preferably being included within a general plan of a finite duration. Only about half is funded by the central authorities, primarily under the budget entry 'finance of the national economy' (which probably includes investment in military as well as civilian branches), but a smaller part within 'social and cultural measures'. The bulk of budgetary financing is for 'centralized' investments (those included in the central investment plan), but some 'decentralized' investment is budget-financed. Non-state investment (wholly 'decentralized') is made by collective farms and individuals (mainly for housing*). The main non-budgetary investment finance within the state sector is from amortization and retained profits, but enterprises are not free to dispose of the bulk of either. During 1930–65 investment within the state sector was funded overwhelmingly by non-repayable grant, in response to claims submitted from below. In 1965 capital charges were introduced (with the aim of curbing over-investment and increasing efficiency), but the share of bank credit in financing investment remains small. *R.H.*

Prices

Prices play a somewhat different role in the Soviet centrally-planned economy than they do in a market economy. Because most goods are allocated administratively, enterprises have very limited scope to choose their inputs and outputs in response to relative prices and profitability. Since the output prices they face have little to do with demand, while their money costs may also bear only a tenuous relation to real relative costs and supplies, it would in any case make little sense to let them decide on a production programme so as to maximize profits. Households, on the other hand, may normally choose freely how to spend their income on the goods which the planners make available at fixed retail prices; but excess demands for or supplies of these goods seldom influence their official prices.

Since workers' and managers' incomes depend only slightly on the profitability of what they produce, the distribution of money incomes* outside agriculture* is also hardly affected by prices. Farmers' incomes (and thus the distribution between workers and peasants) do, however, depend on agricultural prices, both the procurement prices set by the planners and the free prices on the collective-farm market. Moreover, the distribution of real incomes is significantly altered by retail price policy, as the State Committee on Prices generally sets relatively low prices for 'necessities' and high prices for 'luxuries' or products the consumption of which the government seeks to reduce, such as spirits as part of its campaign against alcoholism.*

Although wholesale prices may appear to perform only an accounting* function in the transactions between state enterprises, the planners do use them for more important purposes. These prices permit them to construct plan targets in value terms, to impose a budget constraint on firms and thereby to control and evaluate their performance. Planning itself often requires aggregative magnitudes expressed in values through prices, for the calculation of 'synthetic' macroeconomic balances as well as intertemporal comparisons and analyses of the growth and structure of the economy. Investment* and foreign-trade* decisions must also sometimes depend on comparisons using domestic prices, even if 'corrected' in various ways by the planning authorities.

Wholesale prices have for many decades been set centrally on the basis of the average (over all producers) costs of production, although the rules for determining the average cost of a good have changed from time to time. They have always included the costs of materials, labour and an allowance (relatively small by Western standards) for depreciation, plus a small profit margin, calculated as a percentage of costs (the ratio varying between industries). The 1967 wholesale-price reform allowed for a capital charge (analagous to interest) in profits but not in costs, and for certain rents on land and natural resources* to be in costs; thus these rents were treated as price-determining, rather than as price-determined. Moreover, the profit margin was calculated as a percentage of capital employed. Operationally, the domestic wholesale price system is divorced from foreign prices by a system of taxes and subsidies implemented at the level of the foreign trade enterprises which carry out import and export transactions. In the 1970s, however, the planners have taken account in some instances of world market prices but no significant change is to be made in this direction in the wholesale price reform of 1981–2. Because wholesale prices based on input costs are interdependent, in a price reform the planners must set millions of prices simultaneously. Major comprehensive price revisions of this kind are therefore infrequent, separated by a decade or more. New goods or goods produced by totally new processes require new prices when they appear, and there are continuous minor adjustments, but there is no serious attempt to keep up with short-run or even medium-run cost changes.

A retail price is in principle set so that households buy just that amount available (under the production plan) for sale. Such prices could be flexible, even with fixed wholesale prices, by changes in subsidies or in turnover taxes levied at rates which vary between products (and may differ widely even between highly substitutable goods). In practice, however, the authorities are very reluctant to change any consumer price, responding to excess demand or stocks of unsaleable goods either by tolerating the situation or by adjusting supply rather than price. Similarly, changes in wholesale prices, even in a comprehensive price reform, are normally absorbed in the subsidy or by the turnover tax so that retail prices are unaffected.

Evidently inflation can be abolished by setting prices and wages centrally, allowing incomes to rise only in line with consumer-good supplies. This is what the planning officials have always tried to do, but perfect administration is as rare as perfect markets. Indeed, during the two decades to 1948, there was severe open inflation in the USSR. Following the currency reform of December 1947 consumer prices were annually reduced until 1954, and the official retail price index has remained virtually constant since then. 'Hidden' and 'repressed' inflation in the USSR, however, is often suggested. Hidden price increases might simply involve either false reporting of actual prices (either by sellers, by the statisticians, or by their political masters); or price increases for goods outside the 'basket' on which the reported index is based, including 'new' goods of no higher quality but sold at higher prices than those they replace; or deterioration of the quality of goods sold at fixed prices. Repressed inflation refers to short supply of goods at the fixed prices, so that consumers are informally rationed by having to wait in line and forced either to save more than they desire or to purchase less-preferred but available goods.

Western estimates of the hidden (that is, actual) inflation in the USSR show an annual rate of 0.8–1.2 per cent for 1955–72, and although the rate seems to have accelerated during the 1970s it would be very difficult to argue that it has exceeded an annual 1.5–2 per cent. This is partly because since 1955 disposable money incomes have grown annually at only about 5 per cent per head, while even conservative Western estimates of real consumption per head give growth rates of about 4 per cent a year, leaving little room for price

Queuing for scarce goods

inflation. This last point also partially rebuts allegations of widespread and severe repressed inflation. Of course there are shortages of some goods, as is to be expected when prices are not allowed to respond to excess demand; there are also surpluses of many over-priced goods. Naturally Western visitors perceive inferior quality and low real consumption levels in comparison with their own countries, where real incomes are much higher. But waiting lists and lines for goods such as meat, automobiles, and high-quality varieties of many commodities are not equivalent to a generalized shortage relative to money incomes and desired expenditure.

Nor is there evidence of chronic generally frustrated demand in household savings or labour* supply behaviour. Savings rates do not appear to be abnormally high, and continually rising labour participation rates suggest that people must believe there will be worthwhile ways of spending the extra family income generated by additional earners. Many of the observed lines of people waiting for goods are undoubtedly due to the inefficient and undercapitalized distributive network and to distorted relative prices, and although some shortages do appear to have worsened in the late 1970s, there is little evidence that the over-all retail price level has been too low. For most of the period since the mid-1950s, repressed inflation cannot be verified.   *R.D.P.*

Labour and wages

The allocation of labour is largely determined by market forces. Historically, Soviet labour policy has been dominated by the rapid growth of non-agricultural employment and by the need to absorb large numbers of unskilled peasants and women into industrial employment. This phase has virtually ended; the economy will be faced by conditions of labour stringency for the rest of the century – if not beyond. These factors have restricted the extent to which the authorities have been able to modify the distribution of income in pursuit of socialist objectives. They may also lead to adaptations of existing labour policy and, possibly, to institutional reform.

The vast majority of state employees belong to trade unions.* Before 1956 the role of these organizations was largely confined to reinforcing managerial decisions and participating in the administration of social security.* With the return to a freer labour market their functions have expanded. At the local level they now play a much more active role in the resolution of individual grievances (not through strikes but by negotiation and the courts). At the national level they participate in the formulation of labour policy and the drafting of labour legislation. They still play no significant part in the determination of wages or wage relativities (apart from cooperating in job-evaluation).

Employment

Soviet labour utilization has been dominated by the rapid growth in state non-agricultural employment: 99.2 million in 1979 against 31.2 million in 1940 (including some small non-farm cooperatives), but this trend will not persist. Population projections* suggest that the increase in numbers of people of working age for the rest of the century will be extremely modest. In the RSFSR and the Ukraine (the republics in which the bulk of industrial capacity is located) this age-group will actually contract; only in Central Asia and Transcaucasia will rapid population growth continue. These trends are occasioned by declining birth-rates in the Slav areas, to a considerable extent brought about by the high rates of female employment achieved there. Restricted growth in the population of working age is only part of the problem facing the Soviet authorities. In the past, expansion in urban employment has come from three sources, from new accessions to the labour force, from increased numbers of women workers and from rural-urban migration.* In the 1970s there was little scope for further labour-force recruitment from these latter two sources either. According to the 1970 census, some 65 per cent of the female population of working age was employed (compared with 80 per cent of the male population). But in the most active age-groups the proportion was far higher – between 85 and 90 per cent for those aged 20–40 years. When published, the full 1979 census will almost certainly show an increase in female participation; remaining differences between the sexes can be ascribed to women's responsibilities for child-care (and fewer women employed in areas of labour abundance such as Central Asia). Although agricultural employment in the USSR is large when compared with West European or North American levels, productivity in Soviet agriculture* is low. Without substantial investment in agriculture, it is unlikely that the rate of rural-urban migration could be significantly increased since the USSR is unlikely to be in a position to become a net importer of foodstuffs before the end of the century. Finally, since as many as a third of old-age pensioners* are already in employment, it is doubtful whether this population group could provide a substantial reservoir of labour over that period. Against this background of labour stringency, the efficiency with which existing manpower is utilized and the effectiveness of existing mechanisms for its redistribution become of particular importance, especially in such fields as unemployment and labour turnover, industrial training,* management* and planning.*

After a period (1940–56) of draconian controls on labour mobility and considerable restrictions on freedom of occupational* choice (of which the only relic is three-year obligatory placements for university graduates), the Soviet government reverted to a market-oriented allocation of labour in the mid-1950s. This was associated with an increase in labour turnover about which both policy-makers and specialists have expressed concern. In Soviet statistics, labour turnover is defined to include voluntary separations and dismissals.

In 1967 industrial labour turnover amounted to 22 per cent of the labour force (and total separations to 33 per cent). In the following decade turnover has declined to 19 per cent. The average length of time spent between jobs in the mid-1970s was reported as little more than a month, which would imply unemployment from this cause of the order of 1.5–2.0 per cent. Soviet sociologists considering the problem of turnover identify dissatisfaction with career prospects, with conditions of work and with pay as the primary motives for voluntary separations; among women, the difficulty of reconciling family and career responsibilities also figures largely. These motivation studies should be treated with some circumspection, however, since, for example, improvements in pay or conditions have resulted more often in an increase in the citation of other reasons for leaving than in a fall in the rate of turnover.

These rates of turnover cause concern because they are the source of considerable loss of production time and waste of human capital. This latter results from the frequency with which changes of job are accompanied by changes of occupation – for example, surveys in the early 1970s suggested that some 50–80 per cent of those leaving jobs in metallurgical plants also changed occupation or industry (adding to the need for re-training facilities). In an effort to reduce the costs associated with labour turnover and the length of time spent looking for work, and to improve worker information on job availabilities, labour exchanges were established in some 278 larger industrial centres (mainly in the RSFSR and the Ukraine) during the late 1960s – such organizations had been abolished by Stalin★ as unnecessary in the early 1930s – but they deal with only a minority of local job-seekers.

Industrial training

There is an extensive network of industrial training facilities, which was developed originally to facilitate the incorporation of married women and rural-urban migrants★ into the industrial labour force. Latterly, it has undertaken the retraining of those who change professions, and the expansion of the supply of skilled labour required by labour stringency and redundancies due to technological progress. Whatever the past achievements of this scheme, doubts have been expressed about its present efficacy.

Formally, there are two separate channels for the acquisition of industrial skills, trade schools★ and on-the-job training. The first involves attendance for more than six months at a specialized institution where the worker is supposed to acquire not only practical skills but also an understanding of the appropriate technological processes. In the 1960s the number of trade schools was increased substantially; but even so in the early 1970s only some quarter of skilled workers received their training at them. About 60–70 per cent of qualified workers acquire their skills on the shop floor (the balance reporting a variety of miscellaneous sources such as the army). Trade

Scanning a job-vacancies board in Moscow

Instructor with young technicians at a trade school in Vologda, RSFSR

schools are criticized for limiting training to a few traditional occupations and for technologically backward and narrow curricula. On-the-job training is similarly criticized for its restriction to particular skills and its inability to inculcate theoretical understanding. Certainly trade schools are narrowly specialized, and their curricula are frequently out-dated. But any increase in the supply of qualified manpower must be drawn from among those with adequate general education, and steps have therefore recently been taken to extend the availability of full secondary education. Such changes take time and some of the apparent shortage of qualified manpower is probably due to general labour stringency and to shortcomings in industrial location policy rather than to failures in industrial training itself. Although in need of extension and modernization, the Soviet bipartite industrial training system has played a vital part in the development of the country, and will doubtless continue to do so.

The wage system

Since the mid-1950s, when the movement of labour was decontrolled, wage rates have been determined centrally by the State Committee on Labour and Social Questions (the State Committee on Labour and Wages during 1955–76). Under its auspices the wages system was extensively reorganized during 1957–65 and further revisions in wage scales were adopted during 1970–7. One exception to its prerogative must, however, be noted – the earnings of collective farmers which, for historical reasons, were not classified as wages before 1966. Although, legally, since that date payments to labour have been a prior charge on the assets of the collective farm, the structure and level of members' remuneration have not been controlled by the state committee and collective farms have not been obliged to pay the minimum wage.

The objectives of the 1957–65 wage reorganization (and, to a lesser extent, that of 1970–7) were to simplify and rationalize existing wage scales, to reduce differentials within and between industries and to increase the share of basic wages in take-home pay; basic wages were to be raised at the expense of bonuses of various kinds dependent more on the discretion of local management. The first of these aims was achieved by reducing the number of different wage scales in industry to about 500 (from more than 50 000). Wage scales in other sectors are similar to those operating in industry. The number of wage scales in use after 1977 has been reduced to less than 50. The second objective was achieved primarily through a reduction in the spread of pay differentials.* Before 1957 the top wage paid in an individual sector was frequently as much as four times the lowest wage; by 1977 it was no more than double. Success in achieving the third objective has been more mixed. Immediately after the introduction of the new wage scales (say, in 1960–1) bonus elements accounted for approximately 14 per cent of average earnings; by 1970–2, however, they amounted to about 40–45 per cent, almost as much as in the early 1950s. This is a consequence of the infrequency with which wage scales are changed; but it does mean that central control over the level of earnings in the economy as a whole is weakened.

This rationalization and reorganization of wage rates has been accompanied by (indeed, would not have taken place without) the extensive re-specification and regrading of jobs, both in industry proper and elsewhere in the economy. Thousands of jobs have been subjected to a process of centralized job-evaluation using common criteria. As a result the USSR now has a wage structure that is bureaucratically determined, somewhat rigid and slow to change but, it is hoped, one that is seen to be fair. The process of wage bureaucratization has been accompanied by a sustained growth in nominal earnings. For example, during 1956–79 average monthly earnings in the state sector increased from 73.4 roubles to 163.5 roubles, and the standard working week for manual workers in industry fell from 48 to 40 hours. Increases in the cost of living mean that the growth in real wages will be less than this, but inflation in the USSR has been extremely modest by West European standards (perhaps 1.3 per cent per year, 1955–75). This substantial increase has been the result of three factors: increases in basic wages consequent upon wage reorganization; increases in labour productivity leading to increased bonuses; repeated increases in the minimum wage. In 1955 the minimum wage (state sector) was approximately 22 roubles per month; it was raised to 27–35 roubles in 1956, raised again in 1959–65 to 40–45 roubles (depending upon location and sectoral affiliation of the enterprise), in 1968 to 60 roubles per month and in 1972–6 to 70 roubles. This, more than any other factor, has helped the low-paid (unskilled) worker.

Income distribution

Sample statistics on the distribution of income have been collected for only three post-war years: in 1958 and 1967 the sample was confined to the non-agricultural population but in 1972 was extended to include collective farmers. The material relating to the first two of these surveys that has been released suggests that over the nine-year period, average per-capita incomes increased by almost 30 per cent in nominal terms; inequality, as measured by the ratio of the ninth to the first decile (that is, the ratio of the earnings of the person whose rank in the distribution of income is at 90 per cent of income-receivers to the earnings of the person whose rank is at 10 per cent) also fell by about 30 per cent. Between 1967 and 1974 (the latest year for which comparable data are available) average per-capita income rose by a quarter (again in nominal terms) – but there is some evidence to suggest that inequality did not continue to decline. The distribution of income in the USSR, though more equal than in Western Europe, is less equal than in the East European socialist countries. Also during the 1960s (and, indeed, starting in 1953) the gap between the real incomes of state employees and collective farmers was considerably reduced: successive increases in the prices that the state pays for agricultural output, reform of collective-farm financing and the extension of social security to collective farmers all contributed to this. On the other hand, regional (inter-republican) disparities in living standards seem to have increased, despite a policy objective to the contrary. In 1960–75, there was rapid growth in personal incomes in all republics, but the better-off republics saw the larger increases. The spread between average income per head in the republics also widened because of differences in population growth* rates. It is doubtful whether this objective of Soviet incomes policy will be attained until the government can devise an effective population policy – or until it introduces much more extensive and redistributive family allowance schemes;* changes announced at the XXVI Party Congress (1981) indicate some progress in both respects. None the less, considerable advances have been made since the mid-1950s in raising the standard of living and in reducing inequality.   *A.M.*

Merchandise trade

The foreign trade flows of the USSR are smaller in relation to Soviet gross national product (GNP) than are the foreign trade flows of most other countries in relation to their GNP. In 1977 Soviet merchandise exports were equivalent to about 4.3 per cent of Soviet GNP (the latter being estimated in 1977 US $). This may be compared with equivalent figures of about 20 per cent for most medium-sized West European countries (such as the UK, Italy or the FRG). There are two main reasons for this modest level of trade activity: the sheer economic size and extensive domestic energy* supplies and raw material base of the USSR, and the historically and systematically conditioned tendency towards self-sufficiency in Soviet economic management and policy.

Two basic characteristics of Soviet conduct of foreign trade may be noted: imports and supplies of goods for export are subject to detailed administrative allocation by the central authorities; and the rouble is a strictly domestic currency, not, officially, freely convertible into other currencies. Both these characteristics are closely associated with administrative allocation of resources in the economy generally. An exporter to the USSR cannot spend the proceeds as he can in a market economy and the rouble therefore lacks acceptability outside the USSR. Moreover, the relatively rigid structure of Soviet domestic prices is unrelated to the structure of prices in world trade. Imbalances are settled either in kind or in the convertible currencies of other nations. At the same time the Soviet system endows the central authorities with a degree of direct control over import flows and hence over the balance of payments,* that Western governments lack.

So far as its country-composition is concerned, Soviet merchandise trade may be divided among three groups of trade partners: other socialist countries, and especially the other members of Comecon;* developed capitalist nations; and developing countries. In 1979 the shares of these three groups in total Soviet turnover were 56, 32 and 12 per cent respectively. Within the first group, trade with other Comecon countries accounted for almost all the total: 52 per cent.

The basis on which the USSR conducts its trade is different for each group of partners. In trading with other socialist countries, with Finland and with some developing countries the USSR operates on a bilateral settlements basis. In trading with certain other developing countries and with all developed capitalist countries except Finland, the USSR makes settlement in convertible currencies. The commodity composition of Soviet trade is also different as between the groups of trade partners. In its trade with developing countries the USSR is an importer chiefly of tropical foodstuffs and raw materials, and an exporter of manufactures, especially machinery and armaments. In its trade with Eastern Europe, the USSR operates within a framework of specialization agreements and five-year supply contracts; manufactures account for a substantial share of both exports and imports. In its trade with the industrial West, the USSR derives over four-fifths of its merchandise-export earnings from fuels and other primary products, and imports chiefly sophisticated manufactures and agricultural products (machinery and transport equipment constituting over one-third of such imports).

These structural properties of Soviet trade have shown little sign of radical change since the early 1960s. The growth of Soviet convertible-currency exports has been modest, with few significant increases in market shares in manufactures in the industrial West. Accordingly, rates of convertible-currency import have tended to outrun rates of convertible-currency export.   *P.H.*

The balance of payments

The USSR publishes merchandise trade* statistics but does not publish its balance of payments. Rough orders of magnitude for other components of the balance of payments have, however, been estimated.

The Soviet balance of payments is made up of two balances of a different nature: those with bilateral trading partners and those with convertible-currency trade partners. The latter are those Western and developing countries with whom the USSR conducts trade on a multilateral basis, with settlements in convertible currencies. In bilateral settlements the aim is normally to arrange two-way flows of goods and services so that they balance over any one year. Imbalances that arise are then cancelled out by increased deliveries from the deficit partner in the following period. A major exception is Soviet aid to bilateral partners (for example, Cuba and India), which involves balancing (in principle) over a period of years. The larger part of Soviet bilateral transactions, however, is with East European trade partners, with which merchandise transactions usually show only small imbalances in any one year. This is probably true also for current-account transactions in total. Soviet current-account transactions with multilateral-settlement partners, however, are a different matter. Both country-by-country and in total, they have often exhibited substantial imbalances. The major items in the current account are merchandise trade (including arms), freight transport, tourism and interest on debt. Gold★ sales, though used as an equilibrating device, may also be viewed as part of the current account, in so far as they come from Soviet production.

Foreign equity investment in the USSR is not permitted: convertible-currency current-account imbalances must hence be offset by reserve changes and by foreign borrowing and lending. In the 1970s the USSR, according to Soviet trade returns, generally exhibited a deficit in convertible-currency merchandise trade. It was also making substantial payments of interest on past borrowing. These negative items were usually offset to some extent by hard-currency arms sales (not directly identifiable in the trade returns), net credits on tourism and shipping and gold sales. Net indebtedness also tended to increase.

The Soviet planners, however, retained their ability to control imports and cut machinery orders for convertible currency sharply in 1977–8, precluding any suggestion that the balance of payments might go out of control.   *P.H.*

Foreign borrowing and lending

Since the 1950s, the USSR has extended to various less-developed countries credits in convertible currencies and under bilateral clearing, of which several thousand million dollars are still outstanding (although the flow net of repayments is now small). Only in the 1970s, however, did the USSR itself begin to borrow substantial amounts in hard currency from the industrialized Western countries. Its gross convertible-currency liabilities to the West by end-1979 were estimated at about $17 200 million, against which it held about $7000 million in deposits with Western banks. Soviet debt to the West grew rapidly from 1972 until 1978 (but not in 1979), as finance for a large part of its substantial convertible-currency trade deficits. These deficits in turn resulted from the need for regular imports of large quantities of grain (and extraordinary amounts after the bad harvests of 1972, 1975 and 1979), as well as major purchases of Western capital goods. Western producers were happy to sell these goods in the depressed investment goods markets of the mid- and late-1970s, and Western governments were willing to back them with official export credits. Moreover in the highly liquid Eurocurrency markets of the period, the USSR appeared an attractive borrower to Western banks. Of its total gross debt at the end of 1979, an estimated 45 per cent was in the form of official export credits, while 42 per cent was in short- and medium-term obligations to the Euromarket banks.

Although the absolute amount of this hard-currency debt may appear large, and the suddenness and rapidity of its growth is certainly striking, the USSR has actually followed a relatively conservative borrowing policy. Its hard-currency net debt-to-export ratio of 0.7 and debt service ratio of 0.24 in 1979 were the lowest in Comecon★ (compare also Brazil, with over 2.5 and 0.40 respectively), and its total net debt to the West at end-1979 came to less than 2 per cent of its annual gross national product. Nor is it likely that this conservatism will give way to profligacy, whatever credits may be offered by Western private or public lenders.

Thus with its gold★ and immense natural resource★ base, the USSR should have no difficulty in meeting its repayment obligations. Several of its Comecon partners have been less cautious and under more severe pressures, however, and it is widely believed that the

The International Bank for Economic Cooperation, Moscow

USSR may have to assist them in servicing their convertible-currency debts, as it seems indeed to have done for Poland in the wake of losses caused by the strikes of August 1980. Although it may seem improbable that the USSR would act generally as lender of last resort (as this 'umbrella theory' supposes), it has already broken with previous Comecon practice by converting into long-term loans much of the large balance of trade surpluses it accumulated with its hard-pressed partners in 1975–7. Should this continue, it will change economic relations in Comecon significantly, though not as much as the new financial relationships of the 1970s have broadened and deepened East-West economic interdependence.   *R.D.P.*

Gold reserves and sales

Soviet gold production was not officially published after 1928 nor has the USSR State Bank revealed its reserves of gold and convertible currency since 1935, but its official or commercial agencies have never had to delay payment on a foreign obligation. Its deposits in convertible currency in banks in the industrial West are known from returns collected by the Bank for International Settlements ($8621 million at the end of 1979), although they were more than offset by bank borrowing ($12 922 million at the same date).

An open-cast gold-mine developed since 1969 at Muruntau, Uzbekistan

The State Bank and its subsidiary the Foreign Trade Bank use bullion to make up some of the deficit the USSR normally runs on its convertible-currency balance of payments* (there was a $210 million surplus in 1980) and in some years such sales reduce the reserve. The US Central Intelligence Agency estimates that the gold reserve had been rebuilt from a nadir of 920 tonnes in 1965 to 1581 tonnes at the end of 1979. Curiously, that was not far off the 1913 figure (1566 tonnes). The CIA estimate of 1979 production was 307 tonnes but one made for the Association of American Geographers put output at 336 tonnes and the London-based mining group Consolidated Gold Fields suggested a range of up to 350 tonnes. On such estimates and allowing between 50 and 60 tonnes for jewellery, industrial and decorative uses, reserves would have been reduced by sales to the West in 1976–8 (averaging 367 tonnes annually), but not in 1979 (223 tonnes sold) or 1980 (70 tonnes sold).   *M.K.*

The rate of exchange

The rouble, which dates from the 13th century, was originally of silver; Russia did not adhere to the gold* standard until 1897. Convertibility into gold was suspended in August 1914 and the value of the paper rouble plummeted in wartime inflation and post-war hyperinflation. A phased currency reform during 1922–4 re-introduced a bullion cover (the 1922 *chervonets* of 10 roubles was issued at 8.6g of gold; the 1924 silver rouble was valued at 18g of silver but was replaced by the 1926 silver *poltinik* of 50 kopeks at 9g). The backing became nominal from 1928 (when the import and export of Soviet currency was prohibited); the *poltinik* was formally withdrawn in 1931 and the *chervonets* in 1936; a gold *chervonets* was sold from 1975 against convertible currency (and one million quarter-ounce pieces were minted in 1980). A devalued paper *chervonets* was introduced in 1936 but withdrawn at the 1947 currency reform. The exchange rate of the rouble then introduced was revalued in 1950 but devalued (to its 1980 formal gold content of 0.987412g of fine gold) in 1961, when one new rouble was exchanged for ten old roubles. From 1958 Soviet citizens have been permitted to export and reimport up to 30 roubles in banknotes, but in all other senses the rouble is a strictly national and inconvertible currency. The exchange rate is set by reference to the respective gold contents of the 1961 rouble and the US dollar of 1934–71 (namely, 0.888671g of fine gold). As the dollar has devalued from that formal parity, the rouble has correspondingly revalued; thus the rouble was valued at $1.56 in September 1980; other exchange rates are established by reference to the dollar. The 'transferable rouble' of the International Bank for Economic Cooperation, which is the unit of account for trade among Comecon* members, is at par with the Soviet rouble.   *M.K.*

International economic collaboration

The first recorded Russian economic treaty was that of the year 911 between Prince Oleg of Kiev★ and the Byzantine emperor, but most medieval trade was conducted through the privileged trading establishment (*gostiny dvor*), within which the Hanseatic merchants were the principal foreign group, and through great annual fairs such as that of Novgorod. Peter the Great★ promoted capitalist commercial relations with Central and Western Europe, while the exploration★ and colonization of Siberia, and, later, the Russian occupation of Central Asia, opened up land routes to the Orient. On the eve of the First World War Russia was a major trading nation, exporting one-tenth of its national income.

The renunciation of international bond obligations issued by the tsarist government and the nationalization of foreign assets without compensation in 1918 led to a boycott of trade with the new Soviet state but the signing of a trade agreement with the United Kingdom (1921), coinciding as it did with the resumption of a market system within the USSR (the New Economic Policy or NEP★), ushered in a period of moderate reliance on trade. Severely reduced during the period of extreme self-sufficiency of the inter-war Five-year Plans, the share of exports in national product was in the 1970s the same as it was in the later 1920s, some 3–4 per cent.

The USSR has nevertheless kept itself singularly free of formal commitments to international economic organizations. Briefly as a member of the League of Nations (September 1934 to December 1939) it took part in that agency's economic activities, including the International Labour Office (of which its membership, however, lapsed during 1940–54). A founder member (from 1945) of the United Nations★ (UN) and hence a participant in two regional economic commissions–for Asia and the Far East and for Europe–and in all non-regional work subordinate to the Economic and Social Council, it did not join the General Agreement on Tariffs and Trade, the International Bank for Reconstruction and Development (World Bank) or the International Monetary Fund. It is, on the other hand, a member of all other UN specialized agencies. As the dominant member of Comecon (the Council for Mutual Economic Assistance), formed in January 1949 with five East European states (and an active membership of ten by June 1978 when Vietnam joined), the USSR can block any measure it deems to its disadvantage, but has not been able to carry through certain of its schemes for economic integration. Although refusing to recognize the European Economic Communities (EEC), the USSR encouraged discussions with the European Commission from August 1973 with a view to an EEC treaty multilaterally with Comecon and bilaterally with Comecon members.

In its own bilateral economic relations the USSR has intergovernmental commissions with all members of Comecon and with many Western powers (the most effective being that with France) and favours industrial cooperation with individual capitalist enterprises, whereby the latter are reimbursed for an initial provision of capital and technology in the products of the joint venture ('buy-back', or 'compensation' deals). Equity investment by foreigners (partially permitted as 'concessions' during 1923–9) has not, however, been authorized, as is the case with some other members of Comecon (Bulgaria, Hungary and Romania).   *M.K.*

The Executive Committee of the Council for Mutual Economic Assistance (Comecon) meeting in Moscow, September 1973

SOVIET SOCIETY

Sunday at the home of Boris Samsonov, a pattern maker in the Lyubentsky agricultural machinery factory near Moscow

Social stratification

Social stratification in society may be considered from two major points of view: that of antagonistic social classes and that of various groups of people who stand in a similar position with regard to some form of political power, privilege and prestige. Social mobility* has to do with movement of individuals between these various status positions.

The Soviet concept of class

The first approach is adopted by Soviet philosophers and sociologists, and is based on a Marxist* analysis of society. 'Class' for Marxists is defined principally by a person's relations to the means of production: under capitalism, the owners of property (together with associated strata) form the ruling or exploiting class and those who sell their labour power make up the ruled or exploited class. Since 1936 the Soviet Union has been defined as a socialist society. In Soviet theory, there can be no antagonistic 'classes' in the USSR for social classes are formed on the basis of ownership relations. As private ownership of the means of production has been progressively eliminated, so too have been the property-owning classes, and since political power was held to derive from ownership, it followed that there could be no ruling and exploited classes.

Under the Soviet form of socialism, however, there is stratification in the second sense just defined. Two social classes are recognized: the working class and collective farmers, and one social stratum: the intelligentsia. The working class is no longer a proletariat, because it is not exploited; on the contrary, on the basis of socialist property, it helps to guide Soviet society to communism. The *kolkhozniki* (collective farmers) are engaged in agricultural production on collective farms. They are distinguished as a class from workers because they are in cooperative production. Though the land itself has been nationalized, they collectively own its produce, the seeds used for production and the agricultural implements.

The essential class difference between the workers and collective farmers is one of ownership relations. Even though he does not own the land, the collective farmer still has collective ownership over its produce. The worker, on the other hand, is employed in nationalized state-run enterprises and his work is planned, regulated and defined by the government, whereas these aspects of labour in the collective farm are, at least in theory, under the jurisdiction of the general farm meeting.

The intelligentsia is a stratum technically part of the working class and composed of non-manual rather than manual workers. In this category are included a wide range of employees – engineering and technical, those 'on the cultural front' and 'workers by brain (*sluzhashchie*) in general'. This stratum embraces those in the strategic commanding and creative roles in society, as well as those in the more menial clerical and administrative jobs. The chief

Soviet citizens of all classes and ages may be found in the daily queue at Lenin's Mausoleum in Red Square, Moscow

distinction between manual workers and the intelligentsia is then based on the role each group plays in the social organization of labour. In the Soviet sociologist's description of the country's social structure the working class is given pride of place. It is 'the creator, the builder of a new society of labour'. It has as its aim the 'liquidation of class differences, the creation of a classless communist society'. The 'working class' is divided into manual and non-manual workers; in 1978 manual workers comprised 61.8 per cent of the population, non-manual workers, 23.1 per cent and collective farmers, 15.1 per cent. The working class, it should be noted, includes those employed in agriculture in state farms, as distinct from collectives.

Some analysts in the West argue that a stratum of the intelligentsia, with the support of the police and Party ideologists, forms a new exploiting class by virtue of its control of surplus value created by the working class and peasants. Others regard the Party élite and various government bureaucrats as a new ruling class, having differential access to power, position and education and enjoying a higher standard of living.

The broad classification of non-manual employees, or brain-workers, may be broken down into a number of distinct groups differentiated according to character of work. The total number of brain-workers in the USSR in 1975 was over 30 million and about 70 per cent of this number constitutes the intelligentsia proper, which is made up of those possessing higher or secondary specialist education* (22.7 million). At the other end of the spectrum, performing more routine and theoretically less demanding work, are clerks, draughtsmen and teachers in infant schools.

Pay differentials

Manual workers are also differentiated by the level of skill on which their rates of pay are calculated, there being six grades of pay in most industries. Wage differentials have narrowed over time. The ratio of the highest 10 per cent of all wage earners to the lowest 10 per cent was 8 to 1 in 1956 and fell to 4 to 1 in 1975. In 1979 the average (money) wage was 163.3 roubles and the minimum was 70 roubles per month. In industry, wages* varied from an average of 180.3 roubles for manual workers, 208.9 roubles for engineering technical personnel and 142.9 roubles for non-manual employees. (In 1960 the comparative figures for the last two categories were 89.9 roubles and 73.8 roubles.)

These averages mask high salaries enjoyed by the various élites. For instance, it has been estimated in the West that a top Party secretary will receive 900 roubles per month in money income, a republican government minister 625 roubles and a Marshal of the USSR (the highest military rank), 2000 roubles. In addition, of course, are payments in kind, which are difficult to estimate. The ratio of the money wages between a factory manager and a worker receiving the average wage has been estimated at about 13 to 1.

The changing social structure

The political Revolution of 1917 was followed by an induced industrial revolution which entailed important changes in the occupational structure.* In 1928 only 18 per cent of the population was made up of manual and non-manual workers (and their families); this proportion rose to 50.2 per cent in 1939 and 84.9 per cent in 1978. The total number of employed persons rose from 11.4 million in 1928 to 110.6 million in 1979.

There is very little survey evidence available on the extent of 'exchange mobility' (movement of individuals between statuses). One picture is given by studies of the accessibility of higher education to the children of various social groups. A study of the aspirations and consequent fulfilment of school-leavers' plans showed a differential rate of social access to educational institutions for school-leavers. An extremely high proportion of children wanted to continue to study – an average of 83 per cent ranging from 76 per cent of agricultural workers' children to 93 per cent of those of the urban intelligentsia. Throughout there was very little aspiration to start work immediately (the range being from 2 per cent to 12 per cent). Investigation of the subsequent realization of the children's ambitions showed that there was a definite relationship between social origin and educational opportunity. Eighty-two per cent of the urban intelligentsia stayed on to study; at the other end of the scale only 10 per cent of the children of agricultural workers continued in education; of the children of workers in industry and building, 83 per cent wanted to continue to study and 61 per cent succeeded in doing so. Another study investigated the social background of students entering the different departments (day, evening and correspondence) of the Urals University (named after Gor'ky*) in 1966. In the day and evening departments, over half the students were of non-manual (including specialist) origin. Many more correspondence-course students were from manual and collective farm strata. When the social background of evening class students of higher educational institutions at Sverdlovsk was examined it proved that over two-thirds of those at the university, conservatory, and teacher training college were of non-manual working origin, but at the polytechnic, mining institute, railway institute and economics institute over half the students were from a manual background. More than 52 per cent of evening-class students were manual workers or their children.

While it may be premature to say that the system is becoming more hereditary, over time there has been a tendency towards greater initial recruitment from within given social groups. In the past there certainly has been a great inflow to higher-status positions as a consequence of the very high rate of economic development As this rate falls off, it seems to be the case that the rate of upward mobility likewise falls. It should be emphasized, however, that there is very considerable upward mobility and opportunities are widely available for children of manual workers and of collective farmers. *D.L.*

Occupational structure

Sectoral distribution of the labour force

Although an industrial labour force was building up in the years before the First World War, in 1917 the population of the Russian Empire was predominantly engaged in agricultural activities. This pattern was reinforced during the period of War Communism* and the New Economic Policy (NEP)* when industrial workers, many of whom had been seasonal migrant workers, returned in large numbers to the villages. Even in 1925 85 per cent of the labour force was engaged in agriculture.* The movement out of agriculture over the next years was very rapid, resulting in an immediate absolute decline in agricultural employment, in contrast with the pattern of an initial relative decline, followed only later by an absolute decline, in most countries undergoing industrialization. Between 1928 and 1940 the proportion of the total labour force in agricultural employment declined from 71 per cent to 54 per cent. Concurrently a rapid expansion of the industrial labour force was set in motion with the implementation of the first Five-year Plans.* In contrast with patterns in most industrializing countries, where consumer industries, notably textiles, took the lead in providing expanded employment in industry, the expansion of industrial occupations occurred first and foremost in heavy industry. In spite of the fact that capital-intensive technology was introduced from the West in priority industries (such as metal fabricating, electrical engineering), labour was used very extensively and workers were employed in numbers far exceeding the manning ratios current in the West, especially in auxiliary and subsidiary processes in these industries. The relative neglect of light industry was reflected in the declining proportion of workers in light as compared with heavy industry in the First Five-year Plan period. In the ensuing labour shortage women* workers were taken on in occupations traditionally reserved for men.

As to changes in the sectoral distribution, employment in industry and construction increased from 23 per cent in 1940 to 36 per cent in 1965, growing rather slowly thereafter. Meanwhile employment in agricultural occupations continued to decline markedly to 31 per cent of the total labour force in 1965 and 21 per cent in 1979. Employment in construction rose from a low of 5.1 per cent of the non-agricultural labour force in 1928 to a high of 13.2 per cent in 1932, declining thereafter. Employment in transport* remained rather steady at about 10 per cent of the non-agricultural labour force between 1928 and 1960. Employment in education* and health* expanded rapidly from the early 1930s, increasing from 6 per cent in 1940 to 17 per cent of the total labour force in 1979. However, the other branches of the service sector provided fewer employment opportunities than are commonly found in countries at similar stages of industrialization, partly because of the absence of a private commercial sector. Since the Second World War employment in the service sector* has been expanding rapidly; most of this is accounted for by the growth of education and health services, but recently the need to develop what is described as 'the social infrastructure' of socialism has been advocated. It is stressed by Soviet economists that, although the social infrastructure is not part of the sphere of material production, employment in hitherto neglected 'non-productive' areas is required to facilitate the expansion of production.*

Distribution of workers' skills

The distribution has altered along with the sectoral changes in occupational structure. Handicrafts declined and the skills of the master craftsmen of tsarist industry were no longer required for the new mass-production techniques introduced from the West. A new industrial work-force, recruited mainly from the countryside, was used to man the machinery of the expanding industries. But a large proportion of industrial workers were engaged not in machine operating but in heavy physical labour, especially in auxiliary and subsidiary processes. Even in 1959, 50 per cent of workers in industry and construction were employed in unmechanized manual occupations; by 1965 about 15 per cent of workers in industry were described as skilled; in 1975, 36.5 per cent of manual workers were described as engaged in 'heavy physical labour'. The share of auxiliary workers in the total number of industrial workers was 46 per cent in 1965, and by 1975 it had increased to 49 per cent; among these workers unskilled manual labour predominates. As in earlier periods it is the existence of this group of workers which, in particular, accounts for the overmanning of enterprises, so lowering labour productivity. Soviet economists acknowledge the paradox of increasing absolute numbers of unskilled manual workers in spite of the relative decline in the proportion of manual workers as a whole in the labour force (from 82.8 per cent in 1950 to 75.2 per cent in 1970). Non-manual workers made up almost a third of the labour force in 1977.

The Soviet work-force is characterized by a polarization of skill levels, as in Western economies, but to a greater degree, in part because of the small size of the intermediate non-manual category made up of sales and clerical workers. The relatively small size of this group follows from the prevailing sectoral distribution of the labour force (for example, the small size of the trade sector) and also from organizational patterns in industry and government. The proportion of clerical workers is from one-quarter to one-third of the proportion of the labour force engaged in clerical work in most Western countries. Reported levels of administrative and managerial personnel are also low by international standards. There are ideological objections to the employment of such categories of people since they are regarded as unproductive. It is impossible to assess the proportion of persons actually carrying out administrative functions from the published Soviet statistics; numbers are probably under-reported.

Nevertheless there are various forces at work reducing the actual size of administrative staffs. Organizational patterns in industry and government encourage large numbers of high-level bureaucrats with small subordinate staffs. It is not clear what proportion of the large and expanding body of professional and technical employees are engaged in administrative and clerical tasks rather than the work for which they were trained. However, in medicine, teaching and especially engineering* the number of professionals per head of population is very high by international standards.

Social evaluation of occupations

It is now officially acknowledged that some occupations enjoy greater popular esteem than others; this is held to reflect the unequal contributions made to society by the various occupations. Prestige is seen as a social reward which the authorities should be prepared to monitor and influence to ensure a desirable structure of incentives. Since the 1960s, much of the empirical research in this area has examined the attitudes of school-leavers, where the incentives issue looms large. School-leavers are particularly susceptible, it seems, to the message of the media;* their assessments tend to provide a formal ranking of occupations which corresponds to the informal prestige hierarchy implicit in media portrayal of occupations. On the other hand, some manual workers appear to evaluate skilled manual work more favourably than certain higher professional occupations, basing their assessments on personal experience of the usefulness and accessibility of the jobs concerned. Jobs which are largely held by women tend to be more favourably evaluated by female than by male respondents. Thus different social groups appear to attach importance to different criteria in evaluating occupations. The studies consistently reveal favourable popular evaluation of professional and technical occupations, especially in science, medicine and the arts, while unskilled manual occupations are ranked lowest, as in the West. Prestige ratings appear for the most part to align with relative earnings and benefits associated with specific occupations. There are, however, exceptions; doctors are ranked higher in terms of popular esteem than in terms of earnings. Positions of political power have not been included in Soviet studies.

In contrast with the West, intermediate 'white-collar' occupations are rated less favourably than manual occupations. Official attitudes in part determine the low relative pay and benefits attached to clerical and sales work, which reinforce their low social standing. In contrast, the high evaluation of an occupation such as mining is associated with high relative pay and benefits.* In general the sector of employment has an impact on occupational prestige, in keeping with relative wages* and benefits and independently of the occupational task performed. Agricultural occupations are rated unfavourably as compared with industrial occupations requiring equivalent training. Engineers, technicians and supervisory personnel in certain low-priority industries are in some cases ranked on a level with skilled manual workers in high-priority (high wage) industries. The levelling of earnings between these groups may account in part for evidence of a decline in prestige attaching to certain professional and technical occupations.

Social mobility

It is proclaimed that 'all paths are open' to the hardworking and able Soviet citizen. Empirical studies of social mobility are a recent development and have been attempted on a modest scale as compared with those conducted in some Eastern European countries. Initially Soviet sociologists preferred the concept of social shifts to that of social mobility because they rejected the notion that occupational positions constituted a hierarchy in the Soviet Union. But as the study of occupational prestige has become acceptable, so too has the concept of social mobility.

The rapid transformation of the occupational structure has provided extensive mobility opportunities. An expansion of the social bases of recruitment to new occupational positions was inevitable, given the small size of the urban industrial and non-manual labour force in the tsarist period. The movement out of agriculture into urban industrial occupations has been a major source of social mobility. There have been many fewer opportunities for those remaining in agriculture because of generally low skill requirements. However a high proportion (70–80 per cent according to recent investigations) of those in managerial and specialist positions in agriculture are of rural manual origin.

Comprehensive studies of mobility by age-cohort are not available, but recent small-scale studies document the predominantly peasant origins of older industrial workers. Among younger workers, the proportion drawn from urban families is much greater. New recruits into skilled industrial occupations are now mainly of urban origin, while unskilled jobs in industry are more likely to be filled by recruits from collective and state farms.

In the 1930s the education system began to provide trained cadres to fill the new professional and technical positions; not enough qualified people were available and many jobs were filled by *praktiki* who lacked formal qualifications. The social dislocation of the 1930s and the war years offered further scope for persons of peasant and worker origin to reach positions of responsibility. The effects of social mobility during these years are still much in evidence and give substance to the glorification in the media of 'leaders of Soviet production risen from the ranks of the workers'. In the early 1970s about 70 per cent of government ministers and more than half of the directors of the largest industrial enterprises in the country had started their working lives as manual workers. Mobility studies conducted in the cities of Kazan', Ufa and Leningrad in the 1960s and 1970s showed that 40–50 per cent of those in specialist positions were

SECTORAL DISTRIBUTION OF ECONOMICALLY ACTIVE POPULATION,
USSR 1913–79 (IN PERCENTAGES OF TOTAL LABOUR FORCE)

	1913	1940	1965	1979
Industry and construction	9	23	36	39
Agriculture and forestry	75	54	31	21
Transport and communications	2	5	8	9
Trade, catering and supplies	9	5	6	8
Health, education, culture and science	1	6	14	17
Administration of state and social organizations (credit insurance)	4	3	2	2
Other branches (including community services)		4	3	4

Source: *Narodnoe khozyaystvo SSSR V 1979 godu* (Moscow, 1980)

drawn from worker and peasant families. But the proportion of
praktiki in leading positions has been declining in recent years.
Increasingly, a pool of qualified labour has become available from
which to fill top-level positions; although some of this increase
reflects qualifications obtained on the job through part-time courses,
there are marked differences according to age in average level of
education. In the country as a whole over two-thirds of specialists
with formal qualifications were under 40 years of age in the early
1970s. Between 1939 and 1959 the number of specialists with higher
or semi-professional education increased from 4 million to 9 million,
further to nearly 17 million in 1970 and to 24 million in 1976.
Opportunities to move directly from industrial manual to higher non-
manual occupations have decreased as educational qualifications
have become a prerequisite for promotion.

Since the 1960s successive studies have shown that children of
manual workers are less likely to obtain high-level qualifications than
are their contemporaries from non-manual families. Since opportunities for social mobility are now largely inter-generational,
depending on educational standard reached, the question of access to
further education is of central concern to the authorities.   *E.G.*

Egalitarianism and privilege

The Soviet Union, according to official ideology, is gradually losing
its remaining class distinctions and moving towards a state of
egalitarianism. Undoubtedly industrialization, urbanization and
certain social policies have contributed to such a development. At the
same time important egalitarian principles have been made
unattainable by political and economic circumstance, or deliberately
abandoned by the government. As a result there is a significant gap
between privileged and disadvantaged citizens which is not too
dissimilar from that found in 'capitalist' states.

Incomes

Income* differentials between people in the higher regular salary
brackets and those on the minimum wage are often widened by extra
payments such as a 'thirteenth month' or 'holiday increment' at the
top of the scale. Income tax on earned income in the state sector
reaches a maximum of 13 per cent and is thus hardly redistributive.
Declared money income alone is, however, an inadequate guide to
purchasing power because it may be supplemented by illegal earnings
on the one hand, or lessened in significance by shortages of goods and
purchasable services on the other.

Purchasing power

Persons in the most responsible jobs have the right to purchase deficit
goods, particularly foodstuffs, in 'restricted' shops, take-away
'buffets' in their offices, or through ordering-services at work. The
higher salaries which go with these posts mean that employees can
buy fresh garden produce, when available, at collective farm
markets; prices here, according to observations in 1979, are about
three times those in the state shops. People with access to foreign
currency or the equivalent in so-called 'certificate roubles' may spend
it on foreign or scarce high-quality Soviet goods at special 'currency'
shops. Other Soviet citizens must rely on the goods on public sale;
supplies can be sporadic, shortages are frequent, while durable
goods, including clothing, are expensive; purchasing them can
involve much queuing. Given state prices,* many people on low
incomes have difficulty in making ends meet, and deprivation is a
recognized but unpublicized feature of Soviet life.

The privileged consumer: a customer at a Moscow bar which
accepts only foreign currency or 'certificate' roubles

Living space

The long-term and acute Soviet housing* shortage has meant that the right to extra living space in a publicly-owned apartment, or the chance of buying a private flat in a cooperative, is particularly valuable. This requires either inclusion in a favoured legal category (such as for service to the state), influence (*blat*) with local authorities, or possession of the money for the deposit and repayments on a cooperative flat. The less privileged citizens, on the other hand, still have to share flats with other families, sometimes living in slum conditions. According to one published source, in 1976 only 47 per cent of the families in Leningrad had separate accommodation. Collective farm housing, though more roomy, is frequently primitive because local electricity supplies, sanitation and even roads may be lacking.

Holidays

The most privileged people in Soviet society have the use of better holiday facilities in the form of subsidized, high-grade rest-homes and sanatoria, state-owned or private dachas, and the opportunity, through various channels, of travel abroad. The poorest may not be able to afford to go away at all, or may have to make do with poorer-quality trade union* rest-homes or shared lodgings in private houses.

Medical care*

There is a distinct gradation in the quality of medical facilities, from the special hospitals for people of importance through state clinics where fees are charged, and private consultation down to the ordinary public institutions which tend to be crowded and of poor quality.

Education

The education* system is more differentiated than might appear at first sight. Here one may contrast the state 'special' schools providing additional facilities for languages, science, arts, leading to the more prestigious VUZy, with the ordinary general and vocational schools whose leavers may go straight into unskilled or low-skilled jobs.

Honours

Many titles for meritorious service to the state (for example, Hero of the Soviet Union, Hero of Socialist Labour, Honoured Artist) and a number of orders (such as Order of Lenin) have been established, particularly since the 1930s. These awards can also bring extra accommodation, pension and travel rights, together with holiday benefits. State money prizes are awarded for outstanding achievements in science and the humanities.

Party membership

Membership of the CPSU,* at over 17 million, has now become a mass phenomenon, but the Party is still a differentiating force in society. Since the CPSU endeavours primarily to recruit 'leading' personnel from workers and collective farmers upwards, people in responsible positions have a better chance of joining (if, indeed, membership is not a prerequisite for their occupation). Such membership can mean better promotion prospects, possibilities of useful personal contact with full-time officials, occupancy of Party elective posts, better access to information, or even a chance of a career in the Party apparatus itself. There is evidence that poorer persons rarely become CPSU members.

It is noteworthy that despite the egalitarian ethic, prestige hierarchies of occupations* are openly recognized and discussed: they bear a striking similarity to those of capitalist countries.

The élite

The occupational groups which have easiest access to some or all of these benefits, and thus a relatively élitist life style, comprise leading officials of the Party and state apparatuses, managers of the largest production enterprises, directors of educational, research and medical establishments, leaders of the cultural intelligentsia (editors, writers, artists), senior military,* KGB (Committee of State Security)* and diplomatic personnel. Though numerous in absolute terms they make up only a tiny proportion of the labour force. The least privileged Soviet citizens are to be found amongst unskilled workers, particularly in the less developed branches of industry, low-grade 'white collar' and service staff, poor farm workers and 'marginal' categories (poorer pensioners,* the temporarily unemployed, vagrants and 'deviants'*). Since the mid-1960s a number of Soviet sources have suggested that a third or so of the labour force earns insufficient to bring family cash income up to a recognized minimum requirement.

Despite their relative well-being, privileged groups in Soviet society suffer from marked restrictions as compared to élites in capitalist societies, including an inability to amass great wealth and an almost total dependence on the state for their well-being. The social attitudes of persons at the extremes of the social scale are not easy to determine, but instances of group cohesion and distrust of outsiders have been noted by observers.

Social policy

The policies of successive Soviet leaderships towards social differentiation have varied considerably, albeit within the official egalitarian ethic. Lenin* used Marxist* premises about continued differences of earnings under socialism to justify differentials after the Revolution. His main 'egalitarian' policies were designed to suppress the previous 'exploiting elements' and improve the rights and well-being of the poor. Party and state administrators were expected to forgo a high wage, but the need to reward them (and other key groups) adequately prompted the introduction of many of the material privileges which exist today. At the same time the political and economic tensions of the post-revolutionary years prevented hoped-for improvements in the living standards and status of the poor. Stalin★ was interested in making income and other material benefits more obviously dependent on political loyalty and higher output; he showed little concern for poverty, which was at times exacerbated by the pressures of industrialization and collectivization.★ He widened income differentials, encouraged the growth of 'restricted' supply systems and prestige housing, introduced fees for the non-compulsory years of secondary school and for university, founded separate low-grade schools (the State Labour Reserves) for less privileged children, and was largely responsible for the system of state honours, ranks and prizes. Khrushchev★ was inclined to strengthen egalitarian trends, mainly by improving the supply of consumer goods and housing for the masses, raising low wages, instituting new pensions, improving benefits for the poor, and abolishing payments for education. The Brezhnev★ leadership seems to have continued to reduce some income differentials, while providing more protection for élite life-styles. *W.M.M.*

Marriage

Soviet citizens may marry at 18 without their parents' permission and in certain circumstances, if a baby is expected, marriage may be contracted earlier with permission from parents and local authorities. In Latvia, Estonia, Moldavia, the Ukraine, Armenia, Kazakhstan and Kirgizia women may marry at 17.

In Soviet society the family★ is a strong unit with approximately 83 per cent of the population living within a family. According to the 1970 census 72.2 per cent of men and only 58 per cent of women over 16 were married. Because of the substantial losses of men during this century older women have had a relatively low chance of marrying and most unmarried adults are women aged 50 and over. Among the younger generation the balance of the sexes is now normal. In the 1970 census more women than men reported themselves as married but this can be partly explained by the fact that women are more likely than men to consider unregistered cohabitation as equivalent to marriage. The average age of marriage has been rising, particularly for men; in 1974 it was 25.1 years for men and 23.4 for women.

When a couple decides to marry they declare their intentions at their local register officer where they will be given a date at least a

Top: marriage ceremony in a Leningrad Wedding Palace, once the home of Grand Duke Dmitri Romanov. Right: after the wedding, a young bride lays her bouquet on the Tomb of the Unknown Soldier in Moscow

month in advance to allow them time to reconsider. In some areas the local register office is called a Wedding Palace and the décor justifies the grandeur of the name. Couples are married under chandeliers on a red carpet in front of a portrait of Lenin and the emblem of the USSR. The bride usually wears white and young couples have returned to the old tradition of exchanging rings. In any one Wedding Palace it is not uncommon for between 30 and 40 weddings to be carried out in one day as each ceremony lasts only six or seven minutes. It is performed by a regally dressed woman-representative of the local soviet who addresses the couple briefly on the obligations of marriage. Some wedding parties remain in the palace for champagne and chocolates there, others proceed directly to their own celebration, which usually consists of plenty of food, drink and dancing. This is punctuated by cries of 'Gorko, gorko' ('Bitter, bitter') to which the couple must respond by kissing until the atmosphere is deemed sweet enough for them to stop. Honeymoons are not as traditional as in the West; it is more common for parents to move out of the family home for a few days so that the couple can begin married life in unaccustomed privacy.

In larger cities it is frequently necessary for newly married couples to live with parents, acquiring a home of their own only if they have children. Most married women work outside the home but the burden of the housework still falls chiefly on them rather than their husbands. The relative lack of consumer services* and convenience products makes the wife's burden particularly heavy. *F.O'D.*

Divorce

The tensions of overcrowding and overwork must in part explain the high divorce rate although the main reason cited in divorce proceedings is drunkenness.* The number of divorces has increased in recent years from 0.4 per thousand of the population in 1950 to 3.6 in 1979. Comparable United States figures are 2.6 and 4.8 respectively. The geographical distribution of the Soviet divorces is uneven: the proportion in Central Asia is very low but in Moscow and Leningrad it rose to over 5 per thousand in 1973.

These divorce figures reflect legal changes in the 1960s making divorce easier and cheaper than it was under Stalin. Payment is from 50 to 200 roubles depending on the couple's income and the authorities decide in each individual case which party is to be responsible for payment. If both husband and wife agree in wanting a divorce and if there are no children, divorce can be carried out in a register office; otherwise the case must be heard by a court. In both types of proceeding an attempt will be made to effect a reconciliation but if this fails a divorce will be granted. The court will then decide about alimony and the custody of any children. It is usually felt that

young children need their mother's care although in exceptional cases custody may be given to the father. After the divorce, it is not uncommon for the couple to have to continue living in one room for some time because of shortage of living space. *F.O'D.*

The family

Size

The authorities encourage parents to have children, as for economic reasons they wish to ensure a strong and sizeable future generation. Nor is the Soviet Union as concerned about scarce space and resources as other less well-endowed countries. Parenthood is held in high esteem. Women who produce five or more children are given medals and honorific titles – the Motherhood Medal, second class, for a fifth living child up to the title 'Heroine Mother' for a tenth. Material aid is given to pregnant mothers and to parents with young families; a further aspect of the promotion of childbirth is a tax on unmarried men.

Despite these measures the birth-rate is still low. Most urban families have only one child and, although rural families are larger, the average number of children is approximately 1.7. The over-all net increase in the population* in 1979 was only 8.1 per thousand. Soviet demographers are concerned by the fact that the birth-rate is falling. In 1926–7 the number of births per thousand females was 159.1 whereas in 1973–4 it was only 66.8.

These data vary dramatically from republic to republic. Most of the mothers achieving motherhood medals come from the southern non-Slav republics. Only one per cent of urban families in the RSFSR have four or more children compared to 25 per cent of all urban families in Turkmenistan. The proportion of large families is even greater in the rural areas of Uzbekistan, Tadzhikistan, Turkmenistan and Azerbaijan. The net increase per thousand population as noted above is 8.1 for the USSR as a whole but the figure is 5.0 for the RSFSR, and 30.1 for Tadzhikistan. The Baltic republics, like the Slav, have a low birth-rate. In 1959 the Central Asian and Transcaucasian republics accounted for 15 per cent of the increase in total population. In 1979 their share was as high as 38 per cent. The implications for economic and military planning* are significant.

State assistance

Although parents choose to keep their families small, surveys suggest that many people would like to have at least one more child if they had more living space.* The government wishes to increase the birth-rate and to keep women in the labour market, so that in other ways conditions for pregnant women are favourable. Employers may not refuse jobs to pregnant or nursing women nor may they reduce their pay nor dismiss them. Women have the right to be transferred to lighter work in the later months of pregnancy. They are guaranteed 112 days of maternity leave at full pay and, if they choose to stay at home with their young babies, they have the right to return to the same job for up to one year.

In 1971 the government substantially raised the amount of money to be spent on child allowances.★ Child benefits of 12 roubles a month are given for each child under eight years in low-income families. About 37 per cent of all children under eight are covered by these programmes. Payments are made to the mother if she is working or studying, or to the father if she is not. Although these child benefit payments help the neediest families, the state seems to prefer other ways of helping young families – through, for example, the provision of pre-school★ and leisure facilities for children.

Illegitimacy

Unmarried mothers also receive increased benefits and officially the illegitimate child carries no social stigma. This has not always been the case. Stalinist legislation meant that an unmarried mother had no right to benefits and that a child's illegitimacy was indicated on his internal passport★ – laws abolished only in the 1960s. In practice it seems that high rates of illegitimacy, the prevalence of common-law marriages and the absence of legal discrimination against illegitimate children facilitate social acceptance of the unmarried mother and her child. Official data on illegitimacy are not available but one survey of the situation in Belorussia has shown the rate to have increased dramatically since 1959. For women there aged 20–24 in 1970, 74 of every thousand births were out of wedlock. The proportion of illegitimate births to older women is even higher. An almost complete lack of sex education and of openness about sexual matters is frequently blamed in the press for unwanted pregnancies. However, it seems probable that many illegitimate births are wanted, given the ready availability of abortion in the USSR.

Contraception and abortion

There is very little open discussion of contraception in the USSR; various kinds are available but on a rather unsophisticated level. Condoms are thick and unlubricated; there are diaphragms but jelly or cream is difficult to obtain so they are not comfortable to use. The loop eventually may solve some contraception problems but it has only recently come into use. Birth-control pills are both produced in the Soviet Union and imported from Hungary but they are little used because they are in short supply and there is anxiety about harmful side-effects. Most couples are said to practise the rhythm method or withdrawal. In the light of these facts the low birth-rate perhaps seems surprising. It can be explained by the fact that in practice abortion is used on a large scale as a contraceptive method.

Abortion has had mixed fortunes under Soviet rule. It was legalized in 1920 but became a criminal offence under Stalin. In 1955, after his death, it was re-legalized and is now effectively available on request to any woman who is not more than three months pregnant. It is officially free to any working woman and in 1979 cost only five roubles to any unemployed woman. The medical profession tries to discourage abortion but feels that if a woman is healthy and allows at least six months between abortions there is no lasting damage, and doctors accept that it is the individual woman who must take the decision. In some hospitals the suction method is used but elsewhere the dilatation and curettage process is employed.

Official Soviet data are not available on the number of abortions performed, but it is likely that the rate is the highest in the world. Even on a conservative estimate it is reckoned that at least eight million take place annually and that in some areas there are twice as many abortions as there are live births. Many women seem to have repeated abortions. *F.O'D.*

Women

The emancipation of women and their full and equal participation with men in Soviet life have from the outset been among the official objectives of the government; laws extending rights and obligations of citizenship to women were promulgated in the earliest days of Soviet rule. But competing priorities have until recently prevented the fulfilment of these aims; the gains of Soviet women, though impressive by international standards, remain uneven.

Women's labour

Protective legislation bars women from especially arduous or dangerous work, although they are employed in heavy work in construction and industry to a degree uncommon in the West. The retirement age for women (55) is five years earlier than for men.

Since the 1930s severe labour★ shortages have made for heavy reliance on women's labour. Women made up a quarter of the total labour force in 1922; by 1937 the proportion had risen to a third. In the 1970s women constituted over half the labour force. The high participation rates of women of child-bearing age are striking; in the 1970s over 85 per cent of women aged 20–35 were in full-time employment. Attempts are now being made to introduce part-time work for women on a very limited scale.

Women have been drawn into the labour force both by the extension of employment opportunities and by economic necessity; women's wages were and are essential to family subsistence. Thus in 1971–5 the average wage★ was 146 roubles per month, while the official minimum income★ required to maintain a family of four was 200 roubles a month. Moreover the deficit of males has meant that many households have had no male wage-earner; in 1959 almost one-third of households were headed by women. In 1946 there were 73.4 males for every 100 females; for the age-group 35–59 there were then only 59 males per 100 females. These devastating war losses have had an impact on every aspect of Soviet life, profoundly affecting the conditions of women.

Higher education has been extended to women on an unprecedented scale; by the 1970s they constituted 52 per cent of professionals with higher education. Women made up almost 80 per cent of teachers, 40 per cent of engineers and 70 per cent of doctors in 1970. (The proportion of women doctors is falling, however, and men now make up half of the entrants to medical institutes.) Within these occupations the proportion of women declines at higher levels of responsibility; for example, in 1975–6, 79 per cent of schoolteachers but only 29 per cent of heads of secondary schools and less than half of head physicians and senior health administrators were women. The representation of women in management is low in relation to their numbers in employment. At intermediate non-manual levels of employment, women make up 80–90 per cent of workers. But despite the feminization of clerical occupations, this category of work accounts for a much smaller proportion of the female labour force than in the West because of the nature of the Soviet occupational structure.*

Women make up almost half of all workers in industry, but only one-third of the female labour force is employed in the industrial sector; over one-quarter of women are in agriculture,* while the remainder are in the service sector,* in which they make up the bulk of workers. In the 1970s about two-thirds of women were engaged in manual labour. The low proportion of women in skilled manual occupations is maintained by enrolment patterns in vocational and technical schools; very few girls are being trained in skilled manual trades. The concentration of women in low-priority sectors, at low skill levels, has been rising over the past 40 years.

Occupational segregation is associated with a gap in the average earnings of men and women; precise figures are unavailable but indications are that the average earnings of women are at most only 70 per cent of those of men. Since the 1960s women have accounted for much of the increase in the labour force, but large numbers have entered low-paid jobs in the service sector and light industry. The expansion of the service sector together with the re-establishment of a normal sex ratio in society have not improved the relative position of women in the labour market.

Women's role

Recent Soviet studies suggest that this situation is in part attributable to the continuing heavy domestic work-load of women. Time budgets show that women spend on average two and a half times as long on child care and housework as do men, and have correspondingly less time for leisure and improving their qualifications. Nor is the domestic division of labour changing appreciably. The change in the working week from 6 to 5 days actually decreased the contribution made by men to housework.

The authorities are ambivalent about altering traditional attitudes to women's role, partly because of their concern over the low birth-rate. Women's responsibilities towards family and children are emphasized. Sex-stereotyping of behaviour and occupations persists in the media* and in patterns of upbringing. Girls and boys show marked divergences in occupational preferences, boys finding technical and industrial work more attractive than do girls.

Soviet women are under-represented in positions of political

Women employed in road maintenance

Z. Seidmamedova, Minister of Social Security, Azerbaijan, SSR

influence. They are more active in local than in central government; in 1975 they made up 48 per cent of deputies to local soviets★ but 31.4 per cent of deputies to the Supreme Soviet of the USSR. Women made up 26.0 per cent of members of the Communist Party★ in 1980, but under 5 per cent of first secretaries of urban and district Party organizations and of members of the Central Committee of the CPSU. Very few women have reached the highest levels of the Party apparatus. Party membership is a condition of access to positions of authority throughout society and many women are effectively barred from such positions by their failure to take on the burdens and privileges of Party membership. The low priority accorded by the regime to measures which could reduce women's unpaid labour in the household and family may be attributable in part to the scarcity of women in policy-making bodies. Recognition of the need to raise the birth-rate without reducing women's contribution to the economy may help to alter priorities in the future.   *E.G.*

Children

Children are in many ways a privileged group in Soviet society. The state devotes much money and thought to providing good educational and leisure facilities for them. In addition the average adult's love and concern for children is readily observed; he may, for example, even give up his seat on a bus to a child and he will almost certainly intervene if he notices a child either in difficulties or misbehaving. The atmosphere seems to be primarily one of affectionate discipline.

Upbringing

Most Soviet families★ nowadays have only one child. Babies are usually breast-fed, often for up to a year. This is possible even when the mother quickly returns to work as many workplaces provide crèches. Infants are frequently swaddled, at least while in the maternity home, as this is felt to encourage the development of straight bones. By 18 months toddlers are expected to be toilet-trained. Although nappies or diapers, even disposable ones, are available, and although mothers give themselves enormous washing loads, many choose not to use nappies fearing their children may become bandy-legged. Crèches and kindergartens may serve either a particular living area or a workplace. Approximately half of all children under school age attend such institutions; in urban areas the proportion rises to three-quarters of all pre-school★ children. Children can enter a crèche at a very early age, sometimes even at three months. Despite the extensive network of pre-school facilities there are regular complaints that not yet enough exist and that those available are overcrowded. Many of the young children who do not attend are looked after by their *babushka* (grandmother). A recent

trend seems to be for both family and state to prefer young children to be cared for at home if possible, largely because they then avoid the illnesses which children attending institutions constantly pass on to one another.

The state and the family share the responsibility for the upbringing of children. Parents are constantly told that they must bring up their children to be good Soviet citizens; large numbers of books and pamphlets are published guiding them on how best to do so. If the teachers who are specially responsible for moral education feel parents are doing an unsatisfactory job they will not hesitate to contact the parents' workplaces so that pressure can be put on them from there. A particularly recalcitrant parent may have his photograph displayed at his workplace with a caption referring to his parental inadequacies.

The ideal child from the state's point of view is one who is patriotic, disciplined, loves study, has no religious tendencies and puts the collective before his own individual desires. In practice, although many children assimilate these values from home as well as school, others learn religious habits and less committed attitudes towards work from their families. Schools complain, in particular, that many parents spoil their children, always giving them priority in the home,

so that disciplinary work carried out in the school is undermined. There is very little delinquency among pre-teenagers. Citizens are legally minors up to the age of 16; if a minor is accused of a crime his trial is closed. A particularly difficult child may be transferred to a special boarding-school* for delinquent children. The police devote some time to crime prevention work, for example by visiting local schools and addressing pupils there.

Recreations

The standard of entertainment provided by adults for children is high. There is a wide range of opportunities organized by the youth organizations* and extra-curricular departments of schools. The latter arrange clubs for children with special interests–chess, drama, English, metalwork–in which they can participate after the school day is over. There are also children's theatres, cinemas, libraries, scientific and sports* clubs and so on, often housed in special facilities called Palaces of the Pioneers.* Puppet theatres are particularly popular; the Obraztsov Puppet Theatre of Moscow is justly world-renowned. Facilities are better in urban than rural areas and country children are also less privileged in that they have fewer good specialists to teach them and they are frequently expected to work on the land at harvest times.

The Soviet child's time is moderately full; he is encouraged to participate in organized leisure activities and he also has a substantial amount of homework to do, but children still find time to play informally together, often in the courtyard round which most blocks of apartments are built. Most of the games favoured by Soviet children are universal–dolls, catapults, skipping, tag, hopscotch, football and blind man's buff are as popular in the Soviet Union as elsewhere. More characteristic, particularly in the RSFSR, are carved wooden toys–for instance, the *matryoshka*, which consists of nesting peasant figurines. Large numbers of military toys are produced and children play both their own and organized military games; these aim to develop a sense of patriotism and to train the young in military and sports skills. Children are constantly reminded of the Second World War through visits to war memorials and museums and through films and stories about the war.

Children's literature

It has long been part of the Russian tradition for the best adult authors to write for children; Pushkin,* Tolstoy* and Chekhov* did so and their example was followed by many of the best Soviet writers. Samuel Marshak (1887–1964) and Korney Chukovsky (1882–1969) are two of the most delightful of these. Both are particularly well known for their often humorous poems about animals for small children. Popular Western writers such as Lewis Carroll and A. A. Milne are translated favourites; Mary Poppins, Muffin the Mule and Gerald Durrell's animals are also all familiar to Soviet children.

Top: a *babushka* with her grandson. Left: while their parents work, children play in the yard of a kindergarten. Below: children learn the rules of the road at an 'Autotown' training centre

Adventure and animal stories are popular but school or pony books are rarely found. Large editions of magazines for children are published; these always have some degree of educational content–violence and crime, even naughtiness, are never glamorized–but they are usually amusingly and attractively produced.   *F. O'D.*

The militarization of Soviet society

Even in imperial Russia★ there existed a considerable degree of integration of the military into state affairs at all levels, and military interests took high priority in the consideration of economic and administrative matters. When the Bolsheviks★ came to power, they brought with them to reinforce this tradition an ideological commitment to total involvement in the defence effort–the concept of a nation in arms. The 'militarization of the entire population' to achieve a common identity of civilian and military, advocated by M. V. Frunze, Commissar for War, in 1925, was never practicable. However, thanks to strenuous effort the military is more integrated into civilian life than it is in any Western country, with the possible exception of Switzerland. The citizen is taught to identify himself as part of the military machine; the totally state-controlled media emit a constant flow of publicity for the armed forces,★ as well as a considerable volume of effective propaganda aimed at inciting hatred and fear of the 'capitalist threat'. Schoolchildren do their normal physical training under the banner 'Ready for Labour and Defence' (the standard physical education (PE) test at age 15–16, which qualifies a boy to receive his school-leaving certificate, requires that he be able to throw a 500g hand grenade 25m). Any youth or girl in secondary or higher education who wishes to participate in any sport★ which has even the slightest applicability to the military–such as orienteering, skin-diving, amateur radio operation, driving, shooting–will do so through the Voluntary Society for Aid to the Army, Air Force and Navy (DOSAAF). This is an enormous organization under army-Party control which offers at low cost excellent sporting facilities intended for training Soviet youth in a speciality of direct military value. DOSAAF bears a large share of the responsibility for running the pre-conscription military training programme under which all young men must complete, between the ages of 14 and 17, 140 hours of basic military training–drill, weapons training, military law; the bulk of this is given during the final school years, as part of the normal educational★ curriculum. Conscription at the age of 18 is almost universal in its effect; after discharge from the service, the young man may well find himself called out on reserve training during a major exercise, as part of a civil defence exercise, or on an actual military operation such as the invasion of Afghanistan.★

A second important feature of this militarization is the mainten-ance of a 'war spirit' amongst the population. This is done by constant insistence through the media★ on the existence of a 'capitalist menace' and by the constant reminders of the ordeals suffered during the Second World War. Each major city has its mass cemetery-museums which are popular places of pilgrimage, particularly for schoolchildren, and anniversaries of major battles are celebrated as local holidays. Enormous military parades and 'meet the troops' days are a feature not just of Moscow's Red Square but of every major city when an exercise is held near by, and units often visit farms and villages near exercise areas, providing light entertainment for the inhabitants. The use of up to half a million troops and their lorries every year to assist on collective farms in bringing in the harvest further reinforces this integration.

A third element of civil-military synthesis is provided by the formal organizational structure of the country. The armed forces are directly represented in all industrial or academic enterprises concerned with military production or research.★ In addition, the commanders of military units or garrisons automatically have a seat on the local soviet★ (town or regional council), giving them a direct voice in local civilian affairs. At least at lower levels, this feature–together with the Communist Party★ organization within the armed forces–allows Party and government authorities of a locality formal occasion to put their views to the military in their district. In all branches of the economy,★ the military element takes precedence; for example, a factory producing military equipment will have priority in terms of supply of materials and labour, and will pay higher wages★ and have better facilities for its workers than a factory producing only for the civilian market. In the Ministry of Health, the Military Medical Services are the senior branch, disposing of the best sanatoria and hospitals. The civil airline Aeroflot is commanded by a serving Air Force officer, and its aircraft are on call for military transport and airlift. It is estimated that defence consumes about 14 per cent of the USSR's gross national product, amounting to almost half of public spending. In all, some five million people are employed by the defence industry in production, research and development, military education and so on, in addition to those serving in uniform.   *C. N. D.*

The internal passport system

Every Soviet citizen over the age of 16 carries an internal passport which serves as official identification. In addition to personal data (name, date and place of birth, nationality) the passport has entries recording marriage and divorce, dependent children, military service and place of residence. The passport must be shown when applying for a job, changing address, entering an educational establishment, registering in an hotel, getting married or divorced, collecting mail at the post office, enrolling children in school or nursery, collecting pensions and other social benefits, applying for housing and on many other bureaucratic occasions.

The system was established in 1932 (strictly, re-established, for there had been a passport system in tsarist Russia) when rural-urban migration,* engendered by the industrialization* projects of the early Five-year Plans* and the collectivization* of agriculture, was overwhelming Soviet cities and towns. The passport system at that time was clearly intended to restrict and control population movements. Passports were issued only to urban residents and certain categories of rural wage-earners. Farm workers did not receive passports and therefore could not move about the country without going through a complex bureaucratic (and sometimes unsuccessful) process of application to the local rural soviet.* These mobility restrictions on the *kolkhoz* farmers were in effect until the most recent passport decree in 1974 granted passports to all Soviet citizens.

The Passport, by Oscar Rabin, an artist of the 'alternative tradition'

The administration of the passport system is the responsibility of the Ministry of Internal Affairs (MVD). The passport sections of the militia* in towns and settlements are responsible for ensuring that everyone has the proper endorsements in his passport, and for the issue of residence permits (*propiski*) and residence discharges (*vypiski*). Control over the observance of passport regulations is also exercised by the local soviet's executive committee (*ispolkom*).

A residence permit, compulsory for a stay of longer than one and a half months (or temporary registration for shorter stays) must be obtained from the passport department of the local militia within three days of arrival. These are not automatically issued. Obtaining a *propiska* in Moscow, other large cities or restricted regions is fairly difficult and has led to subterfuges such as marriages of convenience. Some of the regulations governing the issue of *propiski* were published in 1974, but it is still unclear to the average Soviet migrant what criteria are used in decision-making. The regulations specify that, with stated exceptions, no one is given a residence permit unless he can prove he has housing space of at least the designated sanitary norm (9 sq m in the RSFSR and most other republics). Yet most Soviet cities do not boast a housing* stock at this level per head, and a potential migrant cannot be placed in advance on the housing register at his intended destination, because the register is exclusively for those with a local *propiska*. Moreover, he cannot legally be engaged by an enterprise until he has a local residence permit. There are more-or-less legal ways of breaking out of this vicious circle, including private rental of housing with people who have excess space or who are temporarily absent; a housing exchange with someone moving in the opposite direction; residence in a suburb or nearby rural area and commuting to work; living in a dormitory with a temporary *propiska*; or risking the consequences of being caught living and working without this document (an administrative fine of 10 roubles, or criminal prosecution and imprisonment for malicious violation of the passport system).

In recent years the attempt to control the growth of large cities through the restriction of residence permits has been criticized. Undesirable side-effects of the practice have been emphasized, such as the ageing of populations in restricted cities (one in five Muscovites is an old-age pensioner) or the reluctance of specialists to leave these cities even temporarily to take up work in the provinces for fear of losing their *propiska*. Although the commitment to controlling growth in large cities remains, it is conceivable that the passport restrictions will be replaced by more effective regulations.

The information collected by means of the passport system is used for such purposes as providing migration statistics, apprehending criminals, locating missing persons, maintaining a national address inquiry system and enforcing the payment of alimony (a person who has neglected this must have a stamp in his passport, which could authorize an employer to withhold the amount). These uses of passport data are probably more important now than the control of movement. The statistics collected by passport officials will be more valuable than ever under the labour* stringencies envisioned for the remainder of the century.

The machinery remains, of course, and could at some future date re-establish the strict control over migration of the Stalin years. But the individually motivated and, in so many cases, 'irrational' migrants of recent years have demonstrated the inability of passport officials to prevent millions of people from moving where they please. *A.H.*

Trade unions

The trade unions (*professional'nye soyuzy*) are by far the largest public organization in the USSR. Unlike their capitalist counterparts, they do not primarily perform an adversary role, as they claim that under socialism unions can best serve their members by helping management and government to promote economic growth.

The first Russian trade unions date from 1905. Soon after the October Revolution the Menshevik*-dominated union movement was placed under firm Bolshevik* control but the Bolsheviks themselves were divided over its role in the new Soviet system. At one end of the spectrum were Trotsky* and Bukharin, who pressed for 'statification', the incorporation of the unions into the state machine; at the other stood A. G. Shlyapnikov and the Workers' Opposition, who took a syndicalist line. The middle ground was occupied by Lenin,* who envisaged unions as non-governmental bodies that would subsume traditional defensive functions within a policy of collaboration with state and management alike. At the X Congress of the CPSU* in 1921 Lenin's views prevailed and the unions were defined, in words which remain in currency to this day, as 'a school of administration, a school of economic management and a school of communism'. Any hopes of union autonomy were ended in 1929 with the purge of M. P. Tomsky and other independent-minded union officials, and in the next decade the trade unions were reduced to agencies for worker mobilization and welfare* administration.

Reappraisal of the unions' role and performance came in the aftermath of Stalin's* death. In December 1957 a Party Central Committee* resolution called for greater union participation in economic planning* and more effective union protection of workers' rights. The following year union powers were considerably expanded, particularly at enterprise level, and measures were taken to revitalize the whole movement. The economic reforms of the mid-1960s enlarged the scope for union-management negotiation and the 1970 Labour Code and related legislation enabled unions to take advantage of these new opportunities. The balance struck in the 1950s between the unions' production and protection roles has been subsequently confirmed and consolidated. There is no doubt that the unions remain responsible first and foremost for promoting production interests but this is no longer a self-evident truth which totally overshadows all other tasks. The production role is justified in terms of trade unions' obligations to serve their members' interests, and increasing emphasis is being placed on their duty to protect workers against high-handed bureaucrats and negligent managers. Needless to say, only legitimate interests are to be defended and it is the Party that continues to identify these as well as to direct the activity of the trade union movement.

Membership and structure

Union membership is open to all those working in the national economy and all but a handful of the labour force belong – in 1978 total membership stood at 121 million. The explanation for this 99-plus per cent unionization lies as much in material benefits as in organizational pressure. Trade unionists receive free legal aid, higher welfare benefits and access to a whole range of medical, cultural and recreational facilities, all for dues which amount to one per cent of their monthly pay.

Unions are organized on a branch or industrial basis which means that all workers and staff in any one factory or institution belong to the same union. In 1978 there were 30 such industrial or branch unions ranging from the aviation industry and rail transport to health and culture. Operating on the principles of democratic centralism,* each union has a hierarchy of elected bodies from all-Union level to factory and local committees (*fabzavmestkomy*), likewise subordinated to inter-union councils which coordinate and effectively control trade union work at regional, republican and all-Union levels. The All-Union Central Council of Trade Unions, the union equivalent of the Party Central Committee, closely controls the work not only of the inter-union councils but also of the central committees of all industrial or branch unions. Given the strong centralism and executive domination of the trade union hierarchy, there is little scope for democratic control from below despite model provisions in the unions' statute for elections, criticism and the removal of unpopular officials. Only at factory and local level, where 60 per cent of committee members are rank-and-file workers, is any real influence exercised by the membership over union action.

KEY

 Formal election

Authority

Source: based on information in E.C. Brown, *Soviet Trade Unions and Labour Relations*, Cambridge, Mass., 1966; and 'Ustav professional'nykh soyuzov SSSR' in *Materialy XVI sezda professional'nykh soyuzov SSSR*, Moscow, 1977

The union at local level

The local union's general task is to collaborate with management and the Party organization to make sure that the work-force contributes fully to the smooth and efficient operation of the enterprise or institution concerned. The activities undertaken by local committees can be divided into four main areas: mobilization, welfare, participation and control. One of the local committee's main responsibilities is to increase labour productivity and maintain high morale within the work collective. To this end it organizes socialist competition, the movement for a communist attitude towards work; prizes are awarded to individual workers, to teams and to enterprises for achievement of specified goals in the production process. The union also helps management in dealing with those who break factory regulations by, for example, absenteeism.* Much of the union activists' time is absorbed by administering the welfare system. Special commissions are established to deal with the collection and disbursement of social insurance and other benefits. Commissions also run a wide range of cultural and sports* facilities and issue passes to union health* and holiday* centres. In addition to all this, the *fabzavmestkom* supervises catering, housing* construction and the allocation of enterprise accommodation.

Whereas its mobilization and welfare functions cast the union organization into the role of a management and government agency,

The Metallurg trade union sanatorium, Tskhaltubo, Georgia

TRADE UNION STRUCTURE (simplified)

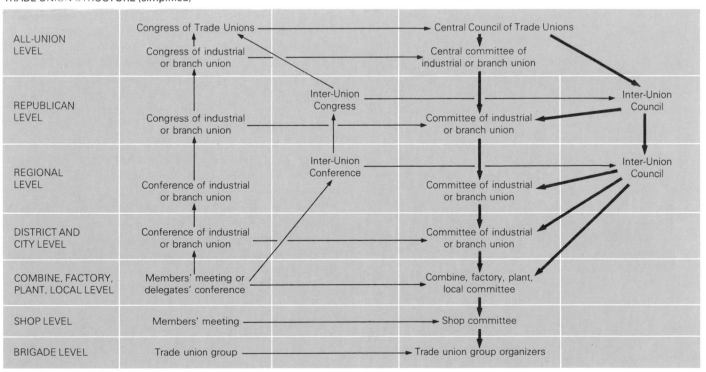

its other rights make it more of an equal partner. According to the 1971 statute on local union rights, the *fabzavmestkom* takes part in the drafting of plans relating to production, the introduction of new machinery, capital construction, housing construction and the social development of the enterprise. The committee also organizes standing production conferences which are supposed to provide a forum for workers' participation and scrutiny of enterprise performance. Given the vague nature of local unions' participation rights, their impact on production plans and strategy is probably small. They exercise greater influence by way of the collective agreement which is drawn up jointly by union and management. Within national guidelines this annual agreement specifies local working hours, vacations, production quotas, bonus distribution and social benefits. Moreover, management decisions on the use of the material incentive

A Party propagandist briefs fellow trade unionists on the shop floor at the Krasny Oktyabr' steel plant, Volgograd

fund, the fund for social and cultural measures and the housing construction fund have to be taken 'in conjunction with the *fabzavmestkom*'. The management also has to obtain union agreement to all overtime, piece rates, job and skill grading, shift arrangements and all dismissals. There is some evidence to suggest that many union committees use these co-decision and veto rights to negotiate advantageous local norms for their members.

A more palpable test of union performance is the ability to control management and combat abuses of workers' legal rights. The *fabzavmestkom* is responsible for monitoring management adherence to the collective agreement and its general legal obligations, particularly with regard to health and safety. The union also helps to protect workers' rights through the disputes procedure. Labour-disputes commissions, comprising an equal number of union and management representatives, exist at shop and enterprise level. Cases are dealt with in the first instance by shop commissions; if there is no agreement they go before the shop union committee. Disputes of enterprise significance go straight to the enterprise commission and, if this fails to reach a unanimous verdict, to the *fabzavmestkom*. Over half the disputes heard are resolved in the workers' favour and union committees seem to treat members' appeals quite sympathetically though many workers continue to take their appeals on to the local courts or to higher union bodies.

While local unions' performance has undoubtedly improved since the 1950s, standards vary greatly within regions and republics and between factories. Workers in large Russian factories and combines are far better served than those in small plants in outlying areas. Furthermore, judging by the number of complaints in the press and the large number of union-condoned illegal dismissals, many *fabzavmestkomy* still strive to get on with managements rather than to keep them in check.

Unions at national level

Formally autonomous, the trade unions at national level are so closely involved with government that they often appear to be quasi-governmental agencies. The all-Union and republican councils are entitled to initiate legislation and since the mid-1950s the Central Trade Union Council has drafted many of the most important labour laws. All government measures relating to labour must be agreed with the trade union bodies concerned and key decrees are often issued jointly by the Council of Ministers and the All-Union Central Trade Union Council. The Central Council and individual unions have some say in the early stages of economic and social planning and it is likely that they put the case for better working conditions and increased living standards, but it is impossible to gauge the impact that any such special pleading may have on Party and government policy. The unions also keep a close watch over the administration to ensure that it fulfils its legal obligations. For instance, Central Trade

Union Council officials have berated some ministries for failing fully to utilize their funds for housing and education. At the same time, the unions work closely with government agencies, such as the Committee on Labour and Social Questions, particularly in the administration of the welfare system. The unions also act as economic mobilization agencies, organizing the vast socialist competition movement which, launched in 1929, involved over 100 million people in 1977. Lastly, the trade unions are charged with raising the educational and political level of the working population and to this end they run courses, publish books and encourage civic participation. Education and propaganda extend to the international arena, where Soviet unions effectively lead the World Federation of Free Trade Unions.

Unions and the Communist Party

Like all public organizations, the trade unions acknowledge the Party's leading role and pay tribute to it as the representative of all working people's interests. It is the Party Central Committee that determines the balance between the unions' production and protection functions and that lays down the way in which these are to be performed. At national and republican levels Party-union collaboration is largely related to policy, whereas lower down the Party may often act as a coordinator and arbiter between union and management. Supervision and guidance of trade union work by Party organs at all levels is underpinned by the presence of communists in strategic positions throughout the union structure. At the higher levels, Party membership* is almost total and top appointments fall within the Communist Party's *nomenklatura*.* The proportion of communists declines in the lower reaches of the hierarchy – they constitute 30–50 per cent of the membership of *fabzavmestkomy* and hold just over half of the chairmanships at local level. All communist unionists form Party groups which ensure that union decisions follow the Party line. Adherence to the Party line does not necessarily make the trade unions the transmission belt they were under Stalin. Their increasing economic weight and the steadily greater role accorded them by the Party give the unions some scope for autonomous action in many areas of labour policy and administration. Nevertheless, this autonomy continues to be delimited by Party directives and by the heavy responsibility for production they still bear.

Given the unions' close collaboration with Party, government and management, it is not surprising that they frequently fail in their protective role. Such shortcomings, and the general weakness that some unions exhibit towards management, prompted 43 workers to try to establish the Free Trade Union Association in late 1977 and early 1978. Although the Association was effectively quashed by police action during 1978, its short-lived existence underlined the need for unions to be more forceful in defence of their members' legal rights.

A.P.

Crime and punishment

Soviet statements – whether for external or internal consumption – invariably assert that crime in general is decreasing. In orthodox communist theory the causes of crime are only two: first, the existence of two hostile systems in the world – socialist and capitalist – and their continuing struggle; second, the relics of past social conditions which bred crime and criminal propensity and whose effect is sustained (though dwindling) by the lag of consciousness behind existence.

Criminal and judicial statistics are strictly secret so that accurate information is unobtainable. What evidence there is suggests that such statistics as exist are unreliable because the local law enforcement agencies* need to keep down the ratio of the number of reported offences to that of arrests and of convictions.

General crime

Offences against persons and property cover much the same ground as in other countries. The Criminal Code, however, classifies offences into those against the state; against socialist property; and against citizens. By and large, greater penalties are prescribed for the first two categories. In the first of them, treason includes flight abroad or refusal to return. In the last, male homosexual behaviour is a crime, as is refusing treatment for venereal disease; blackmail – in the sense of threatening the disreputable truth – is not mentioned.

It seems that over 80 per cent of convictions concern general crime. A number of Soviet sources refer to delinquent contra-cultures, especially among the children of former peasants who have moved to urban surroundings and industrial employment. Their activities are characterized by alcoholism* and vandalism; in response to this and

An offender explains his case at a local militia office

The *Krokodil* cartoonist's aim is to satirize the offender's belief that guilt lies only in detection: the criminal transporting his stolen goods sees militia everywhere

similar delinquency, intensive campaigns are mounted against 'hooliganism' – the Russian word is taken straight from the Irish. It is defined as 'intentional actions which grossly violate public order and express an obvious disrespect towards society' and is now subject to minimum-sentencing prevention techniques.

Organized crime, on the other hand, seems almost to have disappeared. This is partly due to strict repression but also to gang warfare between the 'thieves-at-law' (for whom military service was dishonourable) and the 'bitches', who betrayed their profession by fighting in the Red Army. The consequent mutual massacre (abetted by the authorities) which took place is said to have cost many thousands of lives.

Economic crime

On the one hand, this covers the persistent or large-scale issue of poor-quality products by state enterprises; the managers and officials are criminally liable. On the other hand, it covers a group of offences which infringe the principle that only earned income is the basis of society (1977 Constitution, Article 13). Examples are: 'speculation' – the purchase and re-sale of goods for gain; private entrepreneurial activity in the supply of services (such as selling a place in a queue); and the exercise of a prohibited trade. This last deeply affects the social and economic life of the USSR since a great number of private trades are forbidden – for example, the repairing of television sets in urban areas. Such activity, if carried out on a significant scale or by using hired labour, may be punished by up to four years' imprisonment with confiscation of property.

The converse of criminal economic activity is parasitism – refusal to work and indulgence in an antisocial parasitic existence. This is technically an administrative offence dealt with initially by the assignment of work through the local authority. Deliberate refusal to comply then becomes a crime punishable by imprisonment.

Political crime

Apart from the obvious offences of treason, espionage and terrorism, Soviet law prohibits, as an especially dangerous crime, the possession or circulation, with subversive intent, of 'slanderous fabrications which defame the Soviet state and social system'. In 1966 the conviction for this offence of Sinyavsky★ and Daniel'★ raised certain legal doubts. It was the first public trial for anti-Soviet propaganda of writers of fiction: were, therefore, statements put into the mouths of literary characters to be imputed to the author? and were they circulated with subversive, or merely artistic, intent? Shortly after the trial new offences were added to the Criminal Code. One was the preparation and circulation of fabrications defamatory of the state and social system; it is not necessary to prove subversive intent, merely that the accused knew the matter to be false. Also, in response to the demonstrations which accompanied the trial, it was made an offence to organize or participate in group actions violating public order or in disobedience to the lawful demands of authorized personnel.

Non-criminal sanctions

In a number of cases an offender is subject to sanctioning procedures which do not fall under the Criminal Code or the jurisdiction of the courts. Fines may be imposed by officials for minor traffic violations, public drunkenness, breaches of regulations concerning passports,★ rail travel, fire protection and the like. Disciplinary offences at work may be penalized by loss of salary or dismissal. Finally, Comrades' Courts★ may impose small fines and measures of social pressure.

Volunteers who help to keep public order

Punishment

The purposes of punishment are stated to be chastisement, re-education and general deterrence. There are 12 types ranging from death, imprisonment, exile (which involves compulsory re-settlement), banishment (which does not), corrective labour, confiscation of property and fines to social censure. The death penalty is never mandatory and does not apply to ordinary murder by a first offender; but may be ordered in cases such as treason, espionage, terrorist killing, aggravated rape, large-scale theft of state property, attempts on the life of a policeman or militiaman and in some 16 military offences. In general the sentences imposed are more severe than for similar offences in the West.   *B.R.*

GULag (prison camps)

GULag is the acronym for the Main Administration for Camps, a division of the NKVD (People's Commissariat of Internal Affairs) and, since 1946, the MVD (Ministry of Internal Affairs). In popular usage 'the Gulag' refers to the whole Soviet detention system of labour camps, prisons, special settlement and exile regimes and special psychiatric* hospitals.

This system dates from 1918, at which time penal theory distinguished sharply between reformable and unreformable offenders, the former receiving liberal treatment. The system expanded up to Stalin's* death, developing especially rapidly during the collectivization* of agriculture, the Great Terror,* and the period 1944–53, to accommodate the successive waves of victims of the security* police. While the prisons had about a million inmates, the majority of these victims were imprisoned in 'corrective labour camps' or the less harsh 'corrective labour colonies'. In 1953 all these institutions probably held about 10 million people. Although economic production was an important goal of the system (mining, logging, construction), the death-rate rose rapidly in the late 1930s. Careful estimates indicate that about 15–16 million people died of exhaustion and starvation in captivity between 1930 and 1953. In addition, about one million were executed, and several millions (mostly large deported national groups and *kulaks*–relatively prosperous peasants opposed to collectivization) lived under a punitive regime in special settlements.

In 1953–5 a series of large prisoner revolts reinforced the leadership's intention to dismantle much of the camp system. In 1977, according to secret official figures which leaked out, the camps and prisons held about 1.7 million prisoners, of whom about 10 000 were political. A few hundred more such are held in special psychiatric hospitals, most of them falsely ruled to be mentally ill under a forensic psychiatric system which was greatly developed under Khrushchev.*

In 1956–8 all 'corrective labour camps' were redesignated 'corrective labour colonies', with four regimes of ascending severity,

and GULag became GUITU, or Main Administration for Corrective Labour Institutions. Since 1961 conditions in the camps, which now hold about 99 per cent of convicted prisoners, have been made steadily harsher by a series of changes in the relevant laws and regulations.   *P.R.*

Alcoholism and drunkenness

Russia was known historically as the land of heavy drinking and various forms of alcohol abuse, and the situation has not changed much since the Revolution. After some experimentation in the early 1920s with the prohibition of alcohol and controls of drinking, the Soviet government reinstituted the essentials of tsarist policies–a state monopoly on the production and distribution of alcoholic beverages and high taxation rates to generate significant revenues for the state treasury.

Excessive drinking and the alcoholism which often results from it are highly complex socio-cultural phenomena, for which no single explanation is possible. In the Soviet case, probably one of the most important factors is the cultural tradition which makes drinking a necessary part of socializing and various festivities. This cultural tradition was perpetuated in the USSR by the ready availability of vodka in all localities and at all hours.

Statistics on the production and consumption of alcohol, and on sales, prices, tax-rates and the like are not published in the USSR. However, indirect evidence provided by industrial and trade data, as well as some information appearing from time to time in specialized publications, have made an estimation of at least some key statistics possible. Average consumption of state-produced alcoholic beverages in 1976 per person aged 15 years and older was estimated at between 11 and 11.5 litres of pure alcohol. Of this amount, slightly more than half was consumed in the form of spirits (vodka, cognac), and the rest as grape and fruit wine and beer. In addition to this, some 3–3.5 litres of pure alcohol per head were consumed in the form of *samogon* and other home-distilled varieties. The USSR would, accordingly, rank first in the world (for some 45 countries for which reliable statistics are available) in terms of the consumption of spirits per person aged 15 and over, and third or fourth in the consumption of alcohol in all forms. Consumption per head has been steadily increasing since the end of the Second World War, doubling during the 1960–76 period. It must be noted, however, that average figures are sometimes misleading. Drinking patterns vary greatly by age, sex, profession and nationality (Muslims* and some other ethnic groups, for instance, drink significantly less than the average). Changes in the differentials among groups may thus produce changes in the over-all average. In all probability, the recent rapid rise in average consumption is explained by increased drinking among groups of moderate drinkers (younger people, women,* Muslims) and by increased consumption of alcohol by the traditionally heavy-drinking group – male Slavs* aged 25–50.

The government takes a somewhat ambiguous position on alcohol abuse. Excessive drinking is discouraged by a variety of policies such as stiff penalties for public drunkenness and drunken driving, restrictions of hours and locations of vendors of alcoholic beverages, as well as educational campaigns in the press, public lectures, and the like. Alcoholics and chronic heavy drinkers are denied free medical services and are sometimes forcibly placed in treatment-centres resembling penal camps. Inebriation during the commission of a crime is now treated as compounding a felony. The government also sponsors extensive research programmes on the causes and treatment of alcoholism and excessive drinking; among the most successful of these was the gradual change in the mix of beverages: thus, the share of strong liquor (80 proof and higher) was reduced from some 70 per cent in the early 1960s to slightly over 50 per cent by the mid-1970s.

However, it appears that the various anti-drinking laws and regulations are not very vigorously enforced, and no drastic measures such as a significant increase in the price of alcoholic beverages, reduction in output or the prohibition of drinking in certain places was considered. A partial explanation for the reluctance to raise prices or to cut consumption lies in the fear that such measures would merely encourage illegal home-production.

Probably the main reason for the slack state anti-alcohol campaigns lies in the singularly important role played by the alcohol industry in state finances. Since the 1950s turnover taxes (sales taxes) on alcoholic beverages contributed between 10 and 12 per cent of total state budget* revenues, accounting for some 40 per cent of all direct and indirect taxes paid by the population. Alcoholic beverages comprise about a third of total sales of food in consumer retail trade, and profits on production and sales in industry and trade are also significant. It is, therefore, quite clear that a major cut in the consumption of state-produced and distributed alcohol would entail serious financial repercussions for the entire economy which could not be handled without far-reaching fiscal and monetary reforms.

The social and economic costs of heavy drinking in the USSR are rather high. The press and the specialized medical, sociological and legal literature offer impressive evidence of absenteeism,* reduced labour productivity, industrial and traffic accidents resulting in the destruction of life and property, as well as crime* associated with alcohol abuse. Social effects are equally significant: the explanation offered in a high percentage of divorces* is the excess drinking of one of the spouses, and drinking is often given as the main reason for a decision not to have children. The health* of the population is affected in several ways. The crude death-rate has increased from the low 7.1 deaths per 1000 in 1960 to 9.8 in 1978, and many Soviet and Western demographers cite alcohol abuse as one of the major reasons for this increase.

Adding the cost of medical treatment, rehabilitation programmes and law enforcement to the elements cited above makes the total cost of alcohol abuse very high. The exact rouble figure is virtually impossible to estimate, but in all probability the over-all cost would be between 5 and 7 per cent of Soviet national income. *V.G.T.*

'Drinking Oneself to Death' – the perils of alcoholism in a 1970 cartoon from the satirical magazine, *Krokodil*

САМОУПИЙЦА

Рисунок Е. ЩЕГЛОВА

Absenteeism

Unauthorized absence from work (*progul'*) is the most common breach of labour discipline, accounting for between a third and a half of all disciplinary offences. Official figures, which probably underestimate the problem as many infringements go unreported, show a marked decline in non-attendance over the past 60 years. In 1920 the chaotic state of industry and the emphasis on self-discipline helped to take absenteeism to a record 23.6 man-days, a figure which was reduced to 7.7 man-days by 1927 largely through the introduction of tough penalties for all breaches of discipline. The fall in absenteeism during the 1930s was accelerated by the advent in 1938–40 of draconian measures that made absenteeism a criminal offence and punished even those who were 20 minutes late for work. When in 1956 the most punitive penalties were lifted, improving conditions and more strongly engrained industrial work habits ensured the continued if slow decline of absenteeism from 0.9 to 0.8 man-days between 1955 and 1965. A slight rise in non-attendance (from 0.8 to 0.9 man-days) coincided with the introduction of economic reform in the mid-1960s and it took a sustained campaign to reverse this increase. Only in the early 1970s did levels of absenteeism begin to fall—in 1973 the national industrial figure was 0.6 days per worker.

Low though this figure may appear, absenteeism still constitutes a serious problem on at least two counts. First, the tens of millions of days lost annually impose a mounting burden on the economy at a time when technological progress and manpower shortages make the full use of working time increasingly vital. Second, like other forms of indiscipline, absenteeism is not merely a breach of legal obligations but a dereliction of socialist duties. Many Soviet officials see absenteeism as symptomatic of a general laxness and social irresponsibility that weakens socialism and undermines the authority of Party and state. Because of its dual significance absenteeism has been the object of numerous sociological investigations that shed light on the kinds of worker involved, the roots of the problem and the effectiveness of counter-measures.

Causes

Between 7 and 10 per cent of the work-force absent themselves at least once a year and a third of this number do so more frequently. The typical absentee is a bachelor in his later 20s or 30s; the very young, the old and family men are apparently less prone to break the rules. Women are generally more conscientious even if they tend to arrive late and take time off work to shop. While some absentees are short stayers, changing jobs frequently, the majority are workers with over six years' continuous service. They are often quite well paid but usually belong to the lower-skilled groups, particularly if they work in seasonal jobs or construction where absenteeism has always been much higher than in industry. Unskilled or semi-skilled workers are up to three or four times more likely to take time off than their better-qualified colleagues. Predictably, the typical absentee is also among the less well-educated: two out of three disciplinary offenders in the late 1960s had not completed the seventh form. Those with completed secondary, specialized or higher education are far better disciplined, particularly if they hold non-manual positions. Just the same, rising levels of education* are not a fool-proof answer to the problem, as some evidence suggests that they merely produce better educated absentees. Nor does involvement in voluntary public activities ensure dutiful attendance at work—participants in socialist competition seem to be hardly less prone to absenteeism than are non-competitors. The fact that communists are only half as likely as their non-Party fellows to absent themselves from work may be attributed as much to their higher educational qualifications as to any greater sense of social responsibility.

In trying to explain absenteeism and other infringements of labour discipline, Soviet scholars traditionally referred to capitalist survivals and the influence of bourgeois propaganda. Since the mid-1960s, however, sociologists have assigned a prominent role to the 'objective' factors and problems revealed by their research. By far the most important of these factors is alcohol* which is associated with 80–90 per cent of all cases of absenteeism. One in two offenders put their misdemeanours down to vodka. According to one calculation made in the early 1970s, the 'drying out' of factories would increase labour productivity by 10 per cent by drastically reducing absenteeism and other breaches of discipline. Drinking may itself be a product of personal problems or of the climate at work, both of which emerge as factors making for absenteeism. Management attitudes can also compound the problem, as many directors are willing to overlook minor infringements, such as occasional absenteeism, in order to maintain good relations with the work-force and to avoid conflict.

Sanctions

Managements have a wide array of means at their disposal to deal with absenteeism and other forms of indiscipline. The offender may be reprimanded, deprived of premiums and bonuses, transferred to a lower-paid post for up to three months, or, in the most serious cases and with trade union* concurrence, be dismissed from his job. Alternatively, the management can turn the offender over for discussion and censure by his peers at general meetings or before a Comrades' Court.* The great majority of offenders are merely warned or reprimanded, a small minority are materially penalized or publicly censured; many fewer are temporarily demoted, let alone dismissed. According to the offenders themselves, administrative and material sanctions are far less effective than moral correctives and some of the evidence bears out this assessment. All the same, the most successful campaigns against absenteeism, such as that in the Tula region in the late 1960s, have used administrative and material penalties as well as moral pressure. While such a combination of measures has had some effect on levels of absenteeism, the authorities recognize that the only long-term solution lies in improving material conditions and fostering a more conscientious attitude towards work.   *A.P.*

The health service

Universal, comprehensive, free

Thanks to its main organizational principles, the state-provided health service (*zdravookhranenie*–health protection) makes a unique contribution to the self-image of Soviet society: it is universal in its coverage of the population, comprehensive in its range of provisions and is free, or largely free, at time of receipt. Besides personal medical care the system also embraces environmental health programmes such as those concerned with ensuring the purity of water and food supplies. The service may be considered as dating from 11 July 1918 with the creation of a People's Commissariat of Health Protection. Under central planning,* marked improvements have occurred in the basic indicators of health service development since 1950. The Five-year Plan to 1980 set targets of 123.0 hospital beds, 35.7 doctors and 109.2 intermediate medical personnel per 10 000 of the population. The sums assigned to this sector in the government budget have been increased each year but it should be noted that they represent a broadly stable proportion of total national product. Perhaps paradoxically, health service expenditure per head varies substantially among the 15 Union Republics, as do the ratios of beds and staff to population.

BASIC INDICATORS OF CIVILIAN HEALTH SERVICE DEVELOPMENT: 1950–1979 (END OF YEAR)

	1950	1960	1970	1979
	thousand			
Doctors	236.9	385.4	577.3	960.5
Dentists				
with higher education	10.4	16.2	39.6	
with intermediate education	17.7	30.1	51.5	
Middle grade medical personnel[1]	719	1388	2123	2720
Pharmacists[2]				
with higher education	12.2	26.5	47.7	68.3[3]
with intermediate education	44.9	74.3	120.1	150.2[3]
Hospitals	18.3	26.7	26.2	23.2
Hospital beds	1011	1739	2663	3262
Units providing ambulatory-policlinic care	36.2	39.3	37.4	35.7

[1] This category consists mainly of feldshers, feldsher-midwives, midwives, environmental health officers, nurses, medical laboratory staff, radio-therapists and dental technicians
[2] The totals relate to staff employed in the economy as a whole and not solely in civilian health services
[3] 1977

Source: *Narodnoe khozyaystvo SSSR* for various years

An operating theatre with high atmospheric pressure at the Research Institute of Clinical and Experimental Surgery noted for its pioneering cardiac and vascular surgery

Staffing

Official statements frequently emphasize that the supply of doctors (in Soviet usage the term includes dentists) is at a truly generous level by international standards. However, the high ratio stands in a complex cause-and-effect relationship with the comparatively unattractive salaries for the majority of posts and with the heavy reliance on female labour–nearly 70 per cent of all doctors are women.* The percentage has declined only slowly since 1950, despite discrimination in favour of male applicants to medical school. Evidence indicates that women hold a disproportionately small number of senior positions in the medical-administrative hierarchy: thus in 1975 none of the Union Republics had a female health minister.

Unlike their Western counterparts, Soviet doctors cannot be perceived as members of a high-status, cohesive and independent professional group. In respect of corporate representation they are subsumed within the Union of Medical Workers, which covers all

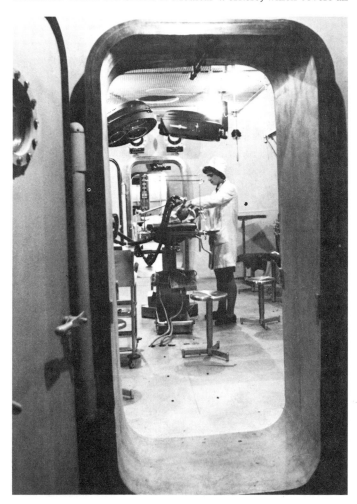

grades of health-care personnel. A sense of separate identity is further inhibited by the long-established policy of permitting staff who have intermediate medical education to acquire a doctor's diploma on easy terms.

Directly relevant to the need for high levels of staffing is a key characteristic of Soviet medical practice – specialization. Even in medical institutes (83 in all) and medical faculties of universities (9) students must opt for a basic specialization, the main fields being stomatology (for dentistry), environmental health, paediatrics and curative medicine. Thus all doctors are specialists although some, by virtue of their post-diploma training and job description, are far more narrowly specialized than others.

Treatment facilities

One consequence of the scientific-technocratic ethos of Soviet medical practice is the dominance of the hospital and in-patient treatment. It is striking that a very high proportion of all out-patient

units (providing care for ambulant patients) are administratively united with hospitals. In many cases these units are actually located within the curtilage of the hospitals whose chief doctor is responsible for them. In the light of this policy, unsatisfactory home conditions (such as crowded housing) and the enlargement of hospital capacity, it is not surprising that there has been a growth in the proportion of the population treated in hospital. In 1974 the national average showed that 22.5 per cent of all patients were treated in hospital; among the rural population the figure has risen especially sharply and now slightly exceeds that for town-dwellers.

Although the large 'multi-profile' hospital is common, many in-patient units cater only for one disease category (cancer, mental illness) or one population group (children, expectant mothers). The same is true of out-patient units, which are known by various names. Most familiar is the policlinic, where the widest range of specialists is encountered. In urban areas policlinics frequently serve populations as large as 30000–60000, which means that some patients have to make long and difficult journeys. The total catchment area is divided up into separate sectors (*uchastki*) for adults and children respectively; in Leningrad in 1976 there were 2020 adults per sector but this average concealed a wide range – from 1500 to 5000. Responsibility for the general over-view of health conditions lies with the sector specialists in internal medicine (*terapevty*) and the sector paediatricians employed in the policlinics. None the less, patients can proceed directly to specialists in certain other fields, for example, ophthalmology and ENT (ear, nose and throat). Thus there is no single 'doctor of first contact' who will attempt to diagnose presenting symptoms in patients of both sexes and all ages.

On the bottom rung of the status and authority ladder, the job of sector doctor is one that lacks attraction. The turnover rate is high and urban policlinics are sometimes reduced to filling posts with paramedical personnel. In rural areas reliance on the latter grade of staff for initial medical care is more explicit; many small units have posts not for doctors but for feldshers (*fel'dshera*), auxiliaries who may be described as semi-trained doctors or super-trained nurses. As recently as 1975 the rural population, on average, had slightly more out-patient contacts with paramedical staff than they had with doctors. The health service planners recognize the undesirability of this situation but in many regions it is not easily remedied.

In order to supply the more remote rural areas with doctors, the state employs both incentives and obligation, the latter being represented by direction of labour. In theory a three-year posting commences after the intern year which now concludes medical training, although in practice many draftees fail to arrive at their

Top: a sector doctor visits shepherds in a remote part of the Turkmen SSR. Left: medical auxiliaries (feldshers) treat an injured tractor driver

destinations, through marriage (in the case of young women) or less acceptable causes such as patronage. Those who serve their time frequently return to the towns as soon as possible, since conditions of work, poor opportunities for specialization and the general socio-cultural ambience provide strong disincentives which are not sufficiently offset by higher pay, earlier retirement and official approbation.

The hospitals and out-patient units serving local catchment areas are duplicated, up to a point, by facilities that have been constructed at the place of work on the basis of funds provided by the enterprise concerned. In 1976 Soviet industry had 925 hospitals containing a total of 209 709 beds, and specialists in internal medicine provided out-patient care to a total of 15 028 'workshop' sectors; there were also 32 124 health points staffed by feldshers and 2485 staffed by doctors.

When treating patients who are in work, Soviet doctors are required to act not only as healers but also as agents of social control.★ They are expected to be alert to detect fraudulent requests for sick-ness certificates, and their issue of such certificates, which validate the change of role from worker to patient, is subject to an elaborate system of hierarchical checks. Reduction of the number of work-days lost due to illness stands as a clearly stated objective of the health service.

For workers in certain sectors of the economy, for example the railways, there are separate health facilities provided outside the general system (which is controlled through the administrative-territorial agencies ranging down from Union-Republican to district level). In the exclusive units reserved for senior Party members and government officials, a very clear association exists between the quality of care and the socio-occupational status★ of the patients. Contrasting starkly with the preferential service for the élite is the deliberate and systematic maltreatment of the dissenters who are in psychiatric★ hospitals as a result of the abuse of psychiatric diagnosis in support of state repression.

Quality of medical care

Although the quality of medical care generally has improved remarkably since 1950, for the average patient it is likely to be inferior to what is available in most of Western Europe. One main reason is the shortage of effective modern drugs resulting from the under-development of the pharmaceutical industry–a defect which is compounded by gross inefficiency in distribution. From patients come complaints about brusqueness and lack of consideration shown by doctors; this may be partly due to the constraint of work norms which recommend a fixed number of consultations per hour. Sometimes unofficial payments are made to staff in health service units to secure better or more prompt attention. In larger towns patients can choose to attend 'self-financing' policlinics and nursing

homes where for payment (made to the unit) they are likely to obtain qualitatively superior care. No purpose-designed units exist for private practice but it seems that many doctors supplement their salaries by means of consultations in the patient's home or their own. This seems to be especially common in dentistry.   *T.M.R.*

Health conditions

Very few morbidity data relating to the whole Union are published on a routine basis. It is clear that the incidence of certain infectious diseases has shown a decline, partly as a result of mass programmes of vaccination and immunization. In 1979 there were, per 100 000 persons, 10 recorded cases of whooping cough, 93 of scarlet fever, 145 of measles, 0.2 of tetanus, 0.1 of diphtheria and 0.08 of acute poliomyelitis. Nevertheless, a major outbreak of cholera occurred in 1970 and gastro-intestinal infections continue to be prevalent. While the incidence of tuberculosis is not recorded, it is revealing that in 1975 as much as 8.5 per cent of the total bed complement was allocated to this specialty. As is well known, the Soviet health service devotes considerable resources to routine examination of specific population groups but the value of this practice must remain in question. Notwithstanding the declared emphasis on preventive medicine, it appears that a major method of birth control is abortion.★

Precise information on deaths from specific causes is also noticeable by its virtual absence. As elsewhere, cancer has become one of the great killers and in 1977 there were 136.5 deaths from malignant neoplasms per 100 000 persons. Diseases of the circulatory system accounted for 484.8 per 100 000 persons. Surprisingly enough, infant mortality★ (deaths of infants under one year) increased from 22.9 to 27.9 per 1000 live births over the period 1971–74; after that year the series of statistics was discontinued but there is indirect evidence that the rise has persisted. The average expectation of life at birth has increased very substantially during this century (from 32 years in the European provinces of Russia in 1896–7 to 70 years in the entirety of the country in 1971–2) but it is clear that this trend results from factors such as a healthier environment, improved housing★ conditions and higher standards of education★ quite as much as from the development of medical care.   *T.M.R.*

Social security and welfare

Origins, objectives and finance

Soviet families have access to an extensive system of welfare benefits designed to provide financial assistance in most of the circumstances in which they suffer temporary or permanent loss of earnings. There are also programmes to alleviate the burden of certain extraordinary needs.

For the urban population, this social security system had its origins in the tsarist workmen's compensation scheme, which was extended and made more egalitarian in the 1920s in accordance with Lenin's* ideas. With the adoption of the First Five-year Plan (1928–32), the system was modified to reinforce the incentives thought necessary for industrialization.* It was recodified in 1956 and since then benefit levels have been raised more or less in line with the growth in average earnings. It was not until 1965 that state pensions* were provided for the collective-farm population and other programmes were extended to this social group over the next five years.

Finance for this welfare system comes in part from an earmarked payroll tax (differentiated by sector) and in part from general budgetary revenue. Since this in turn is derived from indirect taxes as well as from a profits tax, it is difficult to ascertain on whom the burden falls, and whether it falls more heavily on the better-off. There is some evidence to suggest that the absolute value of benefits increases with the income of the recipient household; this, together with the fact that taxation which finances it bears harder on those with lower incomes perhaps implies that the welfare system as a whole does not particularly contribute to making society more egalitarian.

Nevertheless, the Soviet government has made, and continues to make, a major investment in the provision of income support. In 1974 it spent some 43 milliard roubles on various social security transfers, or about 12 per cent of national income; further, expenditure on these programmes has been growing at an annual average rate of 8.7 per cent during the preceding quarter-century (that is, somewhat faster than national income on official definitions).

There are various free and subsidized services that contribute to the material well-being of Soviet households (pre-school* child care facilities, education,* medical care* and housing* subsidies).

Social security payments: entitlement and value

Social security payments fall into two main categories: most are related to employment in some way or another but there are three programmes that are available to the population more generally: child allowances, family income supplement and student stipends. According to Soviet convention, holiday* pay is classified as a social security benefit and is included in Soviet statistics under this heading. The system also makes provision for the payment of burial grants and one or two other minor benefits.

Old-age and long-service pensions

Civilian state employees (that is, everyone in employment other than the armed forces or a cooperative) become entitled to an old-age pension on reaching the age of 60 years (55 years for women) provided that they have a record of 25 years' employment (20 years for women). There are lower retirement ages with correspondingly reduced employment requirements for underground workers and certain other designated categories. Since 1967 collective farmers have been entitled to pensions at the same age and with the same employment record as state employees.

The value of a pension depends upon earnings in the last 12 months before retirement. Those earning the minimum wage (70 roubles per month in 1976) receive a pension of 45 roubles; the ratio then falls by stages until the pension equals 50 per cent of earnings subject to a maximum of 120 roubles per month. Pensions for residents in rural areas (who make up 37 per cent of the population) are set at 85 per cent of these levels. For those with dependants a supplement of 10–15 per cent is paid.

The pension, once granted, is fixed for life unless it subsequently falls below a newly promulgated minimum; in which case it is raised to the new minimum. On the other hand, for most pensioners no deductions are made in respect of other sources of income, and many consequently continue to work (in the mid-1970s between a quarter and a third of old-age pensioners were in employment).

Certain categories of 'white-collar' employee (such as teachers and physicians) receive long-service pensions rather than those described above. Benefit levels are comparable although conditions of entitlement differ; some individuals receive personal pensions for distinguished service to the state or 'the cause of revolution'.

War decorations on display, a chess player in a Moscow home for the elderly

Survivor pensions

On the death of a state employee or collective farmer, his dependent children, grandchildren, siblings under the age of 16, parents and surviving spouse (if above working age) are entitled to a survivor pension. Entitlement also depends upon the deceased having had a sufficient period of employment. The value of the pension varies with the number of dependants (up to a maximum of three) and the earnings of the deceased. In 1973 for a single dependant the survivor pension ranged from 23 to 60 roubles per month; for three or more dependants, the range was 70–120 roubles per month.

Disability pensions

For the payment of disability pensions, distinctions are made between incapacity resulting from industrial accidents or occupational diseases on the one hand and general loss of working capacity on the other. Benefits also depend on the degree of incapacity. Entitlement is subject to a sufficient period of employment, rising with age. Since 1970 the regulations covering the payment of disability pensions to collective-farm workers (*kolkhozniki*) have been broadly similar to those for state employees. Previously, they were less favourable (and before 1965 disability pensions were not paid to this group). Benefit levels are somewhat lower than those of old-age pensions.

In addition to the benefits payable on the presumption of permanent loss of working capacity, there are two major programmes that provide income support during periods of temporary loss of earnings: sickness and maternity benefits.

Sickness benefits

Benefits are payable from the first day of incapacity and continue for as long as the illness lasts (subject to medical attestation); benefits are also payable for seven days to those (mainly mothers) who must remain at home to care for sick children. Benefit levels depend upon earnings, the source of incapacity, type of employment and union* membership. For those with a sufficient record of uninterrupted employment, they are as high as 90 per cent of previous average earnings (without time limit). Non-union members benefit at half the level of members. Benefits are higher in cases of industrial accident or occupational disease than in general sickness. Those dismissed for infractions of labour discipline are not entitled to sickness benefits until they have worked at a new job for at least six months. These benefits were extended to collective-farm workers in 1970, subject to certain limitations on the length of time for which payments would be made.

Maternity benefits

Since 1968 women* state employees have been entitled to a period of 56 days' pre-natal paid leave and a further period of 56 days' post-natal paid leave; they may then take further unpaid leave until their child's first birthday without loss of job or seniority. Since 1973 benefits for all women have equalled previous pay for the full 112 days' leave. Before that date there were complex regulations governing benefits analogous to those for sick pay. Maternity grants are also available for indigent families. Since 1965 both grants and benefits have been paid to collective-farm workers.

Child allowances

Rates have remained unaltered since 1947: mothers of two children are entitled to a payment of 20 roubles on the birth of a third child; those with three children receive 65 roubles on the birth of their fourth and a monthly allowance of 4 roubles between the child's first and fifth birthdays. Rates for both grant and monthly allowance increase until the 10th child. A separate payment of 5 (7.5 or 10) roubles per month is made to single women with one (two or three) children until their child (children) reaches the 12th birthday, is placed in a home or is adopted.

Family income supplement

Since 1974 families with an income of less than 50 roubles a head per month (the Soviet official poverty level) have been entitled to a payment of 12 roubles per month per child until the child's eighth birthday. (Children start school in the autumn after their seventh birthday.) It is estimated that one-third of all children in the relevant age-group were entitled to this benefit in 1974.

Student grants

About three-quarters of registered students in full-time post-secondary education receive stipends or grants, set since 1972 at 40–60 roubles a month for those in institutions of higher learning and 30–45 roubles a month for those receiving secondary specialist training. Rates depend upon the subject studied, the year of study and the student's performance.

Assessment

The various welfare programmes enumerated here make a substantial contribution to the living standards of the average Soviet family. It is estimated, for instance, that welfare payments in cash (including holiday pay) accounted for some 18 per cent of personal income in 1974; adding the value to the individual of government expenditures on such services as health and education, welfare benefits make up as much as 30 per cent of the average total income. More, however, could be done within the same outlay to favour the lower-income groups.

There are three main reasons for this. First, a major part of the system is related to employment. This reflects the subordination of social welfare to the imperatives of industrialization under Stalin.* It means, however, that many households where the breadwinner is not in regular full-time employment (single-parent families, for example) or whose earnings are low, are largely deprived of support. Although the introduction of the family income supplement has alleviated the condition of some, the failure to adopt need as a criterion more widely means that the extensive poverty still existing in both urban and rural society will persist. Second, regulations governing entitlement to various benefits are complex; inevitably some individuals fail to qualify. (For instance, since the collective-farm and state pension schemes are independent, a man who has worked for, say, 15 years on a collective farm and 10 years for a state enterprise will fail to qualify for a pension under either.) The virtual absence of any system of public assistance (supplementary benefits) means that such people are forced to rely upon the charity of their relatives. Finally, the inadequacy of family allowances and the absence, since 1930, of unemployment pay mean that these groups are particularly hard-hit; although unemployment is not widespread, it does exist.

The Soviet system of social security has evolved by a process of piecemeal revision and extension to the programmes devised in the 1930s to serve very different objectives. Although the scale of government expenditure is substantial, the detailed operation of the system is often perverse. The system is permeated by horizontal inequities. It therefore stands in need of extensive reform if it is to act as an equalizing force, if it is to help attain the goal of a socialist distribution of income.   *A.M.*

The education system

Education in the USSR is centrally planned, and is largely the responsibility of two ministries. The Ministry of Education of the USSR is responsible for schools, teacher training and educational research; the Academy of Pedagogical Sciences of the USSR, whose research plays an important part in forming policy, comes under its jurisdiction. The Ministry of Higher and Secondary Specialized Education of the USSR looks after most higher and post-secondary institutions, though other ministries, such as health and culture, are involved where they have special interest in professional training. Vocational training is the responsibility of a committee under the Council of Ministers. The Union Republics have their own ministries but, apart from the language of instruction in non-Russian areas, the differences are not great. Substantially, the organization and content of schooling is very similar in all parts of the country.

Political and moral education – the shaping of the 'new Soviet man'* – is a central feature of the system. Direct political teaching takes place in the senior school years, when there are courses on Soviet government and law, and on basic Marxist-Leninist* theory (*obshchestvovedenie*, or social study); and in all higher educational institutions, all students must take courses in the history of the Communist Party of the USSR, political economy, and Marxist-Leninist philosophy; these account for over 10 per cent of total teaching time. Indirect ideological teaching comes much earlier – through other school subjects, such as history and literature, where values can be clearly conveyed; and through the organization of the school, where discipline is related to the needs of the group and justified on political grounds, and is set forth in the 'Moral Code of the Builder of Communism'. The youth organizations* concern themselves not only with leisure activities but also with socially useful work, take disciplinary action, and generally convey the approved values by statement and symbolism. Attempts to relate education to productive labour are also justified as a means of encouraging 'respect for work and for those who work' (as Khrushchev* put it in 1958).

The youth organizations are, in effect, an adjunct to the educational system. There are three stages: the Octobrists (*Oktyabryata*) for schoolchildren aged under 10; the Pioneers (*Pionery*) for over tens, theoretically voluntary but joined by almost all children; and the Young Communist League (Komsomol) for ages 14 to 28. The Pioneers in particular play a major educational role; apart from mobilizing children for disciplinary and socio-moral purposes, they provide circles (*kruzhki*) in schools or in Pioneer Palaces; some of these are hobbies clubs, but others are really voluntary extra classes, thus permitting the abler or more energetic to add to their curriculum.

Moscow University students

Pre-school education

This stage is neither compulsory nor universally available, but now reaches a majority of the age-group, at least at the older level. Originally organized in two stages – crèches (*yaslie*) for infants aged six months to three years, and kindergartens (*detskie sady*) for ages 3 to 7 – they are now often joined in single institutions (*yaslie-sady*). There is no formal teaching of skills of literacy or numeracy, though the older pupils are prepared for this by means of language and number games to develop their conceptual and oral skills. Pre-school institutions keep the children* for the whole day, including a midday meal and afternoon sleep; parents pay a contribution for the meals, according to their income.

Below: children learning their numbers in a kindergarten in Kishinev, Moldavia. Bottom: French at a Moscow school – girls wear brown dresses and black lace-trimmed aprons

The general educational school

Compulsory schooling begins at age 7 and lasts for a minimum of eight years. There are now very few primary schools (*nachal'nye shkoly*), as this stage has been absorbed into the general educational school, in which the primary stage, when the children are taught by a single class teacher, comprises the first three years. After this, the children simply move on as a group; there is no selection or streaming, though pupils whose work is unsatisfactory may have to repeat the year. (There are few of these; the figure is down to about 2 per cent, and it is government policy to eliminate repeating the year altogether.)

The first eight years are spent in the general educational school, comprehensive, unstreamed and co-educational throughout. Some schools end at this stage, and are thus known as 'incomplete secondary schools' (*nepolnie srednie shkoly*), or simply as 'eight-year schools' (*vos'miletnie shkoly* or *vos'miletki*). After the eighth class at age 15, further study is a virtual requirement, though not strictly compulsory. It can be pursued in three ways (in the order of preference stated by the education minister, M. A. Prokofiev, in 1966).

Pupils may continue in the 9th and 10th classes of the 'complete secondary school' (*polnaya srednyaya shkola*) or 'ten-year school' (*desyatiletka*); about 60 per cent of the age-group do this. There is little specialization at this stage; time for options increases to four hours per week, but all pupils must take the main subjects. The successful completion of the course leads to the award of the 'attestation of maturity', (*attestat zrelosti*), a requirement for entry to higher education, though not in itself sufficient.

'Secondary specialized school' (*srednoe spetsial'noe uchebnoe zavedenie*) provides a combination of general education and professional training. One type, the *tekhnikum*, deals with intermediate technical skills (such as optics, computers, electronics); others, known variously as *uchilishcha* or *shkoly* (both of which might be rendered as 'schools') give qualifications over a wide range— musical, legal, clerical, nursing, pre-school teaching. For students coming in from the eighth class, the courses normally last four years, and include general education up to *attestat* level. It is also, however, possible to enter after completion of ten-year schooling, in which case the course lasts only two years, and is confined to professional training (the general element having been covered already).

'Vocational-technical school' (*professional'no-tekhnicheskoe uchilishche* or PTU) is a trade school, roughly the equivalent of an apprenticeship, training skilled workers. Over 80 per cent of the time is spent on theory and practice of the trade. Courses vary from one to three years, according to the complexity of the skill. There is some general study as well, though not up to *attestat* standard; but students are expected to make this up through part-time upper secondary schools. It is possible (though not common) to proceed to vocational-technical school after complete secondary schooling; this was introduced to raise the status of these schools, and to take pressure off higher and other post-secondary institutions.

Special schools

Although the Soviet system is essentially comprehensive, there are some exceptions to the pattern. The main types of special schools are as follows.

Schools for the physically and mentally handicapped are for children judged quite unable to cope with the normal programme; between two and three per cent of the age-group attend. They are classified according to the kind of disability, and follow the ordinary curriculum as closely as they can; the aim is not so much to compensate for the defect as to correct it if possible.

The Suvorov and Nakhimov schools for army and navy cadets respectively provide the full ten-year course, and are attended by children seeking a career in the officer corps.

Art, music★ and ballet★ schools, often attached to theatres and conservatories, give the full ten-year course plus intensive training in the appropriate art. Entry, at class 1 or later, is highly competitive. There are also sports★ and circus schools.

Science★ and mathematics schools are few in number, for older pupils who have done particularly well in the national competitions (*olimpiady*). Khrushchev advocated these in 1958, but they aroused some controversy as a possible threat to the comprehensive system, hence their limited development.

Mathematics lesson at a boarding-school for the children of shepherds in Kazakhstan

Schools with special curricula in science, mathematics and languages are a much larger category, and provide the ten-year course with additional teaching time in the special field. In the language schools, the language is started earlier (class 2), and some subjects are later taught in the language concerned. Admission is by parental choice or privilege,★ subject to a medical examination.

Boarding-schools (*shkoly internat*) are mainly urban institutions, with children going home (if possible) at weekends. Priority is given to orphans, children of single parents or from overcrowded or problem homes, and children whose parents' work takes them away from home (for example, in the armed forces). The curriculum is the same as in the day-schools. Parents pay a proportion of accommodation costs according to income. A variant, the 'prolonged day-school' (*shkola prodlennogo dnya*), looks after children up to and including the evening meal, but not at night; this is mainly to accommodate parents with awkward working hours.

Higher education

Admission to higher education is highly competitive; proportions vary, but on average one applicant in three secures a place. It is necessary to have the *attestat* but this is not enough; entrance examinations have to be taken as well. In an attempt to balance the social composition of the student body, additional points are given to children of workers and farmers, to those seconded from industry or the armed forces, and to *stazhniki* (those who have spent at least a two-year period in production–*stazh*, hence the term). Most students receive a maintenance grant★ (*stipendiya*); there are no fees.

Part-time study, either through evening and shift classes or by correspondence, is favoured for social as well as economic reasons—it is much cheaper to provide, and students are not taken away from their jobs or environment. The proportion of part-time students has fluctuated, rising to over half in 1965 but dropping to about 40 per cent during the 1970s. Part-time students (along with *stazhniki*) turned out to be the most vulnerable to failure or drop-out, hence the greater state control on their numbers. Attempts are also being made to arrange study methods more appropriate to their needs, and to favour those whose courses have some relevance to their jobs. The system of ten weeks' paid study-leave per year continues. Although no longer dominant, external study still plays a significant role, and helps to alleviate pressure on places and resources.

Higher educational institutions (*Vysshie Uchebnye Zavedeniya*, or VUZy) are not clearly divided into universities and others; all can award a degree (*diplom*), all have the same kind of internal structure, staff nomenclature, and so on. There are some differences in prestige–universities do tend to outrank most other institutes–but status is not clear-cut. The main differences are in function. Universities (*universitety*) concentrate principally on pure sciences and the humanities, while higher professional training (technical,

medical, legal, artistic) is carried out in the appropriate specialist VUZY. Many of these, such as the Moscow Power Institute, the Kalinin Polytechnic Institute in Leningrad and the Gorky Language Institute, have a status and reputation quite as high as many universities.

Most first-degree courses last for five years. Postgraduate study can lead to the Candidate of Sciences degree (*kandidat nauk*), roughly equivalent to a Western Ph.D., or to the higher D.Sc. (*doktor nauk*). Study for these can be undertaken in any kind of VUZ, or in specialist research institutes, the Academy of Sciences,* and so on. Nearly half the postgraduate research students (*aspiranty*) take their degrees in this way. Higher degrees are not awarded by the institutions themselves, but by the ministry's Higher Degrees Commission or VAK (*Vysshaya Attestatsionnaya Kommissiya*).

Teacher training

As it overlaps both the higher and secondary specialized levels, teacher training must be considered separately. The system has been changing for some years, but at present teachers for the various levels of school are trained as follows.

Pre-school teachers:
Pedagogical school (*pedagogicheskoe uchilishche*) at the secondary specialized level.

Primary-class teachers (classes 1–3 of the general educational school): there are two sources:
Pedagogical school, or
Pedagogical institute (*pedagogichesky institut*) at higher level. The appropriate departments offer four-year courses. These were set up with the intention of replacing the primary courses in pedagogical schools; the process is well advanced, but has taken longer than expected.

Secondary-class teachers (classes 4–10; subject specialists):
Pedagogical institute, which gives a four-year course for one special subject, or five years for two combined (such as Russian and history, mathematics and physics, two foreign languages). The latter course is preferred for the greater flexibility of its products in employment.

University: nearly all courses include teacher-training subjects, thus qualifying graduates to teach their single subjects at the end of the five-year course. Although most university students may have other careers in mind, over half find themselves employed in the schools.

In-service training is compulsory, and involves release for one day

Top: main building of the Moscow State University. The central block houses offices and lecture rooms; the wings are student accommodation. Left: a lecture for senior executives on management methods

per week (or equivalent) for one year every five years. Ministries and pedagogical institutes are active in some of these training-courses, but the most important bodies are the institutes for teacher improvement (*instituty usovershenstvovaniya uchiteley*). Continuing education, in this as in other fields, is becoming ever more important as content and methods change.

Achievements and shortcomings

Many serious problems remain in the Soviet system. Some of these can be attributed to the cumbersome administrative machinery and the attempt to run a substantially uniform, centralized system in a large, complex and varied country with communication and transport problems; this difficulty becomes more acute with increased pressure for change and flexibility, to which the central authorities find it difficult to respond quickly. Other problems arise from the nature of the country itself; the most serious, perhaps, is the remaining gap in aspiration and achievement between the urban and rural schools, which remains stubbornly intractable despite labour-direction of teachers, amalgamation of small schools into more viable units, provision of boarding-schools and of special preparatory faculties in vuzy. Another is the attempt to link education and work without falling into the traps of irrelevance on the one hand and premature vocational orientation on the other.

The achievements, on the other hand, have been considerable. Notable among these are a high level of literacy and general culture, the close collaboration between the school and other social agencies, the incomplete but impressive advance in the status of women,[*] and the building-up of a system of mass comprehensive education in a country which, before the Revolution, had an underdeveloped and ill-distributed school provision and a largely illiterate population, and has since suffered both social upheaval and war.   *N.D.C.G.*

PUPIL AND STUDENT POPULATION (THOUSANDS) 1914–80

	1914–15	1940–1	1965–6	1970–1	1975–6	1979–80
TOTAL	10588	47547	71857	79634	92605	99043
General educational school	9656	35552	48255	49193	47594	44412
full-time	9656	34784	43410	45448	42611	39612
part-time		768	4845	3745	4983	4800
Vocational-technical schools	106	717	1701	2591	3381	3935
Secondary specialized schools	54	975	3659	4388	4525	4646
Higher educational institutions	127	812	3861	4581	4854	5186
Further and adult education, re-training, etc.	645	9491	14381	18881	32251	40864

Source: *Narodnoe khozyaystvo SSSR v 1979 godu: statistichesky ezhegodnik* (Moscow, 1980)

Libraries

The earliest libraries in Russia were the collections of manuscripts, and later of printed books, established in some of the Orthodox monasteries[*] from the 11th century onwards, and it was only during the 18th century that secular libraries began to arise on any scale. The Academy of Sciences[*] received as the nucleus of its library the collection begun by Peter the Great[*] in 1714, and the library of Moscow University was founded in 1755. Although the Imperial Public Library was opened in St Petersburg in 1814, early public library development was slow, underfinanced, and hampered by censorship[*] and widespread illiteracy. After the October Revolution in 1917, the Bolshevik government nationalized all libraries, and requisitioned and redistributed many private collections. The growth of libraries was encouraged as an aid to literacy, an educational instrument, and a means of access to approved publications. After extensive destruction during the Second World War, the Soviet library system had by 1979 expanded to some 360000 libraries of all kinds.

Policy and organization

Soviet official policy towards libraries regards them as a service essential to research and industry, and as a means of educating and ideologically influencing the general public. Careful control is exercised over the acquisition of library materials and access to collections. Only a limited number of libraries are allowed to acquire publications from outside the socialist countries; and foreign or Soviet works which do not have, or subsequently lose, the approval of the censorship are available only to readers holding special permission. Particularly in public and children's libraries, the supervision and guidance of users' choice in reading is encouraged. Libraries are also seen as permitting more efficient utilization of the country's book stocks than do collections in private hands, and they therefore receive some priority over individuals in the supply of publications in heavy demand.

In the present organization of Soviet library services, the Ministry of Culture of the USSR is responsible for overall development and coordination, as well as for the public ('mass') library network. Union and republic education ministries are responsible for libraries in schools and in higher and further education[*] institutions. The Academy of Sciences of the USSR controls the libraries in its many research institutes, as well as several important libraries of national status. The State Committee for Science and Technology supervises library services to industry, and also the state scientific and technical information system. The All-Union Book Chamber in Moscow registers all printed matter published in the Soviet Union, and issues current national bibliographies.

National libraries

The Lenin State Library was founded upon the library of the Rumyantsev Museum, opened in 1862, but is now the 'national library' of the entire Soviet Union, holding by far the largest collections and performing many functions in research, methodological guidance and foreign relations for the Soviet library system as a whole. The former Imperial Public Library, now the Saltykov-Shchedrin State Public Library in Leningrad, ranks in many respects as a second national library, and holds the largest collection of manuscripts in the country. Another, and probably unique, national institution is the All-Union State Library of Foreign Literature, in which is concentrated the country's largest holding of publications issued outside the Soviet Union. More-specialized central libraries of national status include the State Public Scientific and Technical Library, the State Central Scientific Medical Library, and the Central Scientific Agricultural Library. Each of the constituent republics, except the RSFSR, has its own 'state library' or 'republic library', serving as the head of the public library network and in particular as a repository of literature relating to that republic. Most libraries of national standing receive by law at least one copy of every work published in the USSR.

Academy libraries

The Academy of Sciences has within its organization the bulk of the libraries intended for the support of fundamental research in most fields of study. The Library of the Academy of Sciences in Leningrad, the oldest and one of the largest in the country, heads the Academy's library network, complemented by the Library of Natural Sciences and the Central Institute of Scientific Information for the Social Sciences (INION), both in Moscow. The rapid expansion of the Academy's research facilities in Siberia from the 1950s onwards led to the establishment in Novosibirsk of the State Public Scientific and Technical Library of the Academy's Siberian Division, which is now the leading research library east of the Urals. Many of the Academy's research institutes, such as the Institute for Russian Literature (the Pushkin House) have very substantial book and manuscript collections of their own. The Academies of each republic, except the RSFSR, all have their own central and institute libraries.

Public and educational libraries

The number of public libraries for general lending has grown from 13 800 in 1914 to about 128 000 in 1979, according to Soviet figures, and virtually all inhabited areas of the USSR now have a public library

One of the reading rooms of the Lenin State Library, Moscow, which has a total stock of over 26 million publications

service. Book acquisition is regulated by recommendations from the Ministry of Culture. Children's* library facilities are provided on a similar scale.

In education,* school libraries have recently begun to assume the task of supplying pupils' textbooks, which had previously to be bought for each child. University libraries, like the institutions they serve, are mostly 20th-century foundations, but a few, for example Moscow and Kazan', date from the 18th century, and those of L'vov and Vilnius Universities date from 1608 and 1570 respectively.

Technical libraries and information services

Soviet industry and construction are served by some 20 000 technical libraries and information centres, mostly in industrial plants, and nearly every branch of industry has its own central specialist library. The State Committee for Science and Technology controls central institutions and services, such as the State Public Scientific and Technical Library and the All-Union Centre for Translations of Scientific and Technical Literature. The most significant national information service is provided by the All-Union Institute of Scientific and Technical Information (VINITI), which in a unique operation prepares and publishes each year Russian summaries of about a million scientific articles from all over the world.   *G. W.*

Book publishing

History

The first dated book known to have been printed in Moscow was the *Apostol* (liturgical acts and epistles) completed by Ivan Fedorov in 1564 – over a century after printing began in Western Europe. Up to the end of the 17th century only about 700 books were printed in Russia, nearly all of them religious. Peter the Great* encouraged printing for official secular purposes, and St Petersburg became the centre of publishing in Russia, which it remained until 1917. Publishing was a monopoly of the state and of state-supervised institutions until 1783, and the very limited means of expression thus afforded by the printed word resulted in the widespread clandestine circulation of works in manuscript which persisted into the 19th century and surfaced again (as *samizdat*★) in the second half of the 20th. A decree of 1804 codified the practice of censorship* for the first time, and censorship of publications was maintained with varying severity throughout the imperial era and up to the present day. The first quarter of the 19th century saw the beginnings of commercial printing and publishing firms. The 40 bookshops in the Russia of 1840 had increased to 1795 by 1893. Measured by copies printed, book output in the later 19th century consisted predominantly of textbooks, popular fiction and religious literature.

For a time after the Revolution of 1917, some private publishing continued to exist beside newly-established Communist Party and government publishers, but the State Publishing House (Gosizdat), set up in 1919, rapidly became the principal book publishing organ. Much printed matter was distributed free, or at very low prices, in the first years after the Revolution, until the New Economic Policy★ (NEP) in 1921 introduced the principle that publishers should aim to cover their costs from sales. Publishing for the non-Russian peoples★ of the USSR was greatly increased during the 1920s. In 1930 the Association of State Publishing Houses (OGIZ) was created to coordinate the work of the reorganized central publishers. The number of titles and copies published dropped markedly during the years of the purges (1933–8). In 1953 the Ministry of Culture assumed responsibility for publishing, but in 1963 it was placed in the charge of a newly-created State Committee for the Press, which in 1972 became the present State Committee for Publishing, Printing and the Book Trade.

The Soviet view of publishing

Publishing, like the other mass media, is regarded by the Soviet authorities primarily as a means for the realization of official policies. The 'right to publish' is granted only by the Party authorities, and only to publishing-houses or other organizations (never to individuals), and may be revoked at any time. Party and government organs assume a very direct responsibility for the nature of what is published and for its dissemination, and the Soviet public is encouraged by low book prices and large edition sizes to read the material produced under these conditions. Publishing enterprises are normally expected to cover their costs from sales income (although book prices are fixed by the state), but subsidies are provided to maintain the output of certain types of book at what are regarded as acceptable prices. This applies especially to school textbooks, and to many of the books published in the minority languages of the Soviet Union. The selection and quantity of books to be issued are heavily influenced by the central authorities' views on the priority to be given to different types of publication, and by available paper and printing resources, which are allocated by the government.

Supervision of the publishing industry by the Communist Party is exercised through the Department of Propaganda of the Central Committee, which also has close links with the main censorship organ (Glavlit). Operational control of the industry is in the hands of the State Committee for Publishing, Printing and the Book Trade, which has the status of a ministry. It directly administers most of the main Moscow and Leningrad publishers, and controls other houses indirectly through its subordinate publishing administrations in the constituent republics. Some important publishers are under the joint control of the State Committee and another public organization, such as the Academy of Sciences or the Writers' Union. The State

Committee is responsible for the economic planning* of the entire industry, and also for overseeing the preparation of all publishers' annual publication plans and for monitoring their fulfilment.

Publishers and authors

In 1977 there were 206 publishing houses in the Soviet Union, and in addition several hundred other organizations (government departments, research institutes) enjoyed a limited 'right to publish'. All publishing houses are under the authority of the local or central state publishing administration or some other parent body, to whom they are answerable for the character and quality of the books issued. Subject to its superior organ's approval, each house has discretion to select topics for treatment, to seek out authors, to negotiate fees (within limits), and to accept or reject manuscripts. Authors' fees are calculated according to the type of work, its length and the number of copies printed – not as a percentage of the price of each copy sold, as in the Western royalty system. The right to publish a Soviet author's work outside the USSR can under Soviet law be granted to foreign publishers only through the All-Union Agency for Authors' Rights (VAAP), and not directly by the author himself.

Character of book production

In 1977, 85395 books and pamphlets were published in a total of about 1800 million copies. The Soviet Union ranks alongside the USA as one of the world's two most prolific publishing countries. Over 81 per cent of the copies printed were in Russian, 14 per cent in other languages of the USSR, and the remainder in foreign languages. Children's books* accounted for 29 per cent of copies issued, school and other textbooks for 22 per cent, and adult fiction for 14 per cent, followed by mass political literature with 8 per cent. The number of mass political publications has been reduced somewhat in recent years, and production of school textbooks is falling as they are loaned instead of sold to pupils, while adult fiction and children's books have been granted enhanced priority after many years of failure to satisfy reader demand.   *G.W.*

Retail publishing outlets range from small kiosks in factories (below) to the House of Books in Moscow, Europe's largest bookstore (bottom)

The media

Newspapers

The Soviet leadership have consistently attached great importance to the development of the mass media—particularly so, perhaps, to newspapers, which played an important part in the Bolsheviks'* conquest of power and were for some time the only effective means of mass communication within the country. The development of newspaper publication over the Soviet period, and that of magazines and periodicals, grew rapidly; although the number of newspaper titles declined somewhat after the early 1960s, the total circulation has steadily increased to a 1979 total of about 173 million copies per issue or 39100 million copies per year. Periodical publications have expanded comparably to their 1979 total of 3203 million copies annually.

'A newspaper', Lenin* observed, 'is not only a collective propagandist and collective agitator; it is also a collective organizer.' Soviet newspapers and periodicals, accordingly, have somewhat different tasks to perform and are rather different in coverage and layout from most Western counterparts. The Communist Party

NEWSPAPERS AND JOURNALS: SELECTED STATISTICS, 1913–79

	1913	1940	1960	1970	1979
Newspapers published	1 055	8 806	9 544	8 694	8 019
Daily circulation (*million*)	3.3	38.4	68.6	140.7	173.0
per 1000 population	20.7	197.8	322.9	582.1	656.8
Periodicals published	1 472	1 822	3 761	5 969	5 265
Annual circulation (*million*)	116.5	245.4	778.6	2 675.0	3 203
per head of population	0.7	1.2	3.6	11.0	12.2

Sources: *Narodnoe obrazonvanie, nauka i kul'tura v SSSR; Statistichesky sbomik* (Moscow, 1977); *Pechat' SSSR v 1978 godu* (Moscow, 1979), *Narodnoe khozyaystvo SSSR v 1979 godu*

Below: *Pravda* on display in a Kiev street. Bottom: an editorial conference of *Pravda*, 1977

daily, *Pravda* (*Truth*), for instance, founded in 1912, normally contains an 'agitational' editorial and reports of production achievements on its front page; its other five pages are usually devoted to Party affairs, correspondence, foreign news (mostly that supplied by TASS, the official Soviet news agency), sports reports and weather (on the back page). About 10.7 million copies of *Pravda* were produced daily in 1978. Other important daily papers, which diverge somewhat from *Pravda* in their coverage but not at all in their editorial orientation, are *Izvestiya* (*News*), the government newspaper, founded in 1917 (8.1 million copies daily); *Komsomol'skaya pravda*, the Komsomol* paper, founded in 1925 (10.1 million copies daily); *Sel'skaya zhizn'* (*Rural Life*), a Party newspaper intended for a rural readership, published under various titles since 1929 (8.5 million copies daily); *Trud* (*Labour*), the trade union* paper, founded in 1921 (8.4 million copies daily); and *Krasnaya zvezda* (*Red Star*), the daily organ of the Ministry of Defence, which was founded in 1924 (2.4 million copies daily). Weekly magazines and periodicals of note include the Party theoretical journal *Kommunist*, published since 1924; the literary monthly *Novy mir* (*New World*), founded in 1925; the illustrated weekly magazine *Ogonek*, founded in 1923; the weekly literary newspaper *Literaturnaya gazeta* (*Literary Gazette*), published since 1929; and the humorous *Krokodil*, founded in 1922.

Sociological studies conducted within the USSR suggest that the majority of the adult population makes considerable use of this substantial diet of newsprint. A study conducted in Leningrad, for instance, found that 75 per cent of those polled read the newspapers every day (a further 19 per cent did so three or four times a week), and even in relatively remote areas at least half the local population normally report reading a newspaper daily, with the younger and better educated more likely to do so than the local population as a whole. People appear also to discuss articles in the press relatively frequently with their family and work-mates, to cut out and keep articles of interest to them, and to place some value upon the paper's ability to deal with local difficulties and shortcomings. More than 500 000 Soviet citizens wrote to *Pravda* during 1979, for instance, and more than 650 000 wrote letters to *Trud*. No more than a small proportion of the letters can be published, but all are supposed to be answered and followed up, and in some cases the newspaper deputes a member of its staff to investigate a particular issue in more detail. A number of dismissals have followed such inquiries.

It remains clear at the same time that most readers take the glowing reports of production achievements in their daily papers with a substantial pinch of salt, and a good deal more importance appears to be attached to personal impressions, foreign sources and rumour than would be the case in most Western countries. Readers appear also to manifest less interest in party-political and economic than in international, cultural and sporting themes. A detailed survey of the readerships of *Pravda* and *Izvestiya*, for instance, found that the most frequently-consulted categories of material in both papers were international affairs (74 and 69 per cent of readers respectively), official communications (81 per cent of *Pravda*'s readers), 'surprising stories' (71 per cent of *Izvestiya*'s readers), moral themes (57 and 75 per cent respectively), and satirical articles (57 and 64 per cent respectively). Only 30 per cent of *Izvestiya*'s readers were interested in its editorials, however; no more than 23 per cent read its articles on economics; and only 18 and 17 per cent respectively read its articles on propaganda themes and on the soviets (councils)–the latter supposedly the paper's main function. Studies of other publications have reached similar conclusions.

Television

Experimental television transmissions were started in 1931, and regular programmes began to be broadcast from Moscow and Leningrad in 1939. The third centre started functioning in Kiev in 1951, since when there has been a rapid expansion to the present total of 117 television centres with programme-making facilities. The number of television sets has also increased remarkably. In 1960, only an estimated 8 per cent of families possessed a television set, and only a relatively limited part of the country could receive television transmissions. Twenty years later, however, there were about 64 million television sets available for use, covering about 85 per cent of families, and 98 per cent of families are resident in areas in which television transmissions can regularly be received. It is planned to extend this coverage still further.

The national television service in 1979 comprised eight main 'programmes' or channels, the total daily output of which averaged nearly 84 hours in 1978. The first channel is the basic national network for informational, socio-political and cultural broadcasting; its daily output averaged 13.5 hours in 1978. The second channel provides similar programmes for Moscow and the Moscow region (about 4.5 hours daily); the third deals with educational and popular-scientific matters and is broadcast to most of the regions of European Russia (about 7 hours daily); and the fourth provides cultural, documentary and sporting features for a national audience (about 5.5 hours daily). Four further channels, 'Vostok' and 'Orbit 1, 2 and 3', relay a number of these programmes to the more remote parts of the USSR (about 13 hours a day respectively in 1978). All central television programmes are now broadcast in colour; television services in regional and republican centres are in the process of transition to this system. In 1979 about one million Soviet television sets were capable of receiving transmissions in colour.

Most urban residents watch television fairly regularly, and for many it is clearly an important source of news and information. The

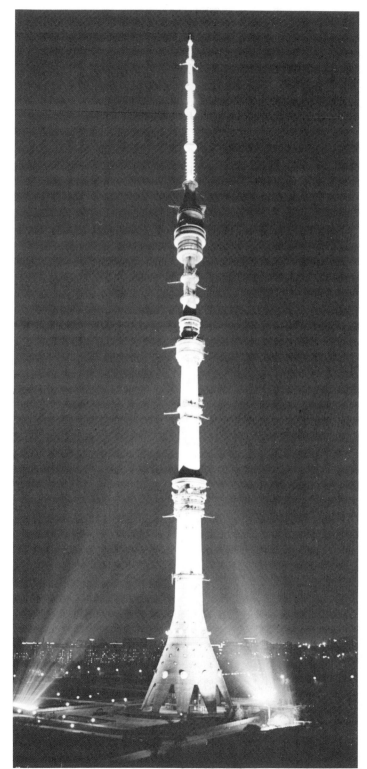

The tower of Moscow's television centre

mass audience, however, displays a pattern of preferences diverging fairly markedly from that which the authorities might be expected to favour. A study in Leningrad, for instance, found that feature films, documentaries and variety programmes were the most popular of all the programmes shown (91.5, 85 and 84 per cent respectively of regular viewers liked most of all to watch such programmes); social and political themes were less popular; and only 4 per cent of regular viewers opted for more programmes on economic matters, the least popular of all the 27 types of programme considered. More than 70 per cent of those polled said that they regarded television as a 'means of entertainment'; more than 41 per cent said that too few entertainment programmes were shown, and 48 per cent believed that their quality should be improved. Current affairs programmes have also been subject to repeated criticism for their tardy and predictable response to developments on the international scene, and an attempt is being made to provide more up-to-date and apparently spontaneous coverage of such matters. Given the requirements of political orthodoxy within which such programmes must necessarily operate, however, it would be surprising if a major improvement were effected. As in other countries the growth of television audiences has diminished those for cinemas, although the decline is smaller than in many other urban societies.

Radio

The first experimental radio broadcasts in the USSR were made in Nizhny Novgorod (now Gorky) in 1919; the construction of a central radio station was undertaken in Moscow the following year, and it began broadcasting in 1922. Further stations were opened in 1924 in Leningrad, Kiev and Nizhny Novgorod, and regular broadcasts throughout the USSR began in the same year. By 1937 a total of 90 radio transmitters were in operation; the present total is approximately 35 000, and 300 radio broadcasting centres are in operation on a daily basis. Radio programmes are made by regional and republican committees for radio and television, of which in 1979 there were 170 throughout the country. These committees come under the over-all direction of the State Committee for Radio and Television of the USSR, whose chairman is a member of the USSR Council of Ministers.

The central radio network broadcasts eight main programmes with a total output which in 1978 exceeded 160 hours daily. The first programme, as with television, is the main national network for informational, socio-political and cultural broadcasts (about 20 hours a day); the second programme, 'Mayak' (Beacon) broadcasts news and music on a 24-hour basis; the third broadcasts educational, literary and musical programmes for about 16 hours daily; and the fourth broadcasts music for about 9 hours daily. The fifth programme provides informational, socio-political and cultural broadcasts for Soviet citizens who are resident abroad; and the sixth, seventh and eighth relay the first programme to Western Siberia and Central Asia,

Eastern Siberia, and the Far East respectively. In 1979 direct radio reception from wired-up speakers was available for areas in which some 97 per cent of the total population were resident. About 60 million people, a substantial proportion of the population, can also receive radio broadcasts from foreign countries, and there is evidence to suggest that this may be a significant source of information for foreign news and for developments to which the Soviet media have not yet themselves had time to react.   *S.W.*

Censorship

Censorship is not a new phenomenon in the USSR, but it has become much more comprehensive and effective in the Soviet period than it was in imperial Russia. First introduced officially by Peter the Great,* censorship was codified in 1804, substantially liberalized after the 1905 revolution and (with the exception of military censorship) abolished following the February 1917 revolution.

Soviet censorship began on the night of the 24 October 1917 (OS) with the confiscation and burning of the latest issue of the liberal newspaper *Russkaya volya* (*Russian Freedom*), said to contain 'libellous concoctions'; the paper's printing press was requisitioned on the following day and immediately used to produce copies of the Bolshevik* *Rabochy put'* (*Workers' Way*). These actions set the pattern for the next few months, and by the end of July 1918 the Military Revolutionary Committees had succeeded in preventing the regular appearance on communist-held territory of all non-Bolshevik newspapers, although a certain amount of new Menshevik* and Socialist Revolutionary political literature circulated in Russia for some time after that. Restrictions on non-Bolshevik publishing were imposed in accordance with the *Decree on the Press* of 27 October 1917 (OS), which stated that 'counter-revolutionary' publications at that juncture were no less dangerous than bombs and machine-guns. This decree (still in force) promised that the 'temporary measures to stop the flood of filth and slander' would be repealed as soon as the new order was consolidated and normal conditions of public life obtained; all administrative interference with the press would then cease and complete freedom within the law would be established. After a decree of 28 January 1918 setting up Revolutionary Press Tribunals, committees of inquiry attached to these bodies were empowered to take swift action against any publications suspected of encroaching on the rights and interests of the revolutionary people (by, for example, printing something critical of Bolshevik policies and practices). In addition, the security* police (then the Cheka–Extraordinary Commission for Combating Counter-Revolution and Sabotage) was given the duty of arresting anyone whose publishing activities could be regarded as 'counter-revolutionary'.

CENSORSHIP SYMBOLS

Cyrillic alphabet

A	Moscow (national publishers on general subjects; recently Academy of Sciences)	N	Ulan-Ude
		NB	Ryazan'
		NE	Irkutsk
AB	Kishinev	NG	Saratov
ACh	Abakan	NK	Smolensk
AG	Barnaul	NL	Tambov
AK	Yaroslavl'	NM	Volgograd
AKh	Magadan	NP	Izhevsk
AL	Krasnoyarsk	NS	Sverdlovsk
AT	Minsk	OD	Novgorod
B	Moscow (national newspapers)	OP	Kemerovo
BB	Uzhgorod	OS	Kurgan
BD	Chernovtsy	P	Ufa
BF	Kiev	PD	Omsk
BG	L'vov	PF	Kazan'
BYa	Simferopol'	PK	Rostov-na-Donu
BK	Kirovograd	PN	Murmansk
BKh	Ternopol'	R	Tashkent
BL	Nikolaev	RCh	Samarkand
BP	Donetsk	RD	Tyumen'
BR	Odessa	S	Makhachkala
BSh	Chernigov	SF	Grozny
BT	Dnepropetrovsk	SL	Archangel
BTs	Kharkov	Sh	Moscow (fields under Ministry of Culture)
BV	Voroshilovgrad		
Ch	Nal'chik	T	Moscow (national publishers on technology and agriculture, and, earlier, USSR Academy of Sciences)
D	Frunze		
E	Yoshkar-Ola		
EI	Sukhumi		
EM	Batumi	TB	Kaluga
ET	Tskhinvali	TS	Kyzyl
FB	Chelyabinsk	Ts	Syktyvkar
FD	Chita	TsP	Tula
FE	Kirov	TZh	Pskov
FG	Baku	UE	Tbilisi
FL	Penza	UG	Alma-Ata
FM	Orel	VE	Blagoveshchensk
G	Defence publishers	VF	Yerevan
GE	Vologda	VG	Stavropol'
GM	Simferopol'	VI	Petropavlov'sk-Kamchatsky
I	Ashkhabad	VL	Khabarovsk
IYe	Kursk	VU	Cherkessk
KE	Ivanovo	Ye	Petrozavodsk
KL	Dushanbe	YeA	Kalinin
KU	Kaliningrad	Yel	Ordzhonikidze
KZ	Tomsk	YeO	Kuybyshev
L	Moscow (republic and city publishers)	Yu	Saransk
		Zh	Vladimir
LB	Perm', Kudymkar	ZhB	Velikiye Luki
LE	Voronezh	ZI	Kostroma
LV	Vilnius	ZM	Ul'yanovsk
M	Leningrad		
MA	Krasnodar		
ML	Yakutsk	**Latin alphabet**	
MN	Novosibirsk		
MTs	Gorky	JT	Riga
MV	Tallinn	LV	Vilnius
		MB	Tallinn

Source: Updated from B. I. Gorokhoff, *Publishing in the USSR*, Bloomington, 1959

Сдано в набор 15/XI 1966 г. Подписано в печать 12/III 1967 г.
Формат 60×90¹/₁₆. Бумага типографская № 1.
Усл.-печ. л. 22,75. Уч.-изд. л. 23,7. Тираж 7000.
Заказ № 1622. Т-03922. Цена 1 р. 67 к.
A-02510

The more routine pre-publication censorship at this time was carried out by employees of the Commissariat for People's Enlightenment and in particular, after its establishment in May 1919, of the state publishing house, Gosizdat, which included a Chief Board for Press Affairs. The remaining private book-publishers (who were able to operate until the end of the 1920s and in isolated cases even longer) were also supervised by Gosizdat functionaries at this stage. The military censorship was separate from the civilian branch, but became part of the 'official' Soviet censorship organ, Glavlit, when this body was finally set up on 6 June 1922. Glavlit (initially meaning Chief Board for Literary and Publishing Affairs – since August 1966 the official title has been Chief Board for the Preservation of State Secrets in the Press, attached to the USSR Council of Ministers) was designated a Chief Committee of the People's Commissariat of Enlightenment and was headed until 1931 by P. I. Lebedev-Polyansky, the author of the first (1924) book on Lenin's literary and aesthetic views, and then (until 1935) by B. M. Volin, both of whom had gained valuable experience for their post as chief censor of the Soviet Union by engaging in Bolshevik underground literary activities in Russia before the Revolution. Volin's successor was S. B. Ingulov, followed in 1957 by P. K. Romanov, a graduate of the Leningrad Institute of Railway Transport Engineering.

The 1922 Statute (*Polozhenie*) states that Glavlit was established to bring together all forms of censorship (*vsekh vidov tsenzury*) of domestic and imported printed works, manuscripts, photographs, drawings and maps that are intended for sale and distribution; it is to compile lists of banned works, and is supplied with broad criteria (such as 'containing agitation against Soviet power') for proscribing harmful items. Publications of certain bodies (the Central Committee,★ Comintern, the Academy of Sciences,★ Gosizdat) are 'freed from censorship', apart from being checked for military secrets. The security police (by then known as the GPU – State Political Directorate) is instructed to cooperate with Glavit to prevent the circulation of banned literature and to 'struggle against' domestic and foreign underground publications. Glavrepertkom (literally, the Main Committee for the Control over Repertoire), was established on 9 February 1923; it was headed by I. P. Trainin, attached to Glavlit, and censored plays, films, circuses, concerts, variety shows, other public performances and, from 1925, gramophone records (both sound track and labels). Slides and photographs had to be submitted to this body for approval before being shown in public, and one or two

Censorship symbols: the colophon (left) from N. K. Gey, *Iskusstvo slova* (*The Art of the Word*), Moscow, 1967, shows that the censor was changed (serial number altered from T–03922 to A–02510) at a late stage of printing

seats no further back than the fourth row from the stage always had to be kept free for Glavrepertkom's requirements.

By the mid-1920s everything was supposed to be submitted to censorship, including sculptures, drawings, handkerchiefs with pictures on them, book jackets, bus tickets and matchbox labels. In the 1930s items were often reinspected upside-down and back-to-front as an extra precaution against accidental unfortunate juxtapositions. The new censorship statute of 6 June 1931 (apparently still in force today) is more wide-ranging than its predecessor. It is now clearly stated that Glavlit (including Glavrepertkom) is concerned also with the pre-publication and post-publication 'control' (this word replaces the term 'censorship' in the 1922 statute) of pictures, radio broadcasts (ballets and television programmes were to be added in due course), lectures and exhibitions, and has its plenipotentiaries not only in publishing houses, printing establishments, editorial offices and radio stations, but also in news agencies, head post offices and customs sheds. Military (as contrasted to state) secrets are barely mentioned, but Glavlit is instructed to draw up lists of secret information (not merely lists of banned titles). Publications of the main state publishing house (now called OGIZ) are no longer free from Glavlit's preventive 'control'. The final loophole appears to have been closed on 28 August 1939 with the obligatory registration and ringing of carrier pigeons, making evasion of the postal censorship even harder than before. Since then, no substantial changes seem to have taken place in this field, apart from the steadily rising educational level of the censors.

It is very important to stress, however, that Glavlit itself was and is largely an executive organ and much less important than: current Communist Party policies controlled by the Central Committee; the wishes and whims of the Party leader (or one or more of his closest associates; the activities of the security police (now KGB*– Committee of State Security) in suppressing and/or provoking manifestations of dissent;* the attitudes of the editor(s) and publisher(s) involved; or the likelihood of self-censorship on the part of the author himself. The Glavlit employee, as a rule, sees not the manuscript but a proof copy, by which stage most of the 'doubtful' passages in the original version have probably been removed, as it is usually fairly clear to all involved what will and will not 'get through' at the Glavlit stage of processing. No edition of Glavlit's book of rules is available in the West, but it is widely believed that special permission is required (and is not very often given) in every individual case before public mention can be made of such matters as earthquakes, explosions and other disasters in the USSR, the salaries of Soviet government and Party officials, price increases at home or improved living standards anywhere outside the socialist camp, and so on. No Soviet publication supplies details about the jamming of foreign radio broadcasts, and the operations of Glavlit itself are also subject to a strict taboo.   *M.D.*

Sport: development

Soviet sport and physical education have their roots deep in Russian history, in the people's traditions, the climate, fears about internal and external foes, the organized sports pioneered largely by Britain, the gymnastics schools of Germany (Jahn), Scandinavia (Ling and Nachtegall) and the Czech lands (Tyrs), and in Prussian military training. The pattern of Soviet sport has been shaped as much by these factors as it has by political ideals.

As an industrial society developed in 19th-century Russia, liberal noblemen and native industrialists, with foreigners resident in Russia, began to set up private sports clubs in the major cities. These embraced sports such as yachting (the Imperial Yacht Club, dating from 1846), tennis (the Neva Lawn-Tennis Circle, from 1860), ice-skating (the Amateur Skating Society, from 1864), fencing (the Officers' Fencing Gymnasium, from 1857), gymnastics (the Palma Gymnastics Society, from 1863) and cricket (the St Petersburg Tennis and Cricket Club, from 1868). Commercial promoters were also providing, for spectators and gamblers, such professional sports as horse-racing (the St Petersburg Horse-Racing Society, 1826), boxing (Baron Kister's English Boxing Arena, 1895), cycling (the Tsar'skoe Selo Cycling Circle, 1880) and soccer (the Victoria Football Club was the first established soccer club in 1894). Various displays of strength were popular in circuses, featuring such world-famous performers as the Estonian Georgy Hakkenschmidt and the Russian Ivan Poddubny and his wrestling wife Masha Poddubnaya.

At the turn of the century, there were several Russian sports associations and on the eve of the First World War as many as 1266 Russian sports clubs existed with an average membership of 60 persons. Although many of these clubs were located in the main Russian cities, the industrializing provinces also accounted for a growing number. For example, the Ukraine had 196 sports clubs with 8000 members, and Belorussia had 1000 members in its Sanitas, Sokol, Bogatyr and the Jewish Maccabee sports clubs (Jews* being barred from entry to many Russian clubs). In 1912 the government set up its quasi-military Physical Fitness Committee under General Voyeikov. The Bolsheviks* were therefore to inherit a developing sports movement that was already largely centrally controlled.

Sport in revolution
The first steps to be taken after the Bolsheviks came to power in October 1917 were by no means clear, for there was no pattern to follow. The change-over from criticism of tsarist sport to action in an 80 per cent peasant country in the throes of a world and civil war presented considerable problems.

However, the crucial question being debated was not what form sport should take, but whether competitive sport should exist at all in the new workers' state. After all, some revolutionaries argued, sports such as athletics, soccer, rowing, tennis and gymnastics were invented by the industrial bourgeoisie for their own diversion and character training for future careers as captains of industry and empire. It was thought perfectly natural by some after the Russian Revolution that a new pattern of recreation would emerge, reflecting the dominant values and needs in the new socialist state.

Hygienists and Proletkultists

The two major groups that regarded competitive sport as debasing workers' physical culture and inculcating non-socialist habits were known as the Hygienists and the Proletkultists (from 'proletarian culture').

To the Hygienists, sport implied competition, games that were potentially injurious to mental and physical health. These included boxing, weight-lifting, wrestling and gymnastics, which were said to

Soviet gymnasts, 1965, by Dmitry Zhilinsky

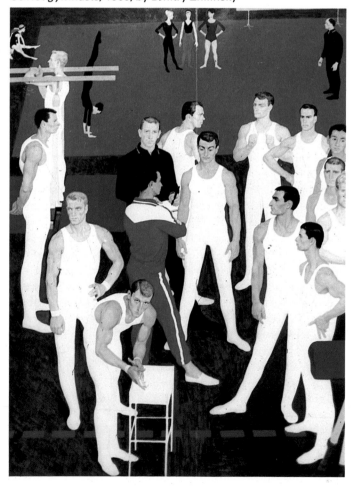

encourage individualist rather than collectivist attitudes. They condemned the emphasis on record-breaking and the professionalism of Western sport, and they favoured non-commercialized forms of recreation that dispensed with grandstands and spectators. Sport, they said, diverted attention from providing recreation for all. Their list of 'approved' sports included athletics, swimming and rowing (all against oneself or the clock, rather than an oppponent). Since the Hygienists had virtual control over the government body for sport (the Supreme Council of Physical Culture), the sporting press, the Ministry of Health and the physical education colleges, they were extremely powerful. They managed, for example, to have physical education excluded from the schools, since they believed that it should be integrated into all lessons rather than tacked on to the curriculum artificially. 'The existence of PE teachers is a sign of pedagogical illiteracy', they claimed.

To the Proletkultists, sports that derived from bourgeois society were remnants of the decadent past and part of degenerate bourgeois culture. A fresh start had to be made through labour exercises and mass displays, pageants and folk games. In the decade after the Revolution, many factory yards and farm meadows could be seen full of muscular men and women rhythmically swinging hammers and sickles, simulating work movements in time to music. The Proletkultists went much further than the Hygienists in condemning all manner of games, sports and gymnastics 'tainted' by class society. They invented new games for children,* had the manufacture of dolls stopped (because they were thought to enforce a maternal instinct among young girls) and organized mass sports activities portraying scenes of world revolution.

Sport for defence, health and integration

Essentially, however, sport during the first few years came to be geared to the needs of the war effort. All the old clubs and their equipment were commandeered for the Universal Military Training Board (Vsevobuch) whose main aim was to supply the Red Army* with contingents of trained conscripts as quickly as possible. It took over the Physical Fitness Committee and coordinated its activities with those of the education and health ministries. A second major consideration then was health. Regular participation in physical exercise was to be a means of improving health standards rapidly and of educating people in hygiene, nutrition and exercise. This campaign could only succeed, in the opinion of Nikolay Podvoisky, head of Vsevobuch, if the emotional attraction of competitive sport were fully exploited.

Competitive sports began to be organized from the lowest level upwards, culiminating in the All-Russia Pre-Olympiads and the

Top: a *kurash* (wrestling) match in the Kirgiz SSR. Right: reindeer-racing at the Festival of the North, Murmansk

First Central-Asian Olympics of 1920. Sports were taken from town to country, from the European metropolis to the Asiatic interior, as an explicit means of involving as many people as possible in organized sport and exercise. A third function of sport was integration. The significance of the First Central-Asian Olympics, held in Tashkent over ten days in early October 1920, may be judged from the fact that this was the first time that Uzbeks,* Kirgiz,* Kazakhs* and other Turkic* peoples, as well as Russians* and other Europeans, had competed in any sporting event together.

Sports activity during the 1920s

Throughout the 1920s, the actual amount of sports activity increased substantially. By 1929, sports club membership had risen fifteen-fold since 1913 (from 0.04 to 0.5 per cent of the population). Furthermore, half the present officially-recognized sports in the USSR had had their national championship by 1929, including 14 women's sports.

The big sports contest of the decade was the First Workers' Spartakiad of 1928, with some 4000 participants, including 600 foreign athletes from 12 countries. In view of the fact that the USSR had few contacts with international sports federations and none with the Olympic* movement, this Spartakiad was intended to be a universal workers' Olympics – in opposition to the 'bourgeois' Olympics held that year in Amsterdam with roughly the same programme. Although Soviet sports performance was understandably below top world standards, in some events the USSR did have world-class athletes. Yakov Mel'nikov (1896–1960), for example, had won the 5000-metre speed-skating event at the Stockholm world championships in 1923.

During the 1920s the Communist Party* made clear its own views on physical culture and took it completely under government control. A resolution of 1925 emphasized that physical culture must be an inseparable part of political and cultural education and of public health. This, then, was the definitive statement on the enhanced role of sport in society to which all subsequent policy statements were to refer. Sport had been given the revolutionary role of being an agent of wide-ranging social change. As a means of inculcating standards of hygiene and regular exercise in a predominantly backward peasant country, its therapeutic role was, for example, widely advertised in the three-day anti-tuberculosis campaigns of the late 1920s. Sport was also expected to combat anti-social behaviour: the Ukrainian Party Central Committee issued a resolution in 1926 expressing the hope that 'physical culture would become the vehicle of the new life . . .a means of isolating young people from the evil effects of prostitution, home-made alcohol* and the street.' The role given to sport in the countryside was even more ambitious: it was 'to play a big part in the campaign against drunkenness and uncivilized behaviour by attracting village youth to more cultured activities. . . In efforts to transform the village, physical culture is to be a vehicle of the new way of life in all measures undertaken by the authorities—in the fight against religion and natural calamities [drought, floods, frosts, erosion, etc].' Participation in sport, therefore, might develop healthy minds in healthy bodies. Sport stood for 'clean living', progress, good health and rationality, and was regarded by the Party as one of the most effective instruments in implementing its social policies.

Sport against the background of industrialization*

The implications for the sports movement of the economic and political processes of the 1930s were extremely important, for it was then that the present organizational pattern of Soviet sport was basically formed–with the sports societies, sports schools,* national fitness programme* and the uniform rankings* system for individual sports. The new society saw the flourishing of all manner of competitive sports with spectator appeal, of leagues, cups, championships, popularity-polls and cults of sporting heroes. All were designed to provide recreation and diversion for the fast-growing urban populace. The big city and security-forces (Dinamo) teams, with their considerable resources, dominated competition in all sports; thus, the Division-1 soccer league of 1938 included nine Moscow and six Dinamo teams from the cities of Moscow, Leningrad, Kiev, Tbilisi, Odessa and Rostov out of its 26 clubs.

The many sports parades and pageants which constituted a background to the sports contests were intended to create 'togetherness' and patriotic feeling. Significantly, sports rallies often began to accompany major political events and festivals (May Day, Anniversary of the Revolution, Constitution Day), thereby linking members of the public, through sport, with politics, the Party and, of course, with their leader.

A relatively close link was re-established in the 1930s between sport and the military, stemming from the conviction that a state surrounded by unfriendly powers must be militarily strong. Sport openly became a means of providing pre-military training and achieving a relatively high standard of national fitness and defence. The two largest and most successful sports clubs in the USSR were (and are today) those run by the armed forces* and the security forces: the Central House of the Red Army (today the Central Sports Club of the Army, TsSKA) and Dinamo respectively. After 1931, moreover, the national fitness programme, the GTO, was expressly intended to train people, through sport, for military preparedness and work—the Russian abbreviation GTO (*Gotov k trudu i oborone*) standing for 'Ready for Labour and Defence'.

Effect of the Second World War

The war years obviously retarded the sports movement, yet had certain far-reaching effects. The war convinced the authorities that they had been correct in 'functionalizing' sport and making nationwide physical fitness a prime target. It also reinforced a belief in a military bias in physical training and sport. The post-war role of organizations such as the army sports clubs, Dinamo and the civil defence* establishment DOSAAF* (*Dobrovol'noe obshchestvo sodeistviya Armii, Aviatsii i Flotu*–'Voluntary Society for Aid to the Army, Air Force and Navy') was to be enhanced and these institutions were to be made the pillars of the entire sports movement. A national physical-fitness programme was to be the main goal, and sports with specific military utility were to become compulsory in all educational institutions and sports societies.

Post-war sports competition with the West

With the conclusion of the war and the setting of a new national target–to catch up and overtake the most advanced industrial powers in sport as in all else–the Soviet leaders felt it possible to demonstrate the pre-eminence of sport in Soviet socialist society. Given the limited opportunities elsewhere, sport seemed to offer a suitable medium for pursuing this goal as an area in which the USSR did not have to take second place. This aim presupposed a level of skill in a wide range of sports superior to that existing in the leading Western states. On the eve of the war, that level was already approached or achieved in several sports. Soviet sources assert that by 1939 as many as 44 unofficial world records had been set, over half (23) of which were in weight-lifting, the rest being in shooting (9), athletics (9), swimming (2) and speed-skating (2).

This trend towards proficiency was strengthened after the war by

Industrial physical training at a L'vov television factory

mobilization of the total, if limited, resources of the entire sports system, by creating full-time, well-remunerated sportsmen and teams, and by giving them considerable backing. Sport is seen as 'one of the best and most comprehensible means of explaining to people throughout the world the advantages of the socialist system over capitalism'.

Effect of changes in urban life on post-war sport

Since the late 1950s especially, there has been a steady increase in public and personal prosperity, and in the range and quantity of consumer goods* available, a reduction in working time* and a continuing shift in population-balance in favour of the towns. All these factors have a qualitative effect on the pattern of sport.

INCREASING PROSPERITY. Soviet sources indicate that both national income and consumption have nearly tripled between 1960 and 1977. Part of the resulting increased personal income is undoubtedly being spent on recreation, on the pursuit of a growing variety of activities, particularly outdoor ones, and on personal durables such as skis, skates, tennis and badminton rackets, fishing tackle, tents and, to a lesser extent, on motor-cycles, canoes, dinghies, yachts and cars.

Higher national income has also resulted in more substantial government allocation to sport and the spread of activities that presuppose a certain level of industrial development and economic surplus. For example, motor-racing and rallying, yachting, karting, various winter sports (bobsleighing, slaloming, ski-jumping), water-skiing, aqua-lung diving, mountaineering, fishing, shooting and the complex of outdoor pursuits that comes under the Russian rubric of 'tourism' all showed appreciable growth in the 1960s and 1970s. Some sports received a new lease of life as industry was able to produce equipment for them—as, for example, in the cases of rugby, archery and field hockey. The most recently-introduced sports for which facilities are at present being constructed are squash, hang-gliding, karate and golf. It is significant that the introduction of new sports comes from above, by government decision, and not from below as in the West. An exception to this was, perhaps, the setting-up of a Soviet pigeon-fanciers' federation in 1975.

State capital investment for the construction of sports facilities grew considerably after the August 1966 government resolutions on sport. For example, some republics increased their expenditure on sport by as much as six to seven times in one year, 1967. The Russian Federation (RSFSR) spent twice as much on sport in 1967 as in all the preceding post-war years put together. As a result of this campaign, between 1966 and 1970 the country gained 319 new sports centres, 185 indoor swimming-pools, 31 indoor athletics stadiums and 16 indoor ice-rinks.

INCREASING FREE TIME. The relationship of work to leisure has also altered radically since the war. Not merely has there been an increase in the absolute amount of free time, but the reduction in the working day has resulted in workers spending less time than previously in such well-defined institutional settings as factory and office. As G. I. Yeliseyev, chief of the trade-union sports societies, has said, 'whereas recreational activities used to take place in urban sports centres, many have now been transferred to out-of-town sports amenities, recreation camps and parks'. As a consequence, the unions have had to 'refit and adapt various buildings, old passenger railway compartments and river steamers, landing-craft, barges and such-like, and to build recreational centres in the countryside'.

The break-through that signals the greatest revolution in leisure, just as in other industrial countries, was the introduction of the five-day week in March 1967. The boom in camping, fishing, hunting, rock-climbing, pot-holing, water-skiing, motoring and boating (and the relative decline in participation rates in chess,* draughts, gymnastics, table-tennis and boxing) is accounted for partly by longer holidays* with pay and partly by the developing cult of the weekend. In 1956, the standard (six-day) week in Soviet industry was

The Central Lenin Stadium, Moscow

46 hours; by 1961, it had decreased to 41 hours, still in a six-day week (most workers having five 7-hour days and one 6-hour day each week). In 1978, the average working week in industry was 40.6 hours and, in state employment in general, 39.3 hours in a five-day week. Altogether, Soviet industrial workers had 95.4 days off during 1978, including paid annual holidays of 15 days for most employees.

INCREASING URBANIZATION.* Nearly two-thirds of the Soviet population lives in a relatively modern, urban, industrial society. Whereas only 18 per cent of the population lived in towns in 1926, in 1978 63 per cent was urban-based–(164 million). Contemporary town-planning* tends to allow for sizeable courtyards for each block of flats and a minimum of sports amenities: one sports centre, one gymnasium and one swimming-pool per 50 000 people. None the less, the problem of providing adequate outdoor amenities for sport is becoming ever greater in the most densely-settled urban areas. For example, despite an instruction by the Moscow city soviet to prevent the commissioning of any new district without the requisite sports

Open-air winter swimming-lesson, Moscow

amenities, Moscow had only a quarter of the prescribed facilities in 1978 and only one-ninth in the new districts constructed since 1960. In the period 1966–71, some 2250 sports grounds should have been built, but only 250 (11 per cent) were actually constructed and it is increasingly difficult to accommodate the casual as well as the serious sportsman.

CHANGING RECREATIONAL PATTERN. Since the war, all these factors have affected the Soviet pattern of sport: people tend to form smaller (family) groups for recreation and holidays; there appears to be an increasing desire to 'get away from it all' rather than to 'get together'. As Soviet writers have admitted, the old production-based sports facilities 'are ill-adapted to family forms of free-time activity or to the leisure activities of the small group linked by personal and friendly rather than formal relationships'.

Public and mass sports activities are giving place to individual, domestic, family and passive leisure–especially televiewing, now reckoned to be the single most time-consuming leisure activity, taking up a third of all time so spent. It is noteworthy that in 1972 as many as 618 hours of television time transmitted sport (40 per cent of which was coverage of soccer or ice-hockey matches) by contrast with 357 hours in 1966; thus, 11–12 hours a week on television* and 14 hours on radio* are now devoted to sport.

'Irrational' leisure activities

One growing problem for the authorities has been to see that this additional free time is used in a 'rational' way. Time given to sports activities is held to be well spent because it contributes to production and to the smooth running of society in general, enriching the individual so that he may enrich his fellows. Nevertheless, a whole set of activities that appear to be at variance with such aims are permitted–for example, horse-racing as a spectators' and gamblers' sport. In fact, it is regarded as the only fully professional sport in the USSR and is extremely popular, attracting more spectators even than soccer. The Moscow Hippodrome Racecourse, for example, is open three times a week all the year round and has an average crowd of 13 000 on a Sunday. Flat-racing, hurdles, steeplechase and trotting races are held. Punters may place a bet of up to ten roubles on any race (for a 'win', 'double' or first or second 'place') through the state totalizator; three-quarters of the receipts are paid out in winnings.

Other sports have nevertheless been attacked and sometimes proscribed because of their alleged 'irrationality' or exhibitionist nature, or because they have lent themselves to commercial exploitation. Such activities include women's soccer and wrestling, male body-building, yoga, karate and bridge, all of which were censured in a government resolution of January 1973. Since then, karate has been included in the list of officially-registered sports, and women's soccer has been once more permitted (if not encouraged).

With more money, more free time and a wider range of recreation to choose from, Soviet people are increasingly able to select the sporting activity that most accords with their personal desires and inclinations, and pursue it 'privately', outside a club, using their own equipment. With improved facilities and opportunities, participation in a sport is being governed less by the utilitarian approach and more by the idea that a game, a sport or outdoor activity of any kind is desirable in itself, for its own sake. *J.R.*

Sport: structure and organization

Over-all direction of the sports movement is today provided by the USSR Committee on Physical Culture and Sport attached to the USSR Council of Ministers;* its chairman is Sergey Pavlov, one-time Secretary of the Komsomol.* Each of the 15 Union Republics has its own Sports Committee. The USSR Sports Committee is the umbrella

ADMINISTRATIVE STRUCTURE OF SOVIET SPORT

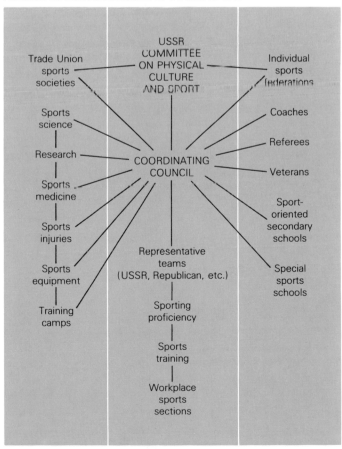

organization for all other elements of the sports movement: the individual sports federations, the various trade-union* sports societies, sports schools, coaching, research, competition, medicine and science.

Sports societies

Actual organization is in the hands of 36 sports societies, all but two of which are run by the trade unions; they comprise an urban and a rural society for each of the 15 Union Republics, four all-Union societies (Burevestnik, representing students; Lokomotiv, representing railwaymen; Vodnik, representing river-transport employees; and Spartak, representing 'white-collar' workers) and two non-trade-union societies, Dinamo and Labour Reserves, the latter representing students at technical colleges. The one major sports organization outside this framework is the Central Army Sports Club with its garrison sports clubs in many parts of the country.

Each sports society has its own rules, membership cards, badge and colours. It is financed out of trade union dues (of the one per cent of each employed person's wages that goes in union dues, a substantial portion is allocated to sport) and is responsible for building sports centres, acquiring equipment for its members and maintaining a permanent staff of coaches, instructors and medical personnel. All members and their families have the right to use the society's facilities for a nominal fee of 30 kopecks a year (in 1977, representing 0.2 per cent of the average monthly wage), to elect and be elected to its managing committee.

Competitions

Contests are held among sports societies and clubs. Each society has its own local and nationwide championships for each sport it practises, and its teams play against teams representing other societies. There exist therefore nationwide sports leagues and cup competitions in a whole range of popular sports like soccer, ice-hockey, basket-ball and volley-ball. All the trade-union sports societies have 'teams of masters' in every major town, as do the sports clubs of the armed services and Dinamo.

Payment to sportsmen

A master sportsman—one who more or less devotes all his time to training for and playing a sport during his active career as a sportsman—is paid by his sports society and the USSR Sports Committee, according to his sports ranking, results and several other factors, so that he can devote time to sport (unencumbered by an external job, though not free from studies and 'social duties') and be coached under the auspices of and using the facilities of the society. In the case of Dinamo and the army sports clubs, the sportsman would normally hold a commission but would not be expected to undertake normal military service. As an example of payment for sport (though details are never published, presumably for fear of accusation that Olympic* rules are contravened), a footballer in the top national league would receive a basic monthly salary from his sports society of 180 roubles. If he has a Master of Sport ranking or has represented his country, he will receive another 30 and 40 roubles respectively, paid to him by the USSR Sports Committee. Additionally, he is likely to receive unofficial payments from various organizations associated with his sports society or town team as bonuses for team success and for playing extra matches outside the normal league and cup programme. A player's utility value may also secure him certain perquisites, such as a good apartment and a car.

Spartakiads

The trade unions are directly responsible for organizing competitions both within their own sports societies and on a nationwide basis, including in the spartakiads.* More recently, the word 'spartakiad' has been used to denote tournaments for schools, farms, factories, Pioneer* camps, and amateur local groups, but the main connotation is the Spartakiad of the Peoples of the USSR, modelled on the Olympic programme and held over the two years preceding each Olympic Games.* How important this sports festival is for popularizing sport may be judged from the numbers of people said to participate. Some 23 million took part in the First Summer Spartakiad in 1956, with 9000 contesting the finals in 21 sports. The Sixth Spartakiad, held over 1975 and 1976, had become so massive that for the first time the finals had to be held in all 15 republican capitals and 12 other major cities; some 55 million people are said to have competed, with 7094 contesting the finals in 27 sports.

Social background of top sportsmen

A survey into the 4294 finalists of the Fifth Spartakiad revealed that 76.2 per cent were men, 4.7 per cent were Communist Party* members, 61.1 per cent were Komsomol* members and 34.2 per cent were unaffiliated. In social composition, only 7.3 per cent were anual workers, 45 per cent were 'white collar' workers, 23.7 per cent students, 4.5 per cent schoolchildren, 18.8 per cent servicemen and the very small percentage 0.8 were collective farmers; 30 per cent had a higher education, 65.2 per cent a complete (up to 17 years of age) secondary education, and 4.65 per cent only a seven-year schooling.

National fitness programme (the GTO)

The two interlinked elements that underlie the whole sports system are the GTO national fitness programme and the uniform rankings* system for individual sports. Both were instituted in the early 1930s and both were intended to serve the twin aims of *massovost* (mass participation) and *masterstvo* (proficiency). While the GTO sets targets for all-round ability in a number of sports and knowledge of the rudiments of hygiene and first aid (for which token gold and silver

badges are awarded), the rankings system contains a whole set of qualifying standards, rankings and titles in individual sports, intended to stimulate the best performers to aim for certain graduated standards.

It is through the GTO that most Soviet people take part in sport and it is regarded as the foundation of the sports system. The targets are not for a single sport, nor even for sporting ability alone, but for all-round ability in a number of events and for knowledge of hygiene, first aid and sports theory. The programme (which is revised every ten years on average) has five stages by age which all necessitate a certain minimum performance in running, jumping, throwing, shooting, skiing and gymnastics. Older people may compete only with a doctor's permission. GTO planning quotas are set for every club, society, region and school, and tests are held throughout the year. The main concern of most sports clubs is, in fact, to see that their members obtain their GTO badges. There seems little doubt that most young people are caught up in this fitness campaign: in the decade 1970–80, an estimated average of 18 million people qualified annually for a badge.

The GTO has as its stated aim to make regular participation in sport a permanent feature of the Soviet way of life; the motives behind the programme would seem to include the following. First, to attract children into sport at an early age, to ensure their later participation and to provide a pool of early talent for development to achieve international success in many sports. Second, the GTO is used for direct military* training: a civil-defence test and gas-mask training are to be found at every stage, and rifle-shooting at three stages. The element of military preparation is especially evident for the 16–18 age-group, many of whose members will thus be entering the armed forces with some training behind them. Third, an oft-stated reason for drawing people into the fitness campaign is to cut down sickness absenteeism* from work by making workers physically and mentally more alert through sport to cope with the changing techniques of industry, and thereby raising productivity. Fourth, the GTO is seen as channelling the zest and energy of young people into relatively healthy recreation.

Sports ranking system

This system is intended to stimulate the best athletes to aim for certain set standards in a particular sport and to help coaches to select promising sportsmen to train with specific targets in mind. A whole complex of qualifying standards, rankings and titles exists for the 80 officially-registered sports. These are up-dated every four years on average to coincide with the Olympic cycle.

The two top titles (Master of Sport of the USSR, International Class, and Master of Sport of the USSR) are honorary and for life. The only higher award to which an outstanding and internationally-successful athlete may aspire is Merited Master of Sport of the USSR, but this is a state honorific decoration outside the classification system (like Merited Artist or Merited Teacher of the USSR). In chess* and draughts (checkers), the title Grandmaster of the USSR is the equivalent of Master of Sport of the USSR, International Class for other sports. In addition, the title Master of Folk Sport exists for a variety of folk games and sports.

Besides these titles and decorations, the top Soviet sportsmen, coaches and officials are regularly included in the country's 'honours list'.* After the Montreal Olympic Games in 1976, for example, a total of 347 Olympic athletes, coaches and officials received awards, ranging from the supreme honour – the Order of Lenin – to the Order of the Red Banner of Labour. The recipients of the Order of Lenin were four athletes – Ludmilla Turishcheva (b.1952), Nikolay Andrianov (b.1951), Levan Tediashvili (b.1950) and Ivan Yarygin (b.1950) (two gymnasts and two wrestlers) – three coaches and the Sports Committee chairman Sergey Pavlov.

The two top titles are awarded mainly on the basis of international success, but an athlete must first meet all the rankings standards for his sport. Sports rankings 1–3 are awarded for results achieved in official Soviet competition (All-Union championships, spartakiads, cups) and are valid for one or two years only, after which they either lapse or have to be renewed—or, of course, the athlete may try for a higher ranking. To obtain a second or third ranking, the athlete must also have satisfied the requirements of the GTO programme for his particular age category. The qualifying standards for each category are high and are regularly revised to keep pace with changing world standards. Junior rankings are awarded to athletes under 18 years of age who have also met the qualifying standards of the appropriate GTO programme for their age.

The physical token of having gained one of the titles is a badge and a certificate awarded by the USSR Sports Committee, plus a financial award (30 roubles a month in the case of a Master of Sport). Ranked sportsmen receive a badge from the sports society to which they belong. All such athletes have the right to take part in official competitions and to receive preference in admission to sports schools and colleges of physical education. Along with these rights, however, go certain duties: to conduct oneself in accordance with sporting ethics; to pass on one's expertise and experience to others; to compete on behalf of one's group or club; to improve one's political and cultural standards; to accept constant medical supervision.

Any violation of these obligations may result in deprivation of the ranking or title—a not-infrequent occurrence. In soccer, several players have been deprived of their awards for receiving under-cover payments or for behaving badly in public or during matches. Leading athletes, therefore, are expected to be models of good behaviour at all times.

Finance and facilities

All sports committees throughout the country (each administrative region has its own) receive cash from the state budget to finance their work. In 1978, state budgetary allocations to sport and health amounted to 12 600 million roubles. This sum is a very small part (0.03 per cent) of the state budget and represents exactly the same proportion as in 1924. However, the sports committees receive finance from the profits of the sports equipment and amenities construction organization Glavsportprom, the state sport publishing agency Sovetsky Sport, and the various commercial enterprises and sports events they run.

SPORTS TITLES AND RANKINGS PYRAMID

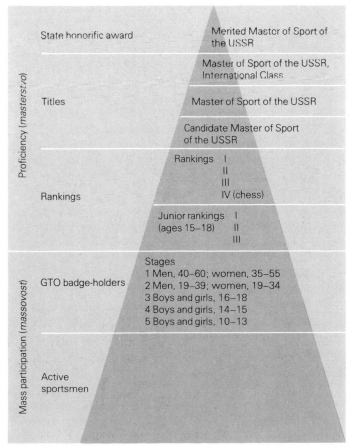

State honorific award	Merited Master of Sport of the USSR
	Master of Sport of the USSR, International Class
Titles	Master of Sport of the USSR
	Candidate Master of Sport of the USSR
	Rankings I / II / III / IV (chess)
Rankings	Junior rankings I / II / III (ages 15–18)
GTO badge-holders	Stages 1 Men, 40–60; women, 35–55 2 Men, 19–39; women, 19–34 3 Boys and girls, 16–18 4 Boys and girls, 14–15 5 Boys and girls, 10–13
Active sportsmen	

Proficiency (*masterstvo*) / Mass participation (*massovost*)

Active sportsmen are officially defined as members of sports groups who engage in sport under the supervision of an instructor not less than twice a week over a minimum period of six months. In 1978, the number was put by the Chairman of the Sports Committee at 60 million people – close to one quarter of the population. By contrast to this global figure, several surveys have indicated one-tenth of the population as a more realistic estimate – 26 million

All state and public organizations which employ labour contribute to the state social insurance fund in the proportion of 4–9 per cent of their wage funds, depending on the branch of the economy. Part of this social insurance fund is used for sport. It is estimated that over half of all sports amenities being built in 1978 were being financed out of the funds of state enterprises and government departments.

The trade unions assign sums of money (out of membership dues and income from various undertakings) to their sports societies and clubs. In 1978, they allotted 580 million roubles to sport, or about a fifth of their total funds.

Sports committees, societies and clubs also receive income from renting out and using sports facilities and from making, lending and selling equipment. Dinamo is in the fortunate position of being the biggest manufacturer of sports equipment in the country, operating over 50 plants and many retail sports shops; most of the 20 million roubles it spent on sport in 1975 in fact came from its own business enterprises.

One means by which the government can raise money for sport is by running sports lotteries. This began in 1964 as one method of helping to finance the Soviet Olympic team's attendance at the Tokyo Games. Since 1970, monthly lotteries have been run to obtain money for more sports amenities. Three different monthly lotteries were running simultaneously in the four years up to the 1980 Olympics,★ called 'Sportloto', 'Sportloto-2' and 'Sprint'. In each lottery, half the revenue from ticket sales went to sport and half in prizes ranging from saloon cars (or 5000 roubles cash) to sports equipment.

It has to be noted that, like the country's industrialization in general, facilities for sport were quite recently at an extremely low and primitive level (many still are), and that much had been destroyed in the war. In just one decade (1960–70) the number of stadiums, soccer-pitches, gymnasiums and tennis-courts roughly trebled; indoor swimming-pools, ski-jumps and indoor athletics stadiums grew from virtually nothing to over 1000, nearly 100 and 50 respectively. By 1978, the country had a total of 3198 sports centres, 66 000 gymnasiums, 1400 swimming-pools, 103 000 soccer-pitches and 600 000 playing-fields.

Much depends on local initiative and the inclination (and ability) of factories, farms, city councils or republics to allocate money for sports purposes; some are much better equipped than others. On the whole, however, the European, more industrialized republics are better off in sports facilities than are Turkmenia, Kirgizia and Tadzhikistan; the towns are, on the whole, much better off than the villages; and some farms have no sports facilities at all.

Special sports schools

All schoolchildren and students are expected to reach certain standards in physical education and sport, and the institutions themselves have to meet official targets. Young people who wish to pursue a sport seriously after school hours may do so in one of several specialized sports establishments. At the base of the pyramid is the children's and young people's sports school which young people can attend outside their normal school hours (they are, in fact, 'clubs' in the Western sense). There were over 5000 such schools with a membership of one and three-quarter million children in 1979. Attempts are made to spread the net as wide as possible both to catch potential talent and to distribute facilities fairly evenly between the republics. Children are normally considered for these schools on the recommendation of their school physical-education teacher or at the request of their parents. Attendance and coaching are free, entry age depends upon the sport—for swimming and gymnastics, 7 or 8 years (or earlier), for cycling and speed-skating, 13–14 years. Moscow Dinamo has a gymnastics section for 4- to 6-year-olds, and the Minsk Dinamo 'soccer nursery' takes young boys aged 6 or 7 years. Coaching is usually intensive and classes are often long and frequent; for example, 11- to 13-year-olds may attend three evenings a week for two-hour sessions; those working for their Master of Sport ranking may attend four or five.

Originally it was intended for the sports schools to cultivate up to ten sports, but today most concentrate on no more than three, some only on a single sport; these are known as specialist children's and young people's sports schools, and all leading soccer and ice-hockey clubs run their own. They are a vital key to Soviet sporting success, especially in the Olympics; in fact, of the 35 sports pursued in the schools in 1976, only six were outside the Olympic programme: acrobatics, chess, modern rhythmic gymnastics, hand-ball, tennis and table-tennis. The most popular were athletics, basket-ball,

Gymnastics lesson at a children's sports school, Moscow

gymnastics, volley-ball, swimming and skiing.

Finance and administration are provided through the local education authorities (over 50 per cent of schools), the trade-union sports societies, and the big sports clubs run by Dinamo and the armed forces.

Full-time 'sport-oriented' day-schools combine a normal school curriculum with sports training, on the model of 'foreign language-oriented' schools; they are said to take children aged 7 upwards from the neighbouring catchment area and offer superior facilities.

The sports proficiency schools (16- to 18-year-olds) and higher sports proficiency schools (18 years and over) provide both extra-curricular training for schoolchildren and students and short-term vacation courses.

In 1967 a new sports society for young people, Yunost ('Youth') was set up to coordinate the activities of all these schools and to ensure that minimum standards were established in regard to facilities, coaches, age and other entrance qualifications. At the apex of the pyramid are the sports boarding-schools of which there were 26 in 1979. The USSR opened its first boarding-school on an experimental basis in Tashkent in 1962, modelled on similar schools running in the GDR since 1949. Others followed in each of the 15 Union Republics, then in some provincial centres, and in 1970 a special government resolution set an official seal of approval on their existence. Only sports in the Olympic programme are pursued; like the mathematical, musical and other special schools they adhere to the standard Soviet curriculum but they have an additional study load in sports theory and practice. Pupils are accepted from between 7 and 12 years, and stay on until 18–a year longer than at normal day-schools; they are served by the best coaches and amenities, nurtured on a special diet, kept constantly under the supervision of doctors and sports instructors, and stimulated by mutual interest and keen enthusiasm.   J.R.

The Olympic Games

Russia was a founding member of the modern Olympic movement and Russian athletes first participated in the Olympic Games in 1908–the Fourth Olympics, held in London. A team of five contestants, sponsored by voluntary contributions, did surprisingly well, winning a gold medal in figure-skating and two silvers in wrestling and taking 14th place over-all out of 22 nations. For the next Olympics, held in Stockholm in 1912, the Russian sports societies were prepared to sponsor a much larger contingent. The government, appreciating the prestige value at home of sports success, set up a Russian Olympic Committee (ROC) headed by Baron F. Meyendorf. With quite generous government backing and organization, a team of 169 athletes (half of them army officers) gathered to take part in 15 sports in the Olympic programme. In fact, half the group failed to reach Stockholm and Russia ultimately shared a disappointing 15th place with Austria, out of 28 countries, and won few medals (in wrestling, gymnastics, shooting and yachting).

Although it was to be another 40 years before Russia was to compete again in the Olympics, the International Olympic Committee (IOC) continued to recognize the old Russian Olympic Committee for several years after 1917, and such ROC notables as Prince Urusov, Count Ribopierre, Baron Villebrand and General Butovsky all served on the IOC in the period before the Second World War.

Soviet participation in international sport

Soviet participation in international sport before the war falls roughly into three periods: 1917–28, when the Soviet authorities pursued a policy of promoting world revolution and proletarian internationalism; 1929–39, when the policy changed towards strengthening the USSR as a nation-state; 1939–41, when the Soviet leaders developed relations with the Axis powers.

On the assumption that world revolution was not far distant and that, until then, the world would be split irreconcilably into two hostile camps, the Soviet authorities after 1917 at first ignored 'bourgeois' sports organizations, refused to affiliate to their international federations and boycotted most of their competitions, especially the Olympic Games, which were characterized as designed 'to deflect the workers from the class struggle while training them for new imperialist wars'.

Initially then, excursions beyond Soviet borders were almost entirely confined to playing against foreign workers' teams, such as the Finnish Labour Team, TUL, and the French communist trade-union CFGT team. As the 1920s wore on, the need to coexist (especially with the USSR's neighbours), a desire to compete against the world's best teams and the consideration that the 'bourgeoisie' in certain backward states were playing a progressive role brought some limited contacts.

For the most part, however, as long as the USSR remained isolated and weak internationally, foreign sports relations were restricted to workers' sports organizations and reflected the policy of the Communist International (Comintern). Soviet foreign sports policy was, in fact, largely identical with and conducted through the International Association of Red Sports and Gymnastics Organizations, better known as Red Sport International (RSI). The RSI was formed at the First International Congress of representatives of revolutionary workers' sports organizations in July 1921. The founders were workers' sports organizations from eight countries: Czechoslovakia, Finland, France, Germany, Hungary, Italy, the USSR and Sweden (by 1924, it included Norway, Uruguay and the USA). After 1928, the former policy changed both in relation to 'bourgeois' states and towards the social democratic countries, and as a result, sports ties developed with the first, but were curtailed with the second. Although the USSR did not try to affiliate to international sports federations, it did send its best sportsmen abroad to compete against the world's best.

When war broke out in Europe and the German-Soviet Non-Aggression Pact was signed, Soviet sports contacts were confined to the Axis powers. In fact, more sports contests took place between Soviet and German sportsmen during 1940 than between the sportsmen of the USSR and all 'bourgeois' states put together in all the years since 1917: some 250 German sportsmen competed in the USSR and 175 Soviet sportsmen in Germany between September 1939 and the end of 1940.

Immediately after the war, Soviet sports associations affiliated to nearly all the major international federations and Soviet athletes were competing regularly at home and abroad against foreign 'bourgeois' opposition. Soviet sport became an instrument of foreign policy, both to advertise the advantages of socialism among socialist states and to influence Third World countries through the provision of instructors and assistance in building sports amenities.

Between 1946 and 1958 the USSR joined 30 international federations and by 1975, 48, thereby embracing nearly all the major world sports. Furthermore, 236 Soviet officials held posts in international sports organizations in 1978.

Not only did affiliations take place, but Soviet athletes quickly established a world dominance, often on their début in world sport. In 1948, Botvinnik won the world chess* title and, in 1949, Ludmilla Rudenko (b. 1904) won the women's world chess title; both have been long held by the USSR with the exception of 1972–4 when the men's title was held by Robert Fischer of the USA. In 1945, Moscow Dinamo football team came to Britain and played four matches without defeat against leading British clubs. In weight-lifting, wrestling, volley-ball and ice-hockey, Soviet teams established a supremacy they have held ever since.

Entry into the Olympic movement

Despite these initial successes, the USSR moved cautiously into Olympic competition. Only in April 1951 was a Soviet Olympic Committee formed and, in May, accepted by the IOC. The USSR made its Olympic début at the 15th Summer Olympic Games, held in Helsinki, in 1952. Soviet athletes contested all events in the programme with the exception of field hockey and, although they gained fewer gold medals than the USA (22:40), they gained more silver (30:19) and bronze (19:17) and tied with the USA in points allotted for the first six places (according to the system used in the *Olympic Bulletin*).

The USSR took no part in the 1952 Winter Olympics and made its winter début only in 1956 at Cortina d'Ampezzo in Italy. There it amassed most medals and points, winning gold medals in speed-skating, skiing and ice-hockey.

From the débuts in 1952 and 1956 up to 1980, the USSR has 'won' every Olympic Games with the sole exception of 1968, when it came second to Norway in winter and second to the USA in summer. It has also provided the most versatile as well as the most successful performance in the Olympics: at the 1976 Montreal Olympics, Soviet athletes won medals in 19 of the 21 sports, coming first in eight sports, second in seven, and third in four; of the 430 Soviet athletes competing, as many as 259 won medals. All these results suggest that the USSR has gone a considerable way to achieving its aim of world supremacy in Olympic sports. Discussing this success, Soviet writers have left no doubt that they see it as a victory for the communist system generally.

SOVIET PERFORMANCE IN THE OLYMPIC GAMES, 1952–80

Year	Summer Games				Nearest rival		Winter Games				Nearest rival	
	gold medals	medal total	points[1]	position	medals	points[1]	gold medals	medal total	points[1]	position	medals	points[1]
1952	22	71	494	1	76	494[2]	—[3]	—[3]	—[3]	—[3]	—[3]	—[3]
1956	37	98	624.5	1	74	498[2]	7	16	103	1	11	66.5[4]
1960	43	103	683	1	71	463.5[2]	7	21	146.5	1	7	62.5[5]
1964	30	96	608.3	1	90	581.8[2]	11	25	183	1	15	89.3[6]
1968	29	91	591.5	2	106	709[2]	5	13	92	2	14	103[6]
1972	50	99	665.5	1	93	636.5[2]	8	16	120	1	14	83[7]
1976	47	125	788.5	1	90	636.5[7]	13	27	201	1	19	138[7]
1980	80	195	1476	1	121	779[7]	10	22	148	2	23	155[7]

[1] The points allocation is that used in the *Olympic Bulletin*: awarding seven points for first place, five for second and so on down to one point for sixth place
[2] USA [3] USSR not participating [4] Austria [5] Sweden [6] Norway [7] East Germany

Outstanding Soviet Olympic champions: (far left) Vasily Alekseyev (b. 1942); (left) Olympic gold medalist Irina Rodnina (b. 1948) with partner Aleksandr Zaitsev (b. 1949); (below) Olya Korbut (b. 1955)

The Moscow Olympics, 1980

The 22nd Olympic Games were held in Moscow from 19 July to 3 August 1980. Yachting events were held in Tallinn, and soccer preliminaries in Kiev, Minsk and Leningrad. This was the first time in the 84 years of modern Olympic history that a communist country had staged the Olympics. Despite a partial boycott led by the USA over the USSR's invasion of Afghanistan,* a total of 68 nations attended the Games (72 attended in Montreal, 1976); notable absentees with the USA were the FRG and Japan. A number of national teams participated against the advice of their governments (including Britain with a team of 322). The USSR affirmed its readiness to take part in the 1984 summer Olympics to be held in Los Angeles.

The central venue of the Games was the Lenin Stadium (seating 104000) where the colourful opening and closing ceremonies took place and the athletics events and soccer semi-finals and finals were held. New sports amenities constructed to accommodate the 21 Olympic sports included the rowing canal and indoor cycling track (6000 seats) at Krylatskoe, the Olympic swimming-pool (10000 seats) and boxing arena (45000 seats) on Prospekt Mira, the field-hockey pitch at the Dinamo Stadium, the equestrian complex in the Bitsa forest park and the shooting-range at Mytishchi. The USSR thus gained several modern sports complexes comparable with the best in the world. The Olympic Village was located to the south-west of Moscow State University; its 18 16-storey blocks of apartments accommodated the Olympic athletes and officials, and after the Games it became a residential cooperative housing* estate. New hotels were built with a total of 27000 beds, including the French-built Cosmos Hotel (3500 beds) and the vast Izmailovo hotel complex (10000 beds). Such modernization should facilitate the future staging of virtually any sports event at any level.   *J.R.*

The Opening Ceremony, 1980 Olympic Games, Moscow

Acrobatic display at the 1980 Olympic Games, Moscow

Chess

Development

The history of chess in Russia goes back more than 1000 years. Recent archaeological researches have established that the game reached ancient Russia from the East as early as the 9th or 10th centuries. By the 16th century chess enjoyed considerable popularity among Russians of many classes, from the tsars Ivan the Terrible,* who is said to have died at the chessboard, and Boris Godunov,* down to the less elevated citizens described by the English traveller George Turbeville in his letters in verse (1568) 'to certeine friends of his in London, describing the manners of the countery and people':

'... The common game is chesse, almost the simplest will

Both give a check and eke a mate, by practise comes their skill.'

In the 17th and 18th centuries Russians who played chess came to Europe from time to time, often impressing with their ability. In a French chronicle, for instance, describing the visit of a Russian embassy to the court of Louis XIV we read: 'These Russians play superb chess. In comparison with them our best players are like schoolboys.'

It was not until the 19th century that Russian masters of chess achieved individual recognition outside their own country. The strongest and most influential master in the first half of the last century was Aleksandr Petrov (1794–1867) whose book *The Game of Chess* (1824) served Russian players as a primer for many years. By the 1860s, however, not only Petrov, but also Karl Jaenisch (1813–72), Ilya Shumov (1819–81) and the two Urusov brothers (Prince Sergey (1827–97) and Prince Dmitry (1830–1903) enjoyed European reputations.

The greatest figure in Russian 19th-century chess and much the most influential was undoubtedly Mikhail Chigorin (1850–1908) who devoted his life to the game as player, writer and organizer. From 1881 until a few months before his death Chigorin competed regularly in international tournaments and twice (in 1889 and 1892) challenged Wilhelm Steinitz (1836–1900) in matches for the world championship, both times unsuccessfully.

Comparatively few international congresses were organized in late 19th- and early 20th-century tsarist Russia, but among them were three of the strongest events of all time: the St Petersburg tournaments of 1895–6, 1909 and 1914. The victor on all three occasions was the world champion, Emanuel Lasker (1868–1941).

By 1914 Russian chess boasted 22 masters, among whose ranks were to be found several of the strongest players in the world, most notably Aleksandr Alekhine (1892–1946) who was to hold the men's individual world championship from 1927 to 1935 and from 1937 to his death in 1946. The First World War and the revolutions of 1917, followed by four years of civil war, brought most official chess-playing in the country to a standstill. In the autumn of 1920, however, an All-Russian Chess Olympiad, now regarded as the first Soviet championship, was successfully organized in Moscow. The winner was Alekhine, who a few months later emigrated from his homeland to settle in France, never to return.

The most significant competition promoted by the Soviet chess authorities in the 1920s was the 1925 Moscow international tournament, in which many of the leading players of the day participated, including the world champion, José-Raoul Capablanca (1888–1942) and the former champion, Lasker. Clearly designed to focus world attention on Soviet chess, this was the first international tournament in the history of the game to be financed by state funds, the Soviet government allocating 30 000 roubles for the event.

During the 1920s and 1930s the Soviet chess authorities strove hard to popularize chess and to raise playing standards. Both these policies met with considerable success. The number of officially registered chess-players rose from about 1000 in 1923 to some 24 000 in 1924; it reached approximately 150 000 in 1929, and around 500 000 by late 1934. At the same time, more Soviet players qualified for the title of master: in 1929 Soviet chess counted 25 masters; by 1934 there were 43, and by the outbreak of the Second World War almost 50. The first player to gain the title of Grandmaster of Chess was Mikhail Botvinnik (b.1911) in 1935; by 1940 he had been joined by Grigory Levenfish (1889–1961) Aleksandr Kotov (b.1913), Vasily Smyslov (b.1921) and two new Soviet citizens, the Hungarian Andrea Liliental (b.1911) and the Estonian Paul Keres (1916–75).

Two more very strong international tournaments were promoted in Moscow in 1935 and 1936. The 1935 event resulted in a tie for first place between Botvinnik and Salo Flohr (b.1908); in the 1936 tournament Capablanca took first prize and Botvinnik second. It was in the 1930s that Soviet masters also began to make their mark in international tournaments abroad. The most consistent results were obtained by Botvinnik, whose shared first place with Capablanca at Nottingham in 1936 inspired a substantial front-page leader in *Pravda* (29 August 1936) propounding that 'the USSR is becoming the classic land of chess'.

World champions

What must be regarded as the golden age of Soviet chess began after the Second World War. The first indication of the potential strength of the Soviet Union in that realm came as early as September 1945 when a radio match against the USA produced a victory for the Soviet team by 15½ points to 4½. It seemed clear, as Botvinnik wrote, that 'the centre of chess thought had passed to the Soviet Union'. For a quarter of a century Soviet players achieved a dominance which has few parallels in any other field of international competition. Soviet masters scored triumph after triumph in international tournaments both at home and abroad; the Soviet Union achieved first place in every one of the world team championships for men in which it competed; and—much the most widely recognized proof of Soviet supremacy—from 1948, when Botvinnik won the title left vacant since Alekhine's death two years earlier, to 1972, when Boris Spassky (b.1937) ceded it to Robert Fischer (USA; b.1943), the world individual championship for men was held exclusively by Soviet players: Botvinnik (1948–57, 1958–60 and 1961–3); Smyslov (1957–8); Mikhail Tal' (b.1936: 1960–1); Tigran Petrosyan (b.1929: 1963–9); and Spassky (1969–72). The women's individual championship also belonged exclusively to Soviet players: Lyudmila Rudenko (b.1904: 1950–3); Elizaveta Bykova (b.1913:1953–6 and 1958–62); Olga Rubtsova (b.1909: 1956–8); and Nona Gaprindashvili (b.1941: 1962–78).

Soviet supremacy was less marked in junior chess, where Soviet competitors only twice won the world individual championship between 1951 and 1972—with Spassky in 1955 and Anatoly Karpov (b.1951) in 1969—but the Soviet team almost invariably carried off the annual world student-team championship. In correspondence play two Soviet players gained the world championship, Vyacheslav Ragozin (1908–62) in the 1956–9 cycle, and Vladimir Zagorovsky (b.1925) in the 1965–8 cycle.

At the same time, during this period of Soviet dominance many of the most significant advances in chess theory stemmed from Soviet research, while Soviet chess literature, which was published in very large editions (by the standards of other countries), came to be regarded as indispensable reading by countless serious chess-players throughout the world. The leading Soviet chess journal, *Shakhmaty v*

Below: world champion Mikhail Tal' (right) playing ex-champion Mikhail Botvinnik in 1961. Bottom: Anatoly Karpov (right) during his match with Boris Spassky, Leningrad, 1974

Nona Gaprindashvili, women's world champion and winner of the USSR women's championship in 1964

SSSR, for example, is published monthly in editions of 65 000.

Valuable contributions were also made by Soviet experts to both the chess problem and the endgame study, particularly to the latter, where Genrikh Kasparyan (b.1910) and Vladimir Korolkov (b.1907), like their older compatriots Aleksey Troitsky (1866–1942) and Leonid Kubbel (1891–1942), achieved world renown.

Organizations and ranking

The communist authorities did not immediately assume control of organized chess-playing in Soviet Russia. Indeed, 1923 saw the re-constitution of the pre-revolutionary All-Russian Chess Federation which had been established in 1914. A year later, however, this apolitical body was replaced by a new organization, the All-Union Chess Section attached to the Supreme Council for Physical Culture. The chairman of the Chess Section was N. V. Krylenko (1885–1938), a Commissar for War in the first Bolshevik* government and later Commissar of Justice for the USSR. The new Chess Section, acknowledging that the game must make its contribution to the nascent socialist society, coined two slogans – 'Chess is a powerful tool of intellectual culture' and 'Take chess to the workers!' – and undertook five main tasks: the popularization of chess among the working masses; controlling the work of chess activities throughout the country; convening conferences; organizing tournaments; and the publication of chess literature. The All-Union Chess Section remained the governing body for Soviet chess until 1959 when a reorganization of physical culture in the USSR led to the establishment of the Soviet Chess Federation.

Most serious Soviet chess-players belong to clubs associated with their work. Clubs are organized by trade unions,* by the armed forces* (where chess is surprisingly popular) and by institutions such as universities and schools. (Almost one-quarter of registered Soviet players are schoolchildren). Competitions are regularly organized for both teams and individuals – men, women and juniors – at various levels: club, town or district, republic and national. The Soviet ranking system* for individual players comprises 8 grades: grand-master, master and candidate master of chess, and categories 1 to 5, the latter being the weakest.

The role of Soviet chess

The importance attached to chess in the USSR is reflected in the status accorded to leading players and the responsibilities imposed upon them; many have received high Soviet honours. Whereas in non-communist countries chess is generally seen as at best a highly skilled game, in the Soviet Union it is regarded as an integral part of Soviet culture with a political and educational role to play.

From the earliest days of the Soviet chess movement commentators have stressed the beneficial influence the game exercises on the individual player. Chess, which is regarded as possessing both scientific and artistic features, is said to enhance the enthusiast's power of logical thought and creative imagination and also to develop in him qualities of endurance and will-power. Moreover, it is emphasized that the characteristics displayed by the ideal chess-player coincide at many points with those of the ideal communist. Both are rationalists with confidence in the power of the mind to solve problems and impose its will on to the environment. (In this context the chess-player is contrasted favourably with the allegedly fatalistic devotee of cards.) The chess-player and the communist recognize the need to be well prepared theoretically and to develop a feeling for both strategy and tactics. They are resourceful and inventive and evince patience and an unshakeable resolve to overcome all obstacles on the path to ultimate victory. Not surprisingly, Soviet writers on the political and educational value of chess never tire of reminding their readers that Marx* and Lenin* were chess-players.

Chess players in Moscow's Gorky Park

During the 1920s and 1930s the allegedly proletarian character of Soviet chess was regularly contrasted with the social atmosphere of the game in the West, where it was said to flourish only among the bourgeoisie. In these circumstances it was inevitable that in 1925 the Soviet chess authorities should decline an invitation to join the newly-formed international chess federation, FIDE (*Fédération internationale des Échecs*) on the grounds that FIDE's apolitical front masked a hostility to the interests of the working class. Instead the Soviet All-Union Chess Section joined the Workers' Chess International which had been founded in Hamburg three years earlier. The USSR became affiliated to FIDE only in 1947.

The Soviet school of chess

In the late 1940s and early 1950s the concept of a distinct Soviet school of chess was formulated. This school was said to have been nurtured in the favourable environment of Soviet society where it enjoyed both a very large membership and the benevolent support of the state. Its players, so the theory ran, were noted for their patriotic fervour, sense of social responsibility and an aggressive and optimistic style of play based on self-confidence and a disciplined, scientific approach to the game in matters of training and research. At the same time, commentators acknowledged the debt owed by the Soviet school to the great Russian players of the past, especially to the influence of Chigorin and Alekhine – though the latter was for many years castigated as a renegade and achieved full recognition only in the mid-1950s.

The Soviet school of chess has undoubtedly exercised a significant influence on the development of the game since the Second World War. It has contributed directly or indirectly to the greatly increased popularity of chess and to the improvement in general standards of play which have been marked in many parts of the world, but especially in Eastern Europe. Within this broad influence two specific features of modern tournament play must be acknowledged as deriving largely from Soviet experience. It was Soviet players, supported by state finance, who first established on any large scale the now widespread practice of disciplined preparation for tournament play through both general training and specific planning for individual games. Secondly, the Soviet concept of chess as a battle of wills meant that great importance was ascribed to possessing the initiative, and this in turn led to the development of many fresh active lines of play for Black, particularly in the asymmetrical defences such as the Sicilian, the French, the Dutch, the King's Indian, and the Semi-Slav, which aim primarily not at parrying White's thrusts and achieving equality, but at wresting the initiative from the first player

as early as possible. Indeed, this counter-attacking style with Black is perhaps the Soviet school's most valuable contribution to chess thinking.

Many reasons may be adduced to account for the impressive achievements of modern Soviet chess-players in both theoretical research and practical competition at the highest levels. In the first place the generous financial support lent by the state since the early 1920s has undoubtedly given Soviet chess organizers a substantial advantage over their counterparts in most other countries. Secondly, as the authorities have long recognized, the size of the Soviet chess movement is of crucial significance, inasmuch as a reservoir of three million players almost automatically engenders a steady stream of masters and the occasional genius. Thirdly, it has also been suggested that chess is particularly attractive to intellectuals living in totalitarian societies. Certainly chess in the Soviet Union has never been subjected to the same degree of ideological control as have activities such as art, literature, philosophy or even science. *

Matches in the 1970s

The era of Soviet supremacy in chess may be seen as ending in September 1972 when Spassky lost the world championship to Fischer. For some years before this, Soviet superiority in international tournament play had been weakening and this trend persisted through the 1970s, in spite of Karpov's success in the world championship. (Anatoly Karpov gained the title in 1975 when Fischer refused to defend it; three years later he retained the championship by winning a match against Viktor Korchnoi (b.1931).) Nevertheless it was still a surprise when the Soviet team finished in second place, behind Hungary, in the world team championships of 1978 – the first time the USSR had failed to win this biennial competition since first entering in 1952.

In spite of these developments – which can be regarded as failures only against the background of superlative earlier achievements – the Soviet Union remains immensely powerful in the world of chess. Even if leading Soviet grandmasters are no longer in a class of their own at the highest levels of international competition, the over-all strength of Soviet chess is still unparalleled: in 1976 among the Soviet Union's three million ranked chess-players were counted 48 grandmasters (37 men and 11 women), 628 masters (559 men and 69 women) and over 3000 candidate masters. This strength in depth is certain to bring enduring competitive success for years to come, while the best creative achievements of Soviet grandmasters will surely long continue to delight millions of devotees of the ancient royal game throughout the world.   *D.R.*

MILITARY POWER AND POLICY

Military ceremonial: early morning in Red Square before a parade

The imperial armed forces

The army

Such military successes as Russia scored in the 17th century must be put down to the enfeeblement and disarray of its main adversary, Poland, rather than to the effectiveness of its own motley armies. At the end of the century, out of 200 000 men who could be put into the field perhaps 20 000 were useful soldiers. The creation of an efficient regular army was made necessary by the territorial ambitions of Peter the Great.* He gave an earnest of his intentions in 1687, when he was 15, by forming from among his 'play troops' the two élite units which later became the Preobrazhensky and the Semyonovsky Guards Regiments. But the establishment of a large standing army organized, uniformed, armed, equipped, trained and provisioned in imitation of the best 'German' (West European) models began in 1699, and was accelerated by Peter's discomfiture at the hands of the boy king Charles XII (Narva, 1700).

Two enactments (1699 and 1705) made all males of the tax-paying classes (that is, all except the gentry) liable to conscription for life. (The obligation of the gentry to serve the state either in the armed forces or in administration, which Peter generalized and tried ruthlessly to enforce, was gradually relaxed by his successors and abolished in 1762.) The duration of conscript service was reduced to 25 years in 1793, 20 in 1834 and 12 in 1855. Selection of recruits was left to their communities, but on private estates landowners rather than peasant communes made the choice, and often abused this power for punitive or mercenary purposes. The custom of avoiding service by purchasing a voluntary substitute was established early, and legalized from the 1840s.

The general overhaul of Russia's antiquated institutions after the Crimean War* produced, as part of the programme of 'Great Reforms', the Military Reform of 1874. Its author, General D. A. Milyutin (1816–1912), among other things introduced universal conscription. Males of all classes became liable to serve at 21, and about a quarter of each annual contingent was picked by lot to serve

Officers of the Chevalier Guards, 1912

for six or seven years with the colours followed by nine or eight in the reserve. The privileged now were not the gentry as a class, but the educated: a university student was required to serve no more than six months.

From Peter's time onwards Russia maintained a larger army in peacetime than any other European country. Its size in the 18th and for much of the 19th century must be explained in part by its role in internal security, and particularly in suppressing peasant disorders. In the later years of the empire Russia (and at times its allies) hoped that sheer numbers would compensate for chronic failure, in spite of strenuous efforts, to keep abreast of the other great powers in military technology. At the end of the 19th century Russia had 850 000 men under arms, and in 1914 was able to mobilize 6 600 000 in a matter of months.

The great successes of the Imperial Army were won in the 18th and early 19th century – Peter's Northern War, the humiliation of Prussia in the Seven Years War, Catherine the Great's* Turkish wars, the Russian contribution to the demolition of Napoleon.* Thereafter, Russia's military history was a tale of disasters (the Crimea, the war with Japan* of 1904–5, the First World War*), intermitted by minor successes too hard won (the war with Turkey 1877–8). Russia owed its great victories not only to the legendary endurance and courage of its common soldiers, and to an occasional genius such as A. V. Suvorov (1730–1800) among its generals, but to its success in the first period in keeping up with and adapting Western organizational and training methods and Western weaponry. Explanations for the disasters of 1854–5, 1904–5 and 1914–17 must include economic and technical backwardness, the inadequacies of the internal transport system, and administrative failures which greatly aggravated difficulties of supply.

The navy

Russia had no navy before Peter the Great: even attempts to police the lower waters of the Volga with foreign-built vessels had failed ingloriously. The first (and archetypal) Russian naval success was the capture of Azov in 1796: Peter's new fleet, operating in support of land forces, closed the ring around the fortress from the sea. Vessels built in newly conquered Baltic ports played a major part in Russia's triumph in the Northern War, and it was the seaborne invasion of the Swedish mainland in 1719 which convinced Western Europe that Russia had firmly established itself as a formidable military power. Although naval ships took a notable part in geographical explorations,* the navy's role throughout the imperial period was largely confined to defence of Russia's shores and support of land-based operations in the Baltic and the Black Sea. As a rule, Russia took naval action further from base – in the Mediterranean in 1770 (Battle of Chesme and blockade of the Dardanelles) and in 1827 (Navarino) – only when other great powers were sympathetic and helpful. Famous

admirals included F. F. Ushakov (1743–1818), P. S. Nakhimov (1803–55) and S. O. Makarov (1848–1904). Imperial Russia's most grandiose naval enterprise was also its most disastrous: the fleet under Admiral Z. P. Rozhdestvensky (1848–1909), after a voyage from the Baltic of over seven months, was smashed by the Japanese off Tsushima in May 1905, and only three out of 38 vessels limped home to Vladivostok.   *H.T.W.*

The Soviet Navy

Development

This century had begun badly for the Imperial Russian Navy* with its virtual annihilation at Tsushima during the Russo-Japanese war* (1904–5). Care for the fleet had long been sporadic, and the navy was relatively ineffective in the First World War.* Sailors of the Baltic fleet played a prominent part in the Revolution* of October 1917, but later mutinied at Kronstadt in 1921. Despite ambitious plans of construction, and although entering the Second World War with the world's largest submarine fleet, the high seas navy achieved negligible results; river flotillas made a useful contribution, however, and many sailors fought on land. In 1945 the much-diminished Soviet Navy barely constituted a coastal defence force.

Development, set back by the war, was resumed at first purely on conventional lines. The next 35 years, while punctuated by many shifts of priority, saw the growth of a huge and modern fleet, able to undertake both defensive and offensive missions, and comparable in size to the United States Navy (larger in numbers of ships, but smaller in tonnage). The USSR immediately concentrated on seaward defence, as if to repulse a D-day style invasion by the Western powers: many small short-range submarines were built. By 1950 Western aircraft-carriers, flying nuclear-armed* aircraft of longer range, began to be seen as the greater danger, and accordingly the accent shifted to producing longer-range aircraft and submarines and missile-armed surface ships. By 1960 the primary threat was perceived to have shifted from carriers to Polaris nuclear-powered ballistic-missile-launching submarines (SSBN), to counter which required more attention to anti-submarine warfare (ASW). The USSR began also to build its own naval deterrent force comprising submarines (both nuclear- and conventionally-powered) equipped with cruise and ballistic missiles and stationed mainly with the Northern Fleet. The aim is a balanced force for exercising sea-denial and to some degree sea-control; while innovative and technically advanced, the Soviet Navy has much less embarked aviation than the US Navy and – aside from the role of nuclear strategic* deterrence – is far less able to project power ashore.

The navy has held exercises on an increasing scale, especially in the final years of Five-year Plans (1965, 1970, 1975), which also have extended into more distant waters. The exercise Okean 1975 involved more than 200 ships (besides aircraft) around Eurasia, in the Indian Ocean and elsewhere. The navy's role in 'protecting state interests' is mentioned increasingly often and signifies that the USSR has embraced a certain 'gunboat diplomacy'. A patrol has been maintained off Guinea, and the navy escorted Cuban and East German troops to Africa. The possibility of acquiring naval (or naval with air) facilities has attracted the USSR towards several African countries. The USSR needs to safeguard its sea lanes to client states and allies (Angola, Cuba, Vietnam) and to protect the growth of its fishing and merchant fleet, now among the largest in the world, but is less dependent on sea links than is NATO, whose communications could be attacked with a Soviet force of conventional submarines several times larger than NATO possesses.

It is a unique handicap that the USSR must divide its navy among four widely separated fleet areas: the Arctic Ocean, Baltic Sea, Black Sea and Pacific Ocean. Internal waterways link the three European fleet areas but permit the passage of small vessels only. Movement between the fleet areas otherwise involves passage through NATO-dominated straits or is feasible (via the northern sea route) only in summer. The Northern Fleet (stationed in the Arctic) is much the largest and most important of the four, the Pacific Fleet the next largest. Shallow waters limit the draught of ships leaving from the Baltic and preclude the passage of submerged submarines, while the Black Sea exit is theoretically regulated by the Montreux Convention of 1936. Generally, the USSR is poorly placed (especially relative to NATO countries) for oceanic access, due to a combination of distance and narrow angles of exit. Principal naval bases are along the (ice-free) Murmansk fjord, Kronstadt and other Baltic ports (including Świnoujście, Poland), Sebastopol in the Black Sea and Vladivostok and Petropavlovsk (ice-free) in the Far East. Since 1964 a naval presence has been maintained in the Mediterranean. A small force is kept in the Indian Ocean.

While current trends of naval strategy as well as of naval design of the USSR and NATO show some convergence, existing construction rates may not swing the balance further in Soviet favour although the Soviet Navy is gaining the ability to pose more diverse threats.

Fleet balance

In cruisers, destroyers and frigates, and in nuclear-powered submarines, both ballistic and attack, the navy approximates in numbers to the US Navy, but it has many more conventionally-powered submarines, patrol boats and mine warfare ships and, on the other hand, fewer aircraft carriers (none nuclear). On the whole, it has many small and medium-sized vessels but few large ones and no leviathans. The reasons are various: historical (an emphasis on mines; interruptions of building programmes); geographical (very

long coastlines and waterways); design difficulties; or internal security considerations (for example, patrol craft can inhibit illegal emigration or entry into sensitive areas). Soviet ships carrying sophisticated detection equipment invariably accompany NATO naval exercises. The USSR also has the world's largest oceanographical fleet, gathering knowledge which is vital for (among other purposes) undersea warfare.

Naval design

The Imperial Russian Navy had been technically innovative: Russians were the first to employ the torpedo in war, and pioneered detonation of mines by remote control; circular ironclads were built to the design of Admiral A. A. Popov (1821–98). Yet in the present century, until the mid-1950s, Soviet warships exhibited little originality. In the 1930s Italian design influence was strong, and immediately after the Second World War German influence. Later designs have shown striking originality: the Soviet Navy installed the first surface-to-surface (SS) guided missiles (in the *Krupny* and *Kildin* classes, 1959–61), the first all-gas-turbine power (*Kashin*, 1963), the first submarine-mounted cruise missile (1958), the first Gatling-type guns to shoot down incoming missiles, and the first sizeable embarkation of vertical take-off and landing aircraft (*Kiev*, 1976). It operates (for amphibious use) the only hovercraft unit. In contrast to their predecessors, present-day Soviet warships tend to be relatively small and fast, and crammed with diversified and partly new weapon systems. This applies to guided-missile destroyers (*Kashin*, *Krivak*), cruisers (*Kynda*, *Kresta I*, *Kresta II*, *Kara*), the helicopter-carriers *Moskva* and *Leningrad*, the missile corvette *Nanuchka* and smaller missile-armed craft such as the *Osa* class. Both nuclear- and conventionally-powered submarines may launch ballistic missiles, whereas Western navies use only nuclear platforms. The Soviet submarine force also includes cruise-missile boats, a class not yet in service in the West. Such originality evidences an unusual design effort, initiated sometimes in haste in order to get to sea some form of counter to an envisaged threat.

Soviet vessels maximize simultaneous firepower, especially for defending the ship itself (whereas in Western task forces protection is partly delegated to escort vessels), but probably carry fewer reloads than Western warships, while earlier long-range weapons may have lacked adequate over-the-horizon guidance. Current Soviet priorities in design may parallel those of allied warships in the Second World War while current Western designs emphasize electronics and habitability. The conspicuous weapon clusters and uncovered radars

---

(1) *Osa* class fast missile patrol boat. (2) *Krivak* class guided-missile destroyer. (3) *Kresta II* class cruiser. (4) The *Moskva* class helicopter-carrier *Leningrad*. (5) The cruiser-carrier *Kiev*. (6) The battle-cruiser *Kirov*

(1)

(2)

(3)

(4)

(5)

(6)

of Soviet surface combatants generate—perhaps intentionally—a menacing look. These somewhat revealing externals partly compensate for the lack of officially published information, but many uncertainties remain. The navy is thought to lag behind NATO in most aspects of ASW, including sonar (though original methods of investigation are known to have been explored), but to lead in electronic countermeasures. Shipborne weapons are primarily guided missiles (SS, ASW or surface-to-air), even the *Kiev* cruiser-carriers mounting eight long-range (probably SS) missiles. Nuclear warheads are probably embarked extensively. Except on obsolescent ships most gun calibres are 76mm or less, although most recently 85mm and 100mm guns are being adopted. Recently-built ships are mostly unarmoured, and the prominent deck-mounted armament may enhance vulnerability. Soviet warships have good sea-keeping qualities and are relatively stable, but tend to be noisy.

Western and Soviet designs now exhibit some convergence, NATO having adopted guided missiles and rapid-fire guns and now tending to build smaller ships. In its turn the Soviet Navy is now building larger ships, including at long last aircraft carriers (though of novel conception) and the huge *Delta* class submarines equipped with 24 transoceanic ballistic missiles. The *Kirov*, a battle-cruiser of 25 000–30 000 tonnes completed in 1980, has no parallel in Western navies and is the largest warship apart from aircraft-carriers to be built anywhere since 1945. The navy's amphibious capability is also growing, the latest vessel (the Polish-built roll-on/roll-off *Ivan Rogov*) resembling US types.

Marines during training emerging from BTR60 PB eight-wheeled amphibious personnel carriers

Construction and maintenance

Apart from certain landing ships all Soviet warships are constructed in the USSR. Gorky (on the Volga) has one of the main submarine-building yards. Large vessels are built in the Leningrad area, at Nikolaev and, recently, at Severodvinsk (near Archangel); the latter together with Komsomol'sk-na-Amure, specializes in nuclear submarines.

The navy keeps more of its ships in port (or if on station, at anchor) than NATO navies do, which lowers fuel costs and wear and tear but must impair training and suggests a fairly low operational readiness. Similarly, the multiplicity of shipborne weapons and sensors may indicate uncertain reliability. Soviet warships are basically factory-maintained, rather than user-maintained which is the Western practice; this reduces spatial and professional demands on board but also efficiency on cruises. The ships can, however, make use of repair facilities in many countries, including Yugoslavia and former British facilities at Singapore.

The navy imposes a considerable economic burden, representing (according to US estimates based on direct costing) almost 20 per cent of total defence spending (that is, nearly as much as the Ground Forces*). Investment (overwhelmingly, procurement of material) comprises about four-fifths of this, calling chiefly on engineering and electronics, design and scientific research.

Naval Aviation

Naval Aviation is fairly equally divided among the four fleet areas and attached to the respective fleets. Bear (reconnaissance) and Badger (missile-armed) aircraft have since 1974 been reinforced by several hundred Backfire (Tu-22M/26) strike planes. Aviation is primarily shore-based, with less use of helicopters than in the US Navy but including some flying boats.

Personnel

Since January 1956 the navy has been commanded by Admiral of the Fleet S. G. Gorshkov (b.1910), who published in 1962 a series of studies on Russian and Soviet seapower. As compared with Western navies, Soviet naval officers provide a larger proportion of narrowly specialized skills and remain longer on the same ship. Their training places less emphasis on readiness to meet unexpected eventualities. Sailors, closely supervised in foreign ports, leave a good impression—yet in recent years one warship (*Storozhevoy*, 1975) has mutinied. Living quarters, though improved, remain cramped and Spartan by comparison with NATO navies. Over four-fifths of Soviet sailors are conscripts (for three years if afloat, as compared with two in the army or air force) and the re-enlistment rate is low.   *R.H.*

The Red Army

Military force has always been crucial to the Soviet system. It was by force that the Bolsheviks★ achieved and retained power, despite the efforts of White and some Allied armies to unseat them. The Communist Party★ devotes much attention to the armed forces, not only because they assure, externally, the defence of the state and, internally, the maintenance of the Party in power, but also because they constitute the only organization capable of overthrowing its rule. From this follows the political involvement and control which constitutes the most distinctive feature of the Soviet armed forces.

Early years

The Workers' and Peasants' Red Army was formed by Lenin★ on 28 January 1918 from the ranks of the Red Guard, the workers' militia with which the Bolsheviks had swept away the Provisional Government★ in the October Revolution.★ It was not a 'national' army but a 'class' army, designed to fight for the Bolshevik cause, and was initially constituted from reliable proletarian volunteers. However, early in the civil war★ its inadequate volunteer strength of 100 000 had to be increased by conscription, and its almost total lack of commanders experienced in formal warfare forced the Bolsheviks to employ ex-tsarist officers as field commanders. The doubtful political reliability of these men was countered by the appointment of Party watchdogs – the political commissars – to positions of equal authority in army headquarters. Trotsky★ was the chief architect of the new army, and within a remarkably short space of time he had transformed the irregular militia into a regular army with strict

formal military discipline. By the end of 1920, the Red Army had grown to almost five and a half million men, but a solid static front on the lines of the First World War was never formed because of the vast spaces across which the fighting raged. The civil war became a war of manoeuvre, and the Red Army's victory was in no small part due to its adaptability and revolutionary spirit uninhibited by any inherited defensive mentality.

After the civil war and the war with Poland, the Red Army was demobilized to provide a work-force for the restitution of the ravaged economy, a mere half-million men being retained for border guard duty, internal security, and as a command cadre for future expansion. This very competent core of command staff was responsible for formalizing the experience of the civil war in a 'Military Doctrine', to be the basis for the future training and development of the army. Many of the senior members of this staff, such as B. M. Shaposhnikov (1882–1945), M. N. Tukhachevsky (1893–1937) and V. K. Triandafillov (1894–1931), had had a tsarist military upbringing and many of the basic military practices adopted – march, deployment, artillery drills – were those of the Imperial Army.★ Combined with this was the experience of the civil war, which gave absolute primacy to the offensive as a means of waging war, for which the dynamic manoeuvre, massing of firepower, and surprise were the requisites. The whole doctrine was dominated and directed by Lenin's concept of war, which itself relied heavily on that of Clausewitz. War and strategy were tools of policy, and the aim was political victory – the complete destruction of the enemy's political system and its replacement with one friendly to the Bolshevik cause. These principles, which remain the basis of Soviet Military Doctrine,★ drove the Soviet Army to develop its organization, equipment and

Conscripts register for the mobilization of the Red Army, Moscow, 1918

Lenin in Red Square, May 1919, viewing the response to his appeal for all to undergo military training

tactics along certain lines. By the late 1920s Triandafillov had fully developed his theories of 'deep war', by which he envisaged thrusts of massed armour penetrating into the heart of enemy territory and bringing about political collapse in the shortest possible time. The Doctrine gives overwhelming emphasis to the Ground Forces.* The navy,* having played only a very small part in the civil war, was in the early years assigned a minor role as coastal defence or as off-shore support to a land operation. Similarly, air power was seen as the third dimension of a land battle, its task being to support ground operations. No independent air force was ever created; the Soviet Air Forces* provide support for other arms of service.

Growth in the 1920s and 1930s

During the 1920s the Red Army was obviously not equipped to put its theories into practice. However, the Party's intense interest in military matters, spurred both by an ideological belief in the use of war as a revolutionizing agent and by a conviction of the implacable hostility of the capitalist powers, ensured that economic planning* would allow for an expansion of arms production as soon as the requisite heavy industrial base had been achieved. A secret provision of the Treaty of Rapallo (1922) with Germany established training and experimental establishments jointly with the Reichswehr, the USSR to train both nations' forces in air, gas and armoured warfare.

By 1930 the Red Army numbered three-quarters of a million; seven years later it had almost doubled. There was a corresponding increase in equipment, particularly aircraft, tanks and artillery. By 1936 the Red Army could boast four mechanized corps, six independent mechanized brigades and six independent tank regiments; foreign military delegations at manoeuvres in the Ukraine were impressed with the technological achievements displayed, such as a light tank being dropped by parachute.

Developments in the late 1930s negated much of this progress towards efficiency. During the 1930s the army became increasingly formalized: ranks – abandoned after the Revolution in favour of 'commander' and 'warrior' – were reintroduced, officers' privileges were reinstated, and the 'officer corps' reappeared. Senior officers were men of considerable standing and power who did not owe their rise to Stalin,* and on several military questions opposed him. In 1936–9 the USSR sent military assistance to the left-wing forces in the Spanish civil war. Their experience in the use of armour in these campaigns led them to the false conclusion that massed armoured formations were not viable on the battlefield. The ensuing debate resulted in the breaking-up of armoured formations and the redistribution of tanks. For political and personal reasons, not wholly unconnected with this debate, Stalin turned the fury of the 1937–9 Terror* on to the army: over 70 per cent (some 35 000) of senior officers were shot or imprisoned, and all tactical and technical experiment and innovation was halted.

The Red Army was gravely weakened by the purges; the poor showing made during the campaign against Finland in 1939–40 highlighted many deficiencies, and the government recognized the need for improvement.

The Second World War

By June 1941, when Hitler* invaded the USSR, it was a much improved Red Army that met the German onslaught. However, the Command's inexperience in handling large forces on the battlefield and the surprise of the attack meant enormous Soviet losses and, by the end of 1941, a retreat to the very gates of Moscow. Despite the appalling position, the Red Army managed to reorganize and launched a successful counterattack which prevented the fall of the capital. There followed two years of warfare of a scale and intensity never before seen. Stalin's total control over Soviet life through the Party and security police, and which he had reinforced with the purges, enabled the entire resources of the country to be massed behind the war effort with absolute ruthlessness and singleness of purpose. The USSR did not come to possess a war machine, it became a war machine. By late 1943 the German offensive effort had been halted, and by 1944 the Soviet armies were on the strategic offensive. Until then the Red Army had been forced into fighting a defensive war for which Soviet Military Doctrine was inadequate preparation. From late 1943 onwards, however, the Soviet forces restructured for offensive operations, which culminated in the fall of Berlin in 1945. With this experience and a plan of operation which owed much to the early Soviet strategists such as Triandafillov, a campaign was

Tank warfare: the battle around Kursk, July 1943, which was decisive in the Red Army's liberation of the western regions from two years of German military occupation

mounted against the Japanese Kwantung Army in Manchuria in August and September 1945. After careful and secret preparation, the Red Army launched a surprise attack on the Japanese, using massed armoured forces to penetrate deep into the country and capture the political centres of the Japanese administration in Manchuria within a mere three weeks.

The change of name from Red Army to Soviet Army that took place after the war was more than a mere matter of form. The Red Army had entered the war in 1941 with uncertain leadership; with its tactics and organization in dispute; with a call to arms based on proletarian internationalism. Despite the enormous military disasters of 1941 and mass desertions to the Germans, the army had survived, succeeded in reorganizing itself, perfecting its military art and smashing the German armies. Proletarian internationalism had very soon given way to plain Russian or Soviet patriotism motivating both soldier and civilian. The entire military system was reconstituted on traditional Russian lines, with officer rank structure, uniforms with epaulettes, military academies and strict discipline.   *C.N.D.*

The Soviet Air Forces

There has never been an independent air force in the Soviet armed forces: the air arm has always been considered as supporting a 'third dimension' of a land or naval battle. This does not mean neglect of air power. From the earliest days the aeroplane was seen as an instrument capable of making a great contribution to victory, but in the 1920s and 1930s the Soviet conviction of the pre-eminence of the land battle, together with the deficiencies of industrial production and the lack of skilled engineers and designers, produced a lag in the development of aviation technology. Soviet experience in the Second World War, while undoubtedly proving the value of the interceptor and ground-attack fighter, did nothing to convince the military leadership of the necessity to develop a strategic bombing wing. The nuclear age led to some development of long-range aircraft, and to greater efforts on the intercontinental ballistic missile (ICBM) system, seen as a more certain method of getting warheads into the enemy heartland. Although aviation technology has lagged behind that of the West, modern Soviet aircraft are no longer as far as they were behind their Western equivalents. The large volume of production which the USSR can maintain goes a long way towards offsetting what technological backwardness still exists. Moreover the USSR now possesses an extremely sophisticated weapons procurement system and extremely skilled design bureaux, producing high-performance aircraft such as the MiG-25 Foxbat with what Western experts considered to be totally inadequate production technology.

The Soviet Air Forces comprise five branches – Tactical Aviation,

Long-range Aviation, Fighter Aviation of the Air Defence Forces of the Homeland, Naval Aviation and Military Air Transport. The Commander-in-Chief of the Soviet Air Forces is responsible for the administration of all these branches, their equipping, training and maintenance. However, in wartime he has direct command only of the Military Air Transport, and even in that his task is to support other arms of service as directed by the High Command. The Tactical Aviation comes under the orders of the Ground Forces Theatre or Front commander; the Long-range Aviation would probably be integrated with Strategic Rocket Forces (SRF); the Fighter Aviation of the Air Defence Forces is, of course, organically part of that arm of service, as is Naval Aviation part of the Naval Command.

The largest of these five branches, which together total over 12 000 aircraft and almost half a million men, is the Tactical Aviation. Four-fifths of its 5000 aircraft are in Eastern Europe or the European USSR in case of confrontation with NATO. It has fighter ground-attack aircraft, interceptors, reconnaissance and strike aircraft, and a large number of reconnaissance, transport and combat helicopters. Really close air support on the battlefield is the task of helicopters rather than fixed-wing aircraft, and helicopters are also used for the transport of air assault troops into the enemy rear. The Air Forces use the same administrative organization and rank structure as the Ground Forces, except at the lower levels of organization, where traditional aviation terms are used for sub-units. The senior Ground Forces commander will use his tactical air force in much the same way as he uses his artillery – terminology is indeed identical for the three basic phases of air or artillery support to an offensive. Aircraft and helicopters will also be used as 'long-range artillery' to destroy targets out of gun range or undetected by ground reconnaissance. The

An-12 Cub long-range general-purpose transports

principles of military art which shape the decisions of the Ground Forces commander apply equally to the Air Forces. Consequently the available tactical aviation will not be dispersed over the wide front of the battlefield but concentrated to support the main axes of attack.

The Long-range Aviation fly mainly strategic strike aircraft carrying nuclear* bombs, primitive cruise missiles (small pilotless aircraft with nuclear warheads) or conventional armaments. Aircraft of this type also fly daily reconnaissance and electronic counter-measures (ECM) missions during peacetime to test Western air defences. Many of the aircraft in use are, like their NATO equivalents, rather old and vulnerable, but the introduction of the Backfire strike aircraft provided the Long-range Aviation with a very up-to-date weapons system which could be used against targets in both Europe and the USA; for although its range, if it is to return safely to base, is only some 4500km, in the event of nuclear war it would probably not be expected even to attempt to return.

The Military Air Transport command has almost 1700 fixed-wing aircraft and 2000 helicopters. Its task is to support operations of the other arms, including conveying airborne forces, supply at all levels, and airlifts. In wartime, during peacetime exercises, and for regular seasonal troop rotation duties, a considerable number of civil machines of Aeroflot come under the command of the Military Air Transport.

The Air Defence Forces of the Homeland have been a separate arm of service in the USSR since 1954, with the task of guarding Soviet air space. The air defence troops whose job it is to provide area or point protection for the Ground Forces in action do not come under this command. However, the Soviet air defence system does utilize national air forces in Eastern Europe, coordinating their activity to provide an integrated and therefore more effective air defence of its western frontiers. The Air Defence Forces comprise four branches. Radio Technical Troops (who man the radar system, the airborne early warning system and ballistic missile early warning system (BMEWS) and the ECM, ECM reconnaissance and electronic counter countermeasures systems); Anti-Aircraft and Anti-Ballistic Missile (ABM) Troops; Fighter Aviation (one of the administrative branches of the Air Forces); and Anti-Aircraft Artillery Troops. Control is exercised at Military District (MD) level, and through ten Air Defence Districts. The USSR now possesses an efficient radar early warning system, a very comprehensive range of rapid-firing guns for low-level defence, and missiles of all types for low-, medium- and high-level defence. In addition, there is an anti-ballistic missile site protecting Moscow. The BMEWS is linked in the USSR to the Civil Defence Command to warn the civil population. The Fighter Aviation has over 2500 interceptor aircraft of various types, and a further 1000 are available elsewhere within the Warsaw Treaty Organization.* In emergency, the interceptors of the Ground Forces air defence could be employed for home defence.   *C.N.D.*

The Soviet armed forces since 1945

Post-war role

The principal role of the armed forces since the end of the war has been to prevent a repetition of the disastrous experience of 1941–2. Consequently in 1945 the government did not demobilize to the same extent as Western governments, but kept very large forces in being, and since the mid-1950s it has allotted more than one-tenth of GNP to keep them up to date and expand their capability. In a secondary but very important role, the Soviet Army has been employed to enforce the communization of neighbouring states–in the GDR in the late 1940s and early 1950s, in Hungary in 1956, in Czechoslovakia in 1968 and in Afghanistan* in 1979–80. Since 1969 the army has been heavily committed on the border with China,* where several minor clashes have taken place. The Soviet Navy* has expanded from virtual insignificance to a worldwide role and Soviet air power* has been greatly increased. When the USSR acquired nuclear* fission and fusion weapons (in 1949 and 1953 respectively), it made strenuous efforts to develop means of employing them against its principal rival, the USA, and disclosed its first intercontinental ballistic missile (ICBM) in 1957. In 1960, in recognition of the development of this strategic weapon, Khrushchev* created a new arm of service, the Strategic Rocket Forces (SRF). Placing his reliance on this arm for defence, he reduced conventional defence spending to finance his attempts to improve the consumer economy. This move was unpopular with the military, and was undoubtedly a contributory factor leading to his removal from office in 1964. Since then the conventional forces of the Soviet Army have been constantly augmented, in accordance with current Soviet Military Doctrine.

Developments in Soviet Military Doctrine

Much of the hard-won experience of the 1941–5 war was thought to have been invalidated by the advent of the nuclear era and throughout the 1950s and 1960s the Soviet armed forces planned, trained and equipped themselves to fight in a nuclear battlefield. In this context, Khrushchev's reduction in the size and role of conventional Ground Forces was logical militarily, however unwise politically.

In the late 1960s NATO adopted the doctrine of 'flexible response', which presumed that the first few days of any war in Europe would be fought with conventional weapons alone. Soviet forces thus needed both conventional and nuclear capacity, and the ability to move from one type of war to the other very quickly. By the mid-1970s there was even the possibility of a war with limited aims being fought in Europe, which it would be in the interests of the Soviet armed forces to win in its initial period (the first few days) before NATO resorted to nuclear weapons. It was for such a lightning war with conventional weapons or a conventional-nuclear mix that the Soviet armed forces were being prepared during the second half of that decade. They are not only very large, but are comparatively well trained for both nuclear and conventional operations, and equipped with weapons systems many of which are as effective as, or better than, those in the West. This Soviet advantage may be contrasted with the parity of the 1960s, when NATO had been able to offset Soviet numerical supremacy with technological superiority. Military problems of the 1970s were not confined to Europe. The Soviet Army had to face the possibility of war with China, and the USSR became militarily involved in several Third World countries on behalf of a left-wing cause. In the late 1950s and throughout the 1960s such aid had been confined mainly to arms and military-training staff, but in the 1970s, in Angola and Ethiopia, the USSR in addition ferried troops of their Cuban and GDR allies, with a decisive effect on the course of both wars. Such intervention, made possible by the growing strength of the naval and air forces and the West's unwillingness to pose opposition must have encouraged the decision to invade Afghanistan in December 1979. Some Western strategists consider that if, by such action, the USSR – self-sufficient in almost all fuels and raw materials – can deny essential commodities to Europe, then it may well be able to come to greater political power in Europe without resorting to war.

The key elements of Soviet Military Doctrine are contained in the Soviet Principles of Military Art – which in a Western army might be called 'principles of war'. Their existence provides a common base not only to instruction and training but also to weapon and vehicle design, making for a remarkably well-integrated military system. The Doctrine is founded on two assumptions: that the offensive is the primary and most effective means of waging war, and that if victory is to be achieved the war, and every battle, must be won *very quickly indeed*. The effectiveness of equipment, tactics and organization must be assessed in terms of their ability to fulfil these principles. To assess them by comparison with British or American equivalents, or by an evaluation of how well such equipment, tactics or organization would suit Western requirements would be a grave error.

The principles of Soviet military art, in order of priority, are as follows: (1) the achievement of mobility and battlefield flexibility, and the maintenance of a high rate of advance; (2) the concentration of effort – careful choice of the location and timing of the main blow on one or several axes, and the creation on those axes of decisive superiority in men and equipment; (3) the attainment of surprise at all levels; (4) the seizure and retention of the initiative by energetic attack, manoeuvre, breakthrough and pursuit; (5) the preservation of the combat effectiveness of troops by (*a*) being properly prepared and efficiently organized to go to war without warning or extra training, (*b*) being able to maintain effective command and control of forces at all times, and (*c*) being able to maintain morale and the will to fight among the troops; (6) ensuring that the aim and plan of the operation are consonant with the forces available; (7) ensuring

cooperation and coordination of all arms of service on the field of battle towards achieving the common goal; (8) attempting simultaneous action upon the enemy to the entire depth of his deployment and upon objectives deep in his rear.

Personnel structure

More of the active population of the USSR are engaged in the armed forces than is the case in the UK or the USA. Some 75–80 per cent of Soviet military personnel are conscripts, the remainder being regular officers, non-commissioned officers or ensigns. Except for those in the ocean-going navy, who serve for three years, all conscripts serve for two years during which they are not entitled to leave or pay, but receive a monthly allowance of 3–6 roubles. Conscription is universal, and takes some 80 per cent of the eligible male population, normally at 18. As well as on health or compassionate grounds, exemption or deferment can be obtained by those attending institutions of higher education, where a certain amount of reserve (officer) training is usually compulsory. Graduates of tertiary education may find themselves conscripted for 12–18 months' service, or as short-service officers for up to three years with officers' leave, pay and allowances.

Conscription takes place every spring and autumn, and posting (principally for reasons of security) mingles nationalities in every sub-unit, to avoid the predominance of any one ethnic group other than Russians. On conscription, priority for high-quality personnel is given to the SRF and then to the navy in terms of technical training, to the frontier and security forces* in terms of political reliability, and to the airborne forces in terms of physical fitness. The best so selected are sent for 6 months to an NCO training school, after which they complete the remaining 18 months' service as conscript sergeants. The remainder go direct to field units for training, and twice yearly a unit will lose a quarter of its trained conscripts and receive an equivalent number of untrained men. It is the task of the regular officer and ensign cadre in the unit to run a continuous training cycle so as to maintain the unit at a constant state of combat readiness. This leads, perforce, to a very intensive and stereotyped training programme with the limited aims of teaching a soldier to do one job very well and several related jobs adequately if necessary. Much time is allotted to physical training; much specialized training is done on training machines or simulators, or with sub-calibre ammunition; and at least 5–6 hours weekly are devoted to political education.

Life for a conscript soldier is coarse and hard, and discipline is severe – extremely so in wartime, when a soldier may be shot as 'company punishment'. However, new disciplinary regulations introduced in 1976 and improved living standards are evidence of a new sophistication in man management, which may be expected to continue. Conscripts wishing to make the armed services their career may opt for extended service as sergeants, or, if they have the necessary educational qualifications, as ensigns. This rank was introduced in 1972 in an attempt to create a class of competent and responsible NCOs in all services, capable of taking over the functions of junior officers, and enjoying the same privileges of accommodation and leave (45 days a year). The move was prompted by, among other factors, a serious shortage of officer candidates, deflected from a military career by the increasing civilian standard of living. All levels of regular officer and ensign are nevertheless paid somewhat more than equivalent professional civilians, and in addition receive free accommodation, access to preferentially-supplied shops, boarding-school* allowances, and better pensions.*

Officers, who constitute about 75 per cent of the regular cadre, start their career with a course at any one of about 150 military colleges, offering general or special-to-arm education for 2–6 years. About 5 per cent attend the Suvorov Academies, élite military secondary boarding-schools on former Imperial Army* lines, taking primarily sons of army officers from their early teens until 18, when they can attend a military college proper for 3–4 years. From there, the officer commands a platoon of infantry, tanks, artillery, motor transport and so on, possibly rising to battalion commander as a captain or major at the age of 30. At this point he may do a three-year training-course at the Frunze Military Academy or similar special-to-

arm academy, or he may obtain a staff qualification through a correspondence course. Formation commanders generally take a two-year course at the Voroshilov General Staff Academy in their 40s or early 50s. A post-war tendency for officers to be drawn from officers' sons (as has also been occurring among other professional establishments in the USSR such as the CPSU* and the Ministry of Foreign Affairs) might have been considered by the Party to represent a threat of military separatism. Party controls within the armed forces, and particularly within the officer corps, however, remain strong, the Party's identity with the army is being constantly reinforced (over 90 per cent of officers are members of the CPSU or the Komsomol*) and the armed forces' political representation on the CPSU Central Committee has been gradually eroded. It may be that less political influence and more political control is what the officer corps will have to expect in exchange for enhanced professional solidarity and greater privileges. The general trend in the army as a whole towards greater sophistication has been linked in the officer corps with initiative, including the extent to which junior commanders might expect some independence of action. Strong though the tendency has always been to curb initiative–which in any case would certainly be at a lower level than that available in comparable situations in the British or US army–the Soviet officer can now undoubtedly display greater initiative than heretofore, and this is potentially a revolutionary development.

Officer cadets taking part in the annual October Revolution parade, Red Square, Moscow

Organization

The Ministry of Defence, which controls the Soviet armed forces, the Ministry of Internal Affairs, which controls the ordinary police (militia★), and the Committee of State Security,★ which controls the security police and the frontier guards are subordinate, through the Council of Ministers, to the Presidium of the Supreme Soviet,★ in which is vested the prerogative of the declaration of war. The effective authority of the Politburo of the Central Committee of the Communist Party★ was traditionally recognized by the Minister of Defence's membership of that body – successively K. Ye. Voroshilov (1881–1969), Stalin★ himself and N. A. Bulganin (b.1895) – but since Stalin's death a Minister of Defence has been in the Politburo in the persons of G. K. Zhukov (1899–1957) briefly in 1956–7, A. A. Grechko (1903–76) – from May 1973 to April 1976, and D. F. Ustinov (b. 1908), since 1976. The Commander-in-Chief of the armed forces and Chairman of the Defence Council of the USSR is Brezhnev,★ who is also both the General Secretary of the Party Central Committee and the Chairman of the Presidium of the Supreme Soviet, with the rank of Marshal of the Soviet Union. The Defence Council, the existence of which was made public in 1975, had previously been known to exist only in wartime (1941–6) and its membership has not been revealed. It probably included the three

relevant ministers and the chiefs of the General Staff and of its Political Directorate. The Council's Military-Industrial Commission is likely to include the nine ministries administering defence production in the engineering★ sector.

The Ministry of Defence operates on a highly-centralized basis and is dominated, despite the impressive naval and air forces, by officers of the Ground Forces (and, more recently, of the SRF) whose doctrines, traditions and practices prevail. Through the Commander-in-Chief of the Warsaw Treaty forces (always a Soviet officer) the Soviet Ministry of Defence controls the policies of the defence ministries of the other member states. As a branch of the ministry the Main Political Directorate of the Armed Forces (GlavPUR) directly controls the political elements present in the command cadre at every level of command, right down to the infantry company, and in every institution and establishment in the Soviet Army. Within the Ministry of Defence, this political involvement is exercised through the Main Military Council. GlavPUR is also responsible to the CPSU Central Committee as the military branch of that Party organization.

The armed forces are divided into five arms of service (plus the Civil Defence Corps): SRF; Ground Forces; Air Defence Forces of the Homeland; Soviet Navy; Soviet Air Forces. The head of the SRF commands land-based strategic missile systems, and directs the employment of (but does not actually administer) naval strategic missiles and those aircraft of the Long-range Aviation carrying strategic weapons. The Chief of the Ground Forces commands all

The then Minister of Defence, Marshal A.A. Grechko, at the leaders' observation point during military exercises in 1975

ORGANIZATION OF THE SOVIET ARMED FORCES

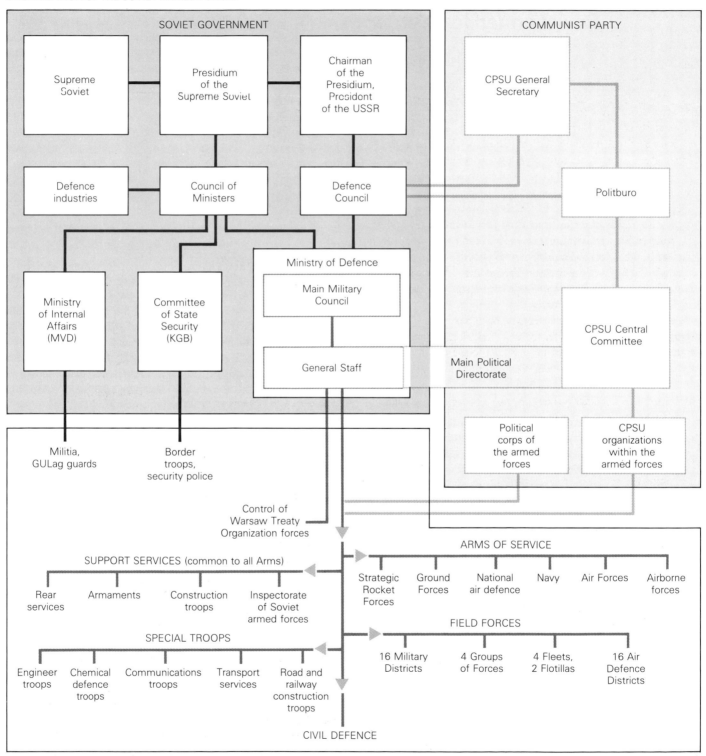

land forces, their tactical aviation and local air defence. The Air Defence Forces of the Homeland command includes all strategic early warning systems, and the associated electronic warfare system; the anti-ballistic missile system; the anti-aircraft missile system; all home-based interceptor aircraft administered by the Air Forces; and all strategic artillery air defence units. The Admiral of the Fleet commands not only naval ships and installations, but all maritime aircraft administered by the Air Forces. Although his submarines and possibly carriers carry strategic weapons, their employment in war is under the direction of the SRF. The Chief Marshal of the Air Forces administers all aircraft subordinate to other arms of service, controls the Military Transport Aviation and has authority over the civil airline, Aeroflot.

Supporting arms within the Ministry are the Rear Services Directorate, responsible for supply and procurement; the Military Construction Troops, who are used on civil or military state projects (such as building barracks or laying the Baykal–Amur Mainline Railway); the Directorate of Arms Production, which coordinates industrial enterprises, research agencies and design bureaux; and the Inspectorate of the Armed Forces.

For the purposes of defence organization in peacetime, the USSR is divided into 16 Military Districts–a tradition inherited from imperial Russia. In addition, those Soviet formations stationed in East Europe are formed into four 'Groups of Forces', each with the status of a Military District. The staff of a Military District administer all the military garrisons, military farms, and factories and installations within the District. The senior officer who would actually command in war all the combat forces of that District is known as the 'Commander of Troops'. Groups of Forces have a Commander-in-Chief, because they are maintained on a war footing. In wartime the activities of several Groups of Forces, or of several Military Districts in a given geographical area, would be coordinated into a Theatre of Military Operations. Military activity planned and executed at Theatre level or above is known as 'strategic'.

In wartime a Group of Forces would probably be reconstituted as, or as part of, a 'front', which can have any number of armies, but in practice probably about four or five. An 'army' is equally composed of any number of divisions, but four or five is usual. Armies with a preponderance of tank forces are called 'Tank Armies'; those with a balance of troops of different arms are called 'Combined Arms Armies'. Military activity organized at front or army level is considered to be 'operational', and in Soviet terminology the word 'operation' when unqualified means specifically activity at army or front level. The commander of an army or front is known as

DEPLOYMENT OF SOVIET GROUND FORCES

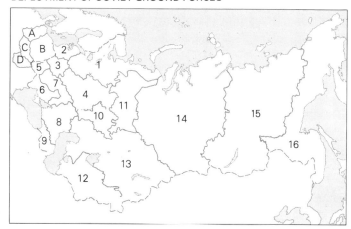

KEY

MILITARY DISTRICTS[1] OF THE USSR	DIVISIONS DEPLOYED	MILITARY DISTRICTS[1] OF THE USSR	DIVISIONS DEPLOYED
1 Leningrad	10	9 Transcaucasian	10
2 Baltic	11	10 Volga	3
3 Belorussian	10	11 Ural	3
4 Moscow	7	12 Turkestan	8
5 Cis Carpathian	11	13 Central Asian	7
6 Odessa	9	14 Siberian	7
7 Kiev	12	15 Transbaykal	9
8 North Caucasian	6	16 Far Eastern	21

GROUPS OF FORCES	DIVISIONS DEPLOYED
A Group of Soviet Forces Germany (GDR)	20 (5 Armies plus Reserves)
B Northern Group of Forces (Poland)	2
C Central Group of Forces (Czechoslovakia)	5
D Southern Group of Forces (Hungary)	4

[1]From 1981 Air Defence Districts were made co-terminous with the 16 Military Districts

Design by C. N. Donnolly

kommanduyushchiy, below which level no independence of action or planning is generally allowed.

The division, led by a Commander (*kommandir*), is the basic formation of the Ground Forces having a fixed establishment of four combat regiments plus support, such as artillery, engineers, reconnaissance, chemical defence and logistics. There are three main types of division: Motor Rifle Divisions of about 13000 men, comprising three regiments of motorized infantry and one regiment of tanks; Tank Divisions of 10000 to 11000 men, with three regiments of tanks and one of motorized infantry; and Airborne Divisions of 7000 men including three or four parachute assault regiments (having light support elements capable of being para-dropped or air-landed). There is also an establishment for Artillery Divisions–the term given to a formation consisting solely of guns (some 200 to 300 weapons)–which in fact comprises the extra artillery complement of a front. The regiment is the basic unit of the Soviet Army: either a mixed force comprising several types of troops and

(1)

(2)

(3)

(4)

(5)

(6)

(7)

(8)

(9)

An airborne reconnaissance unit on a winter exercise

designated by the predominant type (tank regiment, motor rifle regiment) or composed of troops of only one speciality (engineer regiments, artillery regiments). Sub-units which go to make up the regiment are sections (10–11 men, and one armoured personnel carrier (APC) or tank and crew), platoons (about 30 men and three APC, or three or four tanks, or two or three field-guns), companies of three platoons (batteries of two platoons in the artillery) and battalions of three identical companies plus supporting platoons (such as a mortar and anti-tank platoon in the motor rifle battalion, rear supply platoons in most battalions). During combat operations at any level, a unit or a sub-unit may operate with its full complement of men and equipment, or it may be augmented by sub-units attached in support. Similarly, units and formations may well be allotted extra forces from the higher commander's reserves so as to increase the concentration of effort on their sector of the battlefield.

All troops wear the same uniform but are distinguished by epaulettes, gorget and sleeve patches of different colours, and by separate badges special to arm. Some units and formations carry the title 'Guards', an appellation of honour granted to a unit which

(1) BMP multi-role infantry combat vehicle, designed for rapid offensive (especially in nuclear or chemical conditions). (2) T55 tank and armoured recovery vehicle crossing a pontoon. (3) Tactical nuclear missiles (NATO designation Frog), deployed in every Soviet motor rifle or tank division. (4) Mi-24 helicopter gunships, intended as fire support during offensive operations. (5) T55 tank, the most widely used tank in the world. (6) Su-11 close-support aircraft, stationed in the GDR. (7) Tactical operational missiles (NATO designation Scud) capable of carrying nuclear, chemical or high-explosive warheads. (8) SA-9 infrared homing missile providing army regiments with close air defence. (9) Czech-built T55 MTU, designed for assault crossing of narrow rivers – the only major item of foreign equipment used in the Soviet Army

TYPICAL APPOINTMENTS FOR RANKS OF THE ARMY AND AIR FORCES

Unlike Western practice, an appointment to a position of command in the Soviet armed forces does not necessarily carry with it an acting rank; consequentially pay and allowances are predominantly related to appointment: thus a battalion can be commanded by a captain, major or lieutenant-colonel, and in the Second World War a major-general was sometimes placed in command of an army, with a lieutenant-general as his Chief of Staff. The force of command authority is so great in the Soviet system that this is considered neither unusual nor particularly undesirable

Rank	Appointment
Private Private 1st class/lance-corporal	Conscript
Junior sergeant Sergeant Senior sergeant	Conscript or extended service NCO; Section Commander
Sergeant-major	Extended service NCO, CSM
Ensign	Platoon Commander; Battalion Technical Deputy
Junior Lieutenant Lieutenant	Platoon Commander
Senior lieutenant	Platoon/Company Commander; Battalion Chief of Staff
Captain	Company Commander (sometimes Battalion Commander)
Major	Battalion Commander; Regimental Deputy Commander
Lieutenant-colonel	Battalion Commander (occasionally Regimental Commander); Regimental 1st Deputy Commander; Divisional Deputy Commander
Colonel	Regimental Commander; Divisional Chief of Staff; Divisional 1st Deputy Commander; Divisional Political Deputy
Major-general	Divisional Commander; Commandant of a Military College
Lieutenant-general	Army Commander; Commandant of Senior Academy; Ministry of Defence Staff Officer; Deputy Chief Commanding an Arm; Military District Commander
Colonel-general	Army Commander; Military District or Group of Forces Commander; Ministry of Defence Staff Officer; Deputy Commander-in-Chief of an Arm; Commander-in-Chief of a minor Arm
General of the Army	Military District or Group of Forces Commander; Theatre Commander; Ministry of Defence Staff Officer; Commander-in-Chief of an Arm; Deputy Minister of Defence
Marshal of Arm Chief Marshal of Arm Marshal of the Soviet Union	Theatre Commander; Deputy Minister of Defence; Commander-in-Chief of an Arm; Prestige appointment; Commander-in-Chief, Armed Forces; Commander-in-Chief, Warsaw Treaty forces

distinguished itself in action during the Second World War. Units, formations and institutions may carry battle honours in their title or be named after famous personalities and may bear awards for efficiency or outstanding performance. Every unit and formation carries a number by which it is distinguished; sub-units are numbered within their units. Units are never recruited on a territorial basis, although they may have a tradition of being garrisoned in a certain location, and may, therefore, have established close local links.

C.N.D.

The Warsaw Treaty forces

The Warsaw Treaty Organization, comprising Albania, Bulgaria, Czechoslovakia, the GDR, Hungary, Poland, Romania and the USSR, was established in May 1955 ostensibly, and in part actually, in response to the rearming of the Federal Republic of Germany (FRG) and its eventual inclusion in the Western Alliance. Unlike NATO, it is not a free association of nations with equal status, nor could its members withdraw without provoking Soviet action, as France withdrew from military membership of NATO. Albania's withdrawal in 1968 was possible only because its geographic position made it impracticable for the USSR to bring effective military pressure to bear. The USSR has a common border with most Warsaw Treaty countries and the value of this was demonstrated before and during the invasion of Czechoslovakia in 1968.

Initially, the role of the Warsaw Treaty was to offer a legal framework whereby the countries of Eastern Europe would provide men, materials and money for defence. The forces thus available were controlled by the USSR and used in primarily Soviet interests, creating a much more effective buffer zone between it and the West, and reducing the military demand on the Soviet economy. Consequently, there is no independent Warsaw Treaty command structure or General Staff. Such structure and staff as exists is in practice subordinated to the Soviet General Staff, and is in effect an extension of this for directing the war effort of member states.

The Warsaw Treaty Organization has been the vehicle for the independent development, training and equipping of the national armies comprising it, while at the same time acting as a check to prevent any one non-Soviet army from becoming too powerful. The stimulus to develop national arms industries is furthered by the close integration between the Warsaw Treaty and the Council for Mutual Economic Assistance (Comecon*), and has led not only to the growth of those arms factories in Eastern Europe which produce equipment of Soviet design, but also to independent arms developments producing advanced trainer aircraft, armoured personnel carriers, small arms, combat engineering equipment and a whole host of minor military equipment. The independent development of major offensive combat equipment such as fighter-ground-attack aircraft, tanks or field-guns has not been sanctioned by the USSR, either for reasons of political security or in the interest of military standardization.

All the Warsaw Treaty forces are organized, trained and equipped on the Soviet model, so that although it is extremely unlikely that, say, a GDR division would ever be directly commanded by a Soviet officer, it could easily be incorporated into a Soviet army (of 4–5 divisions). The homogeneity of Soviet Military Doctrine* would produce almost complete compatibility. The forces of Treaty states other than the USSR are more likely to be reliable in the Soviet cause than to emerge as guardians of national integrity. Senior officers of such countries, if aspiring to command one of their own national divisions, must first be approved by the Soviet military delegation in the country, and must then complete a two-year course at the Voroshilov General Staff Academy. In addition, a large number of East European officers attend two-year courses at the mid-career Frunze Military Academy. The security services of Eastern Europe, all subordinated to and infiltrated by the Soviet KGB,* infiltrate in turn their own national armies. The East European Communist Parties have representation in their national armies on the Soviet model. Finally, the regular officers in all the armies may be judged to have accepted Soviet supremacy and they probably constitute the least anti-Soviet element in their respective countries.

The Warsaw Treaty forces of prime military importance to the USSR are those of the GDR, Poland, Czechoslovakia and Bulgaria. Hungary and particularly Romania, by virtue of their geo-strategic positions, are of somewhat less importance, and consequently have slightly greater independence in military affairs. In terms of a European confrontation, the 'first-rank' Warsaw Treaty forces would probably support the Soviet forces comparatively willingly if the latter were seen to be winning a war quickly and easily. At the very least, in such an instance, they would reduce the effect of attrition on Soviet forces, and effectively secure the rear area. In any Soviet action contrary to the interests of their respective countries, the national armies could, if surprised, probably be forced to remain inactive as was the Czechoslovak army in 1968. Only in the event of a major Soviet disaster would the Warsaw Treaty armies become a liability rather than an asset, and even then this would probably not be the case if NATO forces, such as those of the FRG, were believed to pose a threat to the national integrity of the country concerned.

In most of the realistic scenarios for war the Soviet armed forces could draw on at least the most effective and combat-ready elements of the Warsaw Treaty forces – in all about one-third of the total strength – and incorporate them as a viable element in a military plan.

C.N.D.

The military use of space

Soviet civil and military space programmes are clearly intermeshed, with many satellites performing dual functions and all launches controlled by the Strategic Rocket Forces (SRF)–a military arm of the Soviet forces. To consider the USSR's space research* and use of space as a means of enhancing the military capabilities of its armed forces involves a somewhat artificial distinction, therefore.

With every year that passes, space platforms of many different kinds are taking over more of the military functions that have hitherto been performed by terrestrial systems. In some cases satellites are able to do things that could not be done at all by land-based means: continuous reconnaissance of continents, the accurate mapping of territory for strategic targeting, and even the establishing of the shape of the earth and the nature of its magnetic field. It is possible to categorize certain satellites as supporting one or more offensive capabilities and others as supporting either solely defensive systems, or both equally. Those satellites which warn of an impending ballistic missile* attack, and those which intercept radio transmissions indicating the emergence of a threat, are clearly defensive. Other satellites support offensive systems: reconnaissance satellites provide targeting information; maritime satellites give the positions of vessels at sea so that naval forces could be directed to strike them; others provide data for missile guidance. A third set of satellites is essentially neutral, providing information valuable for both purposes–communications satellites, 'ferret' (electronic intelligence) satellites and meteorological and geodetic satellites. There is a fourth set unrelated to Soviet military capabilities on land, at sea or in the air which is designed to deny an opponent the use of his space-based systems–'killer' satellites.

The USSR went into space before the USA. Sputnik* 1 was launched on 4 October 1957. Although not directly part of a military programme, this event signalled the beginning of a massive Soviet (and American) investment in spacecraft of increasing sophistication and complexity. There are three groups of Soviet satellites of military interest: Cosmos, Molnya and Meteor. Over 1070 Cosmos satellites have been launched so far and the series is increasing at about 100 launches a year. They have a great many discrete functions and are designed to remain operational for periods ranging from a few days to some thousands of years. Molnya satellites, on the other hand, are all communications satellites (with some 60 launches by 1979). The Meteor series, as the name implies, assists in weather forecasting, which has a clear military use.

Most interest therefore centres on the Cosmos series which has been assessed (but not declared) as having primarily military applications. Of the 72 launches in 1970, 57 were believed to have military roles. In 1975 the comparable figures were 62 out of 85, and in 1976 about 90 out of 101. Of the many functions performed by Cosmos satellites, reconnaissance is probably the most important, whether using optical (visual or infra-red) methods or radar. Most of the optical reconnaissance satellites are recovered after a relatively short time in space, usually 12–13 days. Because they are generally placed in rather low orbits (so as to get high-definition photographs), decay is in any case likely to be rather rapid due to atmospheric drag. They are commanded to re-enter the atmosphere over the USSR with their exposed film, which is then recovered. Capsules of exposed film can also be ejected and recovered during the lifetime of the satellite in order to provide more immediate information if necessary. So far the USSR is not as advanced as the USA in provision of television coverage, but the quality of the photographic record is believed to be very high.

A second method of reconnaissance–mainly maritime–is by radar. Four satellites (three active and identical 'daughter' satellites and one 'mother') are placed close together in space and the correlation of the three radar pictures is carried out, it appears, by the parent vehicle, which can determine both speed and direction by superimposing closely related radar pictures from the three others. This information can either be stored on board and released when the satellites cross Soviet territory or can be passed to an intermediate communications satellite for onward transmission if out of sight of the USSR. A unique feature is that the high power requirements of these satellites (for an active radar uses much more power than any passive system) can be met only by a nuclear power source: neither solar nor chemical power is adequate. But because there is a risk that the radioactive isotopes will re-enter the atmosphere as the satellite orbit decays, the USSR has developed a pattern of boosting the satellite into a high 'safe' orbit at the end of the useful life of the radar–about six weeks–so that the source can decay naturally over time without danger of contamination. The USSR was forced to admit the use of radioactive power sources when something went wrong with Cosmos 954 which crashed in Canada in 1978, spreading radioactive debris over a wide area. It seems that there was a malfunction of the booster which should have raised Cosmos 954 to a higher orbit.

Also in the Cosmos series have been a number of interceptor tests. Target satellites were first placed in orbit and a second satellite was almost immediately launched either to rendezvous with the target or to fly past it at high speed. Some of the interceptors have been seen to explode, clearly indicating an intention to develop an anti-satellite capability. So far such interceptor tests (12 by 1979) have taken place at relatively low levels (250–2000km); American satellites in geostationary orbit would not hence be vulnerable and, since appropriate launch-windows for intercept are infrequent, comprehensive simultaneous attacks using this method would be impossible. Nevertheless the USSR is close to the deployment of a limited anti-satellite capability which would pose a threat to the lower American space platforms in war.

The USSR has consistently aimed at achieving a high degree of redundancy to offset possible malfunction or interference: for example, the military requirement for the Cosmos communications satellites appears to be 36–48 satellites operational at all times. Such redundancy is associated with a lag in progress towards multi-function satellites–not because Soviet technology is inadequate nor because Soviet booster rockets are insufficiently powerful but because it is thought much safer to spread space assets as widely as possible. The USSR is, moreover, geographically at a disadvantage because of its rather northerly position. It is unable to make as much use of geostationary satellites as does the USA–partly because it is not easy to launch into an equatorial orbit from northern sites and because the northern parts of the USSR are not visible from a geostationary satellite. It is therefore sometimes necessary, as with Molnya communication satellites, to use highly eccentric inclined orbits, which allow a satellite to be visible for much of its periodic cycle from the northern hemisphere, maximizing the time when it can be seen from the USSR. Eight hours out of 24 can be achieved, so that only three satellites are needed to provide continuous coverage so long as these are correctly spaced longitudinally. Molyna satellites also handle 'hot line' communications traffic between Moscow and Washington.

Some of the satellites used by both the USSR and the USA are protected to a degree from any interference in peacetime by the provisions of the Strategic Arms Limitation treaty (SALT I),* for much of the verification necessary to assure each of the compliance of the other is done by satellite, and the two governments have agreed not to interfere with national technical means of verification. However, this protection does not, for example, extend to cover communications satellites, early warning or maritime reconnaissance satellites. Therefore there is growing concern that technological innovation may be close to the point where warfare in space becomes a possibility. There appears to be some acceptance of the realization that such a competition would lead to much less strategic stability than now exists for, if one or both were blinded, the margin of permissible error would become very small and the dangers arising from miscalculation unacceptably great. The USSR and the USA are signatories to both the Outer Space Treaty (27 January 1967) which bans the placing of nuclear weapons in free space in orbit, and to the Partial Nuclear Test-Ban Treaty (5 August 1963) which forbids the testing of nuclear weapons in space. There are therefore already some inhibitions, although it must be pointed out that both are now in a position to launch nuclear weapons into space and there to detonate them. The electromagnetic effects of high-altitude nuclear bursts are very undiscriminating but they would certainly provide an effective anti-satellite system in war against any satellite not hardened to withstand the effects of the electromagnetic pulse.

Finally, there is some evidence that the USSR is experimenting with high-energy lasers and particle-beam weapons as a possible means of attacking satellites. Difficulties will persist for many years in harnessing such technologies for military use, such as aiming and focusing the energy release over great distances, and the need for large and vulnerable platforms to assure the very high power requirements for a space-based anti-satellite weapon system.   *J.A.*

Communications satellite Molnya 2 on show at the Paris Salon, May 1973

Strategic nuclear forces

The pre-eminent element of the USSR's offensive nuclear might lies in the Strategic Rocket Forces (SRF), comprising all land-based ballistic missiles with ranges over 1000km. While the USA distributes its strategic deterrent in roughly equal measure among land-based missiles, bombers and missile submarines, something over two-thirds of the Soviet deterrent rests in the missiles of the SRF, and it receives 60 per cent of the Soviet strategic budget. Yet the USSR has steadily improved all its instruments of strategic force; by 1980 it was putting nearly one-fifth of military expenditure* to this purpose, while the USA was spending in the late 1970s under 15 per cent of a smaller budget. The USSR has made great strides in submarine-launched ballistic missiles (SLBM); these still lag behind those of the USA in sophistication and accuracy, but the gap has narrowed.

Strategic Rocket Forces

The SRF is one of five combat services of the Soviet armed forces.* Apparently created in 1959 and elevated to the rank of a separate service in 1960, its formation reflected Khrushchev's* interest in nuclear deterrence (in part as a means of reducing defence spending) and his belief that nuclear missile forces would dominate future wars. At the same time the navy* was deprived of its strategic role. Khrushchev's effort to increase Soviet reliance on nuclear weapons at the expense of conventional forces was shortlived, but the SRF remained of central importance. It is believed to have some 400 000 military and 50 000 civilian personnel; its head, an army general, is (like the heads of the other armed services) a Deputy Minister of Defence.

The SRF is supplied by the so-called Ministry of Medium Machine-building, created in 1953. Three or four design bureaux produce ballistic missiles for the SRF – which contributes to the multiplicity of each new generation of Soviet weaponry (unlike American practice); for instance, the fourth generation of Soviet intercontinental ballistic missiles (ICBM) deployed in the late 1970s consisted of the SS-16, -17, -18 and -19, each having quite different characteristics. The SRF has an active inventory of close to 1400 ICBM; in addition, 600 medium- to intermediate-range ballistic missiles (M/IRBM) are deployed in the western USSR and near the Chinese border, with new SS-20 replacing ageing SS-4 and -5 missiles. The command structure of the SRF is divided between the ICBM and the M/IRBM forces. The SRF commander has, over-all, nine armies, six of them operational and three for weapons testing, and some 300 launch control facilities. The SRF's weapons are deployed in a band that stretches from the region near Moscow to the east of Lake Baykal, with some northward into the Urals.

Under the second Strategic Arms Limitation treaty (SALT II),* the USSR and the USA each would have been limited to 2250 strategic nuclear weapons launchers. Had the treaty been ratified, ICBM with multiple warheads capable of being independently targeted (multiple independent re-entry vehicles – MIRV) would have been limited to 820, the SRF would have reduced its total ICBM force by several hundred, and the USSR would have been limited to the deployment of one 'new' ICBM during the treaty period (to 1985). Some constraints would have been placed on improvements in existing missile systems, mainly as regards missile size, since constraints on improvements in accuracy cannot be verified. With or without the treaty, the USSR may deploy some of the fifth generation of ICBM now being developed, for, provided those have essentially the same size and propulsion characteristics as the missiles they replace, they need not count as a 'new' type under SALT II.

The first three generations of Soviet ICBM were quite crude, with very large rocket motors delivering very large warheads, size and yield compensating for inaccuracy. However, Soviet missiles have

ESTIMATES OF STRENGTH OF SOVIET STRATEGIC FORCES, 1979

Type	Launchers number	Warheads per missile	Yield per warhead Mt^2	Accuracy[1] $nmiles^3$
INTERCONTINENTAL BALLISTIC MISSILES (ICBM)				
SS-9	} 100	1	18–25	0.7
SS-9 modification 4		3 (MRV)	4–5	0.5
SS-11	} 638	1	1–2	0.7
SS-11 modification 3		3 (MRV)	0.1–0.3	0.5
SS-13	60	1	1	0.7
SS-17	} 100	4 (MIRV)	0.9	0.3
SS-17 modification 2		1	5	0.3
SS-18	} 200	1	18–25	0.3
SS-18 modification 2		8 (MIRV)	0.6	0.25
SS-19	} 300	6 (MIRV)	0.55	0.25
SS-19 modification 2		1	5	0.25
MEDIUM- AND INTERMEDIATE-RANGE BALLISTIC MISSILES (M/IRBM)				
SS-4	500	1	1	1.5
SS-5	90	1	1	1.0
SS-20	120	3 (MIRV)	0.15	0.15

Type	Launchers number	Range $nmiles^3$	Warheads per missile	Yield per warhead Mt^2	Accuracy[1] $nmiles^3$
SUBMARINE-LAUNCHED BALLISTIC MISSILES (SLBM)					
SS-N-1	18	350	1	1–2	2.0
SS-N-5	60	750	1	1–2	2.0
SS-N-6	} 528	1750	1	1–2	1.5
SS-N-6 modn 3		2000	3 (MIRV)	..	1.0
SS-N-8	266	4800	1	1–2	0.8
SS-NX-17	12	3000+	3 (MIRV)	..	..
SS-N-18	144	5000+	5 (MIRV)	1–2	..

Type and NATO designation[4]	Deployed number	Maximum range $nmiles^3$	Maximum speed $mach^5$	Weapons load thousand lb
LONG- AND MEDIUM-RANGE BOMBERS				
Tu-95 (Bear)	113	8000	0.78	40
MYa-4 (Bison)	43	7000	0.87	20
Tu-16 (Badger)	613	4000	0.8	20
Tu-22 M/26 (Backfire)	80	5500	2.5	17.5

[1] Circular error probable [2] Mt = megatonnes of conventional high explosive
[3] nmiles = nautical miles [4] There are also 44 Bison adapted as tankers; Badger and Backfire include Naval Aviation planes (some 295 Badger and 30 Backfire) but exclude Badger tankers [5] mach = ratio to speed of sound

Source: US Congressional Research Service and International Institute for Strategic Studies. The Military Balance 1979–1980, London, 1979

improved consistently, especially in accuracy, and have remained considerably larger than those of the USA; the SS-19 is, for example, some three times as large as the American Minuteman III ICBM. The fourth-generation ICBM of the SRF–the SS-16, -17, -18, and -19–are larger (have more 'throw weight') and more accurate than the SS-9, -11, and -13 that they are replacing. The SS-18 is the largest Soviet missile yet deployed. All SRF ICBM are deployed in hardened silos. The SRF also has a fully tested mobile missile, the SS-16, a three-stage version of the two-stage SS-20, but would have been precluded from deploying it by the terms of SALT II. Accuracy is the more important improvement, since the ability to destroy 'hard' targets such as missile silos depends much more on accuracy than on 'throw-weight'. It is hard to know exactly how accurate the missiles of the SRF are. The accuracy or CEP (circular error probable) of the newest missiles is believed to be between 0.2 and 0.3 nautical miles (nm). The SS-17, -18 and -19 all have been tested with multiple independently-targetable warheads (MIRV)–MRV being multiple warheads that cannot be targeted separately from one another–permitting a single missile to attack several separated targets. In particular, there is growing concern in the USA over the possibility that by the early 1980s a fraction of the Soviet large, accurate, multiple-warhead missiles could in theory threaten to destroy all the American land-based ICBM in a first strike. There are a number of technical reasons why that theoretical possibility might not be a serious option, even assuming the USSR had such an intention. One such reason is doubt over reliability–over whether missiles will fly to targets as intended and avoid destroying each other prematurely in flight–which is estimated to be as low as 60 per cent.

Ballistic missile submarines

In the 1950s the USSR began to build submarines especially designed to carry ballistic missiles, the diesel-powered Golf and nuclear-powered Hotel classes (NATO designations). With the creation of the SRF, however, the momentum of Soviet SLBM programmes declined, to revive again in the later 1960s under the spur of the American strategic build-up, in particular the creation of the Polaris submarine fleet, then being built at six per year. The first of the Soviet Yankee class submarines was deployed in 1968, carrying 16 SS-N-6 missiles, similar to early Polaris missiles. The Yankee class was followed by several classes of Delta submarines, which carry SS-N-8 missiles, with a range of well over 6400km. That range added a significant dimension to the Soviet SLBM force because it meant that Soviet submarines did not need to cross the area of sea between Greenland, Iceland and the United Kingdom (which was closely monitored by NATO forces) to gain the oceans from Soviet Arctic ports. Submarines with the SS-N-8 can operate close to home shores (much as is planned for the American Trident submarines). Under the first Strategic Arms Limitation treaty (SALT I) of 1972 both sides were permitted 950 'modern' SLBM. The Soviet SLBM force in 1979 consisted of 34 Yankee class submarines (all but one equipped with SS-N-6 missiles), and about 29 Delta class submarines, most with SS-N-8 missiles but the newer ones carrying SS-N-18, the first multiple-warhead SLBM to be deployed in significant numbers by the USSR. Remaining Golf and Hotel class submarines, some operating in the Baltic, carry obsolescent SS-N-4 and -5 missiles and pose a nuclear threat to Europe. A new submarine, referred to as Typhoon and still larger than the Delta class, is thought to be under development.

Left: intercontinental ballistic missile cold-launch containers on show at the October Revolution parade, 1973. Top: SS-9 intercontinental ballistic missiles (NATO designation Scarp). Centre: *Delta* class ballistic missile submarine. Bottom: Mya-4 bomber (NATO designation Bison), bottom left, shadowed by a British Royal Air Force Lightning

In the past the USSR has kept only a few of its modern missile submarines at sea in firing position at any one time; by contrast the USA keeps about half its fleet on station. That has suggested that the Soviet government has not taken very seriously the prospect of a surprise nuclear attack; however, all Soviet strategic forces gradually have become readier, and with the new longer-range SLBM the percentage of the Soviet submarine fleet on station is likely to rise.

Strategic bombers

The USSR has devoted much less attention to intercontinental nuclear bombers than has the USA – about 5 per cent of its strategic budget versus 40 per cent for America – and the bulk of its long-range fleet are ageing Bison and Bear aircraft. Attention by 1979 had focused on the Backfire, a supersonic bomber which, like the Badger, was being deployed with Soviet Long-range Aviation and Naval Aviation. The Backfire has been excluded from the SALT II agreement on the argument that it is not fully intercontinental in range, but the Soviet authorities would nevertheless undertake commitments on production rates, and possibly on basing and in-flight refuelling to ensure that it cannot strike the USA. However, both the Bear and the Backfire can carry cruise missiles of about 500km range, while reports of cruise missiles of twice that range being tested from Backfires raised questions of whether Backfires carrying such missiles should not have been counted in SALT II. The prototype of a new subsonic bomber with greater range and more payload is expected to replace the Bear in the early 1980s.

The Soviet view of war

The momentum in all Soviet strategic programmes raises the question of how the USSR views nuclear forces. Strategic ballistic missiles, in particular, appear to be seen as a special form of artillery, long the prestige weapon of the Soviet army. Soviet writings do not espouse nuclear war, but neither do they regard it as inconceivable. They emphasize what is often called 'war-fighting': if war occurs, then it will be the task of strategic forces to fight, and if possible to win, that war, even a nuclear war. Nuclear weapons are thus viewed as special weapons but not as something completely apart from other weapons and plans for fighting wars. By contrast, American thinking about nuclear weapons for two decades emphasized deterrence – how war can be avoided – much more than war-fighting. To deter, the essential is the ability to inflict unacceptable damage to the opponent in a retaliatory strike after tolerating a first strike by that opponent. In the logic of deterrence, the ability to destroy the other side's missiles is an evil because it may deprive the other side of its retaliatory forces, hence giving it an incentive to strike first in any conflict. For Soviet military strategists, however, there is little distinction between 'war-fighting' and 'deterrence': the latter is achieved by being prepared for the former.

G.T.

Nuclear survival

The Soviet Civil Defence (CD) organization must be viewed in the context of the particular geographical and social features of the USSR – its great size and low population density coupled with the isolation and backwardness of widespread rural communities (38 per cent of the population in 1979), and the concentration of the urban population in towns likewise far apart. The aim of the CD system is to enable the Soviet state to survive a nuclear war, and to enable the Communist Party* to remain in power to continue the direction of the state. To this end, the organization endeavours to foster the over-all discipline and militarization* of the population so as to facilitate its control by the Party in time of crisis; to increase the speed and efficiency with which the population could then be fully mobilized; to effect substantial limitation of war damage; and to enable the state to recover after a nuclear attack. It seeks to achieve its aims by providing the basic CD training of the entire civilian population; training civilian establishments (such as organs of local government, hospitals factories and farms) for recovery after a nuclear strike, disaster relief and rescue; planning and exercising for the evacuation and relocation of key economic enterprises; and constructing shelters, particularly for the protection of personnel essential to command and production functions. The CD system is a branch of the armed services, with much the same status as other branches. There is a regular Army Civil Defence Corps totalling at least 20 000 men, approximately 20 per cent regular officers and 80 per cent conscripts on a two-year term of service. There is a Civil Defence Officers' Academy, and a large permanent staff in the Ministry of Defence whose task is to integrate the military and civilian elements and to control the entire system. A small full-time and large part-time CD civilian staff work in organs of local government and large factories and administer the system or train to adapt their civilian profession to CD work in wartime. They run the CD system in their town or factory, including the basic CD training course of 6 to 15 hours which every Soviet citizen is supposed to undergo. In the event of war, the civilian CD staff effect the mobilization of the CD structure for military control. The military corps is trained in disaster management, and at irregular intervals combined exercises are held with the civilian CD of a factory or district to test mobilization and operating procedures.

Increasing effort is being put into the CD system which, though it could not as yet hope to guarantee the survival of the Soviet state in nuclear war, could help to mitigate the effects of a nuclear strike. The system has ideological and practical justification, and increasing credibility in the public eye – the more so because no public criticism of it is allowed. There is a large full-time disciplined military core, an impressive potential framework for mobilizing and training the civilian population, and a deep network of shelters in key areas sufficient to protect those in important Party, government, military and production posts. In some towns of military importance, evacuation and protection drill for the general population is practised. The system has not, however, succeeded in giving effective training to all the urban population, and its effort in rural areas has been slight. Officials of the civilian organization do not devote sufficient time or effort to CD training, mainly due to their other responsibilities. Shelter facilities do not exist for the bulk of the population, and the complex evacuation plans from major cities have not been adequately rehearsed. The CD system would certainly help to ensure the survival of the ruling structure in the USSR. The framework for universal protection exists, and could be expanded if sufficient resources were diverted to it.   *C.N.D.*

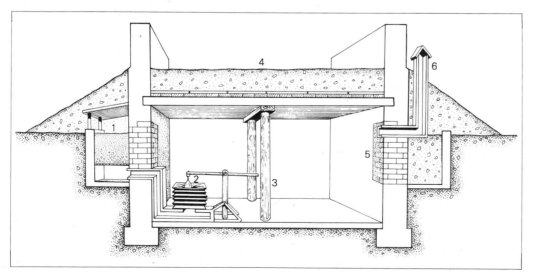

A Soviet civilian nuclear shelter in a cellar: (1) sand filter, (2) bellows for air intake, (3) ceiling support, (4) roof fill, (5) window seal, (6) exhaust box

Strength and deployment of the Soviet armed forces

TOTAL STRENGTH

Total forces under arms, including para-military troops of the KGB and MVD: 4.6 million
Total of civilian personnel employed full-time by defence industries, military research and development and military education: 5 million approximately

EXPENDITURE

1978: Estimated expenditure on defence, including all areas of defence-related spending:

as share of estimated gross national product (GNP)	12–14.5 per cent
as share of public expenditure	40–45 per cent
cost of similar defence effort if purchased in USA at value of $ in January 1981	$210 000 million

1975: Estimated percentage of expenditure on military forces to each arm of service:

	per cent
Strategic Rocket Forces (SRF)	14
Air Defence Forces of the Homeland	8
Air Forces (all types)	20
Ground Forces	22
Navy	18
Command and Support	18

During the 1970s the most dramatic actual increase in expenditure was in the SRF and the Air Forces. The rise in expenditure on the navy was about average–some 4–5 per cent per annum in real terms. The rise in expenditure on the Ground Forces was only half this rate, while the expenditure on air defence fell by some 20 per cent. In 1981 it appeared that greater resources were being devoted to the Air Defence Forces.

PRODUCTION

1978: Estimated production of main items of equipment:

Tanks 2 650; other armoured combat vehicles 3 500; artillery and self-propelled systems 1 700; helicopters 1 100; combat aircraft 950; surface ships and large hovercraft 90; nuclear submarines 6.

STRENGTHS OF THE DIFFERENT ARMS OF SERVICE

1. Strategic Rocket Forces

Land-based ballistic missiles: intercontinental range (ICBM) 1 400; medium and intermediate range (IRBM/MRBM) 690 (including rockets phased out or in store)

Carried by Soviet Navy: 70 submarines carrying 955 surface-fired (SSBN) missiles of intercontinental range; 20 submarines carrying a total of 60 surface-fired missiles of medium range.
Carried by Long-range Aviation (bombers carry nuclear weapons, free-fall or stand-off, capable of engaging land, sea or submarine targets): 156 long-range bombers; 518 medium-range bombers; 45 tanker aircraft; 100 electronic countermeasures (ECM) aircraft.

Source: estimates in International Institute for Strategic Studies (IISS) *The Military Balance, 1979–1980*, London, 1979

2. Ground Forces

Field Formations: 46 Tank Divisions; 119 Motor Rifle Divisions; 8 Airborne Divisions.
Equipment Park: over 50 000 tanks; 62 000 other armoured combat vehicles; 23 000 artillery—guns, mortars and multiple rocket launchers and vehicles with anti-tank guided missiles (ATGM); 8 000 anti-aircraft guns; 7 000 vehicle-mounted missile systems of all sizes; 25 000 hand-held missile systems; 1 300 launchers for tactical and operational nuclear-capable missiles.

Soviet divisions are rated as fully deployed (category 1), partly deployed (category 2) or cadre (category 3). All formations in Groups of Forces in Europe are fully deployed, and the Group of Soviet Forces in Germany has extra-large scales of equipment. In the USSR less than 25 per cent of divisions are fully deployed.

Major items of Ground Forces equipment are shown in the following tables.

ARMOURED FIGHTING VEHICLES

Type	Crew	Passengers	Weight tonnes	Armament	Speed km/h	Range km
T55 tank	4	—	36	100mm anti-tank gun (range 1000m)	48	400
T62 tank	4	—	36.5	115mm anti-tank gun (range 1500m)	50	500
T64 and T72 tanks	3	—	40+	125mm auto-loader anti-tank gun (range 2000m)	63	500
BRDM-2 wheeled amphibious armoured reconnaissance vehicle	4	—	7	14.5 and 7.62 machine-guns in turret	100 (10 afloat)	750
BTR 60 PA wheeled amphibious armoured personnel carrier	2	8	10.3	14.5 and 7.62 machine-guns in turret	80 (10 afloat)	500
BMP tracked multi-role amphibious infantry combat vehicle	3	6–8	12.5	73mm gun, 7.62 machine-gun; anti-tank guided missile in turret	55 (8 afloat)	300

Statistical Estimates

ARTILLERY[1]

Type	Calibre mm	Range km	Weight of shell lb	Maximum rate of fire rounds/min
D-30 howitzer	122	15	48	6–8
M-1943 field-gun	130	27	74	5–6
D-1 howitzer	152	12.4	88	3–4
T-12 anti-tank gun	100	2	..	8
M-1974 self-propelled gun	122	16	55	6–7
M-1973 self-propelled gun	152	17.5	96	4
BM 21 multiple rocket launcher	122 (40 tubes)	20.5	43 (warhead)	3 salvoes of 40 rounds/hour

[1] The following are also in service (NATO designation and range in km): AT–3 (Sagger, 3.0); AT–4 (Spigot, 2.0) with semi-automatic homing; AT–5 (Spandrel, more than 4.0) with terminal homing; and AT–6 (Spiral, 5.0) mounted on the Mi-24 helicopter

TACTICAL OPERATIONAL MISSILES[1]

NATO designation	Range km	Average war-head yield kt^2
Frog-7 unguided rocket on wheeled transporter-launcher vehicle	15–65	20
Scud-B guided missile on wheeled transporter-launcher vehicle	30–280	40

[1] These are in course of replacement by systems deploying warheads of similar yield but with greater accuracy and range (estimates in km); all are guided missiles on transporter-launcher vehicles: Frog replaced by SS–21 (120), Scud replaced and supplemented by SS–22 (1000) and SS–23 (350)

[2] kt = kilotonnes of conventional high explosive

INFANTRY WEAPONS

Type	Calibre mm	Range m	Rate of fire rounds/min
AKM assault rifle	7.62 short	400	90
AK74 assault rifle	5.45	300	120
PKM general-purpose machine-gun	7.62 long	1 000	650
RPG7 light anti-tank grenade launcher[1]	84.5	300	..
120mm mortar	120	5 700	15 (16kg bomb)
Plamya rapid-fire anti-personnel grenade launcher	30	400	90

[1] The RPG16 is almost identical but with greater warhead power

ANTI-AIRCRAFT GUNS

ZSU 23-4 4-barrelled 23mm machine-gun mounted on tracked armoured vehicle, 4 000 rounds/min, integral radar control, range 3 000m

S-60 single-barrelled 57mm gun, 120 rounds/min, remote radar control, range 6 000m.

ANTI-AIRCRAFT MISSILES

Type, NATO designation and date of introduction	Specification and deployment	Altitude ft	Slant range nmiles[1]	Guidance
SA-2 (Guideline) 1958 (many variants)	Mobile or static mounting for strategic defence	High and medium to 80 000	22	Radio
SA-3 (Goa) 1961	Twin mounting on lorry—army/front level	High and medium to 60 000	14	Radio, radar homing
SA-4 (Ganef) 1964	Twin mounting on tracked armoured chassis	High to low 1 000–80 000	40	Complex radar and automatic radar homing
SA-5 (Gammon) 1963	Mobile or static mounting for strategic defence	High 95 000	135	Automatic radar homing
SA-6 (Gainful) 1967	Triple-mounted on tracked armoured vehicle at division level and above	Low to medium 50–60 000	20	Radio, semi-active radar homing
SA-7 (Grail) 1969	Hand-held tube-launched infantry weapon, with platoons and battalions	Low 50–8 000	4	Infra-red
SA-8 (Gecko) 1975	Sextuple-mounted on amphibious wheeled vehicle, at division level	Low and medium 20 000	8	Integral twin radar guidance controls salvoes of missiles
SA-9 (Gaskin) 1971	Quadruple-mounted on armoured reconnaissance vehicle, regiment level	Low 50–15 000	4	Infra-red
SA-10 1979	Strategic defence	Low to medium (possibly for use against cruise missiles)	..	..
SA-11 1979	..	..	..	..

[1] nmiles = nautical miles

3. Troops of the Air Defence Forces

6000 early warning or control radars; 12 AWACS aircraft with warning and control systems (AWACS); 1 anti-ballistic missile system (Moscow) with 64 missiles; 1100 surface-to-air missile (SAM) sites with a total of over 10 000 missiles; 2700+ interceptor aircraft.

4. Naval forces

289 major surface-combat ships; 91 nuclear and 166 diesel attack or cruise-missile submarines. Reserves: 25 major surface-combat ships; 115 attack submarines; 12 000 men in the Naval Infantry; 8000 men in the Coastal Defence Artillery; 770 combat aircraft of the Naval Air Force.

5. Air Forces

Tactical Aviation (subordinated as 16 tactical air armies to Ground Forces Command in Groups of Forces or Military Districts) with 4650 combat aircraft and 2450 helicopters in all branches of the armed forces.
Military Transport Aviation with 1300 military transport aircraft; Reserve: 3500 Aeroflot civil airliners, air freighters or light aircraft.

Major aircraft of the Air Forces are shown in the following tables.

HELICOPTERS

Type and NATO designation	Role	Armament	Payload	Speed km/h	Range (fully loaded) km
Mi-8 (Hip)	General purpose	Rockets, bombs, ATGM	2 tonnes or 24 troops	210	650 (400)
Mi-6 (Hook)	Heavy transport	None	12 tonnes or 61 troops	250	1 400 (250)
Mi-24 (Hind)	Combat and support	Gatling gun rockets, bombs, ATGM	3 tonnes or 12 troops	300	..

FIXED-WING AIRCRAFT (INTERCEPTOR, GROUND-ATTACK AND RECONNAISSANCE)

Type and NATO designation	Role	Armament	Ceiling ft	Speed km/h	Range (combat radius) km
MiG-21 (Fishbed) (several variants)	Fighter ground-attack (FGA) reconnaissance and intercept	Cannon, anti aircraft missiles	59 000	1 800	1 700 (800)
MiG-23 (Flogger) (4 variants)	FGA, intercept	Multiple cannon, missiles, bombs (nuclear)	60 000	1 200	2 200 (900)
MiG-27 (Flogger D) (improved payload)	FGA	Multiple cannon, bombs (nuclear) and Gatling gun missiles	60 000	1 200	2 200 (900)
MiG-25 (Foxbat)	Intercept and reconnaissance	..	80 000	3 000	3 000 (1 100)
Su-7 (Fitter A)	Intercept and FGA	Bombs, cannon	50 000	1 500	1 400 (600)
Su-17 (Fitter C) swing-wing version of Su–7	Intercept and FGA	Bombs, cannon, stand-off nuclear weapon	60 000	2 100	1 200 (500)
Su-19 (Fencer)	FGA	Gatling guns, stand-off nuclear missiles	60 000	2 500	1 300 (600)

Statistical Estimates

FIXED-WING AIRCRAFT (BOMBERS, LONG-RANGE RECONNAISSANCE)

Type and NATO designation	Role	Armament	Ceiling ft	Speed km/h	Range (unrefuelled) km
MYa-4 (Bison)	Long-range bomber, reconnaissance, tanker	Cannon and turrets, bombs (nuclear)	50 000	800	9 000
Tu-16 (Badger)	Medium-range bomber, tanker	Stand-off missiles, cannon	43 000	750	6 000
Tu-95/20 (Bear)	Long-range bomber, reconnaissance	Stand-off missiles, turret, cannon	45 000	800	12 000
Tu-22 M/26 (Backfire)	Medium-range bomber	Stand-off missiles	60 000	2 200	6 000

FIXED-WING AIRCRAFT (TRANSPORTS)

Type and NATO designation	Role	Payload	Ceiling ft	Speed km/h	Range (unrefuelled) km
An-12 (Cub)	General purpose; paratroops	14 tonnes or 90 troops	30 000	620	4 600
Il-76 (Candid)	Heavy jet transport	40 tonnes	50 000	900	5 000

6. Para-military forces

22 000 Civil Defence Forces regular troops; 220 000 KGB, border and internal service troops; 270 000 MVD militia, transportation troops and GULag guards

Civilian complement to the forces (estimated figures, as membership overlaps): 8 million effective regular reserves to the armed forces; 80 million claimed membership of the youth military sports organization (DOSAAF)

7. Civil Defence – civilian resources

45 000 (estimated) full-time civilian staff; 2 million active part-time Civil Defence members

C. N. D.

THE WORLD ROLE

The USSR in its world setting

The expansion of tsarist Russia

Muscovy became an independent state in 1480 when the Tatar* yoke was thrown off by Ivan III* who, after his marriage in 1472 to Sofia, the only niece of the last Byzantine emperor, also initiated Muscovy's claim to be Byzantium's successor as leader of the Orthodox* world ('Moscow is the Third Rome'). Ivan III also asserted Moscow's claim to the former lands of Kievan* Russia, acquired by Lithuania, and gained access to the Baltic. Modest diplomatic contacts with many Western states were started. Muscovite control of northern Russia was completed by Vasily III.* Under Ivan IV (the Terrible),* first to be crowned 'Tsar of All the Russias' (the Russian principates now assembled under Muscovite rule), Muscovy conquered the Tatar khanates of Kazan' (1552) and Astrakhan' (1556), and expanded into western Siberia (1583). The Crimean Tatars, however, remained a great menace, and in the Livonian War (1558–83) against Poland-Lithuania (fully united in 1569) and Sweden, Ivan failed to acquire the lands of the Teutonic Order and lost Muscovy's narrow Baltic coastline. A difficult sea route to the west via Archangel was, however, opened by the English in 1553. Under Fedor I,* an independent Russian Orthodox patriarchate was established (1588). Following the death of Boris Godunov,* violent dynastic and social conflicts erupted, and during the Time of Troubles* Muscovite power was eclipsed. Polish intervention in 1609–12 and the Polish king's ambition to promote Catholicism* provoked a successful national rising, and Mikhail Romanov* was elected tsar in 1613. Under him Muscovy still remained on the defensive. Novgorod was recovered from Sweden (1617), but relations with Poland proved complex; in 1634 Władysław IV of Poland renounced his claim to the Muscovite throne but retained Smolensk. In 1648, however, a Ukrainian Cossack rising against Polish rule, and the Ukraine's incorporation in 1654 by Tsar Alexis,* precipitated a major Russo-Polish war which resulted in the partition of the Ukraine along the Dnieper (1667). A war with Sweden (1656–8) was inconclusive. An 'eternal peace' with Poland (1686) brought the permanent acquisition of Kiev and membership, with Poland, Austria and Venice, of the Holy League against Turkey, but with little success for Russia. A treaty with China excluded Russia from the Amur basin (1689).

The birth of the Russian Empire

By 1696, when Peter I* acquired sole power, Muscovy was no longer isolated and was open to Western cultural and technological ideas. Peter accelerated this process and during the Great Northern War (1700–21) against Sweden altered the balance of power in northern and eastern Europe. Humiliatingly defeated at Narva (November 1700), Peter consolidated his forces while Charles XII of Sweden pursued Peter's ally, Augustus II of Poland and Saxony. Peter conquered Ingria and founded St Petersburg* (May 1703) but failed to secure peace in 1707 and had to face a Swedish invasion from Poland in 1709. Peter's decisive victory at Poltava (July 1709) did not immediately end the war, but Russia's access to the Baltic was now assured. However, Peter fared badly against Turkey, where Charles XII took refuge. An invasion of Turkey (1711) during which Russia, for the first time, sought Balkan Christian support, ended disastrously, and Peter had to relinquish Azov (captured in 1696) and to promise not to interfere in Poland. Despite this promise, Peter restored Augustus II, and in 1716–17 re-established Russian influence in Poland.

The Swedish war was vigorously pursued in Germany, Denmark and Finland; the new Russian fleet defeated the Swedes at Hangö (July 1714), and in July 1719 Russian forces landed in Sweden proper. By the peace treaty of Nystad (August 1721) Russia acquired Ingria, Estonia and Swedish Livonia with Riga. The victorious Peter assumed the title of emperor. Dynastic links with Courland, Mecklenburg and Holstein-Gottorp were also established. However, there was growing concern in England, Germany and elsewhere at the rise of the new northern colossus. In 1722–3 Russia won the south shore of the Caspian from Persia, and although it failed to establish diplomatic and trading relations with China the subjugation of Kamchatka continued.

Although none of Peter I's immediate successors possessed his formidable qualities, Russia's growing international importance was maintained. During 1725–40 Russian foreign policy was largely guided by A. I. Ostermann (1687–1747), who opposed French influence and supported Austria. During the War of the Polish Succession (1733–5) Empress Anne* fought the French-sponsored candidate Leszczyński and helped to install the Saxon Augustus III. In 1732 Peter I's Persian conquests were surrendered, but another Turkish war (1735–9) brought Russia Azov though not the right to enter the Black Sea. Sweden declared war in 1741 only to lose south-eastern Finland in 1743.

In the Seven Years War (1756–62) Russia adhered to the Franco-Austrian alliance (January 1757), fought successfully against Prussia, and in 1760 occupied Berlin. However, the accession of Peter III* brought about an instantaneous reconciliation and an alliance with Prussia which continued under Catherine II* until 1788.

Conquests of Catherine the Great

Under Catherine II Russia's international influence and prestige received a new impetus. Catherine secured the election of Stanisław Poniatowski as king of Poland (1764) but opposed constitutional reform there, and in 1768 imposed a formal Russian protectorate over Poland. An uprising in Poland won Franco-Austrian assistance, and brought Turkey into open war against Russia (1769). The ensuing serious international complications were resolved by the first partition of Poland (1772), which gave Russia Vitebsk and Mogilev. The Russo-Turkish treaty of Kutchuk-Kainardzhi (July 1774) established the independence of the Crimean khanate; Russia annexed Kerch and the territory between the Bug and Dnieper, secured a free passage for its merchant ships through the Turkish Straits, and acquired ill-defined rights to protect Turkey's Christians. Russia's international prestige was greatly enhanced by the victory over Turkey. The Russian protectorate over Poland was confirmed in 1775, Russia became a guarantor of the constitution of the Holy Roman Empire in 1779, and during the American War of Independence lent its weight to the League of Armed Neutrality (1780) against British claims to search neutral vessels in wartime.

Turkey, however, loomed large again. In association with G. A. Potemkin (1739–91) Catherine devised the 'Greek project' to restore Byzantium under her grandson Constantine, and to liberate Orthodox Christians from Turkish rule. This ambitious scheme made necessary a rapprochement with Austria (1781). The Crimea was annexed and a protectorate imposed over Georgia (1783), but the war against Turkey in 1787–92 brought limited success; the situation was further complicated in 1788 by a Swedish attack and by the overthrow of the Russian protectorate in Poland. Although peace was signed with Sweden at Verelä (August 1790), Prussian alliances with Poland and Turkey, and the threat of combined action by the European powers against Russia with British participation in spring 1791 tested Catherine's resilience to the utmost. She refused to budge, the potential anti-Russian coalition disintegrated, and after the Treaty of Jassy with Turkey (January 1792), whereby she postponed implementing the 'Greek project', Catherine turned to deal with Poland whose reformed constitution of 1791 she overthrew in summer 1792. She then proceeded, in collusion with Prussia, with the second partition of Poland (1793). The defeat of Kościuszko's uprising brought about the third and final partition of Poland in 1795; 62 per cent of pre-partition Poland was now in the Russian Empire. Catherine died in November 1796 before another extravagant campaign to destroy the Ottoman Empire could be implemented.

Paul I* was hostile to the French Revolution and after Bonaparte's seizure of Malta (June 1798) joined the Second Coalition against France. Despite Russian successes in the Ionian Islands and Italy, relations with Austria turned sour, as well as with Britain over an expedition to Holland and Russian designs on Malta. Paul abandoned the coalition, organized the second Armed Neutrality against Britain (December 1800) and started negotiations for a French alliance. He turned to planning Turkey's downfall and annexed Georgia, but a Cossack force sent to conquer India was recalled after his murder in March 1801.

The meeting of Alexander I and Napoleon at Tilsit

The zenith of tsarist power

Under Alexander I* Russian influence was to reach its highest point in the imperial period. He restored good relations with Britain and France in 1801. However, the new Anglo-French war (1803), the Duc d'Enghien's execution, and the proclamation of Napoleon* as emperor in 1804 moved him to support the Third Coalition of which the Anglo-Russian alliance (April 1805) was the core. But disaster struck; despite Alexander's warm friendship with the Prussian king and queen, Prussia did not help and the defeat of the Russian and Austrian armies at Austerlitz (December 1805) compelled Austria to sue for peace. Russian military operations resumed when Prussia finally challenged France in September 1806. Prussia's collapse and Russia's defeat at Friedland (June 1807) led to the Treaty of Alliance signed by Napoleon and Alexander at Tilsit in July 1807. Russia severed relations with Britain, helped to enforce Napoleon's Continental System by attacking Sweden and annexing Finland (September 1809), and discussed with France a partition of Turkey, yet again at war with Russia since October 1806. Despite the two emperors' second meeting at Erfurt (September–October 1808), Russia's support of France during the Franco-Austrian war of 1809 was half-hearted, while the enlargement of the Napoleonic Duchy of Warsaw (created at Tilsit) increased Russia's fears for her ex-Polish provinces. In fact the Franco-Russian alliance was under a growing strain. Experiencing economic difficulties, Russia modified the stiff anti-British tariffs demanded by Napoleon. In January 1811 Napoleon annexed Oldenburg, the heir to which was Alexander's brother-in-law. Alexander secured an alliance with Sweden (April 1812) and signed a well-timed peace treaty with Turkey (May 1812),

459

which ceded Bessarabia. A nine-year war with Persia was terminated when that country renounced its claims to a large area in the Caucasus in October 1813.

Napoleon attacked Russia on 24 June 1812 and entered Moscow on 14 September. Alexander's refusal to negotiate, the burning of Moscow, and an early winter compelled the French to withdraw. Disregarding contrary advice and determined to liberate Europe, Alexander pursued them across the Russian border. He was joined by Prussia (February 1813), Sweden and Austria (August), and received the necessary subsidies from Britain. On 31 March 1814 Alexander entered Paris in triumph; he insisted that Louis XVIII could be restored only as a constitutional monarch. At the Congress of Vienna (September 1814–June 1815) Alexander acquired most of the Duchy of Warsaw as a constitutional kingdom of Poland in union with Russia.

The vague Holy Alliance initiated by Alexander in September 1815, which was to commit all rulers to govern according to the precepts of Christianity, had less effect in preserving peace than the periodic international congresses provided for by the renewed Quadruple Alliance of November 1815. At the Congresses of Troppau (1820), Laibach (1821) and Verona (1822) Alexander supported the policy of intervention advocated by Metternich, against revolutions in Italy, Spain and South America, but his offers of Russian troops were politely refused. Diplomatic relations with the USA, which date from 1808, were not strained by the Monroe Doctrine; Alexander admired the American republic and Russia agreed to restrict its territory in America to Alaska (April 1824).

Alexander's new policy of 'legitimacy' proved difficult to uphold when the Greeks rose against Turkey in 1821, and Nicholas I★ finally agreed, in conjunction with Britain, to mediate for Greek autonomy (1826). Turkish indignation after the destruction of the Turkish fleet at Navarino (October 1827) drove Russia into another successful war in April 1828. The Treaty of Adrianople (September 1829) gave Russia the mouth of the Danube, territories along the eastern Black Sea coast and in the Caucasus, guaranteed Russian trade in the Black Sea, and established Russian influence in Moldavia and Wallachia. With Britain and France, Russia established an independent Greek kingdom in 1830, and its domination of Turkey was obvious.

The Caucasus

Russia's strategic position on the Black Sea had been reinforced under Alexander I. The eastern Georgian kingdom–a Russian protectorate since the reign of Catherine the Great–was annexed in 1801. The subjugation of the remaining Georgian principalities, such as Mingrelia and Imeretiya, led to war with Persia (1804–13) which had to cede most of eastern Transcaucasia along the Kura and Araxes rivers (including Baku, and the Azerbaijan lowlands), and to recognize Russia's right to maintain a fleet on the Caspian. Persia

denounced the 1813 Gulistan treaty in June 1826 but was beaten by Field-Marshal I. F. Paske'vich (1782–1856); with the Treaty of Turkmanchay (February 1828) it surrendered the khanates of Nakhichevan and Yerevan (Persian Armenia and the Azerbaijan highlands).

The struggle with Turkey for the western Caucasus started in 1828, but although the acquisition of the eastern Black Sea littoral (including Anapa and Poti) in 1829 completed the formal annexation of the Caucasus, Russia had to face a protracted war from 1834 to 1859 against Muslim★ mountain peoples in the Chechen area and Dagestan under the *imam* Shamil. Russia completed its conquest in Transcaucasia in 1878 when it received Kars, Ardahan and Batumi from Turkey under the Treaty of Berlin.

Russia and the Eastern Question

Revolutions in France, Belgium and Russian Poland in 1830 augmented Nicholas I's fear of subversion and prompted a renewal of the hitherto strained Holy Alliance with Austria and Prussia (1833). But the Eastern Question re-emerged as the dominant problem when the Sultan was obliged to accept Russian help against Mehemet Ali, the Egyptian pasha and France's protégé (1831–3). Although the Russo-Turkish alliance treaty of Unkiar Skelessi (July 1833) did not give Russia new advantages in the Straits, it provided legalistic justification to intervene in Ottoman affairs, to which Britain in particular objected. Nicholas, however, was aware of the dangers of unilateral action and hoped to disrupt the Anglo-French entente. He therefore cooperated with Britain, Austria and Prussia (London Convention, July 1840) in compelling the Egyptians to retreat after the second Egyptian-Turkish war (1839–40), and in replacing the Unkiar Skelessi treaty with the Straits Convention (July 1841), to which a humiliated France also acceded. Palmerston considered the convention a British success since it confirmed that the Straits was an international and not just a Russo-Turkish problem. While Russo-French relations cooled, Nicholas courted Britain with offers of a common policy to preserve Turkey in the short run but to prepare in advance for what Nicholas considered the inevitability of Turkey's disintegration. He obtained an erroneous impression that Lord Aberdeen had committed Britain in 1844 to cooperation with Russia.

The 1848 revolutions in Europe horrified Nicholas, whose subsequent actions were to earn him the nickname of 'gendarme of Europe'. Russian forces overwhelmed the Romanian patriots and restored Russo-Turkish control in Moldavia and Wallachia (May 1849), and in March 1849, fearing Austria's collapse, Nicholas speedily accepted Vienna's request to help crush the Hungarian struggle for independence. He opposed the movement for German unity, successfully supporting Denmark over Schleswig and Holstein (mid-1848), and then Austria in restoring the German Confederation (1850).

RUSSIAN EXPANSION IN EUROPE AND THE CAUCASUS, 1689–1914

KEY

The map also shows the decline of Poland-Lithuania, and the loss of territory by Sweden, the Ottoman Empire and Persia

Poland-Lithuania in 1689, showing lines of partition 1772 and 1793; totally dismembered 1795

Swedish territory 1689

Ottoman Empire (with vassal and allied states) 1689

Persia at the end of the 18th century (the Persian frontier with the Ottoman Empire fluctuated considerably during the 18th century)

— · — · — Eastern frontier of Poland-Lithuania in 1654–67

RUSSIAN FRONTIER: dates of annexation indicated

1689

1725

1796

1815

1914

········· Other international frontiers 1914

SWEDEN Russia's neighbours and other states 1914

Territory held temporarily by Russia with dates of accession (Tarnopol; Danube Delta)

Territory lost by Russia but subsequently recovered (South Bessarabia, Azov)

Territory acquired from Persia in 1723 but lost in 1732

Zaporozhe Cossack territory under Russian control from 1654 to 1667 but disputed with Turkey and fully annexed in 1733–9

Design by W. H. Zawadzki

461

The Crimean débâcle and its consequences

Russia's influence in Europe, now at its peak, was to be drastically reduced by the Crimean War (1854–6). A dispute with France and Turkey over rival Catholic and Orthodox claims to control the Holy Places in Palestine provoked Nicholas to demand of the Turkish government guarantees not only for the Orthodox Church but also for the entire Orthodox population of Turkey–A. S. Menshikov's (1787–1869) mission of February 1853. Nicholas strove for a peaceful settlement of the crisis, but his diplomatic efforts were defeated by widespread Russophobia in France and Britain and by Turkish truculence. Turkey declared war on Russia (November 1853) as did Britain and France (March 1854). Nicholas I died in February 1855 amidst the ruins of his foreign policy; the Crimean War exposed Russia's fundamental weakness and the Austrian ultimatum of December 1855 finally compelled Alexander II★ to sue for peace.

By the Treaty of Paris (March 1856) Russia ceded Bessarabia to Moldavia and, most humiliating of all, accepted the neutralization of the Black Sea region; Ottoman territorial integrity was guaranteed. Though Napoleon III proved less hostile to Russia than Palmerston,

Alexander II disapproved of Italian unification (1859–60) and moved closer to Prussia, a process much accelerated by Bismarck's offers of assistance, in contrast to Anglo-French hostility, during the Polish insurrection of 1863–4. The Russo-Prussian rapprochement benefited both states; it permitted Bismarck to defeat Austria (1866) and France (1870–1), and enabled Russia to repudiate unilaterally in October 1870 the clauses of the 1856 treaty neutralizing the Black Sea. Although resented in Britain, Russia's action was recognized by the London Conference (March 1871). Russia and Germany were soon reconciled with Austria-Hungary, and the Three Emperors' League, reminiscent of the former conservative Holy Alliance, was formed in 1873.

Central Asia and the Far East

Expansion into the nomad-populated steppes between the Caspian and the Aral seas dates from the 1820s, and the Aral Sea was reached by 1846. In 1853 General V. A. Perovsky (1795–1857) took the fortress of Ak-Mechet (Perovsk) on the river Syr Darya along which a line of forts was established. In the east, working from Semipalatinsk, the Russians crossed the river Ili and founded Verny (Alma-Ata) in 1854. The advance on the established khanates of Kokand and Khiva and the emirate of Bukhara, with which Russia already had trading links, began in 1864–5 when General M. G. Chernyaev, acting largely on his own initiative, attacked Tashkent, the Kokand capital, and provoked the emir of Bukhara to declare a 'holy war'. The resulting Russian invasion was accompanied by the creation of a new province of Turkestan under K. P. Kaufman (1866), and led to the establishment of Russian protectorates in Kokand and Bukhara (January and June 1868) and subsequently in Khiva (1873). The latter two states retained this status until 1917, but a rising in Kokand in 1875 brought about its total annexation under the name of the Fergana region (February 1876). Advances in eastern

A modern panorama: the defence of Sebastopol 1854–5

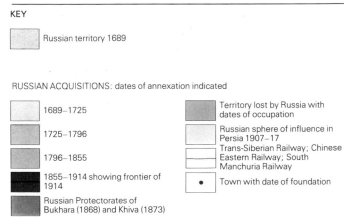

KEY

☐ Russian territory 1689

RUSSIAN ACQUISITIONS: dates of annexation indicated

1689–1725	Territory lost by Russia with dates of occupation
1725–1796	Russian sphere of influence in Persia 1907–17
1796–1855	Trans-Siberian Railway; Chinese Eastern Railway; South Manchuria Railway
1855–1914 showing frontier of 1914	• Town with date of foundation
Russian Protectorates of Bukhara (1868) and Khiva (1873)	

Design by W. H. Zawadzki

Turkestan also involved friction with China over the Kuldja (I-ning) province in Sinkiang, only a small part of which was Russia allowed to retain (Treaty of St Petersburg, 1881).

Next was the turn of the Turkmen tribes east of the Caspian Sea. Although Krasnovodsk was founded in 1869, it was only in 1881 that General M. D. Skobelev took Geok-Tepe. The war scare with Britain, caused by Russia's seizure of Merv (February 1884) and of the Afghan fort of Kushka (February 1885), ended with a joint delimitation of the Russo-Afghan frontier in 1885–7 which left the Zulfikar pass in Afghanistan.* The acquisition of a slice of the Pamir region in 1895 concluded Russia's southward growth which had frequently excited British concern for India.

In the Far East–following the expeditions of Captain G. I. Nevel'-skoy (c.1814–76)–the enterprising governor-general of East Siberia, N. N. Murav'ev-Amursky (1809–81), founded Nikolaevsk near the Amur estuary (1850), led a force up the river and founded Khabarovsk (1854). In May 1858 Russia annexed the north bank of the Amur, acquiring also a share in the administration of the Ussuri region (Treaty of Aygun). Both territories were finally yielded by China in November 1860 (Treaty of Peking). The foundation of

Vladivostok in the same year symbolized Russia's power on the Pacific. Murav'ev also occupied northern Sakhalin in 1852–3 and the island was administered jointly with Japan until 1875 when, in return for recognizing Japanese sovereignty over the Kurile Islands, the whole of Sakhalin passed to Russia.

The end of the 19th century saw a revived interest in the Far East associated with the Trans-Siberian Railway (begun 1891), the colonization of Siberia, and the finance minister S. Yu. Witte's schemes for the economic penetration of China. Growing financial and diplomatic influence led to a secret Russo-Chinese defensive treaty (June 1896) and to indirect Russian control of the broad-gauge trans-Manchurian railway which considerably shortened the journey to Vladivostok. Paramount Russian influence in Korea was accepted by Japan (June 1896) while in March 1898, as a result of the Kiaochow crisis, Russia extracted a 25-year lease on the Liaotung peninsula, including Port Arthur (Lü-shun)–Russia's first ice-free port in the Far East–with a rail link to Harbin. During the Boxer Rising in China (1900) Russian troops occupied the whole of Manchuria where they remained until their defeat at Japanese* hands in 1905 when south Sakhalin and Port Arthur were lost.

RUSSIAN EXPANSION IN ASIA, 1689–1914

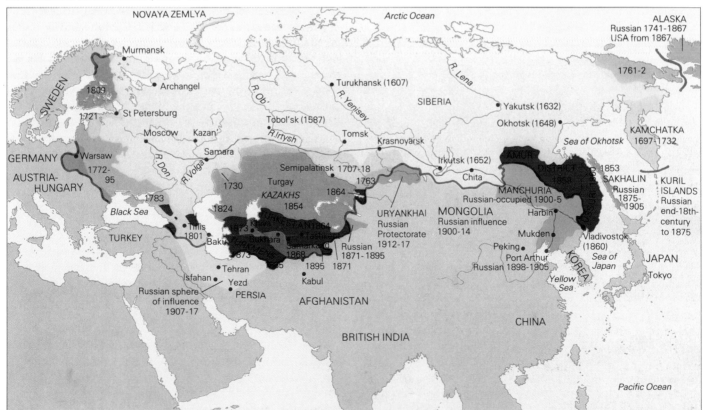

Russia liberates the South Slavs

Anti-Turkish revolts in Herzegovina and Bulgaria in 1875–6, Serbia's defeat at Turkish hands in 1876–7, and growing nationalist and Panslav sentiments in Russia moved Alexander II, after several efforts to secure international intervention, to declare war on Turkey to liberate the Balkan Slavs* (April 1877). The San Stefano treaty (March 1878), which created a large Bulgaria dependent on Russia, met with considerable opposition, especially British; Russia had to retreat over Bulgaria, which was reduced in size and divided at the Congress of Berlin (June–July 1878), although obtaining south Bessarabia* (lost in 1856). Alexander II returned to the Three Emperors' League, formally joined by Alexander III* in June 1881, which sanctioned Austrian control of Bosnia-Herzegovina and checked Panslav tendencies in Russian policy.   *W.H.Z*

Tsarist Russia in decline

The change of alliances

The German and Austrian alliances within the Three Emperors' League proved valuable during a war scare with Britain over Afghanistan (1885), but less so during the crisis, caused by the union of Bulgaria and East Rumelia (1885–6), which ended Russian influence in Sofia. The trilateral agreement was succeeded by a direct 'reinsurance' treaty with Germany only (June 1887). Tariff and financial problems, the end of Bismarck's moderating influence (March 1890), and recognition that the Triple Alliance of Germany, Austria-Hungary and Italy (1882, 1887) was incompatible with obligations to Russia, moved Kaiser William II not to renew the Reinsurance Treaty in 1890. This encouraged Russian rapprochement with France which now provided Russia with loans. After seemingly ominous German behaviour and the renewal of the Triple Alliance in May 1891, and fearing isolation, Alexander III,* although originally hostile to French republicanism, concluded a fateful political and military alliance with France (ratified August 1894).

War with Japan

Divided opinions and pressures in St Petersburg initially led to confusion and some inconsistency in Russian policy under Nicholas II.* Although Russia unsuccessfully proposed the international reduction of armaments at the Hague peace conferences in 1899 and 1907, the construction of the Trans-Siberian Railway and concepts of Russia's 'Asiatic mission' resulted in an aggressive Far Eastern policy. The peaceful penetration of China was facilitated by Russian mediation during the Sino-Japanese war of 1894–5, Russian loans and the subsequent Russo-Chinese treaty (June 1896) granting Russia a railway concession across Manchuria, shortening thereby

the route to Vladivostok (founded in 1860). However, the lease of Port Arthur imposed by Russia (March 1898) and the occupation of Manchuria (July 1900) not only violated the treaty with China but brought Russia into conflict with Japanese ambitions in Korea. Russia's defeat in the war against Japan (February 1904–May 1905), which contributed to the outbreak of revolution at home, forced Russia to recognize Japanese influence in Korea, to evacuate Manchuria and to surrender Port Arthur, south Sakhalin and the South Manchurian Railway (Treaty of Portsmouth, USA, September 1905). To contain Japan's power and American economic involvement in Manchuria, Russia moved closer to Japan, winning its consent to a Russian sphere of influence in north Manchuria and Outer Mongolia (1907, 1910, 1912).

Consolidation of the Triple Entente

Moves to revive a Russo-German alliance and Nicholas II's inept 'private' treaty with William II at Björkö (July 1905) were abandoned as incompatible with the 1894 Russo-French treaty, while improved relations with Japan encouraged Russia to seek an arrangement with Britain (Japan's ally since 1902) on Asian matters, including the division of Persia into zones of influence (August 1907). A Triple Entente of Britain, France and Russia was by no means a certainty but growing suspicions of Germany, and above all Russia's retreat, due to military unreadiness, in the face of Austro-German solidarity during the 1908 Bosnian crisis (Austria-Hungary formally annexed Bosnia and Herzegovina), widened the gap between Russia and the two Germanic powers. In 1908–9 the foreign minister A. P. Izvolsky (1856–1919) also failed to revise the Straits Convention to permit the free passage of Russian warships in and out of the Black Sea.

International relations were further complicated by the two Balkan Wars of 1912–13, which deprived Turkey of most of its remaining European territory. Without abandoning Russia's long-term ambitions for the Straits, and despite considerable Panslav agitation at home, Izvolsky's successor S. D. Sazonov (1861–1927) tried to prevent, and then to localize the Balkan conflict (as at the London Conference, December 1912) and insisted on reducing Serbia's and Montenegro's gains, and on creating an Albanian state. Sazonov's concern to avoid a wider conflict for which Russia was not prepared was probably sincere, but the Balkan Wars and the appointment of a German general to command a Turkish army corps in November 1913 increased anti-German feeling and revived Russia's concern for the Straits; ideas for conquering Constantinople were mooted in December 1913–February 1914.

Notwithstanding occasional Russian disagreements with Britain (such as over Persia), the secret Russo-French naval convention (July 1912), President Poincaré's visits to Russia (August 1912 and July 1914) and Russo-British naval talks (May 1914) illustrated how the states of the Triple Entente had come closer together by the time of

The French president Poincaré with Nicholas II, July 1914, immediately before the outbreak of war

Russia in the First World War

Archduke Franz Ferdinand's assassination at Sarajevo (28 June 1914). Russia was not prepared to see Austria-Hungary defeat Serbia, and the great powers' mobilization systems and interlocking alliances undermined all international attempts to avert a general war. Russian mobilization after the Austrian declaration of war on Serbia (28 July) led to Austrian, and then German and French mobilization. Germany declared war on Russia on 1 August, and on France on 3 August; Britain declared war on Germany on 4 August; Austria declared war on Russia on 6 August.

Russia in the First World War

Although the military fortunes of imperial Russia fluctuated in 1914–17, it remained loyal to the anti-German coalition, formalized by treaty on 5 September 1914, and provided valuable assistance to relieve German pressure on the western front. Badly mauled in East Prussia (August–September), the Russians fared better against Austria in Galicia (September) and checked a German attack in Poland (October–December). A big German-Austrian offensive in 1915, however, pushed the front east of Lithuania and Poland where it roughly remained, except for General A. A. Brusilov's (1853–1926) offensive in June–September 1916, until the Russian collapse in mid-1917.

Russia's war aims, outlined by Sazonov in September 1914, favoured French and South Slav* aspirations at Germany's and Austria-Hungary's expense, and included the Russian annexation of East Galicia and the re-unification of ethnic Poland as an autonomous region under the tsar. Turkey's entry into the war against Russia (October 1914) provided Russia with the opportunity to demand, as a major war aim, the annexation of Constantinople and the Straits, to

which Britain and France, despite their traditional policies, consented in March and April 1915. The general disruption caused by the First World War in Russia contributed to the February 1917 revolution. After Nicholas II's abdication, the Provisional Government* tried to honour all tsarist commitments to the Entente, and the foreign minister P. N. Milyukov (1859–1943) reiterated Russia's claim to Constantinople (March 1917). Although the principle of a defensive war without indemnities or annexations was next adopted, intense war weariness grew, and the attempt by A. F. Kerensky (1881–1970), then Prime Minister, to continue fighting was a major cause of the government's downfall in October 1917.   *W.H.Z.*

The Baltic republics, 1918–40

Estonia, Latvia and Lithuania were declared independent in 1918, after the Russian Empire* had disintegrated. Initially, their independence was endangered by the expansion of socialist revolution from Russia and by repeated German efforts to secure hegemony over them. By 1920, with military and diplomatic support from the Western Allies, these small states overcame such threats. The new Baltic republics adopted broadly similar democratic constitutions, except that Communist Parties* were proscribed. Power resided in their one-chamber legislatures, while executive authority remained weak throughout. Proportional representation produced numerous, usually small political parties, especially in Latvia, where the regional parties that flourished in largely Catholic* Latgalia helped to raise the total to 44. This system led to frequently changing coalition governments and political instability, since no party could consistently command a majority.

Parliamentary democracy did not survive. In 1926 the Populist-Socialist government in Lithuania, unpopular for its conciliatory policies toward the Soviet Union, communists and minorities and for its failure to solve the current economic crisis, was overthrown by an alliance of Nationalists (*Tautininkai*) and army officers, tacitly supported by some leading Christian Democrats. An aggressively authoritarian regime was established. The pretensions to power of more extremist right-wing movements, led by the Prime Minister A. Voldemaras, were crushed by President A. Smetona in 1929, and again in 1934, after which Smetona's government itself became increasingly authoritarian, chauvinist and corporativist. Partial liberalization occurred in 1939, after Lithuania humiliatingly was forced to accept Poland's claim to Vilnius (Wilno) and Germany's to Klaipeda (Memel), but the Second World War curtailed further developments.

In Estonia and Latvia the governing centrist and right Agrarian and Populist Parties steadily gained popular electoral support at the expense of the Socialist Party. In 1934, amidst economic depression, K. Päts in Estonia and K. Ulmanis in Latvia–nationalists like Smetona–supported by the army and the conservatives, staged peaceful, right-wing coups. Authoritarian, self-avowedly nationalistic, semi-corporativist regimes were established, particularly in Latvia, although at the same time more extreme fascist movements were suppressed.

These republics remained ethnically and confessionally heterogeneous. Estonia (1.13 million population, 1934) was the most homogeneous, being 88 per cent Estonian, with, in decreasing importance, Russian,* German,* Swedish, Jewish* and other minorities, and 78 per cent Lutheran.* Lithuania (2.03 million population, 1923) was 84 per cent Lithuanian, with Jewish, Polish,* Russian, German, Lettish and other minorities, and 81 per cent Catholic. Latvia (1.95 million population, 1935) was the most diverse, being 75 per cent Lettish, with Russian, Jewish, German, Polish and other minorities, and 57 per cent Lutheran, with most of the 24 per cent Catholics in Latgalia. While the Germans, Russians and Poles lost their former power, like all minorities they initially were guaranteed linguistic, educational and cultural freedom. In the 1930s their rights were increasingly restricted by the dominant indigenous nations.

The agrarian reforms, which divided up the large estates, strengthened the predominantly agricultural and rural character of these states. The measures were designed to destroy the economic power of the foreign (German, Polish and Russian) landlords, to avert potential peasant unrest resulting from land hunger, and to strengthen the rural communities, regarded as the basis and symbol of nationhood. While many new smallholdings were scarcely profitable, agricultural productivity rose, partly as a result of state aid. The majority, especially the native peoples, were still employed in agriculture in the 1930s–60 per cent of the working population in Estonia, 66 per cent in Latvia and 77 per cent in Lithuania, which remained the least urbanized.

Industry, previously insignificant in Lithuania and devastated by war in Estonia and Latvia, was also built up. Separation from Russia compelled the republics, lacking internal resources and markets, to develop small-scale industries, often offshoots of agriculture and designed to satisfy their own needs–although Estonia and Latvia chose not to rebuild their large-scale industries for fear of producing a revolutionary proletariat. Trade, too, had to be reoriented towards Western Europe, where the bulk of their primarily agricultural exports went. In the 1930s state intervention in trade and industry increased, to keep these sectors under national control and to protect the economy from the vicissitudes of world trade.

Unable to unite, partly since Estonia and Latvia aimed to avoid involvement in Lithuania's territorial disputes with Poland over Vilnius and with Germany over Klaipeda, and lacking effective support from the West, they were incorporated into the Soviet Union in 1940.
R.I.K.

Bessarabia, 1918–44

The lands lying between the rivers Pruth and Dniester formed part of Moldavia, the northernmost of the Danubian principalities, until 1812 when, by the Treaty of Bucharest, they were annexed by the

THE BALTIC STATES, 1917–40

KEY

| | International boundaries in 1937 | | Memel (Klaipeda) Territory occupied by Lithuania, 1923–39 |
| | Vilnius Province occupied by Poland, 1920–39 | | Land ceded to the RSFSR in 1945 |

Source: G. von Rauch, *The Baltic States: The Years of Independence*, London, 1974

Russian Empire★ and called Bessarabia. Three southern districts (Ismail, Cahul and Bolgrad) were returned to Moldavia at the Congress of Paris in 1856, but these reverted to Russia in 1878 at the Congress of Berlin. In effect, Bessarabia was a province of the Russian Empire from the Napoleonic wars★ until the Revolution.★

Five years after annexation a Russian estimate placed the Romanian portion of Bessarabia's population at 86 per cent. A programme of Russification, pursued throughout the century, had a slight impact but migration into the province of Slavs,★ Germans★ and Jews★ from elsewhere in the empire significantly altered the balance of ethnic groups in Bessarabia. The census of 1897 showed only 47.6 per cent of the total population to be Romanians. Almost certainly a distortion, this figure nevertheless indicates the changed ethnic pattern, for the Romanian census of 1930 put that component at 56.2 per cent.

Despite the presence of the Romanian minority, Bessarabia did not become a bone of contention between Romania and Russia until 1917. During the revolution of 1905, Romanians in Bessarabia formed a Democratic Moldavian Party calling for a measure of autonomy for the province, but this initiative came to nothing. In the aftermath of the February 1917 revolution the Bessarabian problem disrupted relations between Romania and Russia, then allied against the Central Powers (Germany, Austro-Hungary and Turkey). In April a National Moldavian Party was established and complemented by Moldavian committees in the Russian army. Encouraged by the prospect of wider provincial autonomy and national self-determination, Romanians from Bessarabia participated in the Congress of Russian Peoples at Kiev in September and held a Congress of Moldavians at Kishinev in October. The Moldavians★ called for recognition of provincial autonomy, confirmation of minority rights and convening of a provincial assembly. The assembly, subsequently known as the Sfatul Tarei, was established in October, but the rest of the Moldavian programme was overtaken by events following upon the seizure of power by the Bolsheviks.★

Not yet despairing of a federal solution to Russia's nationality problem, the Sfatul Tarei declared Bessarabia the autonomous Moldavian People's Republic in December. At once both the Ukraine and the Bolsheviks sought to wrest control of Bessarabia from the Sfatul Tarei, and from one another. The Sfatul Tarei responded to both threats by seeking assistance from Romania which, having reached an armistice with the Central Powers, retained enough troops to occupy Bessarabia in January 1918. Immediately the Bolshevik government declared itself in a state of war with Romania. The Sfatul Tarei, meanwhile, seceded from Russia, proclaiming Bessarabia an independent republic. Opinion in favour of union with Romania mounted in the Sfatul Tarei and was welcomed by the Romanian government. After an overwhelming majority of the Sfatul Tarei had declared itself for union, the incorporation of Bessarabia into Romania was proclaimed on 8 April 1918.

The union was never recognized by Soviet Russia and the Bessarabian issue bedevilled Russo-Romanian relations until the advent of the Second World War. Only in 1934 and 1935 did the two countries exchange ambassadors and move cautiously towards a closer relationship in the face of the threat posed by Germany. Earlier, during the 1920s, the Soviet government sought to infiltrate Bessarabia by smuggling arms and agents across the frontier, an effort that culminated in the rising at Tatar Bunar in 1924. The rapprochement with Romania, engineered by its foreign minister, Titulescu, proved ephemeral. With the fall of Titulescu in 1936, the Romanian government, under the direction of King Carol, shunned collaboration with the USSR in favour of, first, closer ties with its immediate neighbours and then some arrangement with Germany itself. By 1939 Romania, like Poland, found itself isolated between Germany and the USSR. Among the secret clauses of the German Soviet Non-Aggression Pact of 23 August 1939, one referred to the Soviet Union's interest in Bessarabia. After Germany's successes in the west, Soviet intentions to resolve the Bessarabian problem, mooted by the premier V. M. Molotov (b.1890) in March 1940, grew more insistent. In discussions with the German ambassador on 23 June 1940, Molotov revealed that the USSR was ready to demand from Romania both Bessarabia and Bukovina, a neighbouring province not mentioned in the 1939 Pact. In negotiations with Germany the USSR confined its claim to the northern part of Bukovina. On 26 June 1940 the Romanian government was given an ultimatum demanding both Bessarabia and northern Bukovina. Isolated in the teeth of the Russo-German partnership, Romania had no choice but to yield.

Nearly a year later, ranged alongside Germany, Romania invaded the USSR, and advancing as far as Odessa occupied and annexed the region between the Dniester and the Bug. Transnistria, as the province was called, included Bessarabia which, along with the other lands, came under direct military rule. In Bessarabia and northern Bukovina the Romanian occupation forces exacted harsh retribution against the Jews and other minorities who were accused of supporting the Soviet annexation. At the setbacks inflicted on German forces by the Red Army,★ the Romanian government made numerous overtures to the Western Allies for a settlement in which Romania would be protected from the Soviet advance and allowed to retain Bessarabia and northern Bukovina. But the Allies reported all such overtures to the Soviet government, which insisted on the retention of the two provinces. The Western Allies could not intercede on behalf of an Axis ally and when Romania was occupied by the Red Army in 1944 Bessarabia, along with northern Bukovina, was restored to the Soviet Union, where it became the nucleus of the Moldavian Soviet Socialist Republic.   *J.M.K.*

Eastern Poland, 1921–39

At the Yalta Conference in February 1945, Churchill, Roosevelt and Stalin* agreed 'that the eastern frontier of Poland should follow the Curzon Line with digressions from it in some regions of 5–8km in favour of Poland'. As a result, a substantial area which had been part of the Polish state between 1921 and 1939 was finally incorporated into the Soviet Union. This included the provinces of Wilno (Vilnius), Nowogródek, Polesie, Volynia, Stanisławów and Tarnopol and the eastern parts of the provinces of Lwów (L'vov) and Białystok which made up nearly 48 per cent of the surface area of the pre-war Polish state. It was largely agricultural and dominated by great estates, – nearly half of all holdings in 1921 were larger than 50ha. Compared to the rest of Poland, these lands were also rather poor and the state of agriculture was, by and large, primitive. In the northern provinces its progress was hampered by inadequate communications and the rather swampy nature of much of the land, while in the south the abolition of serfdom under Austrian rule had created a plethora of small and unviable holdings. Some industrial development had taken place, particularly the oil and gas wells around Drohobycz and sawmills and wood processing plants in the northern areas which were rich in forests.

Eastern Poland, referred to in Polish as the 'Kresy' or borderlands, was multinational: according to the census of 1931, of the 11.1 million people in the seven eastern provinces, 43 per cent were Polish-speaking, 38 per cent gave Ukrainian as their mother tongue, 13.5 per cent stated that they spoke Belorussian* or the local language, and 8.3 per cent gave Yiddish or Hebrew as their mother tongue. In addition, there were about 70 000 Lithuanians near that border and some

POLAND: FRONTIER CHANGES, 1939 AND 1945

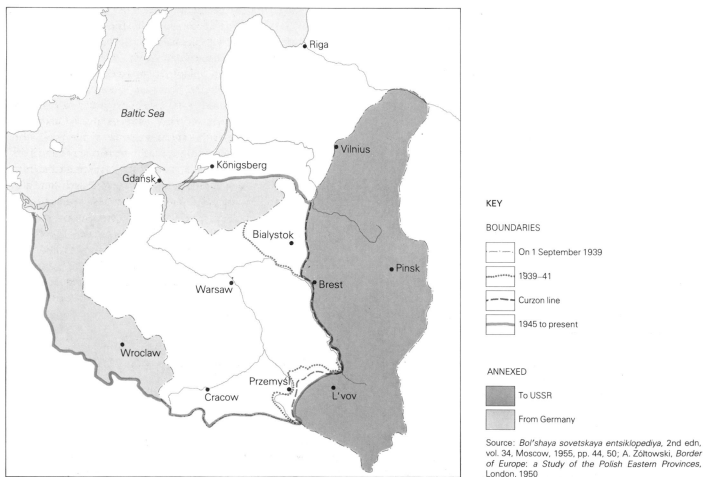

KEY

BOUNDARIES

- – · – · On 1 September 1939
- · · · · · · 1939–41
- – – – Curzon line
- ——— 1945 to present

ANNEXED

- To USSR
- From Germany

Source: *Bol'shaya sovetskaya entsiklopediya*, 2nd edn, vol. 34, Moscow, 1955, pp. 44, 50; A. Zóltowski, *Border of Europe: a Study of the Polish Eastern Provinces*, London, 1950

56 000 Russians scattered across the whole area. These figures were the product of considerable administrative pressure and almost certainly understate the number of Ukrainians* and Belorussians* while overstating that of Poles, who were found everywhere in the Kresy as landowners and officials and formed the majority of the population in the larger towns, above all Wilno and Lwów. There was also a large Polish peasant population in the two north-eastern provinces of Wilno and Nowogródek and in East Galicia. The Ukrainians were the largest group in East Galicia and Volynia and were also found in the provinces of Lublin and Polesie. Those who lived in the former Austrian territories were largely Uniat in religion – Catholics* of the Eastern rite – while in the former Russian areas, Orthodoxy* had struck successful roots after the forced reconversion of 1839. The Belorussians, concentrated in the provinces of Polesie, Nowogródek and Wilno, were also largely Orthodox, though there was a substantial Catholic minority, made up largely of those who had left the Orthodox Church after the Toleration Edict of 1905. The Jews* were almost entirely urban, forming the bulk of the population of the smaller towns and also constituting a significant minority in Wilno and Lwów.

Control of the Kresy had long been a source of dispute between Russia and Poland. Class and national antagonisms also overlapped there, since the peasantry was largely Belorussian or Ukrainian while the landowners were Polish. Religious differences further intensified the bitterness of the land-hungry peasantry, whose national and social aspirations had been greatly stimulated by events during and after the First World War. In the period between 1916 and 1923 when the whole area was definitively recognized as part of the Polish state, it was ruled at times by the Bolsheviks,* by Ukrainian, by Belorussian and by Lithuanian nationalists. Thus it is hardly surprising that the politics of the region throughout the inter-war period were dominated by national questions, and that the Polish authorities were never able to establish a firm basis of popular support for their rule. Among the Ukrainians, the strongest political orientation was nationalist in character, particularly in East Galicia, with its long tradition of semi-parliamentary government. Here the major political party was the Ukrainian National Democratic Organization (UNDO) while more violent para-military groups also had some support. Communist and leftist groups were much weaker, though they had some backing in Volynia. In the Belorussian areas, there was a greater willingness to cooperate with the Poles and the nationalist groupings were generally rather weaker. Pro-Soviet and pro-communist sentiments were strong, however, and from 1921, the Belorussian Revolutionary Organization, which demanded the union of the whole of Belorussia under Soviet rule, began to engage in guerrilla activities.

Until the coup of May 1926, which brought Marshal Piłsudski back to power, Polish policy in the Kresy was marked both by a lack of consistent planning and by the use of officials whose chauvinism was strongly resented by the majority of the population. Piłsudski hoped to initiate a new policy towards the minorities. The goal of national assimilation was to be renounced and instead conditions were to be created to make possible assimilation to the state structure. The inadequacy of many Polish officials, coupled with the strength of local Polish sentiment, made real changes hard to introduce. In addition, the repression which followed an upsurge of communist agitation in Belorussia in 1927 and large-scale nationalist sabotage in East Galicia in the summer of 1930 exacerbated relations. So, too, did the impact of the Great Depression which was felt most acutely by the rural population and which brought to an effective end any attempt to give land on a large scale to Belorussian and Ukrainian peasants.

The 1930s saw some improvement in the situation in the Kresy. Communist strength in both the Ukrainian and Belorussian areas was undermined by the shock caused by collectivization* in the USSR and by splits in the Communist Parties of western Ukraine and western Belorussia. Among the Ukrainians, a feeling also developed that the strategy of a frontal assault on the Polish state had proved unsuccessful and that some accommodation should be sought. This lay at the basis of the policy of 'normalization' adopted by the UNDO in 1935. Some improvement in relations with the Polish government was achieved, but the policy collapsed in the face of the foreign policy successes of Hitler,* whom the Ukrainian nationalists expected to satisfy their aspirations, and it was formally dropped in February 1938. Hitler's abandonment of the Ukrainians in sub-Carpathian Ruthenia to Hungarian rule caused a revival of the pro-Polish orientation, but its exponents did not feel any great conviction in its success. In Volynia too, attempts by the local military commanders to reconvert the Orthodox population to the Uniat Church were also bitterly resented. Pressures for Polonization were stepped up in the Belorussian areas in these years and the government also tried to foster economic development there. This was not very successful, but at the same time the area remained politically quiescent and there was no revival of the terrorism of the mid-1920s. By 1939, although the majority of the population was considerably discontented with its position, support for the incorporation of the Kresy in the USSR was far weaker than it had been a decade earlier.   *A.B.P.*

The Soviet state and the Powers, 1917–45

The revolutionary challenge
L. D. Trotsky,* Soviet Russia's first Commissar for Foreign Affairs, announced that his duties would be to issue a few proclamations and shut up shop. Intended as revolutionary bravado, his words were

none the less prophetic. For nearly four years the new Soviet state had little opportunity to pursue an active foreign policy. Once the belligerent peoples had been urged to conclude a 'peace without annexations and indemnities', once the secret arrangements between Russia and its former allies had been published, Trotsky had only one, far less enjoyable, task to perform before moving on to the Commissariat for War, handing over foreign affairs to G. V. Chicherin (1872–1936). This was to make peace with Germany.

The exorbitant demands put by the German negotiators in the Brest-Litovsk peace talks (22 December 1917 (NS)–3 March 1918) were the occasion of the first major split within the new Soviet leadership. Left Communists, N. I. Bukharin (1888–1938) prominent amongst them, were for defying the Germans and risking a 'revolutionary war' in the hope of raising the proletariat of Western Europe in support of the 'first workers' state'. Trotsky and his supporters, less rash though scarcely less unrealistic, were for breaking off negotiations and adopting a stance of 'neither peace nor war'. A show of force by the Germans in February, and a threat of resignation from Lenin,★ brought the Bolshevik Central Committee to its senses. Under the Treaty of Brest-Litovsk, Russia gave up all claim to Finland, the Baltic states,★ Poland, the Ukraine and parts of Belorussia (areas already outside its control). The government of the drastically reduced Soviet state withdrew to a safe distance, and henceforward Moscow was its capital.

Civil war and intervention

Brest-Litovsk saved the Soviet regime from demolition at the hands of the Germans, and inevitably drew on it the wrath of the Western Allies. France, Britain and Japan landed troops on Russia's coasts in the spring of 1918, originally to prevent the Germans from seizing bases and arms depots, and if possible to reconstitute an Eastern front. Some statesmen and soldiers in the Allied countries would have attempted something more ambitious: a punitive and prophylactic crusade against bolshevism after the collapse of the Central Powers. Such plans were made unrealistic by divisions within and between Allied governments, and by the war weariness of their peoples. In the event, the interventionists could give only logistic and moral support to the White armies and their political appendages, and to anti-Bolshevik regimes on the periphery of the old Russian Empire.★ By doing so they helped to prolong the civil war until late 1920. In the last stages of the civil war the armies of the newly restored Polish Republic thrust deep into the Ukraine. Driven back, the Poles held and defeated the Russians on the approaches to Warsaw ('the miracle on the Vistula', August 1920), and under the Treaty of Riga (March 1921) which concluded the war they were able to extend their frontier eastwards at the expense of the Ukraine and White Russia. For the Soviet state, this was the last aggressive military action it would undertake (outside its own frontiers) until 1939. The last of the White

armies (that of General P. N. Wrangel, 1878–1928) was defeated and evacuated in the autumn of 1920. With organized White resistance intervention also ended, though the Japanese abandoned the Soviet Far Eastern provinces only in 1922, under American pressure.

Diplomacy and disruption

To the Bolshevik leaders the Soviet state's security, its hopes of 'building socialism' fairly quickly, and (to some of them) even its ideological legitimacy depended upon the establishment of kindred, and helpful, regimes in other, more advanced countries. The fires of revolution which sprang up in defeated Germany and Austria-Hungary were, however, quickly extinguished. The attempt to make a prostrate Poland the bridge between the Russian 'proletariat' and its German 'brothers' was frustrated in 1920. Well into the decade, the Soviet leaders fitfully hoped and worked for the revolution which would bring at least one major European or Asian country into the camp of socialism. Soviet Russia, however, was forced to play a dual role: it was the (self-proclaimed) centre of the world revolutionary cause, but it was also a state amongst other states, most of them hostile and suspicious. Backward, impoverished and enfeebled by war and civil war, terribly vulnerable, Soviet Russia for the immediate future urgently needed 'normal' relations with states which, ultimately, it hoped to subvert.

This duality came out clearly in the behaviour and publications of the Third (Communist) International (Comintern), set up in Moscow in March 1919. This body was, in intention, a single political party of which the new Communist Parties in particular countries (formed largely by fission from existing socialist parties) were to be only 'sections', adjusting their policies to a world revolutionary strategy determined in Moscow. At times, this strategy might require a member Party to abate its revolutionary ardour, or even to go out of existence (as happened with the Turkish Communist Party in the early 1920s). In general, communists in other countries were required to prepare themselves for the ultimate overthrow of their governments and simultaneously to persuade those governments to maintain good relations and to trade with the Soviet state.

Soviet Russia began its struggle to normalize relations with the world outside by signing a series of treaties with neighbouring states (with Estonia 2 February 1920, Lithuania 12 July 1920, Latvia 11 August 1920, Finland 14 October 1920, Poland 18 March 1921, Iran 26 February 1921, Afghanistan 28 February 1921, Turkey 16 March 1921 and Mongolia 5 November 1921) which might render them less likely to serve as bases for a renewed imperialist crusade or as a barrier to Soviet trade.★ Commercial relations with major European trading countries were established almost as the civil war ended, but full diplomatic recognition was accorded by the victors of the First World War later, and grudgingly: by Britain, France and Italy in 1924, by the USA not until 1933. The Soviet government's repudiation of pre-revolutionary debts, its failure to compensate foreign owners of nationalized property, its insistence whenever these subjects were raised that Russia too was entitled to compensation for damage done by the civil war and the 'intervention', greatly complicated dealings with the West. Soviet subversive activities, real enough (though Western ill-wishers sometimes saved themselves trouble by trumping up evidence), exacerbated relations with capitalist countries, twice, for instance, resulting in a breach between Russia and Britain (1924 and 1927). To Britain, Soviet support of national liberation movements in the empire, and of anti-British sentiments and actions in the Middle East, was a special source of annoyance. France was preoccupied rather by the Soviet threat to arrangements made at and after Versailles for the containment of a disarmed Germany and the extraction of reparations from that country. No love was lost between Soviet Russia and some of the East European states (Poland and Romania in particular) which France saw as a partial replacement for tsarist Russia as allies to the east of Germany, and also as a *cordon sanitaire* between bolshevism and the West.

Soviet Russia's first big success in breaking out of isolation came in April 1922. Soviet and German representatives, dissatisfied with their treatment at the Genoa Conference, met privately at Rapallo and concluded a Treaty (16 April 1922) which was the foundation of lively commercial relations throughout the 1920s and also provided opportunities for Germany to begin surreptitiously rebuilding its

Comintern poster by S. V. Ivanov, 1921

military strength in defiance of restrictions imposed at Versailles. The weak Germany of the 1920s clung to its special arrangement with Russia in spite of another communist attempt, openly encouraged not only by Comintern but by senior Soviet leaders, to launch a revolution in 1923, and in spite of the development of the German Communist Party in the late 1920s into a threat to democratic government rivalled only by the Nazi Party.

The constant fear of the USSR (as Soviet Russia became in 1924) was that it might be attacked before it had time to construct the economic basis for a war against one or–more likely–several capitalist countries. (The inevitability of such wars was, until 1956, axiomatic.) It viewed apprehensively not merely international agreements with a frankly anti-Soviet slant (until the mid-1930s there were none of importance), but also such attempts to regulate Europe's security problems as the Locarno Treaty of October 1925, which made Germany an equal partner for diplomatic purposes with the Western powers, confirmed that country's western frontiers while not expressly mentioning those to the east, and prepared the way for Germany's admission to the League of Nations.* (The official Soviet view was that the League existed primarily to coordinate imperialist machinations against the 'first workers' state'). To safeguard itself against the implications it read into Locarno, the USSR made a Treaty of Friendship and Neutrality with Germany (24 April 1926), re-embodying and greatly reinforcing the agreements made at Rapallo. It also took an active part in international discussions on arms limitation, to which, however, its main contribution, the proposal for immediate universal and total disarmament put to the Preparatory Commission of the League of Nations in November 1927, was demagogic rather than strictly practical in intent. The USSR showed its eagerness to delay what it regarded as the ultimately inevitable breakdown of peaceful co-existence by associating itself with other international enterprises in whose efficacy it had little faith: thus, it adhered in September 1928 to the Kellog-Briand Pact, and in accordance with this joined a number of neighbouring countries in renouncing aggression as an instrument of policy.

The foreign policy of the USSR in the years 1921–39 was essentially defensive. But self-defence as Soviet leaders understood it was always compatible with, indeed always demanded, active encouragement of foreign Communist Parties with some prospect of seizing power. The tactics urged on such parties by Comintern (which meant in effect by the Soviet faction currently in control of that body) were often misconceived and sometimes disastrous. Perhaps the most serious setback to the cause of 'world revolution' between the wars was the massacre of Chinese communists in 1927, and the subsequent withdrawal of the Chinese Communist Party's enfeebled remnant into remote rural areas. Chinese communists never forgot that they had put themselves at Chiang Kai-shek's mercy by following Soviet advice.

The USSR and the rise of Hitler

Trotsky and his followers in the USSR and elsewhere found the explanation for the Chinese débâcle in Stalin's* pigheaded attachment to policies which they had declared obsolete. The exigencies of Stalin's drive for supremacy clearly distorted the official Soviet interpretation of international developments and Soviet policy in the late 1920s. Thus, a totally artificial war scare, which identified Britain and more particularly France as potential aggressors against the USSR, served to dramatize the urgency of rapid industrialization and of forced collectivization* which, according to Stalin, was the essential preliminary. Comintern urged on its clients everywhere a policy of 'class against class' – of communist struggle against all other political forces – on the grounds that ever acuter contradictions between and within capitalist countries, exacerbated by economic stagnation and collapse, would lead to a new upsurge of working-class militancy. Non-revolutionary social democratic and labour parties were condemned as 'social fascists', and as more dangerous enemies of the workers' cause than the fascists themselves. There can be no certainty that, but for Comintern, German socialists and communists would have joined in resisting the Nazi threat, or that their combined strength would in any case have sufficed. What is certain is that the 'class against class' doctrine ruled out joint resistance in advance, and indeed directed communist militancy primarily against socialists rather than against Nazis.

The USSR was slow to recognize that Hitler* was a much more serious threat to peace, and to itself, than Britain or France had ever been. Indeed, it saw the Nazi regime to begin with as merely an 'alternative instrument' to which capitalism resorted when parliamentary democracy with 'social fascist' (social democratic) participation ceased to serve its purposes. The advent of Hitler, in fact, showed that capitalism was desperate, and the triumph of communism imminent! The USSR, in the meantime, saw no reason why relations with Nazi Germany should be more difficult than with any other 'bourgeois' regime, and for two or three years commercial exchanges between the two countries continued, unaffected by Hitler's persecution of German communists.

Collective security

The increasingly truculent and reckless behaviour of Japan and Germany in the course of the 1930s compelled the USSR to move, tentatively, closer to the Western democracies which it had previously regarded as its main enemies. This modification of Soviet policy should be seen as reinsurance rather than as recognition of a real community of interest. As Stalin put it (at the XVII Congress of the CPSU* in 1934) 'we were not in the past oriented towards Germany, and are not now oriented towards Poland and France. Our orientation, past and present, is exclusively towards the USSR'. Though he went on to speak of rapprochement with 'countries not interested in a breach of the peace' he was clearly serving notice that the USSR would accept whatever alliances its own security seemed to demand.

The Japanese occupation of Manchuria (1931), the departure of Japan (in March 1933) and Germany (October 1933) from the League of Nations, the conclusion of the anti-Comintern pact between Germany and Japan in November 1936 and Italy's adherence to it in November 1937 made the quest for precautionary alliances a matter of increasing urgency. The USSR established relations with the USA (December 1933), joined the despised League of Nations (September 1934) and concluded 'mutual aid' pacts with France and with Czechoslovakia (May 1935), and a Non-Aggression Treaty with China (August 1937). The Soviet-Czechoslovak treaty stipulated that French assistance to the country attacked was a necessary condition of assistance from the other party to the agreement, and Germany had no difficulty in ignoring it.

In support of the Soviet drive for 'collective security' Comintern at its Seventh Congress in July–August 1935 abandoned the 'class against class policy' and called on member parties to establish 'Popular Fronts' with all political forces, of whatever complexion, which favoured resistance to Nazism and to Japanese militarism. 'Popular Front' governments came into being in France, Spain and Chile. It was Spain during its civil war which most vividly illuminated the realities of Soviet policy. Support–in arms, communist volunteers and Soviet military advisers–for the Republican cause went with ruthless (and even murderous) measures to centralize political and military control of the 'Popular Front' in communist hands. Neither the anti-Comintern pact, nor the fact that in 1937 they were intervening on opposite sides in Spain, provoked a final breach

between Germany and the USSR: on the contrary, the two countries in 1937 began discussing in Berlin a possible *modus vivendi*.

The Molotov-Ribbentrop pact

If the Soviet campaign for 'collective security' was never more than a manoeuvre it cannot be said that the Western democracies did much to encourage or deserve a firm Soviet commitment to an anti-Nazi alliance. Even when they abandoned all hope of checking Hitler by appeasement the British and French governments made only cautious and grudging attempts to involve the USSR in joint resistance to further German aggrandizement. Their half-heartedness is understandable: previous Soviet behaviour gave no reason to believe that the USSR would ever take military action unless it was attacked; the Red Army* had, it was thought, been seriously weakened by the massacre of its high command, and a large proportion of its officer corps, in the Great Terror;* and the USSR could put itself in a strong strategic position against Germany only on the territory of Poland and the Baltic republics. Stalin believed that even if he allied himself with them the democracies would leave the USSR to 'pull the chestnuts out of the fire' if war came. He preferred a prophylactic Non-Aggression Pact with Germany (23 August 1939) which gave Hitler a free hand in the West, followed by the Agreement on Friendship and Frontiers (28 September 1939). Germany and the USSR partitioned and occupied Poland, described by V. M. Molotov (b.1890) on this occasion as 'the freakish creation of Versailles.' The USSR also took advantage of the war in Western Europe to attack Finland and annex Estonia, Latvia and Lithuania. In preparation for this rapprochement with Germany, Stalin had executed or consigned to prison camps* many of the European communist leaders in exile in the USSR.

Welcoming demonstration in Barcelona for a Soviet supply ship, October 1936

V. M. Molotov signing the Non-Agression Pact with Germany in August 1939, with Ribbentrop and Stalin looking on

Communists abroad were ordered (not all of them obeyed) to treat the war as a clash between rival imperialisms, to deny their governments support against Germany, and to work for a negotiated peace. Stalin would subsequently claim that the Non-Aggression Pact was intended only to give the USSR a breathing space before the inevitable conflict with Germany. More probably, he hoped for a stalemate which would leave a relatively stronger USSR with its territorial gains. In the two years before the German attack Stalin dismissed as mischievous Western warnings about German intentions, avoided reinforcing forward defences for fear of provoking Hitler, and gave substantial material assistance to Germany. Stalin's description of the German invasion as 'perfidious' makes sense only if we suppose that he expected Hitler to respect his benevolent neutrality.

The German invasion of the USSR on 22 June 1941 instantly converted the 'imperialist war' into a 'people's war against fascism'. Churchill hastened to assure Stalin of British support, and the USA (still neutral) extended lease-lend arrangements to the USSR.

The Grand Alliance

Relations within the Grand Alliance were frequently uneasy. Stalin as a rule found Roosevelt much easier to work with (and upon) than Churchill. The President of the USA believed that the USSR was interested only in guarantees of its own security, that it would work for a world of 'peace and democracy' after the war, and (surely his most memorable statement) that 'Stalin is not an imperialist'. American *naïveté*, Britain's relatively weak position within the Alliance, and the need to encourage and at times placate the country which did in fact bear the brunt of the war in Europe, resulted in a series of diplomatic agreements which greatly extended the area of direct and indirect Soviet rule, and which still in large measure determine Soviet foreign policy. Churchill, in Moscow in October

Churchill, Roosevelt and Stalin at the Yalta Conference, 1945

1944, suggested a division of post-war Europe into spheres of influence which guaranteed Soviet preponderance in Romania and Bulgaria, and equal British and Soviet shares in Greece. At the Yalta Conference in February 1945 the Western leaders accepted as the provisional government of Poland the communist administration installed in Lublin by the USSR: it was to be enlarged to include politicians of other parties, and 'free and unfettered' elections would eventually be held, but the Polish communists and the USSR were only briefly embarrassed by these commitments. At the Potsdam Conference in July–August 1945 decisions were taken which would later result in the division of Germany into two sovereign states, one of them the most useful and loyal of Soviet satellites. Also at Yalta, a bilateral agreement between the USA and the USSR, subsequently accepted by Churchill, awarded the USSR considerable territorial gains at the expense of Japan (and Japanese-occupied China*) in return for its belated, brief and probably unnecessary participation in the war in the Far East.   *H.T.W.*

The cold war

Between 1945 and 1948 the Soviet Union extended its control over most of the European neighbours bordering on its frontier and briefly also over North Korea, Manchuria and northern Iran, giving rise to fears in the West of an ideological conspiracy. It would seem preferable to see such Soviet domination as the consequence of victory in the Second World War. Whatever Soviet intentions may have been, equally important were the interpretations of these events by Western decision-makers. To the American scholar and diplomat George Kennan, Soviet action was a 'fluid stream which moves constantly, wherever it is permitted to move', until 'it has filled every nook and cranny available to it in the basin of world power', and the appropriate response was the vigilant application of counterforce. This was the policy of containment.

The Soviet government, for its part, saw itself as peace-loving. The Red Army* which at its peak in 1945 numbered some 11.3 million men, was reduced to about 2.8 million men by 1947. Until 1949 the USA enjoyed a monopoly of nuclear weapons. One Soviet economist expressed views which appeared to contradict the two-camp image of the world endorsed by orthodox Soviet spokesmen such as Zhdanov* or by foreign communists such as Marshal Tito of Yugoslavia. The economist Ye. S. Varga (1879–1965) wrote that the economy of the United States was not inevitably heading towards a slump and that it possessed the means of reconstruction; he did not believe that the West would pursue an aggressive policy towards the USSR and he discerned the importance of decolonization exemplified in the British withdrawal from India.

The iron curtain

On 9 February 1946, on the eve of the elections to the Supreme Soviet,* Stalin* made his election address. It was a moderate statement of the Soviet view. Although he admitted that the Second World War had been from the outset 'a war of liberation', he also said that it had been the inevitable result of the development of monopoly capitalism and that capitalism might cause a future war. He envisaged an ambitious programme of heavy industrial development to guarantee the USSR 'against all eventualities' – that is, against an 'imperialist assault'. In an obvious reference to a nuclear bomb he promised Soviet scientists such support as would enable them to 'surpass the achievements of science beyond the boundaries of our country'.

The speech caused consternation in the West. Churchill's speech on 5 March at Fulton, Missouri in its turn caused consternation in the USSR. Although Churchill at the time was in opposition to a Labour government, his international reputation, combined with the presence of President Truman in the audience, gave his words the character of an official statement of British policy. He spoke of an iron curtain dividing Europe – and so indeed it was. By 1948 the whole of eastern Europe with the exception of Finland in the north and Greece in the south was under Soviet and communist control. In Poland in January 1947 the communist-dominated bloc received 80 per cent of the votes. In Romania in November 1946 the communist-led bloc won 372 out of 414 parliamentary seats. In Bulgaria the elections of October 1946 placed parliament into the hands of the communists. Only in Hungary and Czechoslovakia was there some delay. In the elections of November 1945 in Hungary the communists polled 17 per cent of the votes, but in the equally free Czechoslovak elections of May 1946 the communists polled 38 per cent of votes. The Hungarian democratic triumph was not to last long: using what the Hungarian communist leader M. Rakosi later described as 'salami tactics', the Hungarian communists, with the active support of the Soviet occupation authorities, destroyed the opposition in one year. Czechoslovakia was to enjoy immunity until February 1948.

Soviet involvement in these events is sometimes, but not always, clearly documented. Thus in Hungary, the secretary-general of the Smallholders Party, I. Kovacs, was arrested, not by the Hungarian police but by the Soviet authorities. Earlier in Romania a government had been forced on King Michael by the Soviet deputy foreign minister himself. More examples of direct Soviet intervention were provided by the correspondence between the Soviet and Yugoslav communists published in the aftermath of the Tito-Stalin split showing that the USSR expected to be consulted on all senior state and Party appointments. The economies of satellite countries were modelled on the Soviet example and exploited by Soviet-controlled joint-stock companies. Control was strengthened and opposition cowed by the judicial murder in 1949 of L. Rajk in Hungary and of T.

Kostov in Bulgaria and by the monster purge trial in Prague in 1952, prepared and conducted with the collaboration of the Soviet security* apparatus.

Outside Europe Soviet control was even more evident. In November 1945 a 'democratic government' of Azerbaijan was set up under the aegis of the Red Army in northern Iran, followed in March 1946 by a Kurdish republic. Reaction from the Western powers, from the Security Council of the United Nations* and even from the Iranian government was firm and by the end of 1946 the Soviet forces withdrew. This incident convinced President Truman that Soviet and communist (to many these terms were interchangeable) imperialists would back down if firmly resisted. There were to be no more Munichs.

Conflict over Germany and Berlin*

Germany became a primary area of conflict. At the end of 1945 the US Secretary of State J. Byrnes had suggested both to the USSR's foreign minister V. M. Molotov (b. 1890) and to Stalin a four-power pact to keep Germany demilitarized, but they showed little interest, being more concerned with the question of reparations. At the Potsdam Conference it had been agreed that each of the four occupying powers should take reparations from its own zone; in addition the USSR was to receive 15 per cent of all industrial capacity removed from the Ruhr (in the British zone) in return for Soviet deliveries of raw materials and food. To the USSR reparations were vital: in February 1946 the leading economist N. A. Voznesensky (1903–50) even formulated the slogan 'Reparations for the fulfilment of the Five-year Plan'.* The Soviet refusal to account for the raw materials exported from their zone or the capital goods and equipment dismantled hampered any attempt to treat Germany as an economic unit, and proved costly to Britain and the USA. Thus in April 1946 all reparation payments from the West to the Soviet zone ceased.

The USSR and the Western powers accepted and consolidated the division of Germany. In the Soviet zone the ruling Socialist Unity Party had been formed by the enforced amalgamation of the Socialist and Communist Parties. Since in the October 1946 municipal elections in Berlin this party had polled only 19.8 per cent of votes, the Soviet authorities were unlikely to hazard the fate of their regime in eastern Germany to the chance of a free election. In March 1948 Marshal V. D. Sokolovsky (1897–1968) left the Allied Control Council on the grounds that a quadripartite basis for governing Germany no longer existed. The Western occupying powers had meanwhile decided on the introduction of a new currency – the D-mark – to be the foundation of economic rebirth. It was not intended to apply to West Berlin. When the USSR in its turn introduced a new mark and applied it to the whole of Berlin the West retaliated by extending the D-mark to West Berlin. As early as March 1948 the Soviet authorities had begun to impede road traffic to Berlin and in

could help to divert or nullify the aggressive tendencies of capitalism. Few concrete results emerged from this new policy in the five months before Stalin's death. To an American journalist he expressed the wish that the war in Korea should be brought to an end, and to two Indian diplomats he voiced his fear of the consequence of war for the USSR. Shortly after his death (5 March 1953) his successors began to implement the policies which had been merely hinted at in the previous two years and one of the first initiatives resulted in the signing of an armistice by the United Nations and North Korean military representatives at Panmunjon on 27 July 1953.   *H.H.*

The 'New Course'

Although Stalin★ left to his successors a strong and united camp with a single centre, it was surrounded by Western bases. The necessary defence expenditure retarded economic recovery from the terrible devastation of the Second World War. Equally, the fissiparous influences within the camp, already visible in Yugoslavia under Tito,★ could not be contained indefinitely. First G. M. Malenkov (b.1902), with his 'New Course', and then Khrushchev★ under the banners of 'peaceful coexistence' and 'separate paths to socialism' tried to break out of the foreign policy constraints imposed both by the Stalinist★ inheritance and by Western containment. Although the June 1953 uprising in East Berlin★ was suppressed by Soviet tanks, the USSR's treatment of its allies did soften: leaders such as Poland's W. Gomułka and Hungary's E. Gerö were released from prison, and the first steps toward rapprochement with Yugoslavia were taken with Khrushchev's visit to Belgrade in May 1955. The signing of the Austrian State Treaty that month produced the withdrawal of Soviet and Western forces from Austria as a prelude to Austria's declaration of neutrality. In the autumn the establishment of Soviet diplomatic relations with the FRG removed the issue of the future unity of Germany from the Soviet Union's immediate foreign policy agenda and seemed to augur well for a period of peaceful coexistence which would allow of more attention to domestic issues.

In the West, however, the memory of the Korean War, the announcement by Malenkov in August 1953 that the USSR possessed the hydrogen bomb, and the French withdrawal from Indochina in 1954, combined with the anti-communist spirit of the McCarthy era to produce an American commitment to large-scale retaliation against any further communist advances which it was feared might produce a chain reaction: the image evoked was of 'falling dominoes'. To this end two alliances comprising the USA and the UK and states in south-eastern Asia and in the Middle East were established – the South-East Asia Treaty Organization (SEATO) at Manila in 1954, and the Central Treaty Organization (CENTO) after agreement in Baghdad

in 1955. In Europe, the decision was taken in May of that year to admit the FRG to the North Atlantic Treaty Organization (NATO).

The Soviet government reacted by setting up the Warsaw Treaty Organization★ which bound the East European states into a close military alliance with Moscow, and by encouraging the nascent non-aligned movement which held its first conference in Bandung (Indonesia) in April 1955. There Tito, China's Premier Chou En-lai, India's Prime Minister Nehru and Egypt's President Nasser emerged as opponents of the rigid division of the world into two camps. Rejected by the US Secretary of State J. F. Dulles as an 'immoral and short-sighted conception', non-alignment was nurtured by the USSR throughout the 1950s and 1960s as beneficial to the achievement of Soviet objectives.   *K.D.*

Crises of the 1950s and 1960s

Beginning with the large supply of arms to Egypt in 1955, the Soviet leaders made clear their willingness to provide military and economic aid to those states not allied with the West. This policy reaped particular benefits after the October 1956 intervention in Egypt by Britain, France and Israel, aimed at the overthrow of Nasser following nationalization of the Suez Canal Company in the previous July. The failure of the invasion, with the Soviet threat of force to bring about a cease-fire, enhanced Soviet prestige in the Third World; the USA in January 1957 in a statement sometimes called 'the Eisenhower doctrine' made known its determination to recover for the West the influence which Britain and France had forfeited.

Poland and Hungary

If the Middle East crisis had the effect of improving Soviet standing in the Arab world, it is also distracted world public opinion from Soviet behaviour in Eastern Europe. Khrushchev's★ speech denouncing Stalin★ to the XX Party Congress in February 1956 sent shock-waves through the world communist movement. Riots which broke out in Poland during the summer led to popular demands for leadership changes. When it became clear both that the Poles would resist any Soviet invasion and that the reforms proposed would not undermine Soviet-Polish relations, the USSR permitted W. Gomułka to become First Secretary of the Polish Party and withdrew a Soviet citizen of Polish origin (Marshal K. K. Rokossovsky, 1896–1968) from his post as Polish Minister of Defence. Developments in Hungary, in particular the far-reaching economic reforms planned and the proposed withdrawal from the Warsaw Treaty Organiza-tion,★ alarmed the Soviet government, despite its acquiescence in the changes of Party leadership in Budapest. Soviet troops entered Budapest to substitute a government under Kádár for that of Nagy.

The Berlin question

Although that invasion halted for 12 years any radical divergence of East European policies from those embraced by the USSR, Soviet attention remained firmly focused on central Europe, where the series of crises over Berlin* between 1958 and 1961 threatened to erupt into another world war. The Soviet Note on the status of Berlin, sent to the USA, France and the United Kingdom in November 1958, proposed making Berlin a free city with access to it governed by the GDR. The Note declared that if after six months no consensus had been reached, the USSR unilaterally would 'carry out the planned measures through an agreement with the GDR', a move designed to force the West to extend *de facto* diplomatic recognition to that government. In the face of a categorical Western refusal to renegotiate the status of Berlin, the situation was defused only when Khrushchev agreed to send A. A. Gromyko (b.1909) to a foreign ministers' conference in 1959. Although that meeting was inconclusive, prospects for a settlement improved after Khrushchev's visit to the USA immediately afterwards, during which President Eisenhower accepted that a solution to the Berlin question had to be found. The following year agreement was reached to hold four-power talks in Paris, with the German question on the agenda. On 4 May 1960, however, only days before the summit meeting was to convene, Khrushchev announced that an American-piloted U-2 high-altitude reconnaissance aircraft had been shot down over Soviet territory, and abruptly curtailed the conference.

The inauguration of J. F. Kennedy as President of the USA in January 1961 brought hopes that a new era in East-West relations might ensue. Yet at their first meeting in Vienna during June, Khrushchev gained the impression that Kennedy was both inexperienced and reckless, judging from his handling of the unsuccessful Bay of Pigs attempt to overthrow Castro's new regime in Cuba in April 1960. As a result, Khrushchev renewed the Soviet threat that if no agreement were reached on Berlin by the end of the year, the USSR would sign a separate treaty with the GDR. When no positive response was forthcoming, the Soviet government allowed the GDR to build a wall around West Berlin, thus achieving the minimum objective of stopping the flow of East Germans to the West via Berlin, but failing either to renegotiate the status of that city or to obtain recognition of the post-war division of Europe.

The Cuban missiles

The crisis over Berlin had both exacerbated, and been exacerbated by, the arms race between the USSR and the USA, initiated by the 1957 Soviet launchings of an intercontinental ballistic missile* and an unmanned space satellite (Sputnik 1*). By 1962, however, the USA had regained strategic superiority which the Soviet Union thereupon attempted to undermine by placing ballistic missiles in Cuba within range of American cities. The Soviet assessment of Kennedy proved to be incorrect, for on 22 October he ordered a full alert and a naval blockade of Cuba. Six days later a crisis was averted when the Soviet leadership acquiesced in the removal of the missiles. In the two years which remained of Khrushchev's tenure in office, a number of important steps were taken to improve East-West relations, including the 1963 agreement to install a 'hot line' telephone between the Kremlin and the White House and the conclusion in the same year of a Partial Nuclear Test-Ban Treaty.

US AND SOVIET WEAPONS EXPORTS, 1967–76

Equipment (units delivered)	Africa		East Asia[1]		Latin America		Near East		South Asia	
	USA	USSR	USA	USSR	USA	USSR	USA	USSR	USA	USSR
Tanks, self-propelled guns, artillery	249	2543	5861	6630	876	771	4662	11916	30	2596
Armoured personnel carriers/ armoured cars	112	1551	2927	500	1250	200	5724	4249	321	544
Surface combatants	6	56	121	5	86	12	13	67	—	16
Submarines	—	1	2	—	20	—	—	5	—	8
Supersonic aircraft	41	328	403	280	16	44	1673	183	—	447
Subsonic aircraft	20	189	456	—	211	—	387	5	—	45
Helicopters	7	112	1257	47	174	41	389	130	—	116
Missiles	135	130	2373	7000	485	111	5512	470	—	324
Total (millions of US dollars at current prices)	404	2051	15413	3204	1022	519	9836	6982	127	1530

[1] Excludes Soviet transfers to North Vietnam and US transfers to South Vietnam

Source: United States Arms Control and Disarmament Agency

China: the split

Khrushchev's management of the crises in Berlin and Cuba had done little to appease opposition within the Soviet Politburo,* and was viewed with equal alarm by the Chinese government. Mao Tse-tung, in response to advances in Soviet power, had optimistically declared as early as 1957 that 'The East Wind is prevailing over the West Wind' and must have hoped that with the acquisition of its own nuclear weapons and with other forms of Soviet military aid, China would soon emerge as an equal partner in a strong revolutionary alliance with Moscow. Soviet refusal to aid China in retaking the off-shore islands of Quemoy and Matsu from Taiwan in 1958 and the cancellation by Moscow of its nuclear cooperation agreement with Peking the following year resulted, by 1960, in the withdrawal of all Soviet technicians from China. At first Albania, which supported Chinese claims against Moscow, was singled out as a proxy for Soviet condemnation of China, but during 1963 the two sides engaged in open polemics. By 14 October 1964, when Khrushchev was replaced as Party leader by L. I. Brezhnev,* therefore, there were very few areas of the world which did not demand the immediate attention of his successors.

The day after Brezhnev and A. N. Kosygin (1904–80) took office, the Chinese tested their first nuclear bomb, thus gaining a place among the nuclear powers. Despite an initial lull in the polemics, it soon became apparent that no long-term rapprochement between Moscow and Peking was possible. The failure of Kosygin's visit to China in February 1965, aimed at agreeing on a common approach to combat the American bombing of North Vietnam, underlined the continuing mistrust by China of Soviet intentions in south-east Asia. Mao also was convinced by this time that the new Soviet leadership would do nothing to prevent the corruption and bureaucratization which he believed characterized Soviet-style regimes. To demonstrate that China would take a different path, he initiated in 1965 the

KEY

USA and its allies

Areas of predominant United States influence

USSR and its allies

Areas of predominant Soviet influence

China

Source: after C. Bown and P. Mooney, *Cold War to Détente*, London, 1976

CRISES IN THE BALANCE OF POWER, 1945–80

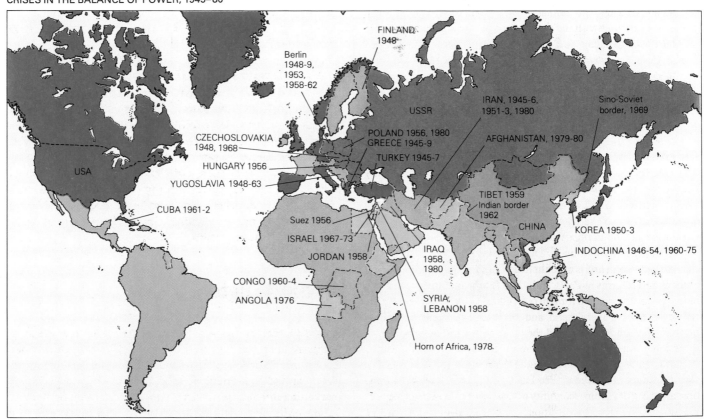

Great Proletarian Cultural Revolution, which had the effect of isolating China from the world arena while at the same time reducing Sino-Soviet relations to their lowest point.

East-West tensions

This was also a time of changes and uncertainty in East-West relations. The escalation of the United States involvement in the Indochina war strained Soviet-American relations, and also exposed the Soviet leaders to criticism within their own camp from those who favoured the concomitant increase in the Soviet backing of North Vietnam. The USSR showed itself to be equally cautious in its response to the June 1967 Middle East war: while providing the Arab states with arms and diplomatic support, it proved unwilling, or unable, to intervene decisively to prevent the overwhelming Arab defeat which followed Israel's pre-emptive strike.

In Europe, de Gaulle's withdrawal of France from participation in NATO in March 1966 produced a positive reaction from the USSR, which welcomed any sign of weakness within the Atlantic alliance. The Soviet leaders did not respond favourably, however, to changes in the foreign policy of the FRG which, beginning with the 'Grand Coalition' government of W. Brandt and K. Kiesinger of 1966, attempted to 'build bridges' between the FRG and Eastern Europe. Romania's decision in January 1967 unilaterally to establish diplomatic relations with the FRG marked the most dramatic gesture thus far of its independence from Soviet policy. It also created a crisis in the East European alliance, only temporarily resolved by a resolution of the Karlovy Vary (Czechoslovakia) Conference of April 1967, which demanded the FRG's recognition of GDR sovereignty as a precondition for the establishment of relations between the FRG and any East European state.

The invasion of Czechoslovakia

The 1968 crisis in Czechoslovakia threatened to weaken bloc unity and undermine Soviet control over East European domestic and foreign policies. Although the USSR did not intervene to prevent the downfall of A. Novotný, the Stalinist First Secretary of the Czechoslovak Communist Party, it soon became apparent that the new leadership, headed by A. Dubček, was planning to introduce reforms far beyond limits thought to be acceptable to Moscow. Cadre changes and reforms in Party and state, freedom of the press, and a more European-oriented foreign policy were some of the issues at the centre of the many bilateral and multilateral negotiations held between the Czechoslovak and the other ruling Communist Parties throughout the spring and summer. Recognition that Czechoslovakia would not willingly abandon its new course, and fear that such reforms would spread into Eastern Europe while at the same time affecting the future reliability of Czechoslovakia as a member of the Warsaw Treaty Organization, were the major factors which

Skirmish between Chinese and Soviet border guards, March 1969

produced the 21 August invasion of Czechoslovakia by the forces of the USSR, the GDR, Poland, Hungary, and Bulgaria. Although the Soviet Union initially failed to install an alternative government in Czechoslovakia it eventually succeeded in suppressing the reform movement, permanently stationing Soviet troops on Czechoslovak territory and – in April 1969 – replacing Dubček with the more conservative G. Husák.

The invasion of Czechoslovakia may have reasserted Soviet dominance in Eastern Europe, but its repercussions on Soviet foreign policy were wide-reaching. Any hope that either Yugoslavia or Romania could soon be brought back under Soviet control was shattered when each denounced the 'Brezhnev doctrine' of limited sovereignty which had been used to justify the invasion. Most of the non-ruling Communist Parties also distanced themselves from the Soviet line after the invasion, and it was from this time that Moscow found it difficult to assert authority over the Eurocommunist movement. The invasion also provoked a sharp reaction in Peking, with the war of words escalating to armed border clashes on the Ussuri River in March 1969.   *K.D.*

Towards détente

The USSR was at pains to limit the effect of the events in Czechoslovakia* on East-West relations. The 1967 Outer Space Treaty (prohibiting the placing of nuclear weapons in space) and the Treaty on the Non-Proliferation of Nuclear Weapons (1968) had marked important stages in attempts to control the arms race. Efforts continued throughout the 1970s with the 1971 Sea-bed Arms Control

Treaty (banning the placement of nuclear weapons on the sea-bed beyond a country's 12-mile limit), the 1972 Biological Warfare Convention (prohibiting the manufacture of biological weapons and toxins), the 1972 Agreement on the Limitation of Strategic Offensive Arms (SALT I), and the 1973 Declaration on the Avoidance of Nuclear War. The conclusion of an Armistice Agreement between the United States and North Vietnam in January 1973, which subsequently resulted in a communist take-over in South Vietnam, removed a further major obstacle to the strengthening of East-West détente, and provided the USSR with the opportunity to extend communist influence throughout south-east Asia.

Yet détente has proved to be both fragile and limited. The marked increase in Soviet military support for the Arabs during the Arab-Israeli war of October 1973 produced a nuclear alert in the USA which threatened to escalate to global proportions. Equally, the USSR's concern to strengthen détente did not prevent it from increasing the supply of arms to the Third World, or from committing military advisers in alliance with Cuban* expeditionary forces to the wars in Angola and the Horn of Africa. The marked improvement in China's relations with the USA, Japan and Europe after the death of Mao Tse-tung in 1976 also produced considerable strains both in East-West relations and in Soviet relations with China,* particularly after the latter's brief incursion into North Vietnam at the beginning of 1979. The Soviet invasion of Afghanistan in December 1979 further undermined the foundations of détente and strengthened American reluctance to ratify the agreement reached following the second round of Strategic Arms Limitation talks (SALT II).

It has been in Europe that the greatest efforts have been made to overcome cold war hostilities. The FRG pursued a more successful

A. N. Kosygin and Chancellor Willy Brandt signing the 1970 Treaty of Non-Aggression; L. I. Brezhnev behind

COMPARISONS OF THE MILITARY EXPENDITURES (1978) OF WARSAW TREATY ORGANIZATION AND NATO COUNTRIES

	$ million	$ per head	percentage of national product[1]
WARSAW TREATY ORGANIZATION			
Bulgaria	438	66	2.5[2]
Czechoslovakia	2 342	153	3.8
GDR	4 238	253	5.8
Hungary	808	76	2.4
Poland	3 335	95	3.0
Romania	1 263	58	1.7
USSR	148 000	574	11–14
NORTH ATLANTIC TREATY ORGANIZATION			
Belgium	3 143	315	3.5
Canada	3 692	156	1.8
Denmark	1 317	258	2.4
France	15 225	285	3.3
FRG	21 366	347	3.4
Greece	1 523	163	4.7
Italy	6 212	109	2.4
Luxembourg	37	102	1.1
Netherlands	4 323	309	3.3
Norway	1 254	308	3.2
Portugal	540	55	2.8
Turkey	2 025	47	4.5
United Kingdom	14 090	252	4.7
USA	105 135	481	5.0

[1] Gross domestic or national product at market prices in national currencies
[2] 1977

Source: International Institute for Strategic Studies, *The Military Balance, 1979–1980,* London, 1979

Ostpolitik after Brandt became Chancellor in 1969: the normalization of relations between the two Germanys paved the way for the 1970 Treaty of Non-Aggression between the USSR and the FRG and the 1971 Four-Power Agreement on Berlin. In 1973, two sets of parallel negotiations were begun on 'mutual and balanced force reductions' in Europe and on 'security and cooperation in Europe', of which the Final Act was signed in Helsinki by 35 states of Europe and North America in August 1975. For the USSR, the Helsinki Agreement represented a major foreign policy victory by finally recognizing the post-war boundaries of Europe. Thus, out of a shattered and devastated state at the end of the Second World War, the USSR had emerged by the end of the 1970s as the leader of a communist bloc racked by internal divisions, yet militarily unrivalled and with global interests and influence. *K.D.*

Participation in international organizations

The Soviet Union sees itself as being, even with its socialist allies, in a permanent minority within international organizations. On these grounds it has always been opposed to allowing any significant expansion in their authority and sees them merely as meeting-places for debate among nations of differing ideology and interests. The commitment to 'socialist internationalism' has therefore never found expression in a policy of support for, or strengthening of, international organizations.

The USSR did not at first become a member of the League of Nations and regarded it during its early years as essentially an alliance of hostile capitalist states. Conversely, its own admission would not have been welcomed nor supported by most members of the League at any time during the 1920s. With the rise to power of Hitler,* and the Japanese attack on Manchuria which threatened the Soviet eastern boundary, both the USSR and Western countries (notably France) were willing to see a closer relationship develop. In September 1934, on the proposal of France, Britain and Italy, the USSR was admitted to the League and became a permanent member of its Council. It used this membership to promote the new Soviet policy, for which the Commissar for Foreign Affairs M. M. Litvinov (1876–1951) was the best-known spokesman, of arousing European states against the dangers presented by the Axis powers. It was, however, a moment when the League's weaknesses were already becoming clear. The USSR supported the somewhat half-hearted action taken by the League in respect of Italian aggression against Ethiopia and opposed the weakening of 'collective security'* obligations proposed in 1938. When the USSR, however, launched its own war against Finland in the autumn of 1939, it found itself, during the League's dying days in Geneva, expelled from the organization: the only country to suffer that indignity, since Germany, Italy and Japan had left of their own volition.

The USSR played a major part in framing the Charter of the United Nations. Although the initial discussions took place between the USA and Britain, both were fully aware of the need to find a basis for the new body acceptable to the Soviet Union. Thus, when the three countries met at the Dumbarton Oaks conference in August 1944 there was soon general agreement about the shape of the new organization. But the Soviet delegation caused some consternation by suggesting separate membership of the United Nations for each of the USSR's republics (the Soviet Constitution* had just been amended to permit each of the 16 Union Republics its own People's Commissariats of Foreign Affairs and of Defence). A compromise was eventually reached, under which only the Ukraine and Belorussia in addition to the USSR were accepted as separate members.

M. M. Litvinov at a press conference following his appointment as ambassador to the USA in 1941

More important was a disagreement about the right of veto to be enjoyed by the permanent members. The Western powers held that this should not apply to measures of peaceful settlement involving a permanent member. Eventually at the subsequent San Francisco Conference they reluctantly accepted that such measures, since they started a 'chain of events' that might ultimately lead to stronger action including the use of force, were subject to the veto.

During the early years the USSR frequently used the veto, needing it as the Western powers, which could normally command a majority for any course they favoured, did not. The great majority of Soviet vetoes were cast on the admission of new members when its own nominees, mainly East European states, were being rejected by the Western majority. Nevertheless, its use of the veto at this time was excessive and included issues over which Soviet interests were scarcely involved at all. It was partly on these grounds that the Western states resorted to new procedural devices: the use of special assemblies, of an 'interim Assembly' when the Assembly itself was not meeting, and eventually the 'Uniting for Peace' procedure under which the Assembly could be called in an emergency to consider threats to peace – an initiative denounced by the USSR as a breach of the Charter.

In January 1950 the USSR abandoned the Security Council and other United Nations organs in protest at the failure of the previous Assembly to accord the China seat in the organization to the People's Republic of China; at about the same time it temporarily abandoned participation in many of the specialized agencies for a period of two or three years, partly on the same grounds. It was consequently absent from the Security Council at the time of the outbreak of the Korean War* in June, and so unable to veto the action then taken. Its resumption of its seat in September was too late to prevent the United Nations operation in Korea, already launched. From then on, the USSR maintained its place in the organization and used its position to denounce the policies of the Western powers, to propose from time to time somewhat visionary schemes for disarmament, and to champion the cause of decolonization. On the last point, it was the initiator of the famous Resolution 1514 of 1960, overwhelmingly adopted, calling for a complete end to the colonial system. On such questions it was often able to create a coalition with Third World countries against the Western powers.

The hostility of the USSR to any strengthening of United Nations authority was shown in its attitude to peace-keeping. Strongly supporting Egypt at the time of the Suez crisis,* it could not oppose the proposals of the Secretary General Dag Hammarskjöld for a United Nations force to help to eject the invaders and keep the peace. The Soviet government nevertheless expressed strong reservations, particularly on the fact that it was the Assembly rather than the Council (as the Charter seemed to provide) that set up the force, and refused to contribute to the cost of the operation. It abstained on the proposal to send a force to the Congo in 1960 and, even though the force was this time established by the Council, once more declined to pay (in common with many other countries) – as it did again for the force in Cyprus. It was not until the establishment of the two new forces in Sinai and Syria in 1973, when a revised framework was established (under which the cost was to be borne by all members though on a special scale), that the Soviet Union for the first time began to contribute to the cost of such measures.

During the 1960s the balance of power within the United Nations and other international organizations changed radically. There was no longer a Western but a Third World majority. The USSR continued to try to mobilize an alliance of Third World countries in its favour, but the strategy became increasingly ineffective as the colonial era drew to an end and as developing countries became concerned mainly with economic aid, on which the Soviet record was even worse than that of the West. Nor did the new balance of power modify Soviet reluctance to see any increase in the authority and activity of these

Khrushchev addressing the 15th session of the UN General Assembly in 1960

organizations. The USSR has consistently declined to contribute significantly to the development work of the United Nations or to the many voluntary funds established for particular purposes, invariably opposing all budgetary increases and sometimes proposing reductions. It has never joined the World Bank, the International Monetary Fund or the General Agreement on Tariffs and Trade, despite participation in them by some of its East European allies. Like other members, the Soviet Union seconds its own nationals to serve as international civil servants, who sometimes operate with distinction, particularly in the technical specialized agencies. None has yet achieved the rank of executive head of any organization, and the most senior post held by a Soviet national so far is that of United Nations Under-Secretary General for Political and Security Council Affairs. Since the Soviet government sees the present structure of the United Nations as practically the most suited to its purposes, it has consistently opposed all proposals for Charter amendment or review, and is unlikely to modify this standpoint.   E.L.

Further reading

TERRITORY AND PEOPLES

W. E. D. Allen, *A History of the Georgian Peoples*, London, 1932

T. E. Armstrong, *Russian Settlement in the North*, Cambridge, 1965

J. F. Baddeley, *The Rugged Flanks of the Caucasus*, Oxford, 1940

R. P. Bartlett, *Human Capital: The Settlement of Foreigners in Russia, 1762–1804*, Cambridge, 1979

L. S. Berg, *The Natural Regions of the USSR*, New York, 1950

A. A. Borisov, *Climates of the USSR*, Edinburgh, 1965

J. C. Dewdney, *The USSR* (Studies in Industrial Geography), London, 1978

M. T. Florinsky (ed), *Encyclopedia of Russia and the Soviet Union*, New York, 1961

R. A. French and F. E. I. Hamilton (eds), *The Socialist City*, London, 1979

I. P. Gerasimov, D. L. Armand and K. M. Yefron (eds), *Natural Resources of the Soviet Union: Their Use and Renewal*, San Francisco, 1971

I.P. Gerasimov and M. A. Glazovskaya, *Fundamentals of Soil Science and Soil Geography*, 1965 (Israel Program for Scientific Translation)

J. R. Gibson, *Feeding the Russian Fur Trade: Provisionment of the Okhotsk Seaboard and the Kamchatka Peninsula, 1639–1856*, Madison, 1969

A. Giesinger, *From Catherine to Khrushchev; The Story of Russia's Germans*, Battleford, 1974

J. S. Gregory, *Russian Land, Soviet People*, London, 1968

M. F. Hamm, *The City in Russian History*, Lexington, 1976

David Hooson, *The Soviet Union: People and Regions*, Belmont, Calif. and London, 1966

G. M. Howe, *The Soviet Union*, London, 1968

C. H. Humphrey (ed), *Peoples of the Earth*, vol. 14: *USSR East of the Urals*, Verona, 1973

Z. Katz, *Handbook of Major Soviet Nationalities*, New York, 1975

D. Kendrick and G. Puxon, *The Destiny of Europe's Gypsies*, London, 1972

L. Kochan (ed), *The Jews in Soviet Russia since 1917* (3rd edn), Oxford, 1978

L. A. Kosinski (ed), *Demographic Development in Eastern Europe*, New York and London, 1977

Lawrence Krader, *Social Organisation of the Mongol-Turkic Pastoral Nomads*, The Hague, 1964

D. M. Lang, *Modern History of Georgia*, London, 1962

D. M. Lang and C. Walker, *Armenians*, London, 1977

M. G. Levin and L. P. Potapov (eds), *The Peoples of Siberia*, Chicago, 1964

R. A. Lewis, R. H. Rowland and R. S. Clem, *Nationality and Population Change in Russia and the USSR: An Evaluation of Census Data, 1897–1970*, New York and London, 1976

P. E. Lydolph, *Geography of the USSR: Topical Analysis*, Misty Valley Publishing, Elkhart Lake, 1979

R. St J. Macdonald (ed), *The Arctic Frontier*, Toronto, 1966

Robert Maxwell (ed), *Information USSR* (trans. from vol. 50, *Great Soviet Encyclopedia*), Oxford and New York, 1962

N. T. Mirov, *Geography of Russia*, New York and London, 1951

Judith Pallot and Denis J. B. Shaw, *Planning in the Soviet Union*, London, 1981

P. R. Pryde, *Conservation in the Soviet Union*, Cambridge, 1972

Paula G. Rubel, *The Kalmyk Mongols: A Study in Continuity and Change*, The Hague, 1967

V. I. Smirnov (ed), *Ore Deposits of the USSR*, 3 vols, London, 1977

T. Sulimirski, *Prehistoric Russia*, London, 1970

D. W. Treadgold, *The Great Siberian Migration*, Princeton, 1957

S. V. Utechin, *Everyman's Concise Encyclopaedia of Russia*, London and New York, 1961

G. E. Wheeler, *Racial Problems in Soviet Muslim Asia*, Oxford, 1962

G. E. Wheeler, *The Peoples of Soviet Central Asia*, London, 1966

HISTORY

Robert Auty and Dimitri Obolensky (eds), *An Introduction to Russian History*, Companion to Russian Studies vol. 1, Cambridge, 1976

P. L. Barbour, *Dimitri, Tsar and Great Prince of All Russia, 1605–1606*, London, 1967

J. Blum, *Lord and Peasant in Russia from the Ninth to the Nineteenth Centuries*, Princeton, 1961

E. H. Carr, *History of Soviet Russia*, 14 vols, London, 1952–78

Stephen F. Cohen, Alexander Rabinowitch and Robert Sharlet (eds), *The Soviet Union since Stalin*, London, 1980

Robert Conquest, *The Great Terror*, Harmondsworth, 1971

E. Crankshaw, *In the Shadow of the Winter Palace*, London, 1976

D. M. Dunlop, *The History of the Jewish Khazars*, Princeton, 1954

J. L. I. Fennell, *Ivan the Great of Moscow*, London, 1963

J. L. I. Fennell, *The Emergence of Moscow, 1304–1359*, London, 1968

M. T. Florinsky, *Russia: A History and an Interpretation*, 2 vols, New York, 1953

I. Grey, *Catherine the Great: Autocrat and Empress of All the Russias*, London, 1961

I. Grey, *The First Fifty Years: Soviet Russia 1917–1967*, London, 1967

G. A. Hosking, *The Constitutional Experiment*, London, 1973

R. C. Howes, *The Testaments of the Grand Princes of Moscow*, Ithaca, 1967

George Katkov, *Russia: February 1917*, London and New York, 1967

George Katkov and Harold Shukman, *Lenin's Path to Power*, London, 1971

George Katkov (ed), *Russia Enters the Twentieth Century, 1894–1917*, London, 1971

W. Leonhard, *The Kremlin since Stalin*, New York, 1962

Philip Longworth, *The Cossacks*, London, 1969

Philip Longworth, *Three Empresses: Catherine I, Anne and Elizabeth of Russia*, London, 1972

I. de Madariaga, *Russia in the Age of Catherine the Great*, New Haven and London, 1981

R. H. McNeal (ed), *Russia in Transition: 1905–1914: Evolution or Revolution?*, Huntington, 1976

Robert K. Massie, *Peter the Great: His Life and World*, London, 1980

Roy A. Medvedev, *Let History Judge*, London, 1972

H. W. Morton and R. L. Tökés (eds), *Soviet Politics and Society in the 1970s*, New York and London, 1974

W. E. Mosse, *Alexander II and the Modernization of Russia*, London, 1958

B. Nørretranders, *The Shaping of the Tsardom of Muscovy*, London, 1964

Dimitri Obolensky, *The Byzantine Commonwealth: Eastern Europe, 500–1453*, London, 1971

M. Raeff, *Imperial Russia, 1682–1825: The Coming of Age of Modern Russia*, New York, 1971

H. Ragsdale (ed), *Paul I: a Reassessment of His Life and Reign*, Pittsburgh, 1978

N. V. Riazanovsky, *A History of Russia* (3rd edn), Oxford, 1977

Georg von Rauch, *A History of Soviet Russia*, New York, 1957

Tamara Talbot Rice, *The Scythians*, London, 1957

M. Rostovtzeff, *Iranians and Greeks in Southern Russia*, Oxford 1922; New York, 1969

S. I. Rudenko, *Frozen Tombs of Siberia* (trans. M. W. Thompson), London, 1970

Leonard Schapiro, *The Communist Party of the Soviet Union* (2nd edn), London, 1970

Albert Seaton, *The Russo-German War, 1941–1945*, London, 1971

H. Seton-Watson, *The Russian Empire 1801–1917*, Oxford, 1967

Harold Shukman, *Lenin and the Russian Revolution*, London, 1977

T. Sulimirski, *The Sarmatians*, London, 1970

M. Tatu, *Power in the Kremlin*, London, 1969

E. A. Thompson, *A History of Attila and the Hun*, Oxford, 1948

D. W. Treadgold, *Twentieth-Century Russia*, Chicago, 1964

A. Ulam, *Stalin: The Man and his Era*, New York, 1973

A. A. Vasiliev, *The Goths in the Crimea*, Cambridge, Mass., 1936

G. V. Vernadsky, *Kievan Russia*, New Haven, 1948

G. V. Vernadsky, *The Mongols and Russia*, New Haven, 1953

G. V. Vernadsky, *Russia at the Dawn of the Modern Age*, New Haven, 1959

G. V. Vernadsky, *The Tsardom of Muscovy*, New Haven, 1969

G. V. Vernadsky *et al.* (eds), *A Source Book for Russian History from Early Times to 1917*, New Haven and London, 1972

B. D. Wolfe, *Three Who Made a Revolution*, New York, 1948

RELIGION

T. Beeson, *Discretion and Valour*, London, 1974

G. Bennigsen and C. Lemercier-Quelquejay, *Islam in the Soviet Union*, New York, 1967

M. Bourdeaux, *Religious Ferment in Russia*, London, 1968

J. Cracraft, *The Church Reform of Peter the Great*, London, 1971

J. S. Curtiss, *Church and State in Russia: The Last Years of the Empire 1900–1917*, New York, 1940

J. S. Curtiss, *The Russian Church and the Soviet State 1917–1950*, Boston, Mass., 1953

G. P. Fedotov, *The Russian Religious Mind*, 2 vols, Cambridge, Mass., 1946–1966

W. C. Fletcher, *Religion and Soviet Foreign Policy 1954–1970*, London, 1973

W. C. Fletcher, *The Russian Church Underground*, Oxford, 1973

G. Florovsky, *The Ways of Russian Theology*, 2 vols, Belmont, Mass., 1977

S. A. Hackel, *The Orthodox Church*, London, 1971

H. M. Hayward and W. C. Fletcher (eds), *Religion and the Soviet State*, London, 1969

W. Kolarz, *Religion in the Soviet Union*, London, 1961

C. Lane, *Christian Religion in the Soviet Union: A Sociological Study*, London, 1978

R. H. Marshall (ed), *Aspects of Religion in the Soviet Union 1917–1967*, Chicago and London, 1971

Dimitri Obolensky, *The Byzantine Commonwealth: Eastern Europe 500–1453*, London, 1971

ART AND ARCHITECTURE

M. Alpatov, *Art Treasures of Russia* (2nd edn), London, 1975

S. Amiranashvili, *Medieval Georgian Enamels*, New York, 1969

M. I. Artamonov, *Treasures from Scythian Tombs*, London, 1969

Robert Auty and Dimitri Obolensky (eds), *An Introduction to Russian Art and Architecture*, Companion to Russian Studies vol. 3, Cambridge, 1980

J. H. Bater, *The Soviet City*, London, 1980

Kathleen Berton, *Moscow: An Architectural History*, London, 1977

John E. Bowlt (ed), *Russian Art of the Avant-Garde: Theory and Criticism 1902–1934*, New York, 1976

M. Bussagli, *Paintings of Central Asia*, Geneva, 1963

David R. Buxton, *Russian Mediaeval Architecture*, New York, 1975

M. Chamot, *Russian Painting and Sculpture*, Oxford, 1963

Norton Dodge and Alison Hilton, *New Art from the Soviet Union*, Washington, 1977

Lydia Dournovo, *Armenian Miniatures*, London, 1961

H. Faenson and V. Ivanov, *Early Russian Architecture*, London, 1975

Sheila Fitzpatrick (ed), *Cultural Revolution in Russia, 1928–1931*, Bloomington, 1978

Igor Golomstock and Alexander Glezer, *Unofficial Art from the Soviet Union*, London, 1977 (*Soviet Art in Exile*, New York, 1977)

N. Gosling, *Leningrad*, London, 1965

Camilla Gray, *The Great Experiment: Russian Art, 1863–1922*, London and New York, 1962; new edn, 1971

G. H. Hamilton, *Art and Architecture of Russia*, Harmondsworth (2nd edn), 1975

C. Holme (ed), *Peasant Art in Russia* (Studio Special), London and New York, 1912

K. Jettmar, *Art of the Steppes*, New York, 1967

Victor and Audrey Kennett, *The Palaces of Leningrad*, London, 1973

I. Lozowick, *Modern Russian Art*, New York, 1925

Yu. Ovsyannikov, *The Lubok*, Moscow, 1968

Tamara Talbot Rice, *The Ancient Arts of Central Asia*, London, 1965

Tamara Talbot Rice, *A Concise History of Russian Art*, London, 1963

D. Sarabianov and J. Bowlt, *Russian and Soviet Painting*, New York, 1977

A. Sonkovitch, jr, *Soviet Architecture 1917–1962: A Bibliographical Guide to Source Material*, Charlottesville, 1974

J. Stuart, *Ikons*, London, 1975

Unesco, *USSR: Early Russian Icons*, Paris, 1958

L. A. Uspensky and V. N. Lossky, *The Meaning of Icons*, Basle, 1952

Elizabeth Valkenier, *Russian Realist Art*, Ann Arbor, 1977

C. Vaughan James, *Soviet Socialist Realism*, London, 1973

A. Voyce, *Russian Architecture: Trends in Nationalism and Modernism*, New York, 1948

N. Zinovyev, *Palekh*, Leningrad, 1975

LANGUAGE AND LITERATURE

Vera Alexandrova, *A History of Soviet Literature*, New York, 1963

Robert Auty and Dimitri Obolensky (eds), *An Introduction to Russian Language and Literature*, Companion to Russian Studies vol. 2, Cambridge, 1977

Jennifer Baines, *Mandelstam: The Later Poetry*, Cambridge, 1976

J. Bayley, *Pushkin*, Cambridge, 1971

F. Borras, *Maxim Gorky the Writer*, London, 1967

Deming Brown, *Soviet Russian Literature since Stalin*, Cambridge, 1978

E. J. Brown, *Major Soviet Writers*, New York, 1973

W. E. Brown, *A History of Eighteenth-Century Russian Literature*, Ann Arbor, 1978

E. H. Carr, *Dostoevsky*, London, 1931

R. F. Christian, *Tolstoy: A Critical Introduction*, Cambridge, 1969

D. P. Costello and I. P. Foote (eds), *Russian Folk Literature*, London, 1967

A. G. Cross (ed), *Russian Literature in the Age of Catherine the Great*, Oxford, 1976

D. Čiževskij, *History of Russian Literature from the Eleventh Century to the End of the Baroque*, The Hague, 1962

C. Drage, *Russian Literature in the Eighteenth Century: The Solemn Ode, the Epic, Other Poetic Genres, the Story, the Novel, Drama*, London, 1978

J. L. I. Fennell (ed), *Nineteenth-Century Russian Literature*, London, 1973

John Fennell and Antony Stokes, *Early Russian Literature*, London, 1974

R. Freeborn, *The Rise of the Russian Novel*, Cambridge, 1973

R. Freeborn, *Turgenev: A Study*, London, 1960

H. Gifford, *Pasternak*, Cambridge, 1977

R. A. Gregg, *Fyodor Tyutchev*, New York, 1965

N. K. Gudzy, *A History of Early Russian Literature* (trans. S. Wilbur-Jones), New York, 1970

R. F. Gustafson, *The Imagination of Spring: The Poetry of A. Fet*, New Haven, 1966

Max Hayward and Leopold Labedz (eds), *Literature and Revolution in Soviet Russia, 1917–1962*, London and New York, 1963

R. Hingley, *A New Life of Anton Chekhov*, London, 1976

A. de Jonge, *Dostoevsky and the Age of Intensity*, London, 1975

Simon Karlinsky and Alfred Appell, jr (eds), *The Bitter Air of Exile: Russian Writers in the West, 1922–1972*, rev. edn, Berkeley, and London, 1977

H. McLean, *Nikolai Leskov*, Cambridge, Mass, 1977

R. Maguire, (ed), *Gogol from the Twentieth Century*, Princeton, 1974

J. Mersereau, *Mikhail Lermontov*, Carbondale, 1962

D. S. Mirsky, *A History of Russian Literature*, London, 1949

V. Nabokov, *Nikolai Gogol*, New York, 1961

R. Peace, *Dostoevsky: An Examination of the Major Novels*, Cambridge, 1971

R. Poggioli, *Poets of Russia, 1880–1930*, Cambridge, Mass, 1960

D. J. Richards (ed), *The Penguin Book of Russian Short Stories*, Harmondsworth, 1980

Harold B. Segal (ed), *The Literature of Eighteenth-Century Russia*, 2 vols, New York, 1967

M. Slonim, *Soviet Russian Literature*, New York, 1967

Y. M. Sokolov, *Russian Folklore* (trans. Catherine Ruth Smith), Folklore Associates, Hartboro, Pa, 1966

Gleb Struve, *Russian Literature under Lenin and Stalin*, London, 1972

M. Valency, *The Breaking String: The Drama of A. Chekhov*, New York, 1966

David A. Welsh, *Russian Comedy, 1765–1823*, The Hague, Paris, 1966

J. West, *Russian Symbolism*, London, 1970

MUSIC, THEATRE, DANCE AND FILM

A. Benois, *Reminiscences of the Russian Ballet*, London, 1941

Faubion Bowers, *Entertainment in Russia*, New York, 1959

E. Braun, *Meyerhold on Theatre*, London, 1969

M. A. S. Burgess, 'The Nineteenth and Early Twentieth-Century Theatre.' In: R. Auty and D. Obolensky (eds), *An Introduction to Russian Language and Literature*, Companion to Russian Studies vol. 2, Cambridge, 1977

M. Calvocoressi, *A Survey of Russian Music*, London, 1944, reprinted 1974

T. H. Dickinson (ed), *Theater in a Changing Europe*, New York, 1938

M. Glenny, 'The Soviet Theatre'. In: R. Auty and D. Obolensky (eds), *An Introduction to Russian Language and Literature*,

Companion to Russian Studies vol. 2, Cambridge, 1977

M. I. Glinka, *Memoirs* (trans. R. B. Mudge), Oklahoma, 1963

A. Haskell, *Diaghileff: His Artistic and Private Life*, London, 1965

Tamara Karsavina, *Theatre Street*, London, 1930, reprinted 1961

J. Leyda, *Kino: A History of the Russian and Soviet Film*, London, 1960

J. Leyda and S. Bertensson, *The Musorgsky Reader*, New York, 1947

J. Macleod, *The New Soviet Theatre*, London, 1943

V. N. Nemirovich-Danchenko, *My Life in the Russian Theatre*, New York, 1936

R. S. Ralston, *The Songs of the Russian People as Illustrative of Slavonic Mythology and Russian Social Life*, London, 1872, reprinted 1970

N. A. Rimsky-Korsakov, *My Musical Life*, New York, 1942

S. E. Roberts, *Soviet Historical Drama*, The Hague, 1965

Princess Romanovsky-Krassinsky, *Dancing in Petersburg: The Memoirs of Kschessinskaya*, London, 1960

Natalia Roslavleva, *Era of the Russian Ballet*, 1770–1965, London, 1966

B. Schwarz, *Musical and Musical Life in Soviet Russia 1917–1970*, London, 1972

G. R. Seaman, *History of Russian Music: From its Origins to Dargomyzhsky*, vol. 1, Oxford, 1968

G. R. Seaman, 'Russian Folk Music'. In: *Grove's Dictionary of Music and Musicians* (5th edn), suppl. vol., London, 1961

M. Slonim, *Russian Theatre from the Empire to the Soviets*, London, 1961

Yu. Slonimsky, *The Bol'shoy Ballet*, Moscow, 1963

Yu. Slonimsky, *The Soviet Ballet*, New York, 1947 and 1973

K. S. Stanislavsky, *An Actor Prepares*, New York

M. G. Swift, *The Art of Dance in the USSR*, Notre Dame, 1968

R. Taylor, *Film Propaganda: Soviet Russia and Nazi Germany*, London and New York, 1979

R. Taylor, *The Politics of the Soviet Cinema, 1917–1929*, Cambridge, 1979

A. Tcherepnin, *Anthology of Russian Music*, Bonn, 1966

T. Tkachenko, *Folk Dances of the USSR*, Moscow, 1954 (trans. Joan Lawson, publ. Imperial Society of Teachers of Dancing, London)

B. V. Varneke, *History of the Russian Theatre* (trans. B. Brasol), New York

E. Wellesz and F. R. Sternfeld, *The Age of Enlightenment 1745–1790*, vol 7 of the *New Oxford History of Music*, London, 1973

THE SCIENCES

M. Adams, *Soviet Genetics*, Chicago, 1980

R. Amann, J. Cooper and R. W. Davies (eds), *The Technological Level of Soviet Industry*, New Haven and London, 1977

V. A. Anuchin, *Theoretical Problems of Geography*, Columbus, 1977

T. Armstrong, *The Russians in the Arctic: Aspects of Soviet Exploration and Exploitation of the Far North, 1937–1957*, London, 1960

K. E. Bailes, *Technology and Society under Lenin and Stalin: Origins of the Soviet Technical Intelligentsia, 1917–1941*, Princeton, 1978

J. S. Berliner, *The Innovation Decision in Soviet Industry*, Cambridge, Mass., 1976

Sidney Bloch and Peter Reddaway, *Russia's Political Hospitals: The Abuse of Psychiatry in the Soviet Union*, London, 1977

R. W. Campbell, *Soviet Energy Technologies: Planning, Policy, Research and Development*, Bloomington, 1980

M. Cave, *Computers and Economic Planning: The Soviet Experience*, Cambridge, 1980

A. C. Crombie (ed), *Scientific Change*, London, 1961

H. J. Eysenck, W. Arnold and R. Meili (eds), *Encyclopedia of Psychology*, vol. 3 ('Soviet Psychology'), London, 1972

F. J. Fleron, jr (ed), *Technology and Communist Culture*, Eastbourne and New York, 1977

D. W. Freshfield, *The Exploration of the Caucasus*, London, 1902

A. N. Frumkin and N. M. Emanuel, 'Fifty years of Soviet Physical Chemistry', in H. Eyring, C. J. Christensen and H. S. Johnston (eds), *Annual Reviews*, vol. 99, 1968

K. W. Gatland, *Robot Explorers*, London, 1972

I. P. Gerasimov (ed), *A Short History of Geographical Science in the Soviet Union*, Moscow, 1976

Raymond Hutchings, *Soviet Science, Technology, Design: Interaction and Convergence*, London, 1976

David Joravsky, *Soviet Marxism and Natural Science, 1917–32*, New York, 1961

David Joravsky, *The Lysenko Affair*, Cambridge, Mass, 1970

Malcolm Lader, *Psychiatry on Trial*, Harmondsworth, 1977

R. Lewis, *Science and Industrialisation in the USSR*, London, 1979

Linda L. Lubrano and Susan Gross Solomon (eds), *The Social Context of Soviet Science*, Boulder, and Folkestone, 1980

R. E. McGrew, *Russia and the Cholera 1823–1832*, Madison 1965

Zhores A. Medvedev, *Soviet Science*, New York, 1978 and Oxford, 1979

B. N. Menshutkin, *Russia's Lomonosov: Chemist, Courtier, Physicist, Poet* (trans. J. E. Thal and E. J. Webster), Princeton, 1952

D. V. Nalikvin, *Geology of the USSR* (trans. N. Rast), Edinburgh, 1973

L. E. Neatby, *Discovery in Russian and Siberian Waters*, Ohio, 1973

L. E. Nolting, *The 1968 Reform of Scientific Research, Development and Innovation in the USSR* (Foreign Economic Report no. 11, United States Department of Commerce), Washington, 1976

L. E. Nolting, *The Structure and Functions of the USSR State Committee for Science and Technology* (Foreign Economic Report no. 16, United States Department of Commerce), Washington, 1979

E. Riabchikov, *Russians in Space*, London, 1972

P. Sager, *The Technological Gap between the Superpowers* (trans. C. Rieser), Berne, 1972

A. D. Sakharov, *Progress, Co-existence and Intellectual Freedom*, London, 1969

S. G. Shetler, *The Komarov Botanical Institute: 250 Years of Russian Research*, Washington, 1967

E. V. Shpol'sky, 'Fifty Years of Soviet Physics', in *Soviet Physics — Uspekhi*, no. 10, 1968

'Sixty years of Soviet Electrochemistry', *Soviet Electrochemistry*, no. 13, 1977

A. C. Sutton, *Western Technology and Soviet Economic Develop-*

ment, 3 vols: *1917 to 1930, 1930 to 1945, 1945 to 1965*, Stanford, 1968, 1971, 1973

J. R. Thomas and U. M. Kruse-Vaucienne (eds), *Soviet Science and Technology: Domestic and Foreign Perspectives*, Washington, 1977

J. L. Turkevich, *Chemistry in the Soviet Union*, Princeton, 1965

A. Vucinich, *Science in Russian Culture*, 3 vols, Stanford, 1965, 1970

J. Wortis and A. G. Galach'yan, in J. G. Howells (ed), *World History of Psychiatry*, London and New York, 1975

E. Zaleski, J. P. Kozlowski, H. Wienert, R. W. Davies, M. J. Berry and R. Amann, *Science Policy in the USSR*, (OECD), Paris, 1969

A. Zauberman, *The Mathematical Revolution in Soviet Economics*, Oxford, 1975

A. Zauberman, *Mathematical Theory in Soviet Planning*, Oxford, 1976

THE SOVIET POLITICAL SYSTEM

Seweryn Bialer, *Stalin's Successors: Leadership, Stability and Change in the Soviet Union*, Cambridge, 1980

Archie Brown and Michael Kaser (eds), *The Soviet Union since the Fall of Khrushchev*, (2nd edn), London, 1978

E. Chekharin, *The Soviet Political System under Developed Socialism*, Moscow, 1977

Paul Cocks, Robert V. Daniels and Nancy W. Heer, *The Dynamics of Soviet Politics*, Cambridge, Mass., 1976

Theodore H. Friedgut, *Political Participation in the USSR*, Princeton, 1979

Ronald J. Hill, *Soviet Politics, Political Science and Reform*, Oxford, 1980

Jerry F. Hough, *The Soviet Prefects*, Cambridge, Mass., 1969

Jerry F. Hough and Merle Fainsod, *How the Soviet Union is Governed*, Cambridge, Mass., 1979

Gayle D. Hollander, *Soviet Political Indoctrination*, London and New York, 1972

George Leggett, *The Cheka: Lenin's Political Police*, Oxford 1981

Wolfgang Leonhard, *Three Faces of Marxism*, New York, 1974

Mary McAuley, *Politics and the Soviet Union*, Harmondsworth, 1977

Roy A. Medvedev, *On Socialist Democracy*, New York and London, 1975

Alfred G. Meyer, *Communism*, New York, 1967

Peter Reddaway (ed), *Uncensored Russia: The Human Rights Movement in the Soviet Union*, London, 1972

T. H. Rigby, *Communist Party Membership in the USSR 1917–1967*, Princeton, 1968

T. H. Rigby, Archie Brown and Peter Reddaway (eds), *Authority, Power and Policy in the USSR*, London and New York, 1980

Rules of the Communist Party of the Soviet Union, Moscow, 1977

R. A. Saifulin (ed), *The Soviet Form of Popular Government*, Moscow, 1972

A. Sakharov, *Sakharov Speaks*, London, 1974

Leonard Schapiro, *The Communist Party of the Soviet Union* (2nd edn), London, 1970

H. Gordon Skilling and Franklyn Griffiths (eds), *Interest Groups in Soviet Politics*, Princeton, 1971

Gordon B. Smith (ed), *Public Policy and Administration in the Soviet Union*, New York, 1980

William Taubman, *Governing Soviet Cities: Bureaucratic Politics and Urban Development in the USSR*, New York, 1973

Rudolf L. Tökés (ed), *Dissent in the USSR*, Baltimore and London, 1975

Boris Topornin, *The New Constitution of the USSR* (trans. M Saifulin and K. Kostrov), Moscow, 1980

Robert C. Tucker, *The Soviet Political Mind*, (rev. edn), New York, 1971

Robert C. Tucker (ed), *Stalinism: Essays in Historical Interpretation*, New York, 1977

Peter Vanneman, *The Supreme Soviet*, Durham, N.C., 1977

Stephen White, *Political Culture and Soviet Politics*, London and New York, 1979

S. Wolin and R. M. Slusser (eds), *The Soviet Secret Police*, New York, 1957

THE ECONOMY

A. Bergson, *The Economics of Soviet Planning*, New Haven, 1964

J. Berliner, *The Innovation Decision in Soviet Industry*, Cambridge, Mass., 1976

W. L. Blackwell, *The Beginnings of Russian Industrialization, 1800–1860*, vol. I, Princeton, N.J., 1968

R. W. Campbell, *Soviet-type Economies*, New York, 1974

R. W. Campbell, *Trends in the Soviet Oil and Gas Industry*, Baltimore, 1976

The Cambridge Economic History of Europe, Cambridge, vols. I, 1966; VI, 1966; VII, 1978; and VIII, 1981

E. H. Carr and R. W. Davies, *Foundations of a Planned Economy*, vol. 1, London, 1969

O. Crisp, *Studies in the Russian Economy before 1914*, London, 1976

R. W. Davies, *The Socialist Offensive: the Collectivisation of Soviet Agriculture, 1929–1930*, London, 1980

R. W. Davies, (ed), *The Soviet Union*, London, 1978

Maurice H. Dobb, *Soviet Economic Development since 1917*, (6th edn), London and New York, 1966

M. E. Falkus, *The Industrialization of Russia 1700–1914*, London, 1972

J. T. Fuhrmann, *The Origins of Capitalism in Russia: Industry and Progress in the Sixteenth and Seventeenth Centuries*, Chicago, 1972

G. Garvy, *Money, Financial Flows, and Credit in the Soviet Union*, Cambridge, Mass., 1977

P. R. Gregory and R. C. Stuart, *Soviet Economic Structure and Performance*, New York and London, 1974

F. D. Holzman, *International Trade under Communism: Politics and Economics*, London, 1976

R. Hutchings, *Soviet Economic Development*, Oxford, 1971

I. Jeffries (ed), *The Industrial Enterprise in Eastern Europe*, New York and Eastbourne, 1981

M. Kaser, *Soviet Economics*, London and New York, 1970

T. Khachaturov, *The Economy of the Soviet Union Today*, Moscow, 1977

L. Kirsch, *Soviet Wages*, Cambridge, Mass., 1972

Alastair McAuley, *Economic Welfare in the Soviet Union*, London, 1979

J. Miller, *Life in Russia Today*, London, 1969

A. Nove, *An Economic History of the USSR*, London, 1969

A. Nove, *The Soviet Economic System*, London, 1977

B. M. Richman, *Soviet Management*, Englewood Cliffs, 1965

G. T. Robinson, *Rural Russia under the Old Regime*, (2nd edn), London, 1967

R. E. F. Smith, *Peasant Farming in Muscovy*, Cambridge, 1977

V. Sobeslavsky and P. Beazley, *The Transfer of Technology to Socialist Countries: The Case of the Soviet Chemical Industry*, Cambridge, Mass., and London, 1980

N. Spulber, *Soviet Strategy for Economic Growth*, Bloomington, 1964

L. Symons, *Russian Agriculture: A Geographic Survey*, London, 1972

L. Symons and C. White (eds), *Russian Transport: An Historical and Geographical Survey*, London, 1975

J. Wilczynski, *Comparative Monetary Economics*, London, 1978

E. Zaleski and H. Wienert, *Technology Transfer between East and West*, Paris, 1980

A. Zwass, *Money, Banking and Credit in the Soviet Union and Eastern Europe*, London, 1979

SOVIET SOCIETY

D. Atkinson, A. Dallin and G. Lapidus (eds), *Women in Russia*, Berkeley and London, 1978

Harold J. Berman, *Justice in the USSR*, Cambridge, Mass., 1963

Harold J. Berman, *Soviet Criminal Law and Procedure*, Cambridge, Mass., 1972

Sidney Bloch and Peter Reddaway, *Russia's Political Hospitals: The Abuse of Psychiatry in the Soviet Union*, London, 1977

J. Brine, M. Perrie and A. Sutton (eds), *Home, School and Leisure in the Soviet Union*, London, 1980

U. Bronfenbrenner, *Two Worlds of Childhood: USA and USSR*, New York, 1970 and London, 1971

G. Chandler, *Libraries, Documentation and Bibliography in the USSR 1917–1971*, London and New York, 1972

E. Clark Brown, *Soviet Trade Unions and Labor Relations*, Cambridge, Mass., 1965

Walter D. Connor, *Deviance in Soviet Society: Crime, Delinquency and Alcoholism*, New York, 1972

Robert Conquest, *Kolyma: The Arctic Death Camps*, London, 1978

M. Dewhirst and R. Farrell (eds), *The Soviet Censorship*, Metuchen, 1973

S. Francis (ed), *Libraries in the USSR*, London, 1971

N. Grant, *Soviet Education* (4th edn), Harmondsworth, 1979

M. W. Hopkins, *Mass Media in the Soviet Union*, New York, 1970

B. J. Jancar, *Women under Communism*, Baltimore, 1978

M. Kaser, *Health Care in the Soviet Union and Eastern Europe*, London and Boulder, 1976

A. Kassof, *The Soviet Youth Program: Regimentation and Rebellion*, Cambridge, Mass. and London, 1965

A. Kotov and M. Yudovich, *The Soviet School of Chess*, Moscow, 1958; New York, 1961

D. Lane, *The Socialist Industrial State*, London, 1976

D. Lane and F. O'Dell, *The Soviet Industrial Worker*, London, 1978

G. Lapidus, *Women in Soviet Society: Equality, Development and Social Change*, Berkeley, 1978

Alastair McAuley, *Economic Welfare in the Soviet Union*, London, 1979

Mary McAuley, *Labour Disputes in Soviet Russia 1957–1965*, Oxford, 1969

Bernice Madison, *Social Welfare in the Soviet Union*, Stanford, 1968

M. Matthews, *Class and Society in Soviet Russia*, London, 1972

F. O'Dell, *Socialization through Children's Literature: the Soviet Example*, Cambridge, 1978

G. V. Osipov (ed), *Industry and Labour in the USSR* (trans. Novosti Press Agency), London, 1966

N. I. Ponomarev, *Social Functions of Sport*, Moscow, 1981

D. J. Richards, *Soviet Chess: Chess and Communism in the USSR*, Oxford, 1965

J. W. Riordan, *Sport in Soviet Society: Development of Sport and Physical Education in Russia and the USSR*, Cambridge, 1977

J. W. Riordan, *Soviet Sport: Background to the Olympics*, London, 1980

Blair A. Ruble, *Soviet Trade Unions: Their Development in the 1970s*, Cambridge, 1981

M. Ryan, *The Organization of Soviet Medical Care*, Oxford, 1978

R. Sharlet, *The New Soviet Constitution of 1977*, Brunswick, Ohio, 1978

Alexander Solzhenitsyn, *The Gulag Archipelago*, 3 vols, London, 1974–8

J. J. Tomiak, *The USSR* (World Education Series), Newton Abbot and North Pomfret, 1962

V. G. Treml, 'Production and consumption of alcoholic beverages in the USSR', *Journal of Studies on Alcohol*, vol. 36, no. 3, 1975

R. G. Wade, *Soviet Chess*, London, 1968

G. Walker, *Soviet Book Publishing Policy*, Cambridge, 1978

G. Walker, *Book Publishing in the USSR: Reports of the Delegations of US Book Publishers Visiting the USSR* (2nd edn), Cambridge, Mass. and Oxford, 1972

M. Yanowitch, *Social and Economic Inequality in the Soviet Union*, London, 1977

M. Yanowitch and W. A. Fischer, *Social Stratification and Mobility in the USSR*, New York, 1973

MILITARY POWER AND POLICY

John Baylis and Gerald Segal (eds), *Soviet Strategy*, London, 1981

R. Bond (ed), *The Soviet War Machine* (2nd edn), London and New York, 1977

Alexander Boyd, *The Soviet Air Force since 1918*, London, 1977

S. Breyer and N. Polmar, *Guide to the Soviet Navy*, Washington and London, 1978

J. Erickson (ed), *Soviet Military Power and Performance*, London 1979

J. Erickson, *The Soviet High Command*, London, 1962

David Footman, *Civil War in Russia*, London, 1961

R. L. Garthoff, *Soviet Military Policy*, London, 1966

K. W. Gatland, *Missiles and Rockets*, London and New York, 1975

Richard Hellie, *Enserfment and Military Change in Muscovy*, Chicago, 1971

A. L. Horelick and M. Rush, *Strategic Power and Soviet Foreign Policy*, Chicago, 1966

Raymond Hutchings, 'Soviet Arms Exports to the Third World: a Pattern and its Implications', in *The World Today*, October 1978

M. MccGwire and J. McDonnell (eds) *Soviet Naval Influence: Domestic and Foreign Dimensions*, New York and London, 1975

M. Mitchell, *The Maritime History of Russia: 848–1948*, London, 1949

J. E. Moore, *The Soviet Navy Today*, London, 1975

W. E. Odom, *The Soviet Volunteers*, Princeton, 1973

Y. E. Savkin, *The Basic Principles of Operational Art and Tactics* (Moscow, 1972) (trans. United States Air Force, Washington: US Govt Printing Office no. 008–070–00342–2, 1975)

G. Stewart, *The White Armies of Russia*, New York, 1933

Norman Stone, *The Eastern Front, 1914–1917*, London, 1975

V. D. Sokolovsky, *Soviet Military Strategy*, Moscow, 1968

P. H. Vigor, *The Soviet View of War, Peace and Neutrality*, London and Boston, 1976

A. K. Wildman, *The End of the Russian Imperial Army: The Old Army and the Soldiers' Revolt (March–April 1917)*, Princeton, 1980

Thomas Wolfe, *Soviet Power and Europe, 1945–1970*, Baltimore, 1970

P. T. Yegorov, *Civil Defence: Soviet Handbook* (trans. United States Air Force, Washington: US Govt Printing Office no. 008 070 00382–1, 1976)

THE WORLD ROLE

M. S. Anderson, *The Eastern Question 1774–1923: A Study in International Relations*, London, 1966

V. A. Aspaturian, *The Union Republics in Soviet Diplomacy*, Geneva, 1960

J. F. Baddeley, *The Russian Conquest of the Caucasus*, London, 1908

M. Beloff, *The Foreign Policy of Soviet Russia, 1929–1941*, Oxford, 1947–9

A. Dallin, *The Rise of Russia in Asia*, London, 1950

A. Dallin, *The Soviet Union at the United Nations*, New York, 1963

Karen Dawisha and P. Hanson (eds), *Soviet-East European Dilemmas: Coercion, Competition and Consent*, London, 1981

J. Degras (ed), *Calendar of Documents on Soviet Foreign Policy*, vols 1–3, London, 1951–3

J. Degras (ed), *The Communist International 1919–1943: Documents*, vols 1–3, Oxford, 1956–65

H. Feis, *From Trust to Terror: The Onset of the Cold War, 1945–1950*, London, 1970

Francois Fetjö, *A History of the Peoples' Democracies*, London, 1974

L. Fischer, *The Soviets in World Affairs*, 2 vols, London 1930; (2nd edn), Princeton, 1951

W. E. Griffith, *Sino-Soviet Relations*, Cambridge, Mass., 1964

Harry Hanak, *Soviet Foreign Policy since the Death of Stalin*, London, 1972

S. Horak, *Poland and her National Minorities*, New York, 1961

G. Ionescu, *The Break-up of the Soviet Empire in Eastern Europe*, London, 1965

B. Jelavich, *St Petersburg and Moscow: Tsarist and Soviet Foreign Policy, 1814–1974*, Bloomington, 1974

N. A. Khalfin, *Russia's Policy in Central Asia, 1857–1868*, London, 1964

D. M. Lang, *A Modern History of Georgia*, London, 1962

Walter LaFeber, *America, Russia and the Cold War, 1945–1975*, (3rd edn), New York, 1976

I. J. Lederer (ed), *Russian Foreign Policy: Essays in Historical Perspective*, London, 1962

A. Lobanov-Rostovsky, *Russia and Asia*, New York, 1933; Ann Arbor, 1951

Evan Luard, *A History of the United Nations*, vol. I, London, 1981

Martin McCauley (ed), *Communist Power in Europe. 1944–1949*, London, 1977

George von Rauch, *The Baltic States: The Years of Independence. Estonia, Latvia, Lithuania, 1917–1940*, London, 1974

Royal Institute of International Affairs, *The Baltic States: A Survey of the Political and Economic Structure and the Foreign Relations of Estonia, Latvia and Lithuania*, London, 1938: Westport, 1970

A. Z. Rubinstein, *The Foreign Policy of the Soviet Union*, New York, 1960

A. Z. Rubinstein, *The Soviets in International Organizations: Changing Policy towards Developing Countries, 1953–1963*, Princeton, 1964

Morton Schwartz, *The Foreign Policy of the USSR: Domestic Factors*, Encino, Calif., 1975

H. Seton-Watson, *Neither War nor Peace*, London, 1961

Marshall D. Shulman, *Stalin's Foreign Policy Reappraised*, Cambridge, Mass., 1963

B. H. Sumner, *Peter the Great and the Emergence of Russia*, London, 1950

A. Ulam, *Expansion and Co-existence: A History of Soviet Foreign Policy, 1917–1967*, Cambridge, Mass., 1968

G. Wheeler, *The Modern History of Soviet Central Asia*, London, 1964

Daniel Yergin, *Shattered Peace: The Origins of the Cold War and the National Security State*, Boston, 1978

A. Zóltowski, *Border of Europe: A Study of the Polish Eastern Provinces*, London, 1950

Acknowledgements

The publishers gratefully acknowledge permission to reproduce the illustrations listed below. Every effort has been made to obtain permission to use copyright materials; the publishers trust that their apologies will be accepted for any errors or omissions.

Reproduced by gracious permission of Her Majesty the Queen 97r; Aid to the Russian Church 323; Ardis Publishers 215br; Dr T.E. Armstrong 68b; Ashmolean Museum 221; The Associated Press Ltd 482, 483; Dr Derek Bailey 360; from M.G. Barkhin; *Mastera Sovetski arkhitekturi*, Moscow, 1975 158; Barnaby's Picture Library 66t, 114, 372, 407; BBC Hulton Picture Library 84l, 102, 103l, 104, 106, 107b, 108l, 110t, 110b, 120, 132tl, 147, 241l, 247r, 310, 330, 465; Jennifer Beeston 355l; Collection of Countess Bobrinskoy/Michael Holford Library 91t, 92b, 94, 97l, 148, 153l; Bodleian Library, Oxford 265r, 270; Professor John Bowlt 174, 178, 180; by permission of the British Library 328; British Library of Political and Economic Sciences 392; Archie Brown 297; Department of Social Anthropology, University of Cambridge 70l; Camera Press Ltd 113, 140t, 252c, 355r, 406b, 432tl, 434; Mary Chamot 154t, 155; Dr J.G. Coates 70r; Dr Catherine Cook 162, 165l; Crown Copyright (Ministry of Defence) 432cl, 432bl, 432tr, 432cr, 451c, 451b; The Daily Telegraph Colour Library/J. Beeston 179; Mike Davis Studios Ltd 249b; Zöe Dominic 249t; Christopher Donnelly 444; Dr K. Eimermacher 182l; Mariamna Fortounatto 150l, 151r, 152, 153r; Marc Garanger 429; Dr I. Golomstock 385; Martin W. Grosnick/Ardea London 43t; Robert Harding Associates 125, 133, 156, 157l, 157r, 238t, 239t, 407b; Dr Caroline Humphrey 68t, 69b; The Illustrated London News Picture Library 473l; S. Jennert 324; *Jews in the USSR* 73; Professor David Joravsky 271; Dr Z. Katz 135r; Keston College 134l, 134r; Keystone Press Agency 302b; Ginette Laborde 32tl, 32cl, 32tr, 36; Lazzarini Collection 247l, 248; P.J. Lineton, Australia 72t; London Weekend Television 313; Marvin Lyons 430; Sir Fitzroy Maclean 234; The Raymond Mander & Joe Mitchenson Theatre Collection 247c; The Mansell Collection 87, 459; John Massey Stewart 32cr, 32br, 39c, 44t, 58, 62, 66b, 122, 149, 182r, 240tr, 241r, 244l, 269t, 346t, 427; Musée de l'Elysée, Lausanne 329; Museum of Modern Art, Oxford 174r; Courtesy of National Film Archive/Stills Library 196, 252b; Novosti Press Agency 38, 39t, 44b, 45, 54, 63t, 63b, 67b, 69t, 72c, 72b, 75, 76, 77, 84r, 86, 88l, 88r, 89l, 90t, 90b, 92t, 93, 95, 96, 98l, 98r, 99, 100, 103r, 105, 107t, 108r, 124b, 128, 132bl, 132tr, 132br, 135l, 136l, 136r, 138l, 138r, 140b, 141l, 141br, 142bl, 142r, 143, 145, 150tr, 150br, 151l, 154b, 158l, 158tr, 158cr, 159b, 160, 161l, 161tr, 161br, 163, 164, 165r, 166tl, 166bl, 166r, 167l, 167r, 170l, 170r, 171r, 172, 175t, 175c, 175b, 176t, 176b, 179b, 183, 195, 197, 198, 199, 200, 201t, 201b, 203, 205, 206tl, 206tr, 206cl, 206cr, 206bl, 206br, 207, 208, 210, 211, 212, 214, 215tl, 215tr, 215bl, 230t, 230c, 230b, 232t, 232b, 235, 236, 237, 238b, 239b, 240tl, 240b, 242, 243, 244r, 245, 251t, 252t, 260t, 260b, 261t, 261b, 263, 265l, 267, 269b, 276, 277, 278, 280, 282, 283, 284t, 284b, 285, 286, 287t, 287b, 290l, 290r, 291, 292, 298, 314, 316, 318, 320l, 320r, 322, 326, 327, 331, 332l, 332r, 333l, 333r, 334l, 334r, 338l, 338r, 342, 344, 345, 346b, 347, 353, 357, 358, 359, 364l, 365r, 368, 369, 370, 371, 376, 378t, 378b, 381r, 382t, 382b, 383, 387, 389, 390t, 390b, 394, 395t, 395b, 397, 399, 400t, 400b, 401, 402t, 402b, 404, 406, 408, 412, 413t, 413b, 414, 415, 416, 420, 422tl, 422tr, 422b, 426bl, 426r, 435l, 436, 437, 445, 450, 451, 462, 471; Dr Felicity O'Dell 302t; Popperfoto 119, 474, 484; Josephine Powell 139b, 141tr, 142tl, 144l; The Press Association Ltd 432br; J.N. Reichel/Agence Top 137; Rex Features Ltd 233, 363, 381l; Professor Gerald Seaman 222, 228, 229; Brian M. Service 448; Mark Shearman 424l; 424r; Society for Cultural Relations with the USSR 31, 116, 126l, 159r, 169tl, 177t, 177b, 255, 289, 315, 435r, 440, 441, 171l; Howard Sochurek/John Hillelson Agency Ltd 341, 352b; Stedelijk Museum, Amsterdam 173; *Der Stern*, Hamburg 219; Tamara Talbot-Rice 139t, 144r; Tass 123, 124t, 253, 352t, 426tl; Dr Richard Taylor 250, 251b; Dr Elizabeth Valkenier 169bl, 169r; Victoria & Albert Museum 67t; Victoria & Albert Museum/Michael Holford Library 89r; Weidenfeld & Nicolson Ltd 91b, 126l; David Williamson 32bl; Xinhua News Agency 481

The publishers are grateful to Times Newspapers Ltd for reference material for the illustration on page 452

Jacket photographs: front: John Massey Stewart; back: top left: Novosti Press Agency; top right and bottom: Susan Griggs Agency

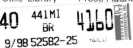